The French Painters of the Seventeenth Century

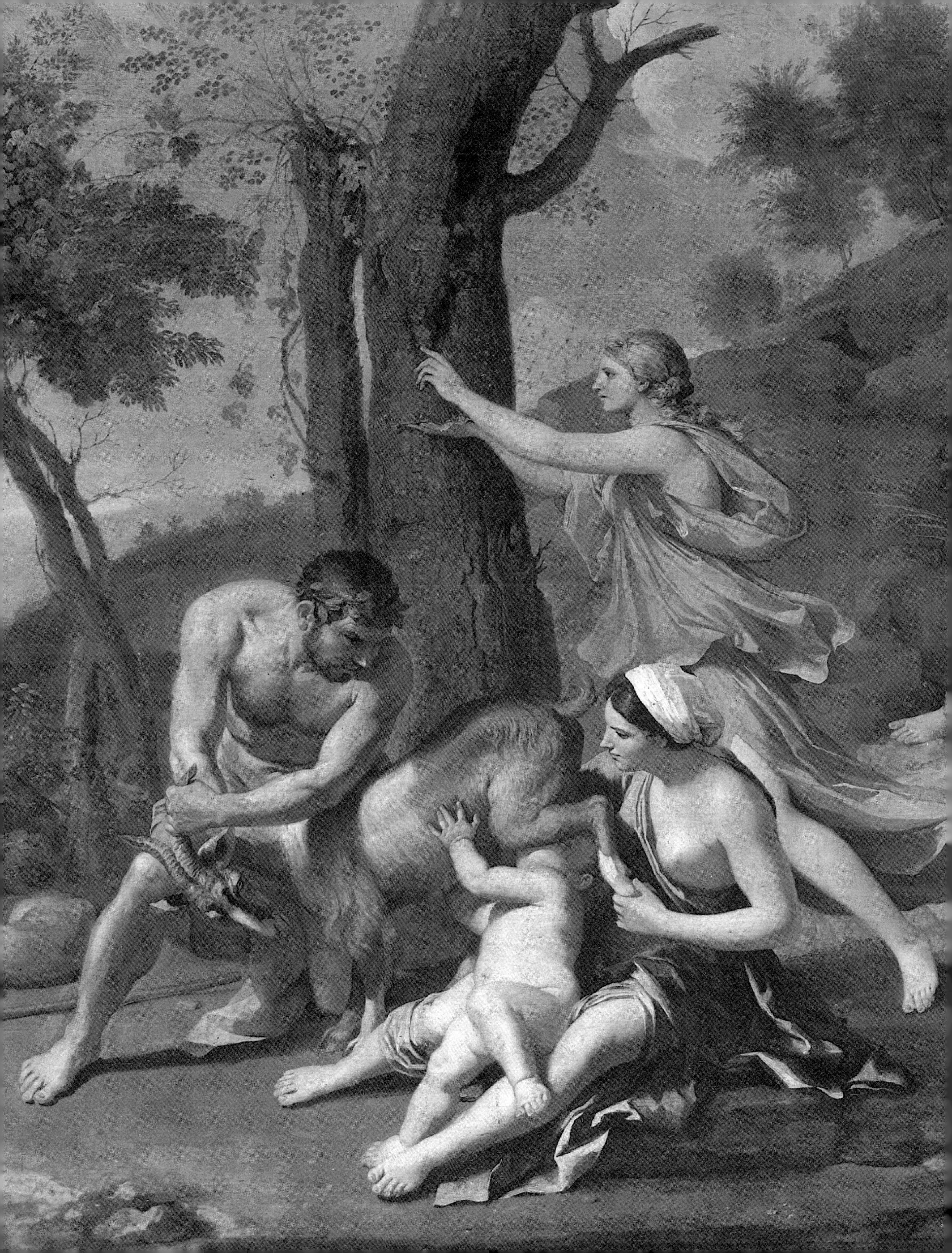

Christopher Wright

The French Painters
of the Seventeenth Century

Orbis · London

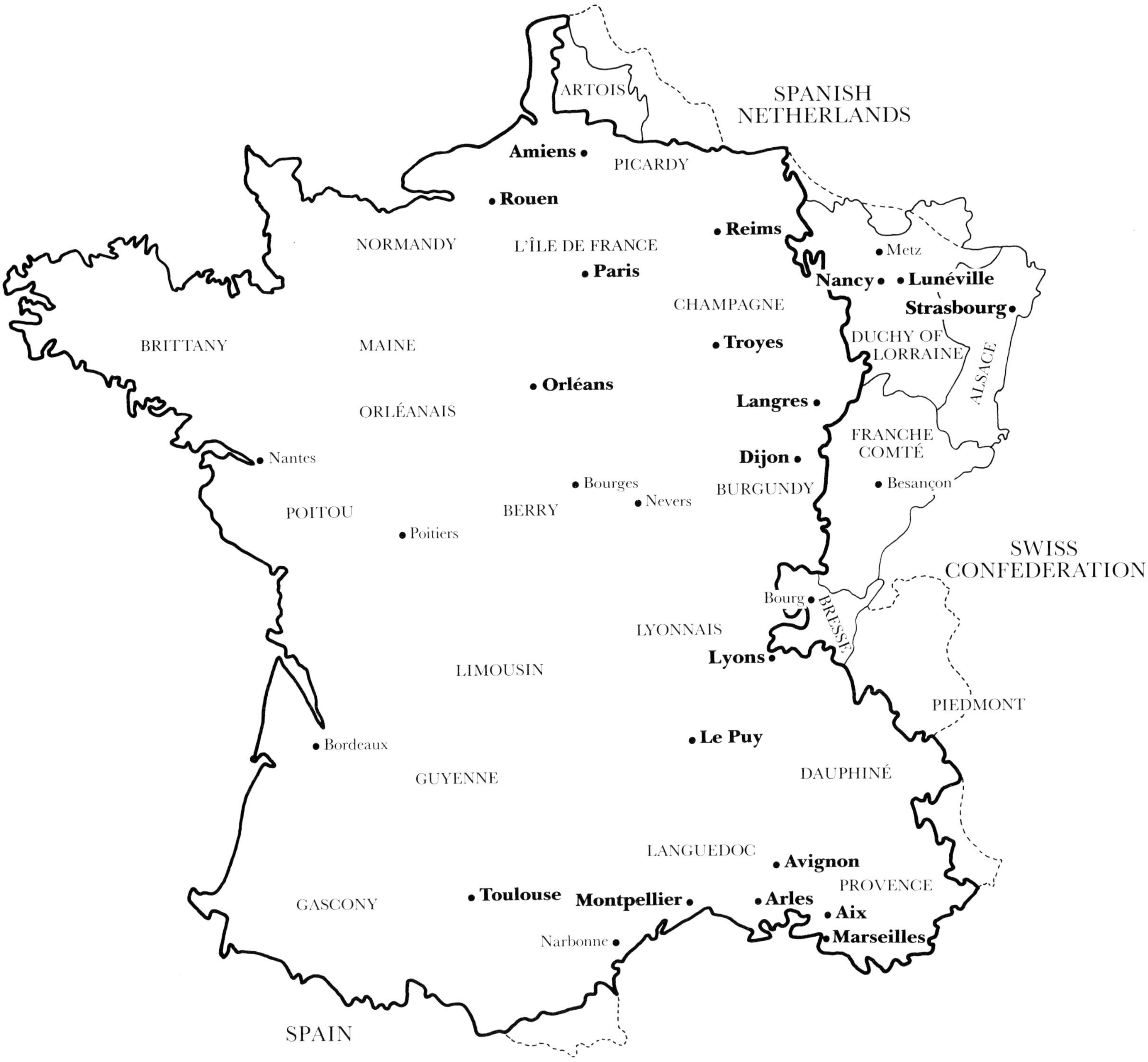

The Kingdom of France in 1600. Artois, the Bishopric of Metz, the Duchy of Lorraine, Alsace, Franche Comté and Bresse were annexed during the course of the seventeenth century. Painting centres are indicated in bold type. The boundaries of modern France are shown by a dotted line.

Frontispiece:
Nicolas Poussin
The Nurture of Jupiter (detail)
London, Dulwich College
Picture Gallery

First published in Great Britain by Orbis Publishing Limited, London 1985

Printed in Italy

Designed by Graham Johnson

ISBN 0-85613-488-0

Contents

Acknowledgments

This book is based on the thirty lectures I gave on the subject of French seventeenth-century painting to undergraduates of the University of California at Santa Barbara in 1973. The course was called rather grandly 'French Baroque Painting', and I spent some of my time trying to define what other art historians had meant by 'Baroque' and then explaining to the students that most French painters were not Baroque at all. My greatest debt is to those students, who challenged what I had to say and made me think again.

The other important debt is to the teaching of the late Anthony Blunt, although we did not always agree, particularly over Nicolas Poussin and Georges de La Tour. During my work on Georges de La Tour in the late 1960s I had many heated arguments with different specialists and I am grateful to them all, even if at times diplomatic relations were strained. The late Benedict Nicolson, the late Vitale Bloch, and the late Georges Isarlo all contributed to my knowledge with their opinions and help.

Over the years I have met with courtesy wherever I have travelled. I owe an especial debt to Robert Rorke for hospitality at Aix-en-Provence, to M. Denis Milhau at the Musée des Augustins at Toulouse, Mlle Guillaume at the Musée des Beaux-Arts at Nancy, M. Claude Souviron at Nantes, and to M. François Bergot at the Musée des Beaux-Arts at Rouen. Dominique de Grunne kindly drove me with Benedict Nicolson all over the area around Le Puy in search of Guy François, as did Pierre Chanel in Lorraine in search of the elusive Le Clerc. In America, people in every museum I have visited have been unfailingly considerate, and I remember with especial pleasure visits to the Toledo Museum of Art, Ohio, the Institute of Arts, Detroit, the Los Angeles County Museum and the Cleveland Museum of Art. Charles Buckley, formerly Director of the St Louis Art Museum, gave me every facility to study the pictures in the collection there. In England, many small museums have been anxious to show me their treasures, even when they were not on view, and I am particularly grateful to David Phillips at Nottingham Castle and Bryan Crossling at the Bowes Museum. As always, the Witt Library and its staff at the Courtauld Institute of Art have provided their unique service in the photographic documentation of works of art.

On a personal level, Caroline Pilkington has, as always, used her sharp eye in looking over my manuscript, and the assistance of Miss Sykes in this respect is acknowledged. Robert Oresko also very kindly read my manuscript, and made numerous helpful suggestions for which I am most grateful. I have had fruitful discussions with Pierre Chanel at Lunéville and also with John Roberts, formerly at Orbis, whose idea this book was. At Orbis now Stephen Adamson, Sarah Chapman and Graham Johnson saw the book through the process of editing and design and I am deeply grateful to them.

This book is dedicated to Barbara (Bobo) Rockefeller in gratitude for that most elusive of qualities—encouragement.

Christopher Wright

Temple Normanton, Derbyshire *December 1981*

Introduction

This book is about a few great painters and a much larger number of others who are either underestimated or recent discoveries. The names of Claude Lorrain, Nicolas Poussin and Georges de La Tour are well known, but the school of painting of which they represent the peak is still obscure. The study of French painting in general has concentrated too much on individual artists and too little on the general background and period relating to them. For instance, the existing literature on Poussin alone is greater than all the rest of the literature on the period added together. There have been too few precursors of this book, and none of them has been in English. This is partly because the pictures from the period are dispersed in museums and private collections throughout the Western world, and there is no single representative collection; even that in the Louvre in Paris is strangely unbalanced. This is in stark contrast to the Dutch, Flemish or Italian schools of painting of the same period, which are comprehensively represented in many great galleries. Another factor is that there has been no major broad-based exhibition of French seventeenth-century painting, with the exception of a showing at the Royal Academy in London in 1958 which encompassed a representative selection from French provincial museums. At the time the exhibition was well received, and many people became familiar for the first time with the real achievement of the Le Nain brothers, and made their first discovery of the rare paintings of Georges de La Tour. The genius of Nicolas Poussin has always been appreciated by connoisseurs, but his rarified art has never been popular with the general public; and even though Claude Lorrain produced some of the most perfect idealized landscapes ever painted, they have not always been appreciated.

The subject-matter of French seventeenth-century painting has often been a stumbling block to a full understanding of its merits: some of it is based on obscure passages in the classics, some of it repeats well-worn religious themes. Landscape and genre represent a much smaller proportion of total output than they do in the Dutch School, and this, too, has contributed to the lack of public esteem. Still-life painting was an important category for French seventeenth-century painters, but it has been almost completely neglected ever since, and it is only in the last few years that the true genius of Louise Moillon and her contemporaries has been recognized.

Sceptics sometimes argue that the neglect suffered by many French seventeenth-century painters has been deserved on purely aesthetic grounds. To some modern eyes the undeniable rhetoric of the painters of Louis XIV seems to have little validity, and it has to be admitted that this type of art is easier for the specialist historian to appreciate than the general public. Perhaps the real reason for the difficulties some people experience in front of so many French pictures is the lack of imagination of so many of the artists: they are so logical in their approach, so clear in their vision and so unambivalent in their message that they leave little or nothing to the spectator's imagination. Nicolas Poussin tried very hard to achieve precisely this effect. Apart from Claude Lorrain, no painter introduced atmosphere into his pictures, and no artists, except for the Le Nain brothers, were interested in daily life.

Among the categories of art in which French painters were *not* interested must be included topographical painting, of which there was little or none, which means that we are denied a visual record of the state of the towns and countryside during the period. (By contrast, it is almost possible to reconstruct Dutch towns as they were in the seventeenth century from the surviving townscape paintings of the Dutch School.) French artists generally confined their interest in landscape to the deliberate idealization of nature, although the exceptions to this are the tantalizing and beautiful backgrounds occasionally seen in the work of the Le Nain brothers. Portraiture was largely formal, and few artists showed their sitters in their homes or at work, but again the exception to this occurs in the work of the Le Nain brothers, which offers touching insights into the daily lives of the better-off peasantry. Still life as a category was largely limited to fruits and vegetables, and there was no flower painter capable of rivalling the Netherlanders. It was in the realm of religious and mythological subject-matter that the French came into their own. Many of Nicolas Poussin's best pictures have subjects taken from Ovid's *Metamorphoses* and those of Claude Lorrain from the poetry of Virgil.

Although so much of the subject-matter of the period is of an admittedly recondite or esoteric nature, it is inexcusable that such a momentous period, part of the inexhaustibly varied cultural past, should be so obscure. The search for so many long-forgotten painters reveals facets of painting unique in the history of art, both on grounds of inventiveness and even spirituality. Jean Tassel's *Catherine de Montholon* (plate 82), Georges de La Tour's *Job Mocked by his Wife* (plate 39), and the Le Nains' *Forge* (plate 51) are unique expressions of eccentric but sensitive minds, contrasting brilliantly with the matter-of-fact achievements of so many Dutch painters who were rarely concerned with the emotional and spiritual effects of their paintings.

The dominating figure in seventeenth-century France was Louis XIV. The momentous events of his reign and the glamour of Versailles have raised his reputation to an artificial height as the one colossus of the period, although he did not begin to rule until 1661, at the age of twenty-three, by which time many of the painters recorded in this book were either old or dead. His reign ushered in a new period in which the art of painting took on a changed role. Easel painting declined as the main form of artistic expression; artists now had to serve the monarch as decorators, and an energetic team of painters under the control of Charles Le Brun began working at Versailles and other royal residences.

No one great painter dominates the century in France (in contrast to the Dutch Republic, where Rembrandt stood out even in his own time as a unique figure). For a good deal of the century Paris was not the predominant city, partly because so many French painters of importance – including Claude Lorrain and Nicolas Poussin – spent their entire careers in Rome. The duchy of Lorraine was also an important centre, almost as far from Paris as the Dutch Republic.

The lack of a unifying thread for the period has had a curious effect: many writers have attempted to create one out of this robust and idiosyncratic century, usually defining this non-existent unity as 'classicism', epitomized convincingly by Nicolas Poussin. Even the realism of Georges de La Tour has been described as imbued with French 'classicism', and, stranger still, the peasant scenes of the Le Nain brothers have been identified as reflecting this trend of classical purity. However, in looking at all the main painters active during the period, a very different pattern emerges from the one that is usually presented.

The purpose of this book is to give an account of the development of French painting in the seventeenth century, as far as can be deduced from the surviving pictures. The French Revolution of 1789 made away with a vast amount of official seventeenth-century portraiture which was either sold or destroyed, and many works of art simply fell to pieces through neglect. No attempt has been made here to reconstruct lost glories such as the great decorative cycles, of which so little now survives, but concentrating on what does survive is not without its problems. Many now obscure painters were prolific, but their work has been reduced to a few uncertainly attributed pictures in small museums in France; the shortness of some of the lists of the existing work of several of the painters in this book speaks for itself.

In recent years some of the minor figures have been rehabilitated, chiefly through the publishing of detailed articles or through exhibitions. Since 1960 there have been exhibitions devoted to the French Caravaggesques, Nicolas Poussin, the Le Nain brothers, Guy François, Jacques de L'Estin, painting in Aix-en-Provence and Marseilles (all in Italy and France), and to Claude Lorrain in Washington, Paris, Munich and elsewhere. In spite of this revival of interest in the field, however, there is still no consensus of opinion over the precise details of individual attributions, or over the broader concept of how the cultural background of these painters fits between that of Netherlandish and Italian artists. Even the main figures such as Nicolas Poussin, the Le Nain brothers and Georges de La Tour are prone to serious problems of attribution. As well as these problems, which give rise to heated discussions among art historians and museum officials, many seventeenth-century French painters are still completely neglected (more than a hundred of them are mentioned in this book).

Even though so many French painters of the seventeenth century are now utterly obscure or forgotten, they were much esteemed by their contemporaries, as is shown by the surviving documents: commissions are often recorded even when the paintings do not survive. Georges de La Tour was rediscovered in the nineteenth century by this method; it was found that the town authorities of Lunéville purchased his pictures, although it was not until 1915 that any surviving painting was attributed to him.

It is surprising that so many writers judge French seventeenth-century art by the standards learned from looking at other schools of painting, whereas, for example, Rembrandt is not judged by the same criteria as Caravaggio, since the two painters have quite different historical and cultural backgrounds. It is because the background of French painters remains so little known and confused that judgments have been clouded. It is of no use to imagine the background to Georges de La Tour, since he worked in isolation in Lunéville with no other artists present. By contrast, Nicolas Poussin's career in Rome spanned the most exciting period of the Roman Baroque, when Bernini, Borromini and Pietro da Cortona transformed the city.

The Historical Background

It requires an enormous stretch of the imagination to turn the clock back to any period of French cultural history before the age of Louis XIV and even to that period itself. Versailles was, after 1789 until it was recently refurbished, a largely empty shell but in its restored state it is now clear testimony to the way in which the most powerful monarch in Europe at the time chose to live. The great Gothic cathedrals of Chartres, Amiens and Reims also speak eloquently of the age of St Louis.

French seventeenth-century history, if it lacks a great monument before Versailles, is even more lacking in an historian: there has been no convenient assessment of the state of France at the beginning of the period. After the death of François I in 1549 the remainder of the century was mainly a period of political and social instability, coupled with religious turmoil, which a succession of weak kings was unable to control. The religious conflict between Catholic and Protestant culminated in the Massacre of St Bartholomew in 1573. France was saved from degenerating into total chaos only by events that occurred after the accession of Henri IV in 1589, which led to a period of relative internal stability. No encouragement was given to the art of painting by the monarch, who was far more interested in establishing religious tolerance, his most important act being the Edict of Nantes in 1598 which gave freedom of worship to both Catholic and Protestant. The king was, however, interested in architectural projects, and attempts were made to modernize Paris; the splendid Place des Vosges is testimony to this.

Following the assassination of Henri IV in 1610, Louis XIII succeeded to the throne as a youth, dominated by his mother, the widowed queen Marie de Medici. There then followed a long period of inefficient royal government which lasted until Louis XIV took over in 1661, but France did not lack leadership during this period. Marie de Medici was a formidable character but incompetent as a ruler, and in the 1630s military affairs were in the hands of Cardinal Richelieu. Both these figures were significant patrons of art. Following the death of Louis XIII in 1643, the main figures of government were his widow Anne of Austria and the wily Cardinal Mazarin, who was one of the most important art collectors of the century.

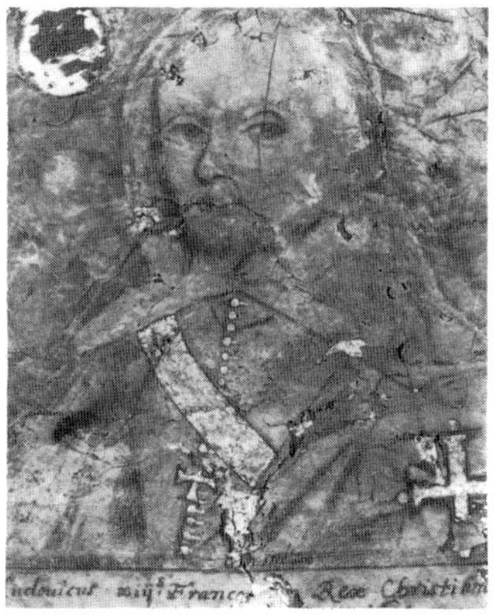

FIGURE 1
Louis XIII of France
Portrait of Claude Deruet
Pastel on paper, 22 × 17 cm.
Nancy, Musée Historique Lorrain

This precious survival shows that the King had learned a certain competence from his teacher, who continued using the bland colours favoured in the 1620s throughout his long career.

The personality of Louis XIII remains relatively obscure against this backdrop of powerful cardinals and queens dowager, but it is wrong to see him simply as a foppish decadent. His interest in the daily events of government was certainly minimal, but he had contacts with artists as diverse as Nicolas Poussin – whom he commissioned, unsuccessfully, to decorate the Grande Galerie of the Louvre – and Georges de La Tour, whose lost *St Sebastian* he may have owned. The king had a drawing master, the Lorraine artist Claude Deruet, and he achieved a modest level of competence (see figure 1).

The country of which Louis XIII became ruler in 1610 was a very different place from the one to be ruled by Louis XIV half a century later. The first half of the seventeenth century laid the foundations, both economically and politically, for the enormous territorial expansion of France under Louis XIV. The wealth of France was concentrated in the hands of the aristocracy, and France was the largest and richest country in Europe with the exception of the enormously powerful Spain, then already in economic and political decline. Like Spain and unlike almost every other European country, France was governed centrally from the capital, Paris, even though some regions had a degree of administrative independence, depending on their histories (but apart from Paris only Aix-en-Provence and Montpellier had universities at this time). Until the reign of Louis XIV France has to be seen without Alsace, Lorraine, the Franche-Comté and Savoy, and the two provinces of Flanders and Artois were still part of the Netherlands. The towns of Arras, Cambrai, Lille, Douai and Valenciennes, all now part of France, were part of the Spanish Netherlands until they were taken by Louis XIV, and therefore for most of the period they too form part of Netherlandish cultural history.

Many of the market towns in different parts of France, including Aix-en-Provence, Dijon, Toulouse and Rouen, were regional administrative capitals, and some of them had been important centres of painting in the Middle Ages. For example, the residence of the popes in Avignon in the fourteenth century had meant that the town had been of considerable importance, the most distinguished artist to work there being the Sienese Simone Martini who died in 1344. In the extreme north of the country as it was then, Amiens had been an important centre in the years around 1500, inspired by artists active over the border in the Netherlands, especially at Bruges and Ghent. In the east, the independent duchy of Burgundy had also been immensely important as an artistic centre in the fifteenth century, controlling the Netherlands for a time. Burgundy's capital was Dijon, and enough remains of painting and sculpture there to testify to its having been one of the most energetic international centres in the late Middle Ages.

In the sixteenth century the prominence of these provincial centres declined. In the reign of François I almost all the artistic activity of significance was concentrated at his palace of Fontainebleau, where several Italian painters of importance had been encouraged to work. After François' death in 1549 artistic activity in France came to a virtual standstill, except for the continuing tradition of court portraiture begun by Jean Clouet, who was the founder of a whole dynasty of portraitists. The reason for this sudden cessation of artistic activity was not only political and economic instability and the continuing religious crises, when the church stopped commissioning pictures all over Northern Europe until the Edict of Nantes in 1598, but also the fact that at this stage in its history France had not evolved a professional middle class used to buying paintings to adorn its houses. This was in direct contrast to Italy and the Netherlands, whose merchant classes were already trading in pictures as commercial commodities, establishing the beginnings of what is today's art market. This demand for paintings from those other than the very rich, or the Church or State, had not yet arisen in France.

The halt in almost all forms of artistic activity in France in the second half of the sixteenth century allows the historian to begin the seventeenth century practically as if it were a clean slate instead of having to draw an artificial line in deciding where to limit the continuum of history. There is more ambiguity at the end of the period under discussion, because it cuts across the long reign of Louis XIV, which was a period of prolific painting activity. His dominating influence, which began on his assumption of personal power in 1661, ended with the century when there was a reaction to the standards he had established. This was not fully expressed, however, until the art of Watteau, which flourished for a brief period just after Louis' death in 1715.

At the beginning of the seventeenth century young French painters had no local traditions on which to rely, and they looked abroad for sources of inspiration. The most exciting development at this time was the return to artistic importance of some of the provincial centres such as Toulouse, which was close to Spain, and the duchy of Lorraine, which was close to the German states. Perhaps significantly, most of these centres were distant from Paris.

Even though there were many anomalies of boundary and local administration, the wealth of France was based on agriculture rather than on trade and manufacture. (Louis XIV later came to realize this, and it was he who first established state-run and subsidized industries in order to rival and even to supersede those of neighbouring countries.) The printers of Haarlem, the tapestry weavers of Arras and Brussels, the textile weavers of Bruges and Ghent and the trading facilities of Antwerp and Amsterdam, none of these had counterparts in France. Instead, towns were regional capitals with a market where produce could be exchanged. Manufactures were usually for local consumption only, there being no elaborate system of distribution like that of the Netherlands, which made goods more easily transportable. Modest artistic activity was possible in each of these centres, but there was no merchant class to buy work on a large scale. The Catholic church seems to have been demoralized by the Protestant challenge to its supremacy, and few could forget the ransacking of such famed monuments as Antwerp Cathedral, over the border in the Netherlands.

Art patronage on the whole has been very little studied, and there are particularly large gaps in our knowledge with regard to France. The collecting tastes of the great figures, Marie de Medici, Louis XIII, Richelieu, Mazarin and Louis XIV, are known, but such knowledge does not in itself constitute an adequate account of patronage over the whole century. Nothing is known of those who bought non-commissioned pictures on the open market. The Church commissioned altarpieces, and owners of châteaux had their property decorated or redecorated from time to time. The only discernible trend during the first half of the century is a gradual change of emphasis: at first, Church and State dominated as patrons all over Europe, with the exception of the Dutch Republic where the merchant class bought more art than any other group, and then in Paris in the 1640s and 1650s it seemed as if the trend was towards the type of patronage familiar in the Dutch Republic. Works of very varied subject-matter, from the exquisite still-life pictures of Louise Moillon to the esoteric pictures of Nicolas Poussin, were bought by middle-class patrons in Paris. In the early 1660s, however, this relative freedom of patronage came to an abrupt end when Louis XIV reorganised the French Academy in Paris which had been founded in 1648. Suddenly, rules about the way in which pictures were to be painted were laid down, and the status of artists was established according to the subject-matter they painted. Still-life and genre subjects were placed on the lowest level, and any painter specializing in these areas was, with very few exceptions, to be denied royal or official patronage.

Though it was the intention of Louis XIV to encourage artistic activity, he effectively stifled it. Almost all the masterpieces of his reign were produced without royal interference. Through his actions the king brought to an effective end a period of artistic emancipation, when an immense variety of artistic style and subject-matter could exist side by side. The century ended as it had begun, with a surprising barrenness of artistic invention.

Chapter One

International Mannerism and its Effect in France, 1600-25

The only time in seventeenth-century France and Lorraine that there was some stylistic unity was during the first quarter of the century. Almost all the surviving pictures of the period, and there are very few of them, fall into the category of what has been defined in the twentieth century as Mannerism. Most art historians today subscribe to the concept of International Mannerism in the same way that they see the unity of style of the Middle Ages in Western Europe as International Gothic. The broad conception of Mannerism is of course subject to widely differing interpretations, often based on the national viewpoint of the writer.

Mannerism is correctly seen as originating in Italy. It has always been understood, even before the term Mannerism was coined in the 1920s, that, following the death of Raphael in 1520, Italian painters turned away from the search for a calm perfection to a more intense style. This change of direction is discernible even in the art of Michelangelo, whose later work in the 1540s and 1550s became more restless and expressionistic. Many other artists of the time in Italy introduced great tensions into their work by exaggerating poses and intensifying colour to an unnatural degree. All ideals of balance and composure were abandoned, to be replaced by eccentricity and even overtones of moral and sexual deviation. The chief exponents of this so-called Mannerist style in Italy were Pontormo and Rosso Fiorentino – the latter worked in France for François I at Fontainebleau. Even Bronzino, the court portrait painter for the Medici, and the art historian Vasari worked in a contorted or exaggerated style in their pictures.

Irrespective of current style, Italy was the Mecca for many aspiring young artists born in Northern Europe. Even in the sixteenth century a very high proportion of young painters went there from the Netherlands and the German states and, for those who did not travel there, the easily transportable medium of engraving enabled them to copy most of the great cycles of paintings on the walls of Italian churches and palaces without ever seeing the originals. Then, suddenly, all over Northern Europe, from Prague to Utrecht, from Fontainebleau to Antwerp, it became the fashion to follow the restless Italian style, even when it had become diluted or gone out of vogue in Italy.

The period of greatest artistic activity in Northern Europe for artists who worked in the Mannerist style, especially in the Netherlands (both in Antwerp and the struggling Dutch Republic further north), was between about 1580 and 1610. Apart from Fontainebleau, where a small amount of work was being done towards the end of the sixteenth century, France was largely left out of this surge of activity. Netherlandish artists were occasionally able to sell their pictures to French patrons, and by the middle of the seventeenth century there was considerable trade in this direction, although the French authorities did their best to prevent it.

By the time the International Mannerist movement was established in Northern Europe, to the point where similar types of pictures were being produced in all the main centres, artists active in Italy had moved away from this style towards a whole series of new experiments, some of them revolutionary in content. France, however, was unaware of this second wave of stylistic experiment led by the Carracci family and Caravaggio, and settled down to a period of isolation, removed from foreign influence and based on what had been fashionable in Italy more than half a century earlier.

No single northern Mannerist seems to have had an effect on French painting of the time, although so little French work survives that it is likely that strong influences were present in work which no longer exists. The arch-Mannerist from Haarlem, Cornelis van Haarlem, spent some time in France, and every northern artist travelling south towards Italy had to pass through France. French artists could repeat compositions easily enough, but could never rival the techniques of the northern painters such as Joachim Wtewael of Utrecht, who was just as much at home painting tiny, minutely detailed and brilliantly coloured copper panels as producing huge tapestry-like canvasses with numerous figures in elaborate poses. Most of the northern Mannerist painters produced figures that were more elongated and muscular than those of their Italian counterparts, and there is always a feeling that they exaggerated for the sake of it. As most art history turns towards the concept of innovation, French painting of this period is always passed over because of its entirely derivative nature. Nothing grew out of these French Mannerist artists; their successors gained new inspiration from Italy rather than building on the experience of the generation which taught them.

In turning to the all-too-few surviving pictures from the first years of the seventeenth century in France, the historian must clutch at straws in order to make sense of the available evidence. Not one artistic personality emerges: the painted output of the Lorrainer Jacques Bellange is totally lost. This is in depressing contrast to so many Netherlandish and Italian painters of the same period, to whom reasonable groups of pictures can be attributed and whose careers can be charted. Nevertheless, the odd anonymous altarpiece in a remote church and the occasional picture in a small museum bear adequate testimony to a robust *naïveté* and an awareness of Italy, albeit at second or third hand.

The most coherent group of pictures from this period is the series of group portraits of the Consuls (magistrates) of Narbonne in the Musée des Beaux-Arts at Narbonne. They are not all by the same artist, and their interest lies not in the portraits themselves but in the setting in which they are placed. The most sensational is the one where the Consuls of Narbonne are before St Sebastian (figure 2). The figures are painted with the kind of gaucheness familiar from Elizabethan England, but in painting the figure of St Sebastian the artist has tried to be up to date. He could not fully understand the drawing which had to underlie such a complex pose, and the result raises a smile because the artist dared not thus modernize his sitters or they would have rejected it out of hand. Indeed, all the surviving portraits from this early period, such as the *Group Portrait* in the Musée Fabrégat at Béziers, show the same hieratic stiffness.

At the other end of France, in Normandy, a few pictures attributed to the painter Quentin Varin survive. Varin worked in the area around Rouen, and

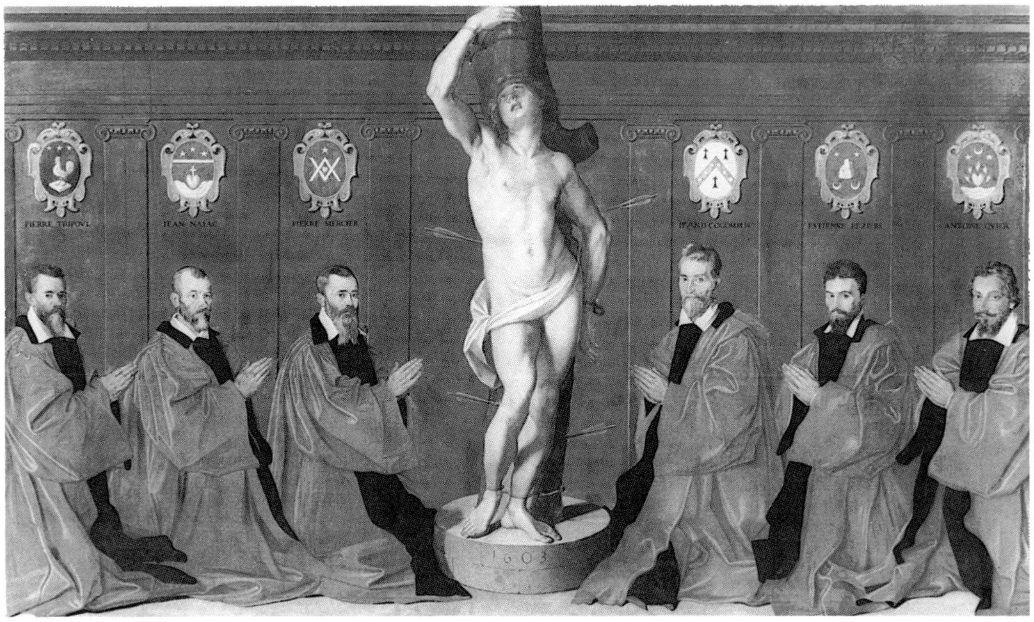

FIGURE 2
French School, 1603
Consuls for the Year 1603
Canvas, 182 × 296 cm. Dated 1603
Narbonne, Musée des Beaux-Arts
In the museum since its foundation in 1833, along with other similar pictures.

This group-portrait of the magistrates (consuls) of Narbonne is one of the extremely rare depictions of middle-class people of the period. The sitters are known; they are, from left to right: Pierre Tripoul, Jean Najac (burgess), Pierre Mercier (doctor of medicine), Jean de Cogomblis (burgess), Etienne Béziers (notary), Antoine Quier (merchant).

there is an altarpiece by him in the church at Les Andelys, the small town where Nicolas Poussin was born in 1593. Varin's pictures look like rather weak versions of altarpieces painted in Antwerp at the same time (about 1600). He is said to have been an influence on the young Nicolas Poussin before the latter finally left for Italy in the 1620s, but this is difficult to prove, owing to the lack of surviving early work by Poussin.

In France proper, excluding Lorraine (a special entity because of the existence of the ducal court), it seems that artists were completely disorganized. When the queen mother, Marie de Medici, had a really important commission to give – that which has come to be known as the Medici cycle, glorifying herself and her dead husband Henri IV – the commission went not to a French artist but to Rubens; and during the early years of the reign of Louis XIII the court portraitist was the Antwerp painter Frans Pourbus the Younger. There were no local artists of suitable talent and energy to provide pictures for the ambitious schemes of Marie de Medici, but examination of the archives in Paris has shown that a large number of churches there were decorated in this period, although very little has survived. The decorators did not, however, have the standing of court artists whose function was to produce effective and usually flattering images of the queen mother and her family.

In only one centre did a whole group of artists use Mannerism as an established style, and this was the court of the duchy of Lorraine. The isolation of the duchy cannot be overestimated in terms of the rest of France, but the painters working for the court there do seem to have been aware of other international trends. Until the 1630s, when the duchy was overrun by the invading armies of Cardinal Richelieu, Lorraine was totally independent, owing allegiance only to the Holy Roman Empire. Its culture was nevertheless largely French-orientated and, although historically a separate entity, as Burgundy had been, Lorraine has always been included in discussions of French cultural history.

The main reason for the artistic independence of Lorraine was the tastes of the court at Nancy. It was luxury-loving, extravagant and given to masques and balls. The only obvious parallel to it was the contemporary Jacobean court in England, served by Inigo Jones. Though painted rather later, Claude Deruet's *Element of Fire* (plate 1) in the Musée des Beaux-Arts at Orléans gives some idea of the elaborate theatrical stage settings indulged in by the court. No painted decorations have survived – they were intended at the time to be ephemeral – but some idea of the appearance of things can be gained from the immense variety of drawings and engravings executed by the Lorraine artist Jacques Callot, at the court during the 1620s and early 1630s. As a graphic artist, Callot played a crucial part in the development of the medium of etching, and as a topographer of the court he is more informative than almost any other artist of his time. From his work we know the way in which the palace gardens at Nancy were laid out, what the ladies at court wore, how fairs were held and even what the low life of the city looked like. Callot also executed a series of beautiful drawings of local views, which are in the library at Chatsworth, in the collection of the Duke of Devonshire.

Even though much visual information survives, almost no paintings have come down to us. Until 1617, when he disappears from the records, the chief painter to the Lorraine court was Jacques Bellange. Only one painting securely attributed to him exists, but since it is a copy of a composition by Albrecht Dürer it is of no use in reconstructing his work. A small corpus of both drawings and etchings survives, however, and their eccentric and original compositions show that Bellange was one of the most inventive artists of his time. His work ranges from the aggressive etching of *Beggars Brawling* to the exaggerated elegance of his *Annunciation* plate. He designed masques for the court, and as every one of his surviving drawings and etchings can be described as Mannerist, it is likely that his painted work was also in this style. It also emerges from the remaining evidence that the court patronized art in quantity: ducal inventories show extensive commissions of paintings and decorations, and each court festivity would require a whole new set of decorations.

The scant evidence available suggests that in France, in these first barren two decades of the century, Mannerism was the general style, there being no evidence of any other form of artistic activity. Curiously enough, one artist, Claude Vignon, was to begin painting in a Mannerist style after it had gone completely out of fashion, and one other painter, Claude Deruet, who served the Lorraine court until the 1660s, painted in a modernized Mannerist style which was to please Cardinal Richelieu.

The artistic scene all over France was to change dramatically in the 1620s. Lorraine, however, was to enjoy a brief period at the centre of the stage once the new wave of influence from Italy had arrived in the mid-1620s, in the form of the dramatic art of painters inspired by Caravaggio.

Chapter Two

Caravaggio and his French Followers

French Painters in Rome

At the beginning of the seventeenth century, the ambition of every aspiring young painter from northern Europe was to go to Italy, and in particular Rome, which had become the chief melting-pot for artistic ideas, while Florence and Venice had lost their pre-eminence in this respect. During this period, Rome looked quite different from the way it looks today. Many of the monuments of classical antiquity were still unexcavated, only their upper parts showing through piles of debris which had accumulated around them. None of the major monuments of the Baroque had yet been built; for instance, St Peter's was still without Bernini's piazza. Most of the major changes of the seventeenth century were to be in architecture, town planning and sculpture, whereas in painting the innovations had begun in the last years of the sixteenth century.

Two totally conflicting types of painting, both of them new, had emerged in the last few years of the sixteenth century in Rome. One was represented by the Carracci brothers and their followers and pupils, the other by the isolated figure of Caravaggio. Both were to be extremely influential on the next generation of painters of all nationalities, although the French were particularly affected. The most important factor concerning these two great influences is that they took place after the artists themselves were dead; the movement now described by some writers as international Caravaggism did not reach its height until the 1620s, and Caravaggio, who left Rome to live in remote Malta and Sicily, had died in 1610; Annibale Carracci died in 1609, and his influence was at its height also in the 1620s.

Annibale Carracci and his assistants Lanfranco and Domenichino were to change the whole course of painting in Italy by the way they decorated one relatively small ceiling in the Farnese Palace in Rome. They have been rightly regarded as the precursors of the Baroque. The chief change they brought about was to employ a variety of methods of decoration on the same ceiling. Scenes were set in panels along the centre and surrounded by elaborate giants and putti supporting them, usually in grisaille. Strong contrasts between monochrome and bright colour and elaborate perspective contributed to a rich but light-hearted effect. Such a combination was to influence most ceiling painters in the seventeenth century in Rome, and this influence is discernible even in Charles Le Brun's decorations in the Louvre and at Versailles, painted more then half a century later, although no other French artist seems to have followed their example.

The other main innovation of the Carracci, Domenichino and Lanfranco, which was also to have a profound effect on French artists, was their evolution of what has come to be known as the 'classical' landscape. For the first time, the picture's story, and even the existence of figures, was subordinated to the landscape setting. The three artists collaborated on a series of landscapes called the *Aldobrandini Lunettes* in the Galleria Doria, Rome. The results now appear conventional enough, with trees on each side carefully balancing one another, yet they were profoundly influential on all the French landscape painters working in Rome, especially Nicolas Poussin, Claude Lorrain and Gaspard Dughet.

Caravaggio, the other main influence at the time of the Carracci, was a completely different personality. It appears that he did not follow the usual custom of working with numerous pupils, but preferred independence. His 'anti-establishment' attitudes gained support amongst a minority of patrons who were sometimes prepared to support him even when his violent nature led him to commit crimes. Caravaggio's approach to conventional religious subject-matter was his real innovation. All through the previous century, Italian painters had been striving to achieve an ideal when depicting the standard religious themes; and even Mannerist artists, in creating their rarefied world, strove towards a weird idealism. As a reaction to this, Caravaggio tried to (and succeeded in) bringing his models down to earth, depicting them with a passionate realism. He used strong contrasts of light and shade in order to achieve a heightened dramatic effect.

It is an over-simplification, however, to see painting in Rome in the 1620s entirely as a conflict and a contrast between the Carracci and Caravaggio. There was a bewildering variety of other forms of artistic expression too, no single one dominant. Inevitably, those that received the most attention are by artists whose work was to be influential either on their contemporaries or on the next generation, but this does not mean that they were necessarily the most successful artists of their time. One of the most influential painters working in Rome in the first decade of the century was Adam Elsheimer, who died there in 1610. Only thirty or so small copper panels survive from his hand, and a few of them are landscapes. His landscapes are among the first 'ideal' ones, and show his interest in the effects of light. Most of Elsheimer's pictures were engraved and his work therefore became well known in northern Europe. He influenced artists as diverse as Rembrandt and Rubens, but in terms of French painters it was his influence on Claude Lorrain which was to be important. Another influential northerner was the Antwerp-born Paul Bril, who specialized in small, brightly coloured copper panels of landscape and seaports. He, too, was to influence Claude Lorrain, but the main significance of both Elsheimer and Bril in their lifetimes was their immense popularity with local patrons. In the second decade of the century, Bril was joined by a host of young Dutchmen from the newly founded Republic, and their experiments also increased the variety of artistic expression taking place in Rome.

At the time of the death of Annibale Carracci in 1609, the dominant figures in Rome were all Italian. The main artists active were Domenichino, Lanfranco, Guido Reni, Guercino and Pietro da Cortona, who together created what has come to be known as the Italian Baroque. In some respects they painted in opposing styles. Domenichino preferred a cold classicism derived from the Carracci; Guercino developed his own warmth of palette and richness of paint; and Pietro da Cortona became the chief decorator, his career culminating in the *tour de force* of the Barberini ceiling. All these painters, whatever their individual characteristics, had various things in common. They were extrovert, broad in their conceptions, uninterested in the nuances of psychological perception. Only one Frenchman, Simon Vouet, ever tried to rival them, and then only after his return to France.

It was within this atmosphere of many types of artistic activity that the first generation of French artists arriving in the years around 1620 had to operate, and the fact that they chose without exception to imitate one type of art is astonishing. In order to understand the profound influence that Caravaggio had on so many different painters, not just the French, it is important to define the particular aspects of his art which beguiled them. It has often been claimed that Caravaggio invented tenebrism – the art of painting the night scene – but there had in fact been a long tradition of night-scene painting before Caravaggio, especially in northern Europe. Italian artists had occasionally tried this difficult genre, but it was to become much more common in the seventeenth century.

Caravaggio rarely depicted his scenes by artificial light. Instead, he preferred strong contrasts of light and shade, with shafts of daylight flooding into dark rooms, as in the justly celebrated *Calling of Matthew* in the church of S. Luigi dei Francesi in Rome. Caravaggio's light illuminates all the relevant aspects of the story, keeping the rest of the scene in shadow. This characteristic is found to an even greater extent in his last works, executed in Sicily, where the lighting becomes unnatural, as if guided by the spiritual demands of the composition. It was not, however, simply the lighting in Caravaggio's pictures that attracted the French and the Netherlanders to him, even though this has often been thought to be his most obvious influential characteristic. Rather, it was his dramatic approach to his subject-matter that was to have such a lasting impact on painters of quite different temperaments and nationalities. Perhaps the two most influential pictures in this respect were the *Entombment of Christ* in the Vatican and the *Death of the Virgin* in the Louvre, in which his use of contemporary dress and settings contributes to their vivid realism and immediacy.

Some of the most obvious Netherlandish debts to Caravaggio's sense of drama are Baburen's *Entombment of Christ* in S. Pietro in Montorio in Rome and Honthorst's *Christ before Caiaphas* in the National Gallery, London. By contrast, the French reacted rather differently to Caravaggio, adopting a specifically homogeneous style with certain important characteristics standing out. Almost all the French painters in Rome whose works survive were steeped in the provincial Mannerist tradition to which they had been born. Simon Vouet came from Paris, Vignon from Tours, Le Clerc from Nancy, Bigot from Provence, and Le Valentin from Coulommiers-en-Brie. All of them, therefore, became aware of the backwardness of their origins. In no instance, unfortunately, has a single piece of their early work been identified. Nevertheless, their backgrounds were much more unified than those of either the Italians or even the Netherlanders, which explains the similarity of their reactions to Caravaggio, and the difficulty of making satisfactory attributions to individual painters.

None of the young French painters who were to turn to Caravaggism was fully trained on arrival in Rome, and almost all of them set about imitating the works of Caravaggio which they could see in the churches around them. Nobody in Rome at the time can have had any idea of Caravaggio's rapid stylistic and psychological development once he had left the city (in 1606) for Malta and subsequently Sicily, and the works executed during his two visits to Naples also remained isolated. It seems as if only Nicolas Tournier, on his return to France and establishment in Toulouse, was able to approach the tragic intensity of mood of Caravaggio's late pictures, although it was extremely unlikely that he knew them. The work of Caravaggio was the catalyst for the continuous experiments made by many of the French painters working in Rome in the 1620s, especially Le Valentin and Simon Vouet.

Caravaggio's was not the only influence, though: Italian followers of Caravaggio in Rome, many of whom had known Caravaggio personally, were themselves extremely influential. The Italians reacted to Caravaggio in much more diverse ways than did the French, and the three most obviously separate streams are characterized by painters as different from one another as Orazio Gentileschi, Carlo Saraceni and Bartolommeo Manfredi. Saraceni was the most eccentric of these three and had the most significant influence on two Frenchmen, Jean Le Clerc, with whom he collaborated, and Guy François, who was to assimilate his style completely. Gentileschi, on the other hand, was a very much more consistent artist than Saraceni, and transformed Caravaggio's brutalism into something of greater elegance and allure, with brighter colours and greater surface polish. Gentileschi seems to have been the main influence on Simon Vouet before the latter left for Paris in 1627. The most severe and pervasive of the three artists was the more obscure Manfredi, who specialized in painting concert parties and gambling scenes in heavy shadow. Many of his works were formerly thought to be by Caravaggio, and their influence can be found in almost all the French painters, including Vignon. (Manfredi was equally important for the Netherlanders, being the stylistic ancestor of an enormous number of Caravaggesque genre scenes painted in both the northern and southern Netherlands.)

In this distinctly international style, it is difficult, but not impossible, to distinguish one French painter from another, and the Italian followers of Caravaggio also show a discernible stylistic unity. It is usually possible to detect the French by their much greater sentimentality and idiosyncratic use of colour, as, for example, in Vignon's *Croesus and Solon* in the Bowes Museum, Barnard Castle (figure 3). Vignon's colour is always irrational, even in his Caravaggesque pictures; cherry reds clash with lime greens, the whole being heightened with pale lilac highlights. Even the severe Le Valentin favoured exquisite smoky blues contrasted with various subtle reds. Vouet's colours were simply brighter and lighter than the Italians' in his Roman period, but after his return to Paris his pink and blue colour schemes seemed to anticipate those of François Boucher in the eighteenth century.

Almost all French Caravaggesque pictures are sweeter in mood than those of the Italians, although there are exceptions, especially with Tournier in Toulouse and even Tassel in Langres. Only Le Valentin stands out as being capable of a certain toughness of sentiment, particularly when his work is compared to the compositions of Simon Vouet (such as the elegant *Martha and Mary* in the Kunsthistorisches Museum, Vienna). Subject-matter was also limited, and not only in pictures whose subjects were dictated by specific commissions from churches. When painting by themselves for sale on the open market, most French painters concentrated on some form of genre on a large scale. The most favoured were low-life concert parties, gambling scenes and fortune tellers. Even religious pictures tended to depict subjects which could be treated in a Bohemian manner, such as *The Denial of Peter*.

It is impossible to reconstruct the artistic background of those painters who

FIGURE 3
Claude Vignon
Croesus and Solon (Croesus Showing Solon his Treasures) (fragment)
Canvas, 82 × 102 cm.
Barnard Castle, Bowes Museum
Bought by John Bowes in Paris in 1861.

Formerly attributed to Rembrandt, the picture is an interesting example of how close Vignon came to the manner of Lastman in Amsterdam in the 1620s. The picture has been cut in half, thus losing the 'treasures' which Croesus is showing Solon. The king is then reminded by Solon that his wealth is worthless when happiness is desired.

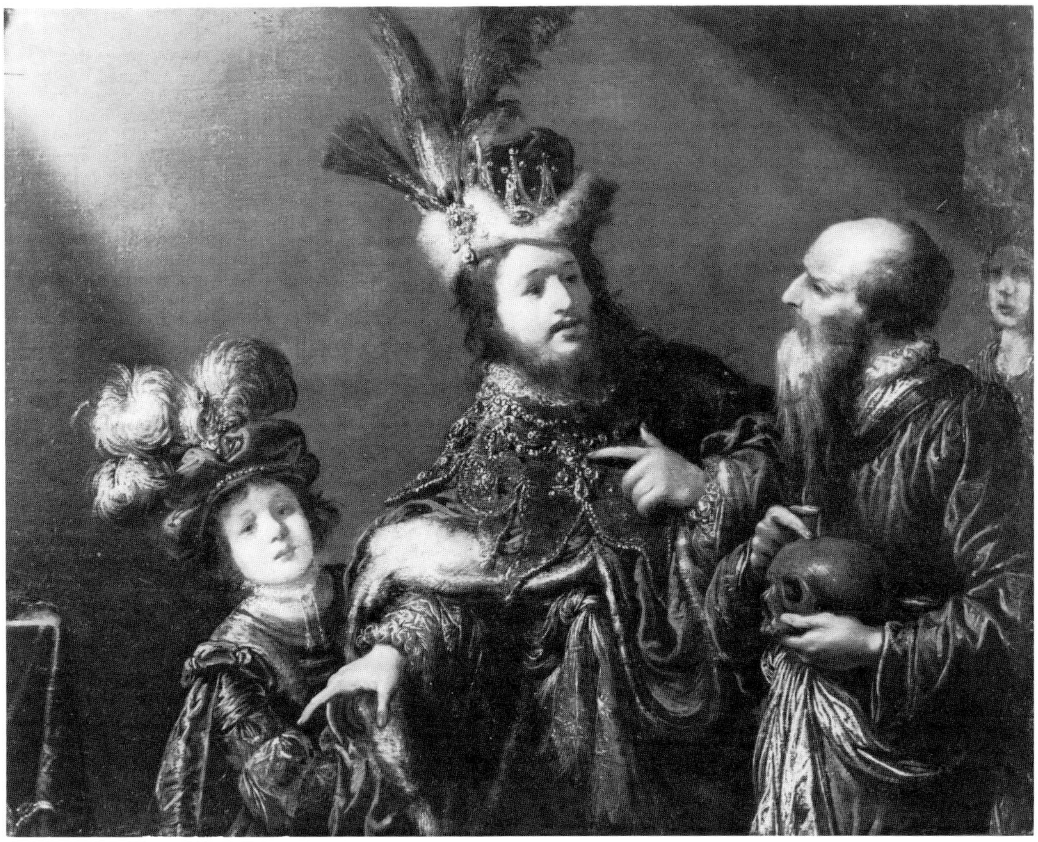

did not receive official commissions, because of the lack of documentation. In almost every instance it is much easier to follow the artists' careers once they had returned to their native France, because of their relative isolation in each of the centres to which they returned. In Rome, there must inevitably be speculation about what went on in the 1620s in their artistic backwater. Certainly most of the painters knew one another (later, Claude and Poussin were to be friendly neighbours), jostled for the few commissions and carried on feuds. It is likely that each national group maintained a certain identity, although Poussin abandoned his French manner of dress following an attack in the street, in which he defended himself with his portfolio. The Dutch, for instance, formed themselves into a group known as the Benteveughels, but the French were not so well organized.

One possible explanation for the consistency of the French painters in following Caravaggio in the 1620s is that they could not hope to rival the achievements of their Italian contemporaries: their provincial backgrounds denied them the complex training needed in order to be able to execute a ceiling painting. They saw that low-life genre in the Caravaggesque idiom still had a certain market which was no longer filled by the active Dutch, for the chief exponents of this style had all returned to the Dutch Republic by 1622.

Virtually no documents survive for pictures that were not official commissions, and surviving inventories of prestigious collections, such as that of the Barberini or of Poussin's patron Cassiano dal Pozzo, are very difficult to interpret after three and a half centuries. It is possible to determine from these early inventories the type of painting favoured by the collector, but often not easy to identify the actual pictures today. From the evidence relating to the very few commissioned pictures which have survived, we know that some time before 1620 Simon Vouet received a commission to paint an important altarpiece for the Roman church of S. Lorenzo in Lucina, and that Le Valentin received one for St Peter's in 1628; and both these works survive. In contrast, no picture by Claude Vignon can be securely fixed by this method, and much of the rest of the work of Le Valentin and Vouet has to be identified on stylistic considerations alone. The confusion is made worse by the fact that numerous records survive of other French painters active in Rome whose work has not come down to us, or is known only from a single inscribed example, like that of Henri Traivoel who painted a superb portrait very much in the manner of Vouet. Sometimes even the documents have been confused, or they have been misinterpreted in their relationship to the pictures which have survived. The most notorious case of this kind is the documentary proof that a picture in a Roman church, consistently given to Bigot on stylistic grounds, is by another as yet unidentified artist, 'Maestro Jacopo'. To compound the error it has been suggested that the pictures attributed to Bigot, and proved to be connected with his activity in France, are also by 'Maestro Jacopo'.

Of all the French painters active in Rome in the 1620s, the most consistent, and the only one who can be claimed to have genius, is Le Valentin. He died relatively young in 1634, without leaving Rome. His influence on other painters was minimal, and he seems to have been a somewhat isolated figure, but later in the century his pictures were collected by Louis XIV, by which time they had already come into the category of old masters. Le Valentin's career has to be reconstructed round his documented Vatican altarpiece, which is a mature work. Many of his earlier pictures, painted when he was much closer in spirit to Caravaggio, have remained unidentified until recently. The best example of his early work is the Dresden *Card Sharps* (figure 6), which is based on a similar composition by Caravaggio (unfortunately missing since the late nineteenth century, when it was recorded in the Rothschild collection). In the Dresden picture Le Valentin has seized on the evil nature of the villain, creating an obvious story completely lacking in subtlety, but delicacy is shown in his handling of the paint which, as always in his work, is very much more refined than that of Caravaggio.

In spite of some slackening of intensity as he grew older, Le Valentin's stylistic consistency makes his chronology difficult. The commission for St Peter's is the only really important one of his whole career, and is of interest because the artist modified his largely tenebrist style to suit the situation. The subject, a gruesome one, is of the *Martyrdom of St Processus and St Martinian* (figure 4). It was subsequently replaced by a mosaic, the original being moved to the Pinacoteca Vaticana. A possible reason for the lightening of the artist's style is the fact that the picture had to match the already completed *Martyrdom of St Erasmus* (figure 5) by the young Nicolas Poussin, who had in turn modified his style towards a much more Caravaggesque approach, especially in his realistic treatment of the gruesome subject-matter. Neither painter received such a commission again, and these two altarpieces stand out in their respective careers, proving that young French artists did appeal to influential people – in this case officials of the Papacy – with the money to give commissions. It could also be argued that this was because by the end of the 1620s pure Caravaggism as such was already out of fashion among all

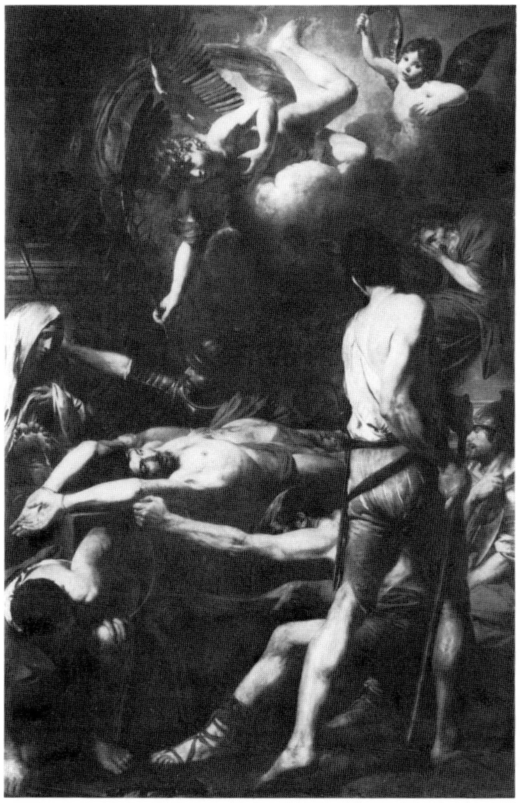

FIGURE 4 (right)
Le Valentin
The Martyrdom of St Processus and St Martinian
Canvas, 308 × 165 cm. Signed
Rome, Pinacoteca Vaticana
Documented 1629–30.
This was Le Valentin's only important commission, and it flanked Poussin's *Martyrdom of St Erasmus*, completed the previous year, in St Peter's.

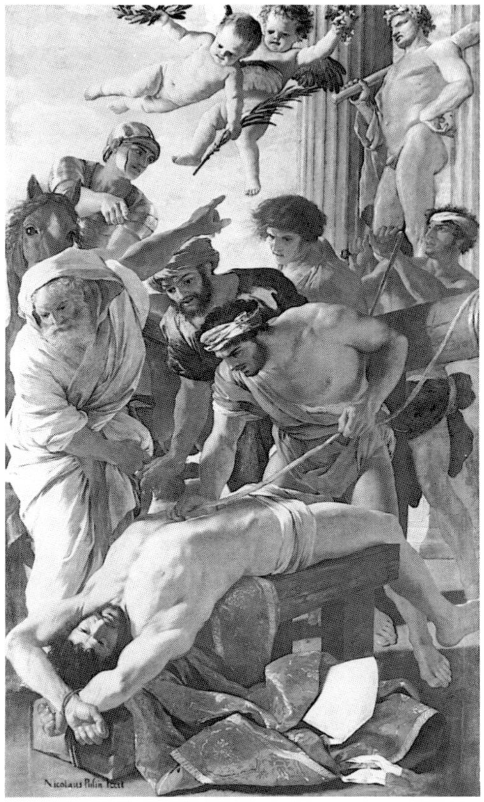

FIGURE 5 (far right)
Nicolas Poussin
The Martyrdom of St Erasmus
Canvas, 320 × 186 cm. Signed: Nicolaus Pusin Fecit.
Rome, Pinacoteca Vaticana
Commissioned for St Peter's in Rome in 1628. Later transferred to the Vatican and replaced by a mosaic.

The subject, an early Christian martyrdom, is one that is rarely depicted.

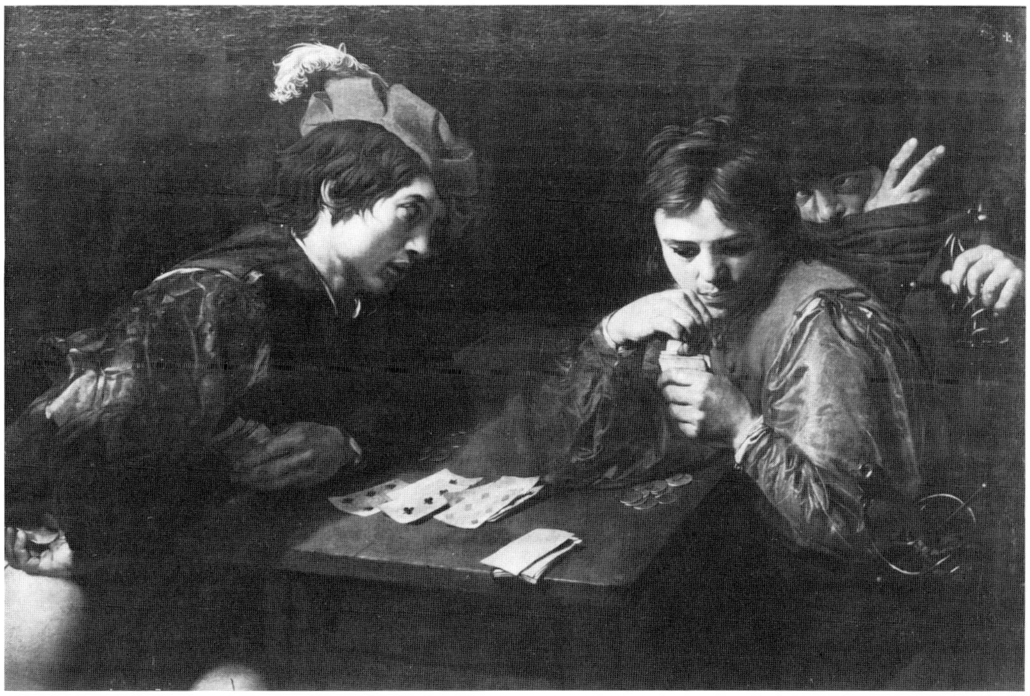

FIGURE 6
Le Valentin
The Card Sharps
Canvas, 94 × 137 cm.
Dresden, Gemäldegalerie
Acquired by the Elector of Saxony from the Imperial Gallery in Prague in 1749.

The subject is derived from Caravaggio's much-copied version, the original of which is now lost.

the successful Italian painters working in Rome. The full Baroque was developing, with Guercino and Pietro da Cortona as two of its leading exponents, and the radical changes among the Italians were to have a far-reaching effect, if only in the form of violent reaction, on some French artists.

Le Valentin's mature style of about 1630 was therefore already slightly out of fashion, but it was at this time that he produced some of his best pictures. One of these is the *Fortune Teller* in the Louvre, a painting which belonged to Louis XIV. The artist has, as usual, concentrated on the low-life aspect of the subject – a gypsy telling fortunes to a hapless youth – yet the refinement of the tones and delicacy of the brushwork raise the painting above those of all his contemporaries in these respects. (The only Italian to achieve such refinement, although it was of a different character, was Gentileschi.) On a much more intimate scale is Le Valentin's *Judith with the Head of Holofernes* in the Musée des Augustins at Toulouse. Though a terrifying subject, the picture has lost all vestige of Caravaggio's brutality, which is replaced by a gentle refinement of both tone and colour.

The only works showing Le Valentin's influence are a coherent group of genre and religious pictures, mostly of concert parties. In recent years they have been detached from Le Valentin, to whom they were mostly attributed, and given to Nicolas Tournier, in the reasonable possibility of representing what he painted when in Rome, but there is no convincing evidence, other than stylistic, either for or against this hypothesis. The main difficulty is Tournier's known development in Toulouse towards a much closer understanding of Caravaggio's mentality. The pictures now given to Tournier take up Le Valentin's compositions and even his models, but are painted in a much more wooden yet polished manner. One of the best examples is the *Concert Party* in the Art Museum of St Louis. Here, the flesh tones are much less realistic and the draperies harder than in the more subtle interpretations of Le Valentin.

In comparing the Roman period of Simon Vouet with that of Le Valentin there may be a sense of disappointment because, although he was prolific and competent, Vouet's pictures lack the mystery of those of Le Valentin. Vouet had no special position of influence during his Roman years; it was only on his return to Paris that he was to assume importance, both in the training of pupils and in the execution of his many extensive decorative cycles for town houses. Nevertheless, Vouet was the most versatile of all the French painters in Rome in the 1620s. As with Le Valentin, his earliest pictures are the closest to those of Caravaggio, especially the brilliant *Liberation of St Peter* in S. Lorenzo in Lucina, but with the exception of this work Vouet's art lacked almost all Caravaggio's sense of drama; nor did he learn anything from Le Valentin's beautiful textures. Instead, he concentrated on flashy and facile effects, which were, of course, to stand him in good stead at the court of Louis XIII, where he was to become the first French painter to be able to understand and interpret the Italian Baroque. He left Caravaggism behind him in Rome. Vouet was good, nonetheless, at lighting effects and sharp contrasts of colour, and an example of this is his *Martha and Mary* in the Kunsthistorisches Museum, Vienna. Also of his Roman period, the *St Jerome and the Angel* (plate 86) in the National Gallery of Art, Washington, is devoid of the drama which marks Caravaggio's *St Matthew and the Angel*. Vouet relied much more on his technique of strong lighting and bold brushwork, and was never interested in penetrating the essence of his subject-matter.

A much more difficult artist to define during his Roman years is Claude Vignon. Chameleon-like, his pictures are still being extricated from the great numbers of Italian Caravaggesque paintings, even though pictures from his later years in France are curiously easy to recognize. In Rome, Vignon seems to have been self-effacing, adopting with competence the mannerisms of his French contemporaries. In his portraiture he was close to Simon Vouet, as is shown in the *Portrait of a Man* that was in the collection of the Earls Spencer at Althorp, Northamptonshire. The only way in which some of Vignon's work differs from that of his contemporaries is in his lighter and more delicate handling of paint.

Although a few masterpieces were produced by Le Valentin and some interesting work was done by Vignon and Vouet, in the general context of Roman painting at the time French artists played a very small part indeed. They were overshadowed by the far more numerous Netherlanders, both Dutch and Flemish, who had a much greater technical facility and were especially good at producing small, highly finished pictures which were much prized by Italian patrons. Only a very few Frenchmen, chiefly those who had not subscribed to Caravaggism, chose to remain in Rome after the 1620s. Notable among them were the illustrious Claude Lorrain and Nicolas Poussin, who in the late 1620s were already evolving highly personal styles that were to find patronage.

One of the less obvious effects upon the French in Italy was their exposure to Italian methods of studio practice. Little is known about these, because at the time few writers thought them worth recording. In Italy the process of producing pictures was more or less controlled: although the guild system had virtually disappeared and had been replaced by the Accademia di San Luca, aspiring painters were subjected to a rigid apprenticeship system in which they learned the complex techniques of their craft. The physical effort and powers of organization required to paint a large altarpiece or to cover a ceiling were enormous, and had to be learned laboriously by means of a fully fledged master teaching his pupil. In northern Europe, including France, such things were less well organized. Pictures tended to be much smaller and the painters' approach more individualistic. The guilds had much greater control in the north, especially when it came to the right to sell completed work. In France itself there was a mixture of systems which only became standardized under Louis XIV. Vouet introduced to Paris an Italian-inspired system of teaching, quite different from what must have prevailed before, when the main efforts of Parisian painters had been directed at stopping the alien Netherlanders from undercutting them. The Netherlanders overcame this problem by installing themselves on the other side of the river in St Germain-des-Prés, outside the jurisdiction of the City of Paris. The rigidity of the Italian system brought to Paris by Vouet is far less obvious outside the capital, although it is known that Georges de La Tour in Lunéville in Lorraine occasionally took on apprentices (none of whom subsequently made reputations as painters in their own right). Parents had to pay La Tour considerable sums for the privilege of having him instruct their sons, but, instead of teaching them how to paint, it seems that he employed them merely as studio assistants.

The tight control of artistic practice which characterized the reign of Louis XIV (discussed in Chapter Six) is well documented, but each case before the 1660s has to be judged on the much more meagre evidence available, and this lack of knowledge makes the task very difficult. It seems unlikely, for instance, that Claude Vignon, in Rome from about 1616 to 1624, followed precisely all the rules governing the making and selling of a work of art while he was there. The Dutch were better organized, as competition burgeoned in the 1620s chiefly because the number of painters active in Rome increased.

The departure of so many painters from Rome was to change the whole course of painting in France and Lorraine, although their disappearance from Italy would have been little noticed at the time.

The Influence of Caravaggio on the French Provinces and Lorraine

Almost all the French painters who returned from Rome in the 1620s went back to the towns or provinces where they had been born. The main exception was Nicolas Tournier, who settled in Toulouse, a great distance from his native Franche-Comté. Bigot returned to Provence, Jean Tassel to Burgundy, Guy François to Le Puy, Vignon and Vouet to Paris, and Le Clerc left Venice and returned to his native Nancy. With the single exception of Paris, into which Vouet imported the new Baroque style instead of the Caravaggism he had been practising in Rome, each centre suddenly received an injection of Caravaggism, which was quite new to France, from an energetic generation of fashionable young artists trained in Rome. It is difficult now to realize the impact this had on the homespun Mannerism of the local painters who were at a stroke rendered obsolete. Lorraine in this case was an exception because of the specific tastes of the court there.

Each main centre of population (and therefore of patronage) had its own special characteristics which are visible even today. Medieval Toulouse, for example, was very different from the modest town of Nancy at the same period; indeed the differences between the main towns in the early seventeenth century were so great that it would have been impossible to predict in which centres the painters influenced by Caravaggio would flourish. However, they had a few characteristics in common. Every centre was isolated from Paris and no influences from the capital are discernible throughout the first half of the century. All the external stylistic influences are Italian or Netherlandish. No town needed to import a Parisian painter; even in the capital the French were having difficulty in gaining commissions, which usually went to foreigners (Rubens, Van Dyck, Fouquières, Pourbus, Gentileschi).

It is also reasonable to suggest, but difficult to prove, that most of the centres where painting was to flourish underwent an increase in prosperity in the early part of the seventeenth century. For Nancy the inventories of the better-off indicate a high standard of living, with table linen and silver vessels being quite common in merchants' houses (such things would have been a rarity in England at that time). Many people had pictures in their houses purely for decoration rather than as part of an art collection: in the hundreds of surviving inventories for Nancy alone in the first half of the seventeenth century, it is rare for an artist's name to be mentioned. That there was considerable wealth even in these quite small places is indicated by the success of Guy François in the environs of Le Puy, and by the patronage of Georges de La Tour by the municipal authorities of the small town of Lunéville, which can have had hardly more than three thousand inhabitants (in significant contrast to the Netherlands, where the town of Delft, by no means the largest town in the Dutch Republic, had a population of some thirty thousand).

The existence of painters in these relatively small communities – Toulouse, Dijon and Aix-en-Provence were larger – is proof enough of a sudden maturity of taste on the part of patrons. This was to disappear equally rapidly after the middle of the century, as every form of artistic activity was then concentrated on Paris. After 1660 there seems to have been little significant artistic activity in any of the main centres, with the exception of Aix-en Provence where the emphasis became increasingly Baroque.

The artistic isolation of each centre is emphasized by the fact that no painter made any radical changes of artistic style after returning from Italy. Some, such as Tournier in Toulouse, died young, but both Guy François in Le Puy and Jean Tassel in Langres and Dijon lived long enough to show that they doggedly continued to turn out what they had learned in their youth. There was to be no sudden burst of genius in old age: instead they watered down their talents to suit a blander era, and no attempt was made to learn new styles. Thus Bigot in Aix and Arles, Jacques de l'Estin in Troyes and Daret in Aix all fell victim to the changing times as they grew older, and their art fell into obscurity even in their own lifetimes.

It is paradoxical that Georges de La Tour, the one artist working in a centre outside Paris and now recognized as a genius, never had the extended Italian experience of his contemporaries. His art, it appears, grew on his native soil and was all the better for it. Yet Georges de La Tour must not be allowed to claim all the limelight: Tournier created a few masterpieces of pure Caravaggism in Toulouse, and the eccentric Tassel was capable of a hypersensitive feeling in his art; and both these painters are underestimated.

Toulouse

Toulouse has been an important city since the Middle Ages, and its wealth of architecture dating from the eleventh century onwards is eloquent proof of this. The art of painting is a much less important factor of the city's cultural history, but a number of painters were active there, especially in the seventeenth , eighteenth and early nineteenth centuries.

The earliest painter of significance in Toulouse for whom there are adequate surviving records is Jean Chalette. He visited Italy as a young man but no work is known from his time there. His few surviving drawings show a provincial Mannerism not unlike that of Jacques Callot, while his paintings seem much more 'modern'. His *Virgin of the Prisoners* (figure 7) in the Musée des Augustins at Toulouse is Italian-inspired in composition and colouring, and the debt to Caravaggio is discernible in the intense realism of the prisoners' heads. It is a rare surviving example of a provincial painter's work of the time.

Chalette's commissioned work was of a very different nature, but it can only be glimpsed through the surviving drawings, which include the elaborate frontispiece he designed for the Aix-en-Provence collector Peiresc (Bibliothèque Inguimbertine, Carpentras). He earned the esteem of his patrons in Toulouse with an astonishing series of group portraits, one executed each year, of the *capitouls* (magistrates) of the town. None of the huge finished pictures survives, but Chalette always provided a miniature of the whole composition which was inserted into the municipal accounts. There most of them escaped the destroyers of all images of the official past at the time of the Revolution of 1789. It is from these miniatures, a drawing (figure 9) and the *Capitouls of Toulouse for the Years 1622-3* in the Musée des Augustins (figure 8),

FIGURE 7
Jean Chalette
The Virgin of the Prisoners
Canvas, 158 × 118 cm.
Toulouse, Musée des Augustins
Originally painted for the Capitole at Toulouse, and transferred to the museum at the time of the Revolution of 1789.

A unique subject, possibly painted for a prison chapel.

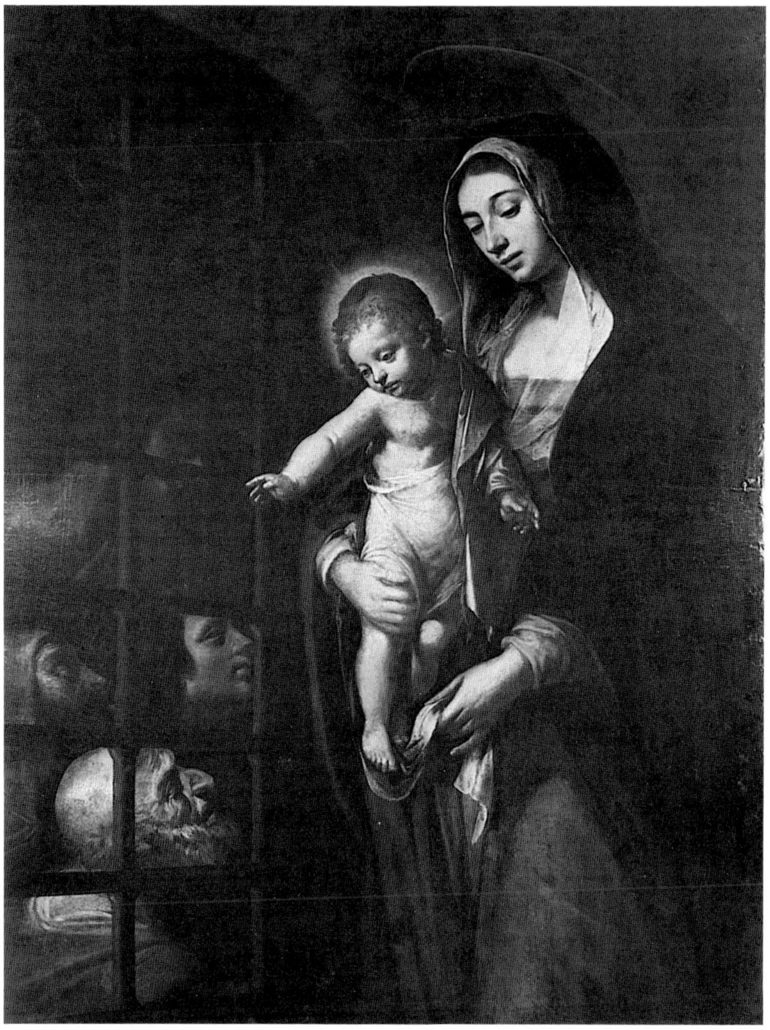

that an idea may be gained of the grandeur of these human instruments of justice. In scale and splendour they would have rivalled the group portraits executed in the Dutch Republic (although Chalette did not have the psychological perception or brilliance of technique of, say, Frans Hals). Chalette's work is especially precious because of the rarity of surviving examples of group portraiture. Apart from earlier works in Narbonne and one inferior picture in the Musée Fabrégat at Béziers, nothing survives except the *Group Portrait of the Échevins of Paris* by the Parisian Georges Lallemant in the Musée Carnavalet in Paris, and the fragment by Philippe de Champaigne in the Wallace Collection, London, from later in the century.

Although Chalette can be described as the most important painter working in Toulouse in the 1620s in terms of the scale on which he was patronized, the painter with the greatest artistic ability was undoubtedly Nicolas Tournier. New information shows that Tournier died relatively young in or before 1639, and not thirty years later as was formerly thought. In the confines of Toulouse, dominated by the hieratic Chalette, Tournier's style was indeed advanced. It seems that he abandoned painting his concert parties – if, indeed, they are by him – and concentrated on religious pictures on the scale of large altarpieces for local convents, and he also painted one large group portrait – *The Entry of Louis XIII into Carcassonne* – which was destroyed during the Revolution.

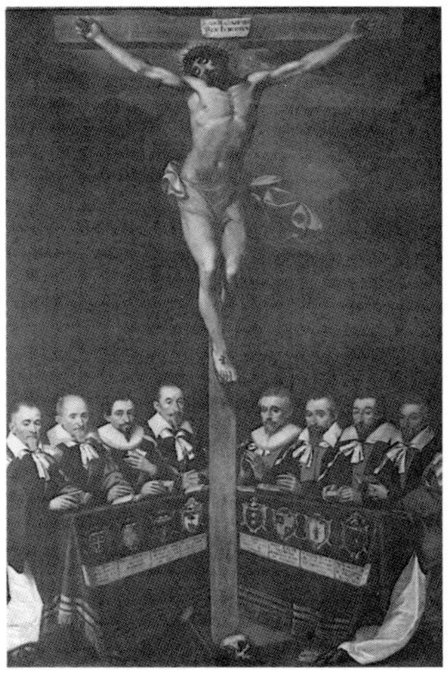

FIGURE 8 (above)
Jean Chalette
The Capitouls of Toulouse for the Years 1622–3 with Christ on the Cross
Canvas, 375 × 245 cm.
Toulouse, Musée des Augustins
Painted by Chalette for the chapel of the Capitole of Toulouse, this is the only large group-portrait by him to survive. It was removed to the museum during the Revolution of 1789.

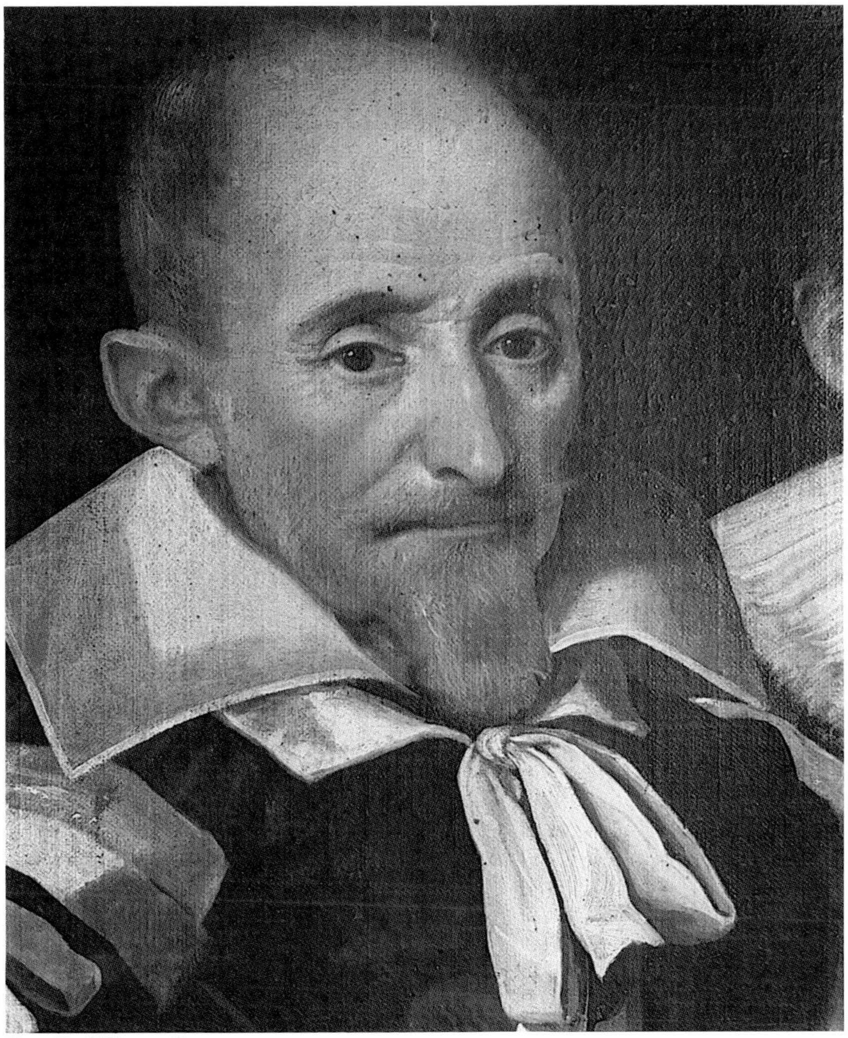

Detail of Figure 8

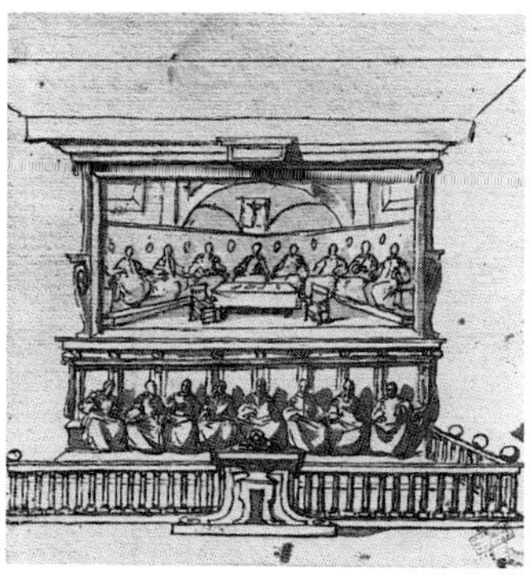

FIGURE 9 (above)
Jean Chalette
The Capitouls of Toulouse in Session before their Portrait by Chalette, 1629–30
Drawing: pen and indian ink wash, 24.7 × 18.2 cm.
Toulouse, Musée Paul-Dupuy
Presumably in the Toulouse collection since it was made.

The painting behind the *capitouls* is lost, but the miniature of it survives in the municipal archives.

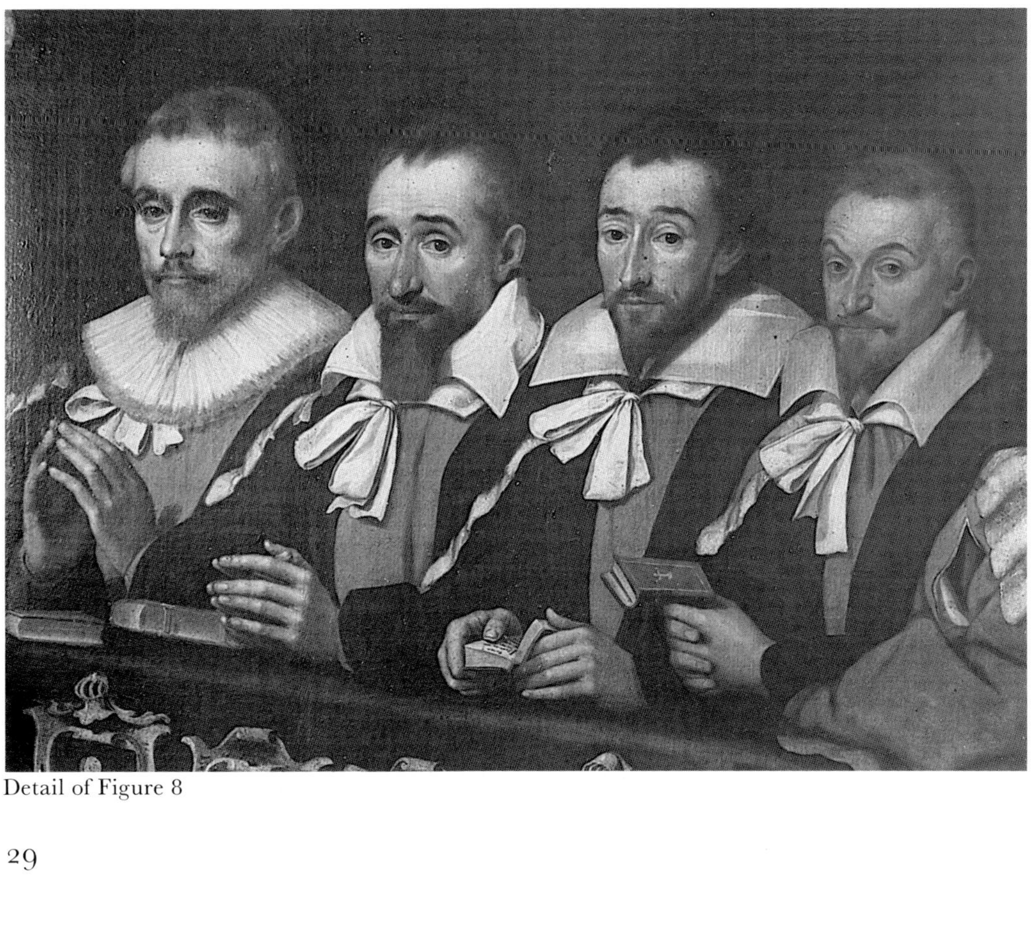

Detail of Figure 8

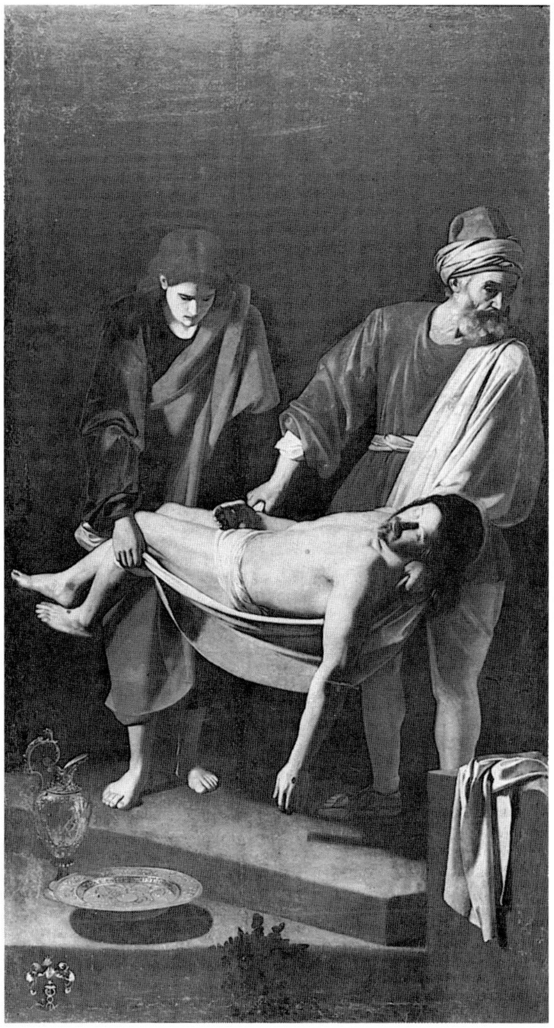

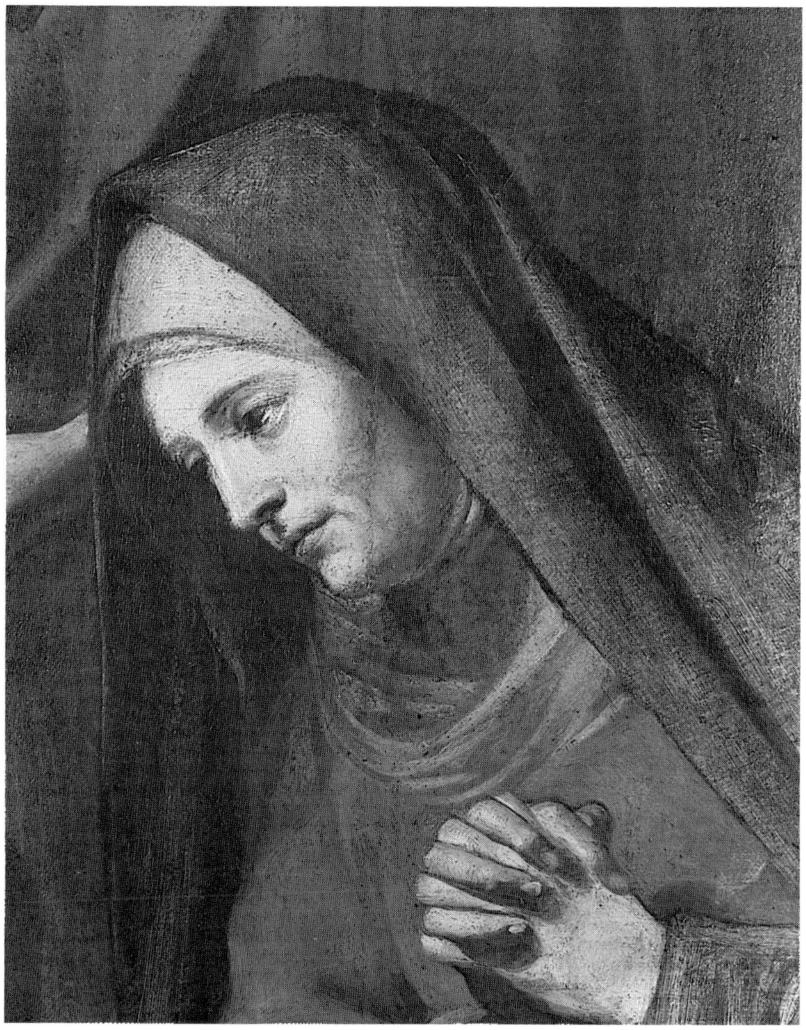

FIGURE 10 (above)
Nicolas Tournier
The Deposition from the Cross
Canvas, 335 × 178 cm.
Toulouse, Musée des Augustins
Presumably painted for the cathedral of St-Etienne at Toulouse. Entered the museum at the time of the Revolution of 1789.

FIGURE 11 (above right)
Nicolas Tournier
Entombment (detail of plate 83)
Toulouse, Musée des Augustins

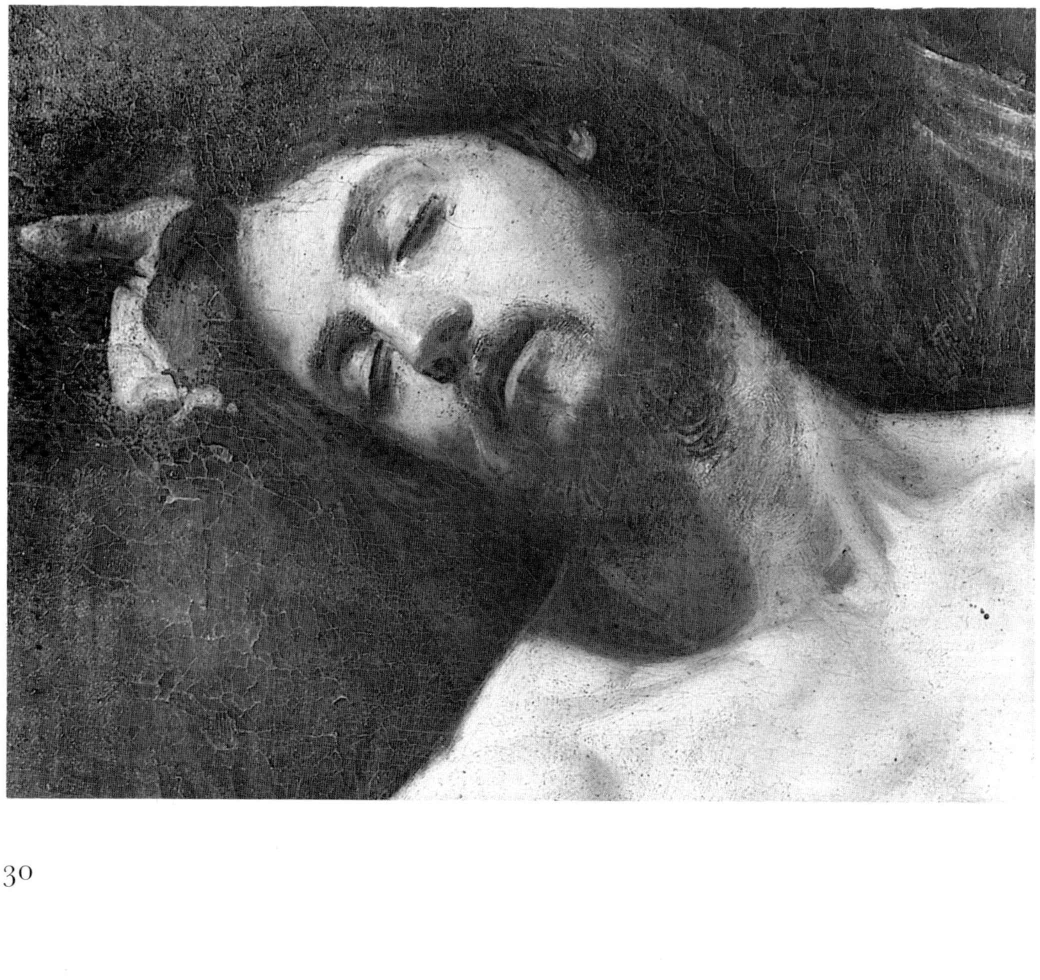

Another detail of plate 83 (right)

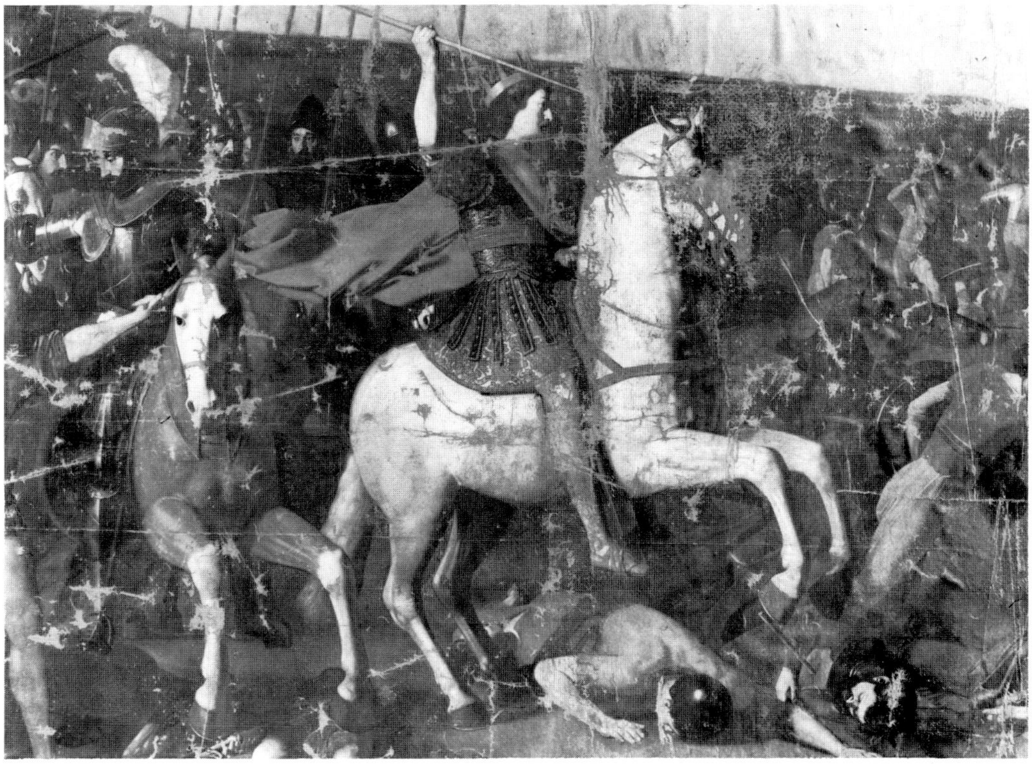

FIGURE 12
Nicolas Tournier
The Battle of Constantine (detail)
Canvas, 260 × 550 cm.
Toulouse, Musée des Augustins
Painted for the chapel of the Pénitents Noirs at Toulouse. Rediscovered in 1861 in the cellar of the convent of the Augustins, Toulouse, in a damaged state.

The treatment here is similar to that in the celebrated fresco by Piero della Francesca in San Francesco at Arezzo.

Tournier was the only French painter to employ a dramatic force equal to that of Caravaggio. Most of his pictures are not in good condition and are often difficult to judge, but it is possible to see that he favoured simple pyramidal compositions with dramatic lighting which seem, surprisingly enough, to be inspired by Caravaggio's last compositions painted in Sicily, which Tournier can hardly have known in Rome. The *Deposition from the Cross* (figure 10), in the Musée des Augustins, lacks the inhibitions and decorative preoccupations found in almost all other Caravaggesque pictures except those by Le Valentin. Tournier imagined the true pathos of the scene: the face of Christ is worthy of Caravaggio, so intense is the expression and so obviously felt the emotion. The surrounding figures relate perfectly to the dominant figure of Christ. The *Entombment* (plate 83 and figure 11) is equally intense, and Tournier's stature can be judged by these two pictures alone.

A little of Tournier's other work survives, and the most interesting by far is the colossal *Battle of Constantine* (figure 12), also in the Musée des Augustins. It comes as a shock to note that the influences on the composition are of the Italian quattrocento, especially those of Piero della Francesca and Paolo Uccello, two painters whose reputations stood extremely low in the seventeenth century. Tournier did not hesitate to borrow compositional elements from different sources in order to create a monumental composition: his own brand of Caravaggism was obviously unsuited to such a large canvas.

The deaths of both Chalette and Tournier in the 1630s left Toulouse with no artistic momentum. There was no new generation of painters trained in Italy to continue their inventiveness and grandeur of scale. The *capitouls* continued to be painted, but not on such a scale, and the tradition died out early in the eighteenth century. That this flash of near-genius was so brief can be explained in part by the fact that, like many other centres, Toulouse had no training system to perpetuate the artistic experience gained in Italy with such effort.

Le Puy

Le Puy is the capital of the Haute Loire, part of a large upland area, the Massif Central, in the southern central region of France. The large number of Romanesque churches in and around the town bear testimony to the fact that it flourished in the Middle Ages. It was never an area noted for painting activity, and the return of Guy François from Rome to his native region was therefore to be of great significance in local terms, much more so than similar events in other centres where there was more than one painter active. Guy François was to work in isolation for more than thirty years, gradually diluting his art as memories of what he had learned in Rome faded. The pictures that he painted in France nearly all remain in and around Le Puy.

It is only in recent years that the Italian period of Guy François has been reconstructed and his Italian pictures disentangled from the work of Carlo Saraceni (though there is still some dispute about the *St Cecilia* in the Galleria Corsini, Rome). Saraceni, a difficult artist to define, was essentially eclectic, with an unusual skill in brushwork almost akin to that of a northener. He assimilated many influences, ranging from Caravaggio to the German Elsheimer. The picture by François that most shows the influence of Saraceni is the *Holy Family with St Bruno and St Elisabeth*, now in the Musée de l'Ain at Bourg-en-Bresse. Like much of François' work, it was intended as a large altarpiece. His altarpieces that have survived in the Le Puy area, in the churches for which they were painted, are often surrounded by a provincial version of a sculptured and stuccoed framework in the Italian Baroque style. Although commonplace in Italy, such pictures *in situ* are rare in France; most seventeenth-century altarpieces by the major painters are now in museums. The *Holy Family* altarpiece has the simplified forms sometimes found in works by Saraceni and also the strong lighting suitable for a prominent position in a church, where the picture would normally be seen from a distance.

The strength of some of Guy François' compositions has led some authorities to suggest that he was influenced by Nicolas Tournier, but the most likely explanations for their superficial similarity are that both artists brought back with them from Italy similar Caravaggesque influences, and that both of them were forced to rely on what they had experienced and learned without renewed contact with their sources. Both painters had a predilection for monumental scale, although François never achieved Tournier's dramatic intensity. Instead he provided, in an area isolated from all artistic contact, a whole group of soundly painted and striking altarpieces.

Aix-en-Provence and Arles

The area of France near the Mediterranean coast is very different from all the other parts of the country, in climate, geography and cultural history, and it is the only part of the country close to Italy that had ties with ancient Greece (Marseilles had been a Greek port). The ties with Rome, and consequently with Italian artists, had been close during the papal exile in Avignon in the fourteenth century. The Gothic style of northern France had never penetrated the area effectively, which meant that the churches of the south had a much greater proportion of wall to glass than did those of the north, and this made them more suitable for embellishment with altarpieces and painted decorations.

The old towns of Avignon, Arles and Aix-en-Provence were the main centres in the region in the seventeenth century. Marseilles was rapidly expanding, but seems to have been dependent on artists travelling from Aix. As might be expected from the pattern shown by the rest of France, the early seventeenth century produced little artistic activity of any consequence. There had been an enormous amount of activity in the same region in the late fifteenth century, when several painters of great ability worked in the area (Enguerrand Charenton at Avignon and the Master of the Aix Annunciation at Aix), but none of this past activity appears to have been relevant to what was happening in 1600, when the only painter to be found working in the area was Trophîme Bigot the Elder. Bigot concentrated on painting altarpieces for churches in Arles in a curiously naïve style, which demonstrated his inability to digest even the most elementary poses from Italian art and to put them together in a coherent composition.

The artistic scene was therefore transformed dramatically by the arrival of Louis Finson (Lodovicus Finsonius) from Rome in 1613. He was obviously proud of his Flemish origins, as his birthplace, Bruges, often appears inscribed on his work along with his signature. The fact that Finson was one of the first followers of Caravaggio to arrive in France is usually overlooked, perhaps because he chose to interpret Caravaggio's art in such a peculiar and personal way. A few of his surviving pictures, such as the copy of a lost Caravaggio, *The Penitent Magdalen* and the *Self-portrait* (equally close to Caravaggio in spirit), both in the Palais Longchamp at Marseilles, are conventional enough, and had only these two works survived Finson would be considered a pure Caravaggesque. However, in the altarpieces Finson painted for the churches in Arles, there appears a self-conscious rejection of all that the artist had learned in Italy. For example, the *Annunciation* in St Trophîme in Arles does not fit into any category, with its primitive forms and hieratic gestures, but shows a stiffness which had already been abandoned in the North in the early fifteenth century. It is just possible that the local patrons wanted pictures that would not seem out of harmony with the large number of earlier works adorning the churches. (These were mostly dispersed at the time of the French Revolution, and only the Madeleine and the cathedral at Aix keep some of their fifteenth-century pictures *in situ*.)

The other two painters active in the area in the first half of the seventeenth century were equally idiosyncratic. The most important was Jean Daret, whose career was centred on Aix. His *Self-portrait* in the Hermitage, Leningrad (figure 13) is convincingly Italianate, and could have been executed by any young Italian painter of the time working under the influence of Caravaggio; Daret's self-analysis has a brooding and melancholic intensity that was the fashion at the time, especially in Rome. The same intensity is found in pictures stylistically as different from one another as Domenichino's *Portrait of Monsignor Agucchi* in the City Art Gallery at York and Bernini's youthful *Self-portrait* in the Galleria Borghese, Rome. The pictures of Daret's Italian period have not been satisfactorily identified, but we know that in Aix-en-Provence he succeeded as a major decorative painter, rather than as a painter of intimate portraits which would have had a very narrow market. Almost all Daret's surviving pictures are elaborate decorations for town houses and

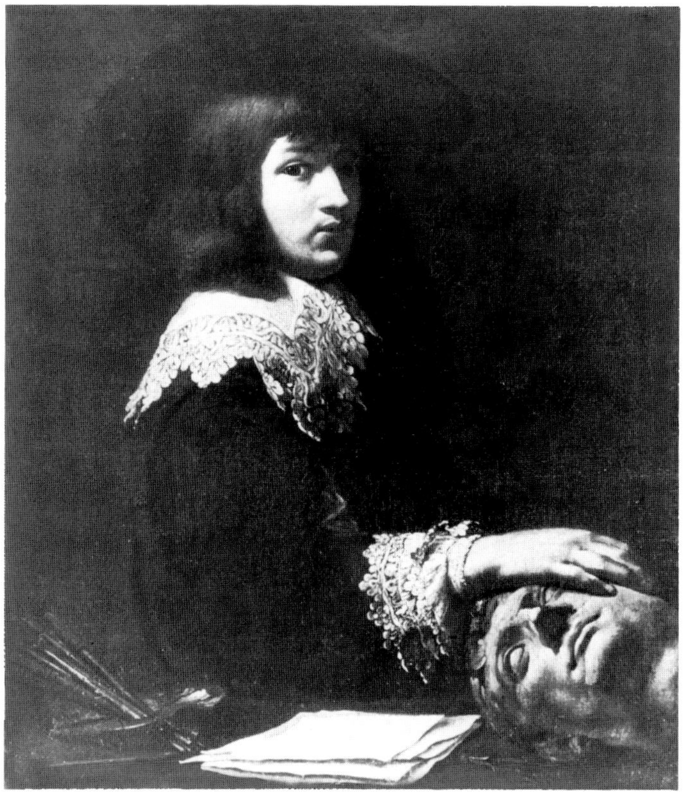

FIGURE 13
Jean Daret
Self-portrait
Canvas, 78 × 66 cm. Signed and dated: J. Daret fecit 1636. aetatis sue 21.
Leningrad, Hermitage.
The Italian influence on this self-portrait is especially strong.

churches in Aix, and are largely based on Italian models, especially works by Domenichino and Guido Reni.

The third painter of significance in this early period is especially interesting because of his bizarre subject-matter. His actual name is still controversial, however; a number of pictures in the Aix area have been identified as by him, and his name appears as Trophîme Bigot in the caption of an engraving of a lost painting of *Christ in the Carpenter's Shop* in the collection of Boyer d'Aiguilles at Aix. The style of this picture appears to have been close to the Netherlandish Caravaggesques, especially Honthorst, which implies that Bigot had worked in Rome. It seems inconceivable, purely on grounds of competence, that this Bigot is the same as the one who worked in Arles, but many authorities are reluctant to accept that there may have been two artists of the same name in the area at roughly the same time. A whole group of pictures, formerly attributed, appropriately, to 'The Candlelight Master', has been assembled round this engraved work. Even though the reconstruction of Bigot/Candlelight Master has not entirely held together because of the recent discovery that one of them is by the otherwise unknown artist 'Maestro Jacopo', there remains a considerable corpus of candlelight pictures that were probably executed both in Rome in the artist's youth and later in the Aix-en-Provence area. They astound by their subject-matter: a child singes a bat's wing (plate 4); St Sebastian collapses in the arms of the Holy Irene. Unique in French art (but common in the North) is the painting of such a subject as *A Doctor Examining Urine* in the Ashmolean Museum, Oxford (plate 3), in which the whole treatment is much closer to Netherlandish than to Italian art, with the artist using brick-red tones for the faces and concentrating on strange facial expressions. A more sympathetic side of the artist's character is to be seen in the *Boy Singing by Candlelight* in the Galleria Doria, Rome, which is much closer to an Italian model.

All three of these painters left little tradition behind them in the south, although Daret was one of the earliest exponents of decorative painting which was to flourish in Aix, reaching its height in the last third of the century. Later in the century, artists changed their styles according to each new wave of influence from Paris, as was to happen in the case of the talented Nicolas Mignard who worked in Avignon in the middle of the century. As it had been for almost two thousand years, the whole area was a receiving ground for each new wave of artistic activity, usually passing northwards from Italy but later in the century descending from Paris. only one native genius emerged, the sculptor Pierre Puget, whose few surviving paintings are sometimes on a level with those of Bernini. Puget is an exception, however: other local painters in the early years of the century were incapable of initiating ideas of their own.

Burgundy

Of all the French provinces, Burgundy had the most significant cultural history in the late Middle Ages. The capital, Dijon, had been the centre of a glittering court which ruled over what had become, by the middle of the fifteenth century, an empire that included much of the Netherlands, encompassing almost all the rich Flemish cities except Liège, which was an independent bishopric. The stability of the region came to an abrupt end with the death of Charles the Bold at the Battle of Nancy in 1477, when Burgundy was immediately absorbed into France. Artistic activity ended equally abruptly, and in the sixteenth century there were no painters of significance in Dijon. Since Burgundy, unlike nearby Lorraine, consequently no longer had a court to commission secular work, almost all the commissions had to come from the Church. In the early years of the seventeenth century Dijon supported only one painter of note, Philippe Quantin, who produced large-scale altarpieces in which there are occasional references to his knowledge of Caravaggio. His few surviving pictures fall into the same category as those of Guy François; they were designed to make a strong impact in a dark church.

On the northern edge of Burgundy, but actually in Champagne, stood the medieval city of Troyes, where the Rome-trained Jacques de l'Estin worked. After painting, probably in Rome, a *Self-portrait* now in the Musée des Beaux-Arts at Troyes (plate 57) which is after the manner of Simon Vouet's Roman style, his art continued in a much lighter vein, with plenty of bright colour and swirling composition. This is precisely what happened to Vouet's art after his arrival in Paris, although Vouet worked on a much grander scale than did de l'Estin. De l'Estin is a rare example of a painter working in the provinces who kept himself up to date without degenerating into provincial naïvety, and some of his pictures have been confused with the work of far greater artists.

Only one other painter of significance emerges in the whole of Burgundy – the mysterious Jean Tassel of Langres. He appears to have been influenced by his father Richard Tassel, and until the 1950s the two painters were totally confused with one another. Richard Tassel's only surviving work of importance is the *Triumph of the Virgin in Heaven* in the Musée des Beaux-Arts at Dijon (figure 14). Since he was working in isolation so early in the century, it is not surprising that the painting is a rather stilted version of an Italian

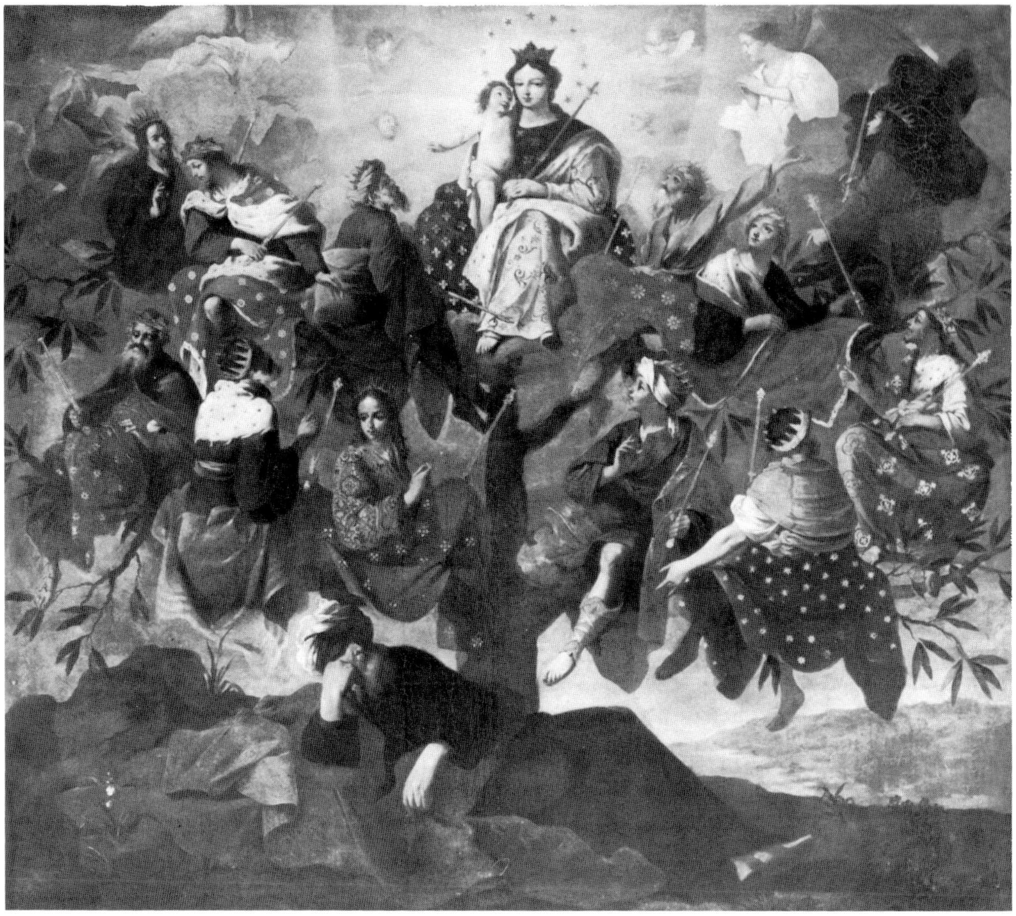

FIGURE 14
Richard Tassel
The Triumph of the Virgin in Heaven
Canvas, 197 × 143 cm. Signed and dated: R. Tassel 1617.
Dijon, Musée des Beaux-Arts
Originally in the Collège des Godrans at Dijon and confiscated at the time of the Revolution.

Depicting an unusual subject in seventeenth-century French painting, it is likely to have been required by a patron. The cult of the Virgin, especially in Dormition, Assumption and Triumph, was much more popular in Spanish and Italian art.

Mannerist picture, showing no knowledge of more recent developments in Italy such as the work of the Carracci. In it can be seen the pinched faces which were to become such a consistent feature of his son's work.

Jean Tassel's art is characterized by bold expressions, cold colour schemes and a generally 'provincial' air which is difficult to define, but in modern terms akin to the wearing of out-of-date garments away from the centre of fashion. Tassel has been left out of anthologies of French painting because his work is so unlike that of his contemporaries, and he is not yet appreciated as a painter of ability in his own right, as are the Le Nain brothers and Georges de La Tour. He was educated in Rome, but no convincing identification of his Roman pictures has yet been made. It may be that a small group of pictures, at present called 'The Master of the Judgment of Solomon', are the missing Tassels. Some of these have the curious slit eyes found in Tassel's work, and one of the pictures is actually at his native Langres, in the Church of St Martin. This may be a coincidence, but the 'Judgment of Solomon' group does show the influence of Le Valentin, as might be expected in the work of a young Frenchman working in Rome in the 1620s.

Apart from a general debt to Caravaggio, there are other influences on Tassel's art. One of the strongest is that of Pieter van Laer and his followers, better known as the Bamboccianti. In Tassel's exquisite *Marauders* in the Musée St-Didier at Langres (figure 15), the composition of the figures is derived from the type of low-life scenes favoured by the Bamboccianti in Rome. Here Tassel was obviously trying his hand at a small, highly finished picture usually known as a cabinet piece, a type of work almost exclusively

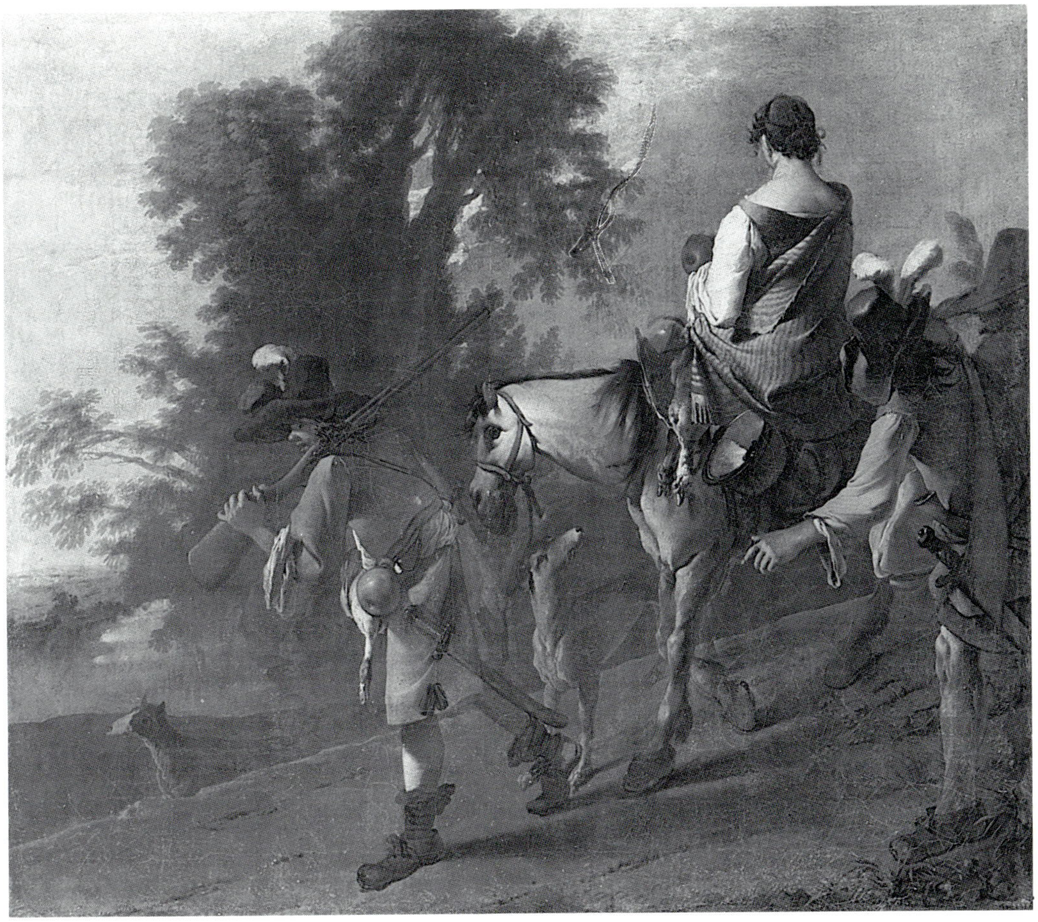

FIGURE 15
Jean Tassel
Marauders ('Les Maraudeurs')
Canvas, 71 × 83 cm.
Langres, Musée Saint Didier

In common with many of the pictures in this much-neglected museum, the early history of this work seems to be unknown. It appears to have been first identified as by Jean Tassel by Charles Sterling in 1934.

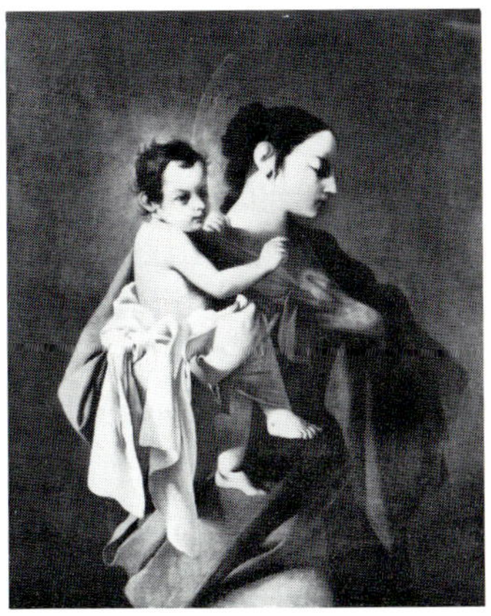

FIGURE 16
Jean Tassel
Virgin and Child
Canvas, 81.5 × 64.5 cm.
Lyons, Musée des Beaux-Arts

This is one of several repetitions of a type favoured by Tassel during his many years in Dijon and Langres.

produced by the Dutch, who dominated the market all over Italy, and even France, because they could produce the much sought-after high finish relatively rapidly. Tassel's attempt is rare in French art, the only other deliberate imitator of the successful Dutch being Sébastien Bourdon. Even though the *Marauders* is Dutch inspired and Italian orientated, Tassel's individuality still shows through. Instead of being merely picturesque, as most Dutch painters aimed to be, there is a feeling of malevolence in these banditti traversing the steep landscape in search of plunder. Tassel's religious pictures are equally bizarre. He produced several versions of a standard *Virgin and Child*, a good example being the one in the Musée des Beaux-Arts at Lyons (figure 16), in which the models have mongoloid faces. These pictures are closer in spirit to the harshness of Caravaggio's last works in Sicily than might be expected from a painter working mostly in Langres, isolated on its high plateau.

Tassel produced one masterpiece which must come from the time he spent in Dijon, the *Portrait of Catherine de Montholon* in the Musée des Beaux-Arts at Dijon (plate 81). The sense of grave austerity which pervades the portrait is usually interpreted by French writers as 'classicism' in the broadest sense of the term. What is most striking about the picture is its lack of reference to contemporary fashions, both in art and life. There is an uncompromising power of observation unadorned by artistic clichés. It is likely that more portraits by Tassel survive. A good candidate is the *Portrait of a Boy* in the Musée Calvet at Avignon, in which the same slit eyes appear. The sitter is young and elegant, but colour is used as minimally as in the *Catherine de Montholon*.

Tassel's *oeuvre* is still not well defined; in recent years *Moses Striking the Rock* in the Museum Bredius at The Hague, long attributed to the German painter Jan Liss, has been identified as being by Tassel. His pictures are difficult to date because of his relative consistency over a long period, and yet, in the very last works from the 1660s, there is a hint of the influence of Vouet, who had already been dead for ten years. As with Daret at Aix and Guy François at Le Puy, it appears that the aged Tassel, after almost two generations of painting better than his contemporaries, had spent his imagination and lost his energy. He was to leave no successor in Langres.

The Duchy of Lorraine: Georges de La Tour

Of all the centres of painting outside Paris from 1620 onwards, Lorraine was the only one with a definite tradition. Only in Lorraine had there been a group of artists active in the first twenty years of the century, notably Callot and Bellange. Claude Deruet continued the Mannerist tradition as started by Callot and Bellange, and the new influences from Italy had to co-exist with his already old-fashioned style.

In the 1620s and until 1633, when the French invaded Lorraine, the ducal court at Nancy was the centre of art patronage. In common with many grander courts of the time, such as those of Madrid, Florence and Prague, the court of Lorraine allowed considerable diversity of artistic style, even though subject-matter may have been limited. The relative splendour of the Nancy court in the 1620s has to be inferred from the drawings and etchings of Callot. Certainly the duchy was as wealthy as nearby France, although it was much smaller, and the dukes had considerable funds at their disposal, payable directly to the painters they commissioned. The position of artists in the duchy was unusually good because the Church also gave commissions, the best-known of which, although the building does not survive, is Deruet's decoration of the Carmelite church at Nancy executed in the years 1626–7. Eighteenth-century descriptions of Nancy record that before the Revolution there were pictures by Jean Le Clerc and Deruet in most of the town's churches.

From the surviving documentation it seems that the most important painter working for the Lorraine court in the 1620s was Jean Le Clerc. Over a short period in the late 1620s he was awarded large sums of money by the duke, far more than Lorraine's greatest painter, Georges de La Tour, was to receive from the municipality of nearby Lunéville in the 1640s. A few of Le Clerc's pictures survive, and it is from them that we must attempt to reconstruct what this court artist was achieving and how he influenced Georges de La Tour, who spent almost all his active career in Lunéville, away from the court. The origins of Le Clerc's art in Italy are clear enough: he collaborated with Carlo Saraceni, who also influenced Guy François. Le Clerc worked with Saraceni on the enormous canvas of the *Doge Enrico Dandolo* in the Doge's Palace, Venice and, so great is Le Clerc's debt to Saraceni, there has been difficulty in sorting out the attributions between the two artists. Le Clerc engraved Saraceni's most successful composition, the *Death of the Virgin*, and may even have painted some of the many surviving versions of that composition. Saraceni died in Venice in 1620 before finishing the doge's picture, and after completing it Le Clerc left Italy and returned to his native

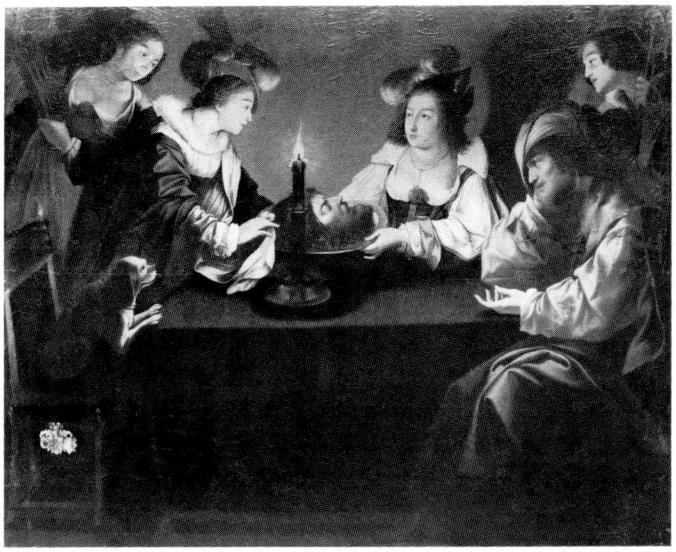

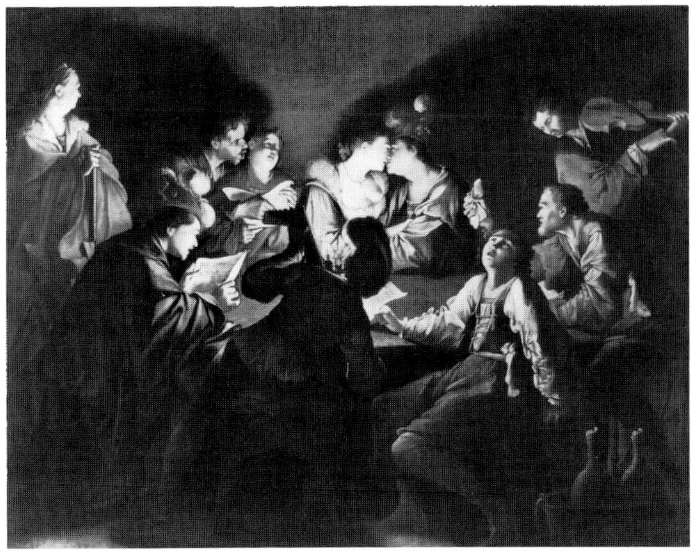

FIGURE 17 (above left)
Jean Le Clerc
The Banquet of Herodias
Canvas, 180 × 225 cm.
Chaumont, Église Collégiale
Probably painted for the church c.1630. First attributed to Le Clerc by Charles Sterling in 1934.
One of the most direct and dramatic treatments of the subject at that period.

FIGURE 18 (above right)
Jean Le Clerc
The Concert
Canvas, 137 × 170 cm.
Schleissheim, Schloss, Staatsgalerie
Long in the Residenz in Munich, and transferred to Schleissheim in recent years. Its importance was only recognized in the 1930s.
The subject is a standard Caravaggesque concert party.

Lorraine. His arrival in Nancy was to change the course of painting in Lorraine, leaving Deruet isolated.

Le Clerc's chief surviving work is the *Concert*, recently removed from Munich to Schleissheim (figure 18). In it the individual figures might be described as 'Saracenesque' in their facial types and poses, but the whole composition is much closer to the concert parties favoured by Caravaggio's Netherlandish followers in Rome, especially Nicolas Regnier and Theodore van Rombouts. It has none of the elegance found in Manfredi and Le Valentin; instead, the emphasis is on the dramatic and vulgar. Significantly, Le Clerc made an etching of the composition, the only known surviving example of which is in the Albertina, Vienna, and he also made an engraving, which meant that the composition became well known. The *Concert* is the earliest surviving candle-light picture from Lorraine, and probably dates from the early part of the 1620s, soon after Le Clerc's arrival in Nancy. Indeed, it has even been suggested that the composition was invented while the artist was still in Venice and that replicas were executed in Lorraine.

Le Clerc's surviving pictures are rare, but they conform to a recognizable pattern, usually being large in scale and dramatic in lighting. His *Adoration of the Shepherds* in the Musée Saint-Didier at Langres was to have some influence on Georges de La Tour but, in terms of scale and the effect it had on La Tour, Le Clerc's most significant surviving picture is the *Banquet of Herodias* in the Église Collégiale at Chaumont (figure 17). In this vast canvas Salome sits at the centre of the table with a lighted candle in front of her, surrounded by other figures. As in the *Concert*, the atmosphere has an almost ghostly quality; Le Clerc was a master of the sinister.

In 1633, two years before Callot's death and in the year in which Le Clerc died, disaster overtook Lorraine. The troops of Cardinal Richelieu invaded, and the duke fled from Nancy into exile. Lorraine was in effect annexed to France, although it was not formally described as such. It is said that the atrocities committed by the invading troops at the time inspired Callot to execute his celebrated set of twelve etchings '*Les Grands Misères de la Guerre*'. What is certain is that the consequence of the French invasion was a massive decline in artistic output.

The most important Lorraine artist to continue working was Claude

FIGURE 19
Claude Deruet
Madame de Saint-Baslmont on Horseback
Canvas, 325 × 365 cm.
Nancy, Musée Historique Lorrain
Acquired by the museum in 1951–2 from the collection of the Château of Aulnoy-sur-Seille. Deruet is documented as having painted this subject.

The large scale of the picture implies that it formed part of an elaborate decoration. The château in the background is that of Neuville-en-Verdunois. It is believed that Madame de Saint-Baslmont (1607–50) was in the habit of adopting male attire, in which she is depicted here, in order to appear less vulnerable to the numerous soldiers crossing her domain as a consequence of the Thirty Years' War.

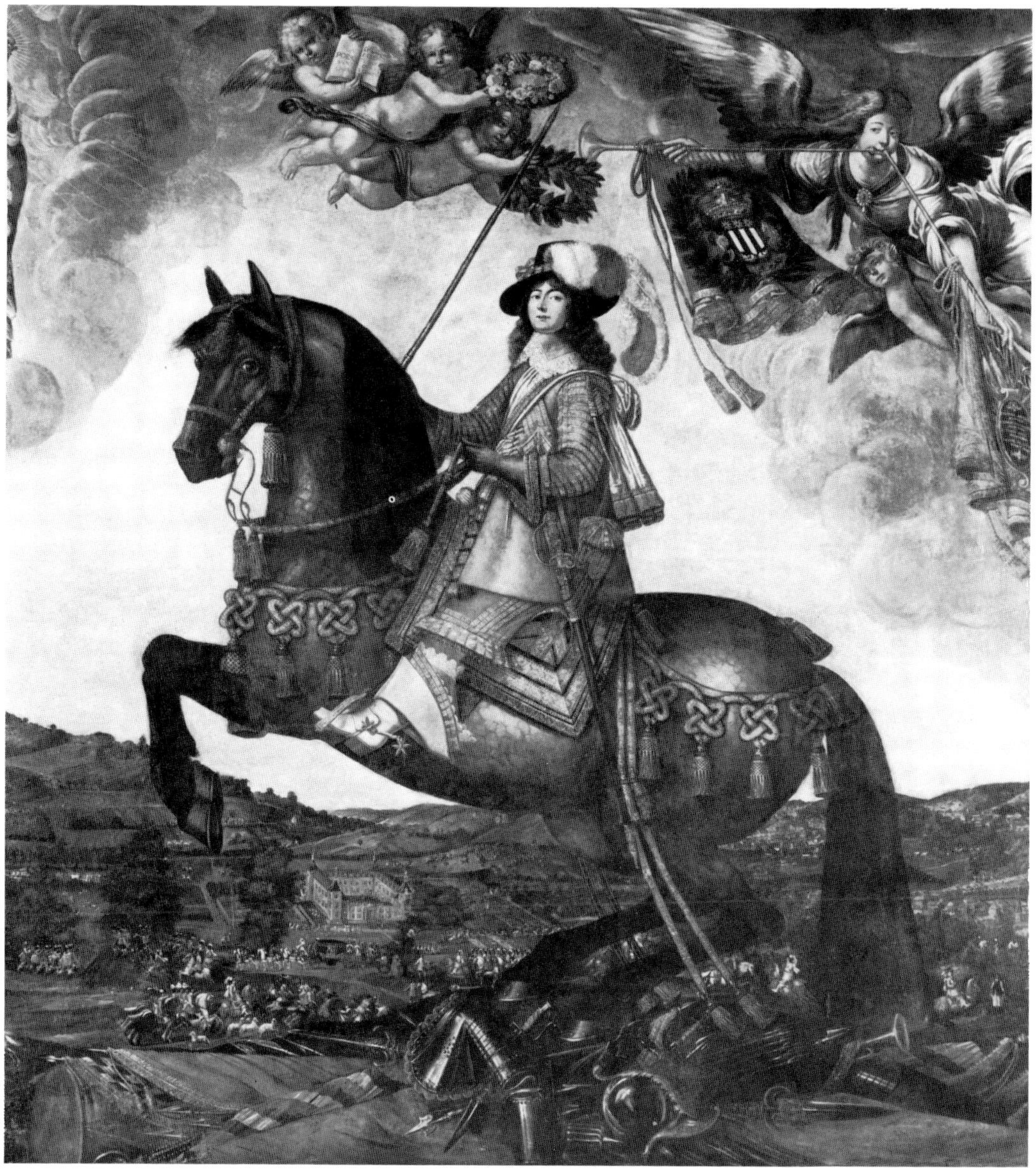

Deruet, who immediately gave his allegiance to the new French regime, which he served for the rest of his long career. In his youth in Rome, Deruet had acquired an attenuated Mannerist style which was already out of date. It was particularly adapted to decoration on a large scale, as he used a technique akin to that of a scene painter, probably developed from executing designs and scenery for masques and balls, exactly as is found in the work of his English contemporary Inigo Jones (from whose hand only drawings survive). Deruet's *tour de force* in terms of scale is his *Portrait of Madame de Saint-Baslmont on Horseback* [*in Male Hunting Attire*] in the Musée Historique Lorrain at Nancy (figure 19). The surface is pale in colour and has the tapestry-like effect of a theatrical backdrop. There is not the slightest attention to or delight in the surface for its own sake; the picture is meant to be seen at a considerable distance, as part of a general scheme of decoration.

The best surviving example of a sequence from Deruet and, indeed, from the whole period, is the series of four *Elements* in the Musée des Beaux-Arts at Orléans (figures 20-23). They were painted for the cardinal's château at Richelieu near Orléans some time before 1642 (in which year the cardinal

FIGURE 20
Claude Deruet
Air
Canvas, 114.8 × 422.7 cm.
Orléans, Musée des Beaux-Arts

This group of pictures comprises the most elaborate surviving Mannerist decoration.

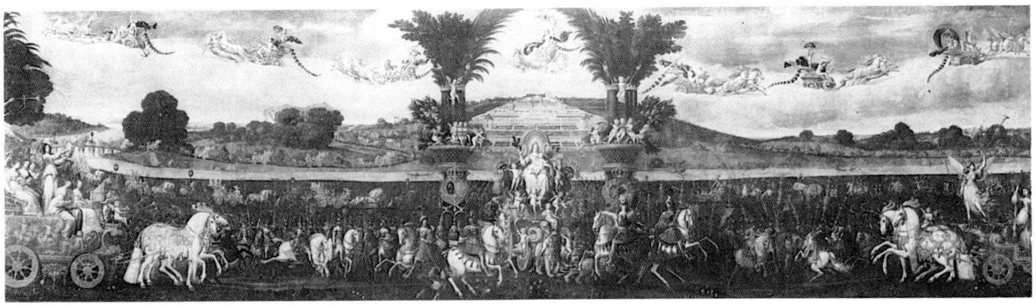

FIGURE 21
Claude Deruet
Earth
Canvas, 194 × 258.5 cm.
Orléans, Musée des Beaux-Arts

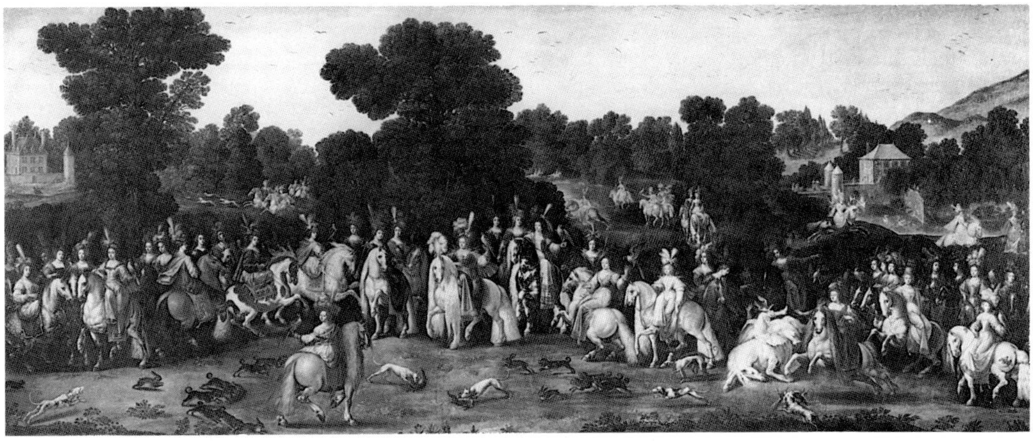

FIGURE 22
Claude Deruet
Fire
Canvas, 114 × 258.5 cm.
Orléans, Musée des Beaux-Arts

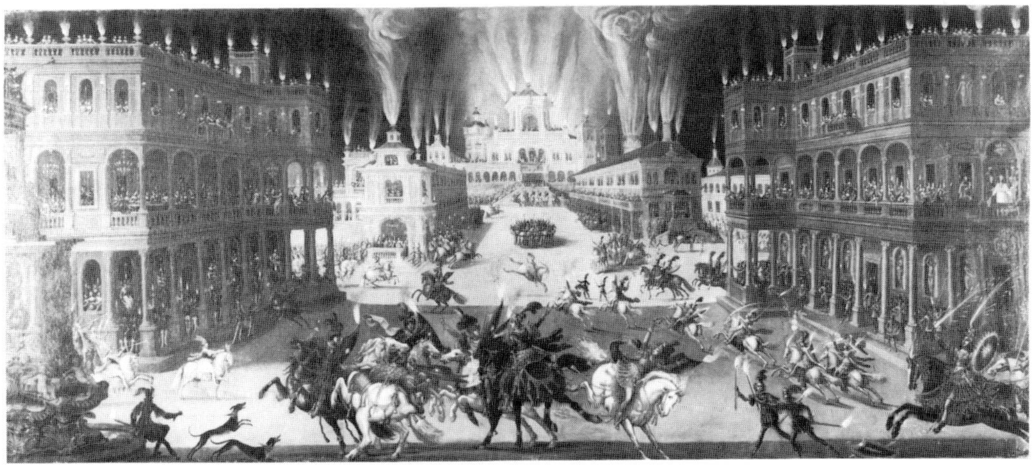

FIGURE 23
Claude Deruet
Water
Canvas, 112.8 × 227.3 cm.
Orléans, Musée des Beaux-Arts
All four pictures were first recorded in the Cabinet de La Reine in the château of Cardinal Richelieu. They must have been painted in or before 1642, in which year Cardinal Richelieu died. The pictures remained at Richelieu until 1822, when the collection was dispersed. They were given to the Orléans museum by a local collector, M. Pilté-Grenet, in 1824.

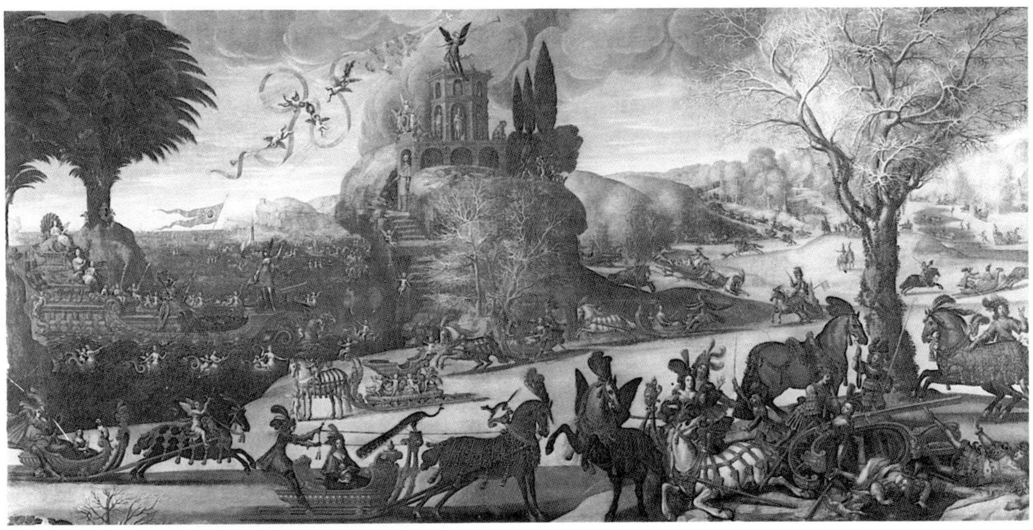

died). They are now in a small room in the museum, detached from their original surroundings, so that little or no idea can now be gained of the complex setting of decorative plasterwork and carved and painted wood in which such pictures were usually placed. The emphasis of the four canvasses is entirely decorative. The *Element of Fire* (detail, plate 26) is particularly dramatic, and depicts one of the elaborate firework displays popular at the time. The *Elements* conform very closely to the aesthetic spirit of the last years of the reign of Louis XIII, who died in 1643. There were a few painters active – such as Poussin in Rome and Georges de La Tour in Lorraine – who did not conform to the general spirit of the age, but the artists who achieved the greatest success in official circles were those who were able to decorate (rather than execute easel paintings) with a minimum of effort, and these were Claude Deruet and Simon Vouet.

Two other contemporaries of Deruet, François Nomé and Didier Barra, left Lorraine at an early age and so do not fit into the context of painting either there or in Paris, because they worked exclusively in Naples. Both came from Metz, and until recently their work was confused, being known under the generic name 'Monsù Desiderio'. Their style has its roots in the same tradition which allowed Deruet to develop along such unusual lines. Their work can be divided into two main categories, architectural pieces and topographical works, usually bird's-eye views. The latter are of little interest, but the architectural scenes are among some of the oddest pictures ever painted, exceeding in extravagance even Deruet's *Elements*. Most of them are scenes of fantasy, with buildings which would fall down if actually constructed according to the pictures. The *Martyrdom of a Saint* in the Musée des Arts Décoratifs in Paris (plate 27) is relatively restrained, but even in this architectural piece a gruesome martyrdom is taking place. More extreme is the *King Asa of Juda Destroying the Idols* in the Fitzwilliam Museum, Cambridge (plate 28): no other painter of the period managed to depict the event with such a sense of theatre, while at the same time removing all sense of moral seriousness from the occasion. It seems as if the artists were more interested in the pyrotechnics of an event than the moral of the story. Such flippancy with regard to subject is perhaps one of the reasons for the artists' long neglect. Neither painter seems to have exercised any influence in Naples, where there was an unusual flowering of Caravaggism at the time, led by the Spanish painter Ribera who worked there for much of his long career.

It is against this background of artistic activity at the court at Nancy that the art of Georges de La Tour has to be placed. La Tour is now considered to be one of the greatest painters of seventeenth-century France, and his work has undergone, in the last twenty years, a rise in popular esteem. He worked from 1620 onwards in Lunéville, which was isolated from any artistic tradition.

Few facts are known about La Tour's career, and they appear in any case to have little bearing on the development of his art. He was born in 1593, the son of a baker in Vic-sur-Seille in the bishopric of Metz. He married the daughter of a Lunéville bourgeois in 1617 and moved to that town three years later, living there for the rest of his life. He died at the age of fifty-nine in 1652. It is not known where La Tour obtained his artistic education, and there has been much speculation on this matter, most of it derived, unfortunately, from looking at pictures attributed to him and then working out the locations of the

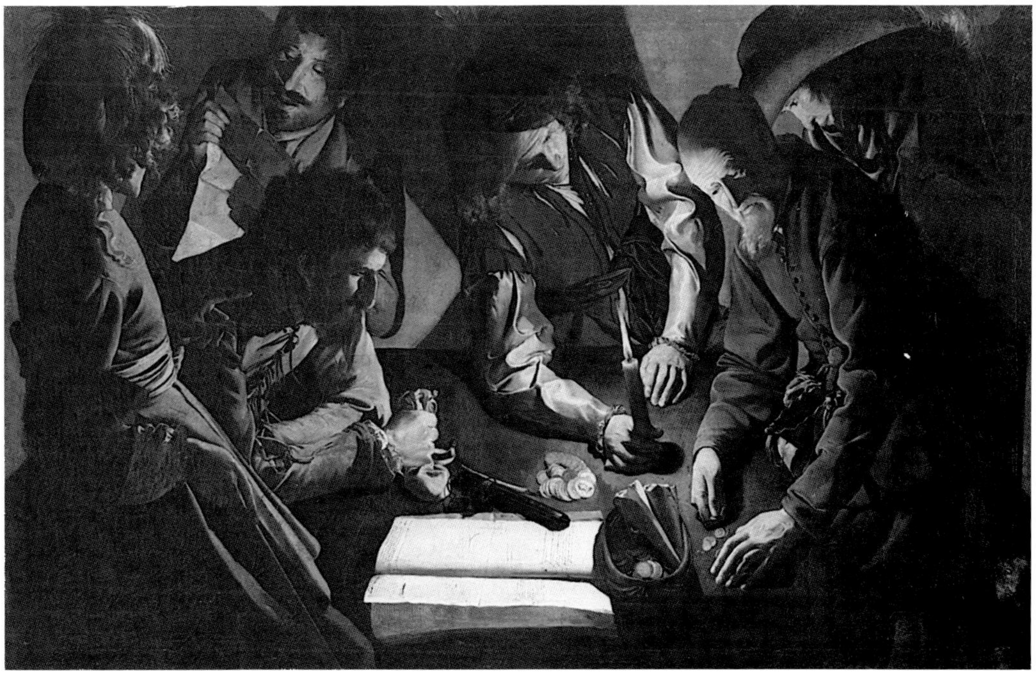

FIGURE 24
Georges de La Tour
The Payment of Dues
Canvas, 99 × 152 cm. Signed and dated halfway up on left: Georges de La Tour 1634
Lvov, Museum
First recorded at Lvov in the early nineteenth century. Only identified as by La Tour in 1970. The signature and date, still controversial, appeared after cleaning in 1973.

The subject may well be a 'Calling of Matthew', since Matthew was a tax-gatherer.

possible influences. In fact, now that Le Clerc is better defined, most of the sources of La Tour's art can be seen to be local, derived from Deruet and Le Clerc, exactly as was thought by the earliest of the La Tour scholars, François-Georges Pariset, in his study *Georges de La Tour*, published in 1948.

La Tour's mature pictures, mostly dating from the second half of the 1630s and the 1640s, are now recognized as some of the greatest pictures ever painted showing the effect of candlelight. The fact that they are unique in art presents problems for some connoisseurs. The pictures do not fit into any defined tradition, particularly since Lunéville was isolated from the principal centres of European painting at the time.

No artist of La Tour's stature and individuality matures without a struggle, and much of the time and effort of recent scholarship has been spent in reconstructing his early development. In this quest many mistakes have been made, partly because insufficient attention has been paid to the small amount of surviving evidence. La Tour began by painting small pictures of saints. An *Image Saint-Pierre* was acquired by the Duke of Lorraine in 1623 and another unspecified picture the following year, both for modest sums. What these pictures looked like can be guessed at by the survival of an engraving of one that was in the collection of the Archduke Leopold Wilhelm in Brussels, and an attributed picture in the Royal Collection at Hampton Court, *St Jerome Reading*. These pictures are small in format and are provincial in every respect, but their technique is highly skilled, especially in the Hampton Court picture, where the light is seen reflected through the paper the saint is reading.

Much more important than these two pictures is the surviving *Payment of Dues* (figure 24), only identified in 1972, even though it has been in the museum at Lvov since at least the early nineteenth century. The picture was cleaned soon after its debut in Paris at the time of the La Tour exhibition in 1972, and a date was revealed. This date, thought to be 1634, has caused a great deal of controversy. If 1634 is correct, a drastic reassessment of La Tour's stylistic development must be made. The early pictures of saints remain from the 1620s, and then in the early 1630s La Tour moves towards

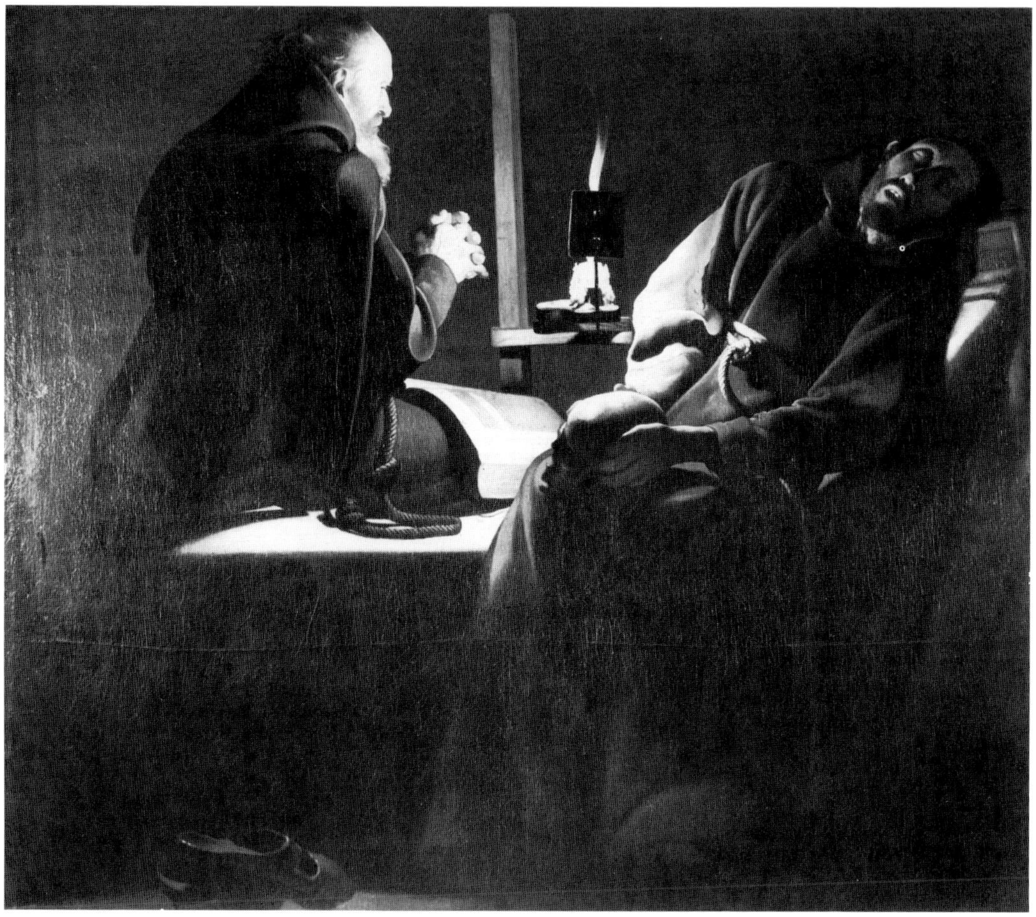

FIGURE 25
Attributed to Georges de La Tour
The Two Monks
Canvas, 154 × 165 cm.
Le Mans, Musée de Tessé
First recorded in the museum in 1892. Not identified as a La Tour until after 1945. The attribution is still controversial.

The subject is sometimes identified as the ecstasy of St Francis, although it appears as if one of the monks is dead.

his second phase, basically a Le Clerc-influenced period. The swaying figures and flickering lighting of the *Payment of Dues* are especially reminiscent of Le Clerc's *Concert* at Schleissheim. There is a certain ambiguity—often present in La Tour – in the subject, which appears to have been little studied. At first sight it is a simple peasant scene of the rich extracting money, ruthlessly, from the poor, but it could be a depiction of the 'Calling of Matthew' (the tax collector).

Three engravings exist after La Tour compositions, and are accepted by every authority as having been engraved by the same hand that engraved Le Clerc's *Concert*. These compositions do not all survive in the form of paintings, although related works exist in each case. The exquisitely melancholy *Penitent Magdalen* is reflected in the full-length picture in the National Gallery of Art, Washington. The closest of these to Le Clerc is, however, *The Two Monks*, which is known in a similar but not identical composition in the Musée de Tessé at Le Mans (figure 25). In the Le Mans picture there is extraordinary passion, an emotion which has led many writers to reject the attribution, forgetting that at this stage La Tour was still under the spell of Le Clerc. The related Le Clerc composition is the attributed picture of *St Francis* in the church at Bouxières-aux-Dames near Nancy, which is in fact a replica of a Saraceni.

Le Clerc died in 1633, and thus a major rival was removed from the scene. The French invasion of Lorraine was then at its height, and La Tour seems to have retreated into further isolation, although he was to have contact with Louis XIII who acquired a *St Sebastian* by him which, according to an eight-

Detail of Figure 25

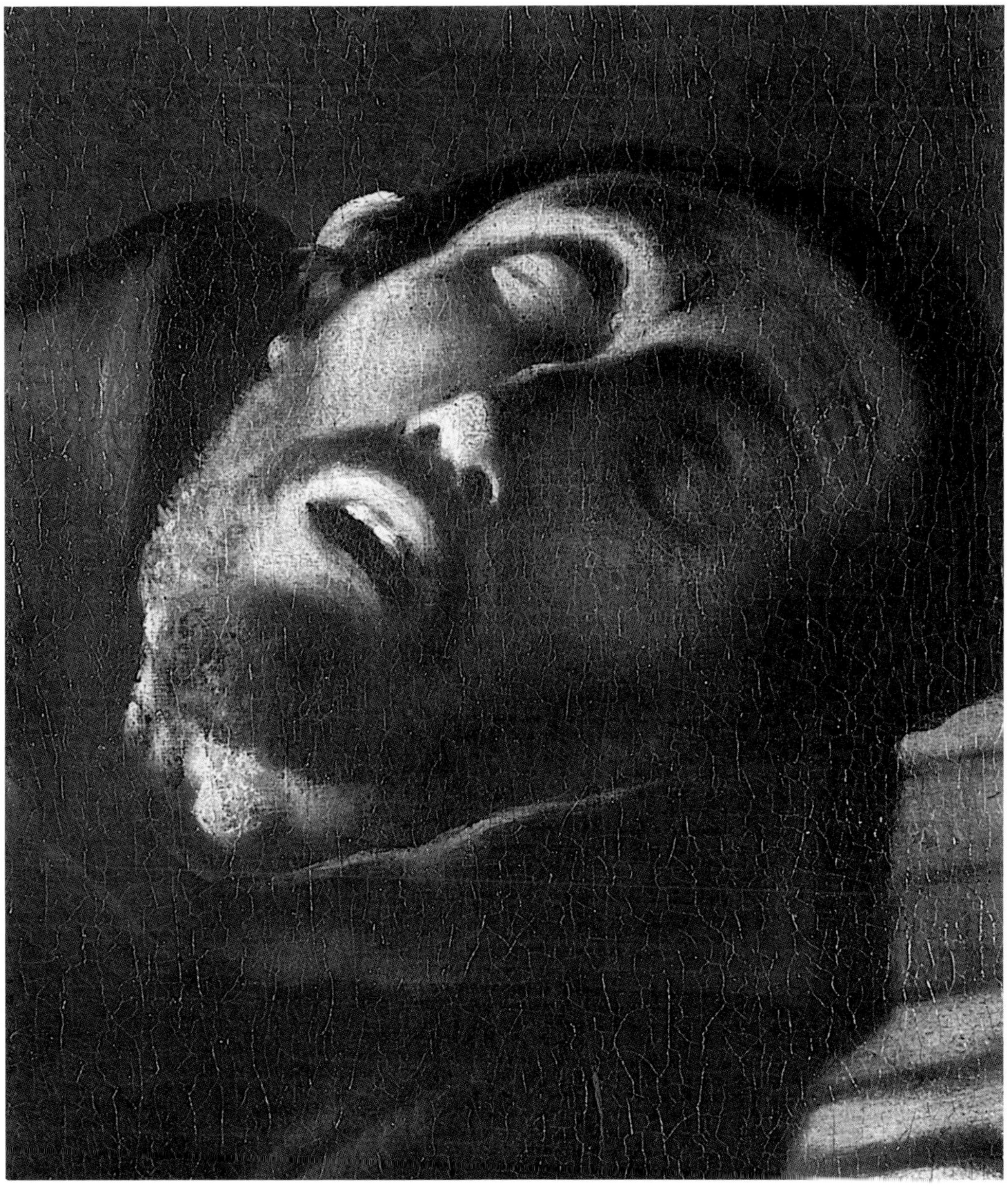

eenth-century source, was so much admired by the king that he ordered all other pictures in the room where it was hung to be removed. It is not easy to explain what brought about the change from the morbidity and mystery of such pictures as the penitent Magdalen contemplating a skull and a monk watching over his dead or dying companion, to works of a much calmer and more distilled air. The transitional pictures, also datable to the 1630s, are *Job Mocked by his Wife* (plate 39) at Épinal and the so-called '*Woman with the Flea*' (plate 38) at Nancy.

The composition of the *Job* is immediately striking. There is the same flickering movement that is found in the *Payment of Dues*, even though there are only two figures. It is derived from Bellange's etching of *The Annunciation*, an unexpected source, especially when it is considered that *The Annunciation* by Caravaggio was already in the ducal collection at Nancy by 1616 (this much-damaged picture is now in the Musée des Beaux-Arts at Nancy where it is accepted by most authorities as authentic). No influence on La Tour is discernible in the Caravaggio, although it is virtually certain that he knew it.

Although its composition is a complex amalgam of the Bellange *Annunciation*, the mood of the *Job* is entirely original. La Tour has concentrated on a dialogue between the unfortunate Job and his ill-tempered wife, and has allowed us a glimpse of a rarely painted subject, a husband tormented by his wife. Her cruel mockery of him comes over with great force as Job sits helplessly contemplating his sores (the potsherd he uses to scrape them is on the ground). The spectator is forced to realize that this painter's genius lies chiefly in his ability to observe the human condition; his skill in painting candlelight is only part of his brilliance. Such a depiction of the complex relationship between two people is rare indeed in French art of the period, and in his maturity La Tour was to develop the concept of dialogue between people to ever-increasing heights of subtlety.

The '*Woman with the Flea*' (plate 38), in the Musée Historique Lorrain at Nancy, is enigmatic in both composition and subject-matter. It strikes an uneasy note because of its stark simplicity, which has usually been interpreted as a genre scene of low life – a woman crushing a flea between her fingernails – but no authentic La Tour depicts such an obviously banal theme without a deeper meaning. The only symbol in the picture is the solitary candle burning on the chair, and it is surely not too speculative to suggest that the picture might represent the pregnant Virgin, isolated by Joseph when he discovers that she is with child, the candle thus symbolizing the forthcoming Christ as the Light of the World.

La Tour's mature pictures form a close-knit group which must date from the years immediately before and after 1640. None of them is documented, although some of them are signed. The most typical and one of the best preserved of them is the so-called *Dream of Joseph* (plate 40) at Nantes, which in many respects forms a microcosm of La Tour's art and the problems which surround it, in terms of both history and the interpretation of the subject. It was first recorded as early as 1810 when it entered the Nantes Museum as part of the Cacault collection, but it was largely ignored in the nineteenth century. As recently as 1913, when a full catalogue of the museum was issued, it was attributed to Rembrandt, although the picture was clearly signed La Tour in the top right-hand corner. It is interesting that an illustrious name should have been sought for so magical a picture, and the subject, even now, is as elusive as was the former difficulty of attribution. A youth in biblical costume is making a beckoning or announcing gesture before an old man who has fallen asleep reading a book. The traditional interpretation is that it is a Dream of Joseph, even though Joseph is normally shown as a carpenter (as he is in La Tour's Louvre picture described below). The youth is hardly the angel Gabriel either, coming to warn Joseph to flee to Egypt in order to escape the impending massacre of all the children in Bethlehem by Herod's soldiers. A possible explanation for this enigmatic picture is that it depicts the moment when the young Samuel, having been, he thinks, summoned by the elderly priest Eli, finds him asleep. This surprises Samuel, who at that instant realizes that it is God's voice calling him. If this interpretation of the subject is correct, La Tour has with characteristic subtlety and understatement shown the exact moment when the youth Samuel arrives before the sleeping old man, with a 'here I am' gesture. Samuel's pose is unforgettable. All attempts at the naturalism with which La Tour is so wrongly credited have been abandoned, leaving a Mannerist twisting of the fingers and the caprice of shielding most of the candle flame. Above all, there is an exquisite stillness, which pervades not only this picture but also the other all-too-few masterpieces from this period.

On the same deep level, in a similar vein but more complex in composition, is the *Christ in the Carpenter's Shop* (plate 41) in the Louvre. As in the *Job*, one of the figures is arched over the top of the canvas, and again the attention to mood is shown in the minute observation of the effects of light in certain areas, especially that of the translucency of the child's hand silhouetted against the candle, revealing even the dirt in the fingernails. As usual, La Tour tells the Bible story in the simplest of terms. Only items essential for identifying the subject, in this case the paraphernalia of the carpenter's shop, are included. The picture can exist on the level of a genre scene without religious overtones, and its realism makes it one of the greatest genre paintings of the seventeenth century, rivalling Velasquez's *Water Seller of Seville* and Rembrandt's *Jewish Bride* (the latter has also been interpreted as a religious or mythological subject).

In 1983 the County Museum and Art Gallery in Leicester acquired a previously unknown work, *The Choirboy*. The boy's hand is poised in the familiar gesture of shielding a candle flame and diffusing the light. As is usual for La Tour, the theme of the painting is a compromise between a religious and a genre subject, and the atmosphere of the picture is one of perfect stillness, as the boy's singing seems frozen on the canvas.

The precise order in which La Tour's pictures were painted remains undetermined. By common consent, however, his best picture is the *New-born* at Rennes (plate 43). At first sight this now-famous work seems starkly simple, a refinement of the already-familiar mannerisms and abbreviations, and only close inspection of the relatively small-scale picture reveals its complexity. The technique is almost pointilliste: the intense red of the mother's dress is achieved by minute dots of colour of varying hue, and the same is true of the lilac garment of the servant (or St Anne, if the subject is the Christ Child). The whole surface is thus the product of an intensely concentrated effort, and a large amount of detail is concealed in the stark simplicity of the forms. The collar of the mother's dress is elaborately decorated, and the profiles are painted with an exceptional delicacy of line. A total calm pervades the picture, in which the faces have been described as almost Buddha-like in their serenity. The sentiments which characterize almost all the rest of seventeenth-century painting are avoided, and this picture alone justifies La Tour's reputation. Just as Vermeer's *View of Delft* is exceptional, even for Vermeer, so the *New-born* rises above all the conventions of its time.

The contrast between the Rennes *New-born* and the *Adoration of the Shepherds* in the Louvre (plate 45) could not be greater. The composition of the latter work is much more complex, and the paint is handled with much more freedom, great attention being paid to the surface texture. Some of the elements are familiar: the figure of the old man Joseph, on the right, recurs throughout La Tour's art, and one of the shepherds in the background is taken from Le Clerc's *Adoration of the Shepherds* at Langres. There are some especially sensitive passages, including the depiction of the sleeping Christ Child, which are much softer in treatment than any of La Tour's pictures so far discussed. This picture, with all these observable differences, marks the beginning of La Tour's last phase. The final years of his career in Lunéville

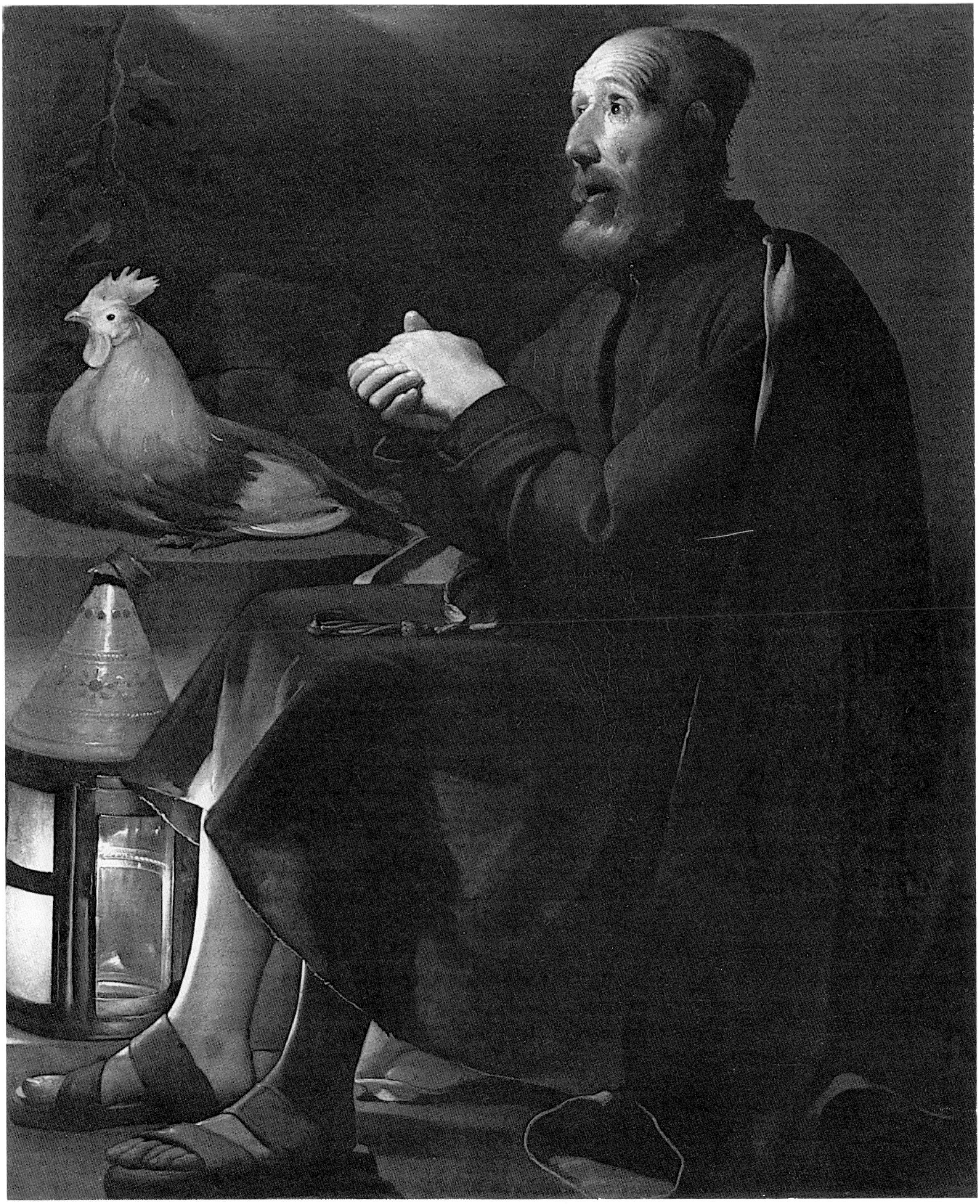

FIGURE 27 (right)
Georges de La Tour
The Dice Players
Canvas, 92.5 × 130.5 cm. Signed along the table, left: Georges de La Tour Inve[t] et Pinx
Stockton-on-Tees, Preston Manor
First recorded in 1930 in the collection of Annie Elisabeth Clephan of Leicester, who bequeathed it to the museum in the same year. Not identified as by La Tour until early in 1972.
One of La Tour's rare genre scenes, it could well depict the soldiers gambling for Christ's garments.

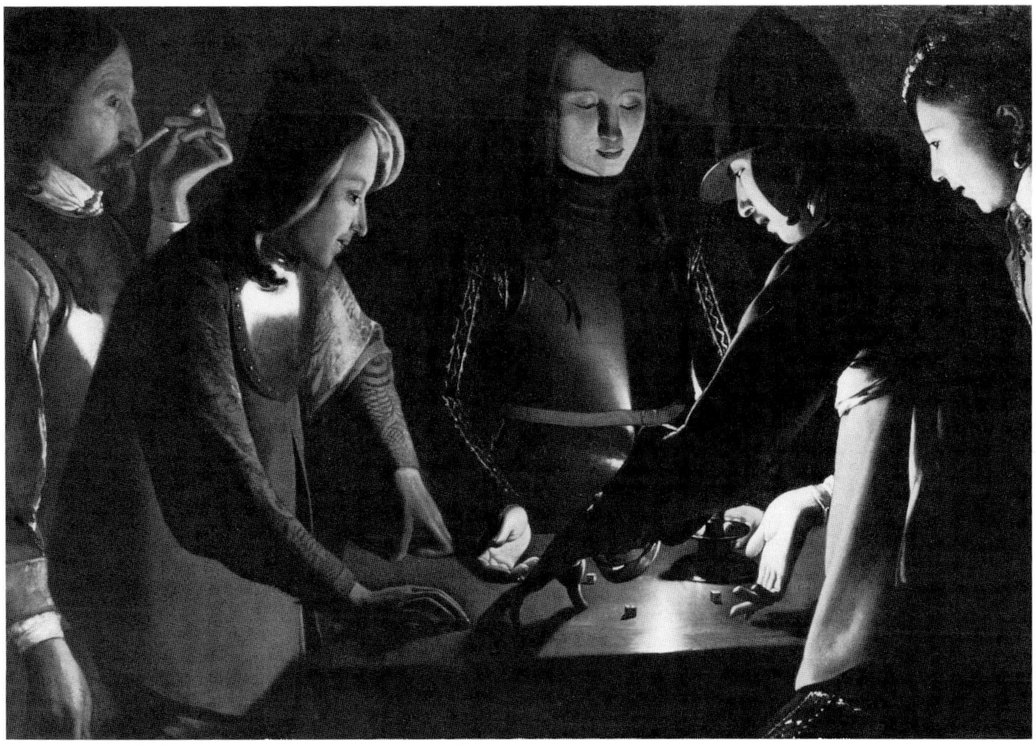

are much better documented than his earlier years, and we have a clearer idea of his later stylistic development because of the survival of two dated pictures, the Cleveland *Penitent St Peter* of 1645 (figure 26) and the Nantes *Denial of Peter* of 1650. The change in La Tour's art in these last years is so great that it has to be seen in terms of a decline and a rapid increase in studio participation. This has given rise to much speculation, and bitter controversies have raged over the different surviving versions of the same composition. The facts for this period are as follows. From 1644 onwards the municipality of Lunéville made an annual purchase from La Tour of a large and expensive picture, intended for presentation each new year to the French occupying governor at Nancy, the Marquis de La Ferté. (Later, these pictures were inventoried by none other than Deruet, who placed a good deal less importance on them than had Lunéville, which paid so dearly for them.) In most cases the subjects of these pictures are known – a *Nativity*, a *St Sebastian*, a *St Alexis*, and a *Denial of Peter*. All these subjects are identifiable in pictures known today.

Among several dozen surviving problem pictures (including ten horizontal versions of the *St Sebastian* composition), the key picture is the Cleveland *Penitent St Peter* of 1645, because it is dated. It follows on quite logically from the Louvre *Adoration of the Shepherds*, which is usually identified with the 1644 payment by the town of Lunéville. The Cleveland picture is more than usually sentimental for La Tour: tears pour down St Peter's face as he contemplates the cock, symbol of his betrayal of Christ. The lighting, reflected from the lantern on the floor, is one of La Tour's triumphs. Far from being a weakening, the Cleveland picture represents a change in La Tour's art towards a more fluid and less stylized approach.

Problems arise with the Nantes *Denial of Peter*, dated 1650. The payment for such a subject by Lunéville is recorded for 1651, and it has always been assumed that this is the picture concerned. It has become totally stylized;

FIGURE 26 (left)
Georges de La Tour
The Penitent St Peter
Canvas, 114 × 95 cm. Signed and dated upper right:
Georgs de La Tour Inve et Pinx. 1645.
Cleveland (Ohio), Museum of Art
First discovered on the English art market in 1950 by Marshall Spink. Acquired by the museum the following year (gift of Hanna Fund)
Although the theme of the penitent St Peter is a common one in seventeenth-century art, La Tour's showing of his tears of regret is unusual.

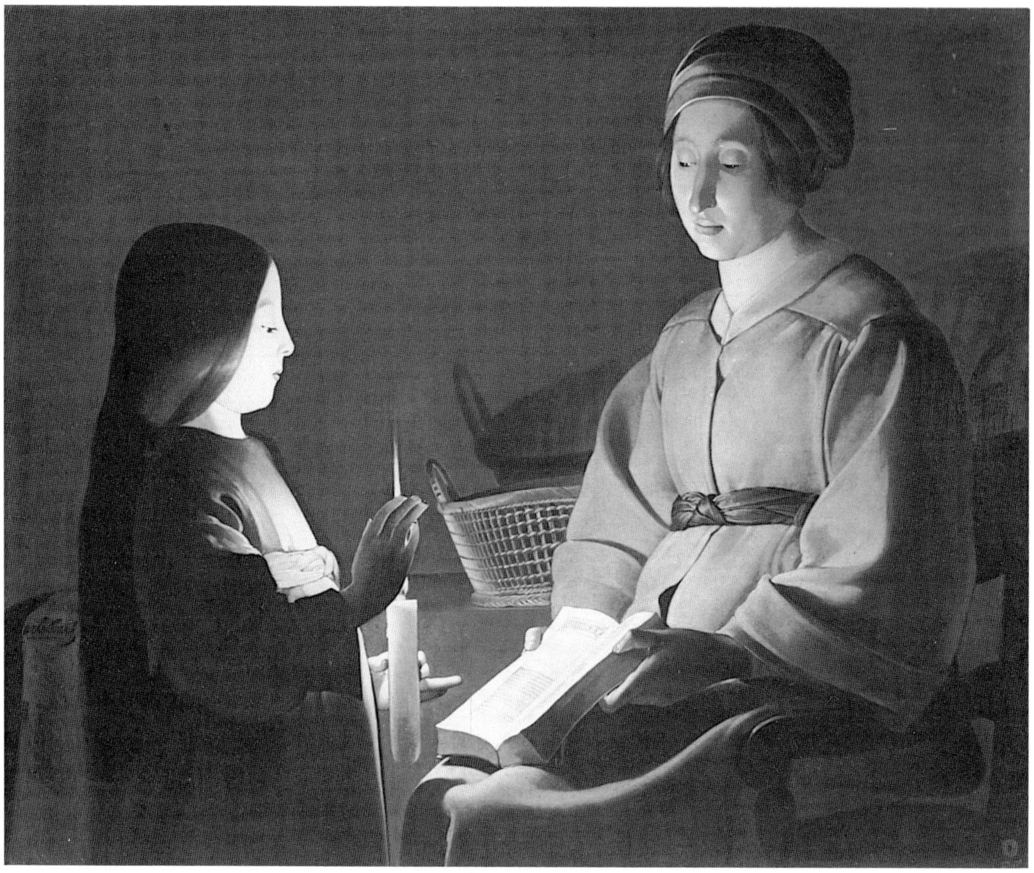

FIGURE 28
Étienne de La Tour
The Education of the Virgin
Canvas, 83.8 × 100.4 cm. Signed behind the Virgin on the left: de la Tour f.
New York, Frick Collection
Acquired by the museum in 1948 from a private collection in Nice.

St Anne, the Virgin's mother, is teaching her daughter to read. There is no reference to this in the Bible.

the poses of the figures have largely been taken from an engraving after an obscure composition by the Flemish artist Gerard Seghers. The disappointment the spectator must feel in front of the *Denial of Peter* may in part be due to the poor condition of the picture and the unwillingness of critics to admire the cruelly vulgar faces of the soldiers gambling for Christ's clothes.

Fortunately, another recent discovery, the *Dice Players* (figure 27) at Preston Manor, Stockton-on-Tees, has given us some insight into La Tour's achievements in his decline. The composition disconcerts at once: there is a feeling of awkwardness in the placing of the figures, and the handling of the three central characters is of a cold precision; and yet the androgynous figure on the right with the pearl eardrop is treated quite differently, with a softness also associated with the *Penitent St Peter*.

La Tour's genius petered out as rapidly as it had emerged from the aegis of Le Clerc. His achievements were noted by his local contemporaries, as is shown by the high prices that La Tour demanded and got from the town of Lunéville. By 1660 his pictures were in the collections of Charles II of England (the Hampton Court *St Jerome*, previously misidentified as a Dürer) and the Archduke Leopold Wilhelm, as well as in the French royal collection (Louis XIII's *St Sebastian* cannot be traced) and the ducal collection of Lorraine (the two pictures recorded in the 1620s have also never been found). It is therefore not true that La Tour and his art were unknown in their time. More is known about his patrons than those of Vermeer (who were limited to a local bookseller and a baker taking a picture in lieu of bills), and only the fact that La Tour was forgotten in the eighteenth and nineteenth centuries has led to the mistaken idea that he was totally obscure.

The recent identification of Étienne de La Tour, Georges de La Tour's son and pupil, rests on one signed picture and some documentation. The *Education of the Virgin* (figure 28) in the Frick Collection, New York, cannot match the Rennes *New-born* to which it is close in style and spirit, as it lacks Georges de La Tour's consummate skill with detail and subtle outline. Yet the Frick picture has a quiet dignity of its own, and it is characterized by a curious simplification of the forms. Indeed, it was the chiselled quality of this painting which made La Tour almost a cult figure amongst an educated French minority in the 1930s, although they did not realize that they were largely admiring the work of La Tour's main pupil.

Étienne's work is also characterized by a tendency to repetition. Three other versions of the Frick picture exist, and it is tempting to attribute to him a further group of pictures until now hesitantly attributed to Georges. One of the most controversial is the horizontal *St Sebastian* composition, where the model of one of the figures is a familiar La Tour type. Most of the versions are curiously incompetent, only three of them having pretensions to quality: the one in Kansas City, the one with Wildenstein and, best of all, the one in the Poggi collection in Rome. There are pentimenti in this picture, whose execution is fluid enough for it to be considered an original. It ought to be by the elder La Tour, but recent observations on the possible dating of the costumes have left little doubt that the picture is rather later than the artist's lifetime. The same is true of the two celebrated upright versions of the same subject, one in the Louvre (plate 37) and the other in Berlin. Again, the composition, as in the Frick picture, is curiously monumental, as if the painting were depicting a sculptured tableau. The Louvre composition is especially moving, with the mourning figure in a blue cowl (in the Berlin version the cowl is black) looking as if she were taken from a piece of Burgundian tomb sculpture. A suggestion that these pictures are probably by Étienne de La Tour will not at first be welcomed, but their quality is undiminished by a change of attribution. Étienne de La Tour is actually documented as being required to continue his father's style, should the latter die inopportunely, and it is likely that he continued long into the 1660s and even the 1670s, painting ever-weaker versions of the *Smokers* and *Girls with a Brazier* which eventually became mockeries of his father's genius.

With the death of Étienne de La Tour at almost the end of the century, this particular tradition of painting came to a close, never to be revived. Nancy was to witness a glorious period in the early eighteenth century, as was Lunéville, when the town La Tour knew was completely rebuilt. We can therefore no longer wander in the old streets, musing on an enigmatic past: the seventeenth-century pictures executed here, now scattered in many museums in the western world, must speak for themselves.

Chapter Three

Painting in Paris, 1600-35

The Work of Rubens and other Flemish Artists

In the first half of the seventeenth century Paris failed to dominate the rest of France in terms of artistic activity; the painters there were not influential elsewhere. It was not until the 1660s that Paris became the dominant centre of the whole country, to the extent that painting almost everywhere else, with the exception of the extreme south, all but ceased. Nevertheless, at the beginning of the century Paris was a large city by the standards of the time, although it did not possess the colossal wealth of Netherlandish cities such as Amsterdam and Antwerp (whose significance was entirely based on trade). Paris was already an important administrative centre, and a considerable amount of patronage was to come from government officials, both major and minor, from Richelieu at one end of the scale to all the anonymous bourgeois who bought still-life pictures and patronized the Le Nain brothers at the other.

There had long been a tradition of art patronage by the French crown, but (as in England) most of the main commissions had gone to foreigners. François I, the most energetic sixteenth-century monarch, had persuaded even Leonardo da Vinci to come to France, and some of Leonardo's most significant pictures were acquired for the French royal collection, where they were to be profoundly influential on later generations of artists who had access to royal patronage and could therefore see them. Later in his reign François I had his palace at Fontainebleau decorated by three of the most avant-garde Italians of the time, Primaticcio, Rosso Fiorentino and Niccolò dell'Abbate. After the death of the king in 1549, royal patronage ceased for some years, but the example was there and when the time came to request new schemes, foreigners were again often chosen. In the second half of the sixteenth century the French monarchy had shown no interest in painting on a grand scale; there was too much political uncertainty and religious strife. Even after the Valois dynasty had come to an end with the assassination of Henri III, the much more stable reign of Henri IV was nevertheless troubled, and the king himself was in any case much more interested in encouraging architecture than in commissioning more ephemeral paintings.

In 1610 Henri IV was assassinated and Louis XIII came to the throne as a minor. He was too young to be interested in grand designs, and his artistic tastes as well as the political scene were dominated by his formidable mother Marie de Medici, Henri IV's widow. Even as Louis XIII grew older it became clear that he was not interested in the complexities of ruling a prosperous nation emerging from religious conflict and set on a course of economic expansion. Military matters were thus left to the brilliantly skilled Richelieu, whose ambitions succeeded in expanding the boundaries of France, especially eastwards with the annexation of Lorraine.

The capital city of the young Louis XIII lacked the artistic cohesion of many other European centres, particularly those of the Italian states and in the Netherlands. The immigration to France of painters from the north, chiefly from the Netherlands, had begun in the reign of Henri IV, in response to French patrons, who admired the immense skill of the Netherlanders, especially in portrait painting. Since official portraiture of the ruling class was very much more prolific in the Catholic southern Netherlands than in the Dutch Republic, where it was orientated more towards the merchant classes, it was to the southern Netherlands that the French court was drawn, as patrons wanted rather formal, elaborate portraits of themselves for positions of prominence in palaces and public buildings.

The most important Netherlander to work in Paris in the early years of the seventeenth century was Frans Pourbus the Younger. Though skilled, he was no innovator in his portraiture, but copied the idiom favoured half a century earlier by Anthonis Mor. Like Pourbus, Mor acquired an international reputation through painting Spanish and English sitters as well as local sitters from Antwerp. His style was easily recognizable: its studied stiffness was combined with acute observation of character, sometimes worthy of the previous generation of Holbein and Dürer in its power of perception. Pourbus was heir to this style, though his treatment of sitters lacked Mor's intensity; but because of the skill he showed in such pictures as the *Portrait of a Man* of 1591, at Temple Newsam, Leeds, French patrons saw him as a rival to their own Clouet dynasty of portraitists, who had served the court all through the middle years of the sixteenth century.

Pourbus's importation into France of what was, in the Netherlands, already an outmoded style was to have great importance for the whole subsequent development of court portraiture in France in the seventeenth century. Just as Van Dyck influenced the course of English portrait painting for a century and a half after his death, so Pourbus gave rigidity to a formula that was never abandoned, even during the period of great artistic freedom in the middle years of the century. The French court never employed an artist of the stature of Velasquez; instead, it preferred Pourbus to depict the elaborate court costumes and to give his sitters an icon-like quality (as had occurred in Elizabethan England, where there had been a positive denial of realism in portraiture, even though artists of Flemish origin working in the country were quite capable of it). A typical example of Pourbus's court art is the *Portrait of Marie de Medici* in the Louvre, in which the stiffness and formality are exceptional even for the period. The fleurs-de-lis emblazoned on her copious skirts are repeated in a monotonous rhythm. The result is a cold grandeur (which the sitter surely cannot have possessed if Rubens's interpretations of her are taken as evidence); it rivals the images favoured by the Spanish court in the early years of the century, before Velasquez was employed there. Pourbus's religious pictures were also to be influential. For example, his *Last Supper* in the Hermitage, Leningrad, was to serve as the model for Philippe de Champaigne's treatment of the same subject in the Louvre. (Although Champaigne arrived in Paris in 1621, the development and maturity of his art belong to a later era.)

Marie de Medici virtually ruled France, and it was typical of her grandiose ideas that she should want a large decorative cycle of paintings for the newly reconstructed Luxembourg Palace. In 1622 there was no local painter to whom she could turn, and so her natural choice was Rubens, who was inventive, efficient, and above all able, as a professional diplomat, to understand the needs of his patrons. (Lack of local painters was to prove a similar problem for Charles I of England, who also commissioned Rubens in 1629 or 1630 to decorate the ceiling of his new banqueting hall at Whitehall.) It was inevitable that Marie de Medici should choose a political theme – her career and that of her assassinated husband Henri IV, whose reputation stood high at the time. Such a broad theme suited Rubens's expansive mentality, affording him plenty of excuses to paint elaborate arrivals and departures and to include a large number of allegorical allusions. For the Medici cycle Rubens made sketches of all the compositions (most now in the Alte Pinakothek, Munich), then the studio set to work, to produce the colossal cycle of tapestry-like decorations. In spite of a certain heaviness of handling, the sequence of twenty-four canvasses was a decorative triumph. Seen now in the Louvre, they overwhelm by their sheer force of energy in composition and narrative. They actually belong to the history of Flemish painting, but their presence in Paris as the largest artistic creation before the work of Le Brun was to have a profound influence on several generations of painters. This influence was not to be apparent until much later; clearly all the painters working outside Paris were totally oblivious to Rubens's achievement but, more important, it appears to have had no effect on painters working in Paris at the time. There was no sudden move to imitate Rubens's colour, compositions, or energy; that was not to come until later when the whole cycle had acquired an academic respectability under the aegis of Le Brun in the 1660s and after.

The other major decorative cycle in Paris from these years is now lost and its effect can only be guessed at. The now-obscure Flemish painter from Brussels, Jacques Fouquières, was entrusted by Louis XIII to paint a series of views of the major French towns along the entire length of the Grande Galerie of the Louvre. The commission was to be paid for by the simple strategem of persuading each town in the series to contribute the necessary payment for the privilege of having itself depicted. If the Fouquières scheme had been completed, it would have formed a unique record of the appearance of early seventeenth-century French towns, but nothing appears to survive. It is reasonable to assume, in the light of Fouquières's other work, that each picture would have been relatively small in scale and minutely detailed, and that such an extensive project would have taken far too long for one person ever to hope to complete. The artist's few surviving pictures are, not surprisingly, entirely in the Flemish manner, derived from the late sixteenth-century Antwerp painter Joos de Momper. A good example of Fouquières's work is the *Winter Scene* in the Fitzwilliam Museum, Cambridge. Curiously enough, his type of art had little or no influence on the subsequent development of landscape painting in France; Dutch or Italian models were preferred.

Little is known about the work of painters in Paris in the first quarter of the century. The surviving documentation shows that artists there were both numerous and prolific, but little of their output survives. The most important of them was undoubtedly Georges Lallemant, who maintained a studio, and trained the young Nicolas Poussin before he left for Rome. Lallemant's few surviving pictures include the impressive *Échevins of Paris Praying before St Geneviève* (plate 36) in the Musée Carnavalet, Paris, in which the treatment of the figures is realist enough to suggest that Lallemant was influenced by such Flemish artists as Pourbus. In spite of the fact that he ran the major Parisian studio, Lallemant's importance was overshadowed by the arrival of the new generation of artists trained in Italy, led by Simon Vouet.

Simon Vouet's Career in Paris and his Contemporaries Blanchard and Vignon

Simon Vouet arrived in Paris in 1627, having already pursued a successful career in Rome. His art seems to have appealed immediately to Louis XIII, who gave him more commissions than he accorded other artists. Vouet's main achievement was in bringing a fully developed Baroque style back from Italy, which shows his extraordinary ability to change direction: he had been totally preoccupied with Caravaggism in his Roman years. He must, however, have been absorbing all the fashionable trends in Rome (Caravaggism had already become old-fashioned among Italian painters in the 1620s), and he was able to bring them almost unadulterated to the court of Louis XIII.

The Parisian court's preoccupation with foreign styles of painting was already obvious, and Vouet, although a Frenchman, found that he could provide an up-to-date approach to what the court wanted without any local rivals. The combination of Italian influences is seen to perfection in his *Presentation in the Temple* (plate 87) in the Louvre, given by Cardinal Richelieu to the Jesuit church in Paris. Only certain of the facial expressions suggest that the picture might not be Italian. In scale and composition it is a flawless altarpiece of the type then being commissioned for newly decorated or reconstructed churches all over Rome. The main influences in the picture are derived from the cool order of Domenichino and the much softer, more sensual approach of Guido Reni, and in it Vouet reached the level of accomplishment found in the work of Orazio Gentileschi, who had been working successfully for the Parisian court for two years. Only one picture can be with certainty identified as by Gentileschi from this period, and it has to be assumed from it that the Italian painter made no changes to his mature style when in Paris.

A few pictures by Simon Vouet, connected with Louis XIII, do show that he made a few concessions to his patron's whims, in the sense that they are less obviously Italianate. *Louis XIII between France and Navarre* (figure 29) in the Louvre is an elaborate allegory based on the fact that Henri IV had successfully united the two kingdoms. To modern eyes the whole composition seems a little stilted and completely lacking in the fluidity of Rubens's work glorifying the reign of Henri IV, yet it shows Vouet's ability as a portraitist in its formal interpretation of the king's features, revealing his unattractive character. Louis XIII's problem as a monarch was that he took little interest in the daily affairs of government when it was one of a monarch's functions to do so. On the other hand, although he remains an obscure and enigmatic figure, it seems that his artistic taste was well defined. For instance, Vouet's *Diana* (figure 30) at Hampton Court has always been considered to have formed part of a now-dismembered decoration for Louis XIII. The figure of Diana is both languid and elegant, foreshadowing much eighteenth-century taste in France, even in the bright blue and yellow colour scheme, and such a painting shows that the king was abreast of the tastes of his time, and not living statically with outdated ideas, as was the court of Lorraine.

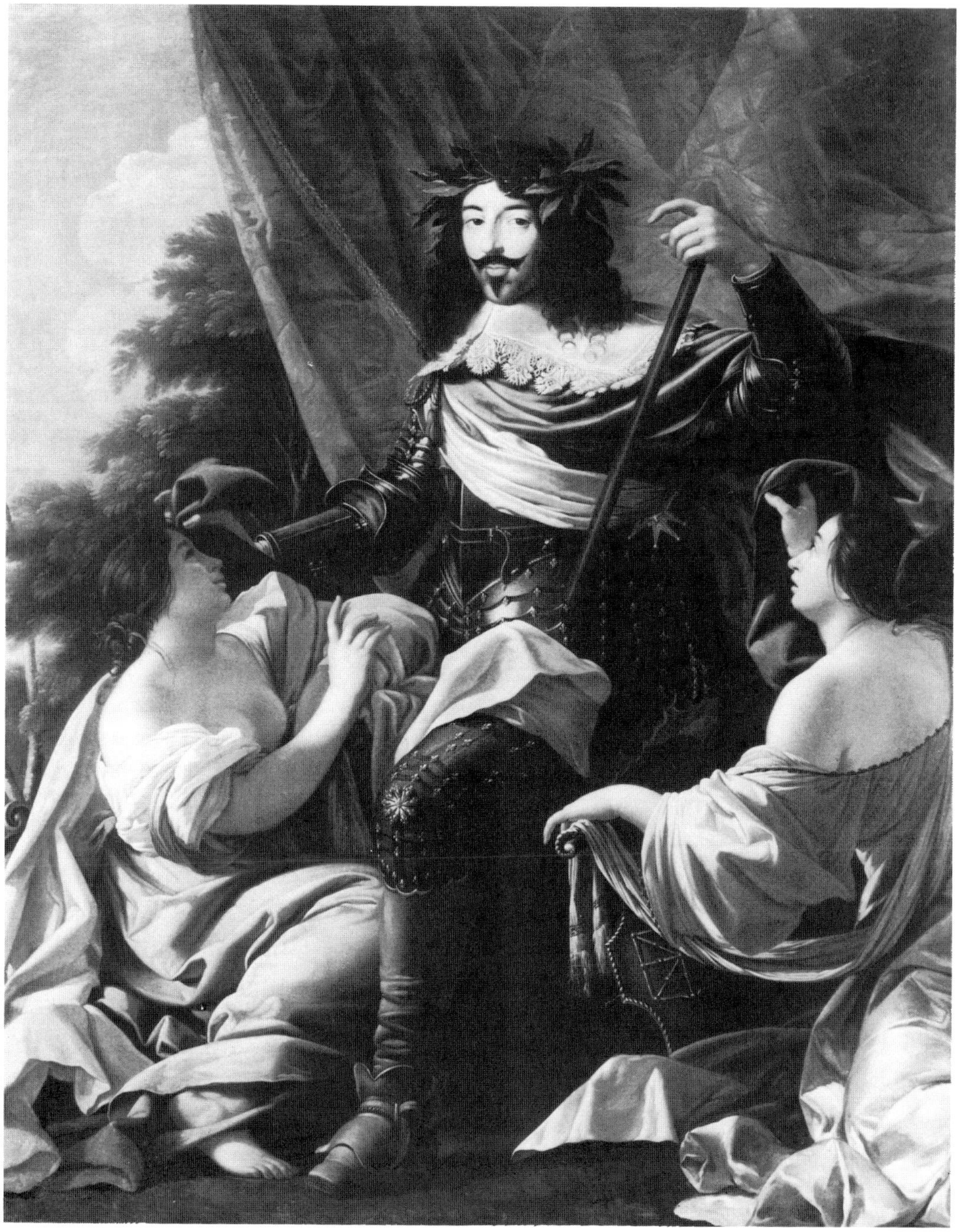

FIGURE 29
Simon Vouet
Louis XIII between France and Navarre
Canvas, 163 × 154 cm.
Paris, Louvre
From the collection of Louis XIII, who commissioned it.

Vouet was aided by his considerable studio, and his output was enormous. His pupils on the whole did not reflect his style, preferring other influences from Rome, but it seems that Vouet kept training young artists to turn out anonymous decorations in his manner, exactly as Rubens was doing on a much larger scale in Antwerp. This explains the large number of pictures now attributed to Vouet, many of which may be the work of the competent studio. He rarely painted small-scale pictures which would be prized by collectors, but he did make modellos (small versions) of his larger pictures, many of which survive. They are often extremely skilled and show how much Vouet had assimilated the Italian method of working, on a scale not to be repeated until Charles Le Brun's time, thirty years later. In common with many Italian artists in Rome in the early part of the century, Vouet had concentrated on achieving a specific style which was, in the final analysis, anonymous:

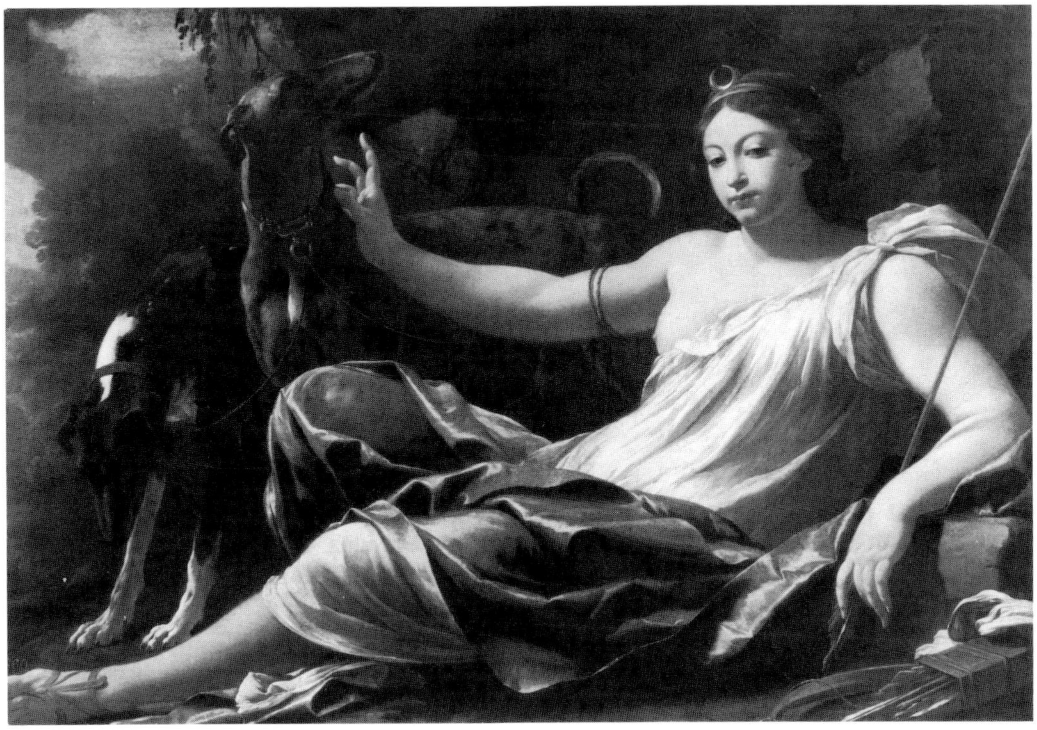

FIGURE 30
Simon Vouet
Diana
Canvas, 102 × 141 cm. Signed and dated in the quiver, lower right: Simon Vouet F. Paris 1637 (this is sometimes read as 1627).
Hampton Court Palace, Royal Collection. Reproduced by gracious permission of Her Majesty the Queen.

It is likely that the picture formed part of an elaborate decorative cycle, now lost.

the Caravaggesque pictures of the time were painted to conform to a set of rules as rigid as the standards against which their creators rebelled.

Vouet's contemporary Claude Vignon had also worked in an 'anonymous' style, which he abandoned as soon as he returned to Paris. Indeed, his ability to merge into the background in Rome has led to great difficulties in defining his Roman *oeuvre*. A superb portrait of a sultry-looking man, now in the Royal Collection at Kensington Palace, reveals Vignon's unmistakeable hand only in the treatment of the jewellery; the style of the rest of the picture is purely Italian. It would seem logical that, in Paris, Vignon would have taken the same path as Vouet and tried to rival him, especially as Vignon had great facility with brushwork, but instead he close a path which turned his art into a total anachronism: he returned to a modified form of Mannerism. This *volte face* produced a marvellously interesting painter who has been neglected precisely because he does not fit into the pattern of the development of painting at the time (whereas the mainstream was led by Vouet because he was such an efficient teacher).

The earliest Mannerist influences on Vignon, which probably occurred before he left for Rome, must have been submerged while he was in Italy, as in fact happened with all French artists there with the exception of Deruet. That Vignon's Caravaggism was perfectly competent is shown by the fact that his work effectively merged with that of his contemporaries. After his return to Paris in 1624, he suddenly became enormously prolific; a huge number of pictures, several hundred in all, were documented at the time of his death, but since then only a hundred or so have been identified, many of them quite recently. One of the most extravagant in terms of its composition is the *Martyrdom of St Matthew* in the Palais Saint-Vaast at Arras. The colour is still rather subdued, but the forms have taken on a twisted exaggeration, exactly as in the Mannerist etchings of Bellange.

One of the most curious aspects of Vignon's work in the 1620s, which has

FIGURE 31
Claude Vignon
Croesus Receiving Tribute from a Lydian Peasant
Canvas, 105 × 149 cm. Signed and dated: Vignon Inª Faª 1629
Tours, Musée des Beaux-Arts
Deposited in the museum in 1872 from the Louvre.

There is some doubt about the identification of the main figure as Croesus, but the story fits well enough. The moral is clear —great wealth is amassed by cruel methods. The story is continued in the picture in the Bowes Museum (figure 3).

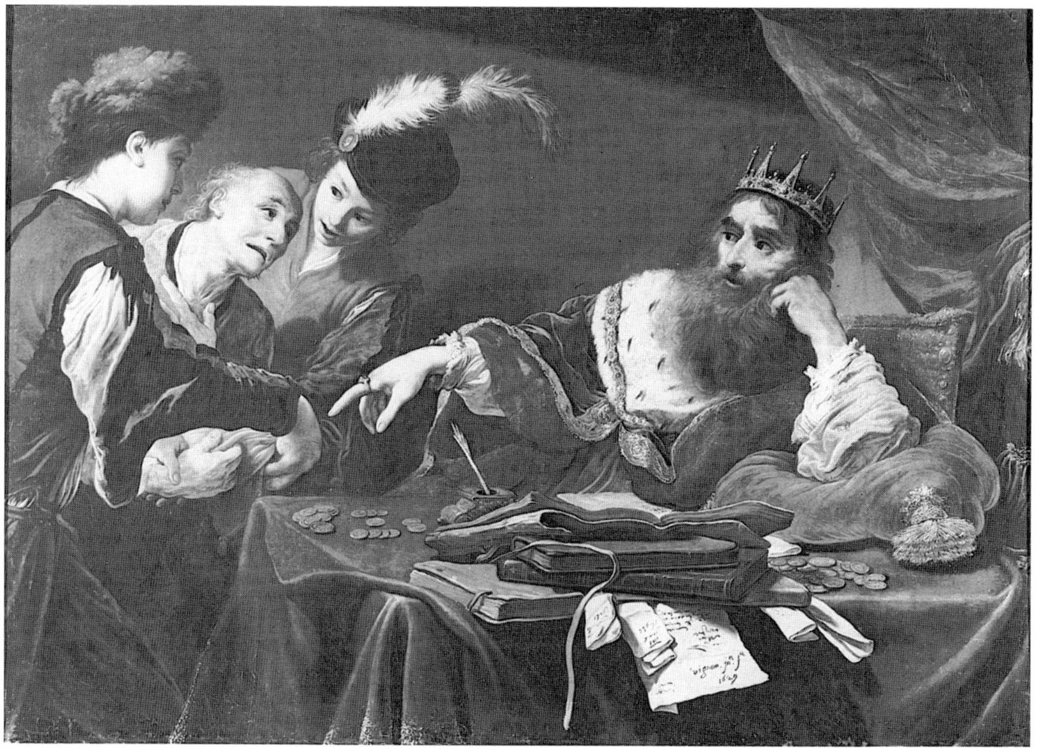

FIGURE 32
Claude Vignon
Solomon Adoring the Idols of Baal (fragment)
Canvas, 76.2 × 77.5 cm.
Signed and dated 1626
Los Angeles, Solomon collection
One of Vignon's unusual Old Testament subjects.

It is interesting to imagine how Vignon depicted the grotesque idols.

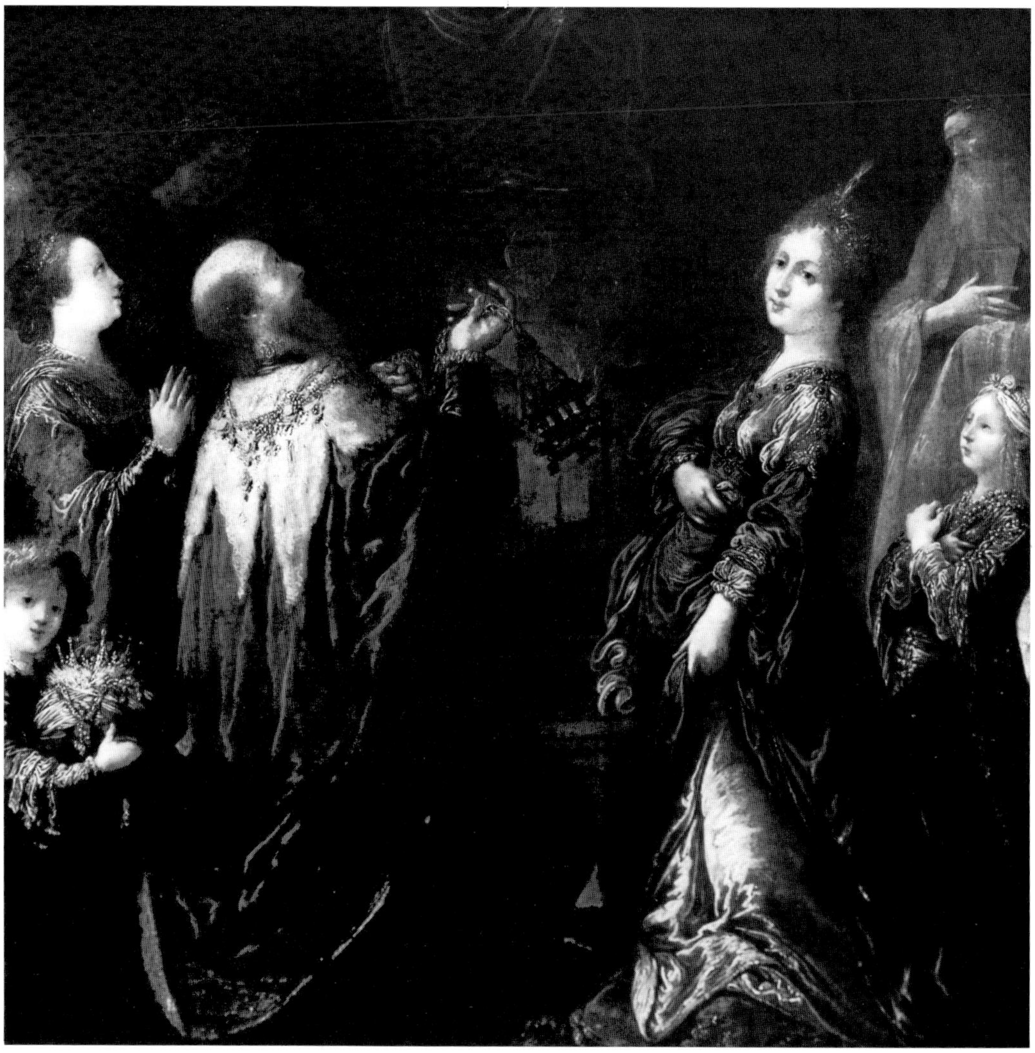

often been noted but not adequately explained, is his affinity with the early works of Rembrandt. It is known that Vignon owned a Rembrandt from that artist's youth in Leiden, *The Ass of Balaam*, now in the Musée Cognacq-Jay in Paris, and it is likely that he was impressed by Rembrandt's curious technique of using highly coloured impasto at that time. Especially close to Vignon is a newly discovered Rembrandt, the *Baptism of the Eunuch* in the Rijksmuseum 'Het Catharijneconvent' at Utrecht. Most French writers have suggested that Vignon, the older artist, influenced the young Rembrandt, but this seems unlikely, since influences were coming south to Paris from the Dutch Republic rather than travelling northwards.

Vignon's pictorial extravagance is also illustrated in *Croesus Showing Solon his Treasures* (figure 3) in the Bowes Museum at Barnard Castle. This picture was long thought to have been a copy after an unidentified Rembrandt, so similar was the technique, but the use of colour, unique in seventeenth-century painting, gives Vignon away (although such contrasts of acid lime green, cherry red and pale lilac are to be found in Italian Mannerist pictures of the previous century). No other painter of Vignon's period used such combinations of impasto and colour. Vignon's passion for over-elaboration is also seen in *Esther before Ahasuerus* of 1624 (plate 85) in the Louvre. It seems that Vignon enjoyed painting awkward human situations: Esther confronts Ahasuerus, just as Solon confronts Croesus, with the awful truth that worldly wealth is of little importance.

One of the attractions of Vignon's work is his preoccupation with unusual subject-matter, which he often treated in an anecdotal way. Unfortunately, many of his pictures have been cut: Solon and Croesus have lost the treasures they are discussing, and the still-life from this picture is also missing (the whole composition is known from a copy). In the same way, *Solomon Adoring the Idols of Baal* of 1626 (figure 32), in the Solomon collection in Los Angeles, has lost the idols, leaving the lower figures in heavy shadow. In all these pictures there is an atmosphere of mystery, and it seems as if Vignon must have known and admired other early works by Rembrandt such as the *Simeon in the Temple* in the Mauritshuis, The Hague.

As he matured in Paris and lightened his palette a little, Vignon still maintained his sense of drama. For example, in his *Croesus Receiving Tribute from a Lydian Peasant* of 1629 (figure 31), in the Musée des Beaux-Arts at Tours, there is a lessening of interest in bizarre surface texture, and the poses of the figures round the table show a return to the conventions of Caravaggism. After 1630 or so the precise chronology of Vignon's pictures is unknown, but they show no radical changes of style. Instead of developing further, Vignon's style remained static for the rest of his forty-year-long career.

The other important painter to arrive in Paris from Italy in the 1620s was Jacques Blanchard. He died young in 1637 and so exerted little influence on his contemporaries, and his considerable achievements have often been ignored. The influences on his art were entirely different from those of any French painter of the time, except possibly Nicholas Poussin. These were an infatuation with Venetian sixteenth-century painting, especially the work of Titian and Veronese. His *Bacchanal* of 1636 (plate 6) in the Musée des Beaux-Arts at Nancy is particularly Titianesque in mood and composition, but the palette is rather lighter than was usual in the Venetian master. There is a concentration on movement in the composition, and a delicacy that foreshadows the eighteenth century in France. At Nancy the picture is often hung among the French paintings of the eighteenth century, unnoticed as a seventeenth-century work of art. Blanchard's refinement is also found in *Allegory of Charity* (plate 5) in the Toledo Museum of Art. Here, the technique is especially delicate, showing careful attention to the effects of various silvery tones making up the draperies. Such subtlety is found in Veronese but is rare in the work of French painters of the seventeenth century.

Unfortunately only one picture survives from Blanchard's final year, 1637. This is the *Charity* in the collection of the Courtauld Institute, London, which reveals that Blanchard was losing his Venetian-inspired manner and turning to the much more fashionable classicizing tendencies already popular with Vouet's pupils. This was symptomatic of the reaction to the old standards, which was taking place in the mid 1630s. Such rapid changes, although meaning that Blanchard's success was to be short-lived, were evidence of a great increase in painting activity in Paris. No longer was one style either required or preferred: in the 1630s artistic activity in the city suddenly matured. Vouet had taught a generation of painters; Rubens's Medici cycle was present in the Luxembourg Palace as an example; and the next twenty years were to be the most exciting and inventive period of painting, scarcely to be rivalled until just before and during the French Revolution.

Chapter Four

French Painters in Rome: the Classical Tradition

All the French painters in Rome in the 1620s were working against the current of the fashions of the time, as set by their Italian contemporaries. They were still following Caravaggio, while the Italians were evolving the most significant artistic style of the century all over southern Europe – the Baroque. The term 'the Baroque' is often used to cover the whole of seventeenth-century painting irrespective of its style, which can be misleading, and in this context it is used to define a specific type of painting, to which the term was originally applied as one of abuse (baroque means misshapen, as in a 'baroque' pearl).

In the last years of the sixteenth century there had already been signs of the development of new trends in Italy, especially in Rome, although it is only with hindsight that it is possible to pick out which painters were to be the most significant in their influence on successive generations. The chief innovators at the end of the sixteenth century were Annibale Carracci and those who worked for a time in his entourage on the Farnese ceiling, especially Domenichino. The Carracci concentrated on brilliantly drawn ceiling decoration, but also executed a few easel paintings in which the main influence was the drawing style of Michelangelo, combined with a greater richness of colour derived from Correggio. The result, however, was always subtle and restrained. Today the Farnese ceiling seems modest in scale and quiet in tone, especially when compared with what was to come later in the century. The dual nature of the Carracci, their combination of dryness and sensuality, was to be extremely important to the next generation of artists, who built on both these characteristics but took them in opposite directions. Domenichino, for instance, kept his colour schemes simple and his compositions Michelangelesque, and thus became the main exponent of what is now termed 'Baroque classicism'. Pietro da Cortona and Guido Reni, on the other hand, developed much more extravagant styles, where strong emotionalism was dominant. They respected the lessons they learnt from the Carracci about drawing and perspective, but applied them with a much greater vigour and with less regard for what could be termed academic correctness.

The developments towards the Baroque style were extremely rapid in the first decades of the seventeenth century in Rome, and the Caravaggesque movement, taking place at the same time, was of very much less importance. An immense number of commissions went to the developing generation of artists – such as Lanfranco, Guercino and Pietro da Cortona – who, in the ceiling of the Barberini Palace glorifying the Barberini family, created the greatest piece of decoration of the whole period.

Nicolas Poussin

When Nicolas Poussin, already in his thirties, arrived in Rome in the middle of the 1620s, he was without connections and without an accomplished style. He was ill-equipped to rival any of the current styles through lack of adequate training; no young painter, however talented, would have been able to adopt the fashionable methods without years of studio apprenticeship. Only then was it possible to master such complexities as painting in perspective on a ceiling and the difficult technique of painting in fresco. Nor did the young Poussin have the skill to concentrate on small cabinet pictures, at which the Netherlandish painters in Rome were so successful. Nevertheless, within ten years he had established himself as the most distinguished French painter living in Rome, and was beginning to gain patrons in France, which culminated in his being summoned to Paris in 1640 by Louis XIII. That such success was achieved in so short a time was partly due to Poussin's determination to pursue his chosen ends, and partly to the fact that he evolved a unique form of art which appealed to intellectually minded collectors.

In spite of the clarity of almost all Poussin's pictures, in terms of their composition and even the moral principles they depicted, much of his work is curiously ambiguous, and his pictures have been subjected to many different interpretations. Poussin's own explanations of his art, in his letters, are often unsatisfactory because they reveal deep meanings behind many of his major paintings, which are not always apparent when one stands in front of them. Except to the scholarly, Poussin is on the whole incomprehensible, and he is thus deprived of appreciation on a general level. This is a pity, because a few of his pictures are so charged with emotions and ideas that they are among the strongest of the whole period. The reason so many of Poussin's complex ideas and emotions are no longer understood is because they reflect a totally different moral ethic. Only a very few people today are educated in the subtleties of the Greek way of thinking, which was what Poussin was attempting to put over in many of his pictures. Thus the modern viewer has to be educated into an understanding of much of Poussin's art, a problem which did not occur in his own time. The result can be extremely rewarding for those who are prepared to broaden their tastes from the overtly emotional and sensual in art, to include the unashamedly intellectual.

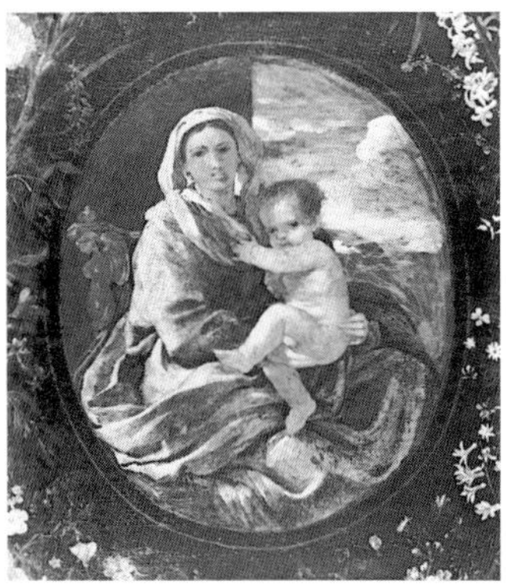

FIGURE 33
Nicolas Poussin
The Virgin and Child (with Daniel Seghers)
Canvas, 58 × 50 cm.
Brighton, The Royal Pavilion, Art Gallery and Museums (Preston Manor)
First recorded in the collection of Cassiano dal Pozzo. Bequeathed to the museum in 1930 but not correctly identified until 1974.

Almost as soon as he arrived in Rome, Poussin was fortunate enough to come into contact with the scholarly and benevolent Cassiano dal Pozzo, who was to be his patron for the next thirty years until his death in 1657. Their relationship in its early years seems to have consisted mainly of Pozzo collecting a number of Poussin's first works, almost out of charity for the struggling young artist, as the pictures vere indeed of modest pretensions. The best examples of these early efforts are a pair of pictures which were originally garlands of flowers painted by the Antwerp Jesuit monk and specialist flower-painter Daniel Seghers. The centres of these garlands were filled in by Poussin, a *Pietà* in one and a *Virgin and Child* (figure 33) in the other. In the nineteenth century the flowers were cut away and the pair of small canvasses was split up (one is now in the Musée Thomas Henry at Cherbourg, the other at Preston Manor at Brighton). The *Virgin and Child* perfectly illustrates Poussin's amateur status. The brushwork is hesitant, though fluid, and no definable style is yet apparent, but there is already a certain intensity in the feeling of the picture, an intensity which was to become Poussin's dominant preoccupation during his first ten years in Rome.

So much has been written about Poussin's maturity during the thirty years from the mid-1630s onwards that it is not often realized that almost half his surviving output dates from the first ten years of this period, and therefore demands discussion. The changes in his style are rapid, and it has been difficult to establish a reasonable chronology because Poussin was capable of adopting several different styles at once. He both reacted against and was deeply influenced by the fashions of the time, but after the late 1630s he renounced all variety and concentrated on painting one specific type of picture, for which posterity has both praised and blamed him.

The first important commission Poussin received was from Cardinal Francesco Barberini at the end of 1626, for the *Death of Germanicus*. The picture, now in the Minneapolis Institute of Arts, was completed early in 1628 and immediately became famous. This was the first of the deathbed scenes that Poussin was to favour throughout his life. The figures are arranged in a frieze-like composition which was almost certainly derived from the arrangement of figures on classical sarcophagi. Already, too, there is a preoccupation with classical antiquity and its intensely moral approach to life. In his pictures Poussin was to become obsessed by morality, and with man facing the supreme trial: how to face death with equanimity.

As soon as the *Germanicus* was completed, an even more important commission was received, this time for the Basilica of St Peter's. It was for a large altarpiece depicting the *Martyrdom of St Erasmus* (figure 5). The picture was not a success and, with the exception of the *Virgin with St James* (Louvre, Paris) which was probably painted for a church in Valenciennes, Poussin painted only one more large altarpiece for a prominent position. The *Erasmus* is nevertheless important in several ways: it shows Poussin's temporary preoccupation with the Caravaggesque idiom (already referred to under the discussion of Le Valentin in Chapter Two) and also his weaknesses as a composer of large altarpieces, demonstrating that he was temperamentally unsuited to the painting of a single picture on a grand scale. Almost all the greatest pictures of his maturity form part of a pair or a series: the first set of *Sacraments*, the *Seasons*, and the *Crossing of the Red Sea* paired with the *Adoration of the Golden Calf*.

Many of the other pictures painted at this period show such a variety of influences that it would not have been possible at the time to say in which direction Poussin was developing. There was certainly a preoccupation with the richness of Venetian sixteenth-century colouring, especially as shown by Titian and Veronese, and an example of this is the still-immature *Venus and Mercury* at Dulwich. There is also an early preoccupation with landscape, seen in pictures such as the sombre *Landscape with Venus and Adonis* in the Musée Fabre at Montpellier, which once belonged to Cassiano dal Pozzo.

By 1630, Poussin was moving towards the uncompromising statements about the moral condition of humanity that were to characterize his work. In that year he painted the *Plague of Ashdod* (Louvre, Paris), which sets the style and mood of his work for the next five years. The figures are interlocked in an extremely complex composition which appears somewhat disorganized; in depicting the Old Testament theme, in which the spectator is spared none of the horror, Poussin was trying to achieve accuracy. The following year he painted the *Triumph of Flora* (Dresden, Gemäldegalerie), a more cheerful subject but with a similarly interlocking frieze of figures. It is round these two pictures, datable through documents, that the rest of Poussin's pictures supposedly painted around 1630 have to be grouped.

One of the most effective of these early works is the *Lamentation over the Dead Christ* in the Alte Pinakothek, Munich. The treatment of the subject is both passionate and austere, and anticipates the painting of the same subject now in the National Gallery, Dublin (figure 37), painted almost thirty years later. Two pictures that are very much more Venetian in their inspiration are the Munich *Apollo and Daphne* (plate 64) and the Louvre *Triumph of Flora*, whose subjects are taken from Ovid's *Metamorphoses*. Throughout his career Poussin liked to dwell on themes of transformation, especially those found in stories from classical antiquity. Apollo pursues Daphne, and to escape his clutches she is transformed into a laurel tree. The theme has a poetic melancholy, and this melancholy is also present to a certain extent in the much more cheerful *Flora*. In the *Bacchanal: the Andrians* in the Louvre (plate 65), the mood is even lighter, although the colours retain a Venetian richness. In these pictures, Poussin was trying to express his personal vision of the lushness and extravagance of antiquity, tinged with a certain sadness. In some cases he succeeded, although in a number of others his use of a dark ground has caused excessive darkening and the pictures have sometimes lost their brilliance.

The most poetical and moving of all the early pictures is the *Narcissus* in the Louvre, where the excessively beautiful youth Narcissus is changed into the flower that bears his name, while admiring his own reflection in the water. A similar melancholy is seen in the exquisite *Arcadian Shepherds* (figure 34) in the Devonshire collection at Chatsworth, Derbyshire. The shepherds, wandering in Paradise, come across a tomb on which is the inscription 'Et in Arcadia Ego' ('And I, too, was in Paradise'). On the tomb is a skull, a reminder of death. The precise idea behind the picture has been much discussed, and it seems that it is the strong contrast between lusty life and the stillness of death that Poussin wished to stress. The shepherds, in the full vigour of life, are forced, by accidental contact, to contemplate their ultimate destiny. The picture's pendant, on a similarly sombre theme, has now been identified: Midas bathing in the waters of the Pactolus in order to rid himself of the curse of turning everything he touched into gold.

There are instances of pictures by Poussin whose specific literary theme has not been identified. One of the best, the dating of which is controversial, is the *Inspiration of the Poet* (plate 67) in the Louvre, Paris. It is unusual in that the figures are almost life-size: a more modest format was usually favoured by Poussin, whose pictures, intended for middle-class collectors without great palaces, had to be contemplated in the intimacy of a small room. In the *Inspiration of the Poet* Poussin has used the idea that poetry was inspired by the Muses, in order to create a dreamy composition of figures interlocking in an unusually elegant way.

Among several controversial pictures dating from the early 1630s is the *Triumph of David* at Dulwich in London. Its attribution to Poussin has been denied, in spite of the existence of preparatory drawings for the composition by him. X-ray photographs prove that he made many alterations to the positions of the figures, and this fact has given rise to problems of dating. On the grounds that the picture reveals a tendency to a much more theoretical

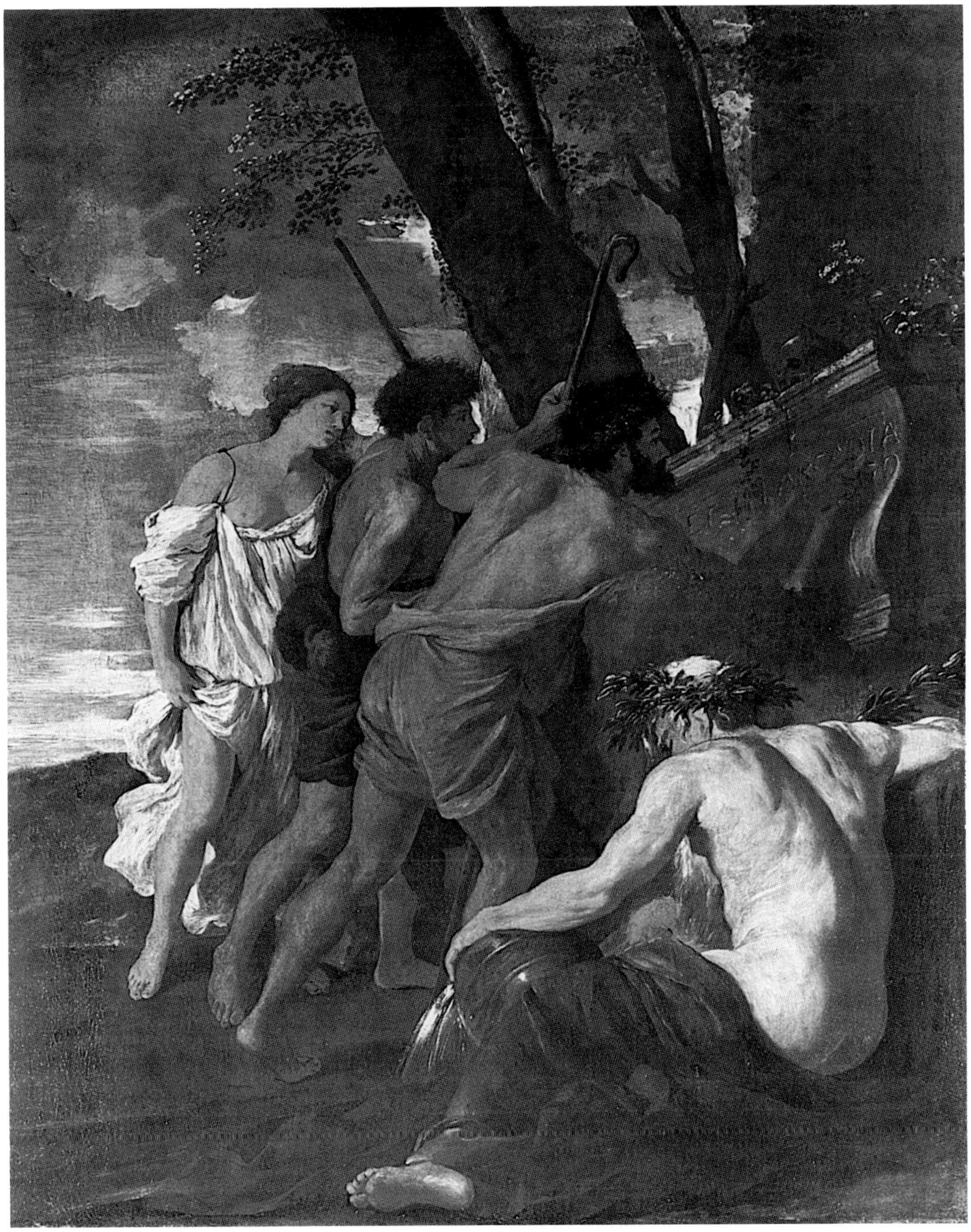

FIGURE 34
Nicolas Poussin
The Arcadian Shepherds
Canvas, 101 × 82 cm.
Chatsworth, Trustees of the Chatsworth Settlement
Probably painted for the Massimi family. Acquired by the Duke of Devonshire in or before 1761, thence by descent.

The exact literary source for this poignant reminder of the presence of death has not been discovered.

and calculating approach, a dating in the early 1630s can be favoured. The line of figures at the lower level has a rhythmic change of colour which then repeats itself on the other side. There is in addition a certain coolness of handling, also found in the little-known *Adoration of the Kings*, signed and dated 1633, in the Gemäldegalerie at Dresden.

The emphasis on rhythm in Poussin's art in the mid-1630s is nowhere better shown than in the *Nurture of Jupiter*, also at Dulwich (detail, frontispiece). This picture is important because it shows how Poussin was able to integrate his figures into the landscape, a reminder that much later in life he was to evolve the purely classical landscape. The landscape background is perfectly balanced with the rhythmic figures. It is known that Poussin went into the countryside near Rome and made drawings on the spot, although few of them survive. He was able to use the information from these drawings for

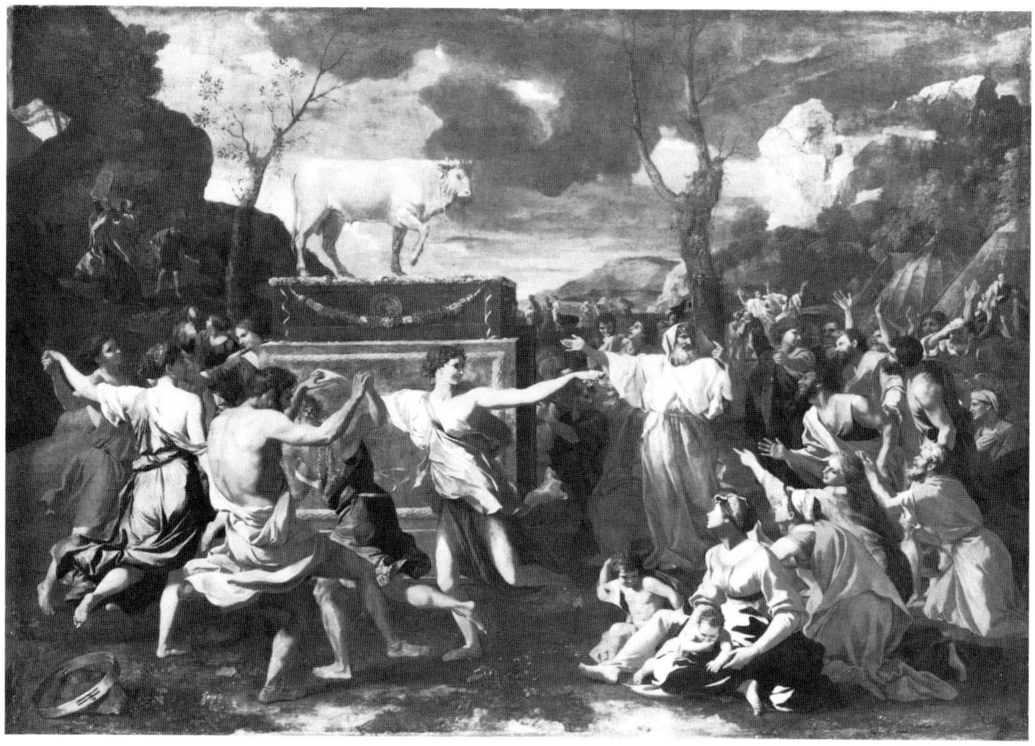

FIGURE 35
Nicolas Poussin
The Adoration of the Golden Calf
Canvas, 154.5 × 214 cm.
London, National Gallery
Probably painted for Amadeo dal Pozzo, the cousin of Cassiano dal Pozzo. Acquired by the National Gallery in 1945 from the collection of the Earls of Radnor.

This subject was also painted by Claude (see figure 45).

landscape backgrounds such as this. The treatment of the draperies is noticeably harsh and brilliant, and anticipates the almost metallic effects he created in his mature years.

During the mid-1630s Poussin was especially productive, as he gained more prestigious patrons. The precise order in which the major pictures were painted is not known. Among the most significant are two works painted as a pair: the *Crossing of the Red Sea* in the National Gallery of Victoria, Melbourne, and the *Adoration of the Golden Calf* (figure 35) in the National Gallery, London. It was not until after 1945 that the pair was separated. They were intended to complement one another, especially in the rhythms created by the figures as they dance round the golden calf and struggle across the exposed sand of the sea-bed.

At the same time, Poussin was working on a major series of *Bacchanals* for Cardinal Richelieu which were designed to adorn his château near Orléans. The earliest of Poussin's bacchanals (not one intended for Richelieu) is the *Bacchanalian Revel before a Term of Pan* in the National Gallery, London. The colours are conspicuously light, with pink and pale blue predominating. The lightness of tone is also seen in the *Triumph of Neptune* (plate 68) in the Philadelphia Museum of Art, a picture almost certainly painted for Richelieu and probably rather earlier than the three large *Bacchanals* for the château. The composition of the *Triumph of Neptune* is derived from Raphael's fresco in the Villa Farnese, but the result is unfortunately a little pedantic; when looking too closely at other art, Poussin forgot to relax and somehow stopped letting his own special intensity dominate. The result is light-hearted and decorative, and its subject has been interpreted in many different ways.

The three main canvasses executed for Richelieu, the *Triumph of Pan* (National Gallery, London), the *Triumph of Bacchus* (Nelson Gallery, Kansas City) and the *Triumph of Silenus* (known from a good old copy in the National Gallery, London), are clearly decorative in intent. As a result of the recent cleaning of the *Triumph of Pan*, one can see that its colours were intended to be light and delicate, with a strong predominance of pinks and blues, and that Poussin was entering into the light-hearted spirit of antiquity. Even at this stage in his development, he was moving away from his contemporaries; his isolation from current trends was beginning to take hold and was at the same time bringing him a very specific type of success – that of patronage by collectors with an academic or literary turn of mind. In the end, however, this was to prove Poussin's downfall, because it led him to pursue certain extremes in his approach to his subject-matter, which meant that some of his later compositions became dry, cold and unfeeling.

The catalyst for this development towards an extreme in the later 1630s was undoubtedly Cassiano dal Pozzo, who commissioned Poussin to paint his first set of *Sacraments*. The dates of execution for this first set are unknown, but they were not completed until 1642, when the final one was sent by Poussin from Paris to Rome. Cassiano owned a Poussin executed in the late 1630s, a *Baptism of Christ* now in the Getty Museum at Malibu, and it may well have been this carefully calculated composition which spurred Cassiano on to commission Poussin to create the *Sacraments*, one of the most important single commissions of his career. The seven pictures, though executed over several years, were intended to be seen together, presumably in a relatively small room. Five of them – *Marriage*, *Extreme Unction*, *Confirmation*, *Ordination* and *Eucharist* – are now at Belvoir Castle, Leicestershire, hung in different places in the house; the sixth, *Baptism*, is in the National Gallery of Art, Washington; and the seventh, *Penance*, was lost in the fire which destroyed Belvoir in 1816. It is difficult to know whether Poussin worked out his artistic theories after he had solved his problems on canvas, or whether he thought in the abstract and tried to prove his point by painting to a chosen formula. Whatever the explanation, the result was an extremely cerebral approach, epitomized by this first set of *Sacraments*.

Poussin's basic premise was that painting should appeal to the mind as well as to the eye; in other words, the picture should provoke thought in the spectator. Poussin believed that the best method of achieving this was to create pictures according to an elaborate series of self-imposed rules, which he never properly explained, although he hinted at them. His ideas were adopted as standards for the newly reformed academy in Paris, and the result for the next generation of painters, especially under Louis XIV, was much misunderstanding, unnecessary pedantry and ultimately a rigid formula to which pictures for official positions were supposed to be painted. Among the many of Poussin's precise statements that have given rise to speculation is his idea that painting should be related to the Greek theory of the modes in music, where each specific mode was designed to be related to a particular mood. Poussin thought that such rules could be applied to painting. This was a very personal point of view, and it has never been satisfactorily explained. Poussin was also very strongly influenced by the Greek philosophers, as is obvious from his themes such as the *Phocion* landscapes which are taken from Athens in the heroic days of the Republic of the fifth century BC.

In spite of his great rigidity of theory, and in spite of some very dry pictures in which there seems to be little feeling of any kind, a surprisingly large number of Poussin's best pictures are tense with emotion. This is nowhere better seen than in the first set of *Sacraments*: it is as if all Poussin's energies and

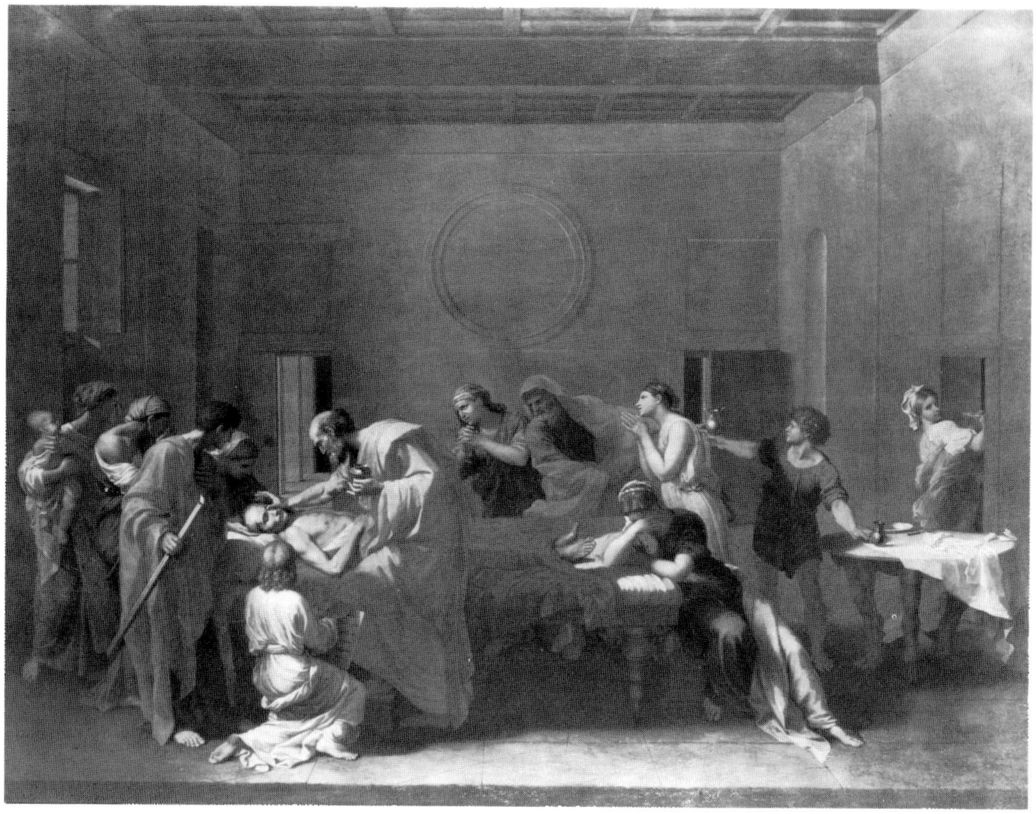

FIGURE 36
Nicolas Poussin
The Sacrament of Extreme Unction
Canvas, 95.5 × 121 cm.
Belvoir Castle (Leicestershire), Duke of Rutland
Documented 1636–40; one of the set of *Sacraments* originally acquired by the Duke of Rutland in the late eighteenth century.

This is the most austere of the six surviving canvasses of the seven *Sacraments* executed for Cassiano dal Pozzo, c.1636–40.

ideas are concentrated in these relatively small canvasses. They exist on many different levels. First, they are a gravely beautiful decorative ensemble. Seen together, as they were uniquely at Edinburgh in 1981, the rhythmic nature of the colours in the figures becomes obvious, and makes Poussin's achievement in this respect all the more astonishing when it is remembered that the pictures were executed over a period of several years. On a second level they exist almost as archeological reconstructions of the rites of the early Christian Church and also in some instances as scenes from the life of Christ when the Sacraments were instituted, such as in the *Baptism*, showing the baptism of Christ and the *Eucharist*, which depicts the Last Supper. As reconstructions they are free of pedantry, and the scenes seem perfectly natural even though they were originally formal occasions. The third level is the emotional and spiritual one, and it is in this area that Poussin has been misunderstood. Few of his later pictures, with the exception of the very last works such as the *Seasons*, show such an intensity of emotion. In the *Extreme Unction* (figure 36) we are made to contemplate the frailty of human life in a deeply moving manner. We are not meant to feel sorry for the dying but to admire the stoicism with which the last rites are being received. For Poussin there seems to have been no conflict between the Stoic philosophy of the Greeks and the Early Christian Church; in fact, there is never any conflict in his art between the treatment of Classical mythology and religion. Significantly, with few exceptions he kept away from contemporary religious iconography as favoured by Guido Reni and Guercino, and reconstructed religious themes to be as close as possible to what he believed had actually taken place.

The *Sacraments*, a microcosm of Poussin's art, reveal his working methods. It is known that he kept a small box rather like a miniature theatre, in which he arranged wax models and altered the lighting in order to help him with the layout of his complex compositions. He then made numerous rough drawings, trying out the compositions until the final solution was reached. It is easy to see that all the interior scenes of the *Sacraments* are arranged like a theatrical tableau, which gives them their curiously static quality and enhances their gravity.

In the last part of the 1630s, at the time he was painting the *Sacraments*, Poussin's art underwent a rapid metamorphosis. One of the best examples of this is the *Destruction of the Temple at Jerusalem* (plate 69) in the Kunsthistorisches Museum, Vienna. It is dry in handling and agitated in composition, and has that peculiar unattractiveness of surface on which Poussin was to dwell so much in his later years. His denial of the sensual quality of painting was deliberate: this preoccupation with surface texture is found in all his pictures of around 1630. Yet the Vienna picture succeeds by the mood it creates. The subject is one of prime importance for Jewish as well as Christian history – the final and irrevocable loss of the Jews' holiest place – and Poussin has concentrated on the mood of wanton destruction. Another equally dry picture, now also usually placed at the end of the 1630s, is the Louvre version of the theme of *Et in Arcadia Ego* (plate 70). The contrast with the earlier Chatsworth version (figure 34) could not be greater. All sense of surprise has been removed, and instead, the shepherds are arranged in attitudes of contemplation round the tomb in the countryside. The artist has lost all interest in story-telling, and has concentrated on a totally static scene. No pleasure is taken in surface texture, and the whole is hard and cold, with the figures in statuesque poses.

Poussin had completed six of the seven *Sacraments* for Cassiano dal Pozzo when the momentous summons to Paris came. Poussin's reputation had grown so much even outside Italy that he had the honour of being asked by Louis XIII himself. He arrived in Paris in 1640, immediately provoking by his very presence a crisis among the painters then working for the court. Less than two years later Poussin had returned to Rome, defeated by the intrigues of Simon Vouet and his friends, and by the unsuitable demands made upon him.

The court of Louis XIII can hardly have been aware of the great change in Poussin's style, and it is significant that the pictures he executed in his brief two years in Paris are entirely different from the Louvre *Et in Arcadia Ego* and the Vienna *Destruction of the Temple at Jerusalem*, mentioned above. The most important commission, to decorate the whole of the Grande Galerie of the Louvre, was not completed, and only drawings for it have survived. After it had become clear that Fouquières' scheme of continuous small landscapes for the Galerie would never be finished, Poussin was asked to take on the project. He applied himself to the task with great determination, designing a whole series of Herculean figures to decorate the full length of the room. Their style was derived from Annibale Carracci's Farnese ceiling, if the drawings are to be taken as evidence. It is difficult to visualize the effect of the finished result, even though the Grande Galerie remains undecorated. Poussin was not temperamentally suited to large decorative schemes, as had already been shown by his altarpiece the *Martyrdom of St Erasmus* (see page 63).

Most of the easel paintings executed during Poussin's stay in Paris were on a large scale because of the positions for which they were destined. The most important of these works was the *Miracle of St Francis Xavier*, executed for the

Jesuit church, and the *Pentecost*, painted for Louis XIII's chapel at St Germain. In these pictures the composition is at once much more Baroque and consequently much closer in general style to the successful compositions of Simon Vouet. The figures seem agitated, almost swaying. Even more Baroque, and clearly executed in rivalry with Vouet, is the *Victory of Time over Envy and Discord* in the Louvre, painted for Cardinal Richelieu in 1641. Only a certain stiffness in the figures reveals Poussin's unease with this large composition, which was intended as a ceiling decoration. The only small-scale picture reasonably attributed to the time of his Paris sojourn is the *Roccatagliata Madonna* in the Detroit Institute of Arts. In this picture the treatment is especially Raphaelesque, but Poussin has worked hard at the depiction of the tender relationship between the Virgin and Child.

After Poussin, defeated in a sense, returned to Rome in 1642, his output declined considerably. There were probably several reasons for this. His health seems to have deteriorated, and in his drawings an increasing shakiness of hand can be seen. In his paintings there is evidence of a greater effort to prepare the composition, and painstaking work on draperies and landscape backgrounds in order to pull the whole into an utterly calm, dry unity. Each picture was intended to be a unique and uncompromising statement on the chosen theme. This aim led Poussin in a direction which on one hand terminated in a cul-de-sac and on another led him to develop a completely new type of art, in the form of his evolution of the classical landscape.

Soon after his return to Rome, Poussin was asked by another important patron, Paul Fréart de Chantelou, to paint a duplicate set of *Sacraments* to the ones for Cassiano dal Pozzo. Refusing to repeat himself, Poussin created a totally new set. These pictures have always remained together, and are on loan from the Duke of Sutherland to the National Gallery of Scotland in Edinburgh. Their current fame is much greater than the earlier set's, but this is perhaps unjustified. They very clearly show the slow changes that took place in Poussin's art during the second half of the 1640s. Most of them can be precisely dated through Poussin's letters, and indicate that he must have been working on other pictures simultaneously.

Some of Poussin's other pictures painted in the latter half of the 1640s can also be dated. They include *Rebecca at the Well*, painted for Pointel in 1648, where the large scale and almost frozen quality of the figures is the same as that of the Edinburgh *Sacraments*. In such pictures Poussin seems to have lost the art of charging each figure with a living emotion, as he had done in the first set of *Sacraments*, and there is an increased gravity at the expense of humanity; but some people see this as the summit of Poussin's achievement just because it is such an extreme.

At the same time, Poussin was embarking on one of the most significant asides in his art, the painting of landscape. His earliest attempts at pure landscape are, as with all Poussin's early pictures, at the centre of heated controversy. The argument is concentrated round a group of small wooded landscapes formerly thought to be by Gaspard Dughet, but removed from his *oeuvre* in the 1950s and placed in an anonymous group called 'The Silver Birch Master'. It is now thought that these pictures represent Poussin's earliest attempts at pure landscape, since they can be compared with the landscape backgrounds of his pictures of the early 1630s. This style, however, must have been very short-lived, as by 1640 Poussin had painted two perfectly severe landscapes, the Chicago *Landscape with St John on Patmos* and the Berlin *Landscape with St Matthew*. His few non-Classical landscapes, including the two in the National Gallery in London, are likely to date from before 1640.

Poussin was the innovator of Classical landscape, although only about a dozen of his pictures of this type survive. Their stylistic source was the *Aldobrandini Lunettes* by Annibale Carracci, assisted by Domenichino and Lanfranco. Poussin abandoned many of the Italians' concessions to realism and retreated into a totally artificial world devoid of subtle light or atmosphere. Again, this can be proved to be deliberate: in the Chicago *St John on Patmos* the treatment of the Roman Campagna dotted with ruins is especially sensitive; there is not the slightest hint of the stage-like setting which was to dominate the later *Phocion* landscapes. The earliest of the truly Classical landscapes is probably the *Landscape with a Man Killed by a Snake* (plate 74) in the National Gallery, London. In this picture a drama is taking place, but it is not immediately apparent. It was Poussin's aim to bring about this realization slowly in the spectator, through contemplation. A man lies dead in the foreground in the coils of a snake, and another man has come across the spectacle and is fleeing in terror. In the background a woman reacts to the terror of the man in flight, and in turn her reaction is noticed by a fisherman. Poussin has depicted a series of emotions in this extensive panorama which is painted in dense blues, greens and browns. The gloom of the scene is intended to provoke the spectator to contemplate the triumph of nature over man.

Whereas the mood of the London *Landscape with a Man Killed by a Snake* is intentionally severe, the *Landscape with Diogenes* (plate 77) in the Louvre is much lighter in tone and mood. In it the well-known story of Diogenes, the humble philosopher, is depicted. Rejecting all worldly goods, he even throws away his last remaining possession, his drinking cup, when he sees a man drinking water from a stream by cupping his hands. The philosopher's final return to and communion with nature are expressed perfectly in the naturalistic landscape, and although there is a good deal of calculation in the placing of the tree silhouettes, it is the delicacy of each element and the subtle tonality of yellows and greens which dominate. Of all Poussin's work, this type of picture was imitated the least.

From 1648 come the two *Phocion* landscapes, the *Funeral of Phocion* (Earl of Plymouth loan to the National Museum of Wales, Cardiff) and the *Gathering of the Ashes of Phocion*, now in the Walker Art Gallery, Liverpool. Painted as a pair, both pictures are constructed exactly like a stage set. Perhaps it was because this way of creating a landscape was very theoretical that such compositions were imitated so widely; they were seen as the proper way to paint landscape – by construction rather than by observation. The scenes are of great tragedy: in one the good General Phocion has been wrongly accused by the citizens of Athens and sentenced to death, and in the other his grieving widow collects his ashes. The deep melancholy of these two pictures again indicates Poussin's determination to make the mind exercise thought rather than imagination.

The two Phocion landscapes are extreme, but Poussin was to take his ideas even further, in such almost black pictures as the *Landscape with Pyramus and Thisbe* in the Städelsches Kunstinstitut at Frankfurt and the *Stormy Landscape* recently acquired by the Musée des Beaux-Arts at Rouen. In these pictures the thoughts of the artist are so prominent that the spectator is denied any form of visual pleasure, and it requires a great deal of mental effort to contemplate them. Less severe is the *Landscape with Orpheus and Euridice* (plate 75) in the Louvre. Here the artist was dealing with a much less solemn subject, but even so the forms are rather hard. The whole has the feeling of having been put together in pieces like a jig-saw puzzle, rather than composed as a single entity as was the *Diogenes*, surely one of the most perfectly ordered but naturalistic landscapes ever painted.

The beginning of Poussin's final phase came after the completion of the second set of *Sacraments* and the landscapes of about 1648, with the *Self-portrait* of 1650 in the Louvre. Here he is seen at the height of his powers, and his severe face is set in a half-frown as he looks at the viewer. Poussin has shown himself as he wanted to be – a thinker and an intellectual. This is in contrast to many of his Italian contemporaries, whose intellectual pretensions, if any, were subordinated to the needs of their patrons. Much of what is termed 'Baroque' art was very carefully programmed by the church authorities that commissioned it, and the artist had to use his imagination in order to create the required scenes of martyrdom or ecstasy. Poussin's early work, such as the *Martyrdom of St Erasmus*, followed these dictums, but in his maturity he worked out many of these themes for himself and did his own research in order to set the scene in antiquity correctly. This provoked Reynolds's famous comment that his was 'a mind naturalized in antiquity'. All these pretensions are visible in the Louvre *Self-portrait*, in which Poussin's own pictures appear in the background, stacked up behind him to emphasize his profession. Self-portraits by other artists of this period are rare, and it is particularly instructive that Poussin should have presented himself in an image to command respect, instead of following the more usual Dutch pattern of showing the artist at work, or at least in some modest dress.

The last phase of Poussin's career is the most rewarding and yet the most difficult to understand. A few particularly severe pictures stand out, almost all of them on morbid themes. The *Last Testament of Eudamidas* in the Statens Museum for Kunst at Copenhagen is the grimmest by far of all the death-bed scenes. Great store was at that time laid on the significance of the words of the dying, and Poussin manages to make the spectator shudder without introducing anything gruesome. This is perhaps one of the secrets of his genius – his ability to transmit certain thoughts to canvas without depicting the event in a narrative way. Such pictures as the *Last Testament of Eudamidas* require a great degree of participation from the spectator, and are thus some of the most demanding in all art.

Even more extreme than the *Eudamidas* is the *Lamentation over the Dead Christ* (figure 37) in the National Gallery, Dublin. Here the mood can almost be termed expressionist. The colours, ultramarine blue, lime green and deep crimson, are used almost pure. There is none of the realism of the *Eudamidas*: the poses are exaggerated in exactly the same way as in late Gothic sculpture, and it is possible that the ageing Poussin was thinking of the images in the Gothic churches of France that he would have known as a young man. Even with this combination of extremes, Poussin avoids banality by means of his intensity of expression, which overcomes all his exaggerations of form and colour.

In his last years Poussin, revered by an admiring circle of friends, did not lack patrons, even though Cassiano dal Pozzo had died in 1657. For Cassiano's

FIGURE 37
Nicolas Poussin
Lamentation over the Dead Christ
Canvas, 94 × 130 cm.
Dublin, National Gallery of Ireland
Acquired by the museum in 1882 at the Hamilton Palace sale.

Poussin has treated the subject in an almost expressionist way: both form and colour are exaggerated.

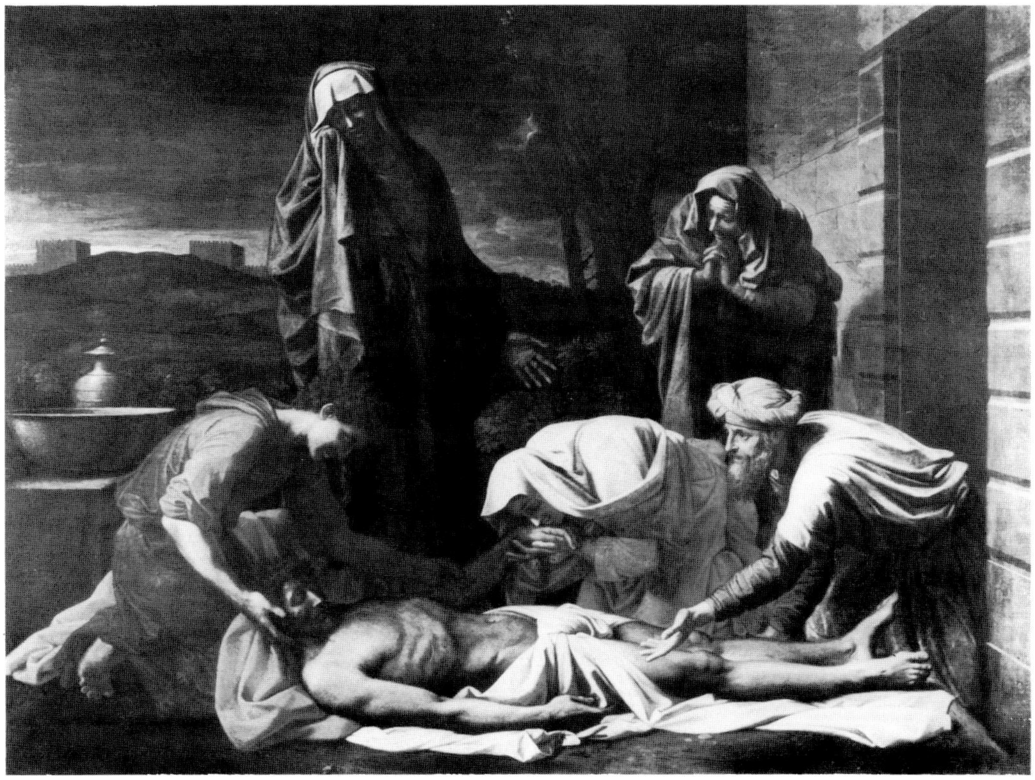

tomb Poussin had painted the uncompromising *Annunciation* now in the National Gallery, London. (This austere composition makes sense when it is realized that it was intended to hang over his patron's tomb in a dark church.) In these years, the 1650s and early 1660s, Poussin gradually lost control over his brush as his hand became shakier. During this period he produced a series of *Holy Families*, all set in rather similar landscapes. When his subject-matter is simple and unemotional as here, the modern spectator is more than usually bewildered by the dryness of the technique and the lack of subtlety in the colours: the whole seems too calculated, without producing a compensatory mood. Some of the compositions were even close to Raphael, and the reaction of Poussin's contemporaries, who admired them just because they were so erudite and close to that much-esteemed master, was very different from modern reactions to what now seem to be pedantic pictures.

Poussin in old age was the grand old man of French painters in Rome. Esteemed by all and collected by discerning connoisseurs, he was revered as the man who had elevated painting to a much more serious plane than many of his Italian contemporaries, whose stature was often that of decorator. In the early 1660s, however, a great change, which has to be described as a totally new phase, came over Poussin's art. Only a few pictures from this period survive, the earliest of which is probably the *Landscape with Diana and Orion* (plate 76), which is in the Metropolitan Museum of Art, New York. The change is in the completely different handling of paint, which shows his preoccupation with surface texture, and a relaxation of mood. His sense of severity and order has disappeared and been replaced by a mood much more akin to the last works of Titian, such as the *Diana and Actaeon* in the National Gallery, London. In the New York picture the forms are less rigid than previously, and there is a return to the sense of rhythm last seen in his work of the 1630s. The landscape becomes a much more sensual interpretation of such

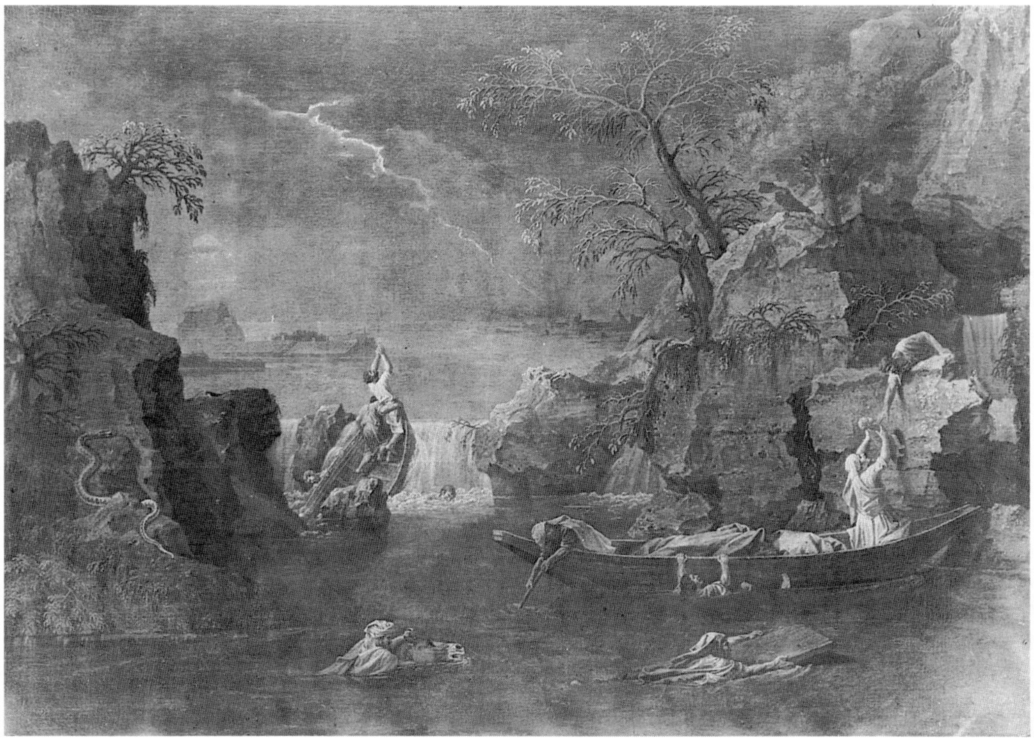

FIGURE 38
Nicolas Poussin
Winter (The Deluge)
Canvas, 118 × 160 cm.
Paris, Louvre
Documented 1660–64; acquired by Louis XIV from the duc de Richelieu in 1665.

Both this and plate 78 form part of the *Four Seasons*, all in the Louvre. They have several levels of meaning.

types of painting as the *Diogenes*.

The *Seasons*, the four canvasses of this period now in the Louvre, are an even more extreme personal statement than the New York picture. All Poussin's severity and pessimism seem to have disappeared in these paintings, to be replaced by a fusion of all the poetical leanings in his nature. They are the supreme expression, not in this case of mind over eye, but of praise for the beauty and grandeur of nature, now ordered by man, and now defeating man. *Spring* is luxuriant, *Summer* (plate 78) a fecund harvest, *Autumn* the gathering of mellow grapes and *Winter* (figure 38) the terrible deluge in which all mankind is overwhelmed and destroyed. These pictures exist on a complex series of levels, and even the most unscholarly spectator must be aware that Poussin was trying to balance moods and ideas in a much more subtle and intricate way than usual. Firstly, the pictures are a sequence, and they are hung in this way in the Grande Galerie of the Louvre. *Spring* is cool in tone, *Summer* and *Autumn* are warm, and *Winter* is cold. Even this obvious modulation of tones has its own rhythm. In all but *Winter* man is seen in harmony with nature, especially in *Spring*, surely one of the most perfect evocations of Paradise since the subject was attempted by fifteenth-century Netherlandish painters.

The last picture to survive from Poussin's hand, and unfinished at his death, is the *Apollo and Daphne* in the Louvre, of which he had painted a version more than thirty years earlier. The theme is one of a gentle melancholy: Daphne, in order to escape from the clutches of Apollo, is transformed into a tree. The composition of the many figures is agitated, and if completed the painting would no doubt have been even more detailed.

Poussin thus ended his career with a short sequence of pictures of the most deeply personal nature, far removed from any of the tastes and ideas of his contemporaries. These last pictures were not to be influential until many generations later. The *Deluge* (*Winter*) came into its own in the nineteenth century, when the dramatic events of nature were a popular subject for artists in England as well as in France; even the apocalyptic extravagances of such Romantic landscape artists as John Martin owe their inspiration to Poussin's composition. It was the Classical landscapes of 1648 which were to be the most imitated by other artists from the 1660s onwards. The imitators included Johannes Glauber of Utrecht, who took back to the Dutch Republic with him a whole repertoire of classicizing landscape which was to be an influence on Dutch painting even during the eighteenth century. Artists from the Southern Netherlands such as Jan Frans van Bloemen and Francisque Millet made their own versions of Poussin's landscape style, and the most important and original of the followers was of course Poussin's own brother-in-law, Gaspard Dughet.

Poussin's achievements as a painter are curiously difficult for the modern viewer to assess. So much has been written over the last hundred years in his praise, but his art suffers from the not uncommon problem of being admired by a small circle of connoisseurs and academics and underestimated by everyone else. To the eye unaccustomed to Poussin's eccentricities, his figures do seem stilted, his colours lacking in refinement, and his compositions pedantic, being taken too often from Raphael or Classical antiquity, and the apologist for Poussin is thus forced back to the old argument that he has to be appreciated on an intellectual level. In fact, Poussin's struggles with his doctrine that the picture should appeal to the mind rather than the eye led him to produce some very curious paintings.

Poussin's intellect has also been misunderstood. It is implicit in most writings on the artist that Poussin had a mind of great profundity which placed him on a level with contemporaries such as Pascal, but this is not the case. His ideas and morals were simple ones; his complexity comes from trying to put them over in paint. For example, one of Poussin's most often-repeated themes, as we have seen, is of the courage and dignity required in the face of death; the *Germanicus*, the two *Extreme Unctions* and the *Last Testament of Eudamidas* are all deathbed scenes in which stoicism is required (combined in the *Extreme Unctions* with Christian virtue), and this is an extremely difficult message to paint.

Poussin was painting for a specific and very erudite audience, much more used to discussing pictures as moral examples than we are today, and to these patrons he was highly successful in achieving his aims. This type of audience no longer exists, and it is often necessary to learn of all these intricacies before the pictures can assume their intended meaning. Even the best-informed spectator, however, will not wish to carry dictionaries of classical mythology and other reference works every time he chooses to look at a Poussin, neither can he spend hours of careful research into the seventeenth-century concept of Stoic philosophy. The picture must stand or fall on its visual impact, along with all other works of art. In this respect Poussin succeeded much more often than his detractors will admit. It is easy enough to dwell only on the cold, dry pictures he produced and be conscious of their failings, but Poussin's best work achieves a fine balance between his oppressive subject-matter and his delight in expressing it. His *Narcissus* in the Louvre is a truly lyrical picture – we are made to sympathize with the ill-fated Narcissus; and, although on quite a different scale, the figures in the *Inspiration of the Poet* in the same collection are entirely free from pedantry in their relaxed poses.

More difficult to appreciate, but equally rewarding, are Poussin's 'extreme' pictures, such as the Dublin *Lamentation over the Dead Christ*, which displays the qualities of excessive pathos admired in so many other artists, such as Goya, but seldom in Poussin. In this picture he went further in terms of expression than any other artist before the nineteenth century. The result is not agreeable, any more than are Goya's so-called 'black paintings', but Poussin has succeeded in conveying not only an incident of grief but the sorrow and sin of the whole world. Even such pictures as the *Annunciation* in the National Gallery, London, have a strange power to move. The mistake is to be aware of the other pictures in the room: Poussin's pictures were painted for individual contemplation, and not intended to be seen in large galleries alongside the works of his contemporaries. He never attempted a purely decorative effect unless it was specifically required, as for example in the Richelieu *Bacchanals*.

If Poussin's achievement as a painter is judged on the basis of his influence over his contemporaries and on later generations, he is one of the most important artists of the seventeenth century, exceeded in stature in this respect only by Rubens and Rembrandt. This was the verdict of a good number of Poussin's contemporaries; criticism of his infelicities of drawing and difficulties in handling colour relationships was raised only occasionally. Judged from a modern standpoint, however, Poussin still needs apologists. His art was uncompromising and out of touch with the tenor of his age. Delight in beautiful paint surfaces was one of the main preoccupations of seventeenth-century painters in all the main centres of artistic activity, and it is just these surface qualities which have always been admired in a Velasquez, a Rubens or a Rembrandt. It therefore seems perverse of Poussin that he should have tried so hard to deny such pleasures to the viewer in so much of his work.

Poussin's emotional power can be seen in probably half his pictures. Only the learned will fully appreciate the remainder; for the rest of us, able to appreciate just half the *oeuvre*, a large proportion of Poussin's work must remain obscure in cultural terms. This is not as élitist as it may sound: just as it is difficult today to understand the fervour which created Gothic cathedrals, and therefore to have a full understanding of the buildings themselves, so Poussin is to some degree alien, and he has thus achieved the status of antiquity. However, he would no doubt have been proud of that.

The French Followers of Poussin in Rome: Gaspard Dughet, Jacques Stella and Sébastien Bourdon

The idiosyncratic nature of Poussin's art, his deep sense of moral purpose and his obsessive preoccupation with formulating his ideas make it unlikely that he worked with a large number of studio assistants and pupils. A few painters, however, do seem to have been admitted to his circle, and it is virtually certain that he collaborated with them on occasion. His earliest proven association with a totally different type of painter was with Daniel Seghers, whose *Garlands of Flowers* were formerly round the Brighton *Virgin and Child* and the Cherbourg *Pietà*. These must date from before the end of 1627, when Seghers left Rome for Antwerp. In 1630 the fifteen-year-old Gaspard Dughet was admitted to Poussin's studio, shortly before Poussin married Dughet's sister, Anne-Marie. Dughet remained in the studio for several years, and throughout his long career – he lived until 1675 – was closely associated with Poussin with regard to artistic style. This association has given rise to much controversy over their respective roles in the development of landscape painting. Far from being a specific battle of connoisseurship, the Poussin-Dughet problem lies at the heart of the whole concept of the development of seventeenth-century landscape painting and, by extension, that of the next two centuries.

The landscapes by Poussin are few, and they have a precise if rapid development from the naturalistic works from before 1640, such as the pair in the National Gallery, London, to the set-pieces of 1648 such as the *Phocion* pair. The first problem focuses on the mid-1630s, by which time Dughet was old enough and well trained enough to create pictures independently. Unfortunately, there are no pictures that can be proved to be by Gaspard from this period. The 'Silver Birch' group (discussed on page 70) are arguably so close to Poussin, and fit so sensibly into his development during the 1630s, that those who insist that they are by Dughet must also conclude that Dughet added the landscape backgrounds to Poussin's pictures of the 1630s, right up to the first set of *Sacraments*. The definition of Dughet's early development must therefore await further discoveries, although a number have been made in recent years, such as the documentation of the landscape frescoes in the Roman church of San Martino ai Monti. The most important series of landscapes securely attributed to Dughet are the series of gouaches in the Palazzo Colonna, Rome. Conceived in a purely decorative manner, they are light in tone because of the gouache medium, and based on an elegant interpretation of the Roman Campagna, utterly alien to the severity of Nicolas Poussin or even to early attempts at naturalism.

All Dughet's documented pictures are decorative cycles for Roman patrons. Neither Claude nor Poussin was able to supply this demand, probably because they were temperamentally unsuited to working on a large scale, although both had tried it. One unifying thread runs through the hundreds of easel paintings at present associated with Dughet: they are all more or less related to Poussin's own approach to landscape, although none of them is signed, dated or documented. Dughet often comes close to such naturalistic Poussins as the pair of landscapes in the National Gallery, London, even though the Dughets concerned are often dated twenty or even thirty years later. Sometimes Dughet's debt to Poussin is obvious, as in the *Landscape with Dido and Aeneas* (figure 39) in the National Gallery, London, which is very close in mood and style to Poussin's *Pyramus and Thisbe* landscape at Frankfurt. If anything, Dughet is even more dramatic and gloomy than Poussin, a fact that led Ruskin in the nineteenth century to complain of Dughet's lack of respect for nature. In some respects Ruskin was right, because Dughet's response to nature was limited compared with Poussin's. In his many drawings of the Roman Campagna, he often avoided naturalistic elements, preferring the landscape style of Poussin.

Not all Dughet's work falls into the category of Poussin imitation, however. There is a category of much more naturalistic pictures, which have proved almost impossible to date. They often include views of Tivoli, as in the excellent example in the Wallace Collection, London, and also show a preoccupation with the picturesque. The ruined circular temple of Tivoli on top of

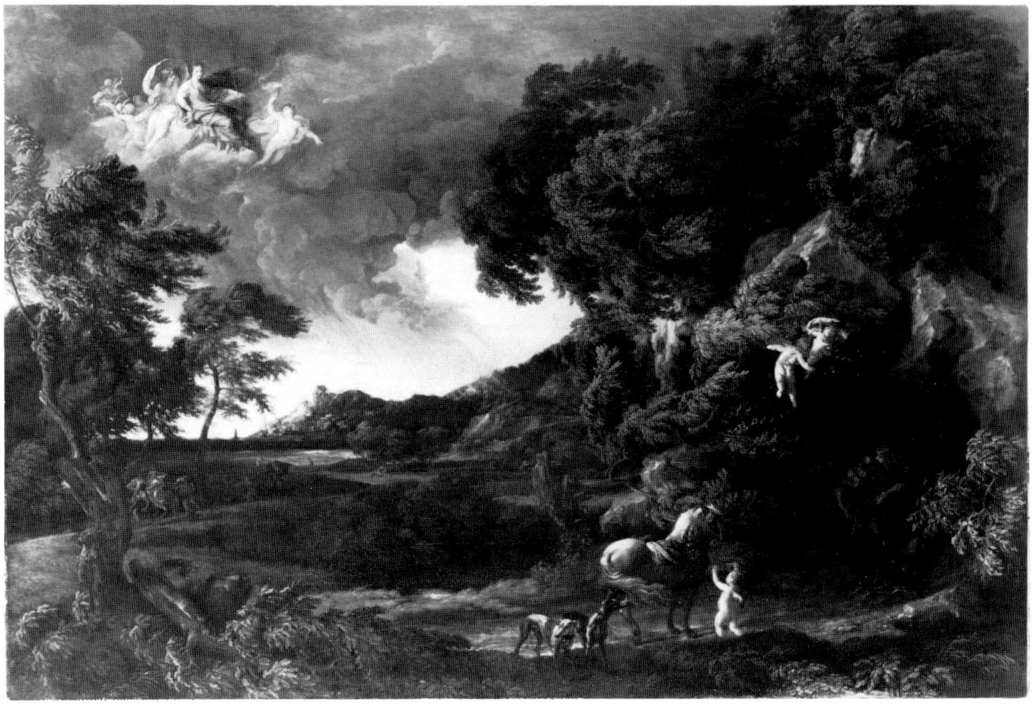

FIGURE 39
Gaspard Dughet
Landscape with Dido and Aeneas
Canvas, 152.5 × 224 cm.
London, National Gallery
In the Palazzo Falconieri, Rome, until 1804, when brought to England. Bequeathed to the National Gallery by the Rev. W. Holwell Carr in 1831.

The subject is taken from Virgil's *Aeneid*, a source rare in Dughet's art but common in that of Claude Lorrain. The artist is much more interested in the effects of the storm than in the mythology.

its very steep slope inspired painters interested in nature at its most romantic, and some of Dughet's best pictures are of this subject, in which the waterfalls trickling over the rocks are painted with great naturalism. Another good example of this type of landscape is his picture in the Molinari Pradelli collection, Bologna (plate 29). Many of these pictures found their way to Britain, where they were to be extremely influential, not only on the tastes of connoisseurs but also on eighteenth-century British landscape artists who often saw Italy through Dughet's eyes, developing his picturesque interests even to the extent of depicting the British countryside in a Dughet-like manner.

Dughet's sensitivity is clearly seen in the *Landscape with a Pool* in the National Gallery of Scotland, Edinburgh, where the effect of cool water in the tree-covered landscape verges on the naturalistic. Yet Dughet was rarely interested in atmosphere, and therefore in this respect always leans more towards Poussin than to Claude. In his best pictures Dughet attempted a gentle truth to nature within the classical idiom. He never aspired to the grand designs of Poussin, and many of the landscapes at present attributed to Dughet reveal a misunderstanding of Poussin's methods of constructing a landscape and of the reasons behind his extreme attitude.

The only other painter close to Poussin was the enigmatic Jean Lemaire. A typical work is the *Pasiphae* (figure 40) formerly in the Anthony Blunt collection in London. His figures are usually inept compared with those of Poussin, but Lemaire's speciality was the painting of classical architecture, and in this he excelled. It is believed that he painted the background (i.e. most of the picture) in Poussin's *Theseus Searching for his Father's Shield* in the Musée Condé at Chantilly, and that he also collaborated in the *Architects Sketching amongst Ruins* in the Victoria and Albert Museum, London. Lemaire's reputation is now totally obscure, but he is an interesting example of a painter who collaborated with an artist of much greater talent. Poussin must have thought highly of Lemaire to allow him to work with him.

FIGURE 40
Jean Lemaire
Pasiphae
Canvas, 66 × 94 cm.
London, formerly Anthony Blunt collection

The subject plays a relatively unimportant part in this picture, which is essentially a detailed depiction of an architectural capriccio.

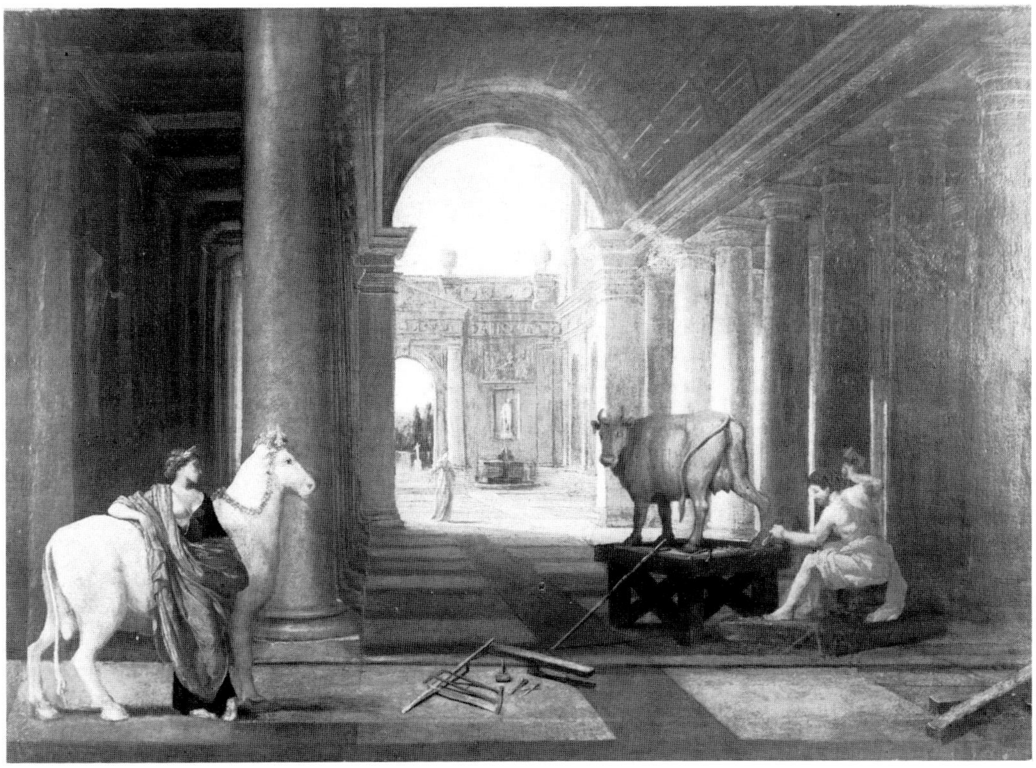

FIGURE 41
Jacques Stella
Adoration of the Child
Canvas, 65.5 × 78 cm. Signed and dated: I. STELLA F. 1639
Barnard Castle, Bowes Museum
Part of the collection of John and Josephine Bowes given as a museum in 1871.

This is one of Stella's earliest surviving pictures, in which the influence of Poussin is already discernible.

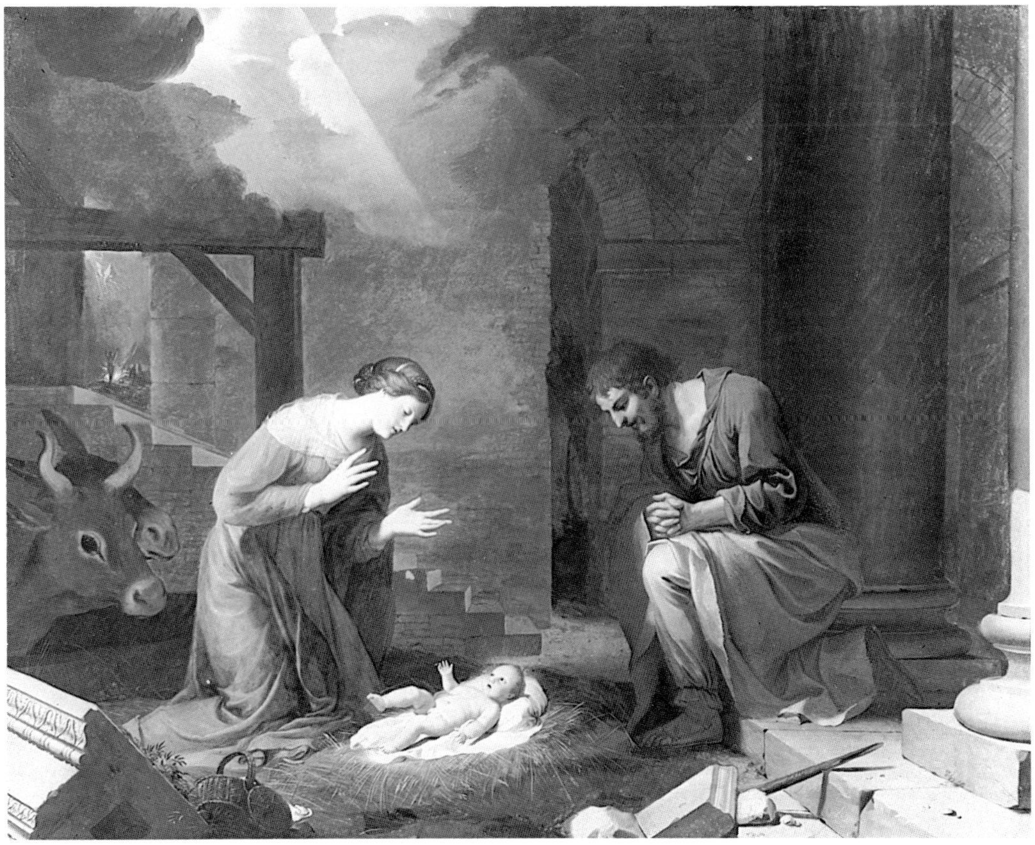

One of Poussin's most surprising patrons in Rome was the French painter Jacques Stella, who commissioned from Poussin the extremely austere *Venus Giving Arms to Aeneas* in the Musée des Beaux-Arts at Rouen. Stella's own art, although sometimes influenced by Poussin in terms of its composition, was often very much more light-hearted. Stella had a good grasp of minute technique, akin to that of Dutch artists, and sometimes worked on a tiny scale on semi-precious stones such as lapis-lazuli and on rare marble. Such pictures would be eagerly sought after by patrons with cabinets of curiosities, or by collectors of cabinet pieces. Very small pictures became known under this title as they were locked up in a cabinet especially designed for this purpose, or, later, kept in a small room which would be opened for favoured guests to marvel at the skill of the painters who worked on such a tiny scale.

One of Stella's earliest surviving works is the *Adoration of the Child* (figure 41) in the Bowes Museum at Barnard Castle, Co. Durham. Painted in the late 1630s, it already shows the influence of Poussin's recently developed dryness of handling. In subject-matter Stella's approach is conventional enough: he concentrates on the sweet side of the event, exactly as had been the tradition for a hundred and fifty years in Italy, from the time of Correggio's *La Notte* at Dresden, which was so much admired and imitated in the seventeenth century. Correggio's influence is always strong in Stella's art, especially the Italian's sweetness. This is particularly obvious in the small *St Cecilia Playing the Organ* in the Musée des Augustins at Toulouse. Although he sometimes used Poussinesque figures in his larger compositions, Stella never interested himself in the moral and intellectual side of Poussin's art. St Cecilia is simply a charming lady making music, rather than the patron saint of music as she so obviously is in Raphael's representation of her.

A number of other minor painters in Rome came under Poussin's spell. Some of them, like François Perrier, have had their reputations undeservedly eclipsed, partly because they could not resist including Poussin's poses in their pictures even though they did not understand the reasons behind Poussin's adoption of the poses in question. This must not cloud our judgment of the abilities of such painters as Perrier, however, as they believed that they were following the correct models which would lead them to perfection.

The one painter who came under the influence of Poussin in Rome but who also retained his individuality was Sébastien Bourdon. He is one of the few French painters of the whole century who was equally adept at portrait, landscape, mythological and genre painting. This versatility, noticed by his contemporaries, has meant that only in recent years have a number of his pictures been identified. His mythological pictures are confused with those of other Poussin followers, his landscapes with those of Dughet, and his genre pictures with those of the Netherlandish Bamboccianti and even Jean Tassel. The pictures by Bourdon which follow Poussin are the least successful because they lack Poussin's emotional intensity, and yet, in the seven large canvasses of the *Seven Acts of Mercy* in the Ringling Museum, Sarasota, Bourdon's ability to conceive a convincing series on a large scale is revealed, although the works are now much damaged and difficult to read as an effective sequence. It is interesting to compare his Poussinesque *Finding of Moses* (plate 9) in the National Gallery of Art, Washington, with Poussin's interpretation of the same subject in the Louvre. Bourdon's colours are lighter and more delicate than Poussin's, and although his figures adopt Poussinesque poses, they do not relate to each other in the intense way characteristic of Poussin. On the other hand, Bourdon was good at narrative and anecdote, as his guardroom scenes (such as the one in Dulwich College Picture Gallery, London) show.

It is thought that Bourdon imitated other artists of his time with the deliberate intention to deceive; certainly he succeeded. He did make an original contribution to the development of portrait painting in France, however. The home of experiment had been Italy, while in France the basic tradition had been the Flemish style of Pourbus, which was later to be complemented by the intense, realistic style of Philippe de Champaigne, all this being entirely removed from Italian influence. In Rome the young Bourdon was exposed to some of the greatest portraits of the Renaissance in the collections there, as well as to the constant experiments of artists as diverse as Bernini, Lanfranco and Domenichino, who all painted portraits. The great Velasquez *Portrait of Innocent X* (Doria Gallery, Rome) was also well known. From all these influences Bourdon compounded his own style, which inevitably became a formula, but a successful one. He often painted his sitters three-quarters on, in a soft and even light, and preferred waist-length portraits and a feeling of relative informality, even for the portraits of his grandest patron, the redoubtable Queen Christina of Sweden, at whose court in Stockholm he spent a short period.

Queen Christina of Sweden (plate 7) in the Nationalmuseum, Stockholm, is surprisingly frank for a royal portrait. The French court preferred a complete stiffness even as late as the 1650s, when artists such as the Beaubruns were employed during the minority of Louis XIV (see figure 42). It is difficult to know whether Bourdon evolved this style specifically for his royal patron, a style which then became standard for his middle-class portraits, or whether the influence was the other way round, with the monarch wishing to be seen in a less formal pose, after the fashion of her humbler subjects. What is important is that, with this curious mixture of Italian influences, Bourdon set the style for middle-class French portraiture for almost the rest of the century. One of the best examples is his *Portrait of a Man* (plate 8) in the Musée Fabre at Montpellier, which is a *tour de force* of subtle modelling and lighting. Indeed, almost all the surviving middle-class portraits of the time in France, that are not by Philippe de Champaigne and his followers, copy this type. Complex sumptuary laws were in force which prevented people wearing clothes out of their social station so that, unless the portrait is a work of the imagination, it is possible to deduce the sitter's status. Curiously enough, later in the century, all over Europe, sitters were no longer being painted in everyday dress, preferring to be seen either in their shifts or in some sort of allegorical pose and clothing.

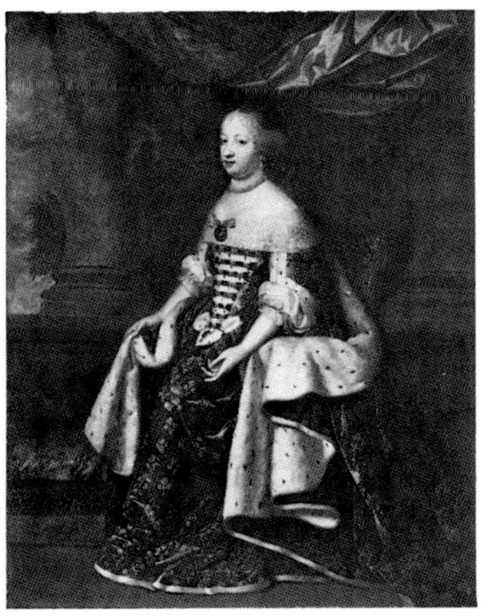

FIGURE 42
Beaubrun cousins
Marie Thérèse, Wife of Louis XIV
Canvas, 180 × 140 cm.
Versailles, Château

This formal portrait of the ineffectual Austrian wife of Louis XIV has presumably been in the French royal collection since it was painted.

The difficulty of attributing unsigned portraits from this period proves the popularity of Bourdon's style. For example, the *Man Holding a Bust of Caracalla* in the Louvre, probably depicting an antiquarian or a scholar, is painted in the manner of Bourdon without being definitely attributable to him. Bourdon's very success in his own time has been his undoing in terms of his later reputation, because his artistic individuality has been lost. He is an example of a French artist who formed his style exclusively in Rome and then transported it both to France and to Sweden, a country which was to retain strong links with French artists, especially in the eighteenth century.

Claude Lorrain

Claude Lorrain was Poussin's junior by seven years and he outlived him by seventeen, dying at the age of eighty-two in 1682. Poussin and Claude knew one another and were virtually neighbours in Rome, but they have too often been placed together because of the accident of their nationality, although Claude's native Lorraine was several hundred miles from Poussin's native Normandy. In spite of their differences, these two titans of French art shared a few common factors. From their maturity onwards, after the mid-1630s, they were both totally out of touch with the trends of their time and uninfluenced by the later developments of the Baroque, which culminated in such extravagances as Pozzo's illusionistic ceiling for the church of Sant'-Ignazio in Rome.

Claude's career spans almost the entire century – his earliest datable works are from the end of the 1620s – and he witnessed almost all the main changes of artistic style during his long stay in Rome. Some details of his early life are known, but they add up to very little in the search for his artistic origins. Leaving his native Lorraine for Rome at the age of thirteen in 1613, Claude spent the next decade of his life learning his art. Nothing survives from this period. In 1626 he returned to Lorraine and was apprenticed to Claude Deruet for one year. Re-examination of the documents at Nancy now suggests that Claude may have returned to Rome after completing this one-year apprenticeship, as he is not mentioned in the contract drawn up with Deruet for the decoration of the Carmelite church at Nancy (Deruet's only surviving decoration is the small ceiling in the Villa Borghese in Rome).

Claude's earliest surviving pictures have usually been dated to around 1630, although he did not begin to keep accurate records until the mid-1630s. By this time he was already mature, and so it is from the evidence supplied by the undated pictures that his first hesitant steps have to be reconstructed. The fact that he developed so rapidly from his first unpromising topographical scenes to become the virtual inventor of the atmospheric and poetical landscape is evidence of his genius. In the early pictures, considerable reference is made to a wide variety of painters, all of them landscapists. By about 1630 an enormous amount of landscape painting was going on in Rome, soon to be increased by the innovations of Poussin and Dughet. Claude therefore had to contend with many other artists working in mature styles, either influencing or ignoring one another. He drew almost casually from this varied background, now leaning on one, now on another, and then discarding them all, to achieve total self-confidence by the time he was thirty-five.

One of the most influential landscape painters in Rome was the German Adam Elsheimer, and Claude could well have known Elsheimer's *Aurora* landscape in the Herzog Anton-Ulrich Museum, Brunswick, as it was engraved. Elsheimer's composition is bold and unusual, with a strong diagonal, but his real achievement was his observation of the effect of Italian light which is quite different from that of the North. Elsheimer's sky is pale blue with tiny golden clouds floating in it, and lower down the copper panel there is a warm yellow which merges into the blue almost imperceptibly, without passing through green, a difficult technical achievement. A number of Claude's small early pictures follow this formula, and are sometimes painted on copper, like almost all Elsheimer's works.

Claude was also influenced by the Dutch painter Cornelis van Poelenburgh, who was working in Rome in the first half of the 1620s. The latter copied Elsheimer's pictures on several occasions, and Claude took from Poelenburgh a preoccupation with the topography of antique ruins, transforming them into picturesque small elements in his landscapes. At this stage Claude was working in the same format as his Dutch rivals, and his pictures were appreciated by the collectors of cabinet pieces.

A very different and simultaneously discernible influence on Claude's art was Annibale Carracci's *Aldobrandini Lunettes*, whose effect on Poussin has already been mentioned (page 71). Claude took from them quite different elements from those used by Poussin, being interested in Carracci's sense of scale. The *Lunettes* concentrate on the broadest of panoramas; like all Italians, Carracci was trying to create a balance in nature by elaborate artifice. The landscapes by Italian painters often had a specific subject, such as St George and the Dragon, but the figures were on the smallest possible scale in relation to the panorama. The Italians had not yet learnt to paint a 'pure' landscape, and with very few exceptions Claude followed their dictums, always including some figures on which an interpretation of the subject could be based.

A further influence was the fashion for painting seaports, the main exponents of this being the Antwerp-born artist Paul Bril and the Italian Agostino Tassi. Bril either worked on small copper panels or, late in life, produced much larger-scale works. His observation of water and ships' rigging was perfectly accurate, although his pictures were rarely strictly topographical. Tassi, less competent at minute detail, was much more interested in the picturesque possibilities of ships' silhouettes against the sky. Claude combined all these elements in his earliest seaport scenes, which became rarer as he grew older. Because he was also a passionate observer of nature, his ability to fuse all these styles and subject types is remarkable.

A good example of Claude's early hesitancy is the *Landscape with a Rock Arch* in the Museum of Fine Arts, Houston, Texas. Probably painted in about 1630, the composition is already deeply romantic. The rocks are dark and silhouetted against the blue sky. The handling of the paint is devoid of subtlety, as Claude had not yet matured his technique of infinitessimal gradations of tone. The same lack of subtlety is seen in one of Claude's rare topographical scenes, the *View of the Trinità dei Monte, Rome*, in the National Gallery, London, where the emphasis is on the picturesque grouping of the buildings in a landscape made rather more rural than it would have actually appeared, even at that time.

Claude's direct debt to Elsheimer can be seen in a series of small copper panels. Two of them, in the Louvre, the *Seige of La Rochelle* (figure 43) and the *View of the Pass of Susa* (figure 44), are especially luminous and show that even at this early stage Claude was mastering his technique of depicting light. Claude's earliest surviving *Seaport*, in the collection of the Duke of Buccleuch at Bowhill, Selkirkshire, dated 1633, is one of his best. In dramatically positioning the boats behind the port buildings his debt is to Paul Bril, but in other respects the picture is original in conception, especially in the fall of the light, and Claude has already been able to give the scene a unique feeling of serenity.

A growing number of pictures is now being attributed to Claude for the period of the first half of the 1630s. As well as the small-scale works on copper,

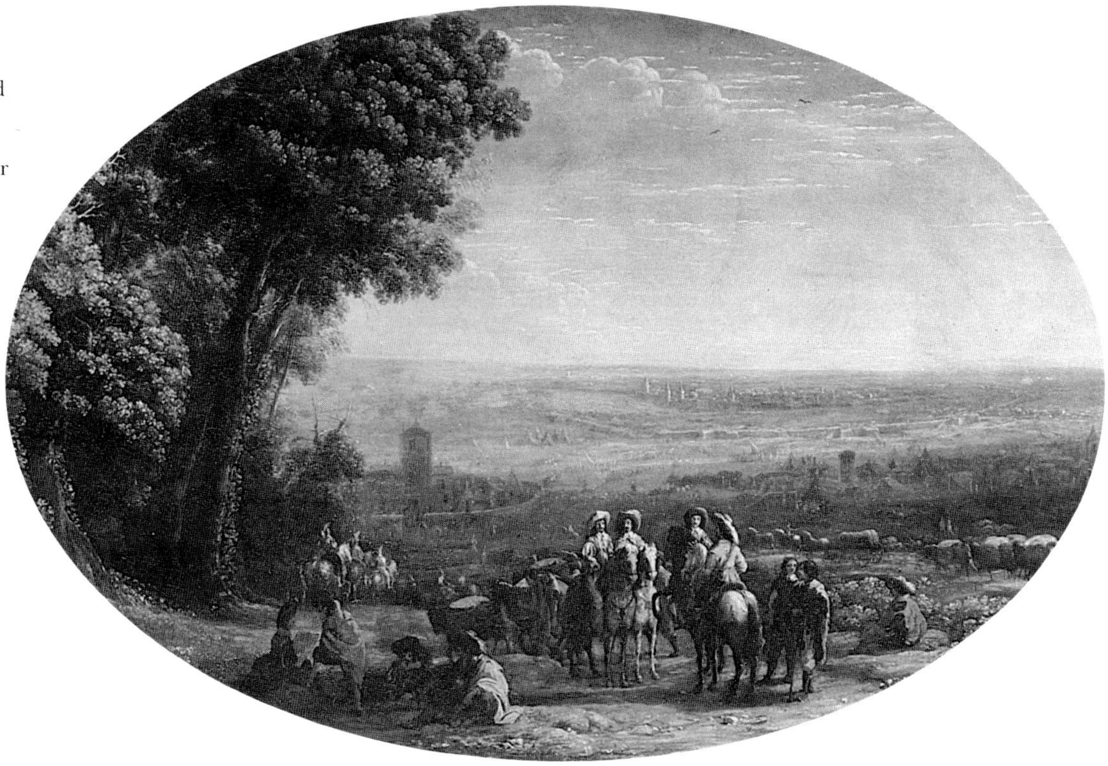

FIGURE 43
Claude Lorrain
The Siege of La Rochelle
Copper, 28 × 42 cm. Signed and dated 16..
Paris, Louvre.
Acquired by Louis XIV no later than 1709.

there is a considerable group of large canvasses where the elements are clearly Claudian, but the treatment often lacks the luminosity of the securely authenticated works. It was in the mid-1630s that Claude decided to keep a record of every picture he painted, in the form of the *Liber Veritatis* (London, British Museum), in which, after he had completed a painting, Claude made a careful drawing of the composition and noted the buyer on the back. He thus documented some two hundred pictures over almost fifty years. The traditional reason for the introduction of this system was that it guarded against the proliferation of forgeries, but it seems astonishing that a relatively obscure artist could have his business interests damaged by unscrupulous imitators, and this reason has now been somewhat discredited by modern scholarship. Nevertheless, there are rather too many 'early' Claudes not included in the *Liber Veritatis*, and this is especially obvious when Claude's relatively slow working methods are taken into account.

The year 1635 marked the beginning of Claude's maturity, when his pictures were steadily increasing in refinement but had not yet become hallmarked by his unique style, being still too much influenced by the sources already mentioned. One of the most striking early works of this period is the *Port Scene with the Campidoglio, Rome*, now in the Louvre, in which Claude has transposed the well-known Roman landmark and set it by the water, even though it is obvious that such grand architecture – by Michelangelo – could hardly sit so close to the water without proper foundations. However, Claude was uninterested in a convincing reality; this was an idyll, designed to be picturesque and pleasing without reference to the logic of architecture. Only part of the boat on the left can be seen, as its only purpose is as a decorative prop. (This is the total antithesis of almost all the Dutch seascapes, which were evolving as a national preoccupation at the same time. The Dutch painted their ships as portraits of the vessels, the decorative elements being

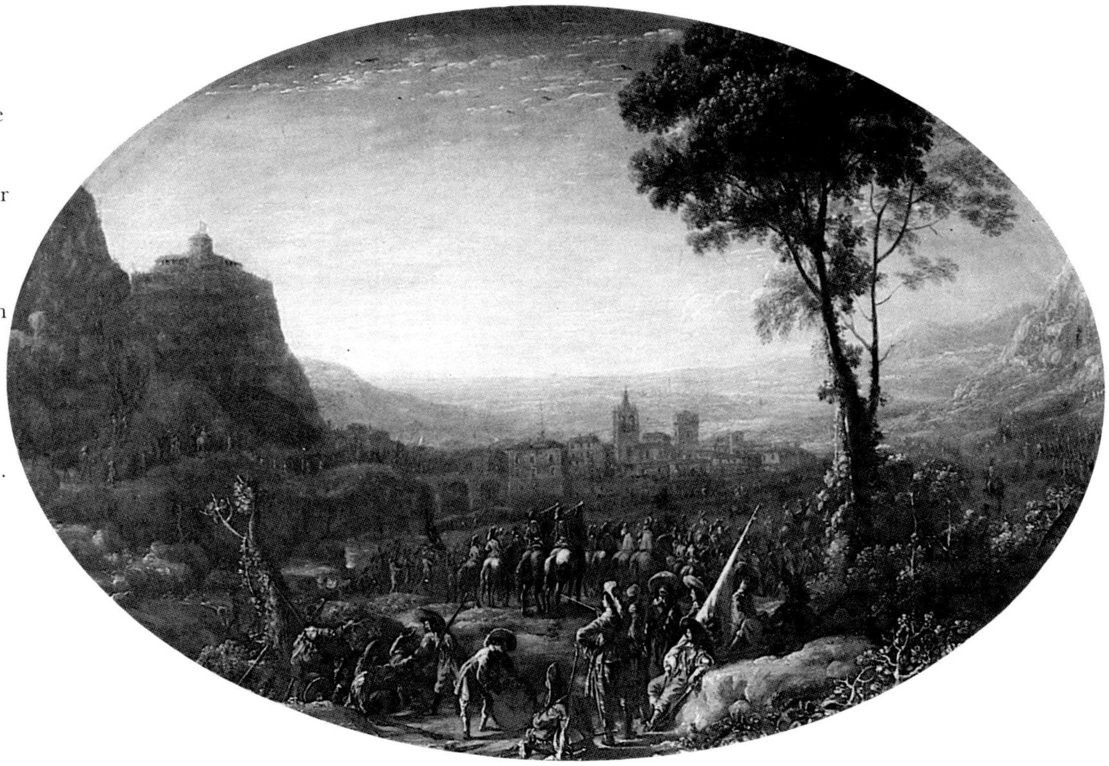

FIGURE 44
Claude Lorrain
View of The Pass of Susa
Copper, 28.5 × 41.5 cm. Signed and dated: Claude Lo . . Romae 163 . .
Paris, Louvre
Acquired by Louis XIV no later than 1709.

These two pictures form a pair. They are unusual because they depict specific military events in the career of Louis XIII. It is likely that they were commissioned, probably by Henri-Auguste de Loménie, comte de Brienne, who was Minister of State to Louis XIII.

secondary.) In the Louvre picture Claude produces a perfect example of his famous 'golden glow'. How this was achieved remains a mystery, and it is one of the technical marvels of Western painting. Close examination reveals many small and extremely painstaking brushstrokes. Claude was no wizard with the brush, in the sense that he had none of the freedom of many of his Italian contemporaries or even of Poussin in the first half of the 1630s. Instead, Claude built up his pictures in many careful layers, lovingly observing every minute detail but without ever losing sight of the tonal unity of the whole.

Claude's 'golden glow' has given rise to a good deal of art-historical speculation, because it became a feature of certain Dutch paintings, and was deeply influential in the eighteenth and early nineteenth centuries, especially on British painters ranging from Richard Wilson to Turner. The Dutchman Jan Both, who left Rome in about 1640 to return to his native Utrecht, took with him Claude-like compositions and a preoccupation with golden light. Both certainly knew of Claude's work, but it is also likely that each artist was influenced by the same natural phenomena.

In the 1630s, in direct contrast to Poussin whose experiments continued to take him in many different directions, Claude sought gradually to refine his chosen themes. Only in his old age did a new feeling develop in his art, but there was no radical change as there was in Poussin's late work. By about 1640 Claude had fully mastered all his themes. His seaports, although fewer in number, became increasingly splendid. His landscapes broadened and became more poetical, and were sometimes even without a specific subject, although to his contemporaries they would have been interpreted as illustrating the pastoral poetry of Virgil.

The advance in skill from the *Port Scene with the Campidoglio* is especially obvious when one compares it with the *Port Scene with the Embarkation of St Ursula* of 1641 in the National Gallery, London. This picture is entirely concerned with the phenomenon of light; the golden tone fills the whole surface and envelops each of the individual elements. The actual subject, St Ursula embarking with her retinue of virgins, seems lost in this paean of praise for the sun, which shines directly at the spectator from the middle of the canvas. In this picture Claude perfectly observed an effect which eluded most painters before the nineteenth century – the convincing depiction of direct sunlight. Few of Claude's pictures go as far as this one, as he usually preferred to portray the softer light of early morning or late evening.

The best example of his direct response to nature, although not topographically accurate, is the *Landscape with Shepherds – the Ponte Molle* (plate 21) of 1645 in the City Museum and Art Gallery, Birmingham. Each element in the picture is perfectly observed from nature; nothing is obviously artificial, but Claude arranged these elements – cabbage-like plants on the ground, classical ruins, a large pine tree – in a way which later generations came to regard as picturesque. To those unfamiliar with the actual landscape he painted, Claude's pictures seem even more artificial than they are. The Roman Campagna has changed little since the seventeenth century, especially the area around Tivoli; the terrain is dotted with the ruins of classical antiquity and there are numerous scattered pine trees which seem, especially when one is walking through them, to take on a 'Claudian' aspect when juxtaposed with ruins. The light is marvellously clear, with the sky changing from blue to yellow in the morning and evening. Claude achieved a near-perfect depiction of this atmosphere in the Birmingham picture: instead of the brilliant sunshine of the *St Ursula* there is a soft glow, in which the artist produces an almost milky light. He manages to capture atmosphere not by blurring the edges of each object depicted but by juxtaposing infinitesimal gradations of tone without losing the slightest detail. In all Claude's mature landscapes, and signally in this one, there is a sense of infinite distance in which the spectator can wander at will.

Compared with Poussin, Claude had a relative lack of interest in his subject-matter, and his attitude in this respect was much more akin to that of his contemporaries. This was that the subject should be obvious to those who looked for it but that it should not spoil the viewer's appreciation of the beauty of the landscape. From the 1640s onwards Claude invented a perfect compromise between subject and landscape: instead of repeating his favourite earlier subjects such as the *Flight into Egypt* (which was used merely as a vehicle for a landscape) he began to use the poetry of Virgil as a major source of his subject-matter. Unlike Poussin, who tried to imitate his source in as accurate a manner as possible, Claude used the poetry as a source of general inspiration for his pictures, which remained landscapes first and foremost. Virgil's pastoral poetry, the *Eclogues* and the *Georgics*, had already been used by Claude in a generalized way for his many scenes of shepherds resting, dancing or simply minding their flocks in an ideal landscape. The almost wistful verse of Virgil could be translated into paint by Claude without any pedantic references to specific passages, and without arousing any argument over the precise passage illustrated.

In the 1640s Claude produced many of his most ambitious pictures, such as the two versions of the *Landscape with Dancing Figures* (sometimes called *The Mill*) in the Galleria Doria in Rome (plate 20) and the National Gallery, London. They are wide in scale and the atmosphere is of broad daylight.

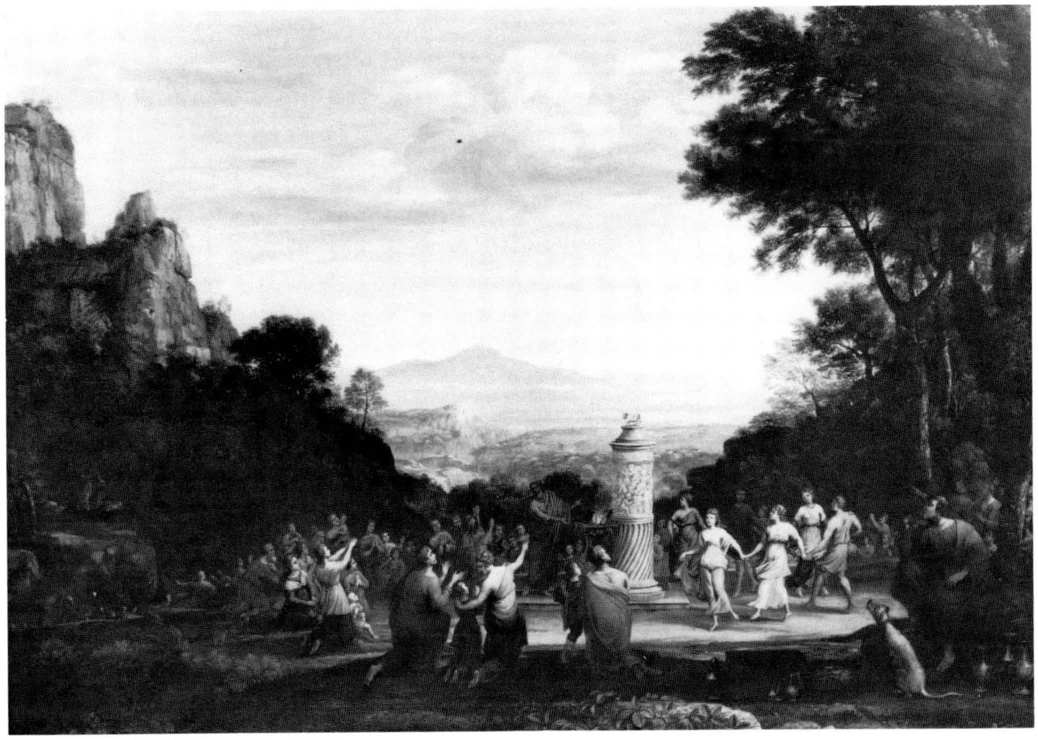

FIGURE 45
Claude Lorrain
Landscape with the Adoration of the Golden Calf
Canvas, 114.5 × 158.5 cm.
Signed and dated 1660.
Liber Veritatis No.148
Manchester, City Art Gallery
Original patron not known. In England by the end of the eighteenth century. Acquired by the museum in 1980.

There is a complete balance between careful observation of the reality of the Roman Campagna and the need to produce an organized composition. Unfortunately both versions of the picture suffer from a problem afflicting a number of Claude's works, the darkening of the greens in the trees. This gives them a much greater solidity than the artist intended. Moreover, in Claude's later pictures there is also sometimes a fading out of the fugitive yellows he used, which gives the pictures a much stronger bluish hue than he intended. Painted in 1648, these two pictures sum up Claude's mature art. He had arrived at this maturity by degrees, almost imperceptibly, refining and perfecting his technique. He had for many years been drawing from nature almost obsessively, and several hundred of his sensitive and often atmospheric drawings survive. He was therefore able to combine the more naturalistic approach seen in the *Ponte Molle* of 1645 with an increasing desire to turn the landscape into an idealized world. He had tried dramatic atmosphere in some of his early compositions, and had succeeded with direct sunlight but had not pursued it; but he developed in his later years the soft and subtle light effects which were the most difficult of all to achieve convincingly. As he grew older Claude became even more meticulous, and his pictures never acquired the looseness sometimes seen in the works of painters in their old age, even Poussin.

Inevitably for a painter who appears so easily to have achieved perfection, there have been criticisms and invidious and unnecessary comparisons with Poussin. One of the most frequent observations about Claude's art relates to his treatment of figures. They certainly lack naturalism and there is a virtual abandonment of anatomy, which seemed to intensify as he grew older. It is in these strange elongated figures that Claude reveals his Lorraine background: his mannerisms are exactly those of his fellow-countryman and teacher Claude Deruet. In spite of their bizarre attitudes and unnatural colours Claude's figures fit well into his landscapes, and it is only when he introduces a large number of them that the spectator becomes aware of their characteristics. For example, in the *Landscape with the Adoration of the Golden Calf* (figure 45) in the Manchester City Art Gallery, the figures are integrated perfectly into the setting and do not demand individual inspection and contemplation. In this the picture is totally different from Poussin's treatment of the same subject of some twenty years earlier.

Although so much of Poussin's art was guided by logic, and Claude's by intuition, it is Claude's art which was to pursue a more logical development in the second half of his career. It is likely that Claude maintained his much more consistent style because of the demands of his patrons, who were largely aristocratic and rich, but without the intellectual pretensions of Poussin's patrons. All they required was refinement, and Claude's pictures were intended to hang in their large private picture galleries as part of decorative ensembles. Only in the Galleria Doria in Rome can any idea be gained today of how Claude's pictures would originally have appeared, hanging cheek by jowl with the works of artists as diverse as Raphael and Caravaggio.

The gradual increase in poetic intensity in Claude's art can be seen in the *Seaport with the Departure of Aeneas* of 1650, now in the collection of the Earl of Radnor at Longford Castle, Wiltshire. The sun is low in the sky and a gentle melancholy pervades the perfectly calm scene. In pictures of this type Claude was aiming at a certain definition of peace which is only apparent when his landscapes are compared to most of those of his contemporaries, whose aim was to excite the senses.

Claude painted fewer pictures during the 1660s and 1670s, but his output was still considerable, and every Claude admirer has a favourite or favourites among them. The mood of these landscapes is even softer, and the compositions, with odd exceptions, are even less dramatic. Claude's most poetic picture is the *Landscape with Psyche at the Castle of Amor*, better known as *The Enchanted Castle* (figure 46). It is one of the tragedies of art that it has suffered so much from abrasion, but even in its present state the poetical content of the picture is its most obvious characteristic. The story seems irrelevant: the diminutive Psyche in the foreground appears to be almost an afterthought. The castle rises from the water, taking the form of an architectural fantasy of Gothic and Renaissance motifs, and the water is deep turquoise, the trees dark olive green. In short, the landscape is designed to evoke a mood. It was only in the eighteenth century that Claude's intention was fully understood, and its most famous outcome was John Keats' verse-letter of 1818 to his friend John Reynolds, which is usually taken to refer to the picture, which the poet might well have known:

> You know the Enchanted Castle – it doth stand
> Upon a rock, on the border of a Lake,
> Nested in trees, which all do seem to shake
> From some old-magic like Urganda's Sword.
>
> You know it well enough, where it doth seem
> A mossy place, a Merlin's Hall, a dream;
> You know the clear Lake, and the little Isles,
> The mountains blue, and cold near neighbour rills . . .

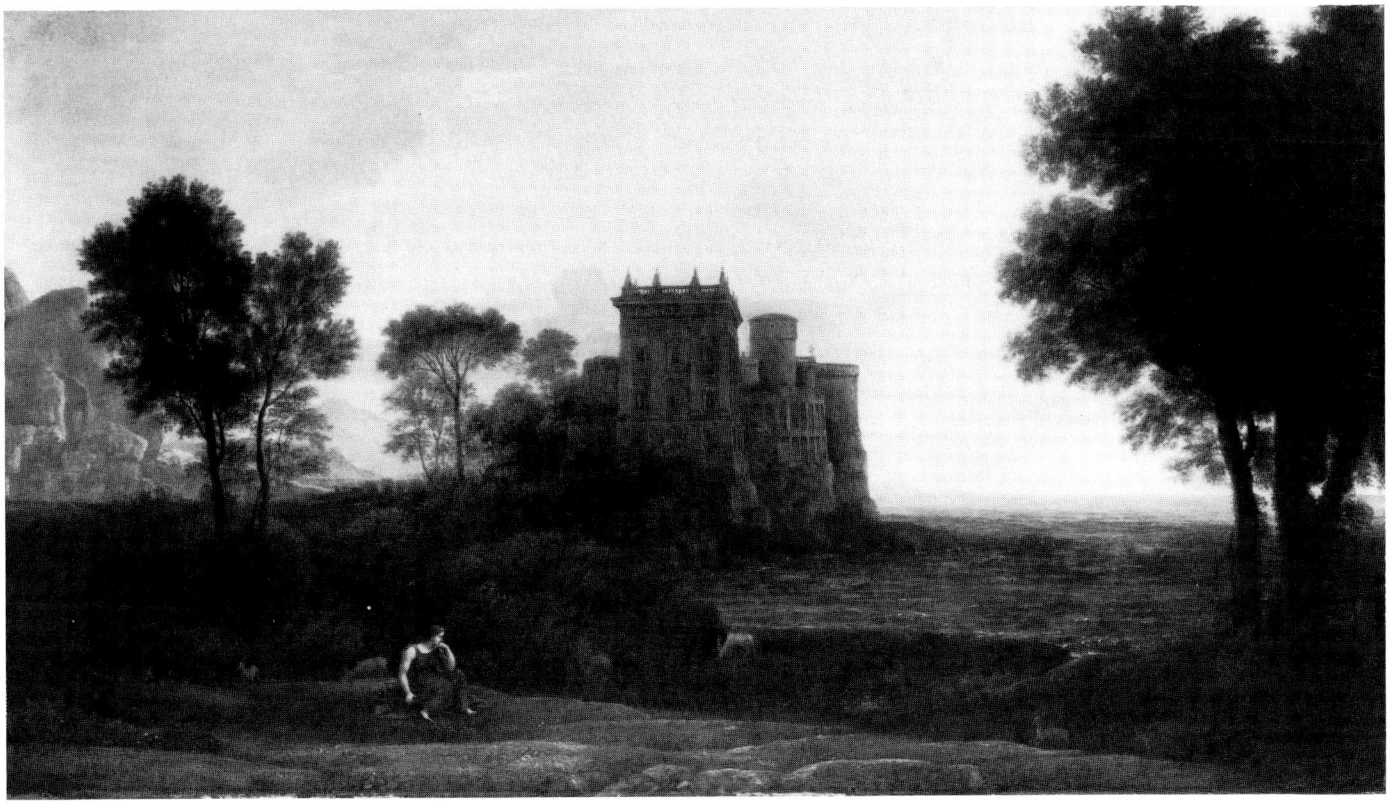

FIGURE 46
Claude Lorrain
Landscape with Psyche at the Castle of Amor (The Enchanted Castle)
Canvas, 87 × 151 cm.
Liber Veritatis No.162
London, National Gallery
Painted for Lorenzo Onofrio Colonna. In England by 1777. Long in the Loyd collection at Wantage until acquired by the National Gallery in 1980.

The pair to this picture is the *Landscape with Psyche Saved from Drowning Herself* in the Wallraf Richartz Museum, Cologne.

Keats' reference to 'Charm'd magic casements, opening on the foam/Of perilous seas, in faery lands forlorn' in the *Ode to a Nightingale* may also be an evocation of the painting.

A pair of landscapes, the *Expulsion of Hagar* (plate 22) and the *Landscape with Hagar and the Angel* of 1668 in the Alte Pinakothek, Munich, are further examples of Claude's often-repeated essay on the theme of the morning and evening landscape. Again, the figures play a tiny and almost insignificant part in the picture, although in the *Expulsion* there is a feeling that they are reacting to the inhospitable nature of the cool morning. Such pictures, or pendants as they came to be known, were a great favourite with collectors because they were easier to hang in a room whose design was formal. A surprising number of painters of all schools in the seventeenth century painted pictures in this way, although an informality of hanging which developed in the nineteenth century has often obscured this.

In the last decade of his life, Claude concentrated on a limited number of themes, many of them from Virgil's *Aeneid*. The *Apollo and the Muses on Mount Helion (Parnassus)* of 1680 (plate 23) in the Boston Museum of Fine Arts is a good example of his use of idyllic mythology during his last years. His technique remained as refined as in his earlier years, but his compositions often lost the earlier sense of perfect balance in the trees of different sizes and densities on each side of the picture. Sometimes, as in the Boston picture, the whole appears rather awkward, especially in reproductions which tend to emphasize the patterns made by the landscape against the sky. In front of the original, however, these awkwardnesses disappear because one becomes aware that the artist is concentrating entirely on atmosphere, to the exclusion of everything else.

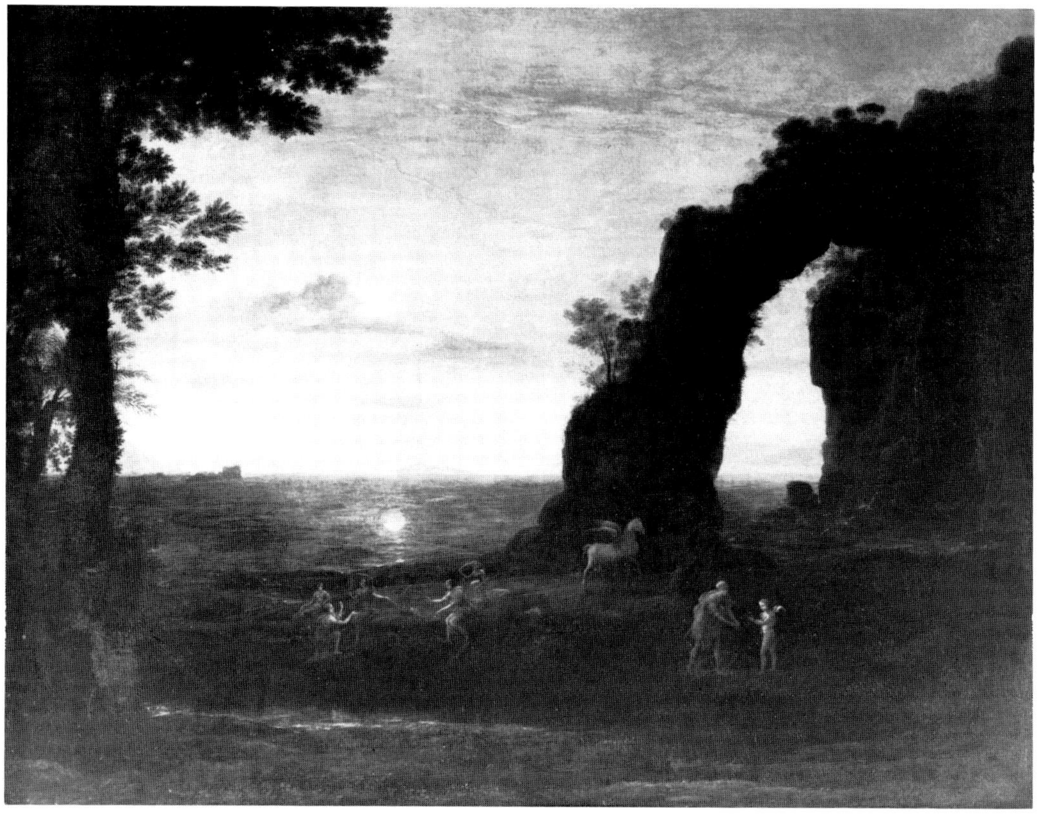

FIGURE 47
Claude Lorrain
Marine with Perseus and the Origin of Coral
Canvas, 100 × 127 cm. Remains of a signature lower centre
Liber Veritatis No. 184
Holkham Hall, Norfolk, Earl of Leicester
Painted for Cardinal Massimi. Brought to England by 1746. By 1759 in the collection of the Earls of Leicester, Holkham Hall, Norfolk. Thence by descent.

One of the most dramatic and unusual of the late compositions is the *Marine with Perseus and the Origin of Coral* (figure 47) of 1673, in the collection of the Earl of Leicester at Holkham Hall, Norfolk. The subject gave Claude an excuse to paint a coast scene with a rock arch and a sunset, and those who have witnessed this type of light effect on the Mediterranean coast will be able to understand Claude's truth to nature within his chosen classical format. He had to close the composition on the left with a balancing tree in order to produce the correct sort of formal arrangement required by his patron. The rock arch, used early in the artist's career in the Houston *Landscape with a Rock Arch* (see page 83), is here transformed into an almost abstract idea. It is this unique combination of the ideal and the natural, in perfect balance, which gives Claude the edge over every landscapist of the time seeking to idealize nature. Those who sought drama, like the Italian Salvator Rosa, achieved a different level of sublimity.

Most of the late Aeneas subject pictures are large in scale. The most splendid by far is the *Landscape with Aeneas Landing at Pallanteum* at Anglesey Abbey, Cambridgeshire. Much darker is *Aeneas Hunting in Libya* in the Brussels Musée Royal des Beaux-Arts. They cannot have been conceived as an exact sequence, however, because some twenty years elapsed between the earliest and the latest, and they were nearly all for different patrons.

As with Poussin, the pictures from the last two or three years of the artist's life transcend all that he had achieved before. With Claude the change was less dramatic than with Poussin, but it seems as if, in the last months of his life, the artist set out to please himself. The *Landscape with Christ Appearing to the Magdalen* of 1681 in the Städelsches Kunstinstitut at Frankfurt-am-Main is in better condition than many of the others, although it is not the most successful composition, and from it we can work out the artist's intentions in his very last picture, the *Landscape with Ascanius Shooting the Stag of Sylvia* of 1682 (plate 24) in the Ashmolean Museum, Oxford. Here the yellows have faded completely, leaving a bluish tinge over the whole, and the entire surface has been abraded. As a result the picture has an unnatural and ghostly feeling. The composition is one of Claude's most calculated, with trees, distant landscape and figures in total harmony. The Deruet-like figures are more prominent than usual, with their bright blues and reds. The story is a tragic one: Ascanius accidentally shoots the stag of Sylvia, which unleashes a brutal war of revenge. It is fitting that Claude should have ended his career on this theme without depicting brutality, as it sums up his gentleness of temperament as an artist. In a large number of Claude's late pictures there is a strong sense of the artist's mind at work. There are no precise intellectual pretensions as in Poussin, but there is a clear determination to persuade the spectator to feel a mood, rather than simply to contemplate the beauties of nature as presented by the artist. In other words, Claude was expressing intuitively the much more cerebral approach of Poussin.

Many misconceptions have grown up about both artists. Despite claims by French writers that they epitomize French culture of the seventeenth century, it is safe to assume that had they never left France for the artistic stimulation of Rome, their painting would not have achieved such great heights. Neither of them was close to the French court, and Poussin's relations with it were disastrous. The achievements of these two artists were on a highly individualistic level, unlike those of the Italian painters of the Baroque, who were part of a great decorative tradition. The causes of these misconceptions are twofold. The first relates to nineteenth-century nationalism, when each European country with its post-1815 boundaries sought to write its own cultural history. France was no exception, and it was to these two unique painters that it turned, rather than to the court art of Louis XIII and Louis XIV. The second reason is that their far-reaching influence has tended to cause historians to overestimate their real abilities. Poussin's influence was the more obvious, and affected a number of French painters working in Rome as well as later in Paris. Claude's art had a less immediate effect, although there were a few imitators of his landscapes working in Paris in the second half of the century, such as Pierre Patel the Elder. Because they were both imitated, Claude and Poussin became part of the subsequent history of art, but this cannot hide the fact that for the whole of their lifetimes, and for two centuries after their deaths, it was for their uniqueness that they were so highly esteemed.

Claude's achievement as a pioneer in landscape painting has earned him a place in the pantheon of art history. He was widely imitated for almost two centuries, and therefore often produces in the popular imagination a feeling of *déjà-vu*, especially in his best-known compositions. Claude's powers of innovation were in fact limited – he concentrated on a very narrow range of tones in a very narrow landscape type. Once he had perfected his technique, he did not develop much further deliberately; his work was too eagerly sought after by powerful patrons for him to need to do so.

It is difficult, therefore, to sweep away the debris of the eighteenth and nineteenth centuries when looking at Claude, and to see him with the freshness that was his own vision of the Roman Campagna. Less learned than Poussin, he never let the subject of his painting interfere with his treatment of the landscape, although he paid careful attention to the relationship between the general mood of the subject and its pictorial setting: thus the *Expulsion of Hagar* (Munich) takes place in a morning landscape.

Another difficulty for the twentieth-century spectator looking at Claude's landscapes is that he does not belong to the naturalistic tradition of landscape painting. During the twentieth century, respect for nature has taken precedence over its idealization in art, since the whole concept of idealization was abandoned during the middle of the nineteenth century, in the artistic revolution begun by Courbet and continued by the Impressionists. Claude epitomized all that the latter half of the nineteenth century was struggling against, in trying to order nature rather than to record it faithfully in all its imperfection. The fact remains, however, that Claude's ordering of nature arose from the most profound understanding of it, as is shown in the hundreds of totally naturalistic drawings by him of the Roman Campagna that have survived. These are as adventurous in their treatment of the fleeting effects of nature as some of the drawings by Constable a hundred and fifty years later. Claude was no mere theorist working out his ideas in the studio without first-hand experience, but his naturalism was always combined with a deep desire to rearrange nature into something more perfect.

Almost all Claude's mature pictures achieve greatness by stealth. They never dazzle and they never provoke. To the eye accustomed to action in a picture or to an obvious story, it is a surprise to find that there is none; and any figures present seem strange and elongated. Instead, an appreciation of Claude's magic must come from standing still and silent in front of the picture, in order to allow its mystery to penetrate the imagination. Claude is never explicit: his distances melt into infinity, and his world is one of an unattainable idyll, an earthly Elysium, unsurpassed by any other painter seeking the ideal.

Chapter Five

Painting in Paris, 1635-60

The 1630s saw rapid changes of artistic style, not only in French artists working in Rome but also in painters working in Vouet's studio in Paris, and there was also an enormous increase in output and a proliferation of painters active in Paris. This was a direct result of the expansionist policies of Louis XIII, masterminded by Cardinal Richelieu, whose ambition was to secure the boundaries of France against the Spanish Netherlands, the Holy Roman Empire (which included Lorraine) and, further south, the Franche-Comté and the duchy of Savoy. Not all these ambitions were achieved by Richelieu – they had to wait until Louis XIV – but after 1633 the occupation of territory such as Lorraine brought in its wake economic expansion. After such acts of aggression the whole system of government became of much greater importance. For the previous half-century the monarchy had been trying to protect itself from minorities of its own subjects, but now the nation was united behind these expansionist policies.

Painters were to benefit from this brief period of optimism, which effectively came to an end with the death of Richelieu in 1642. The untimely death of Louis XIII the following year ushered in the long minority of the infant Louis XIV and another period of political instability, which culminated in a virtual civil war known as the Fronde, which was at its height in the late 1640s and 1650s. Painters, however, seem to have suffered few setbacks during this politically difficult period; indeed, the 1640s were for Paris the most prolific decade of the whole century.

Little is known about the day-to-day nature of artistic activity during this period. Georges de La Tour took apprentices into his studio at regular intervals and the parents had to pay the artist considerable sums for the education of their teenage sons, but there is no evidence that these apprentices ever became artists in their own right. Certainly there was no rigid system of tuition or an application of either practical or theoretical standards, as was to be found in the Academies of Bologna or Rome. It was not until 1648 that the first Academy was founded in Paris, and it seems to have been a largely informal association of a dozen artists with similar aims. There is no evidence that it offered any theoretical approach to art until the early 1660s, when Louis XIV reorganized it.

The only truly Italian-style system of art education was that imported by Simon Vouet, who seems to have trained his pupils in the manner expected of an Italian. Evidence for this takes the form of the survival of drawings clearly intended as preparatory to large compositions: it required a good deal of specific training to design pictures in this way. There are drawings of this type also surviving from one of Vouet's most distinguished pupils, Eustache Le Sueur. The methods of artists outside Vouet's orbit were, on the other hand, entirely dictated by personal taste. Some of these painters were obviously methodical, such as Philippe de Champaigne, whose compositions were based on preparatory drawings. Others, such as the long-lived Claude

Vignon, worked directly on canvas with great facility. The Le Nain brothers, too, must have worked directly on canvas, as there are no surviving preparatory drawings by them. This lack of organization was immensely beneficial, because it permitted a wide variety of artistic styles. When Louis XIV reorganized the Academy and laid down strict rules whose intentions were to encourage the art of painting rather than to discourage it, he in fact caused an immediate end to these expressions of individuality.

The period 1635–60, then, was one of great diversity of both style and subject-matter, in which parallels are to be found in the main Dutch cities rather than in Italy. Groups of specialist painters established themselves, to work exclusively on still-life, flowers, landscape, portraiture or genre painting. Only the painters with large studios, such as Vouet, could diversify and at the same time satisfy the considerable demands of their patrons for decorations. The other consequences of this great burst of activity was a lack of clear stylistic development. It is impossible to chart any main trend running through the 1640s and 1650s, quite unlike the 1620s and 1630s, when Caravaggio's influence spread through the provinces. The painting activity in Paris in this period can, however, be divided into the main subject categories, because within each group – especially still-life, genre and portraiture – very specific standards and styles were maintained.

Still-life Painting: the Paris Artists and Stoskopff in Alsace

The most neglected area of French seventeenth-century painting is that of still life. The researches of Michel Faré, summarized in *Le grand siècle de la nature morte en France* (1974), his comprehensive book on the subject, have only rarely been incorporated into general surveys of the field. It is still sometimes mistakenly assumed that the work of still-life painters was insignificant in their time compared with the grand designs of, say, Claude and Poussin but, with one major exception, all the main still-life painters worked in Paris; they were not provincial artists working in obscurity away from the mainstream of the development of painting.

The exception was the obscure Sébastien Stoskopff, whose *oeuvre* has only recently been reconstructed. He was isolated in Strasbourg, the main town of the province of Alsace, which did not come under French rule until 1648 (although Strasbourg itself was not occupied until 1681). In the Middle Ages the artistic traditions of Alsace had their own flavour, being subjected to influences from central Europe, Italy and, to a lesser extent, France. Stoskopff, however, was influenced by none of these traditions, being a totally isolated painter working in a style verging on the naïve. Influences from such German still-life painters as Georg Flegel are discernible, but they may merely be caused by a similarity of subject-matter rather than by any stylistic affinity.

Stoskopff's art is unique. One of the best examples of his work is the *Still Life with Glasses in a Basket* (plate 80) in the Musée de l'Oeuvre de Notre Dame at Strasbourg. The tonality is monochrome, and the glasses in the basket are positioned in disarray. To this day, waitresses in restaurants in the region collect the empty drinking glasses by placing them heaped up in a basket rather than balancing them on a tray. There is therefore no complex

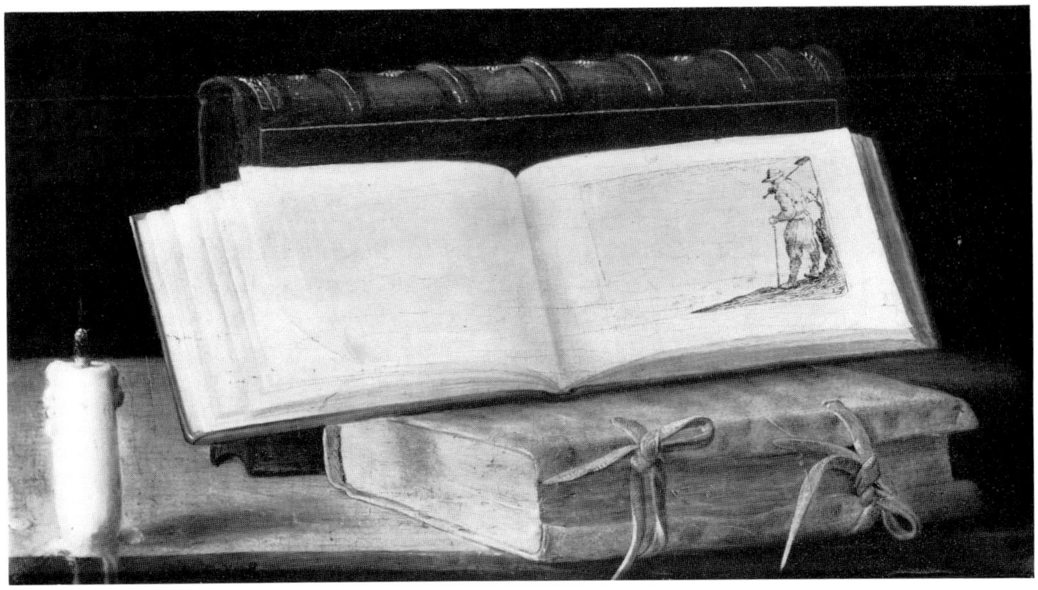

FIGURE 48
Sébastien Stoskopff
Open Book with a Callot Etching and Candle
Panel, 20.5 × 35 cm. Signed and dated lower left: STOSKOPFF 1625
Rotterdam, Museum Boymans-van Beuningen
Acquired in 1958, along with the rest of the van Beuningen collection.

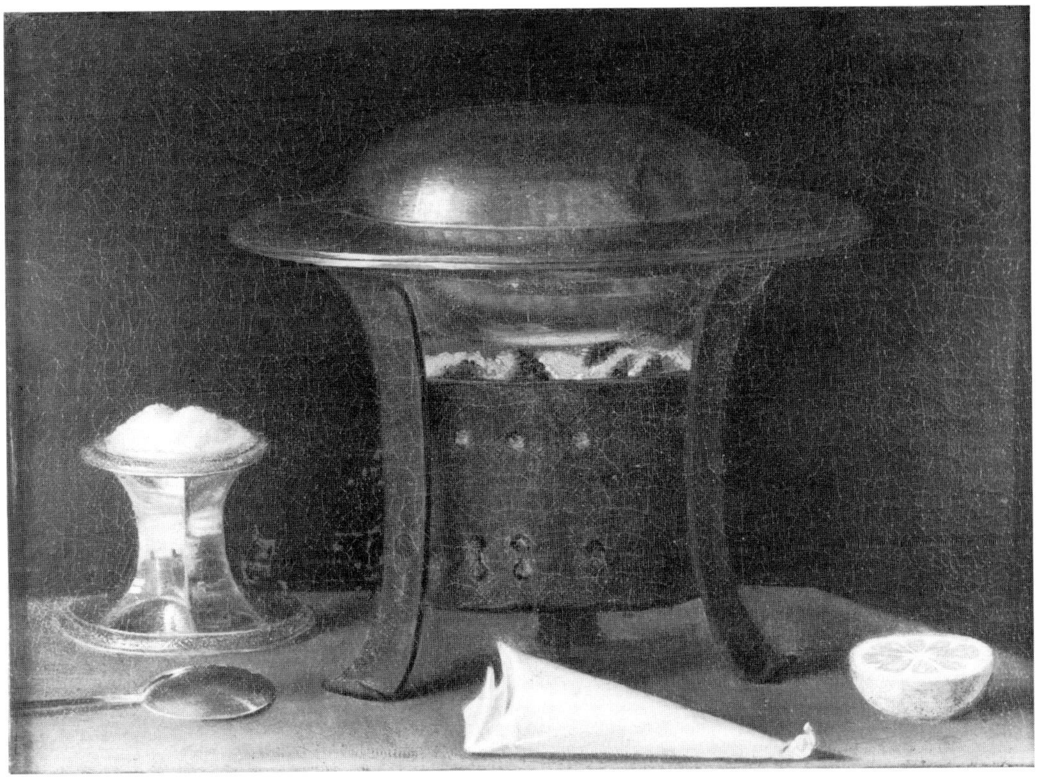

FIGURE 49
Sébastien Stoskopff
Warmer, Salt Pot and Cornet of Pepper
Canvas, 39 × 51 cm.
Chaumont, Musée Municipal
Date of entry into the museum unknown.

iconography behind such a depiction; it is just a careful record of an everyday sight. Even more bizarre is his *Warmer, Salt Pot and Cornet of Pepper* (figure 49) in the Museum at Chaumont, only recently attributed to Stoskopff. The glowing coals in the warmer had led to the suggestion of a Lorraine origin for the picture (La Tour painted similar glowing coals in his *Girl with the Brazier*, now in a private collection in Bremen), but the attribution to Stoskopff seems to be correct. It would appear that pepper, being a very precious spice at the time, was kept in small cornets. This newly established tradition of painting objects from everyday life in a naturalistic way was to be perfected in France by Chardin in the eighteenth century. A more conventional work by Stoskopff is the still life (figure 48) in the Museum Boymans-van Beuningen at Rotterdam. It has as its main element an open book of etchings by the Lorrainer Jacques Callot. Even though the subject was local, the stylistic influence, which produces the more conventional approach, was from the Dutch, who specialized in painting still lifes depicting open books, which often contained a deliberate moral message displayed on the open page.

Stoskopff only achieved a local reputation. A few of his compositions were more ambitious, especially the large *Allegory of Summer, or the Five Senses* at Strasbourg, but there is no evidence that his reputation suffered in local circles because he was a still-life painter. Nevertheless, whereas in the Dutch Republic still-life painters were held in just as much esteem as landscapists (indeed, so minute and skilled was their work that still-life painters were often held in especial esteem), the situation was quite different in France, and this is one of the reasons for the neglect of French still-life painting even today, and the lack of surviving biographical information. In France, formally after 1661, and informally before that, the status of an artist depended not on his ability but on his subject-matter. The newly reformed Academy laid down rules that had been crystallizing over a long period, chiefly through the influence of Italian art and those who wrote about it. The painting of history pictures (and that included religious themes) was considered to be the highest form of art; it was of course the one branch of painting which could be used by those in power for propaganda purposes, as it was by Marie de Medici, who employed Rubens to this end so successfully for her Luxembourg Palace decorations.

The other subject areas in painting were placed on a much lower level, with still-life painting at the very lowest. No still-life painter, however talented, could therefore achieve high social or academic status. It is likely that the proliferation of still-life painting provoked Pascal's famous comment that it was pure vanity to ask the spectator to admire in painting what was certainly not worthy of admiration in life. The deeply religious Pascal subscribed to the idea that art should take on a moral purpose, to uplift and bring the spectator towards the realization of higher spiritual values. (Although he did not put it this way, this was also Poussin's view.)

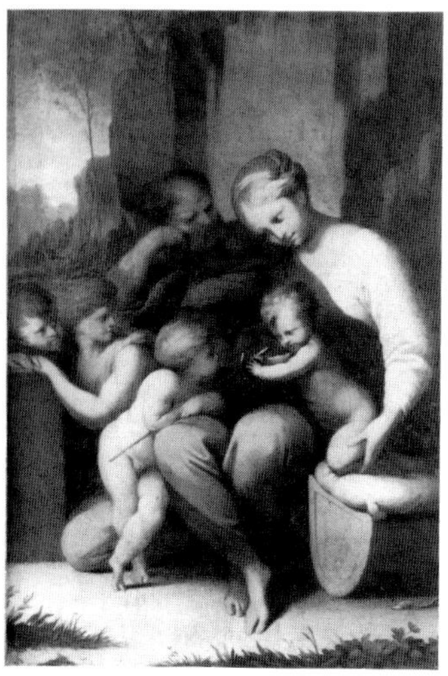

FIGURE 50
Lubin Baugin
Holy Family
Panel, 32 × 22 cm.
Dijon, Musée Magnin
This is one of a huge collection of pictures, mostly bought at public auction in the years 1880–1930 by the Magnin family.

The development of still-life painting in France is difficult to chart because of the lack of dated examples from the first thirty years of the century. As often happens, however, the earliest surviving pictures from the whole field are among the best. Perhaps the most spiritual of them are the three or four surviving still-life pictures by the enigmatic 'Baugin'. All the pictures are signed with the surname, and they have in recent years been equated with Lubin Baugin, a religious painter of pictures on a small scale. These were heavily influenced by Italian models, especially Correggio, and earned him the nickname of 'Le petit Guide' (after Guido Reni). Lubin Baugin's pictures are sentimental and sweet, with pretty pinks and pale blues, as in such delightful works as the *Holy Family* in the Musée Magnin at Dijon (figure 50).

Unfortunately there are no linking pictures between the religious scenes and the still-life pictures, but many authorities insist that they are all by the same artist. The two best still-life pictures, both in the Louvre in Paris, are the *Still Life with a Chequer Board* (plate 1) and *The Dessert of Gaufrettes* (plate 2), and they show a level of skill equal to anything produced by the Dutch at that time. Baugin's colours are subdued, exactly as in the still-life paintings of such artists as his contemporary Pieter Claesz., who worked in Haarlem and specialized in monochromatic pictures. Verging on the monochrome is Baugin's *Still Life with Writing Implements* in the Galleria Spada, Rome. Baugin's pictures are curiously international in feeling; there is no specifically 'French' flavour about them, and the only element in all these pictures that reveals that the artist was not Dutch is the lack of narrative anecdote. Each element is observed with meticulous care and without emotion. The spectator is not invited to participate, to join in the game of chequers or to scribble with the pen, unlike Claesz., who tempts us with his half-eaten pies and half-peeled lemons. Baugin seems to take no pleasure in the objects he depicts; they sit in utter stillness.

Like Stoskopff in Alsace, Baugin was isolated, whoever he was and wherever he worked. Most other French still-life painters had rather more defined personalities, although it is difficult to reconstruct the careers of even the most talented of them. It is not known what kind of patrons commissioned so many pictures from these artists, who proliferated in the middle years of the century, but they were probably very similar to their Dutch contemporaries. Many Dutch artists were able to work in Paris, and French collectors liked their small and highly finished pictures. It was only in the realm of still life that the French were successful in rivalling the Dutch, who dominated the market in small genre and landscape pictures (which explains the lack of such pictures by French artists of the time). Even if too little is known to generalize, it is possible to surmise, from inspection of the inventories taken after the death of middle-class inhabitants of the Lorraine capital, Nancy, that it was usual for such people to have several dozen paintings in their houses; a few had several hundred. The middle classes collected such pictures as decoration, not as 'art', and their subject-matter covered all the genres. From the evidence of this one centre it can be assumed that the pattern in Paris was similar.

There was some still-life painting in the south, where the leading painter was Meiffren Conte who favoured extravagant scenes of gold and silver

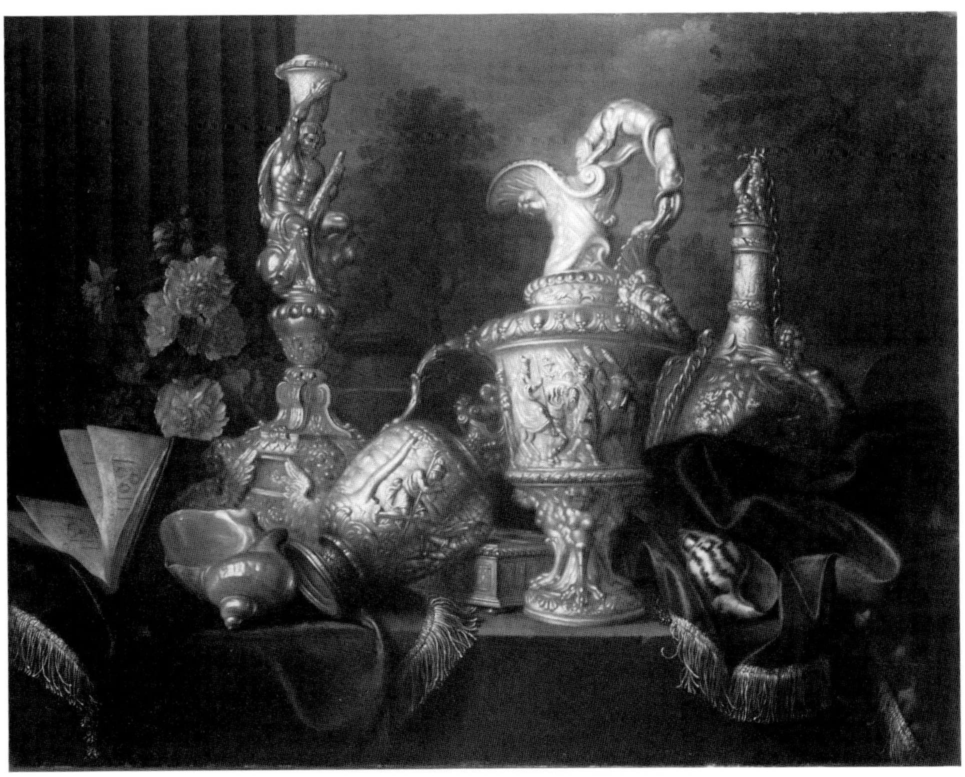

FIGURE 51
Meiffren Conte
Pitcher, Flambeau of Hercules, Armorial and Shells against a Landscape Background
Canvas, 105.4 × 129.5 cm.
Karlsruhe, Staatliche Kunsthalle
Acquired by the museum in 1965 from the American art market.

Similar elements appear in Conte's pictures in the Musée des Arts Décoratifs in Paris and in the Musée de Toulon.

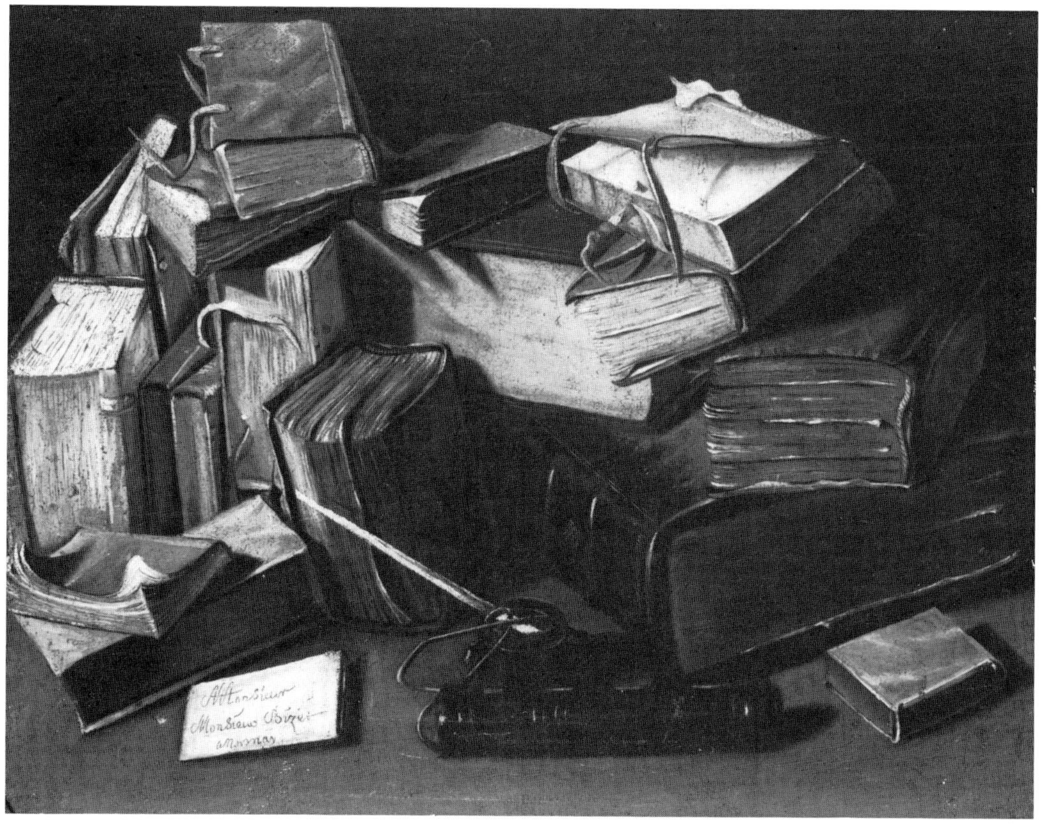

FIGURE 52
Charles Emmanuel Bizet
Still Life of Books
Canvas, 50 × 60 cm. Signed on the letter: A Monsieur, Monsieur Bizet Anonnay
Bourg-en-Bresse, Musée Départemental de l'Ain
Acquired by the museum in 1851 from the Lorindonnet collection.

vessels, a good example of which is in the Staatliche Kunsthalle in Karlsruhe (figure 51). Much more obscure is the remarkable Bizet, whose *Still Life of Books* in the Musée de l'Ain at Bourg-en-Bresse (figure 52) displays an energy worthy of Rubens and seems to have been derived from a Flemish source. Such painters left no school or influence behind them.

The 1630s saw the development of the one unexpected genius of the period, Louise Moillon. Her long career was spent entirely in Paris, and enough of her work survives to justify her being placed among the greatest of all still-life painters. Inevitably this claim will be challenged by those who do not accept that genius can exist outside the grand manner of painting but, in the context of the art of depicting fruit and vegetables, Moillon had few superiors.

Certain influences can be detected in Moillon's art, but these are superficial. A few of her genre pictures are of the type reflected in the market scenes painted in Antwerp at the end of the sixteenth century by Joachim de Beuckelaer, but Moillon's market scenes owe a debt to Antwerp only in subject-matter. A recently discovered picture is the *Market Scene with a Pickpocket* (plate 61) in a London private collection. In many of the Antwerp pictures, the humble activity of vegetable selling was transformed into a religious theme by small scenes in the background such as Christ in the house of Martha and Mary, always a popular addition because it could be classed as 'genre'. In Moillon's work there is no such concession. Instead, in the London picture, the artist reveals her modernity by telling an anecdote: a prosperous housewife buys fruit and vegetables, while an urchin picks her pocket; the vegetable seller is likely to be part of the plot. The whole unfortunate scene is painted with a complete sense of detachment, producing a snapshot effect rather than an elaborately posed and worked-out theme. The figures are observed as if they were part of the still life themselves. Each still-

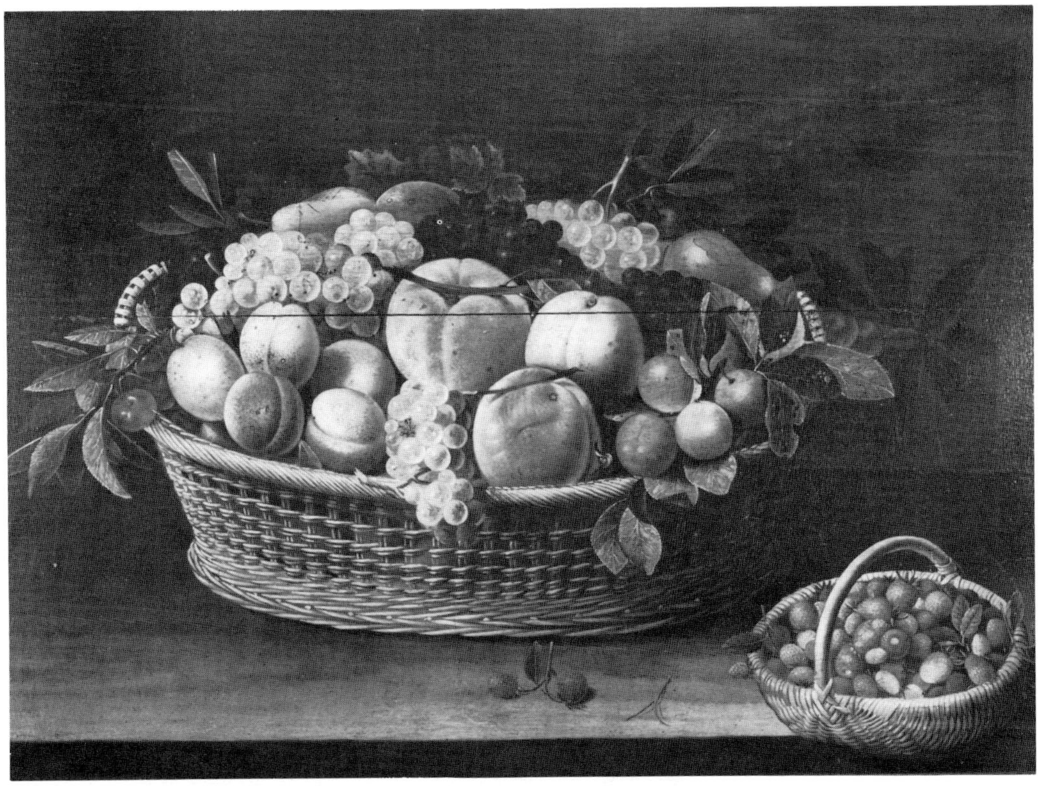

FIGURE 53
Louise Moillon
Peaches, Apricots, Grapes and Strawberries
Panel, 47 × 59 cm. Signed and dated: Louyse Moillon 1672
Toulouse, Musée des Augustins
From the collection of Le Tonnelier de Breteuil, Bishop of Montauban. Acquired by the museum in 1799.

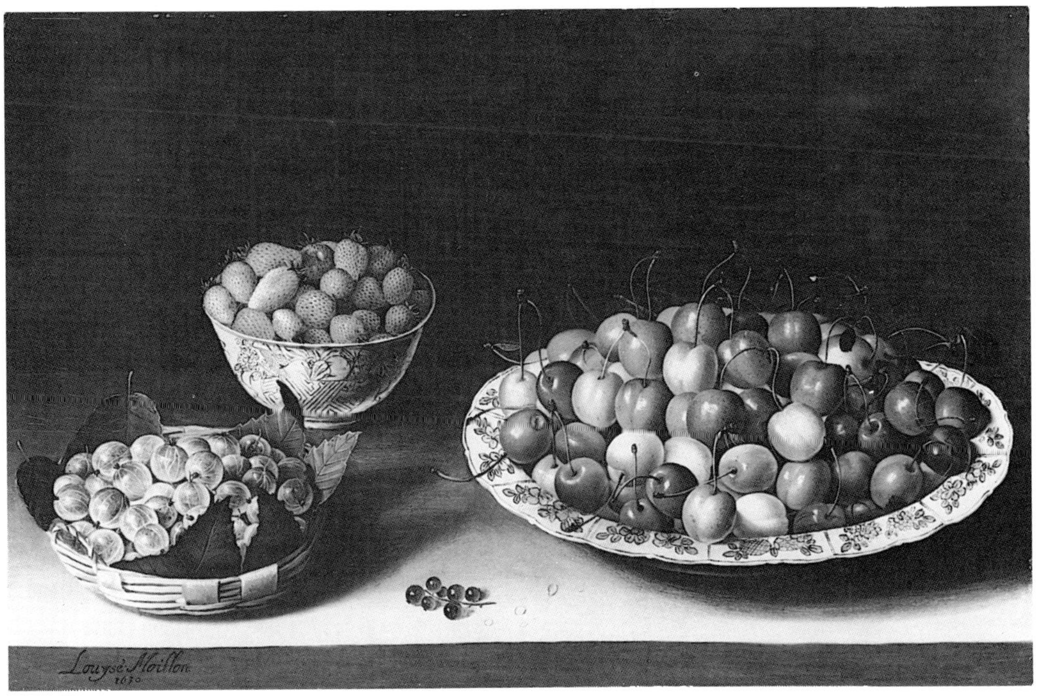

FIGURE 54
Louise Moillon
Cherries on a Plate, Basket of Gooseberries and a Bowl of Strawberries
Panel, 32.4 × 48.9 cm. Signed and dated lower left: Louyse Moillon 1630
Pasadena (California), Norton Simon Museum

life element in the picture is painted with enormous skill: the bloom on the fruit is beautifully recorded. Each object has an almost surreal isolation (similar to that in the celebrated *Still Life* by her contemporary, the Spanish painter Zurbarán, in the Norton Simon Museum, Pasadena). Moillon's still life of *Cherries on a Plate* (figure 54), also in the Pasadena collection, shows the humbler side of her art. Again, there is no emotional or romantic involvement with the subject, only an obsession with the appearance of ripe fruits. They are not even made appetizing, as were the sumptuous banquets depicted by the Dutch. Most of Moillon's other pictures are of baskets and

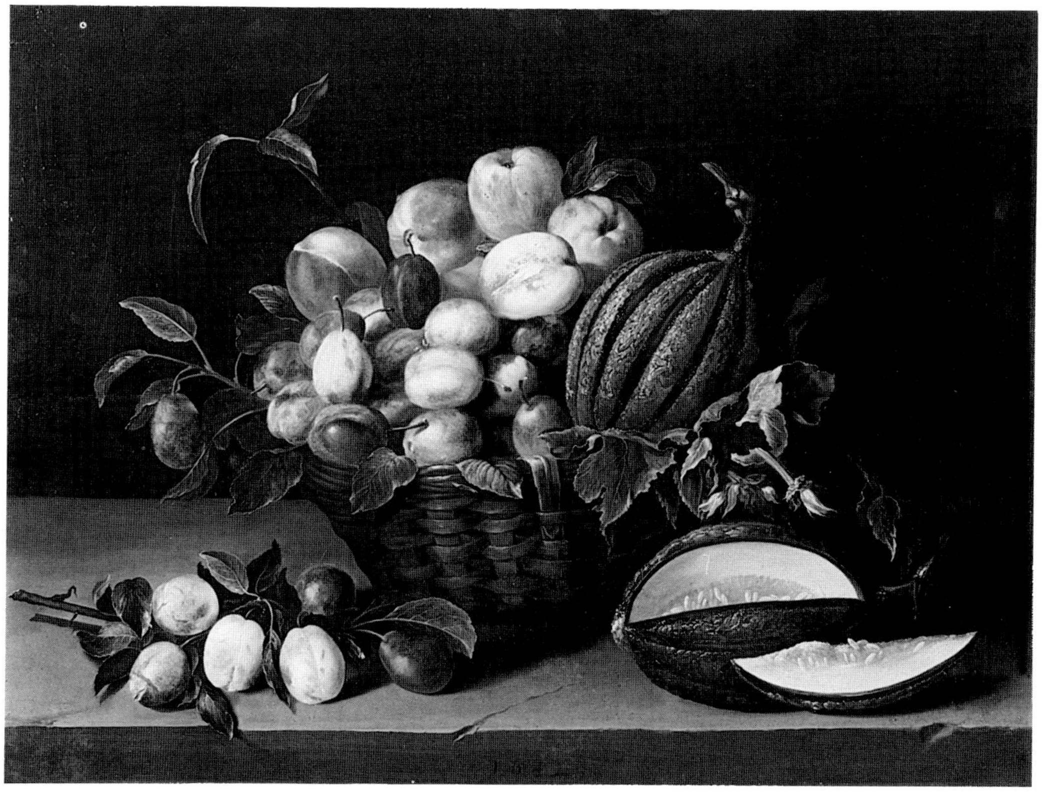

FIGURE 55
Jacques Linard
Still Life of Peaches, Plums and Melon
Panel, 56.5 × 75.2 cm. Dated 1642
Barnard Castle, Bowes Museum
Part of the enormous collection given as a museum by John and Josephine Bowes in 1871.

Not identified as by Linard until recently.

bowls of fruit, occasionally of exotic varieties. Her work is still rare in museum collections, the only museum to hold a group of them being the Musée des Augustins at Toulouse (figure 53). Moillon's unswerving sense of detachment in her art has inevitably led to questions about her Frenchness, but in fact she was simply a courageous individualist, unlike most French still-life and flower painters, who were happy to imitate, usually in a weaker manner, the styles and compositions that were typical of Dutch and Flemish artists.

Jacques Linard and François Garnier were Moillon's contemporaries, but they never achieved her greatness. Garnier comes close to Moillon in his *Cherries and Gooseberries on a Table* (plate 32) in the Louvre, Paris, but his sense of the picturesque quality of the fruits and leaves hanging from their branches is obvious, whereas Moillon never allowed such charm to intrude on her distillations of banal subject-matter. Linard painted both fruit and flower pieces. In his *Peaches, Plums and Melon* (figure 55) in the Bowes Museum, Barnard Castle, he also comes close to Moillon, and it is at times difficult to differentiate between them. Linard's passionate concern is with the surface of the fruit, and he shares Moillon's refusal to be side-tracked by the picturesque possibilities of arrangement. His *Basket of Flowers* (plate 59) in the Louvre shows how relatively unskilled he was, compared to Netherlandish contemporaries (especially the earlier generation that included Roelandt Savery and Ambrosius Bosschart the Elder). Linard could draw with precision, and presumably followed the Netherlandish method of making very precise drawings of individual flowers from nature, but was unable to place the whole in a convincing ensemble. Such achievements came only much later in the century, with Jean-Baptiste Monnoyer.

A large number of minor specialists in still life were working in Paris in the 1630s and 1640s, and all of them are meticulously recorded by Faré. A good example is the prolific Pieter (Pierre) Boucle from the Netherlands, who specialized in dead fish. His style is crude when compared to that of other Dutch artists, and his reputation is deservedly modest.

Still-life pictures by artists who were not specialists in the genre are rare indeed. There are a number of anonymous pictures which have never been identified, such as the perfectly painted *Still Life with Books* in the Musée des Beaux-Arts at Nantes, and the equally skilled *Still Life with Books* in the Louvre, which is often thought to be eastern French in origin. For Philippe de Champaigne, who spent the first twenty-one years of his life in his native Brussels, a captioned engraving of a *vanitas* piece helps to identify a unique work by him: a similar but not identical painting in the Musée de Tessé at Le Mans, *Still Life with a Skull* (plate 15). A skull, an hour glass, and a single tulip in a glass are shown. The picture has great severity: the skull is seen frontally and the other objects are placed on either side without any thought of making an interesting arrangement. The skull is treated with the maximum realism, and it appears as if recently exhumed rather than bleached. The artist was interested in the moral meaning of his *Vanitas* and not, as the Dutch would have been, in its picturesque qualities.

Still-life painting was so self-contained as a category that it shows none of the stylistic changes which took place in other areas of painting. The artists remained oblivious to the impact of Poussin on history painting in Paris, and did not notice the developments taking place in the Netherlandish centres, and they therefore embody as a group one more piece of evidence that France remained a backwater, away from the traditions of the North and of Italy. This was to change completely, even in still-life painting, after Louis XIV took control in 1661, when Monnoyer became one of the most advanced still-life painters in all Europe, setting the fashion in almost every important centre for half a century afterwards.

The Pupils of Simon Vouet: Eustache Le Sueur and Laurent de La Hyre

The efficiency of Simon Vouet's teaching is shown by the large number of surviving pictures in his manner but which are certainly by his pupils. There are far too many of them to have been painted by one person. Two of his pupils, Le Sueur and La Hyre, stand out. They asserted their independence relatively young in the 1630s, and then changed their styles to accommodate changes in fashion. Both painters achieved the peak of their powers in the 1640s, Le Sueur with the St Bruno series and La Hyre with his mythological pictures and elaborate, classically inspired landscapes. They both preferred bright colours and precise drawing, were uninterested in texture and on the whole avoided dark shadows. Their palettes – and they have often been confused with one another – are derived from the later work of Vouet, whose art became very much lighter in his last years. Their drawing owed much more to Poussin, however; they must have seen and been impressed by his first series of *Sacraments*. Le Sueur's *Annunciation* (figure 56) at Toledo, Ohio, is close in mood and treatment to Philippe de Champaigne, not because they were influenced by one another, but because they used the same source material. The reputations of both Le Sueur and La Hyre have suffered in the last hundred years, for reasons not easy to understand. In the nineteenth

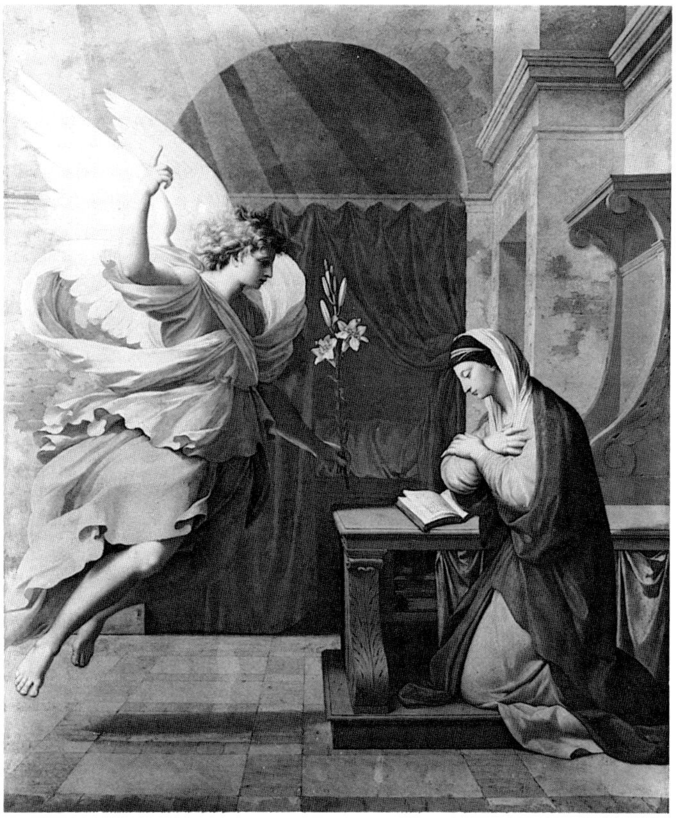

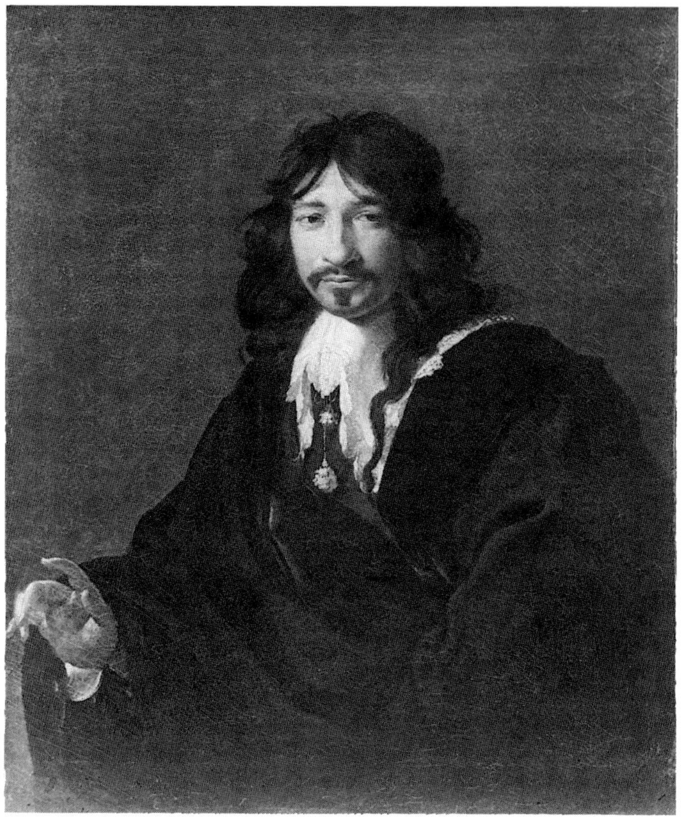

FIGURE 56 (above left)
Eustache Le Sueur
The Annunciation
Canvas, 156.2 × 125.7 cm.
Toledo (Ohio), Museum of Art
Known since the seventeenth century when the picture was recorded by the Charles Briçonnet collection in Paris. Acquired by the museum in 1952.

A little earlier, c.1650, than Poussin's treatment of the same subject in the National Gallery, London.

FIGURE 57 (above right)
Eustache Le Sueur
Portrait of M. Albert
Canvas, 89 × 73 cm. Inscribed on the back and dated 1641
Guéret, Musée Municipal
Given to the museum from the Fayolle collection, 1852.

The realistic treatment of the sitter, identified from an inscription on the reverse, could well have been derived from Simon Vouet.

century, for instance, Le Sueur's name was coupled with that of Poussin, and Delacroix wrote respectfully of him.

Le Sueur was the less sensual of the two and the more energetic. He died young and it is likely that his art would have developed towards further extremes. He was exceptionally versatile, as is shown in his few surviving portraits. His *Monsieur Albert* (figure 57) in the Museum at Guéret shows how well he had assimilated Vouet's Italian period portraits with their romantic overtones, but he was also able to add his own, far greater talent for observing character, instead of copying the superficial elegancies of Vouet (a number of rather similar pictures, such as the *Portrait of a Man* in Toledo, Ohio, has in recent years been attributed to Jacques Blanchard, who died in 1637).

The central act of Le Sueur's short career was the painting of the *St Bruno* series, now in the Louvre. This long sequence of canvasses immediately became famous, and remained so until the nineteenth century. In almost all the scenes, which survive in a perished condition through long exposure in a church cloister, there is a grave austerity that must in part be derived from Poussin. Le Sueur never went to Italy and could only have known Poussin's work through engravings and through first-hand knowledge of the pictures Poussin painted in Paris in the years 1640–42. The treatment of each scene is slightly more anecdotal than Poussin would have preferred, but in each picture Le Sueur has avoided unnecessary detail, concentrating entirely on the main figures in the drama.

His *Muse Terpsichore* in the Louvre (plate 58) is in a much more light-hearted vein. It is obviously part of an extensive decoration, but the artist made no concessions to decorative charm, and the figure conforms closely to the ideals of classical antiquity. However, when it came to painting a large religious picture, Le Sueur had the curious trait of emasculating Poussin's intellectual severity without giving up any of his austerity of composition. This is best seen in the unique *Annunciation* (figure 56) in the Toledo Museum of Art, Ohio. Every vestige of Vouet's influence has disappeared, and that of Poussin, so superficially obvious, has been transformed. Painted before Poussin executed his own uncompromising *Annunciation* of 1657 (in the National Gallery, London), the picture shows that Le Sueur took from Poussin the idea of placing each figure in total isolation from the others, thus immediately achieving a static effect. The setting is painted as if it were a theatrical backdrop. Here the similarities to Poussin end: Le Sueur has chosen a light-hearted colour scheme, unthinkable in Poussin.

La Hyre was very much more sensual than Le Sueur in approach. As in Le Sueur, the influence of Vouet was slight, even in the earliest surviving pictures; indeed, La Hyre's early works, such as the large *Dog* in the Palais Saint Vaast at Arras, betray some Flemish influence. Although La Hyre's career spanned some twenty years, he showed relatively little stylistic change once he had reached maturity. Instead of portraits, there are a few genre pictures from his hand, as well as the more usual mythologies and landscapes. The few mythological pictures are close in style to Le Sueur but painted in stronger colours, with reds and blues prevailing.

Almost all La Hyre's best pictures are of figures in classical landscapes. *The Children of Bethel Mourned by their Mothers* (plate 34) in the Palais Saint-Vaast at Arras corresponds to a type already perfected by Poussin, namely a strong moral content with figures carefully arranged in an equally carefully balanced landscape or architectural setting. Even though La Hyre's result was totally different from that of Poussin and it would never be possible to confuse the two, they fall into the same general category and would have appealed to the same types of patrons. The *Peace and Justice Embracing* (plate 35) in the Cleveland Museum of Art, Ohio, is an example of the great refinement of La Hyre's art. The background landscape, with its delicate trees and golden light, is almost Claudian in its inspiration. The landscape dominates the figures in this instance, also as in Claude. The subject, with its elaborate allegorical intention, shows Poussin's influence.

Neither La Hyre nor Le Sueur is likely to return to the position of esteem they once enjoyed, because both of them are too derivative. They fell under the spell of Claude and Poussin (in differing amounts), which to their contemporaries would have been a mark of distinction, but more than three hundred years later poses a great difficulty in understanding. These two painters, in the final analysis, have to be appreciated in terms of the artists who influenced them.

The Le Nain Brothers

The Le Nain brothers hold a unique place in the history of French seventeenth-century painting because they perfected a style that would have been more at home in the Netherlands. With one or two exceptions, they did not influence their contemporaries, and they are usually classified, quite wrongly, as 'provincial' painters, although all their best work was painted in Paris. Their training took place, it appears, in the North, yet they worked for most of their highly successful careers in Paris instead of in their native Laon, which was at that time close to the northern border with the Spanish

Netherlands. The conquests of Louis XIV in the 1660s and 1670s were to add to France a considerable piece of the old Netherlands, including Kamerijk (Cambrai), Atrecht (Arras), Rijssel (Lille) and Douai. This area was subsequently also absorbed culturally into France. Before the 1660s the area was still under Netherlandish domination, and the Le Nain brothers cannot have been unaware of influences across a border that was so close. Before they came to Paris, they were thus in a very similar position to Georges de La Tour, isolated from Paris but close to another main centre of artistic activity, the Netherlands.

In identifying the individual works of the three brothers, Antoine, Louis and Mathieu, who collaborated, surprisingly little progress has been made by modern art historians. The problem does not become acute until their maturity in the 1640s, when all the surviving pictures are signed cryptically LE NAIN, implying collaboration. All the works associated with their earlier period are unsigned, and no real attempt has been made to separate them.

It seems that the peasant genre pictures for which they are justifiably famous were not painted until the late 1630s, and that most of their earlier output was of religious or allegorical pictures. A few of these survive, most of them identified only in recent years. They present many problems for the historian, as most of them appear to be the work of relatively unskilled provincials, while the peasant pictures are among the highest achievements of that genre. No dates can definitely be given for these early religious and mythological pictures. Known only since the 1950s is the *Bacchus and Ariadne* in the Musée des Beaux-Arts at Orléans. As might be expected from an artist or artists brought up in the relative isolation of Laon, the picture is gauche in composition, but its execution is refined. Especially felicitous is the sleeping figure of Ariadne, who appears languid in a manner suggesting that the artist was familiar with Italian Renaissance poses. The background figures are, however, awkward in the extreme, revealing a lack of training.

The problem of the collaboration of the three brothers and their artistic development is highlighted in the *Venus at the Forge of Vulcan* in the Musée Saint-Denis at Reims (plate 50). It is dated 1641, which was during the last period when all three brothers were alive. Stylistically it is an advance on the Orléans *Bacchus*, but there is little surviving evidence of the activity of the Le Nain brothers in the 1620s and 1630s (as with Georges de La Tour, most of the surviving pictures seem to have been painted at the end of the artists' lives). In this painting the figure of Venus herself seems an uneasy adaptation of a Renaissance model. Perhaps including an obvious quotation was the artist's way of making it plain to the client that the picture had a well-known precedent. The rest of the picture, however, reveals, instead of the gaucheries of the *Bacchus*, great powers of observation. Especially perceptive are the two figures in the background, silhouetted against the light of the furnace. In all the French art of the seventeenth century, this is the first time that a painter has been able to observe nature without adding mannerisms of his own; even Georges de La Tour at his most realistic created an artificial world in which everything was secondary to his fascination with candlelight. Here, the figure on the left glances towards Venus in a completely natural way, and it is this naturalism, which occurs again and again in parts of their pictures, that sets the Le Nain brothers apart from all their French contemporaries.

The Reims *Venus* and the *Forge* in the Louvre (plate 51) are close in style;

in the latter the artists simply removed Venus and painted a straightforward genre picture, in which they could concentrate on the most sympathetic rendering of men working in a forge. The smith himself looks towards the spectator as if he has been disturbed by the artist and asked to hold the pose while a photograph is taken. The other figures look in different directions, exactly as a group of people will do today when caught unawares by the camera. Especially perceptive is the depiction of the seated old man on the right – he is staring into space exactly as many old people tend to do, particularly when they are preoccupied with something which is not part of the event in front of them. The gazes of the three children are alert but lacking the concentration of the adults. Thus the painters of this picture have observed, for the first time in French painting, a 'slice of life'. The depiction of the better-off peasantry is interesting from a sociological point of view because there are so few renderings of that class, but, even more important, it showed that masterpieces could be produced from humble material. This realistic treatment of 'low' subjects was not to be found again in French art until Courbet in the nineteenth century. The Le Nain brothers were in fact rediscovered in the nineteenth century by Champfleury, the champion of Courbet, just as Georges de La Tour was the exciting rediscovery of the middle years of the twentieth century. Such dramatic reappraisals are only possible in an area which is little studied and where the pictures are scattered: any large surviving corpus will be noticed sooner rather than later. In the case of French seventeenth-century painting, so many of the best pictures remain dispersed in the smaller provincial museums of countries other than France that reappraisal has always been difficult.

The peasant genre scenes, the best ones set in the open air being given to Louis Le Nain, fall into several categories. Again, they make new statements about figures and landscape which set them apart from the work of their contemporaries in France. Even in the Dutch Republic few parallels to them can be found. The realistic approach of the Dutch to landscape, especially in Haarlem in the 1620s, remained strictly local in its expression, and did not generally influence French painters; the similarity of the backgrounds in the Le Nain brothers' peasant scenes to those of Dutch landscape painters may well be coincidental.

Like their peasant scenes, the landscapes of the Le Nain brothers are careful observations of what they saw, rather than derivations from other painters' work. An example is the *Landscape with Peasants and a Chapel* (plate 54) in the Wadsworth Athenaeum, Hartford, Connecticut, in which, although figures dominate the foreground, the main effort has been concentrated on the landscape. In the distance there is a large village with traces of its decaying fortifications, and a small Gothic chapel outside its walls. Such a sight may still be seen today, in the remoter parts of northern and eastern France. Again, the Le Nain brothers have told us what the people and the landscape of the time looked like. Few records of middle-class life in painting exist (although the engravings of Abraham Bosse give us some idea of how houses were decorated and what the more prosperous classes wore) and the surviving pictures of the Le Nain brothers are the only evidence we have of a common way of life at the time, that of a prosperous peasantry living off the riches of the land. Without them, all we have are the great official portraits of the monarch and his court.

FIGURE 58
Le Nain brothers
Peasants before their House
Canvas, 55.2 × 70.5 cm.
San Francisco, California Palace of the Legion of Honor
Acquired by the fourth Duke of Rutland (d.1787). Acquired by the museum in 1941.

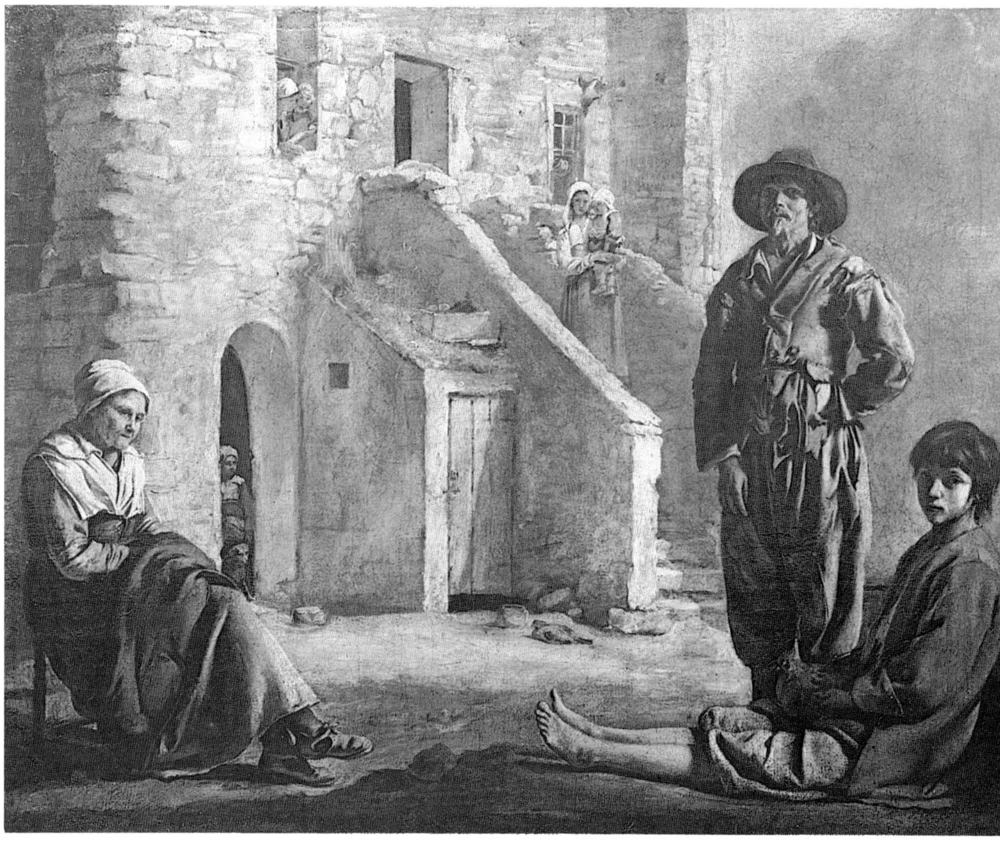

In the *Peasants before their House* in the California Palace of the Legion of Honor, San Francisco (figure 58), the approach is unusually stark for the Le Nain brothers. Instead of a landscape background, there is a two-storey house belonging to the peasants, whose relative prosperity is indicated by the glass in the windows (all over Europe at this time many of the poorer classes lived in conditions far more primitive than those recorded by the Le Nain brothers). This unassuming picture is one of the most perceptive paintings to be produced in the 1640s. As in the *Forge*, the treatment of the low-life subject is given a totally unexpected dignity. The boy on the right and the old man next to him stare through us into space, and together they counterbalance the large area of pale stone of the house behind them. Into their expressions the artists have distilled a timelessness as far removed from anecdote as possible. Whereas in Georges de La Tour this timelessness is easier to understand because of the spiritual content of his subjects, in the depiction of a peasant's face it is rare for the artist not to be interested in telling a story, but simply to be observing what he sees. This approach, which was to preoccupy many of the most important painters of the nineteenth century, from Courbet to the Impressionists, was an anachronism in the seventeenth century and the reason why the Le Nain brothers were so untypical of artists of their time.

In the pictures of peasant interiors there is as much diversity as in the exterior scenes, and again attempts have been made to group them round each of the brothers. The categories into which they have been divided make sense, even if no name can convincingly be attached to each one. Closest to the Dutch models, especially to the art of Jan Miense Molenaer, is the group of peasant scenes painted on a minute scale. One of the best is the *Peasant*

Interior (plate 52) in the National Gallery, Washington, signed 'Lenain fecit' and dated 1642. Although exquisitely painted, the figures seem to be in a very curious spatial relationship with one another; the mother seems far too small and the children far too big. All their expressions are lively and alert and, as is usual in Le Nain, they look in different directions, as if caught by surprise. Yet more disconcerting, because the viewpoint is even closer, is the *Saying Grace* in the Frick Art Museum, Pittsburgh, Pennsylvania. It may be that the composition has been cut at the edges, but there is again the feeling of a camera taking a close-up shot of the sitters unawares. The three children, who are supposed to be attending while their mother says grace, are shown in contrasting attitudes: the one on the right appears to be laughing out loud and cocking a snook at the formality of the occasion; the child in the middle is well-behaved; and the third one looks on inattentively. Even at their most direct, none of the Dutch artists managed such closeness to life, except perhaps in roistering tavern scenes, and even then there is often a sense of theatrical pose although the individual characters are painted with the utmost realism.

There are considerable differences between the small-scale peasant interiors and those of larger dimensions. In the larger works the handling is more fluid and there are indications of a greater temptation to tell a story. Two examples are the *Card Players* in the Musée Granet at Aix-en-Provence and the *Brawl* in the National Museum of Wales, Cardiff. The Aix picture has only three figures, and in this it is reminiscent of the work of Le Valentin, whose pictures the Le Nain brothers may have seen in Italy. Even the dramatic lighting is Caravaggesque. As in Le Valentin's Dresden *Card-sharps*, there is a consciousness in the Le Nain picture that the card game has reached a dramatic moment. Nonetheless, overstatement has been avoided, and the spectator is left to guess the reasons for the sudden halt in the game. The Cardiff picture is much more explicit: one of the players has drawn his sword and the other is about to do so; but again, the reason for the drama is left unstated and the spectator is left to speculate upon the causes of the trouble. (This is in direct contrast to the work of the Dutch, who went to great lengths to explain the story depicted in a painting.)

Not all the Le Nain genre scenes depict peasants. Some of them show middle-class sitters, even rarer in art than the depiction of the poor. Fortunately, some of the best are signed and dated, but it is impossible to discover whether they are the work of one brother or of two or all of them. The *Musical Company* of 1642 in the Louvre is small in scale like the *Peasant Interior* and *Saying Grace*, yet the treatment is quite different. Although the critical eye can detect a certain gaucherie in the placing of the figures, there has been an enormous increase in sophistication, as if the social position of the sitters demanded it. Nevertheless, it is hard to believe that this work was a commissioned group portrait, although this is possibly the case in a few of the larger bourgeois compositions.

It is one of these larger 'bourgeois compositions' which admits the Le Nain brothers into that small group of painters capable of creating a masterpiece. This is the *Smokers in an Interior* (plates 55 and 56) in the Louvre, dated 1643. It was in a private collection until 1969, and so it has never been properly assessed in the older literature. Its technique must have been learned during the painting of the *Forge*, but the brushwork is far more precise. The composition is much less original, being closer to the type familiar from the

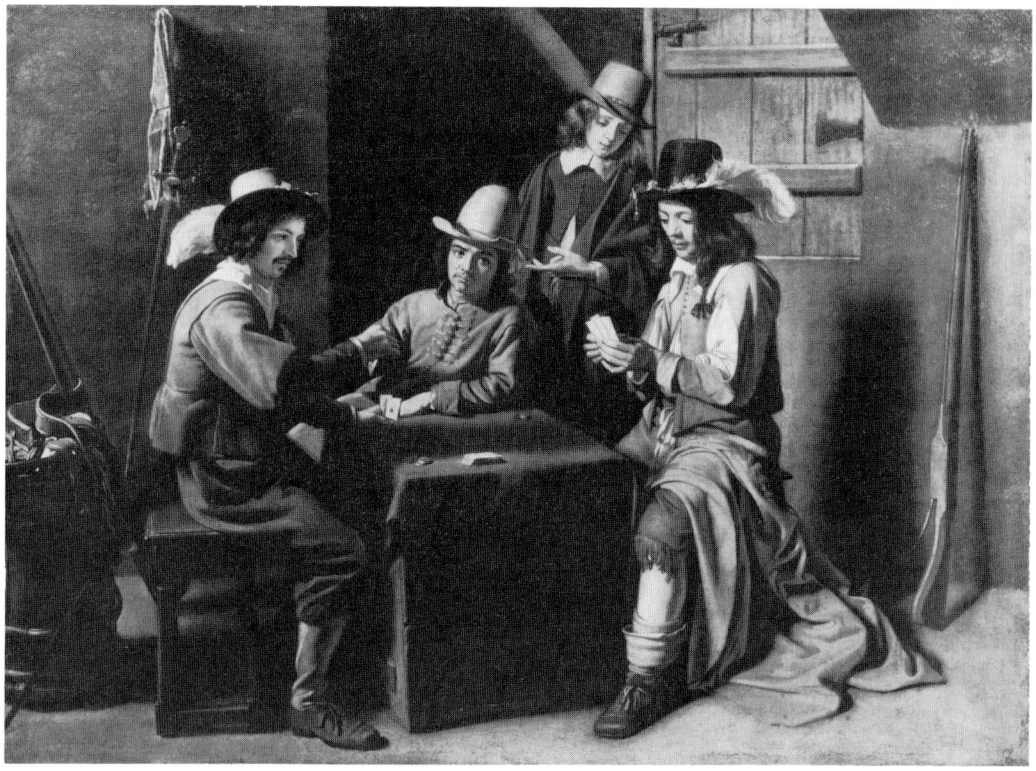

FIGURE 59
Le Nain brothers
Soldiers Playing Cards
Canvas, 85 × 114 cm.
Birmingham, Barber Institute of Fine Arts
Probably at Broadlands, Hampshire, since the end of the eighteenth century. Acquired from Countess Mountbatten by the museum in 1941.

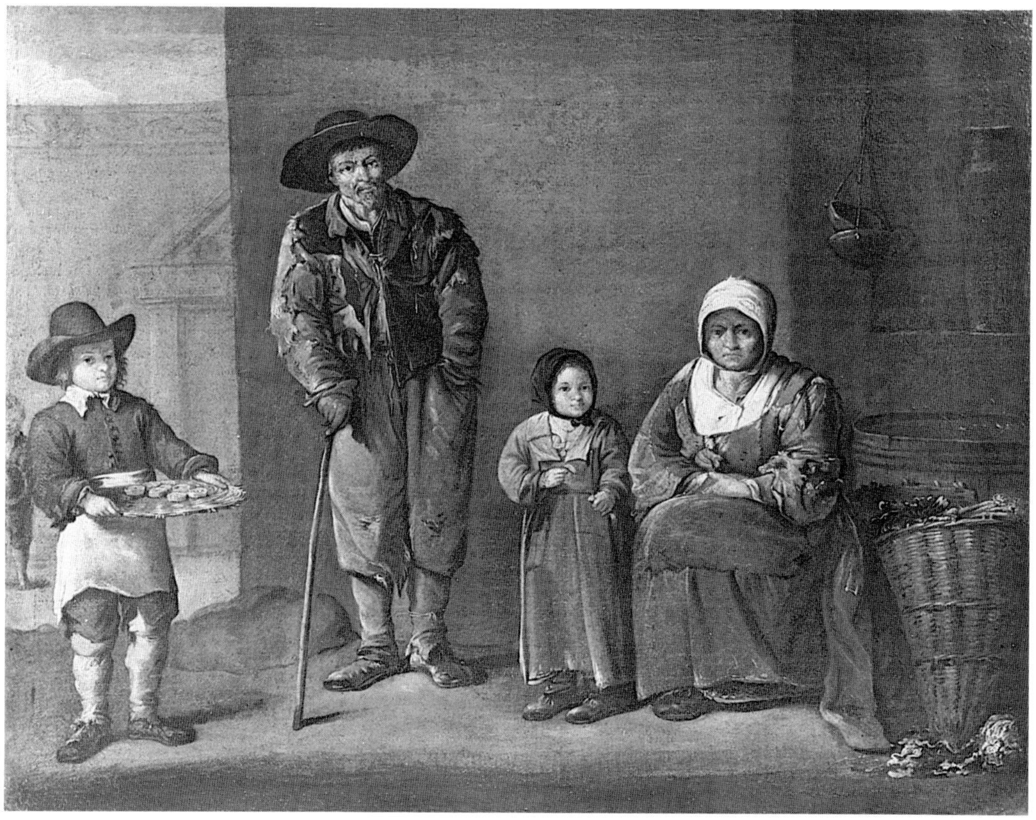

FIGURE 60
Jean Michelin
The Baker's Cart
Canvas, 98 × 125 cm. Signed and dated lower right: Michelin f. 1656
New York, Metropolitan Museum of Art
First recorded in an English collection in 1918. Bought by the museum in 1927.

Dutch, but only one Netherlandish artist, the much-travelled Michiel Sweerts, achieved the same atmosphere (in his *Interior with Boys Smoking* in the Alte Pinakothek, Munich, which has the same mood of calculated nonchalance). The figures are grouped round a table illuminated by a solitary candle, and the figure on the left has fallen asleep at the table. In this painting it seems that the depiction of low life – here, middle-class men smoking in an interior – has risen beyond its normal pictorial limitations to create a masterpiece which is, perforce, unexpected. While Nicolas Poussin was obsessed with the concept of beauty and with the need to be able to paint exactly what he thought, here the painter's desire arises from an opposite need, the need to observe. Each of the models appears to be a portrait, although it is difficult to explain why the sitters should have chosen to be depicted with such casualness. There is no clue to the possibility of a confraternity, although the curious emblems on the carpet on the table could be symbols of some secret society. The eerie quality of the picture is emphasized by the fall of the shadows on the faces and by the way in which the figures stare into space just like the peasants in other pictures and the seated figure on the right has all the appearance of being under the influence of some drug. There is no satisfactory explanation for such a picture; it is as if this trio of painters, observers of a small fragment of their times, never intended the meanings of their pictures to be divined.

The 1640s were the most productive years for the Le Nain brothers. Louis and Antoine both died in 1648, leaving Mathieu to continue working alone. It is thus possible to separate the work of Mathieu in the 1650s and 1660s, when he was without the inspiration and encouragement of his two brothers. All sense of mystery and symbolism then disappeared from his work and there is just a delicate competence; but this is not to say that his powers were declining. Attitudes towards art were changing during these two decades and were on the point of crystallizing into the artistic programme of Louis XIV, so it is not surprising that Mathieu Le Nain began to paint more innocuous conventional interior scenes, such as the *Soldiers Playing Cards* (figure 59) in the Barber Institute of Art at Birmingham. This picture shows that all the fire went out of Mathieu Le Nain's compositions once the collaboration had ended. One could easily believe that this is an inferior Dutch picture, albeit with an unusual colour scheme and curiously alert faces.

The Le Nain brothers were imitated on a modest scale, and copies of their work survive; but far more numerous are pictures of obvious ability that modern scholarship nevertheless does not include in the canon. Some of these have been grouped unsatisfactorily under the name of the Maître des Cortèges, and even more are described as anonymous. Most of these are outdoor scenes of peasants, painted in greys and greens, and the majority probably date from the 1650s or later. It was at this time that one of the Le Nains' main imitators, Jean Michelin, was active. His style is distinctive, however, even though, in his *Baker's Cart* (figure 60) in the Metropolitan Museum of Art, New York, his models may look similar to those in paintings by the Le Nain brothers.

Michel Corneille the Elder does not appear to have been influenced by the Le Nain brothers, but in one memorable picture his approach was very similar. The narrative in *Esau Selling his Birthright to Jacob* in the Musée des Beaux-Arts at Orléans (figure 61) is treated as a contemporary and realistic

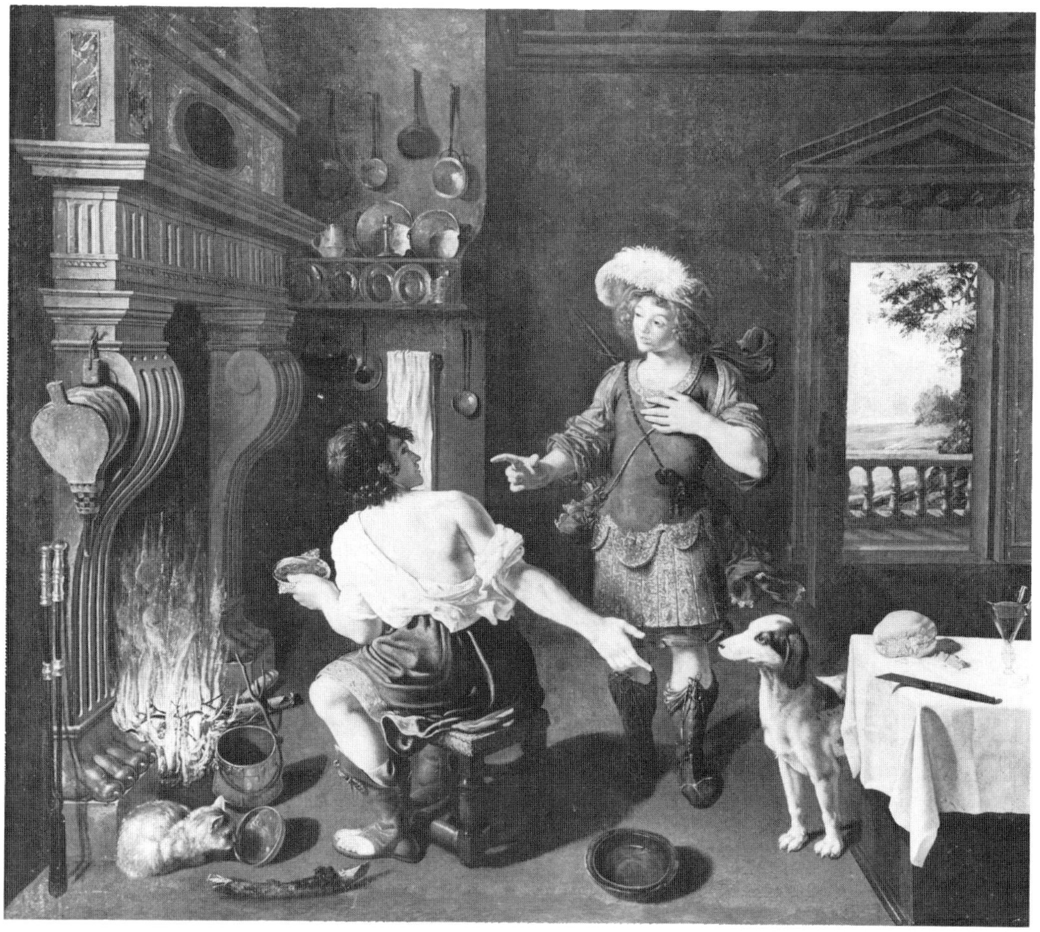

FIGURE 61
Michel Corneille I
Esau Selling his Birthright to Jacob
Canvas, 115 × 125 cm. Signed and dated: M. Corneille pinxit, 1630
Orléans, Musée des Beaux-Arts
Given to the museum by Madame de Limay in 1825.

This treatment of the famous Bible story is a rare one: the artist has depicted it as a genre scene.

event, and the picture tells us more about the appearance of a French seventeenth-century kitchen-cum-dining-room than it does about the story of Jacob and Esau. Unfortunately, Corneille did not produce any other work so revealing.

Philippe de Champaigne

Philippe de Champaigne was undoubtedly the most successful and important painter in Paris in the middle years of the seventeenth century. He was extensively patronized by Richelieu and by the Church, and also painted many portraits of the higher ranks of the administrative classes. Philippe de Champaigne's style conflicted with that of his contemporaries, rarely losing its Flemish origins even when he was also under the influence of Poussin, whose brief visit to Paris was to have an all-important effect on almost all the artists active in the city (both his colours and his compositions were enormously influential).

Although Philippe de Champaigne was the most competent and successful painter in Paris for almost forty years, he was relatively uninfluential during his lifetime. His pictures show a huge variety of sources which are easily identified, and yet, for all his easily defined characteristics, Champaigne was able to paint a subtle masterpiece of observation at almost all stages of his career. His chronology is notoriously difficult and hypothetical; dating is particularly dangerous when a career of this length is being discussed. Because his artistic education took place in Brussels, his early work is totally

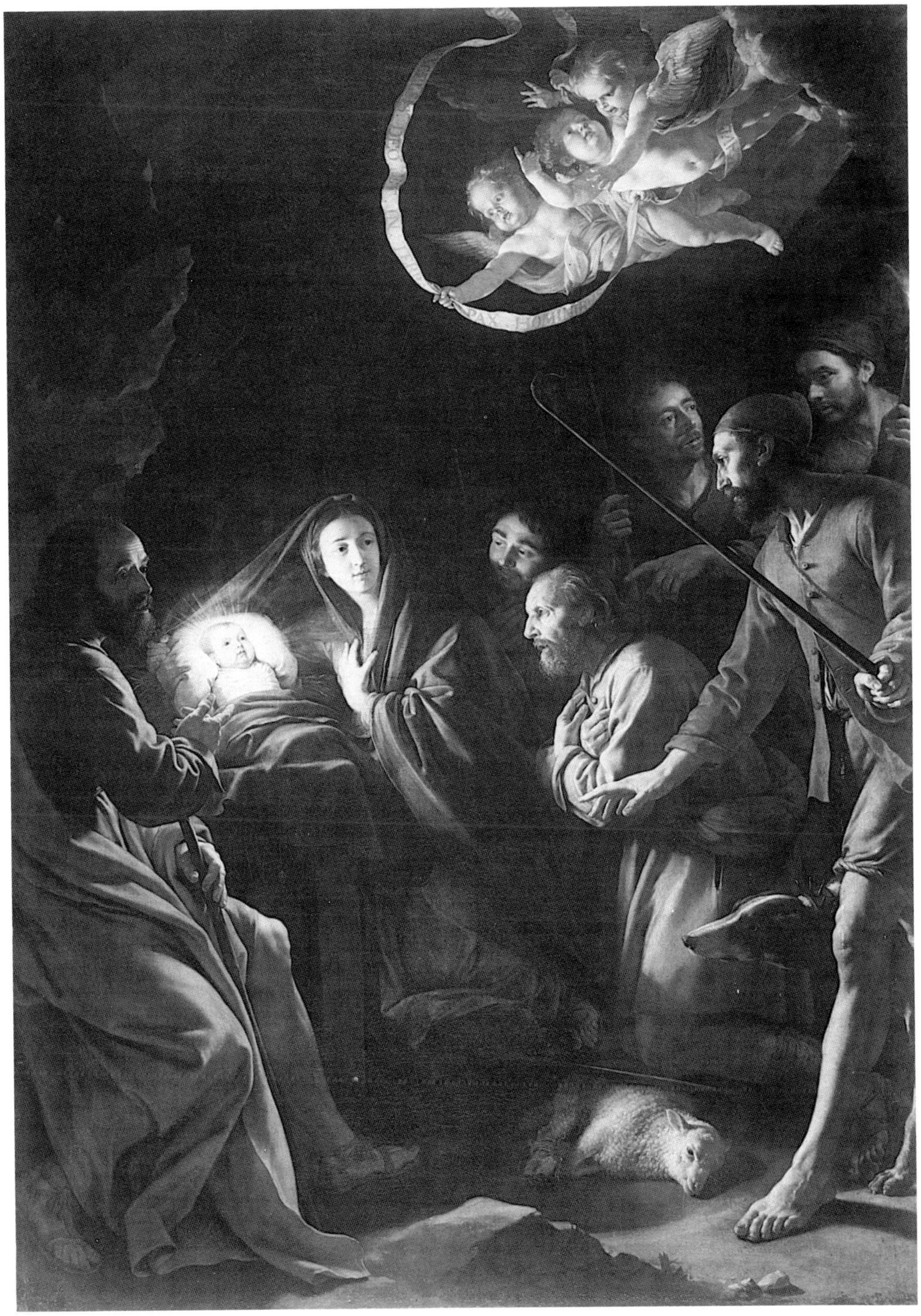

FIGURE 62
Philippe de Champaigne
Adoration of the Shepherds
Canvas, 233 × 163.2 cm.
London, Wallace Collection (reproduced by permission of the Trustees)
Commissioned by Cardinal Richelieu for the abbey at Quincey, near Poitiers, in 1628. Bought by the fourth Marquess of Hertford from the celebrated Montcalm collection at Montpellier in 1849.

Flemish in character, stylistically and compositionally close to Pourbus, who also achieved success at the court of Louis XIII. He must already have been teaching in the 1620s: it is recorded that the young Nicolas Poussin spent a short time in his studio before leaving for Rome.

Champaigne frequently repeated similar compositions at different times in his career. Inevitably there were modifications, as the artist's attitudes changed, and without the evidence of a few engravings and certain provenances there would be great confusion. One of the best examples of this habit is the series of pictures devoted to the Nativity. The earliest is probably the large canvas in the Wallace Collection, London (figure 62), because it is so strongly influenced by Rubens. The treatment is almost luxuriant in both colour and texture, and the picture fits perfectly into the concept of the Baroque altarpiece, whose motive is religious propaganda, to educate and inspire the faithful by magnificence and even rhetoric. Rubens was the supreme master of this (although, of course, this was only one aspect of his genius). Champaigne was able to translate Rubens's dramatic emotion into something calmer, and yet there is still an element of agitation and drama in the lighting. Later in his career, Champaigne returned with equal bravado to the theme of the Nativity, in the version in Rouen Cathedral probably painted in 1644, in which there has been very little change.

Champaigne was in the habit of producing highly finished small versions of his large pictures, unusually for a French artist of his time, and the Rouen Cathedral picture is duplicated in miniature at Narbonne. It is not clear whether these versions were finished modellos in the Italian manner, designed to be shown to the client before the expensive large picture was begun (as was often the custom in Italy) or whether they were replicas painted afterwards. Another example of two versions of one picture is the *Annunciation*, the small version of which is in the Ferens Art Gallery, Hull (plate 11). Although the modelling, colour and line are precise, there is a certain sensuality in their treatment, again clearly marking the artist's Flemish origins. In the large version in the Wallace Collection all trace of this has disappeared and, instead, a grandeur is achieved by a large amount of space in the composition and a treatment of the draperies as if they were metal foil or even sculpture. Indeed, this *Annunciation* has all the appearance of a coloured, sculptured tableau with dramatic lighting added. Champaigne arrived fairly quickly at this style of austere but highly coloured grandeur, and a good number of his *Annunciations* could well date from the 1640s, when they would have fitted into the context of the pictures of the rapidly maturing Eustache Le Sueur and Laurent de La Hyre, who were moving away from their master Vouet's version of the Baroque and becoming increasingly severe.

Champaigne was by far the most prolific artist of his time, and the diversity of his compositions and subject-matter was immense. Fortunately he received patronage from different types of people, and as a record of the times his portraits of the intellectual bourgeoisie, the group portrait of the *Échevins of Paris* (Louvre) and the many portraits of Cardinal Richelieu are perhaps the most interesting. His most important sitter, the King, was depicted as part of a complex religious picture called the *Vow of Louis XIII*, in the Musée des Beaux-Arts at Caen, in which Champaigne was not encouraged to use his analytical brush on the monarch's features. It seems incongruous to twentieth-century eyes that the king, dressed regally and holding crown and sceptre, should be depicted before a severe representation of the Virgin lamenting the body of the dead Christ, but at that time such votive pictures were the fashion, accepted as part of official paraphernalia.

Richelieu was painted by Champaigne in several different guises, all of them with unwavering accuracy and concentration, and these portraits are a vivid record of that statesman's determined and brilliant personality. Unique in French art of the time, but familiar from Van Dyck, is the *Triple Portrait of Richelieu* (figure 63) in the National Gallery, London. This was painted for the same purpose as the Van Dyck triple portrait of *Charles I of*

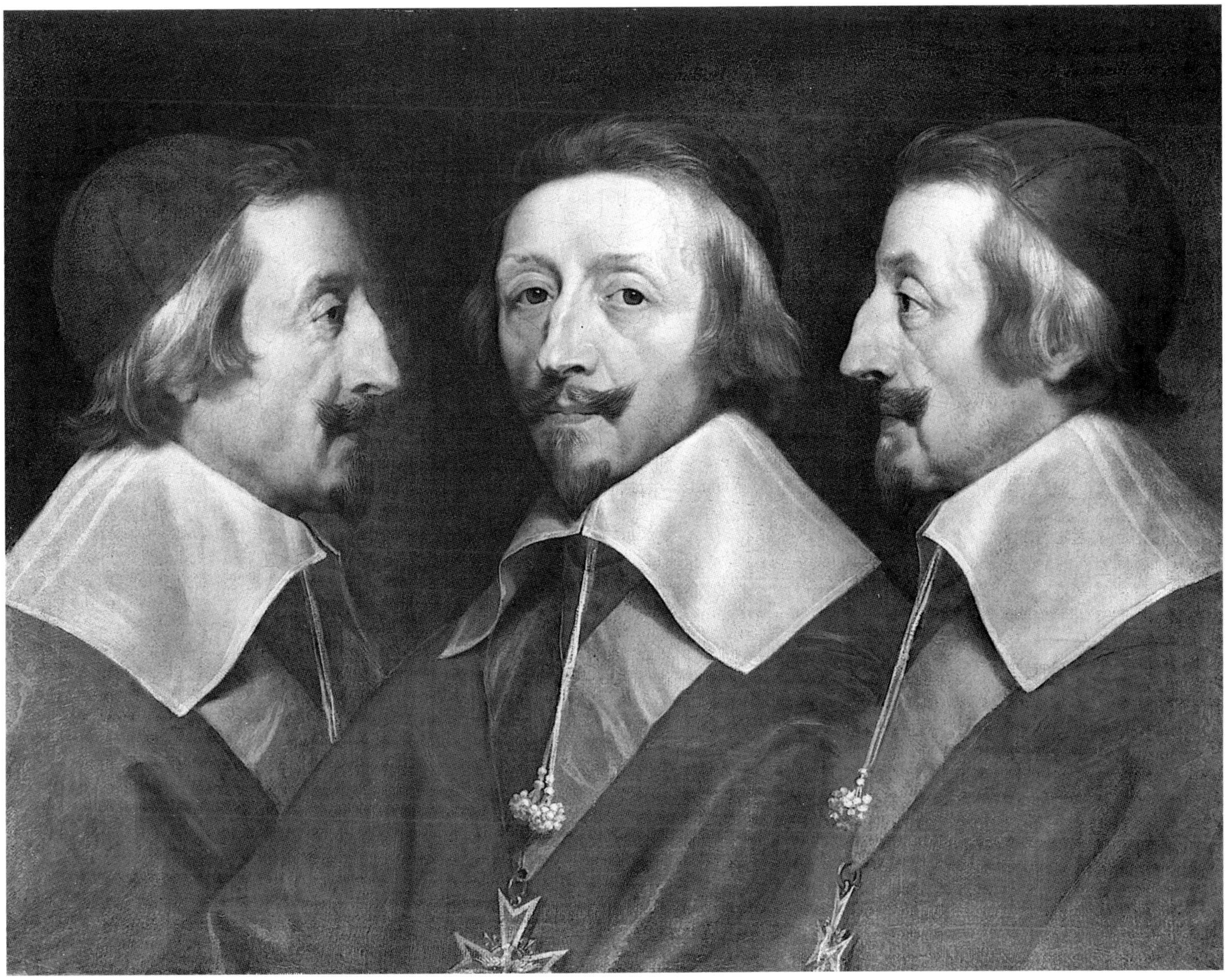

FIGURE 63
Philippe de Champaigne
Triple Portrait of Cardinal Richelieu
Canvas, 58 × 72 cm.
London, National Gallery

It is likely that this triple portrait was intended to serve as the model for the bust of the cardinal executed by Bernini in Rome in 1640–41.

England (Windsor Castle) – to serve as the model for the sculptor Bernini to make a portrait bust in distant Rome, which explains the unusual level of accuracy. Because the painter was conducting an exercise for a specific purpose, all the rules and conventions normally used when painting portraits were omitted, and it is precisely because the trappings of dignity and social position are ignored that this is such an impressive portrait. If this were true of all Champaigne's portraiture, he would be among the most outstanding portraitists of his time. In its powers of perception there are reminiscences of Poussin's Louvre *Self-portrait* (plate 72), which must be rather later – the *Richelieu* is usually dated about 1640. Since being cleaned, the painting has revealed a much greater subtlety of tone; the sitter is treated objectively, exactly as if he were a still life. Most of Richelieu's career is well documented, and since more has recently been discovered about his activities as an art collector and patron, it is now more likely that an accurate assessment of Champaigne's ability to describe character can be made than previously. Richelieu was politically adept, ruthless, successful, and the chief power in the state because Louis XIII allowed him such latitude, and most of this is obvious in the National Gallery *Triple Portrait*. There is hardly any need to turn to the full-length *Portrait of Richelieu* in the same collection. In the full-length, of which there are many versions, all the cardinal's strength of character is revealed, as might be expected in a grand state portrait. His red robes allowed the artist to introduce a richness into an otherwise utterly cold composition. This lack of warmth is one of the reasons why Champaigne has never attracted a popular following.

Midway through his career, Champaigne satisfied the needs of middle-class patrons. In works such as the *Portrait of a Man* (plate 14) in the Louvre, Paris, and the *Group Portrait of the Montmort Children* in the Musée Saint-Denis at Reims, he recorded his sitters faithfully and well. In the Louvre portrait it is easy to see Champaigne as a painter who epitomized French art at the time, but although there is a superficial 'classical' restraint, there are no classical overtones. Champaigne's austerity in fact predated that of Poussin, and its source was the portrait painting of the fifteenth-century Netherlandish masters (it has already been mentioned that Tournier of Toulouse had even earlier influences). Painters of this period had no particular reason to ignore the art of the immediate past, but most of the painters working outside Paris were too remote to be aware of it, or were swayed by popular fashionable trends such as Caravaggism. By contrast, Champaigne did not hesitate to use the conventions of almost two hundred years before, simply because they were successful ones. The convention of the man behind a ledge, typical of Van Eyck and the generation including Memling and Bouts that came after him, is made freer by Champaigne, who permitted a greater degree of realism in his work: for instance, moisture is visible on the slightly open lips of the sitter in the Louvre picture. The *Montmort Children* also has a formal arrangement of the kind acceptable a century before for a group portrait of burghers, but it shows a much greater naturalism in the treatment of the faces than would have been the case in an earlier portrait.

In the only other surviving group portrait by Champaigne, the *Échevins of the City of Paris* of 1648 in the Louvre, the hieratic nature of Champaigne's art comes to the fore. The composition is utterly rigid, the colour scheme based only on black and red, and although the faces are well observed and true to life, there is no interaction between them. It is very rare in Champaigne's art for a dialogue to take place, and in some of his religious pictures he hides this inadequacy in complex action. In the *Échevins of Paris* it is only by analysing each portrait that one becomes aware of the artist's abilities. Much more successful, because it is of one person, is the *Portrait of Omer Talon* (plate 12) in Washington. The sitter was a prominent lawyer and member of the Jansenists, an austere Catholic sect that believed in predestination, but the artist has shown him in the full panoply of his profession rather than recording the more sombre religious side of his character. The splendour of portraits by Van Dyck, such as his *Cardinal Bentivoglio*, spring to mind; once again Champaigne is revealing his Flemish origins.

The most interesting and complex aspect of Champaigne's art did not develop until after 1643, when he was influenced by the teaching of the Jansenists. Always austere and moral, Champaigne was drawn towards the high-minded principles of this religious sect which contrasted strongly with the behaviour of the court, even though he never became a member. The seventeenth century was an age of paradox: violent changes of moods and attitudes, repentences after excesses, and tears of regret when signing death warrants were regarded as normal by the minute group of people who ruled;

and the existence of the severe Jansenist sect in France at the time was no aberration, but a normal facet of such a society. Champaigne's reticence was combined with his new-found religious intensity towards the end of his life, and it resulted in a series of uncompromising masterpieces.

In 1662 Champaigne's crippled daughter, a nun, was miraculously cured through the nuns' prayers at the Jansenist convent of Port-Royal near Paris, and to commemorate the event Champaigne painted his most celebrated picture, the *Ex-Voto* (plate 16) now in the Louvre. Like most pictures that achieve greater fame than their creators, the picture is untypical of the artist. (Hobbema's *Avenue* and Hals's *Laughing Cavalier* are other examples of this.) Champaigne presented the *Ex-Voto* to Port-Royal as a record of the miracle. He had always resisted Baroque excess, largely because his main influence, fifteenth-century Netherlandish paintings, recorded truth to nature rather than rhetoric (when Baroque rhetoric was successful, as in Rubens or Guercino, it posed no problem, but as a hybrid style imported by Vouet it sat uneasily on native traditions). Rhetoric was thus far from Champaigne's mind when he painted the *Ex-Voto*, and there is a deliberate avoidance of the usual religious paraphernalia such as angels and elaborate symbols. Light from Heaven is indeed shining down, but it is restrained and realistic, like a shaft of sunlight in a darkened room. It shows the artist's daughter in the company of Mère Agnes, who was painted several times by Champaigne. It is very rare in his art that we feel any relationship between the sitters, but he achieves this here through their intense spirituality, and yet they both remain absolutely natural.

It is perhaps significant that two of the masterpieces of the age, Champaigne's *Ex-Voto* and Georges de La Tour's *New-born* (plates 43 and 44) should have a deep, almost indefinable spirituality. The success of the artist in both cases is based ultimately on his profound religious belief. Such intensity was rare in the France of Louis XIII, and in the France of Louis XIV it disappeared altogether after the death of Champaigne in 1674.

Chapter Six

Painting under Louis XIV, 1660-90

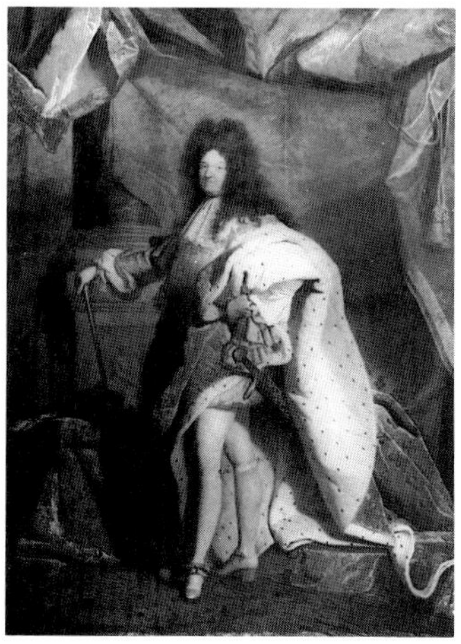

FIGURE 64
Hyacinthe Rigaud
Portrait of Louis XIV
Canvas, 313 × 205 cm.
Versailles, Château

Epitomizing the monarch's pretensions to grandeur, this is one of the most famous pictures of the period.

The history of painting in France under Louis XIV is the history of royal patronage and little else. Through his ministers, the monarch controlled almost all the artistic activity of the country, of which there was in fact relatively little outside the main centre, Paris, and the nearby palace of Versailles. The main reason why this state of affairs came about seems to have been the young monarch's determination, especially in the early part of his reign in the 1660s, to encourage all the arts. At this time France was much less efficient than the Netherlands at manufacturing luxury goods such as tapestries and silks, and so Louis established factories or improved existing ones. His concern extended to painting, and he commissioned a large amount of ceiling decoration, especially at the Louvre and at Versailles, which could be seen to rival the great Italian decorative cycles, though in France there had been little precedent for such ambitious undertakings earlier in the century.

The most important instrument used by the monarch to control painting was the Paris Academy. In the 1650s the importance of the Academy, founded in 1648, was modest, and there is little evidence that its small group of members sought to lay down specific standards of organization. In 1661 Louis XIV reorganized it, making dramatic changes. The members were to adhere to a strict set of rules governing the theory of painting, and the hierarchy of the genres was established, with history painting the most important. The model for all this was of course Italy, but there were far fewer young painters in France who could give the Academy a healthy diversity. So determined was the organization, however, that in 1665 a French Academy in Rome was founded, a sister institution which allowed young French painters, if they were considered competent enough, to work in Rome, the centre of artistic activity in Europe.

Although the Academy in Paris was regimented on Italian lines, with pupils being taught the newly devised rules of art, an unforeseen controversy immediately occurred among the members that was to dominate artistic attitudes for the rest of the century. This was what has been described as the 'battle of the styles', the conflict over whether Rubens or Poussin was a suitable model to follow. Poussin's art from his mature period was an ideal model for an academic teacher because his pictures followed such a precise sequence of rules in the placing of figures and in facial expressions. (However, if he were imitated too closely, the resultant picture from another artist could easily be lifeless.) On the other hand, the sensuality of Rubens, both in form and colour, was an ideal model to imitate when painting on a grand scale was required, especially for a palace decoration. The two sides were never reconciled in theory: the views of the Rubenists and the Poussinists were too opposed; but a surprising number of painters combined the characteristics of both sources, to produce a hybrid art that set the standard for the rest of the century.

Almost all the painters involved in the battle of styles are easily recognizable. One of the earliest and best of them was Charles de La Fosse, whose work falls chronologically within the scope of this book but whose style already looks forward to the next century. La Fosse's colour is Rubensian, but his compositions are classically inspired. Few painters of the time had La Fosse's energy, and his most important achievement was the decoration of the interior of the dome of Les Invalides in Paris towards the end of his career in the 1690s.

Another reason for the change in the role of painting was that Louis XIV organized almost all painting activity around his court. In the earlier part of the century the emphasis had been on a diversity of patronage, which ranged from the monarch – although there were no commissions of any importance after 1643 because of the minority of Louis XIV, who was an infant on his father's death in that year – to the ever-growing demands of the rising professional classes, for whom official portraiture had been an important branch of patronage. Louis XIV changed this emphasis at a stroke by the establishment of the court at Versailles: what had once been a hunting lodge of Louis XIII he enlarged into what was to become by far the largest palace in the world at the time. The change in the nature of patronage was due to the social system that Louis XIV set up at Versailles. The aristocracy, formerly spread all over France on their estates, were encouraged to reside at Versailles where the king could keep an eye on them. All the important government officials were also there. Inevitably there was a tendency to follow the king's tastes rather than to strike out on an independent path, and the one wealthy courtier who did so, the king's minister Fouquet, met with royal displeasure: it was said that Fouquet's fall was caused by the king's rage and jealousy on seeing his minister's great château at Vaux-le-Vicomte, which had been decorated by Charles Le Brun.

Before discussing Charles Le Brun, the one major painter of the first part of Louis XIV's reign, it is useful to note the few painters who did not conform to the pattern set by Le Brun and later by his rival Pierre Mignard. There are few painters in this category of independents, and many of these painters of individual talent in Paris under Louis XIV have been neglected because they did not play a significant role in the all-important royal circle. One of the best of them was the portraitist Claude Lefebre. His work has never been satisfactorily defined, through lack of documentation, but one work attributed to him is the delightful *Portrait of a Teacher and his Pupil* (plate 49) in the Louvre. It is a rare French example of a double portrait, with none of the stiff formality found in court portraiture. The probable reason for Lefebre's obscurity is that he failed to paint sitters of any importance. The *Portrait of La Chapelle* in the Musée Condé at Chantilly (figure 65), traditionally attributed to Lefebre, is an especially sympathetic treatment of an unassuming face, entirely devoid of the rhetoric of official portraiture.

Closer to the court was the still-life painter Jean-Baptiste Monnoyer. Often known as 'Baptiste', he was, in his prime in the 1670s, the foremost still-life painter in Europe, but his skill has been much underestimated in recent years, due to the proliferation of incorrect attributions to him. He specialized in flower pieces of most elaborate design, although in the early part of his career he produced more conventional still-life paintings, such as the one in the Musée Fabre at Montpellier (plate 62). His flower pieces are characterized by his ability to subordinate each flower to a complete en-

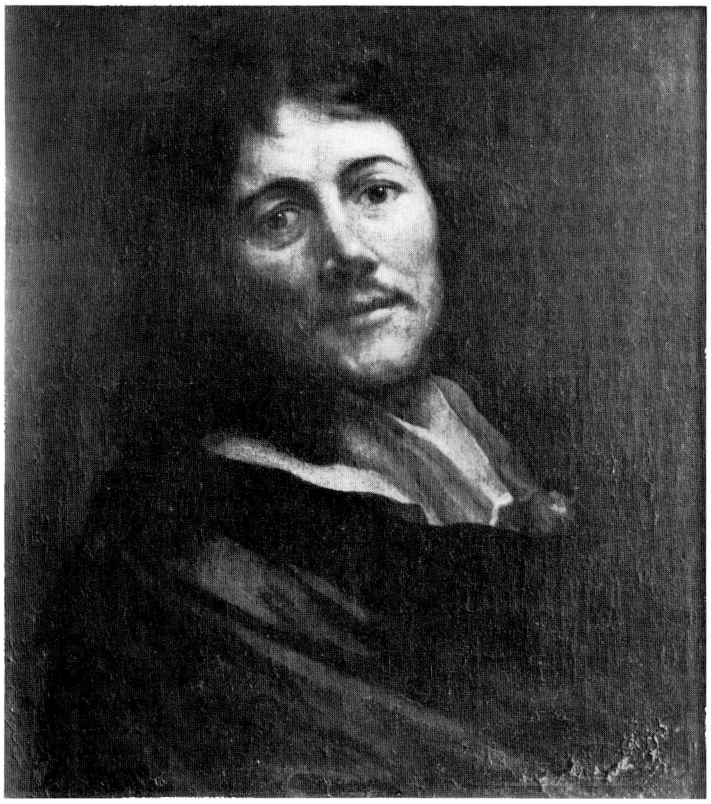

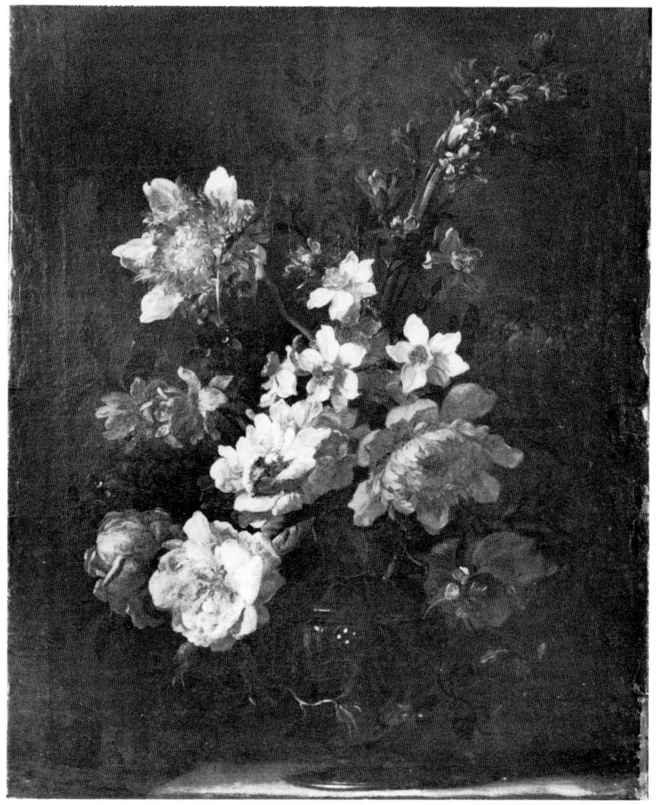

FIGURE 65 (above left)
Claude Lefebvre
Portrait of La Chapelle
Canvas, 52 × 46 cm.
Chantilly, Musée Condé
The picture was first recorded in 1817.

The identification of the sitter as the poet Claude Emmanuel Luillier, called La Chapelle, is possible but by no means certain.

FIGURE 66 (above right)
Jean-Baptiste Monnoyer
Vase of Flowers
Canvas, 45 × 34 cm.
Toulouse, Musée des Augustins

One of the many hundreds of conventional flower pieces by Monnoyer which are both lively and opulent.

semble. Each one is perfectly drawn, exactly like those of his Dutch and Flemish contemporaries, but Monnoyer managed to envelop them in deep-toned shadow that emanates from the background. The result is both mysterious and luxuriant. A good example of a small-scale work of this type is in the Musée des Augustins at Toulouse (figure 66). Monnoyer, whose subsequent influence was immense, spent the latter half of his career in England, working for the Dukes of Montague, and most of his surviving flower pieces are in the collection of the Duke of Buccleuch at Boughton House in Northamptonshire.

It is in the field of landscape painting that some measure of continuity is observable under Louis XIV. The two main painters of the time, Pierre Patel and Francisque Millet, were largely derivative in their styles, but this was the secret of their success. Both of them are relatively little known today. Patel derived almost all his ideas and inspiration from Claude, specializing in idyllic classical landscapes, usually with a golden light. His best pictures, such as the example in the Springfield Museum of Fine Arts (plate 63), are elegant interpretations of Claude, but lack Claude's poetry, being much more akin to the Dutch interpretation of the Italian landscape; and sometimes there is a more antiquarian approach where the ruins are prominent, as in the example in the Fitzwilliam Museum, Cambridge (figure 67). It was precisely his lack of imagination which brought Patel success: he conformed to the accepted standard of landscape format. Such art is particularly difficult to appreciate today, when so much significance is attached to originality.

Francisque Millet, the other important landscapist, was more talented than Patel, though his present reputation is also obscure. Flemish in origin like Philippe de Champaigne, he worked mainly in Paris, specializing in classical landscapes inspired by the works of Dughet and Poussin. Millet had imagin-

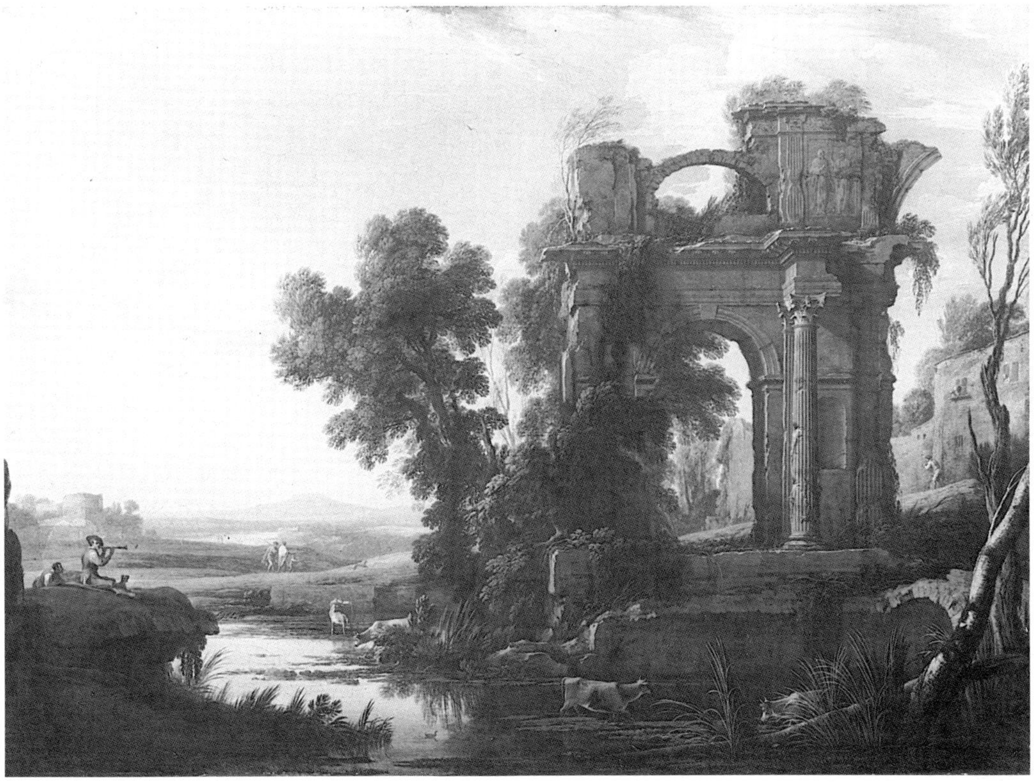

FIGURE 67
Pierre Patel
Landscape with Classical Ruins
Canvas, 64.8 × 85.7 cm.
Cambridge, Fitzwilliam Museum (reproduced by permission of the Syndics)
Given to the museum by A. A. Van Sittart in 1864.

This picture is close in composition to the one in the Musée des Beaux-Arts at Poitiers. Unlike the works of Claude, where the figures usually have some mythological or religious significance, this composition is entirely without a subject.

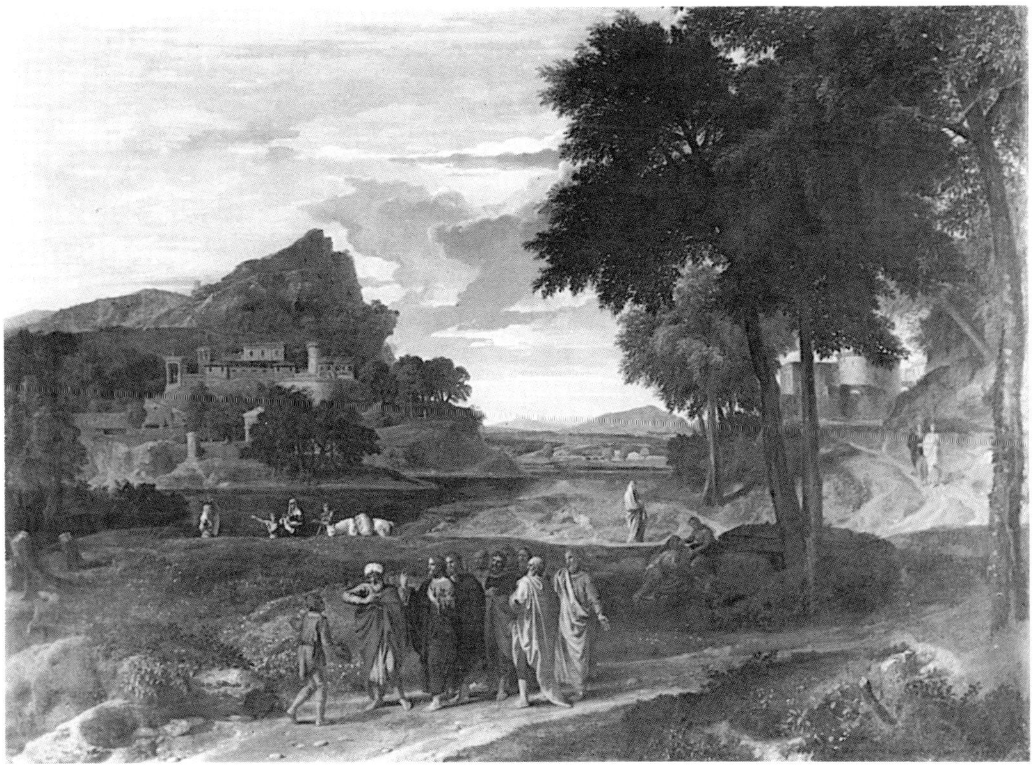

FIGURE 68
Francisque Millet
The Noblemen of Capernaum
Canvas, 104.7 × 140 cm.
York, City Art Gallery
Given to the museum by F. D. Lycett-Green in 1955.
First recorded in England in the late eighteenth century.

ation and good powers of observation, but he never painted anything without a classical format. His recently cleaned *Storm Landscape* in the National Gallery, London, is one of the very few successful depictions of lightning. Millet preferred an intense blue for his landscapes (as did Poussin), which gives them an unnatural air. One of his best pictures is the *Noblemen of Capernaum* (figure 68) in the York City Art Gallery, in which the figures are worthy of Poussin in their correctness, and the landscape is sensitively depicted.

Outside the stylistic conformity of the period is the obscure Michel Gobin, who is believed to have worked in Orléans in the 1680s. His only still-life picture, entitled *Still Life with Flowers and Silver*, is similar to a Monnoyer, but his one genre painting is an astonishing candlelight work whose style is half-way between that of Georges de La Tour and the Dutch artist Godfried Schalcken. We will never know whether this truly provincial picture is an unusual work by a minor artist or an accidental survival from a much larger output that has been lost.

Several artists, whose careers and styles form a transitional period between the seventeenth and eighteenth centuries, enjoyed enormous success under the patronage of Louis XIV. By far the best of them was Hyacinthe Rigaud from Perpignan near the Spanish border. There is a strident quality about many of his best portraits which suggests a familiarity with Spanish painters like Zurbarán. Rigaud rigidly provided the court with exactly what it wanted – a splendid, opulent and yet tasteful glorification of its new-found power and wealth. Rigaud's celebrated *Portrait of Louis XIV* at Versailles (figure 64) sums up the age: the artist has become subordinated to the precise desires of the patron. The result is none the worse for this; it is only a pity that Rigaud was not a Velasquez in his measure of talent. Court art is not necessarily bad, and Louis XIV was fortunate in having an artist of the competence and appropriateness of Rigaud.

Another important figure of the time, and Le Brun's rival, was Pierre Mignard. Much of Mignard's art consisted of portraiture, derived from the Bourdon type but rather more polished. The same is true of his large religious pictures, which often have the polish of the Florentine Carlo Dolci (1616–86). Mignard's *Portrait of Molière* in the Musée Condé at Chantilly (figure 69) reveals the artist's abilities as a portraitist: the intelligence and wit of the sitter are successfully captured. The rapidly brushed draperies show Mignard's adherence to the style of Rubens at a time when the battle between the Rubenists and the Poussinists was at its height. A host of other painters surround Le Brun and Mignard, and many of their careers extend into the eighteenth century. The careers of Louis de Boullongne the Younger and Nicolas de Largillière, which bridge these two periods, have been neglected because historians of the eighteenth century prefer to begin their accounts with Watteau (who died young in 1721), whose *Enseigne du Gersaint*, showing the portrait of Louis XIV being consigned to a packing case, is considered to epitomize the new generation.

One reason for the scant treatment of the reign of Louis XIV by art historians is that painting became subordinate to and part of the other arts, and thus very difficult to isolate. Nowhere is this better shown than at Versailles, where the whole ethos of the interior is that of a decorative ensemble. There is no place for the individual easel painting, to be cherished as an isolated object. Louis XIV was an avid collector of the old masters, but the interiors he inhabited seem hardly to have been designed for the purpose of displaying such pictures. The king's attitude to Dutch paintings is summed up in his famous remark 'Otez-moi ces magots' – to him such pictures inevitably distracted from a grand design and gave the atmosphere of bourgeois clutter.

Thus, art at the court of Louis XIV seems to have become merely a decorative necessity. There is little evidence that many of the painters of this period, apart from Poussin and Claude, were collected by patrons as the masters of

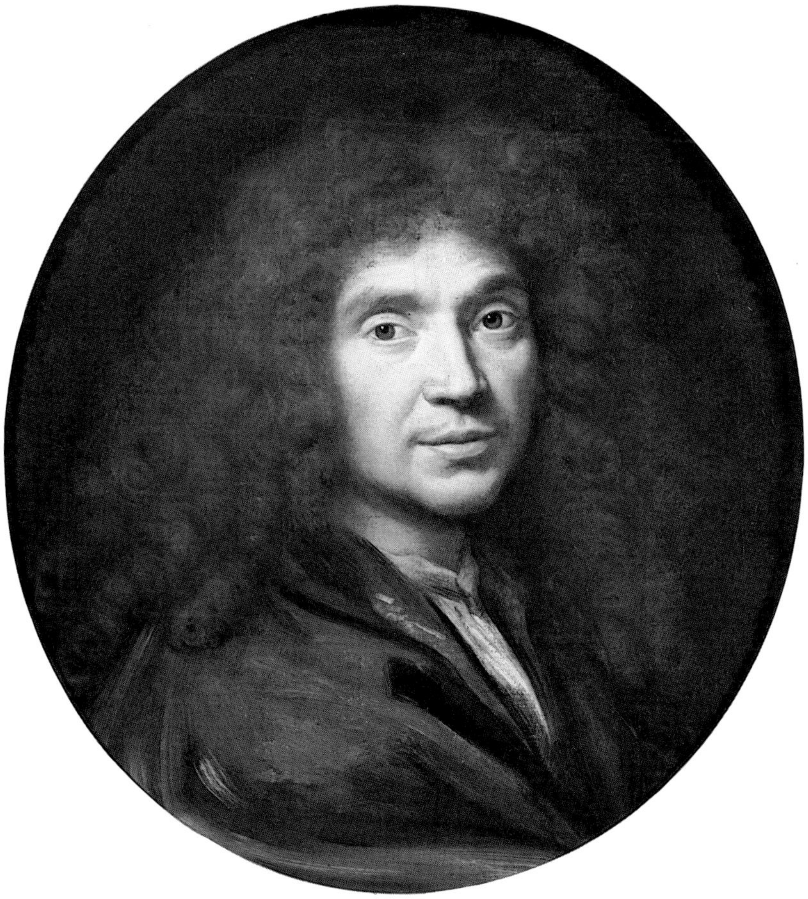

FIGURE 69
Pierre Mignard
Molière
Canvas, 55 × 48.5 cm.
Chantilly, Musée Condé
An old inscription on the back reads: peint par Pierre Mignard en 1671.

Mignard rarely relaxed enough to give his sitters any sense of realism, but in this case the celebrated playwright has been recorded with unusual sensitivity and liveliness.

the Italian Renaissance were collected in their time. The French were considered too minor and, as most of their pictures had been painted for a specifically decorative purpose, they were *in situ* and therefore not marketable commodities. So it is a mistake in historical terms to try to isolate the art of painting, even of a Rigaud, since it tends to merge into a splendid background of stucco and gilt, silvered furniture, sculpture, and the minor decorative arts. Much, too, has been lost, even from Versailles, and a good deal of imagination is needed to recreate the dazzle of the time.

The most significant result of the court's attitude to art at this period was the calamitous decline in easel painting. Apart from a very few and very minor exceptions, the whole art of easel painting disappeared from the provinces, not to be revived until the following century. It is as if all the energy of the country was suddenly sucked towards Paris and Versailles. In addition, the wars of Louis XIV were on an entirely new scale, demanding much more money and resources than the comparatively modest campaigns of Louis XIII had done. Many of the provinces then on the edge of France (parts of Flanders and Artois especially) were overrun by invading armies, and huge taxes had to be raised in order to pay for these expansionist policies. So great was the expenditure that the king had to melt down the silver furniture made for Versailles in order to raise more money.

In searching the provinces for signs of artistic life, it has to be remembered that much official portraiture must have disappeared during the Revolution of 1789, when objects from the reign of Louis XIV were destroyed by the revolutionaries even more avidly than those of earlier epochs, because they symbolized the hated *ancien régime*. Also, everything was drawn towards Paris and Versailles both administratively and economically, as the king's power increased, and the painting of the period reflects this. There was thus very little artistic activity outside the orbit of the court, which is a total reversal of the position up to approximately 1660. However, there was certainly no decline in general painting activity, as the prodigious efforts of Charles Le Brun and his pupils well show.

Charles Le Brun

In his lifetime Le Brun was the most influential artist in France although, in marked contrast to Poussin, that influence did not long survive him. Significantly, for the first part of his career Le Brun was in Rome, where he acquired a thorough training. He then became the official artist for Louis XIV, and thus for most of his career had to execute what was required of him. His inordinate skill meant that he was equally adept at ceiling decoration, portraiture and religious painting. In assessing Le Brun's early easel pictures, therefore, there is a danger that what came later may cloud our judgment. The number of pictures from his years in Rome in the 1640s is relatively small; indeed, Le Brun's total surviving output of easel paintings, while full of variety, is not large.

A young painter arriving in Rome in 1642, and not under the spell of Poussin (that came later, for a short time), would logically turn to the Baroque, and this is precisely what Le Brun did. In the *Hercules and Diomedes* (figure 71) in the Castle Museum, Nottingham, he produced one of the masterpieces of French Baroque painting. Its recent cleaning has revealed much more intense colour and has emphasized the swirling movements of the figures engaged in destruction. It seems that everything for which Vouet had been striving, and had ultimately failed to achieve, is summed up in this picture. The Baroque elements were clearly intended to stun and impress, and the young Le Brun had already acquired the technical facility to do this. Indeed, throughout the varied range of Le Brun's easel paintings there is the

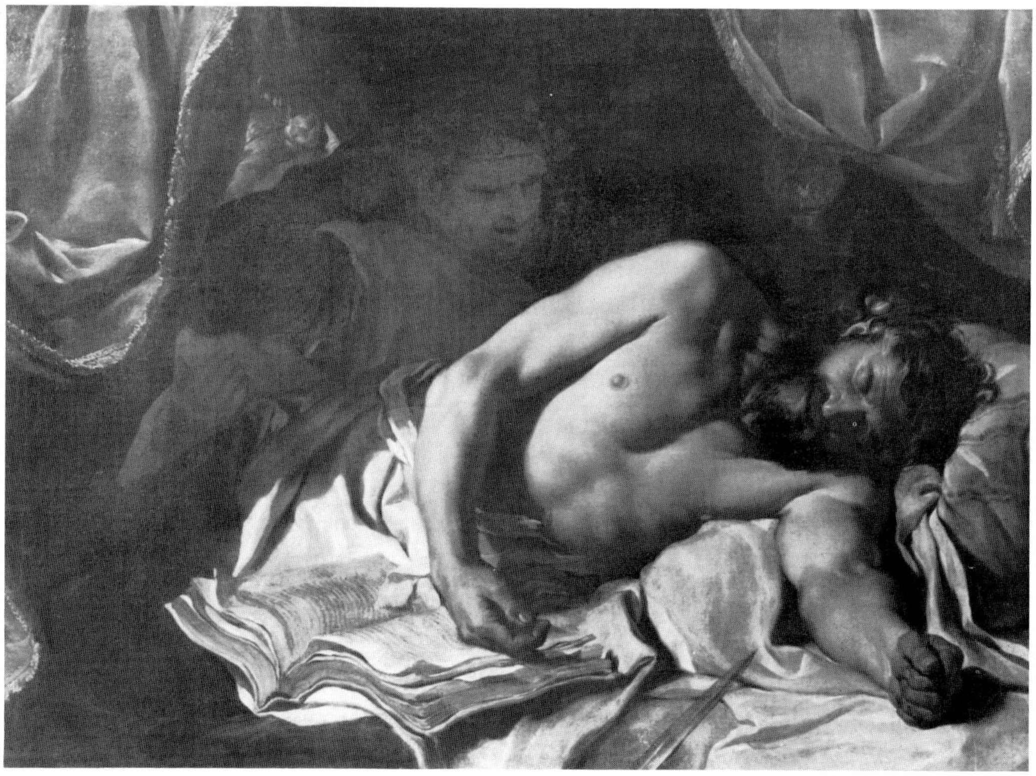

FIGURE 70
Charles Le Brun
The Suicide of Cato
Canvas, 96 × 130 cm.
Arras, Palais Saint-Vaast
Painted in Lyons in 1646. Given to the Academy in Paris in 1763. Deposited by the Louvre in 1896 at Compiègne and in 1953 transferred to Arras.

An unusually gruesome depiction of Cato's suicide by disembowelling, its effect is in total contrast to Poussin's idea of a deathbed scene.

FIGURE 71
Charles Le Brun
Hercules and Diomedes
Canvas, 290 × 188 cm. Signed lower left: LEBRUN F.
Nottingham, Castle Museum
Painted for Cardinal Richelieu for his Paris residence, the Palais Cardinal (now the Palais-Royal), as a chimney-piece. Sold at the time of the Revolution of 1789 and brought to England. Given to the museum in 1893 by Colonel C. J. Wright of Mansfield, Nottinghamshire.

One of the less frequently depicted of the twelve labours of Hercules, here seen vanquishing the horses of Diomedes which are fed on human flesh.

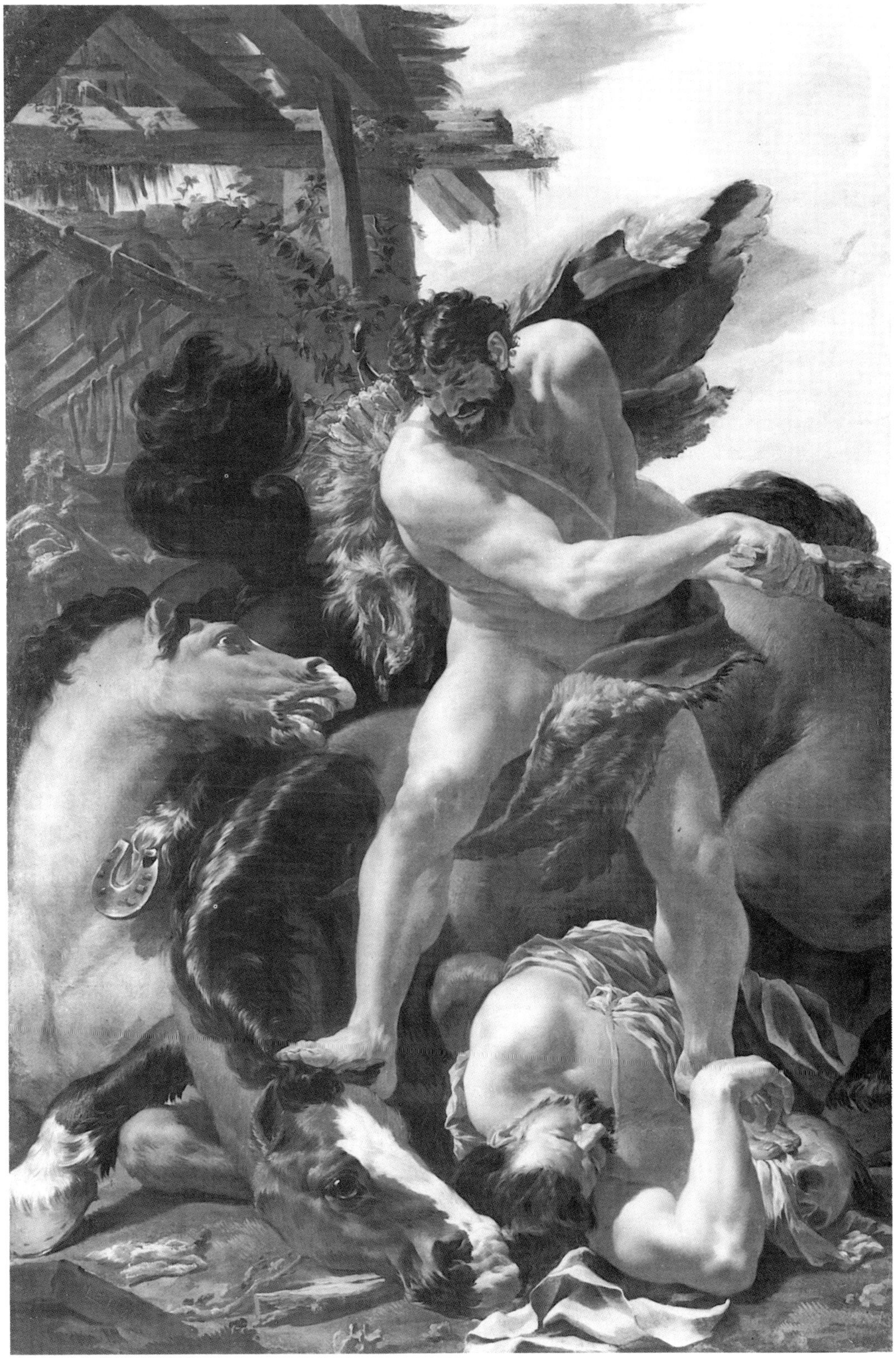

feeling that each picture is an exercise, always perfectly achieved, of a whole series of different styles and moods. On a much smaller scale, but equally impressive and even more violent, is the *Suicide of Cato* (figure 70) in the Palais Saint-Vaast at Arras. Again, the artist has tried to depict the event with maximum effect, and he has succeeded.

The change that took place in Le Brun's art after his return to France in 1646 is admirably illustrated in the *Brazen Serpent* (figure 72) in the City Art

FIGURE 72
Charles Le Brun
The Brazen Serpent
Canvas, 95.2 × 133.3 cm.
Bristol, City Art Gallery
Given to the museum by the Rt. Hon. Lewis Fry in 1905.

This is an early example of Le Brun's dependence on Poussin, where all the elements are recognizable as Poussinesque without any specific copying.

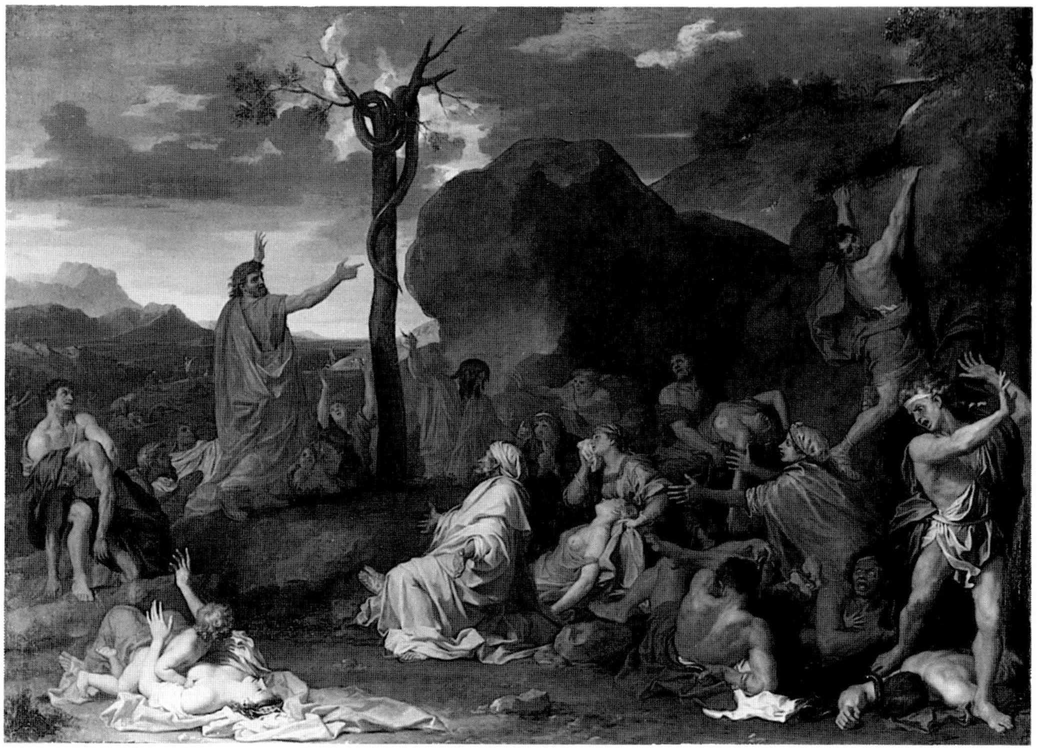

Gallery, Bristol. Suddenly, both the individual figures and the whole composition have become Poussinesque, instead of having the overtones of Rubens which are found in the *Cato* (whose fleshy quality is reminiscent of Rubens's *Samson and Delilah*). The *Brazen Serpent* is on a small scale, exactly as in Poussin's first series of *Sacraments*, and its colour scheme is on the hot side, with reds and purples. The conclusion that Le Brun was at this stage working in Poussin's manner is unavoidable. The general style is, of course, also close to Bourdon's pictures of this type.

Le Brun pleased the young Louis XIV because he was able to carry out the king's ambitious projects satisfactorily. Le Brun's role was that of both administrator and organizer and, ultimately, artistic director. The history of decorative painting in France is beyond the scope of this book (before Le Brun, only Vouet was a decorator of significance), but it was Le Brun's early and important contribution in this field – the ceiling decorations at Vaux-le-Vicomte for Fouquet – which caused the king such jealousy against his minister because of their splendour and led ultimately to Le Brun being given the post of chief royal decorator.

Le Brun continued to execute easel paintings throughout his career, and they were much esteemed by his contemporaries. The *Family of Darius before Alexander* at Versailles, begun by Le Brun for the king in 1660, shows the stage he had reached at the beginning of the long relationship between the two men. It is an enormous magnification of a Poussin-type composition, softened and modernized in order to produce a more palatable account of the incident of Alexander's magnanimity towards the vanquished. Poussin would have painted the same scene with very much more severity, even though a number of the models in the Le Brun seem straight out of Poussin. It appears that the king was interested in the story of Alexander because his own special type of megalomania could see itself reflected in the Greek past. Le Brun accordingly executed the truly colossal series of four canvasses depicting the *History of Alexander*, in the Louvre. Like so many Herculean undertakings, they impressed everybody by their sheer size. Later history has not been kind to them, but even so, tremendous energy bursts out of every corner of these pictures, some of which are more than twelve metres long. The source, without any doubt, is Rubens. This is not the exuberant Rubens of the Medici Cycle, but the Rubens of the vast hunting scenes and tapestry cartoons. Le Brun had in effect changed sides, as he moved from modest echoes of Poussin (in the *Brazen Serpent*) to a full-blown eulogy of Rubens.

The later changes in Le Brun's art can best be seen in the *Resurrection of Christ* in the Musée des Beaux-Arts at Lyons, completed in 1676. It is a modernization of Champaigne's *Vow of Louis XIII* (see page 112) and, inevitably, compared with Champaigne, a much more erudite picture. Champaigne treated this difficult subject with crispness and a certain naïveté of vision, whereas Le Brun has been grandiloquent, and as a result has produced a totally vapid exercise in the glorification of his master; but never does he allow his competence to flag. The picture, as might be expected of a work of such colossal dimensions, is in fact one of the summits of this type of art.

At the end of the 1670s Le Brun began the most exacting of his tasks – the decoration of the ceiling of the Galerie des Glaces at Versailles. Many of the sketches for the main compositions survive, and allow an assessment, on a small scale, of his inventiveness, which is usually lost in the vastness of the decorated ensemble. A typical example is the *Resolution of Louis XIV to Make War on the Dutch Republic*, 1671 (plate 47), in the Musée des Beaux-Arts at Auxerre, depicting an event which was to have enormous repercussions. The handling, rapid and sure, is taken almost completely from Rubens, and yet the composition is original and dramatic, and demonstrates that Le Brun conformed to the grand tradition of Rubens and Pietro da Cortona in Italy. His work at Versailles shows that he belongs among the great decorative painters on the grounds of his energy, originality and appropriateness of setting, but even in France his reputation is not as high as it should be.

Le Brun's *Self-portrait* in the Uffizi, Florence, though formal, offers a rare glimpse of the more personal and intimate side of the artist. The pose is academic, as would be expected, and is based on Italian Renaissance tradition in the placing of the sleeve, familiar from Titian's portraits. The face is severe but sensitive, and is just as revealing in its own way as Poussin's *Self-portrait.*

Le Brun must not be rejected as a mere decorator, even though so much of his other art is relatively inaccessible, deposited in provincial museums or surrounded in the Louvre by so much more exciting and exacting painting. There was no sense of his inferiority at the time – on the contrary, his art was highly esteemed by his contemporaries – and the ambivalent attitude towards him came about only in later centuries when the art of the period came to be assessed as history. Le Brun was in fact the most important painter in France in the second half of the century, and the *Portrait of the Chancellor Séguier* (plate 48) in the Louvre justifies a high estimation of his talent. The composition forms an enormous pyramid with the figure of Séguier at its apex. The scale is almost life-size, and the characterization of the sitters is worthy of Champaigne. Acknowledged as a masterpiece even though the name of Le Brun is forgotten, it is a unique record of an important official surrounded by his attendants. The date is uncertain, but it is likely to be from the 1660s.

The century by no means came to an end with the death of Le Brun in 1690, but as happened in so many other periods, the new age did not coincide with the turn of the century. In the case of the last years of the reign of Louis XIV – roughly the period 1680–1715 – there was a definite decline in the quantity of artistic output centred round the court. The reason for this was the vast increase in military expenditure, culminating in the long wars of the early years of the eighteenth century, which ended with the humiliating Treaty of Utrecht in 1713.

Changes in the general character of painting during the last years of the seventeenth century were taking place behind the scenes, as it were, as artists began to be a little more experimental but still within the rules laid down by the Academy. Portraiture was dominated by Rigaud and Largillière, whose consistent style epitomized the mood of the early eighteenth century rather than that of the seventeenth. There is a need for a whole book on the age of Louis XIV from an artistic point of view, beginning with the achievements of Le Brun and ending before the all-too-brief maturity of the great Watteau, before his death in 1721.

Epilogue: the Reputation of French Seventeenth-century Painters

The history of taste is a complex subject, and many of its chapters have hardly yet been sketched in; it is only in the twentieth century, as a direct result of nineteenth-century nationalism, that a precise distinction has been made between the different national schools of painting in the seventeenth century. In old inventories and sales catalogues, a distinction was made only between the Italian and Northern schools, whose differences are easily recognized, based as they are on both subject-matter and style. The dependence of the French on both Italian and Netherlandish models has led to problems in the past about categorizing French painters, and only in modern times has there been a concerted effort to define French painting earlier than 1700 as a distinct national school. Such an attempt is now justified on historical grounds, since, as this book tries to show, these painters were individual enough to warrant their being seen separately from their Italian and Netherlandish counterparts.

A notable fact about the reputations of many of the main painters discussed in this book is the great difference between their past reputations and their present position. The painters who achieved the greatest success in their lifetimes are not necessarily the ones we most admire today: no one now would place Vouet above Champaigne or Le Brun above Poussin, even though their respective careers warrant this in historical terms. The historian working on an individual artist rather than an epoch normally uses the double criteria of critical acclaim and market price. For Nicolas Poussin this is an effective method because on both counts there is enough evidence from the last three centuries to form a complete picture. Furthermore, Poussin can then be placed in the context of other artists such as Rembrandt, and by this means a whole series of interesting conclusions can be drawn. For Poussin, the general trend is critical acclaim in most quarters and esteem from collectors prepared to pay reasonably high prices for his work. When criticism was levelled at him – for instance, by Ruskin – it could be dismissed as mere churlishness, and against the general trend. Poussin has always been admired by academics and intellectuals, who have thus secured him an impregnable position in the history of taste.

Poussin is, however, only one artist, and in trying to discover more general trends, few consistent facts emerge. A very large number of the painters discussed in this book, even the most idiosyncratic such as Georges de La Tour, were esteemed by their contemporaries in the narrow circles in which they lived. It cannot be overemphasized that, until Louis XIV, Paris was in relative cultural isolation; painters there, including artists as diverse as the Le Nain brothers, Vignon, Vouet and Champaigne, could thus have considerable local reputations, without being known to the outside world.

A reputation in Italy would have been impossible for them, because of the competition from the huge number of painters working there, and relatively little art was imported into Italy from France. This isolation was even more extreme in the centres outside Paris, and many once-esteemed provincial painters, from Daret in Aix-en-Provence to Jacques de L'Estin in Troyes and Tournier in Toulouse, were soon forgotten after their deaths. No new commissions were forthcoming, which might have encouraged artistic continuity.

The eighteenth century saw the rapid centralization of France, but a great proportion of the art produced in the seventeenth century remained *in situ* rather than being bought and sold on the open market. Small pictures, mostly genre scenes by the Le Nain brothers and landscapes by Claude and his followers, did change hands from time to time as part of mixed collections of pictures, but nobody collected exclusively French work because, until very recently, there was no concept of the French school as a distinct entity. Therefore, in direct contrast to the Dutch, the saleroom fortunes of most French artists give an inaccurate record of the esteem in which they were held. A little information can be gleaned from the series of exhibitions held in the eighteenth century in the Academy at Toulouse, when many pictures by seventeenth-century artists were shown. (This is remarkably early for such a custom, which became usual in all the main European cities only in the nineteenth century, when the many newly founded museums began exhibition programmes.)

The greatest single factor affecting taste in this field was the French Revolution. The destruction and upheavals of that time explain why there are so few existing works by most of the major artists working in France, except Le Brun and Philippe de Champaigne. Le Brun's work survived because much of it was in the French royal collection, and therefore became the property of the Republic (most of it remaining either in the Louvre or at Versailles), and Champaigne's pictures, mostly in religious institutions, were thought large enough and important enough to confiscate and place in the new museums. The revolutionary authorities, in order to cope with the vast influx of works of art confiscated both from the aristocracy and the Church, created many new museums, one in each major provincial town. Some eighteen were created in the 1790s; and seven other towns, not originally chosen, soon followed suit. The royal collection survived largely intact in the Louvre, where it can still be studied in detail, although it is necessary to remove from the mind's eye all the later gifts and purchases that have enhanced the collection since then. The monarch's taste in seventeenth-century pictures was mainly for the grand and classical. Poussin had always been collected, as had the early work of Claude, and there is a fine series of pictures by Vouet, Champaigne and Le Brun, but the Le Nain brothers are scantily represented. In sum, the French royal family was little interested in the bizarre or out-of-the-way in French painting, although they were prepared to be much more catholic in their taste where foreign painters were concerned, even admitting Rembrandt in the eighteenth century.

The revolutionary confiscations did not simply gather into any one place all the important pictures from the surrounding region, but caused a massive upheaval with regard to locations. The large holdings of altarpieces by Rubens and Jacob Jordaens (1593–1678) in the museums of Lille and

period by travelling round the French provinces, where many of the key works are to be found. The rewards for such efforts are great, because of the unusual nature of many of the best pictures of the period, and it is their refusal to be categorized which makes the painters of the period so interesting. They have in the recent past been justified by elaborate literary and philosophical allusion, but this aspect of academic enquiry cannot sustain a bad painter. Comparison with the flowerings of music and literature of the period are always tempting, because they lead to the assumption that all these cultural phenomena are somehow interrelated, but this is true only inasmuch as they were produced by people living together in the same time and place. Literary allusion is usually relevant only to artists who were deliberately erudite, such as Poussin. There has been a recent fashion in art history to enquire deeper into the meaning that pictures would have for contemporaries, especially if the work of art has a literary source. With Poussin this has been done brilliantly, but such an enquiry is difficult to justify for painters such as the Le Nain brothers, whose work is unsuited to such treatment. The erudition of Poussin's work may be daunting, but for those with that type of mind, such an enquiry is eminently worth while; whereas for those who admire the matter-of-fact approach of many of the Dutch painters, the art of the still-life painters and much of the work of the Le Nain brothers will be more rewarding. For devotees of the Baroque there are Le Brun and Vouet, who at their best are hardly inferior to their Italian contemporaries.

A good deal of French art can therefore be justified by comparison; to justify it on grounds of individuality the final analysis is bound to be personal. The so-called detached point of view actually balances other people's unashamedly personal judgments. Poussin's contemporaries who admired him were expressing an opinion or preference and not reiterating some provable theoretical value, and today one can admire the detached coolness of Poussin only when it is not laboured. In the Louvre *Seasons*, painted in his old age, Poussin has become so much less self-conscious and more at peace with himself than he was when young, and his earlier, deliberately stilted figures have been replaced by a lilting poetry.

The best pictures of the period were produced by painters who, once they had assimilated their polyglot sources, were able to forget them. For example, a good number of the pictures of Claude's maturity, some of which hang in great galleries where the competition is severe, can stand comparison with the work of any other great artist. Claude's vision was much more sensitive on the whole than that of Poussin, and his refined sensibility permitted him to reach unprecedented heights in such pictures as the Dulwich *Jacob and Laban* and the Munich *Expulsion of Hagar*.

For Georges de La Tour, the other painter who has risen to prominence in recent years, there is a danger of overpraise; too much has been claimed for this passionate but remote individual. As with Claude, there is something lacking in the whole artist: the personality cannot sustain a searching analysis, as can that of Rembrandt or Vermeer; La Tour eludes our grasp when we try to define him. What remain, however, are the few masterpieces such as the so-called *Dream of Joseph* in Nantes and the Rennes *New-born*. Such pictures are outstanding by any standards, and they caught the attention of critics and museum cataloguers even when it was not known who painted them.

While praise and respect for Claude, Poussin, Le Nain, Champaigne and La Tour need no elaborate justification, a much stronger plea must be made for the lesser masters. Tournier is difficult to see in the shadows of the museum at Toulouse (though admirers of Caravaggio's followers should journey there); and Tassel is concentrated at Dijon and Langres, where his pictures are also much neglected. A considerable effort is even required to see enough of Le Brun's work to obtain a rounded view of his art. In recent years the administrations of the French provincial museums have varied enormously, some shutting down completely, others revealing new displays and cataloguing. Rennes, Rouen and Orléans stand out as institutions that facilitate the study of their holdings.

It seems certain that almost all the main artists of the period will go through a time when their reputations are enhanced. A gradual opening up of enquiry is taking place, both on a scholarly level and on the level of exhibiting pictures to the public. Nevertheless, much remains to be done in purging the field of the meretricious and the spurious. The French seventeenth century has never been broadly reassessed; discoveries have been plentiful, but have often increased the confusion. The definition of the *oeuvres* of so many of the painters in this field is far from complete, and as more pictures come to light there will have to be radical reappraisals of artists, even those as apparently secure as Poussin, Gaspard Dughet and La Tour. The study and appreciation of even the best French masters of this period is thus at an auspicious beginning rather than at a tired and overpraised end.

The Artists

In the following alphabetical guide to seventeenth-century French painters, each entry is divided into three parts.

The first part is a brief account of the artist's career, with particular attention to movements and places of artistic education. (The position of more important artists in relation to their contemporaries and artistic development is fully discussed in the main text.)

The second section comprises a list of the artist's main oil paintings in public collections. Privately owned pictures have been included where information is available, especially if the picture is signed or dated, or if a large proportion of the artist's work is still privately owned. These lists, though incomplete, are a reasonable guide to the extent of the artist's surviving work. A code has been used after some picture titles: 'signed and dated' is self-explanatory; 'documented' means that there is a good reason for ascribing the picture to the artist; and 'attribution' means that there is, or has been in the recent past, dispute as to the picture's status. Inclusion of pictures of this latter type is limited to those works which by general consensus are of high quality, although they may well be by another painter.

The third section of each entry is a bibliography, which concentrates on the main available literature about the painter. In some cases works of considerable obscurity have been cited where they are the only text on the particular artist. By far the most useful achievements of recent years have been the exhibition catalogues, both from Paris and the provinces.

Claude Audran II

Lyons 1639–Paris 1684

A minor painter, Audran was able to assimilate the style of Charles Le Brun and as a consequence received important commissions for ceilings at Versailles. His large canvas of *The Beheading of St John the Baptist* in the Louvre shows the influence of Caravaggio in its dramatic use of lighting, and must have been especially impressive in its original position in Notre Dame.

Collections

Narbonne, Musée des Beaux-Arts
The Arms of Aeneas

Paris, Louvre
The Beheading of St John the Baptist (signed and documented 1674)

Versailles, Château
Decoration of the Salon de Mars and the Salon de Diane

Bibliography

There is no recent literature on this artist.

Didier Barra

Metz 1590–working Naples until 1644

Apart from one signed work in the Museo di San Martino, Naples, this artist has not yet been isolated from his compatriot François de Nomé. They are therefore both included under the better-known but not strictly correct name of Monsù Desiderio (see page 175).

Claude Bassot

Working Épinal 1608–14, last dated picture 1627.

Bassot worked in the isolation of the Vosges in the early years of the century, and is an example of extreme naïvety in an artist.

Collections

Épinal, Musée Départemental des Vosges
St Gorgon? St Barbara and a Donor (signed and dated 1611)

Bibliography

André Philippe in Épinal, Musée Départemental des Vosges, *Catalogue*, 1929, p.46.

Nicolas Baudesson

Troyes c.1611–Paris 1680

Received into the French Academy in 1671, Baudesson seems to have achieved a considerable reputation with his contemporaries as a specialist flower painter. His work is still confused with Monnoyer and even with Blin de Fontenay.

Collections

Albi, Musée Toulouse-Lautrec
Flowers in a Vase

Arras, Palais Saint-Vaast
Vase of Flowers (attribution)

Belgium, J. Jakovliu-Warsage
Flowers in a Glass Vase

Brussels, private collection
Flowers in a Glass Vase

France, private collection
Flowers in a Glass Vase

France, private collection
Flowers in a Glass Vase

New York, with Paul Drey
Flowers in a Glass Vase

Paris, with Cailleux
Vase of Flowers

Paris, with Pardo
Flowers in a Glass Vase

Paris, private collection
Basket of Flowers

Paris, private collection
Flowers in a Basket

Rouen, Musée des Beaux-Arts
Flowers in a Crystal Vase (attribution)

Private collection, whereabouts unknown
Flowers in a Vase (signed on the reverse)

Salt Lake City, Utah Museum of Fine Arts
Flowers in a Vase (attribution)

Bibliography

Michel Faré, *Le grand siècle de la nature morte en France*, 1974, pp.277–90.

There is a useful summary in the exhibition catalogue, Paris, Petit Palais, *Peintres de fleurs en France du XVIIe au XIXe siècles*, 1979, nos.1–4.

Bauguin

No information survives on this painter. It is still frequently believed that he is identical with Lubin Baugin, even though in 1934 Charles Sterling convincingly separated him from his namesake.

Collections

Paris, Louvre
Still Life with a Chequer Board (signed) (plate 1)
The Dessert of Gaufrettes (signed) (plate 2)

Rennes, Musée des Beaux-Arts
Still Life of Fruit (signed)

Rome, Galleria Spada
Still Life with a Candle (signed and dated 1630)

Bibliography

A lengthy summary of the problem of Baugin's identity is given by Charles Sterling in the exhibition catalogue, Paris, Orangerie, *Les peintres de la réalité*, 1934. The literature on the problem has continued to grow, the most important article being Michel Faré's 'Baugin, pentre de natures mortes', *Bulletin de la Société de l'Histoire de l'Art français*, 1955, pp.15–26.

All Baugin's work was excellently reproduced, continuing the identification with Lubin Baugin, in Michel Faré, *Le grand siècle de la nature morte en France*, 1974, pp.106–15.

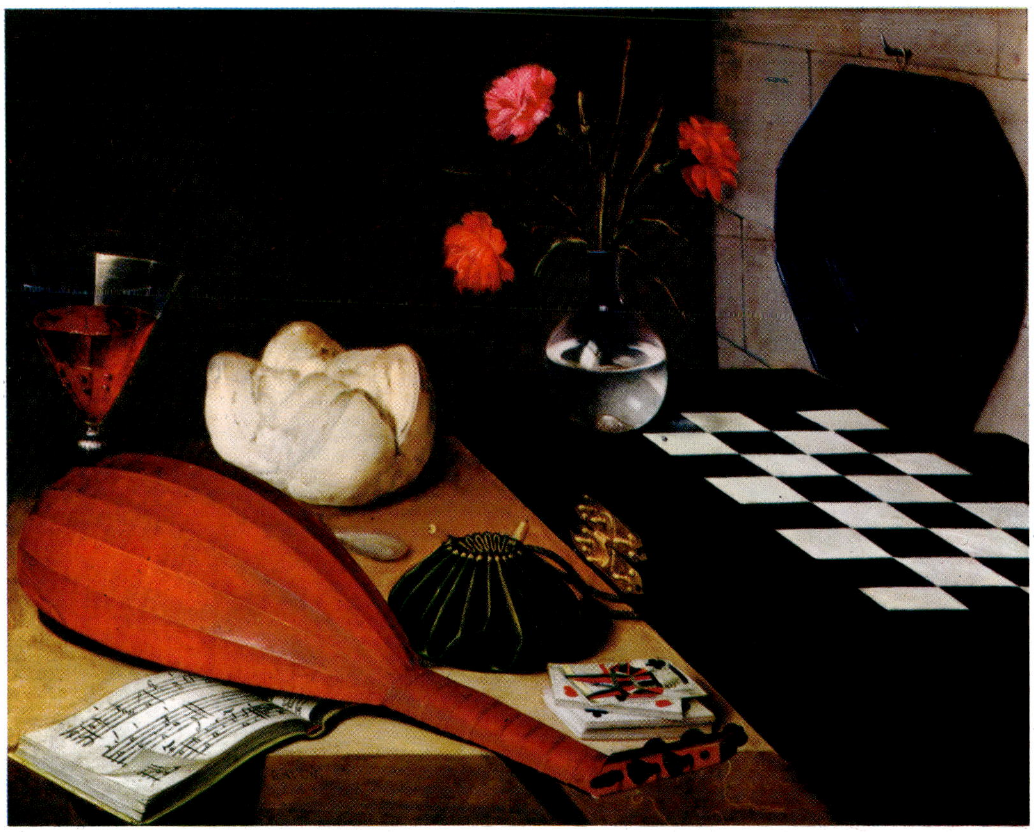

PLATE 1
Baugin
Still Life with a Chequer Board
Panel, 55 × 73 cm. Signed: Baugin
Paris, Louvre
Gift of M. van Gelder, 1935.

There seems to be no specific moral in this still life, but a game (such as a chequer board) was often included in *vanitas* pieces by Netherlandish artists.

PLATE 2
Baugin
The Dessert of Gaufrettes
Panel, 41 × 52 cm. Signed: Baugin
Paris, Louvre
Acquired by the museum in 1954.
There is unlikely to be a specific moral in this still life, which seems to be simply an exercise in accurate observation.

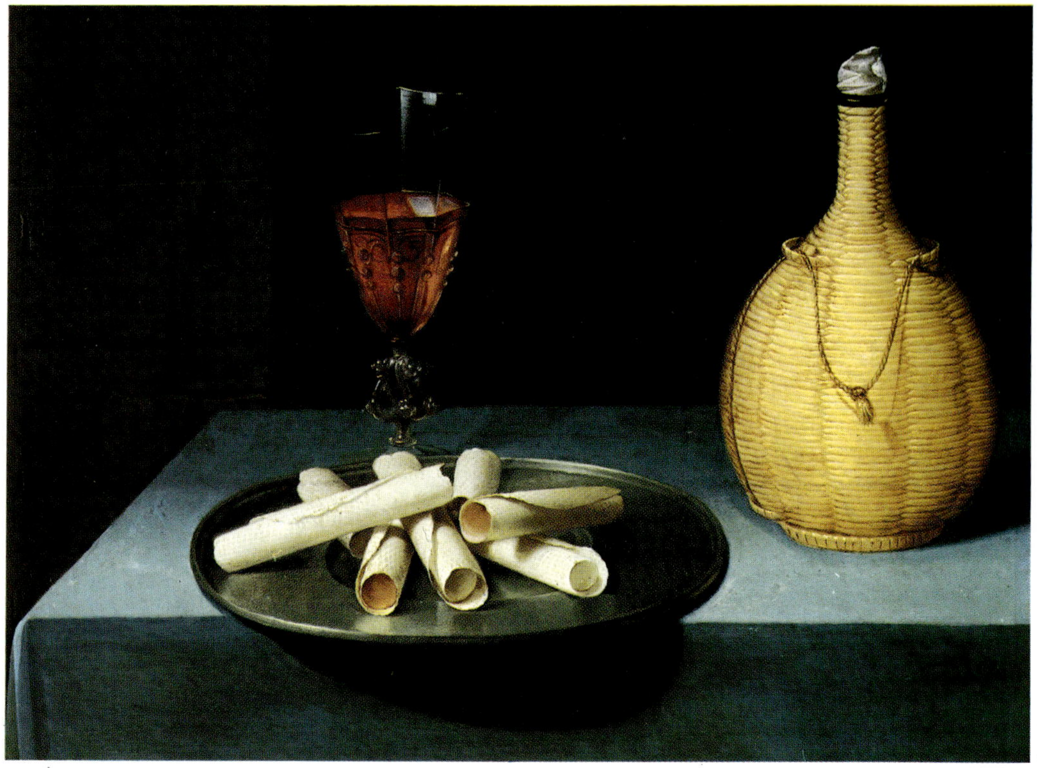

Lubin Baugin

Pithiviers c.1612–Paris 1663

Almost all Baugin's surviving pictures are small, highly finished and brightly coloured religious works. He was given the nickname 'Le Petit Guide' after Guido Reni. It is assumed that he visited Italy, although there is no documentary proof of this. He is recorded in Paris (Saint Germain-des-Prés) in 1629, and from then on seems to have pursued a successful career in the capital, especially with his important altarpiece *The Martyrdom of St Bartholomew* for Notre Dame. In recent years there has been a tendency to attribute the small group of still-life paintings signed 'Baugin' to Lubin Baugin. There are, however, no obvious stylistic links between the two artists.

Collections

Aix-en-Provence, Musée Granet
Presentation of the Virgin in the Temple
Birth of the Virgin

Biberach an der Riss, Stadtisch Sammlungen
Virgin and Child (attribution)

Caen, Musée des Beaux-Arts
St Jerome (signed)

Chantilly, Musée Condé
Allegorical Portrait of the Grand Condé (attribution)

Dijon, Musée Magnin
Holy Family (fig. 50)
The Rape of Helen

Karlsruhe, Staatliche Kunsthalle
Holy Family (attribution)

London, National Gallery
Holy Family with St Elizabeth, St John and Angels

Montargis, Musée Girodet
Death of Cleopatra

Nancy, Musée des Beaux-Arts
Virgin and Child and St John

Norfolk (Virginia), Chrysler Museum
The Virgin (monogram)

Orléans, Musée des Beaux-Arts
The Carrying of the Cross (signed)
The Dead Christ

Paris, Louvre
The Sleep of the Infant Christ
Lamentation over the Dead Christ

Paris, Notre Dame
Martyrdom of St Bartholomew
Virgin of Pity

Rennes, Musée des Beaux-Arts
Virgin and Child and St John

Rouen, Musée des Beaux-Arts
Martyrdom of St Bartholomew

Saltram Park (Devon), National Trust
Holy Family with the Infant St John (attribution)

Vienna, Diözesanmuseum
Virgin and Child

Bibliography

Pierre Auzas, 'Lubin Baugin, dit "Le Petit Guide"', *Bulletin de la Société de l'Histoire de l'Art français*, 1957, pp.47–54.

Pierre Auzas, 'Nouvelles oeuvres réligieuses de Bauguin', *Bulletin de la Société de l'Histoire de l'Art français*, 1967, pp.67–72.

Charles Beaubrun

Amboise 1604–Paris 1692

Henri Beaubrun

Amboise 1603–Paris 1677

Louis Beaubrun

Working 1610–27

Beaubrun was the name of three cousins who worked together, becoming indistinguishable stylistically from one another. They worked in a curiously naïve style, and were influenced by the Flemish artist Frans Pourbus the Younger. They had marked success at court, especially with Anne of Austria, wife of Louis XIII. Except for the series of portraits in the Prado and at Versailles, little of their work has been identified.

Collections

Barnard Castle, Bowes Museum
A Lady in a White Dress with a Bouquet

Béziers, Musée Fabrégat
Marie Thérèse, Wife of Louis XIV

Bussy-Raboutin, Château
Isabelle Hurault de Cheverny
Catherine de Bonne, Marquise de La Baume (attribution)
Louise Antoinette de La Châtre, Marquise de Humières
Isabelle de Harville Paloisveau
Gilonne de Harcourt, Marquise de Piehnes

Chambord, Château
A Woman as Diana

Chantilly, Musée Condé
Mme de Longueville (attribution)
Mlle de Longueville (attribution)

Créteil, Carmelite Monastery
Marie-Thérèse of Austria as St Helen

Florence, Galleria Pitti
Henrietta of England, Duchess of Orléans

Le Puy, Musée Crozatier
La Duchesse de Savoie

London, Victoria and Albert Museum
Jeanne de Marigny (attribution)

Madrid, Prado
Marie Anne de Bourbon
Marie Thérèse, Wife of Louis XIV
The Grand Dauphin of France (signed and dated 1663)
Anne of Austria (signed)
Anna Maria Luisa of Orléans (signed and dated 1655)

Montpellier, Musée Fabre
Julie d'Angennes

Oiron, Château
Virgin and Child with St Dominic and Catherine

Omaha (Nebraska), Creighton University
Marie Thérèse, Wife of Louis XIV (attribution)

Sigy, Chateau
Marquise de Haut de Sigy
Edme de Régnier de Guerchy (signed and dated 1622)

Versailles, Château
Marie Thérèse, Wife of Louis XIV (fig. 42)
Louise Ollier de Nointel, née Ardier
Marie Thérèse, Wife of Louis XIV
Marie Thérèse, Wife of Louis XIV (replica)
Anne of Austria
Madame de Montespan as Diana
Anne of Austria (replica)

Bibliography

Georges Wildenstein, 'Les Beaubrun', *Gazette des Beaux-Arts*, November, 1960, pp.261–74.
Jacques Wilhelm, 'Quelques oeuvres oubliés ou inédites des peintres de la famille Beaubrun', *Revue de l'Art*, No.5, 1969, pp.19–32.

Pierre Bedau

Paris c.1647–Marseilles 1707

From his only surviving work it is easy to see how Bedau made a considerable reputation with his contemporaries, as it shows that he was working under the influence of Le Brun.

Collection

Aubagne, Church
The Beheading of St John the Baptist (signed and dated 1695)

Bibliography

All the known information is summarized in the exhibition catalogue, Marseilles, Palais Longchamp, *Le peintre en Provence au XVIIe siècle*, 1978, pp.1–2 (entry by Nathalie Volle).

Jacques Bellange

Working Nancy c.1600–Nancy 1616

Bellange worked as a painter, designer of masques and graphic artist at the ducal Court at Nancy in the early years of the century. Several dozen surviving drawings and a limited number of etchings testify to his brilliance in these media and show why he was held in such esteem by his patrons. His painting activity can only be surmised, as his one signed work is a copy after Albrecht Dürer. The other picture is a modern attribution.

Collections

Karlsruhe, Staatliche Kunsthalle
Diptych: *Angel of the Annunciation, The Virgin Mary* (signed)

Leningrad, Hermitage
Pietà (attribution)

Bibliography

For Bellange's graphic work the literature is extensive, but the only sensible comments about his paintings are made by Jan Lauts in the catalogue, Karlsruhe, Staatliche Kunsthalle, *Alte Meister*, 1966, pp.42–3.

The following Mannerist pictures, clearly not all by the same hand but probably French in origin, have in recent years been attributed to Bellange. The Nancy picture could well represent his style.

Munich, Alte Pinakothek
Bouquet of Herodias

Nancy, Musée Historique Lorrain
The Ecstasy of St Francis

New York, Metropolitan Museum
Holy Family with St Anne

Sarasota (Florida), John and Mable Ringling Museum
Scene from the Commedia dell'Arte

Washington, Michael Straight collection
A Beggar

Pierre Bergaigne

Maroeuil (Pas-de-Calais) 1652?–Lille 1708

This modest painter was strongly influenced by Flemish genre painting, and his work shows few specifically French characteristics.

Collections

Arras, Palais Saint-Vaast
The Card Players (signed and dated 1699)

Flers-bourg, Church
St Peter Punishing Sapphira (dated 1705)

Geneva, Musée d'Art et d'Histoire
The Supper (attribution)

Bibliography

Charles Sterling in the exhibition catalogue, Paris, Orangerie, *Les peintres de la réalité*, 1934, pp.5–6.

Jacques-Samuel Bernard

Paris 1615–Paris 1687

One of the fourteen founder-members of the French Academy in Paris in 1648, Bernard was excluded from it in 1681 because he was a Protestant. His work in still life is elaborate and probably influenced Jean-Baptiste Monnoyer, who also became an Academician. Bernard later abjured his faith and was reinstated into the Academy in 1686. He executed many engravings after the paintings of his contemporaries, and was also a miniaturist.

Collections

Amsterdam, formerly with De Boer
Flowers in a Vase (signed and dated 1663)

London, formerly with Richard Green (1970)
Still Life of Flowers (signed and dated 1679)

New York, formerly Silberman, now private collection
Fruit, Violin, Flowers and Ewer on a Carpet (signed and dated 1657)

Paris, sale Hôtel Drouot, 24 April 1974
Still Life of Flowers (2) (signed and dated 1662)

Bibliography

Michel Faré, *Le grand siècle de la nature morte en France*, 1974, pp.256–60.
Pierre Rosenberg in the exhibition catalogue, Paris, Grand Palais, *La peinture française du XVIIe siècle dans les collections américaines*, 1982, pp.221–2.

Trophîme Bigot I

Arles 1579–d. after 1649

It is inconceivable that the pictures listed under Trophîme Bigot II (formerly called 'The Candlelight Master') were painted by this artist, whose Mannerist pictures were produced for churches in and around Arles. He seemed unaware of the stylistic developments around him, even those of Louis Finson who worked for the same churches.

Collections

Arles, Saint-Césaire
Martyrdom of St Lawrence (signed and dated 1635)

Arles, Saint-Trophîme
Assumption of the Virgin (signed and dated 1635)

La Tour d'Aigues, Church
Assumption of the Virgin (signed)

Pertuis, Church
The Saviour of the World (signed)

Bibliography

Earlier articles were admirably summarized by Jacques Thuillier in the exhibition catalogue, Marseilles, Palais Longchamp, *La peinture en Provence au XVIIe siècle*, 1978, pp.4–5.

Trophîme Bigot II (the Younger?)

?c.1600–?after 1650

Bigot, who was probably born in Arles, has just one picture certainly attributed to him, and it survives only as an engraving made towards the end of the seventeenth century. It is a *Christ in the Carpenter's Shop*, at that time in the Boyer d'Eguilles collection at Aix-en-Provence. Round this lost painting Benedict Nicolson grouped a whole series of Caravaggesque pictures, apparently French in origin although derived from Honthorst in colour and general composition, but recent research has proved that this group is not coherent. Two large pictures painted for (and still in) the Church of San Maria in Acquiro, Rome, are documented as being by a certain 'Maestro Jacopo', although they were formerly attributed to Bigot. The theory that there were two painters of the same name is borne out by the fact that the other Trophîme Bigot (who was born in Arles in 1579 and also worked there and in Aix-en-Provence) had a totally different style, as a signed picture by him in Arles demonstrates.

Although the following list of pictures under Bigot's name is tentative—not one is signed, dated or documented—they are likely to be French in origin and are not inconsistent in style with the lost picture known from the engraving.

Collections

Aix-en-Provence, Musée Granet
Denial of Peter

Amsterdam, art market, 1929
Hermit with a Lamp

Arras, Saint-Jean-Baptiste
St Jerome Praying

Baltimore, Walters Art Gallery
Judith and Holofernes

Bologna, Pinacoteca Communale
St Sebastian Tended by the Holy Irene

Bologna, Guglielmo Maccaferri collection
St Francis and St Clare

Bordeaux, Musée des Beaux-Arts
St Sebastian and the Holy Women

Brussels, D. Coeckelberghs
Cupid and Psyche

Burghley House (Northamptonshire), The Marquess of Exeter
St Peter Visiting St Paul in Prison

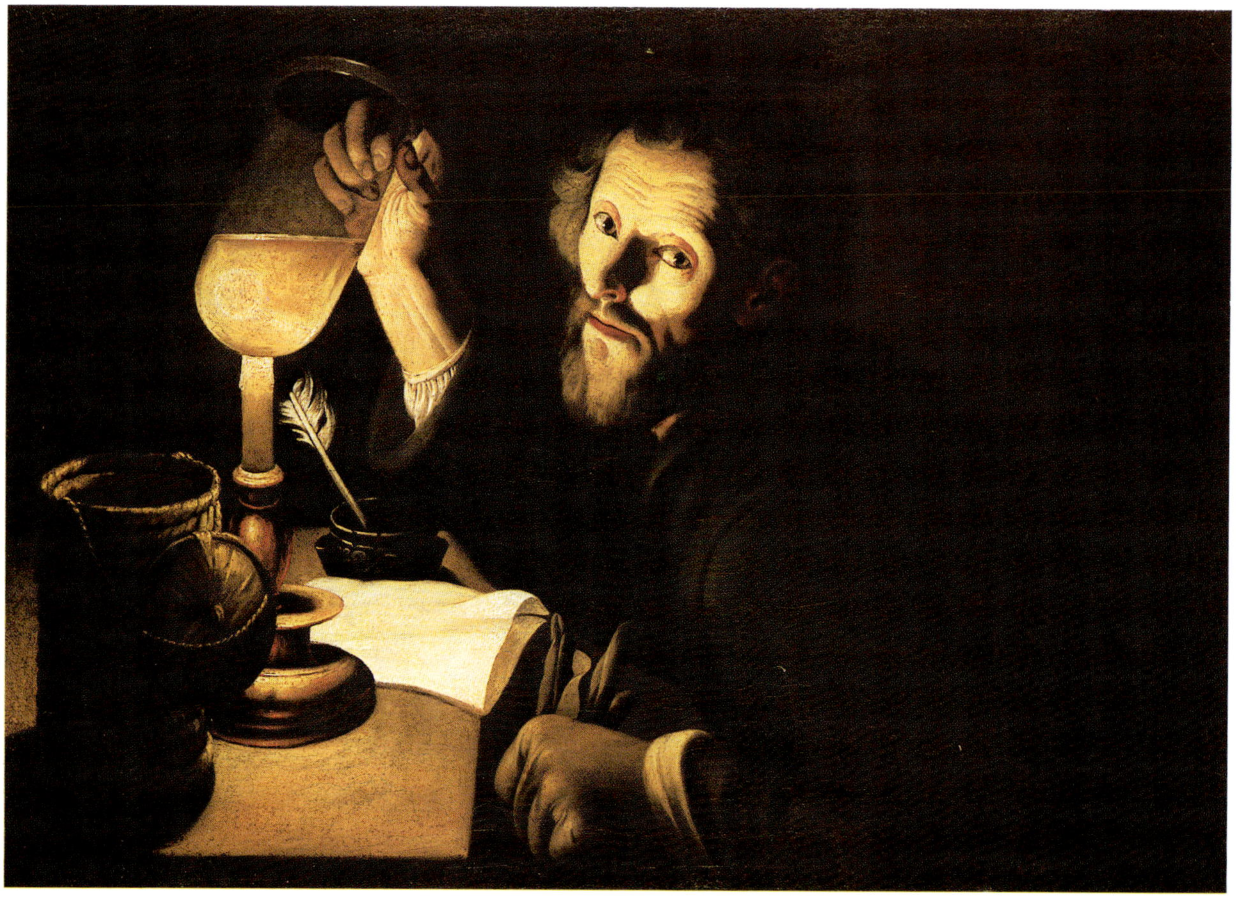

PLATE 3
Trophîme Bigot II
A Doctor Examining Urine
Canvas, 72 × 99 cm.
Oxford, Ashmolean Museum
Given to the museum by Percy Moore Turner in 1942.

(cf. Georges de La Tour, *Christ in the Carpenter's Shop*, plates 41 and 42)

Chantilly, Musée Condé
The Supper at Emmaus

Devonshire, art market, 1975
Tavern Scene

Dublin, formerly Judge Murnaghan
A Man

Éguilles, Hôtel-de-Ville
Denial of Peter

Florence, Florentine Galleries
Tavern Scene

Florence, Longhi collection
A Saint

France, private collection (near Riom)
Man with a Pipe

Greenville (South Carolina), Bob Jones University
St Sebastian Tended by the Holy Irene

Hampton Court Palace (Middlesex), Royal Collection
Christ in the Carpenter's Shop

Jerusalem, Leib Herman collection
Drinking Scene

Leeds, Miss E. Cawthorne collection
Conversion of the Magdalen

London, formerly Miss Grete Ring
Tavern Scene

London, Sotheby sale 19 March 1975
St Jerome Listening to the Trumpet of the Last Judgment

Macerata, Palazzo Marefoschi
Arrest of Christ

Madrid, Museo Cerralbo
Man Masking a Flame with a Paper Shade

Milwaukee, Dr Alfred Bader collection
Man Masking a Flame with a Paper Shade

Montefortini, Pinacoteca
Smoker

Montepulciano, Marchese Ricci collection
Coal Heaver

Montpellier, M. Chappert collection
Mocking of Christ and Crowning with Thorns

New York, with Victor Spark
Liberation of St Peter

Ottawa, National Gallery of Canada
St Jerome

Oxford, Ashmolean Museum
A Doctor Examining Urine (plate 3)

Paris, Saint-Leu Saint-Gilles
St Jerome Reading

Paris, Saint-Severin
St Luke

Paris, private collection
Angel with the Dead Christ

Paris, private collection
The Denial of Peter

Parma, Galleria Nazionale
Judith with Holofernes

Pesaro, Museo Civico
The Mocking of Christ

Philadelphia, La Salle University
Conversion of the Magdalen

Ponce (Puerto Rico), Museo de Arte
The Magdalen

Prato, Palazzo Communale
Christ

Quebec, Hôtel Dieu
Holy Family and Two Angels

Rome, Casa Depositi e Prestiti
St Jerome Reading

Rome, Palazzo Corsini
St Jerome Reading
Vanitas

PLATE 4
Trophîme Bigot II
Boy Singeing a Bat's Wings
Canvas, 45 × 39 cm.
Rome, Galleria Doria
Presumably in the Doria collection since the seventeenth century.

This painting is one of a series of similar pictures in the collection.

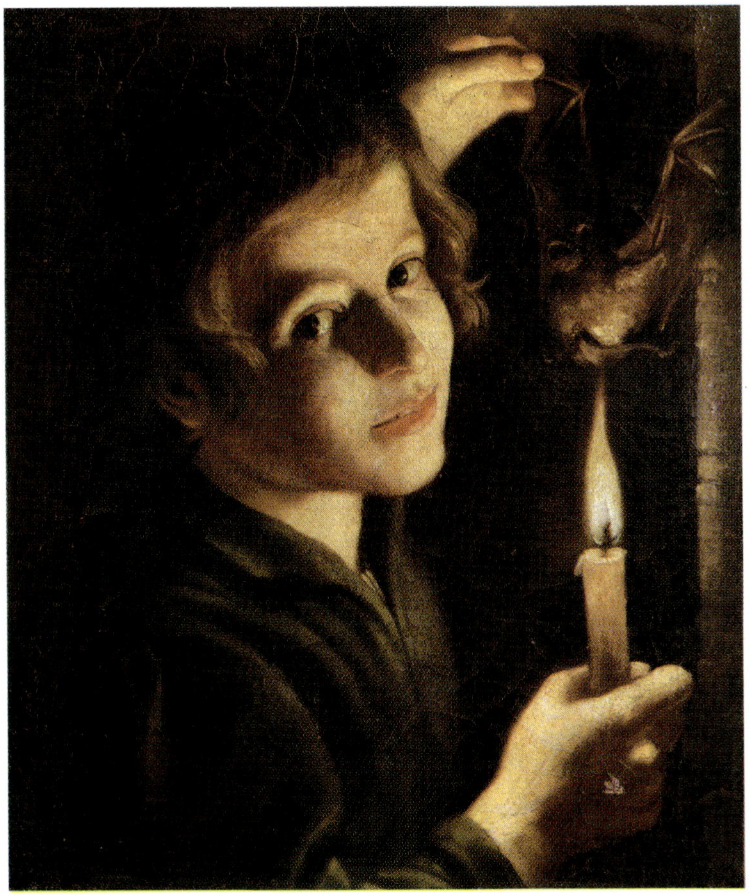

Rome, Galleria Doria
A Girl Flea-Catcher
Boy Singeing a Bat's Wings (plate 4)
Boy Putting Oil in a Lamp
A Young Girl Singer
Boy Singing by Candlelight

Rome, Museo Francescano
St Francis in Ecstasy

Rome, Vatican
St Sebastian Tended by the Holy Irene

Rome, with di Castro
Cupid and Psyche

Rome, sold Christie's 15 October 1970
St Jerome Reading

Rome, with Galleria Vangelli
Doctor Examining a Sample of Urine

Saint-Anthonin (near Aix-en-Provence), Church
St Jerome Praying

San Francisco, California Palace of the Legion of Honor
Young Singer

Southbury (Connecticut), private collection
Denial of Peter

Teramo, Museo Civico
Cupid and Psyche

University Park (Pennsylvania), State University
Denial of Peter

Urbino, Galleria Nazionale
Tavern Scene

USA art market
Denial of Peter

Valencia, private collection
St Francis and St Clare

Valletta, Malta, Major Edward Scicluna collection
Tavern Scene

Verona, Cav. Uff. Comm. Domenico Fraccaroli collection
Lighting a Candle from an Oil Lamp

Bibliography

The creation and subsequent demolition of 'The Candlelight Master' and the recent emergence of Trophîme Bigot, first one, then two, places all the previous literature on the subject into the category of an art-historical curiosity, rendered obsolete by the very recent literature. The longest list of pictures—the one adopted here with reservations—is that of Benedict Nicolson in *The International Caravaggesque Movement*, Oxford, 1979, pp.21–3. However, the biographical text of the entry is confused, owing to the fact that the editors of the book misunderstood the interpretation of the documentation of 'Maestro Jacopo', whose pictures are at present limited to those in S. Maria de Acquiro and are presumably not French. For a recent summary of the problem, see the exhibition catalogue, Marseilles, Palais Longchamp, *La peinture en Provence au XVIIe siècle*, 1978, p.6.

Charles Emmanuel Bizet

Mechelin (Malines) 1633–Breda 1710

Only one signed picture survives from the hand of this mysterious but talented artist, whose depiction of books, with their tattered edges, is reminiscent of Netherlandish *Vanitas* pieces. It has been assumed that he worked at Annonay in the Ardèche as well as in Paris, before returning to his native Netherlands.

Collections

Algiers, Musée des Beaux-Arts
Still Life of Books (attribution)

Bourg-en-Bresse, Musée de l'Ain
Still Life of Books (signed) (fig.52)

Nantes, Musée des Beaux-Arts
Still Life of Books (attribution)

Bibliography

Charles Sterling, in the exhibition catalogue, Paris, Orangerie, *Les peintres de la réalité*, 1934, pp.6–7. This was brought up to date by Michel Faré in *Le grand siècle de la nature morte en France*, 1974, pp.149–50.

Gabriel Blanchard

Paris 1640–Paris 1707

Son of the painter Jacques Blanchard and pupil of his uncle Jean-Baptiste Blanchard, Gabriel Blanchard nevertheless painted in the tradition of Le Brun rather than in the manner of his family. He became a member of the Academy in 1663. Although he must have been prolific, few paintings are now ascribed to him.

Collections

Bergues, Musée Municipal
Copy of the Versailles Ceiling

Lyons, Saint Polycarpe
Annunciation (dated 1683)

Paris, Louvre
St Andrew on his Knees before the Cross (documented 1670)

Rouen, Musée des Beaux-Arts
The Triumph of Diana (sketch)

Toulouse, Musée des Augustins
Presentation of Christ in the Temple (signed)

Tours, Musée des Beaux-Arts
Holy Family (dated 1686)

Versailles, Château
Ceiling Decoration of the Salle de Diane
Allegory of the Birth of Louis XIV 1638 (documented 1663)

Bibliography

See Charles Sterling, 'Jacques Blanchard', *Arte de France*, 1961, for basic information.

Jacques Blanchard

Paris 1600–Paris 1638

Nothing seems to be known of Blanchard's work before he left for Rome at the age of twenty-four. After two years the artist moved to Venice, where he remained for two more years. It was there that his style was formed; the chief influences were the sixteenth-century painters, especially Titian and Tintoretto with their rich, warm colours. After 1628 Blanchard went back to France, and it is from the brief but productive period after his return that all his dated works survive. They show him to stand quite apart from his contemporaries, not only in his painting style but also in his choice of sensual subject-matter, for example the *Bacchanal* at Nancy. His very last pictures, such as the *Charity* in the Courtauld Institute, London, have some affinity with the work of Simon Vouet, who also seemed to look back to Venice in his later work.

Collections

Albi, Cathedral
Virgin and Child and St Peter (signed and dated 1628)

Amsterdam, Rijksmuseum
St Sebastian

Bar-le-Duc, Musée Barrois
St Jerome

Bourges, Musée du Berry
Pierre Tallier presented to St Stephen by the Virgin (attribution)

Budapest, Szépmüvészeti Múzeum
St Jerome (signed and dated 1632)

Cherbourg, Musée Thomas Henry
Holy Family

Chicago, Art Institute
Virgin and Child with St Elizabeth and St John

Cognac, Saint-Leger
Assumption of the Virgin

PLATE 5
Jacques Blanchard
Allegory of Charity
Canvas, 108 × 138 cm.
Toledo (Ohio), Museum of Art (Gift of Edward Drummond Libbey)
First recorded in the Prince de Carignan's collection, 1765. Acquired by the museum in 1975.

This painting depicts a common subject in seventeenth-century painting throughout Europe. Its meaning would have been interpreted in both a religious and secular way.

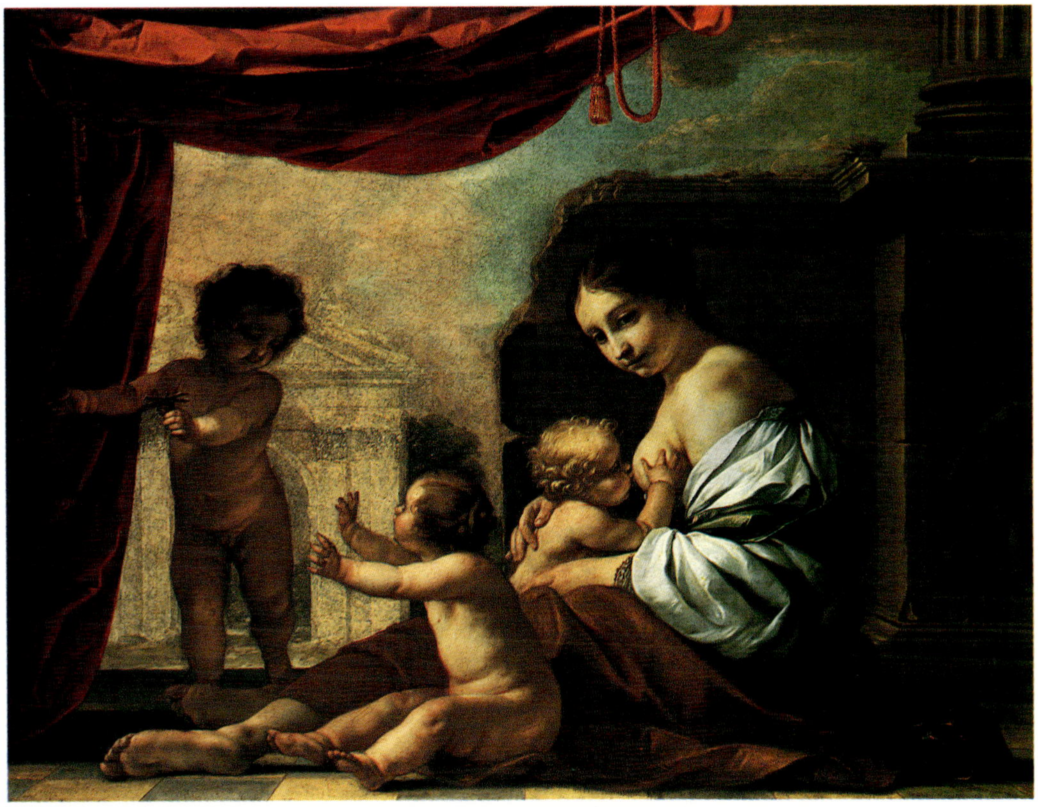

PLATE 6
Jacques Blanchard
Bacchanal
Canvas, 138 × 115 cm. Signed and dated: Blanchard f.1636.
Nancy, Musée des Beaux-Arts
Acquired by the museum in 1884.

There is a much more sensual approach to the subject in this work than in that of Poussin, but still the same longing after the Elysian world of classical antiquity.

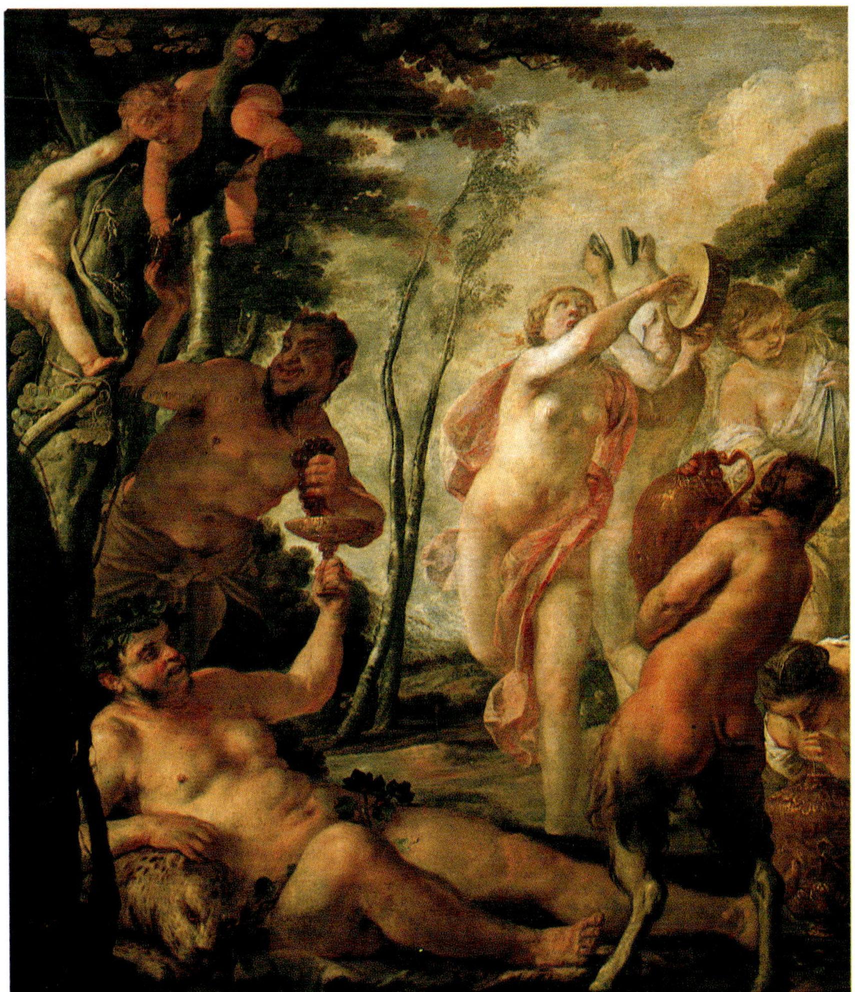

Detroit, Institute of Arts
Portrait of a Man Aged 27 (dated 1631, attribution)

Greenville (South Carolina), Bob Jones University
Charity (signed)

Heidelberg, Kurpfälzisches Museum
Hercules and Omphale

Karlsruhe, Staatliche Kunsthalle
The Meal of the Infant Christ

Leningrad, Hermitage
St Veronica

London, Courtauld Institute
Charity (signed and dated 1637)

Lyons, Saint-Denis
A Bishop and a Woman Holding a Newborn Child before the Virgin (attribution)

Malibu (California), J. Paul Getty Museum
Virgin and Child (attribution)

Moscow, Pushkin Museum
Danaë

Nancy, Musée des Beaux-Arts
Bacchanal (signed and dated 1636) (plate 6)

New York, Metropolitan Museum
Angelica and Medor

Orléans, Musée des Beaux-Arts
Pope Nicolas V in the Grotto of St Francis of Assisi

Paris, Louvre
Holy Family with St Elizabeth
Venus and the Graces Surprised (signed)
Charity
Virgin and Child and St Anne

Paris, Notre Dame
Pentecost (documented 1634)

Paris, with Pardo
St Jerome (signed)

Providence, Rhode Island School of Design
Portrait (attribution)

Rennes, Musée des Beaux-Arts
The Flagellation

Salzburg, Residenzgalerie
Portrait of Duquesnoy

Toledo (Ohio), Museum of Art
Portrait of a Sculptor (attribution)
Allegory of Charity (plate 5)

Tours, Musée des Beaux-Arts
St Anthony Abbot (attribution)

Bibliography

Charles Sterling, 'Jacques Blanchard', *Art de France*, 1961. In this remarkable article in a short-lived periodical, Sterling gave all the known facts, a succinct biography and a fully documented *catalogue raisonné* including all the pictures only known from engravings. The article has not been superseded.

Jean-Baptiste Blanchard

?–Paris 1665

Jean-Baptiste Blanchard travelled to Rome with his brother Jacques in 1624. In 1663 he became a member of the Academy, and his few surviving pictures show him to have been influenced by his brother. Two unsigned pictures have been attributed to him, both genre subjects.

Collections

Indianapolis, Museum of Art
Kitchen Scene with a Hare (attribution)

Paris, Louvre
Virgin and Child with St John the Baptist and St Simon (signed and dated 1640)

Paris, private collection
Beggar in a Ruin (signed)

Rennes, Musée des Beaux-Arts
Soldiers in the Ruins of a Church (attribution)

Bibliography

A brief summary of the available information is found in Charles Sterling, 'Jacques Blanchard', *Art de France*, 1961.

Thomas Blanchet

Paris 1614 or 1617–Lyons 1689

Blanchet was an enormously prolific painter and decorative artist from whose hand relatively little survives. His style was close to that of Le Brun. He was especially active in Lyons, where he decorated numerous palaces and churches.

Collections

Arras, Palais Saint-Vaast
The Taking of St Philip (signed and dated 1663)

Lyons, Hôtel de Ville
Numerous Decorations

André Bodan

Mulhouse 1654–Zerbst 1696

After visiting Italy, Bodan worked for Hans Ludwig von Anhalt at Zerbst. From the *Self-portrait* in the Uffizi it appears that he was working in a style more akin to the Caravaggism of Toulouse than to the Baroque.

Collections

Basle, Öffentliche Kunstsammlung
Portrait of the Painter Wereugeb

Florence, Uffizi
Self-portrait (signed and dated 1679)

Mulhouse, Musée des Beaux-Arts
Justice

Bibliography

Pierre Rosenberg in the exhibition catalogue, Florence, Galleria Pitti, *Pittura francese nelle collezione pubbliche fiorentine*, 1978, p.36.

André Boisson

Aix-en-Provence 1643–Aix-en-Provence 1733

Most of this artist's work was executed in and around Aix-en-Provence. His style was robust and Baroque in manner, with especially exaggerated movement in the figures.

Collections

Aix-en-Provence, Saint-Jean-de-Malte
Annunciation
Death of the Virgin (signed and dated 1678)

Aix-en-Provence, La Madeleine
Birth of the Virgin (signed and dated 1678)
The Visitation (signed and dated 1667)

Marseilles, Palais Longchamp
Moses Saved from the Water

Saint-Maximin, Basilique
Penitent Magdalen
The Magdalen at the Sepulchre
The Magdalen with the Pot of Ointment

Bibliography

Henri Wytenhove in the exhibition catalogue, Marseilles, Palais Longchamp, *La peinture en Provence au XVIIe siècle*, 1978, p.10.

Jean Boucher

Bourges 1563?–1633?

Boucher's few surviving pictures show considerable Italian influence, and the *Vow of Pierre Tullier* of 1628 at Bourges shows that the artist was already aware of Simon Vouet's Italian style, brought to France on his return in 1627.

Collections

Blois, Château
Virgin and Child

Bourges, Musée du Berri
The Vow of Pierre Tullier, 1628
Adoration of the Kings
Beheading of St John the Baptist

Bourges, Carmelite Convent
Lamentation over Dead Christ (1630)

Dijon, Musée des Beaux-Arts
The Eleven Apostles (dated 1618)

Dijon, Musée Magnin
The Presentation in the Temple (signed and dated 1620)

Bibliography

There is no recent literature on this artist.

Pierre Boucle (Pieter van Boeckel)

Antwerp? c.1610–France 1673

Boucle is an interesting example of a painter whose formation was entirely in the Flemish tradition but who spent his active career in Paris. The main influences on him were the Antwerp painters Jan Fyt and Frans Snyders, but Boucle lacked their sureness of composition, and his pictures are reminiscent of Sébastien Stoskopff in the awkward way the objects are juxtaposed. Like Stoskopff's, his colours are usually subdued.

Collections

Atlanta (Georgia), High Museum of Art
Dead Game and Fruit

Bloomington (Indiana), University Art Museum
Bowl of Fruit and Fish

Bordeaux, B. collection
Still Life of Fish and Onions (monogrammed)

Brussels, private collection
Kitchen Still Life (signed by Baugin)

France, Michelson collection
Tails of Fish and Carp

France, private collection
Lobster and Fish
Carp and Oysters

Geneva, Musée d'Art et d'Histoire
Still Life (dated 1648)

Le Mans, Musée de Tessé
Still Life of Fish with a Cat and a Dog

Munich, P. Griebert collection
Fish, Warmer and Copper Vessels

Narbonne, Musée des Beaux-Arts
Fish, Cat and Cauldron

Notre Dame (Indiana), University Art Gallery
Still Life with a Dead Turkey

Paris, Aubry collection
Fish, Cabbage and Bowls of Fruit

Paris, formerly with Cailleux
Carp, Oysters and Mussels (monogrammed and dated 1652)
Fish and Dead Game (monogrammed and dated 1652)

Paris, Countess P. de M. collection
Carp, Bread and Bowl of Fruit (signed and dated 1662)

Paris, private collection
Carp and Warmer

Paris, private collection
Carp and Flask (monogrammed and dated 1651)

Paris, private collection
Chicken, Pumpkin and Dead Birds (monogrammed)

Toledo (Ohio), Museum of Art
Basket of Fruit (monogrammed and dated 1649)

Bibliography

Michel Faré, *Le grand siècle de la nature morte en France*, 1974, pp.98–106.

Louis de Boullongne I

Paris 1609–Paris 1674

One of the first painters in Paris to work in a classically oriented style, Boullongne worked both at the Louvre and at Versailles. He was one of the fourteen founder-members of the Academy in 1648.

Collections

Arras, Palais Saint-Vaast
The Martyrdom of St Simon
The Miracle of St Paul at Ephesus (signed and dated 1646)

Bordeaux, Musée des Beaux-Arts
Baptism of Constantine

Le Mans, Musée de Tessé
Calypso and his Companions
Jupiter and Semelé

Paris, Louvre
The Beheading of St Paul

Paris, École des Beaux-Arts
Minerva Appearing to Cadmus After the Defeat of the Dragon (completed 1681)

Bibliography

There is no recent literature on this artist.

Jan Bouman

Strasbourg 1601/2–Amsterdam after 1653

Although he left Strasbourg for Amsterdam at an early age—he married there in 1626—Bouman took with him a style close to the work of Stoskopff, who worked in Strasbourg. Thus he has a recognizable 'Strasbourg style', in which there is almost always a certain naïvety in the placing of the objects.

Collections

France, private collection
Dish of Fruit

Karlsruhe, Staatliche Kunsthalle
Bowl of Fruit

Paris, C.B. collection
Apples and Pears

Paris, A. Kotie collection
Basket of Fruits (attribution)

Rome, private collection
Basket of Fruit (signed)

Saarbrücken, Saarland-Museum
Bowl of Strawberries and Rummer (signed and dated 1653)

Strasbourg, Musée de l'Oeuvre de Notre Dame
Apples and Pears (signed and dated 1635)
Still Life with a Monkey (signed)

Bibliography

Michel Faré, *Le grand siècle de la nature morte en France*, 1974, pp.136–42.

Augustin Bouquet

Working Paris mid-seventeenth century

Bouquet painted still life and flowers in a naïve style, halfway between the austerity of Stoskopff and the realistic tendencies of Linard.

Collections

Paris, private collection
Basket of Fruit and Maize

Paris, private collection
Vase of Flowers

Paris, private collection
Flowers in a Glass Vase

Valence, Musée des Beaux-Arts
Basket of Fruit with an Artichoke (signed)

USA, W.S. Franckel collection
Basket of Fruit and Vegetables

Bibliography

Michel Faré, *Le grand siècle de la nature morte en France*, 1974, pp.80–84.

Sébastien Bourdon

Montpellier 1616–Paris 1671

Bourdon was one of the most complex French painters of the seventeenth century because he imitated many other artists, ranging from Pieter van Laer (Bamboccio) to Nicolas Poussin himself. His exposure in Rome to so many different styles led him to develop his own immense variety of style. In 1637 he returned to Paris, where he appears to have specialized in small genre pictures with a strong Dutch influence. At the same time he could compose pastiches of the classical landscapes of Poussin and Gaspard Dughet with great facility, the main difference from his models being his use of a seductive, smoky blue tonality.

In 1648 Bourdon became one of the founder-members of the Academy in Paris. In 1652 he went to Sweden, where he entered the service of that redoubtable monarch Queen Christina, who eventually gave up politics for art. During his years in Sweden, Bourdon mostly executed portraits, characterized by their elegance and subtlety. They are usually bust length with the face slightly turned, a type of portrait that was to be extremely influential on the next generation of painters, especially Le Brun and Mignard, and a whole host of more minor portraitists.

Collections

Althorp, formerly Earl Spencer
Self-portrait (attribution)

Aix-en-Provence, Musée Granet
Halt of the Troops
St Sebastian

Algiers, Musée National des Beaux-Arts
The Tric-trac Players

Amiens, Musée de Picardie
The Guardroom

Amsterdam, Rijksmuseum
Mystic Marriage of St Catherine

Arras, Palais Saint-Vaast
Sacrifice of Noah
The Beheading of St Protius

Aschaffenberg, Schloss
Entombment of Christ

Avignon, Musée Calvet
Two Mythological Sketches

Beauvais, Musée Départemental de l'Oise
Esther and Ahasuerus
The Five Senses

Béziers, Musée Fabrégat
Death of Dido
Queen Christina of Sweden

Blois, Museum
Eleazer and Rebecca

Boston, Museum of Fine Arts
Eleazer and Rebecca (attribution)
Christ and the Samaritan Woman (attribution)

Brest, Musée des Beaux-Arts
Holy Family

Budapest, Szépmüvészeti Múzeum
Bacchus and Ceres

Caen, Musée des Beaux-Arts
Triumph of Bacchus (attribution)
Minerva Protecting the Arts
Bandits' Cave

Cambridge, Fitzwilliam Museum
Classical Ruins with Figures

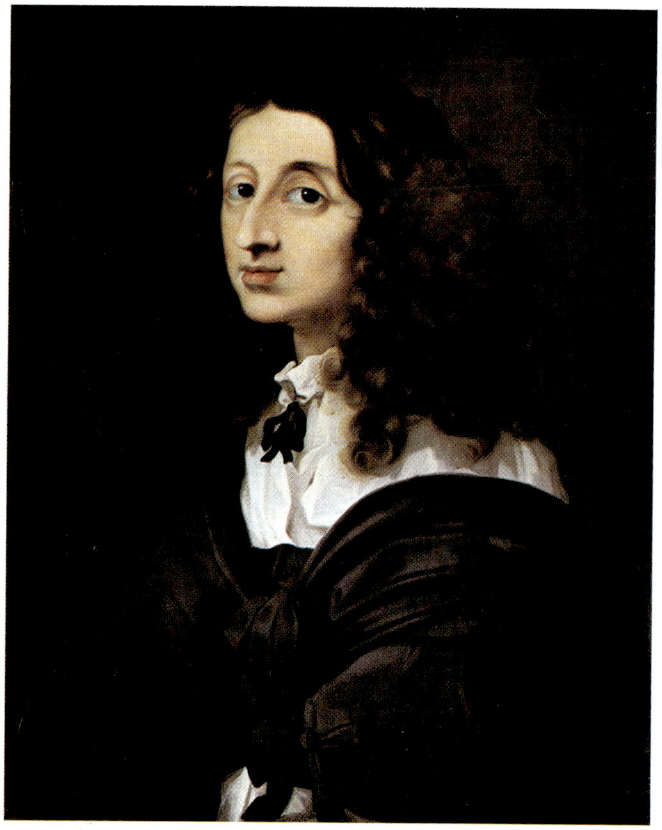

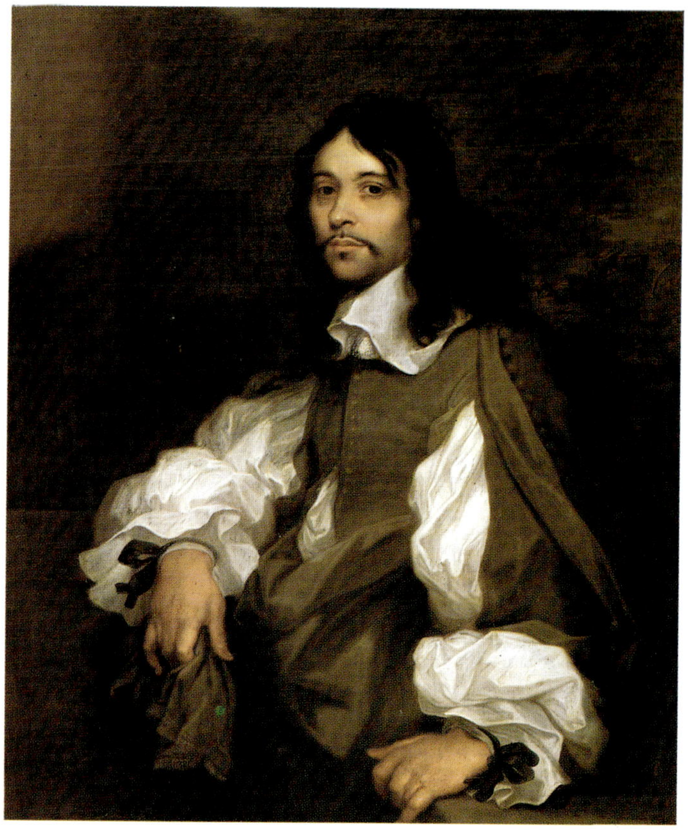

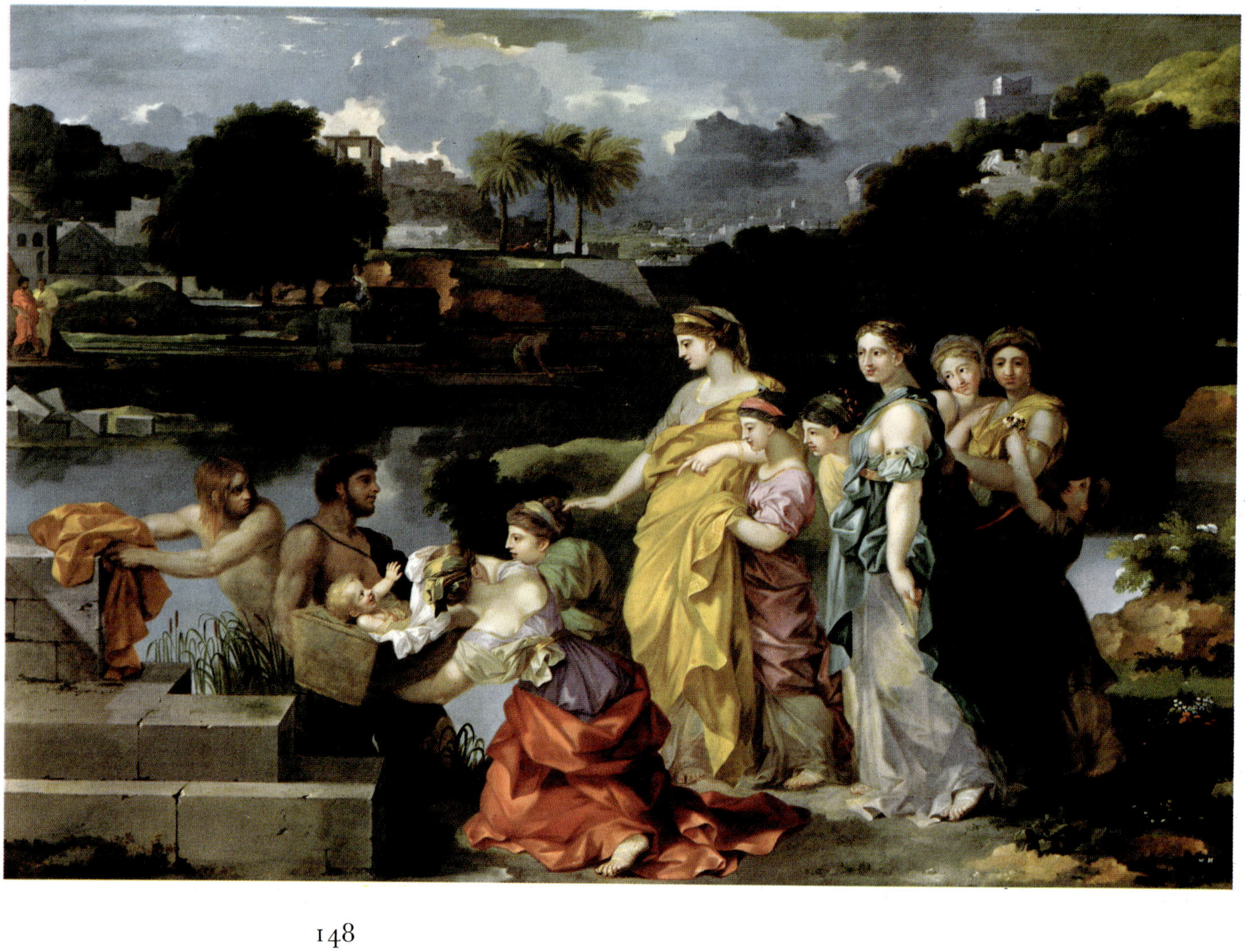

PLATE 7 (top left)
Sébastien Bourdon
Queen Christina of Sweden
Canvas, 72 × 58 cm.
Stockholm, Nationalmuseum
Acquired by the museum in 1869.

The informality of the treatment of the sitter is striking.

PLATE 8 (top right)
Sébastien Bourdon
Portrait of a Man
Canvas, 105 × 85 cm.
Montpellier, Musée Fabre
Acquired by the museum in 1836 from the collection of Madame Campredon.

The sitter is unknown.

PLATE 9
Sébastien Bourdon
The Finding of Moses
Canvas, 119.6 × 172.8 cm.
Washington, National Gallery of Art
Given to the museum as part of the Samuel H. Kress collection in 1961.

Depicting a favourite subject of Nicolas Poussin, this picture sets out successfully to imitate his style.

Champaigne (Illinois), Krannert Art Museum
Jacob and Rachel at the Well

Chantilly, Musée Condé
A Man (attribution)

Chartres, Musée des Beaux-Arts
Deliverance of St Peter

Chicago, Art Institute
A Man
Suffer Little Children to Come unto Me

Dayton (Ohio), Art Institute
Holy Family (attribution)

Dijon, Musée des Beaux-Arts
The Rest of the Holy Family

Dijon, Musée Magnin
Holy Family
A Miracle of St Gregory
Resurrection of Lazarus

Drumlanrig, Duke of Buccleuch
Portrait of an Architect (dated on reverse 1657)

Dunkirk, Musée des Beaux-Arts
Attack on Travellers
The Ecstasy of the Magdalen

Épinal, Musée Départemental des Vosges
Holy Family

Florence, Uffizi
The Fortune Teller

Freiburg im Breisgau, Augustinermuseum
Rest on the Flight into Egypt

Greenville (South Carolina), Bob Jones University
The Exposition of Moses (attribution)
Moses Striking the Rock

Grenoble, Musée de Peinture et de Sculpture
The Continence of Scipio

Hartford (Connecticut), Wadsworth Athenaeum
The Smoker

Houston (Texas), Museum of Fine Arts
The Departure of Jacob

Kassel, Staatliche Gemäldegalerie
Guardroom Scene
Pietà

Kiel, Stiftung Pommern
The Soldier

Leningrad, Hermitage
Venus Giving Arms to Aeneas
The Massacre of the Innocents
The Death of Dido

Lichfield (Staffordshire), Benson collection 1934
Double Portrait with the Artist (signed and dated 1651)

Lille, Palais des Beaux-Arts
The Bandit's Rest
Christ Surrounded by Angels

London, Dulwich College Picture Gallery
Brawl in a Guardroom

London, National Gallery
The Return of the Ark

Lons-Le-Saunier, Musée Municipal
Eleazer and Rebecca

Lyons, Musée des Beaux-Arts
The Ambush
A Young Soldier

Madrid, Prado
Queen Christina on Horseback
St Paul and St Bernard

Marseilles, Palais Longchamp
Country Scene

Minneapolis, Institute of Arts
Moses and the Daughters of Jethro

Montpellier, Cathedral
St Peter and Simon the Magician

Montpellier, Musée Fabre
Halt of the Gypsies
Portrait of a Man (plate 8)
The Count Palatine, Adolf Johann I
The Fall of Simon the Magician
Descent from the Cross

Morlaix, Musée des Jacobins
Martyrdom of St Bartholomew

Munich, Alte Pinakothek
A Roman Chalk Oven
Perseus and Andromeda

Nantes, Musée des Beaux-Arts
Martyrdom of St John (attribution)

Narbonne, Musée des Beaux-Arts
An Abbé (attribution)
Almsgiving (attribution)
François Bon
The Caravan (attribution)

New Haven, Yale University Art Gallery
'Et in Arcadia Ego'

Northampton (Massachusetts), Smith College
Landscape

Oberlin (Ohio), Allen Art Museum
The Encampment

Orléans, Musée des Beaux-Arts
The Sacrifice of Iphigenia

Paris, Louvre
Travellers amongst Ruins
The Beggars
Halt of Soldiers
Interior Scene
The Descent from the Cross
Solomon Sacrificing to the Idols
Presentation in the Temple
Augustus before the Tomb of Alexander
Presumed Portrait of Descartes
Christ and the Little Children
Adoration of the Shepherds (attribution)
Man Holding a Bust of Caracalla (attribution)
A Magistrate (attribution)

Paris, Notre Dame
Crucifixion of St Peter (documented 1643)

Paris, Saint-Jacques-du-Haut-Pas
Martyrdom of St Felicity (attribution)

Paris, Val-de-Grâce
Christ and the Blind man of Jericho (attribution)

Paris, F. M. collection
Still Life in Kitchen

Petworth House (Sussex), National Trust
The Selling of Joseph

Philadelphia, La Salle College Art Gallery
The Flight into Egypt

Pittsburgh, Art Museum
Landscape (fragment)

Providence, Rhode Island School of Design
Landscape

Reims, Musée Saint-Denis
Landscape

Rouen, Musée des Beaux-Arts
The Farewell of Dido and Aeneas

Saltwood Castle (Kent), formerly Lord Clark
Holy Family with St Elizabeth and St John the Baptist

San Francisco (California), Art Museums
Landscape (attribution)

Sarasota (Florida), John and Mable Ringling Museum
Seven Acts of Mercy:
Feeding the Hungry
Giving Drink to the Thirsty
Clothing the Naked
Welcoming the Stranger
Freeing the Captive
Healing the Sick
Burying the Dead

Schleissheim, Schloss
The Rest on the Flight into Egypt

Stockholm, Nationalmuseum
Queen Christina of Sweden (plate 7)
Holy Family
Self-portrait
Carl Gustav X

Stuttgart, Staatsgalerie
Eleazer and Rebecca at the Well

Toulouse, Musée des Augustins
St John the Baptist
Martyrdom of St Andrew

Turin, Galleria Sabauda
Massacre of the Innocents

Valence, Musée des Beaux-Arts
Tobias Burying the Dead

Versailles, Château
Martin Bourdon
Self-portrait
Self-portrait
Called Nicolas Fouquet (attribution)

Washington, National Gallery of Art
Countess Ebba Sparre
The Finding of Moses (plate 9)

Worcester (Massachusetts), Art Museum
Massacre of the Innocents

Bibliography

The last monograph was Ch. Ponsonailhe, *Sébastien Bourdon, sa vie, son oeuvre*, 1886.

Charles Sterling, in the exhibition catalogue, Paris, Orangerie, *Les peintres de la réalité*, 1934, pp.10–17.

Much research by both Jacques Thuillier and Pierre Rosenberg remains unpublished, owing to the last-minute cancellation of the projected Bourdon exhibition in 1971.

Jean Boyer

Working first half of seventeenth century

No biographical information seems to be available about this painter.

Collection

Boulogne-sur-Mer, Musée des Beaux-Arts
St Jerome (signed)

Bibliography

The existence of this picture is noted in the exhibition catalogue, Dunkirk/Valenciennes/Lille, *La peinture française aux XVIIe et XVIIIe siècles*, 1980, p.167.

Louis Brocard

Paris 1646?–Avignon 1676

The directness of his Narbonne portrait implies that Brocard was familiar with the painting of Pierre Puget as well as that of his contemporary Laurent Fauchier. Only in the provinces could such an unaffected style continue at this late date.

Collections

Avignon, Saint-Pierre
St Peter Raising a Man from the Dead (signed)
St Peter Raising a Woman from the Dead

Narbonne, Musée des Beaux-Arts
Portrait of a Man (signed and dated 1672)

Bibliography

Henry Wytenhove in the exhibition catalogue, Marseilles, Palais Longchamp, *La peinture en Provence au XVIIe siècle*, 1978, p.12.

Jean Chalette

Troyes 1581–Toulouse 1644

The first part of Chalette's career was spent in Italy, and he had returned to France by 1611. In that year he was working for the collector Peiresc at Aix-en-Provence: a drawing of 1611, *Astra Medicea*, in the Bibliothèque Inguimbertine at Carpentras, was executed for Peiresc. Later in 1611 Chalette is recorded in Toulouse, where he spent the rest of his life. Most of Chalette's commissions were for large group portraits of the *Capitouls* (municipal magistrates) of Toulouse, who were different every year. All but one of these annual portraits disappeared at the time of the Revolution of 1789, but a record of the appearance of these important pictures survives in the form of miniatures, which Chalette himself executed for the municipal accounts. A number of pages was torn out of these during the Revolution, but a few survive in Toulouse (in the Archives Municipales, the Musée Paul Dupuy and the Musée des Augustins), and another example is in the Musée des Beaux-Arts at Troyes. Chalette's few surviving portraits and religous pictures affirm by their quality that he was the leading painter in Toulouse until the arrival of Nicolas Tournier (who was recorded there from 1632 onwards).

Collections

Toulouse, Musée des Augustins
Portrait of a Man as a Poet (signed and dated 1635)
The Capitouls of Toulouse for the Years 1622–3 with Christ on the Cross (documented 1623) (fig.8)
Portrait of a Priest (signed and dated 1635)
Holy Family
The Virgin of the Prisoners (fig.7)

Toulouse, Musée Paul Dupuy
The Capitouls of Toulouse in Session before their Portrait by Chalette, 1629–30 (fig.9)

Troyes, Musée des Beaux-Arts
The Capitouls of Toulouse

Bibliography

The most recent summary of Chalette's career is contained in the exhibition catalogue, Paris, Orangerie, *L'age d'or de la peinture toulousaine*, 1947. The whole question of the miniatures was dealt with in detail by Robert Mesuret in the exhibition catalogue, Toulouse, Musée Paul Dupuy, *Les miniaturistes du Capitole, 1610–1790*, 1956.

Jean-Bernard Chalette

Working Rennes 1668–78

Chalette worked for local patrons in Rennes in the 1660s and 1670s in a manner influenced by Charles Le Brun, both in his pictures' large scale and their general style.

Collection

Rennes, Musée des Beaux-Arts
Allegory of the Revolt of the Papier Timbré (signed and dated 1676)
Tatila, King of the Goths, Prostrating Himself before St Benedict (dated 1678)

Bibliography

François Bergot and Patrick Ramade in *Bulletin des Amis du Musée de Rennes*, 1979, p.10.

Jean-Baptiste de Champaigne

Brussels 1631–Paris 1681

The work of Jean-Baptiste de Champaigne, nephew of Philippe de Champaigne, remains obscure. His identifiable pictures are close in style to those of his uncle, even though his artistic education was in Italy. Even more so than those of Philippe de Champaigne, his pictures retain a strong Flemish character. He was received into the Academy in 1663, and in 1667 painted the *Stoning of St Paul* for Notre Dame in Paris (now in Marseilles), which was one of the annual commissions for the church, known as the 'May'.

Collections

Brussels, Musées Royaux des Beaux-Arts
Assumption of the Virgin

Detroit, Institute of Arts
The Last Supper

Dijon, Musée Magnin
The Stoning of St Paul

Elmira (New York), Arnot Art Museum
The Stoning of St Paul

Lyons, Musée des Beaux-Arts
Adoration of the Shepherds

Marseilles, Palais Longchamp
The Stoning of St Paul (1667)

Nancy, Musée des Beaux-Arts
St Paul

Paris, Louvre
Philippe de Champaigne (dated 1668)
The Education of Achilles (*Lesson of Arms*)
The Education of Achilles (*Lesson of Equitation*)

Tourcoing, Musée des Beaux-Arts
St Theresa

Versailles, Château
Ceiling Decoration of the Salon de Mercure
Mercury on his Chariot Carried by Two Cocks
Angélique Arnaud (copy after Philippe de Champaigne)

Bibliography

Pierre Rosenberg in the exhibition catalogue, Paris, Grand Palais, *La peinture française du XVIIe siècle dans les collections américaines*, 1982, pp. 231–2.

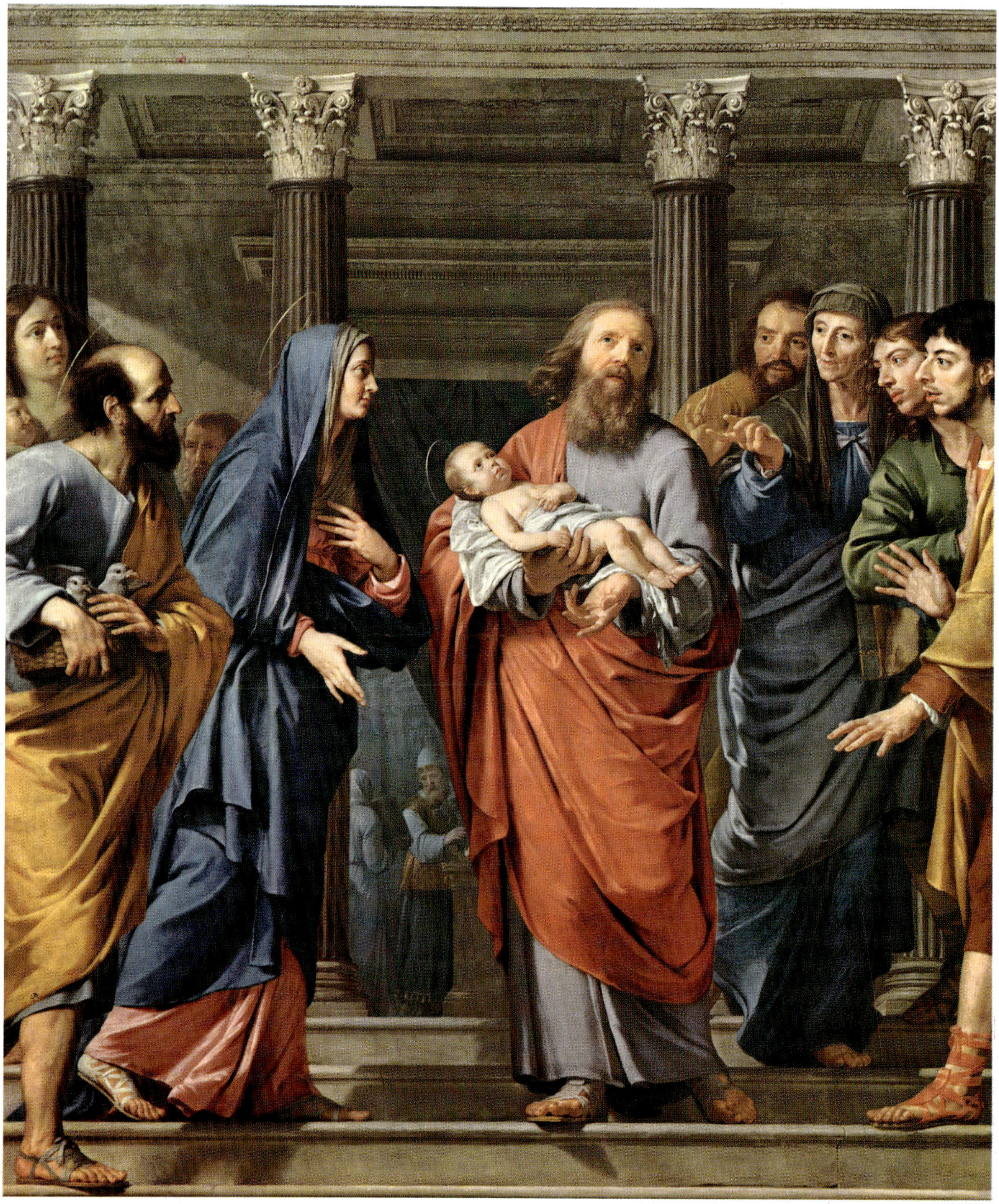

PLATE 10
Philippe de Champaigne
The Presentation in the Temple
Canvas, 257 × 197 cm. Dated 1642
Brussels, Musées Royaux des Beaux-Arts
Executed for the church of Saint Honoré in Paris. Sent to Brussels during the French Revolution.

Philippe de Champaigne

Brussels 1602–Paris 1674

Apart from Vouet, Champaigne was the most important painter active in Paris in the middle years of the century. He arrived in the capital in 1621, already having trained under Jacques Fouquières. Throughout his career Champaigne had many official commissions, for monasteries, for the Church and for Louis XIII. His art has not been studied in depth until recently, and has undergone radical reassessment: instead of being seen as an exponent of dry Classicism, he is now seen to epitomize the whole epoch. As a portraitist, his vivid depictions of Cardinal Richelieu show how he was able to seize on the essential characteristics of the autocrat, while his portraits of other, now unidentifiable contemporaries are much more sympathetic.

In the first part of his career, as a painter of religious pictures, he executed a number of large altarpieces that show his Flemish origins. This is especially true of such Rubens-inspired works as the *Adoration of the Shepherds* in the Wallace Collection, London. Later in life, Champaigne changed his art dramatically when he came under the influence of the Jansenist movement. His paralysed daughter was miraculously cured in the Jansenist nunnery of Port-Royal, and to mark the event Champaigne painted his celebrated but untypical *Ex-Voto* (Louvre). Champaigne's art was much more varied than is usually thought, and his achievement spans almost fifty years, from the mid-1620s to his death in 1674. He was one of the fourteen founder-members of the Academy in 1648.

Collections

Aix-en-Provence, Musée Granet
Pompone de Bellaire
An Échevin of Paris (fragment dated 1648)
A Man

Alençon, Musée des Beaux-Arts
Assumption of the Virgin
The Trinity

Althorp (Northamptonshire), formerly Earl Spencer
A Man

Amiens, Musée de Picardie
Moses
Mgr de Harlay

Angers, Musée des Beaux-Arts
The Supper at Emmaus
Christ in the Temple (1663)

Ann Arbor (Michigan), University
Landscape: Christ Healing the Deaf-mute

Arras, Palais Saint-Vaast
Tapestry cartoon: *The Birth of the Virgin*
Tapestry cartoon: *Presentation of the Virgin in the Temple*

Avignon, Musée Calvet
A Man

Baltimore, Walters Art Gallery
An Échevin (attribution)

Barnard Castle, Bowes Museum
A Lady in Black (formerly called *Henrietta Maria*)

Basle, Öffentliche Kunstsammlung
A Man

Bayeux, Musée des Beaux-Arts
Virgin and Child
Heads of St Peter and St Paul

Berlin, Staatliche Museen, Berlin-Dahlem
A Man

Besançon, Musée des Beaux-Arts
A Man Aged Fifty-seven
A Man
An Échevin

Birmingham, Barber Institute of Fine Arts
St Julienne de Cornillon

Boston (Massachusetts), Museum of Fine Arts
Self-portrait

Brighton, Art Gallery
The Veil of St Veronica

Brussels, Musées Royaux des Beaux-Arts
The Presentation in the Temple (plate 10)
St Ambrose
St Stephen
St Genevieve
St Joseph
Self-portrait
St Charles Borromeo
A Man
St Germain d'Auxerre

Brussels, Saint-Michael and Saint-Gudule
Assumption of the Virgin

Budapest, Szépmüvészeti Múzeum
Henri Eroulart (signed and dated 1654)

Burleigh House (Northamptonshire), Marquess of Exeter
Adoration of the Shepherds

Caen, Musée des Beaux-Arts
Christ and the Woman of Samaria
The Veil of St Veronica
Louis XIII Adoring the Dead Christ

Cambridge (Massachusetts), Fogg Art Museum
St Joseph (1658)
The Virgin

Chalon-sur-Saône, Musée Denon
Double Portrait

Chantilly, Musée Condé
Cardinal Mazarin Seated
Mère Angelique Arnaud (dated 1648)

Chartres, Musée des Beaux-Arts
Turenne

Chaumes-en-Brie (Seine et Marne), Church
Crucifixion

Cherbourg, Musée Thomas Henry
A Man
Assumption of the Virgin

Clermont-Ferrand, Musée Bargoin
A Man

Cleveland (Ohio), Museum of Art
King Charles II of England

Darmstadt, Hessisches Landesmuseum
A Man

PLATE 11
Philippe de Champaigne
Annunciation
Canvas, 74.3 × 54.6 cm.
Hull, Ferens Art Gallery
Given to the museum anonymously in 1963.

This is a carefully finished modello for the large picture in the Wallace Collection, London, which could well have been painted for the Palais Royal in about 1644.

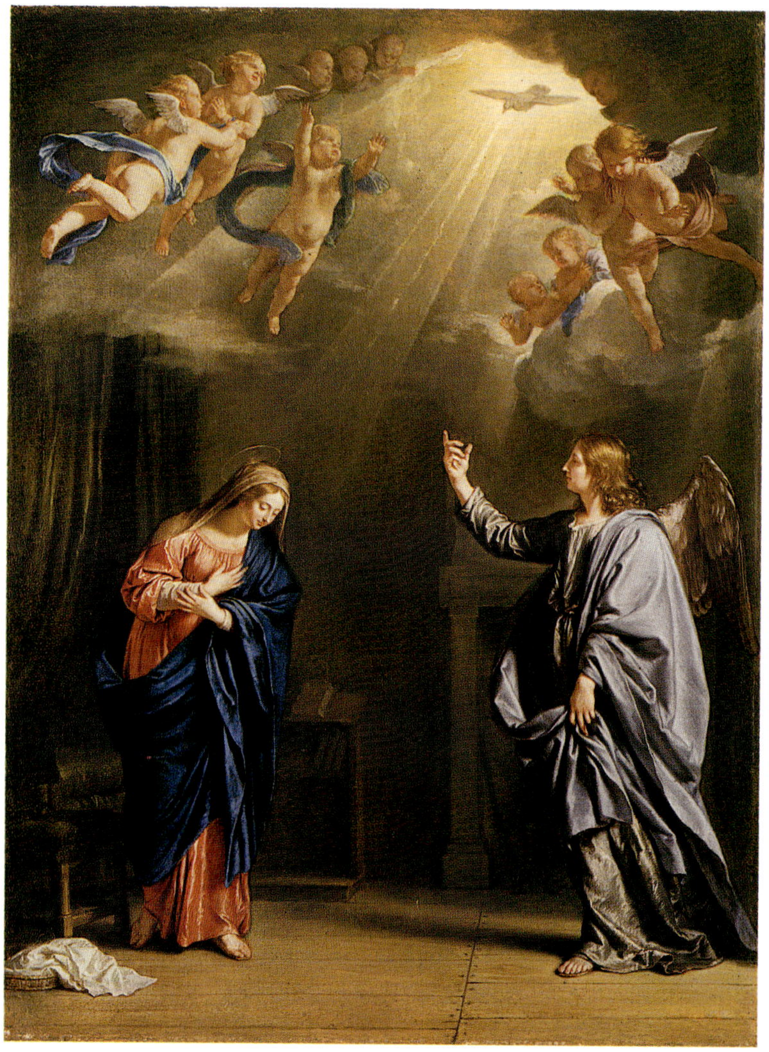

Dijon, Musée des Beaux-Arts
The Presentation in the Temple
Study of the Heads of Old Men

Florence, Galleria Pitti
Nicolas Fouquet, Marquis de Belle Isle

Geneva, Musée d'Art et d'Histoire
The Visitation

Ghent, Museum voor Schone Kunsten
Pierre Camus

Greenville (South Carolina), Bob Jones University
Christ as the Man of Sorrows

Grenoble, Musée de Peinture et de Sculpture
St John the Baptist
Abbé de Saint Cyran
Louis XIV Receiving the Knight of the Holy Spirit
The Crucifixion (1655)
Assumption of the Virgin
Self-portrait

Hamburg, Kunsthalle
Adoration of King Louis XIV (1643)

Hampton Court Palace (Middlesex), Royal Collection
Cardinal Richelieu

Houston (Texas), Museum of Fine Arts
The Penitent Magdalen (plate 13)

Hull, Ferens Art Gallery
Annunciation (plate 11)

Jassy (Rumania), Art Museum
Self-portrait

Kansas City, Nelson Gallery
Christ on the Cross

Karlsruhe, Staatliche Kunsthalle
Man in an Armchair (signed and dated 1668)

Knole Park (Kent), Lord Sackville
Claude de Bullion

Leamington Spa, Art Gallery
Penitent St Peter (signed)

Le Mans, Musée de Tessé
The Sleep of Elijah
Still Life with a Skull (plate 15)
Adoration of the Kings

Leningrad, Hermitage
Moses Receiving the Tablets of the Law

Liège, Musée des Beaux-Arts
A Man

Lille, Palais des Beaux-Arts
Christ as the Good Shepherd
The Nativity

London, National Gallery
Cardinal Richelieu
Triple Portrait of Cardinal Richelieu (fig.63)
The Dream of Joseph

London, Wallace Collection
An Échevin (fragment)
The Marriage of the Virgin
Adoration of the Shepherds (fig.62)
The Annunciation
Abbé de Saint Cyran

Lyons, Musée des Beaux-Arts
The Last Supper
The Finding of the Bodies of St Gervais and St Protius (1660)
A Man
The Nativity (1629)

PLATE 12
Philippe de Champaigne
Portrait of Omer Talon
Canvas, 225 × 161.6 cm. Signed and dated lower left:
P. Champaigne F. A°. 1649
Aeta s 54
Washington, National Gallery of Art
Acquired by the museum as part of the Samuel H. Kress collection in 1952.

The sitter was a Jansenist and in 1641 he became First Lawyer of the Paris *Parlement*. He died in 1652.

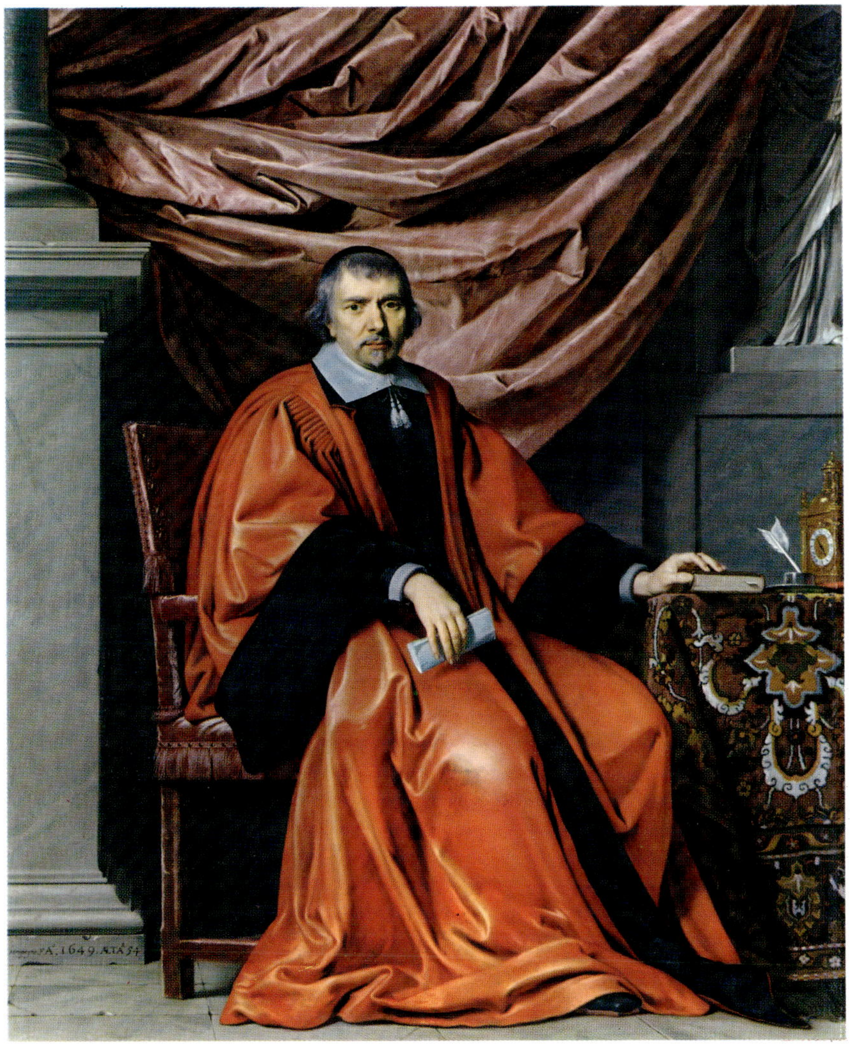

Lyons, Musée des Arts Décoratifs
Three Children (1655)

Madrid, Prado
Louis XIII (signed and dated 1655)

Magny-lès-Hameau, Musée du Port-Royal
Head of St John the Baptist
Ecce Homo
The Good Shepherd

Mainz, Mittelrheinisches Landesmuseum
Landscape with a Carthusian Monk

Marseilles, Palais Longchamp
Assumption of the Virgin

Metz, Musée Central
The Magdalen

Milwaukee, Art Center
Moses

Montigny-Lemcoup (Seine-et-Oise), Church
St Genevieve

Montrésor, Church
Annunciation

Munich, Alte Pinakothek
Turenne

Nancy, Musée des Beaux-Arts
Charity

Nantes, Musée des Beaux-Arts
Supper at Emmaus

Narbonne, Musée des Beaux-Arts
A Man
Adoration of the Shepherds
Presumed Portrait of the Artist's Daughter

New York, Historical Society
A Man with a Dog (lent to Metropolitan Museum, New York)

New York, Metropolitan Museum
The Virgin (attribution)
The Angel Gabriel (attribution)
Colbert (dated 1655)

Orléans, Musée des Beaux-Arts
St Carlo Borromeo (signed)

Ottawa, National Gallery of Canada
Crucifixion

Paris, Musée Carnavalet
Colbert

Paris, Musée Jacquemart-André
Colbert

Paris, Institut Français
Richelieu on his Deathbed

Paris, Louvre
Two Angel Musicians (documented 1648)
Assumption of the Virgin
Louis XIII
Louis XIII Crowned by Victory
Cardinal Richelieu
The Dead Christ
The Prevôt des Marchands and the Échevins of the City of Paris
St Philip the Apostle (documented 1649)
A Man (signed and dated 1650) (plate 14)
The Last Supper
The Last Supper (small version)
Jean-Antoine de Mesme (signed and dated 1653)
Mère Angélique Arnaud (dated 1654)
Paphnucis Liberating Thais (documented 1656)

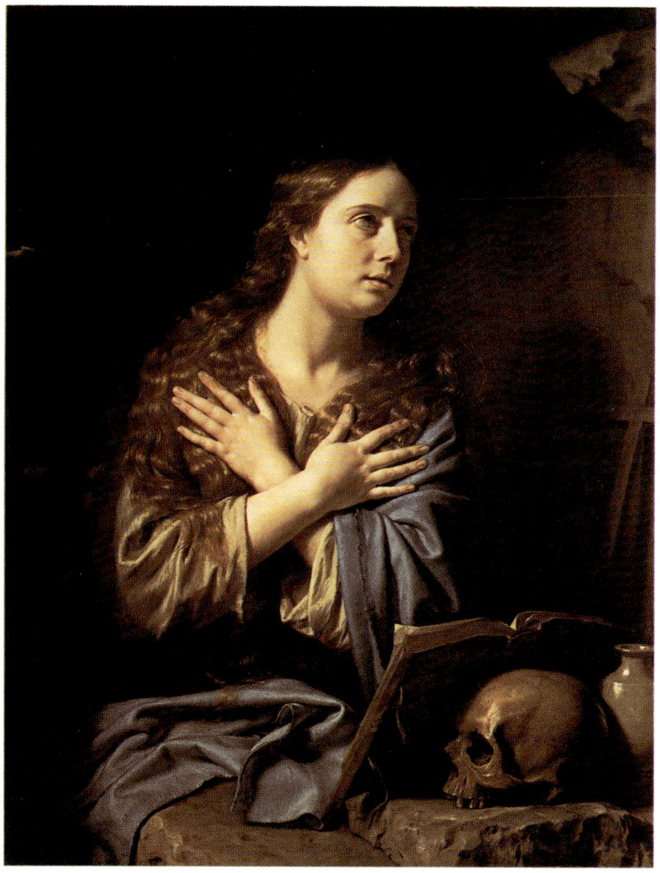

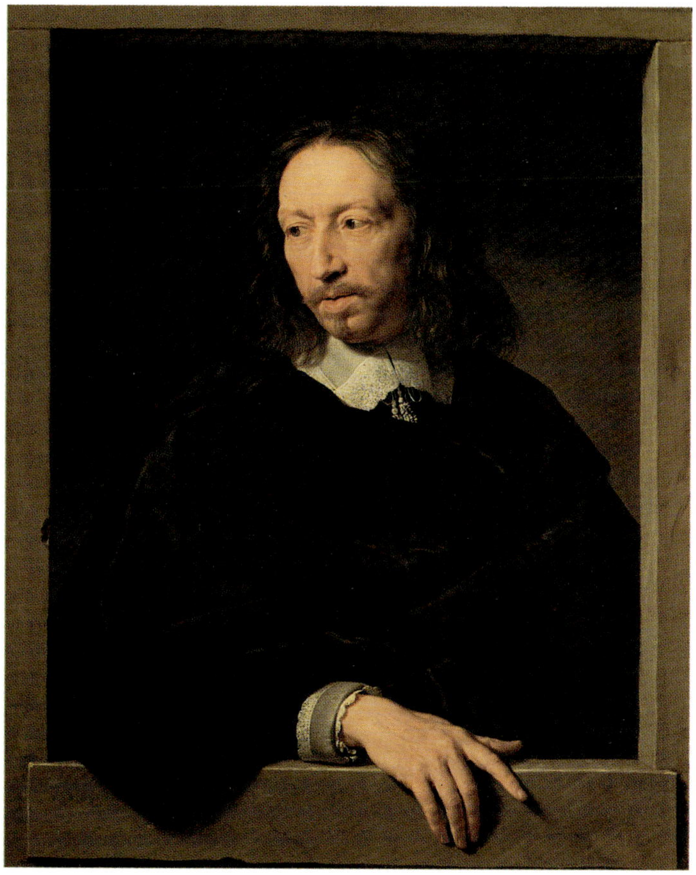

PLATE 13 (top left)
Philippe de Champaigne
The Penitent Magdalen
Canvas, 115.5 × 87 cm.
Houston (Texas), Museum of Fine Arts (purchase Agnes Cullen Arnold Endowment Fund)
Acquired by the museum in 1970 after having been in several different English private collections.

Probably painted for the convent of the Dames du Saint-Sacrement in the Marais, Paris.

PLATE 14 (top right)
Philippe de Champaigne
A Man
Canvas, 91 × 72 cm. Signed and dated: Phi[l] Champaigne F. A° 1650
Paris, Louvre
Acquired by the museum in 1806.

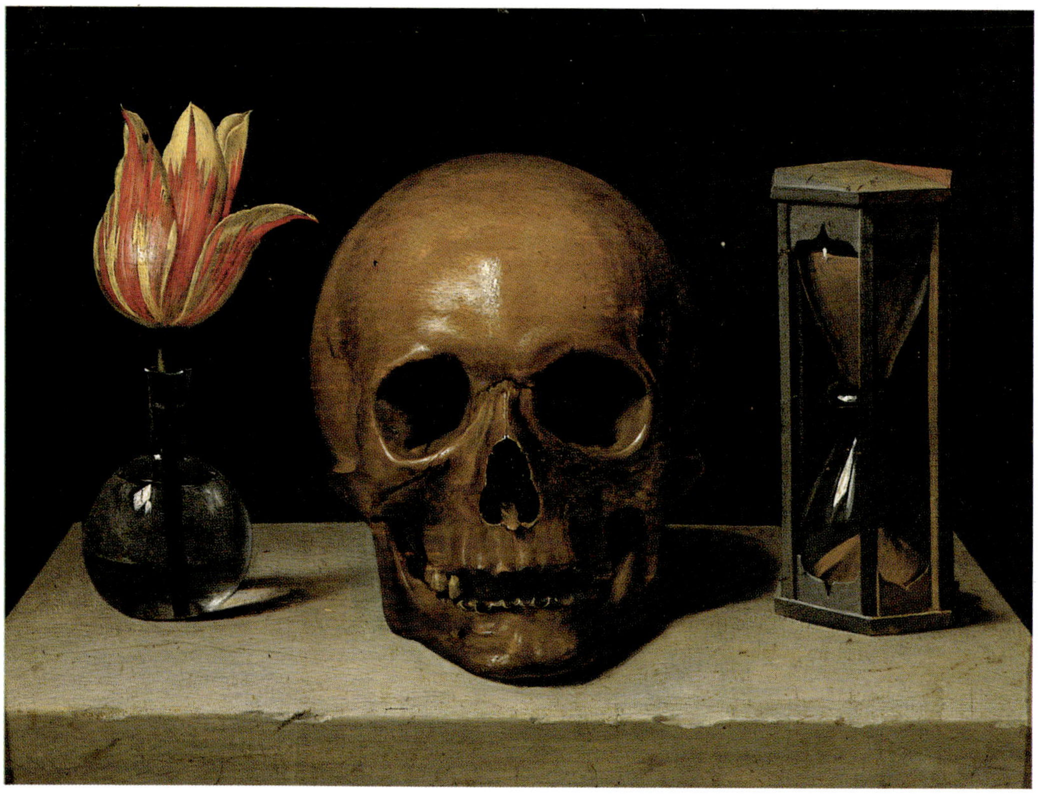

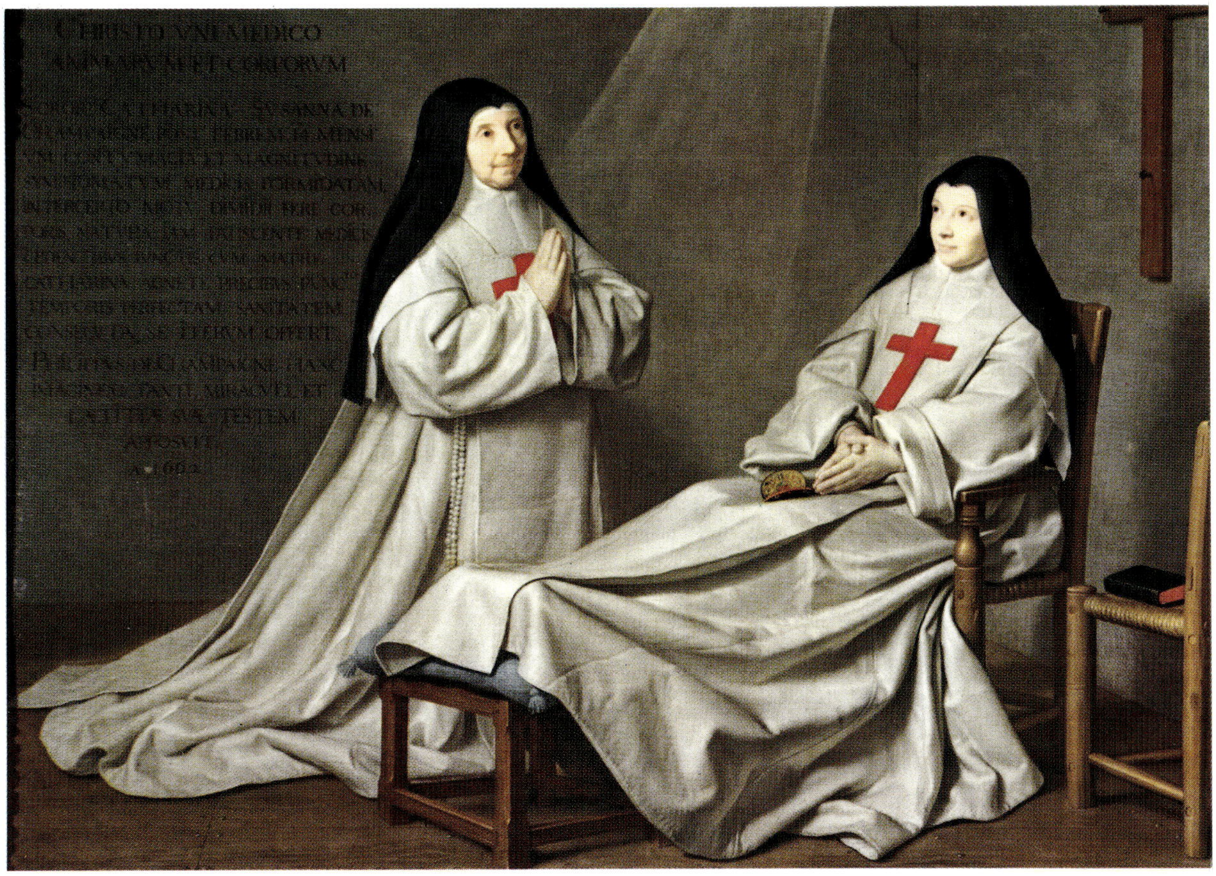

PLATE 15 (left)
Philippe de Champaigne
Still Life with a Skull
Panel, 28 × 37 cm.
Le Mans, Musée de Tessé
First recorded as early as 1720 in the Bonnaire collection.

The artist reveals his Flemish origins in this picture, since *vanitas* pieces are extremely rare in French art, though common in the North.

PLATE 16 (above)
Philippe de Champaigne
Ex-Voto (Catherine-Agnès Arnaud and Catherine de Sainte Suzanne Champaigne)
Canvas, 165 × 229 cm. Dated 1662
Paris, Louvre
Given by the artist to the nunnery of Port Royal in Paris, 1662. Confiscated at the Revolution of 1789.

Painted as a thank-offering for the miraculous cure of the artist's daughter from paralysis.

The Penitent Magdalen (documented 1656)
Christ in the House of Simon the Pharisee
Translation of the Bodies of St Gervais and St Protius (documented 1661)
Ex-Voto (dated 1662) (plate 16)
Christ on the Cross (signed and dated 1674)
Christ on the Cross
A Girl
A Child (attribution)
A Man (dated 1648, attribution)
Two Men (dated 1656)
A Man

Paris, Saint-Étienne-du-Mont
The Gathering of the Manna

Paris, Saint-Geneviève-du-Mont
St Geneviève

Paris, Saint-Leu Saint-Gilles
A Man on his Deathbed

Paris, Saint-Médard
Dead Christ

Paris, Saint-Roch
Head of Christ

Pasadena (California), Norton Simon Museum
Visitation

Périgueux, Musée du Périgord
A Boy with a Feather

Ponce (Puerto Rico), Museo de Arte
Presentation of Christ in the Temple

Portland (Oregon), Art Museum
Adoration of the Shepherds

Reims, Musée Saint-Denis
The Montmort Children (1649)
A Man

Rennes, Musée des Beaux-Arts
The Penitent Magdalen (dated 1657)

Rouen, Musée des Beaux-Arts
Concert of Angels

Sacramento (California), Crocker Art Museum
Christ among the Doctors (attribution)

St Louis (Missouri), Art Museum
Louis XIII (or St Louis)

San Diego (California), Timken Art Gallery
Landscape with the Healing of the Blind Men of Jericho

São Paolo, Museu dé Arte
A Man

Senlis, Cathedral
St John the Baptist

Strasbourg, Musée des Beaux-Arts
A Man
A Man

Stuttgart, Staatsgalerie
Christ in the Garden of Gethsemane

Toledo (Ohio), Museum of Art
An Échevin of Paris (fragment)

Toulouse, Musée des Augustins
Christ with the Souls in Purgatory
Christ Nailed to the Cross
Louis XIII Giving the Order of the St Esprit

Tours, Musée des Beaux-Arts
Landscape with St Zosimus Giving Communion to St Mary of Egypt

Troyes, Musée des Beaux-Arts
Louis XIII Giving the Order of the St Esprit
Claude Jolly

Turin, Galleria Sabauda
A Man with a Lace Collar

Versailles, Château
Abbé de St Cyran
Angélique Arnaud (replica)
Anne of Austria and her Children
Gaston de Foix, duc de Nemours

Mère Agnès (study)
Jacques Tuboeuf (dated 1663)
Lemercier (signed and dated 1644)
Cardinal Richelieu (replica)
Denis Talon (replica)

Vienna, Kunsthistorisches Museum
Adam and Eve Mourning the Death of Abel
A Man

Warsaw, National Museum
Cardinal Richelieu

Washington, National Gallery of Art
Portrait of Omer Talon (signed and dated 1649) (plate 12)

Bibliography

The only monograph with *catalogue raisonné* is Bernard Dorival, *Philippe de Champaigne, 1602–1674*, 2 vols., 1976. This immensely long book was not well received, even though the documentation is exceptionally thorough.

Nicolas Chaperon

Châteaudun 1612–Rome 1656?

A pupil of Vouet in his early years in Paris, Chaperon then visited Italy. He always remained under the influence of his master, although some of his compositions of the 1630s are related to those of Poussin.

Collections

Chapel Hill (North Carolina), Ackland Art Gallery
The Nurture of Bacchus

Compiègne, Saint-Nicolas
Presentation in the Temple

Dallas (Texas), Museum of Fine Arts
Venus and Bacchus

Dijon, Musée Magnin
Bacchanal

Florence, Uffizi
The Drunken Silenus

France, private collection
Bacchus and Ariadne

Houston (Texas), Museum of Fine Arts
Presentation in the Temple

Leningrad, Hermitage
Two Pictures

Bibliography

Pierre Rosenberg in the exhibition catalogue, Florence, Galleria Pitti, *Pittura Francese nelle collezione pubbliche fiorentine*, 1977, p.124.
Pierre Rosenberg in the exhibition catalogue Paris, Grand Palais, *La peinture française du XVIIe siècle dans les collections américaines*, 1982, pp.237–8.

Claude Lorrain(e) (Claude Gellée)

Champagne (Vosges) 1600–Rome 1682

The inventor of the ideal landscape, Claude was isolated stylistically, as a painter whose entire productive career was in Baroque Rome. He left his native Lorraine as a youth and travelled to Italy in about 1613, then returned to Lorraine for a year in 1625/26 when he was apprenticed to Claude Deruet in Nancy. In 1627 he was again in Rome, where he lived for the rest of his life. From 1635 onwards he kept an exact record of each picture he painted, in the form of a drawing of the finished painting. This book, known as the *Liber Veritatis* (London, British Museum), forms the basis from which the artist's work can be reconstructed. In it some two hundred paintings are recorded, although modern scholarship adds to his *oeuvre* a considerable number not recorded in it.

Claude's development as a painter falls into distinct phases. During the more than fifty years he lived in Rome he was a neighbour of Nicolas Poussin, whom he counted as a friend, but the sources of their art were quite different. Claude's earliest pictures are eclectic, deriving from the landscapes of many artists in Italy at that time, ranging from the local Agostino Tassi (whose pupil and assistant Claude was) to foreigners like Adam Elsheimer and Paul Bril. In the 1630s Claude specialized in small panels similar to those of the artists who influenced him, which were either landscapes or port scenes. In the late 1630s his art matured, and for the next forty years he concentrated on the ideal landscape. In his later years, although his output declined, the lyrical poetry and harmony of his compositions increased. In his own lifetime, the exceptional quality of the light and atmosphere depicted in his work was recognized, and his pictures were much sought after by collectors. His work became even more influential in the eighteenth century, when his treatment of light was imitated in France by Claude-Joseph Vernet and in England by Richard Wilson. Claude's reputation declined in the nineteenth and early twentieth century because his pictures were then thought to be too artificial, but in recent years his outstanding ability to seize on poetical mood has been once more appreciated, and his pictures are once again held in high esteem.

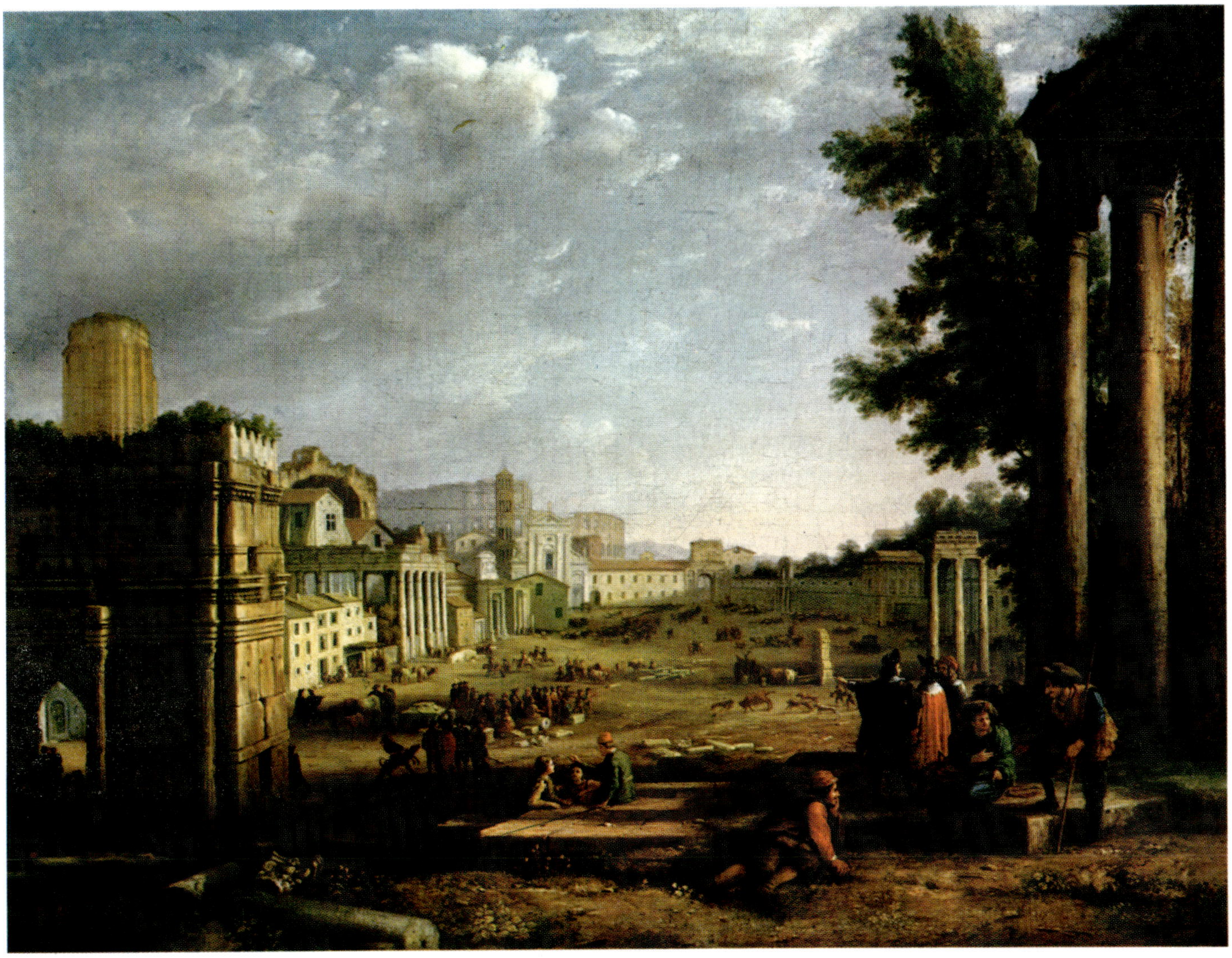

PLATE 17
Claude Lorrain
The Campo Vaccino, Rome
Canvas, 56 × 72 cm. Signed
Liber Veritatis No.9
Paris, Louvre
Confiscated from the duc de Brissac during the Revolution.

This composition shows the state of the Roman Forum in the early seventeenth century, with many of the famous monuments half buried by debris.

Collections
LV = *Liber Veritatis* number

Alnwick Castle (Northumberland), The Duke of Northumberland
Port Scene (signed and dated 1637, LV 14)

Anglesey Abbey (Cambridgeshire), National Trust
Landscape with Psyche Sacrificing at the Temple of Apollo (signed and dated 1663, LV 157)
Landscape with Shepherds (LV 176)
Landscape with the Arrival of Aeneas in Latium (signed and dated 1675, LV 185)

Belvoir Castle (Leicestershire), The Duke of Rutland
Landscape with the Flight into Egypt
Landscape with Shepherds (LV 155)
Landscape with a Boat (signed and dated 1662, LV 156)

Berlin-Dahlem, Staatliche Museen
Landscape with Cephalus and Procris Reunited by Diana (signed and dated 16..)
Landscape with Shepherds (signed and dated 1642, LV 64)

Betchworth House (Surrey), Major General Goulburn
Landscape with Apollo and the Herds of Admetus (LV 170)

Birmingham, Barber Institute of Fine Arts
Landscape with Shepherds (signed and dated 164.., LV 93)

Birmingham, City Art Gallery
Landscape with Shepherds—the Ponte Molle (signed and dated 1645, LV 90) (plate 21)
Marine with the Embarkation of St Paula (LV 132)

Boston, Museum of Fine Arts
Landscape with a Ferry (signed and dated 1637, LV 22)
Apollo and the Muses on Mount Helion (Parnassus) (signed and dated 1680, LV 193) (plate 23)
The Mill (signed and dated 1631)

Bowhill (Selkirkshire), The Duke of Buccleuch
Landscape with the Judgment of Paris (signed and dated 1633)
Marine (signed and dated 1633)

Brocklesby Park (Lincolnshire), The Earl of Yarborough
Landscape with Dancing Figures (signed, LV 13)

Brussels, Musées Royaux des Beaux-Arts
Aeneas Landing on the Libyan Coast (signed, LV 180)

Budapest, Szépmüvészeti Múzeum
Landscape with Shepherds (LV 107)

Cambridge, Fitzwilliam Museum
Landscape with Castel Gandolfo (LV 35)

Cardiff, National Museum of Wales
Landscape with St Philip Baptising the Eunuch (signed and dated 1678, LV 191)

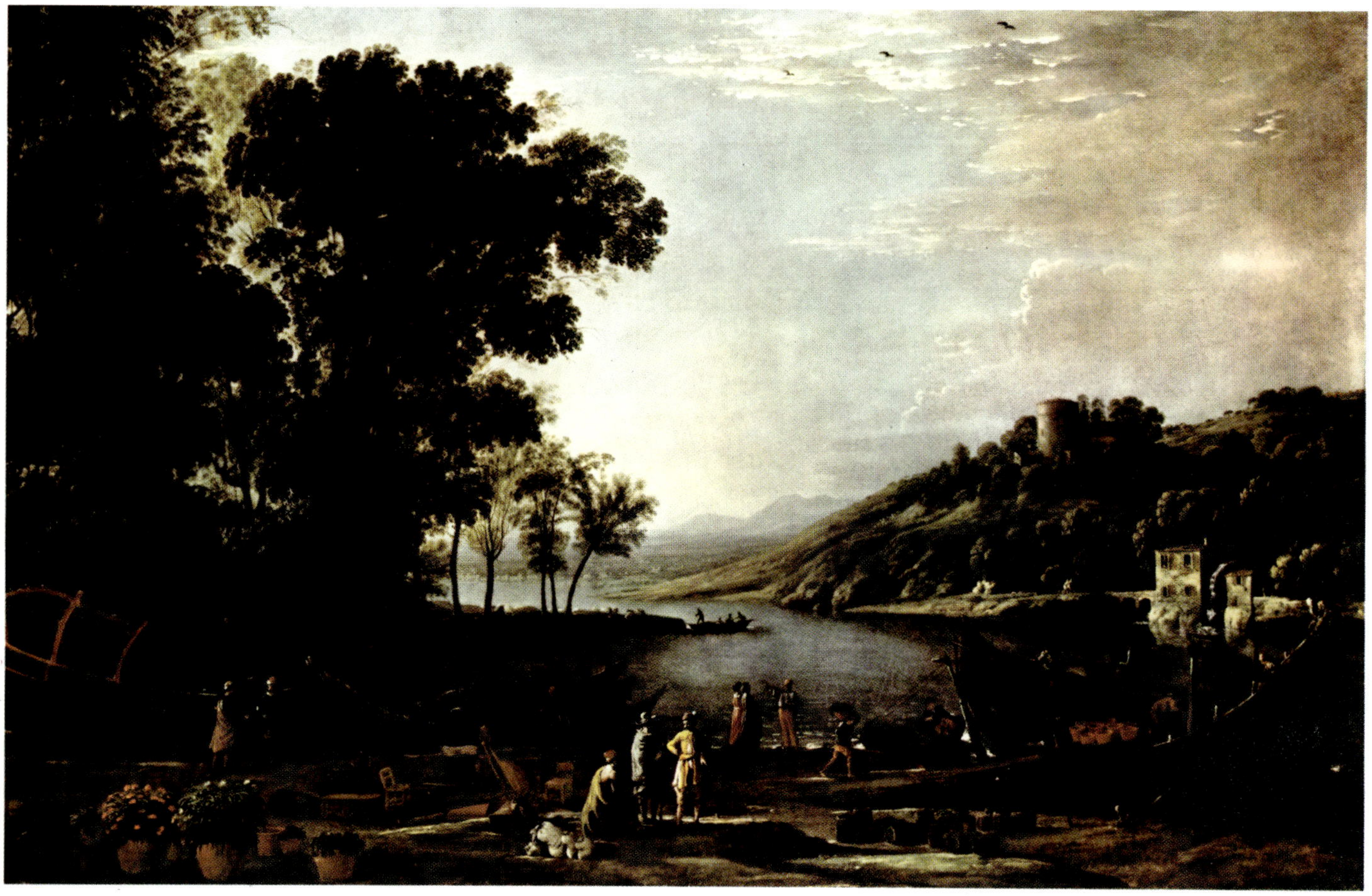

PLATE 18
Claude Lorrain
Landscape with Merchants
Canvas, 97.2 × 143.6 cm.
Signed on the boat, left:
CLAVDIO
Washington, National Gallery of Art
Given to the museum by the Samuel H. Kress Foundation, 1952.

An early work by the artist, probably from about 1630 before he began the *Liber Veritatis.*

Castle Howard (Yorkshire), formerly George Howard collection
Landscape with Shepherds (LV 56)

Chatsworth (Derbyshire), The Duke of Devonshire
Landscape with Mercury and Battus (LV 159)

Chicago, Art Institute
View of Delphi with a Procession (signed, LV 182)

Cincinnati (Ohio), Art Museum
Coast Scene (signed and dated 1639, LV 44)

Cleveland (Ohio), Museum of Art
Landscape with Figures (signed and dated 16..)
Landscape with the Rest on the Flight into Egypt (LV 88)

Cologne, Wallraf-Richartz Museum
Marine (signed)
Landscape with Psyche saved from Suicide (LV 167)

Copenhagen, Statens Museum for Kunst
Landscape with Shepherds

Corsham Court (Wiltshire), Lord Methuen
Landscape with St John the Baptist and Angels (signed and dated 1647)

Detroit, Institute of Arts
Landscape with Shepherds (signed and dated 1637, LV 12)
Marine (signed and dated 1638)

Dresden, Staatliche Gemäldegalerie
Landscape with the Flight into Egypt (signed and dated 1647)
Marine with Acis and Galatea (LV 141)

Dublin, National Gallery of Ireland
Landscape with Juno, Io and Argus (signed and dated 1660, LV 149)

Dumfries House (Scotland), The Marquess of Bute
Landscape with Shepherds
Port Scene (signed and dated 1638, LV 31)

Eaton Hall (Cheshire), Duke of Westminster
Landscape with the Flight into Egypt (signed and dated 1631)
Landscape with Dancing Figures (signed, date illegible)
Landscape with the Arch of Constantine (signed and dated 1651, LV 115)
Landscape with Shepherds (LV 124)
Landscape with the Arch of Titus (LV 153)

Edinburgh, National Gallery of Scotland
Landscape with Parnassus (signed and dated 1652, LV 126)

Elmira (New York), Arnot Art Gallery
Marine with Bacchus and Ariadne

Épinal, Musée Départemental des Vosges
Marine with the Embarkation of St Paula (LV 120)

Florence, Uffizi
Landscape with Dancing Figures (signed)
Port Scene with the Villa Medici (signed and dated 1637, LV 28)

Fort Worth (Texas), Kimbell Art Museum
Landscape with Shepherds (signed and dated 1677, LV 190)
Landscape with the Rape of Europa (signed)

France, private collection
Landscape with Shepherds

Frankfurt-am-Main, Städelsches Kunstinstitut
Landscape with the Appearance of Christ to the Magdalen (signed and dated 1681, LV 194)

Garrowby Hall (Yorkshire), Earl of Halifax
Landscape with Shepherds (signed, LV 23)

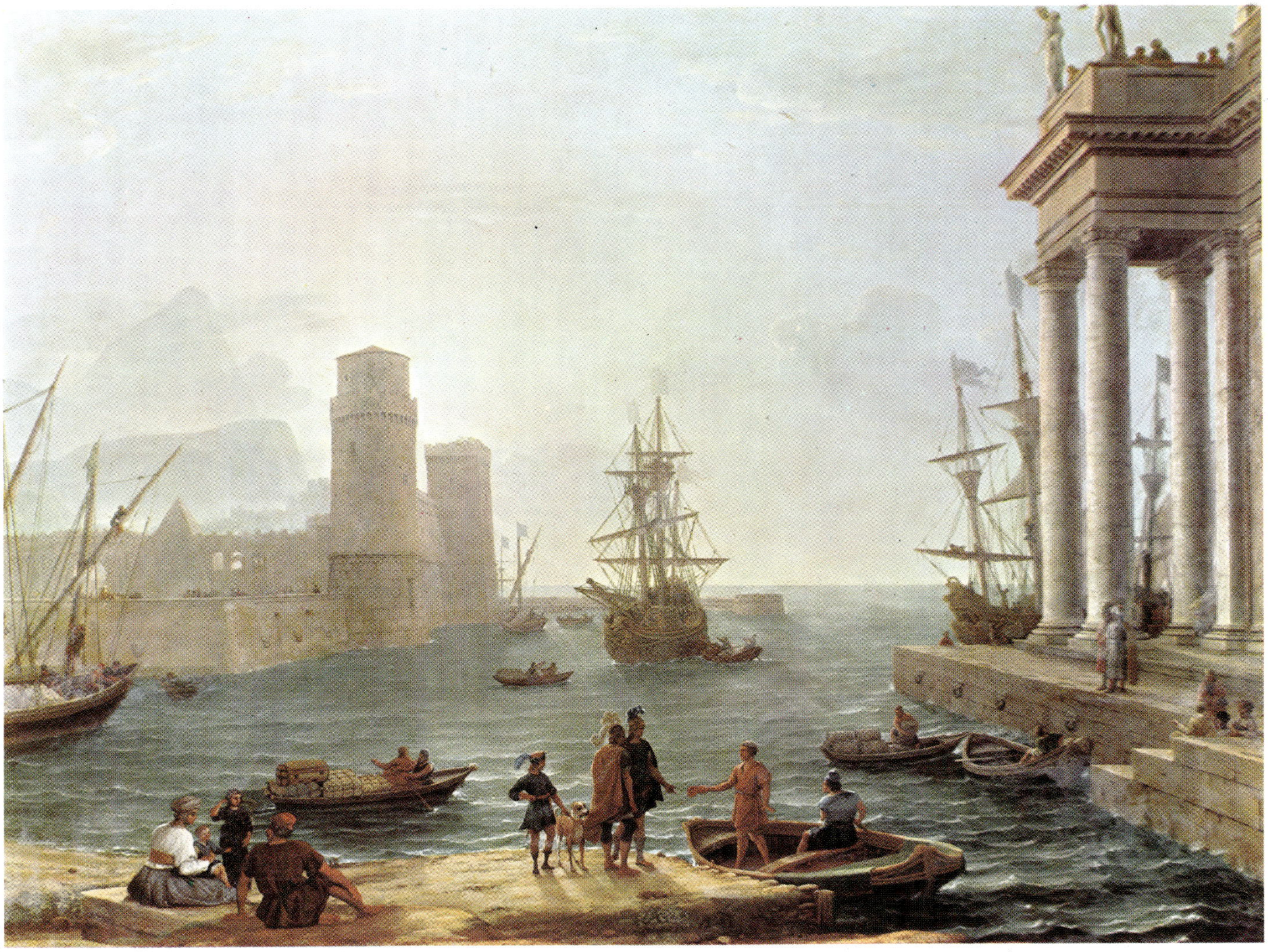

PLATE 19
Claude Lorrain
Port Scene with the Departure of Ulysses from the Land of the Feaci
Canvas, 119 × 150 cm. Signed and dated: CLAVDE IN. ROMA 1646
Liber Veritatis No.96
Paris, Louvre
Acquired by Louis XIV before 1695.

Great Britain, private collection
Port Scene (LV 19)

Great Britain, private collection
Landscape with Shepherds (signed and dated 1638, LV 25)

Great Britain, private collection
Landscape with Brigands (LV 34)

Great Britain, private collection
Landscape with Shepherds

Grenoble, Musée de Peinture et de Sculpture
Landscape with Shepherds

The Hague, Schilderijenzaal Prins Willem V
Marine with the Rape of Europa (LV 111)

Hamburg, Kunsthalle
View of Carthage with Dido and Aeneas about to Set out for the Hunt (signed and dated 1676, LV 186)

Hartford (Connecticut), Wadsworth Atheneum
Landscape with St George (signed, LV 73)

Holkham Hall (Norfolk), Earl of Leicester
Landscape with Shepherds
Landscape with Argus Looking after Io (LV 86)
Landscape with the Flaying of Marsyas (LV 95)
Landscape with Shepherds (LV 105)
Landscape with Apollo Guarding the Herds of Admetus (signed and dated 1654, LV 135)
Landscape with Esther Entering the Palace of Ahasuerus (fragment, LV 146)
Landscape with Erminia and the Shepherds (LV 166)
Marine with Perseus and the Origin of Coral (LV 184) (fig.47)
Landscape with the Rest on the Flight into Egypt (signed and dated 1676, LV 187)

Houston (Texas), Museum of Fine Arts
Landscape with a Rock Arch

Indianapolis, Museum of Art, Clowes collection
Landscape with the Flight into Egypt (signed)

Ireland, Lady Dunsany collection
Landscape with Hagar and the Angel (signed and dated 1656)

Jacksonville (Florida), Cummer Gallery
Perseus with Minerva Visits the Muses (signed and dated 1680, LV 195)

Kansas City, Nelson Gallery of Art
Landscape with Shepherds (LV 123)
Landscape with Shepherds (LV 172)

Karlsruhe, Staatliche Kunsthalle
Landscape with the Adoration of the Golden Calf (signed and dated 1652, LV 129)

Lawrence (Kansas), Art Museum
Landscape with a Draughtsman (attribution)

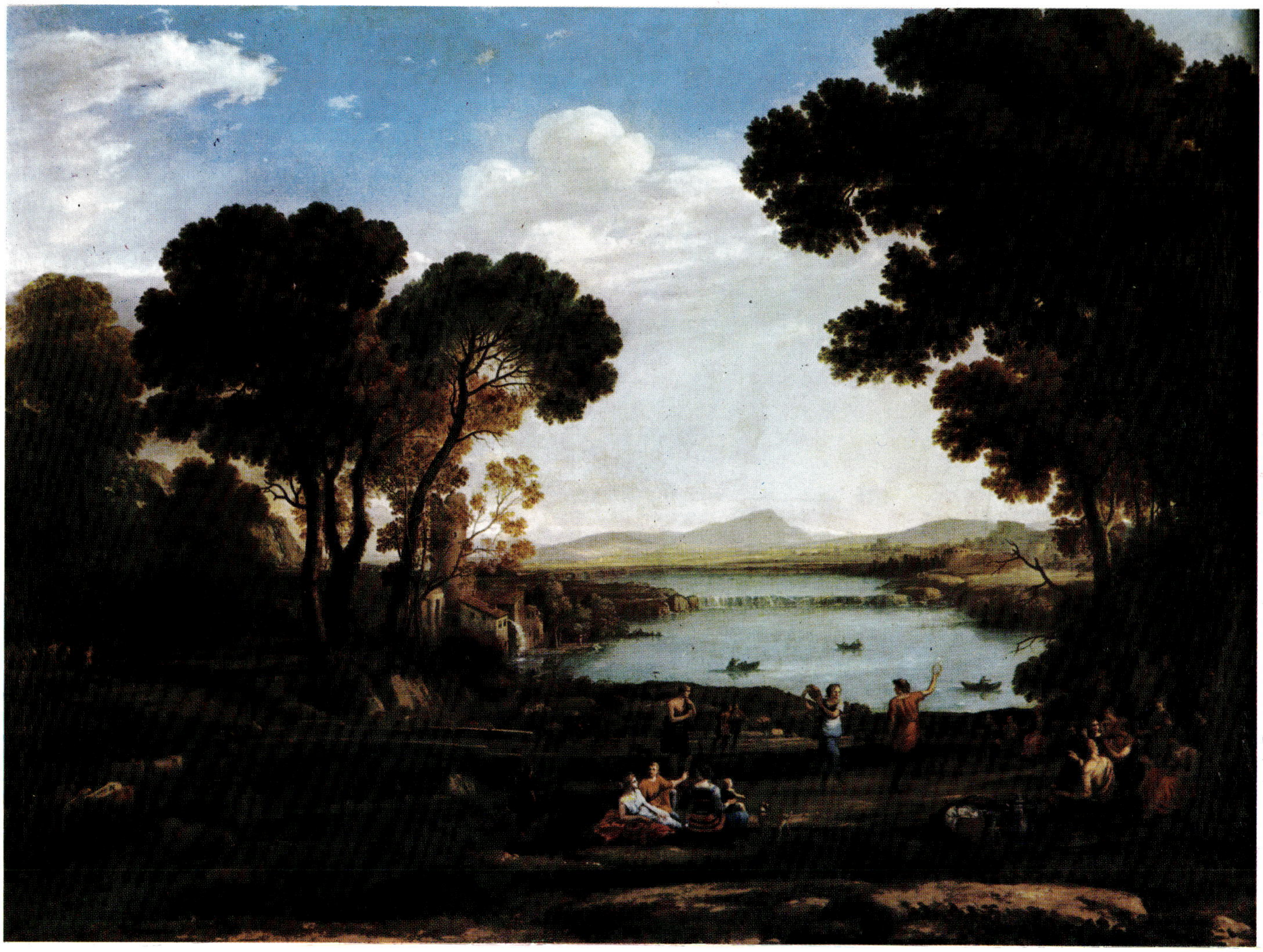

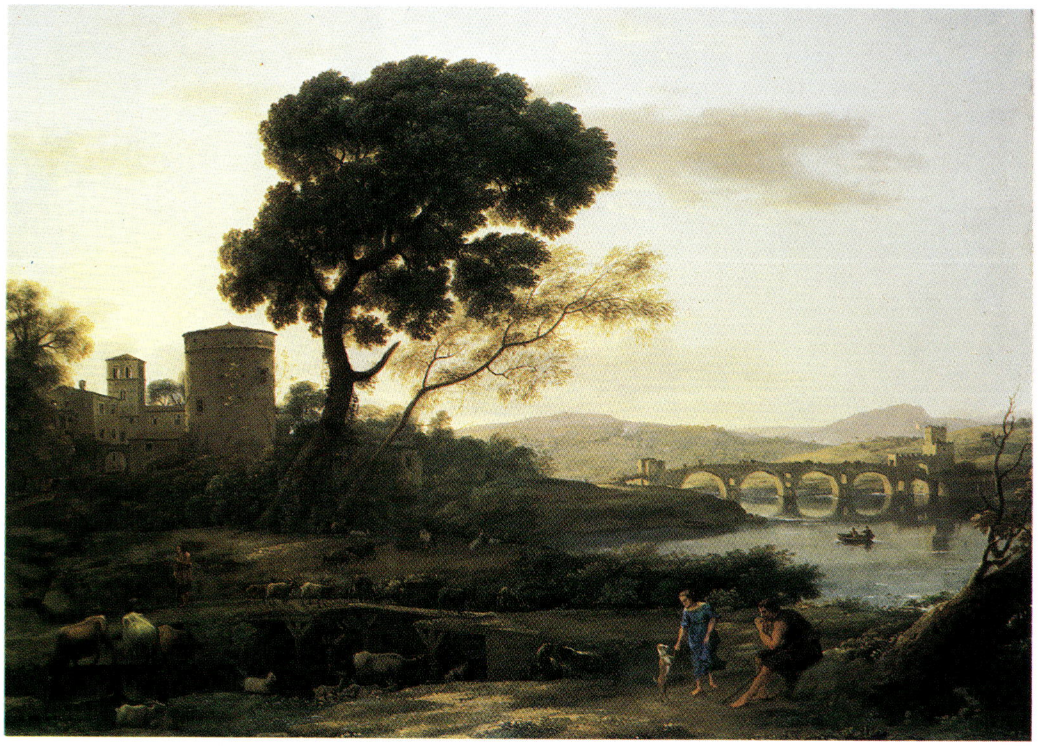

PLATE 20
Claude Lorrain
Landscape with Dancing Figures (The Mill)
Canvas, 150 × 200 cm. Traces of signature on rock in centre
Liber Veritatis No. 113
Rome, Galleria Doria
Painted for Prince Pamphili and by descent in the Doria-Pamphili family.

PLATE 21
Claude Lorrain
Landscape with Shepherds—the Ponte Molle
Canvas, 74 × 97 cm. Signed and dated below the shepherd: CLA... ROM... 1645
Liber Veritatis No. 90
Birmingham, City Art Gallery
According to the Liber Veritatis, painted for a Parisian collector, and first recorded in England in the Bragge sale in 1743. From 1760 in the celebrated Ashburnham collection. Bequeathed to the museum by Ernest Cook of Bath in 1955.

The picture is one of the rare works of Claude's maturity that depict an identifiable site.

Leningrad, Hermitage
Marine (LV 5)
Marine with Apollo and the Cumean Sybil (LV 99)
Landscape with Shepherds
Landscape with the Journey to Emmaus (LV 151)
Landscape with the Rest on the Flight into Egypt (signed and dated 1661, LV 154)
Landscape with Tobias and the Angel (LV 160)
Landscape with Jacob, Rachel and Leah at the Well (signed and dated 1666, LV 169)
Landscape with Dancing Figures
Landscape with Jacob Wrestling with the Angel (LV 181)

London, Courtauld Institute
Imaginary View of Tivoli (signed and dated 1642, LV 67)

London, Dulwich College Picture Gallery
Landscape with a Harvest Scene (LV 58)
Landscape with Jacob and Laban (signed and dated 1676, LV 188)

London, National Gallery
View of the Trinita dei Monti, Rome (signed and dated 1632)
Landscape with Shepherds (LV 15)
Port Scene (signed and dated 1639, LV 43)
Port Scene with the Embarkation of St Ursula (signed and dated 1641, LV 54, 198)
Landscape with Echo and Narcissus (signed and dated 1644, LV 77)
Landscape with Cephalus and Procris Reunited by Diana (signed and dated 1645, LV 91)
Landscape with Hagar and the Angel (LV 106)
Marriage of Isaac and Rebecca (signed and dated 1648, LV 113)
Port Scene with the Embarkation of the Queen of Sheba (signed and dated 1648, LV 114)
Landscape with David at the Cave of Abdullam (signed and dated 1658, LV 145)
Landscape with Psyche at the Castle of Amor (The Enchanted Castle) (LV 162) (fig.46)
Marine with Aeneas at Delos (signed and dated 1672, LV 179)

London, Wallace Collection
Landscape with Apollo and the Herds of Admetus (signed and dated 1660)

London, de Beer collection
Landscape with Hagar and the Angel (signed and dated 1654, LV 133)

London, Royal Collection, Buckingham Palace
View of the Countryside near Tivoli (signed, LV 89)
Marine with the Rape of Europa (signed and dated 1667, LV 136)

London, Mrs David Silver collection
Landscape with a Distant View of the Roman Campagna

Longford Castle (Wiltshire), Earl of Radnor
Marine with the Embarkation of Aeneas (signed and dated 1650, LV 122)
Landscape with the Arch of Titus (signed and dated 1644, LV 82)

Lugano, Thyssen collection
Landscape with the Flight into Egypt (signed and dated 1663, LV 158)

Madrid, Prado
Landscape with Shepherds
Landscape with Shepherds
Landscape with the Penitent Magdalen
Landscape with an Anchorite
Landscape with the Temptation of St Anthony (LV 32)
Landscape with the Finding of Moses (signed, LV 47)
Landscape with the Burial of St Serapia (LV 48)
The Port of Ostia with the Embarkation of St Paula (LV 49)
Landscape with Tobias and the Angel (signed, LV 50)
Landscape with Shepherds (signed and dated 1644, LV 85)

Manchester, City Art Gallery
Landscape with the Adoration of the Golden Calf (signed and dated 1660, LV 148) (fig.45)

Melbourne, National Gallery of Victoria
Landscape with the Temple of the Sybil at Tivoli

Merion (Pennsylvania), Barnes Foundation
Landscape with Shepherds (LV 87)

Mertoun (St Boswells), Duke of Sutherland
Landscape with Shepherds (LV 101)
Landscape with the Apulian Shepherd
Landscape with Moses and the Burning Bush (signed, LV 161)
Marine with Ezekiel Lamenting the Ruins of Tyre (LV 171, 200)

Milton Park (Peterborough), Earl Fitzwilliam
Landscape with Shepherds

Moscow, Pushkin Museum
Landscape with the Flaying of Marsyas (LV 45)
Marine with the Rape of Europa (signed and dated 1655, LV 136)
Marine with a Battle on a Bridge (signed and dated 1655, LV 137)

Munich, Alte Pinakothek
The Expulsion of Hagar (signed and dated 1668, LV 173) (plate 22)
Landscape with Hagar and the Angel (LV 174)
Landscape with Shepherds (signed and dated 1670, LV 176)

Nancy, Musée des Beaux-Arts
Landscape with a Shepherd

Naples, Capodimonte
Landscape with the Nymph Egeria (signed and dated 1669, LV 175)

New Bern (North Carolina), Tryon Palace
Landscape with Shepherds and Hunters (LV 40)

New Haven (Connecticut), Yale University Art Gallery
Landscape with Shepherds (LV 116)

New Orleans, Museum of Art
Imaginary View of Tivoli (LV 81)

New Orleans, private collection
Port Scene

New York, Frick Collection
Landscape with the Sermon on the Mount (LV 138)

New York, Metropolitan Museum
Landscape with Figures (signed and dated 1636, LV 8)
Landscape with Shepherds (signed and dated 1639, LV 42)
Marine with the Trojans Burning their Boats (signed, LV 71)
Landscape with Shepherds (signed, LV 109)
View of Crescenza (LV 118)

New York, Mrs Rush H. Kress
Landscape with Shepherds (signed and dated 16.., LV 121)

New York, Kauffman collection
Landscape with Shepherds

New York, Suida-Manning collection
Landscape with Shepherds

New York, with Wildenstein
River Landscape (LV 21)

New York, Mr and Mrs J. Seward Johnson
Landscape with Mercury and Battus (LV 131)
Marine with a Battle on a Bridge (LV 27)
Pastoral Landscape with a Watermill

New York, private collection
Landscape with Oenone

Nivagaard, Denmark, Hage collection
Landscape with the Flight into Egypt (signed, LV 104)

Norfolk (Virginia), Chrysler Museum
River Landscape (attribution)

Nostell Priory, Wakefield, Lord St Oswald
Landscape with the Flight into Egypt (signed)

Notre Dame (Indiana), University Art Gallery
Landscape with the Rest on the Flight into Egypt (LV 38)

Oakley Park (Shropshire), Earl of Plymouth
Landscape with Cephalus and Procris Reunited by Diana (signed and dated 1664, LV 163)

Omaha (Nebraska), Joslyn Art Museum
Landscape with the Rest on the Flight into Egypt

Ottawa, National Gallery of Canada
Landscape with Shepherds (LV 78)

Oxford, Ashmolean Museum
Landscape with Shepherds
Landscape with Ascanius Shooting the Stag of Sylvia (signed and dated 1682) (plate 24)

Paris, Louvre
The Siege of La Rochelle (signed and dated 16..) (fig.43)
View of the Pass of Susa (signed and dated 163.) (fig.44)
Marine
Landscape with Shepherds
View of Genoa
The Campo Vaccino, Rome (signed, LV 9) (plate 17)
Port Scene with the Campidoglio (signed, LV 9)
Landscape with Dancing Figures (signed and dated 1639, LV 13, 36, 37)
Port Scene (signed and dated 1639, LV 14)
Landscape with Shepherds (LV 41)
Port Scene with the Embarkation of Cleopatra for Tarsus (signed, LV 63)
Landscape with Samuel Consecrating David, King of Israel (LV 69)
Landscape with Ulysses Restoring Cressida to Crise (signed, LV 80)
Port Scene with the Departure of Ulysses from the Land of the Feaci (signed and dated 1646, LV 96) (plate 19)
Landscape with Paris and Oenone (LV 117)

Paris, Petit Palais
Landscape with the Port of Santa Marinella (LV 146)

Paris, private collection
Port Scene (signed and dated 163., LV 26)

Pasadena (California), Norton Simon Museum
Landscape with Shepherds (signed)
Landscape with Jacob and Laban (signed and dated 1659, LV 147)

Petworth (Sussex), National Trust
Landscape with Jacob and Laban (signed and dated 1654, LV 134)

Philadelphia, Museum of Art
Landscape with Shepherds (signed and dated 1629)

Raleigh, North Carolina Museum of Art
Landscape with Shepherds (LV 20)

Richmond, Virginia Museum of Fine Arts
Marine with a Battle on a Bridge (signed and dated 1655, LV 137)

Rome, Palazzo Crescenzi
Eight landscape frescoes (attribution)

Rome, Galleria Doria
Landscape with the Rest on the Flight into Egypt
Landscape with Apollo Guarding the Herds of Admetus (signed, LV 92)
Landscape with Cephalus and Procris Reunited by Diana
Landscape with Dancing Figures (The Mill) (LV 113) (plate 20)
View of Delphi with a Procession (signed and dated 1650, LV 119)

Rome, Galleria Pallavicini
Landscape with Shepherds (signed, LV 15)
Marine with Mercury and Aglaurus
Landscape with Bacchus at the Palace of Staphilus (LV 178)

Rotterdam, Museum Boymans-van Beuningen
Landscape with Figures

Saint Louis, Art Museum
Landscape with Dancing Figures (traces of signature)

San Diego (California), Timken Art Gallery
Landscape with Shepherds (LV 103)

San Francisco (California), Palace of the Legion of Honor
Landscape with Shepherds

San Marino (California), Huntington Library
Marine (LV 2)

Springfield (Massachusetts), Art Museum
Capriccio with the Ruins of the Roman Forum (LV 1)

Strasbourg, Musée des Beaux-Arts
Landscape with the Flight into Egypt (signed and dated 1645)

Strathfield Saye (Hampshire), Duke of Wellington
Port of Ostia with the Embarkation of St Paula (signed, LV 61)
Landscape with Shepherds (LV 62)

Tokyo, Imperial Museum (lost since 1872)
Port Scene (signed and dated 1636, LV 6)

Toledo (Ohio), Museum of Art
Landscape with Dancing Satyrs and Figures (LV 55)

Toronto, Art Gallery of Ontario
Marine with the Embarkation of Carlo and Ubaldo (LV 168)

Vienna, Akademie der bildenden Künste
Landscape with a Satyr
Landscape with Sheep (formerly signed and dated 1656)

Washington, National Gallery
River Landscape (signed and dated 1630)
Landscape with Merchants (signed) (plate 18)
Landscape with the Judgment of Paris (LV 94)

Welbeck Abbey (Nottinghamshire), Duke of Portland
Landscape with Shepherds (LV 18)

Williamstown (Massachusetts), Sterling and Francine Clark Art Institute
Landscape with the Rest on the Flight into Egypt (signed and dated 1646, LV 84)
Landscape with Jacob's Journey (signed and dated 1677, LV 189)

Windsor Castle, Royal Collection
Port Scene (LV 19)
Landscape with Shepherds (LV 83)

Woburn Abbey, Duke of Bedford
Landscape with Dancing Figures (signed and dated 1640, LV 53)

Unlocated private collections in roughly chronological order:
Landscape with Ruins (attribution)
Landscape with Shepherds (attribution)
Landscape with Shepherds (attribution)
Landscape with Shepherds (attribution)
Wooded Landscape with a Waterfall
Marine (signed and dated 1630)

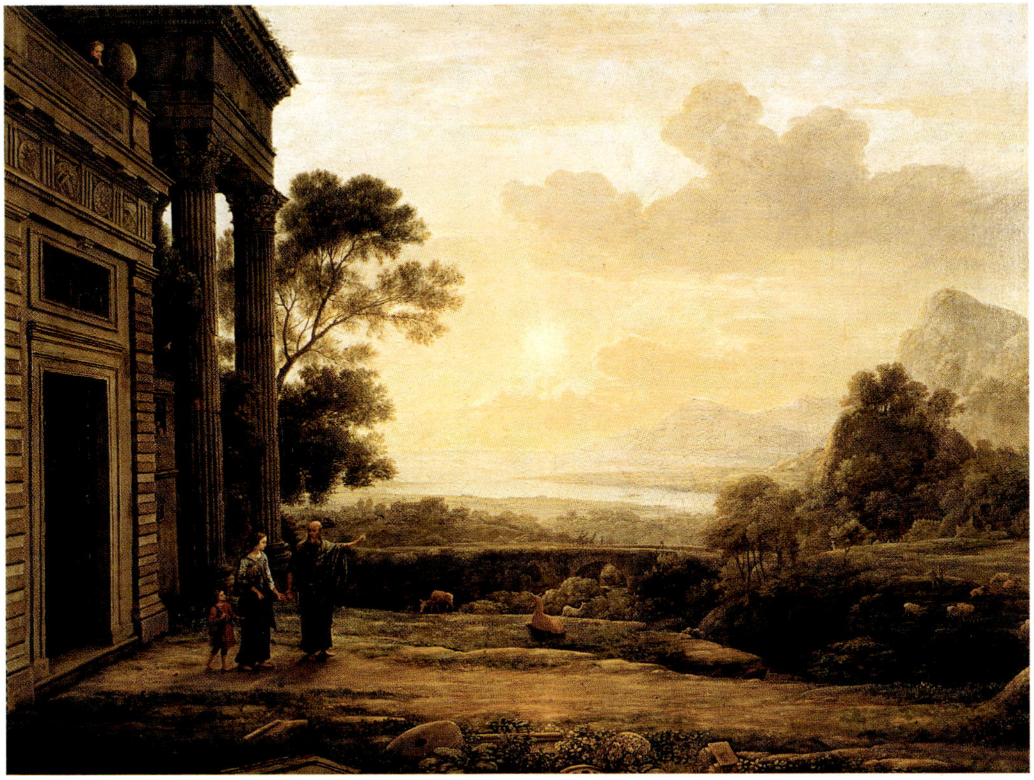

PLATE 22
Claude Lorrain
The Expulsion of Hagar
Canvas, 107 × 140 cm. Signed and dated lower left:
CLAVDE GELLE IVF ROMA 1668
Liber Veritatis No.173
Munich, Alte Pinakothek
Along with its pendant, in the Electoral picture gallery at Zweibrücken. Transferred to Munich in 1799 and to the Pinakothek in 1836.

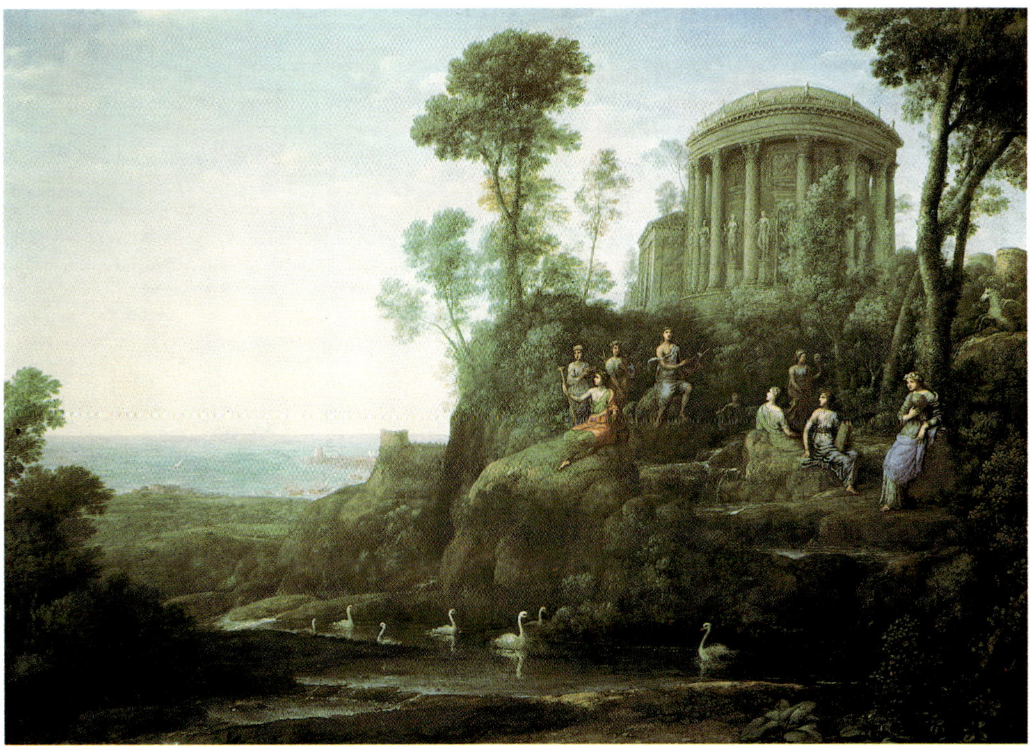

PLATE 23
Claude Lorrain
Apollo and the Muses on Mount Helion (Parnassus)
Canvas, 98 × 135 cm. Signed and dated lower centre:
Claudio IV fecit 1680.
Liber Veritatis No.193
Boston, Museum of Fine Arts
Acquired by the museum in 1890.

This work was painted for the Principe Colonna, and was in the family collection until at least 1783.

Landscape with Shepherds
Landscape with the Journey to Emmaus
Landscape with a Shepherd
Landscape with the Rest on the Flight into Egypt (signed)
Landscape with Shepherds (LV 11)
Landscape with Shepherds and a Ruined Temple
Landscape with Shepherds (signed LV 39)
Landscape with the Journey of Eleazer and Rebecca (LV 52)
Landscape with Satyrs and Nymphs Dancing (signed and dated 1646, LV 108)
Marine with Apollo and the Cumean Sybil (LV 164)
Landscape with Apollo Guarding the Herds of Admetus
Landscape with Juno Confiding Io to Argus (signed and dated 1668)

PLATE 24
Claude Lorrain
Landscape with Ascanius Shooting the Stag of Sylvia
Canvas, 120 × 150 cm. Signed and dated lower centre: CLAVDIO. I.V.F. A ROMAE 1682 Come. Asciano. saettà il. Cervo di Silvia figliuola di. Tirro lib. 7. Vig.
Oxford, Ashmolean Museum
Like the Boston *Apollo and the Muses on Mount Helion*, painted for the Principe Colonna. Still in the collection in 1783. Brought to England by 1798/9 and given to the museum by Mrs. F. Weldon in 1926.

One of Claude's purest inspirations from the poetry of Virgil, this painting shows the accidental shooting of the precious stag that unleashes a bitter war.

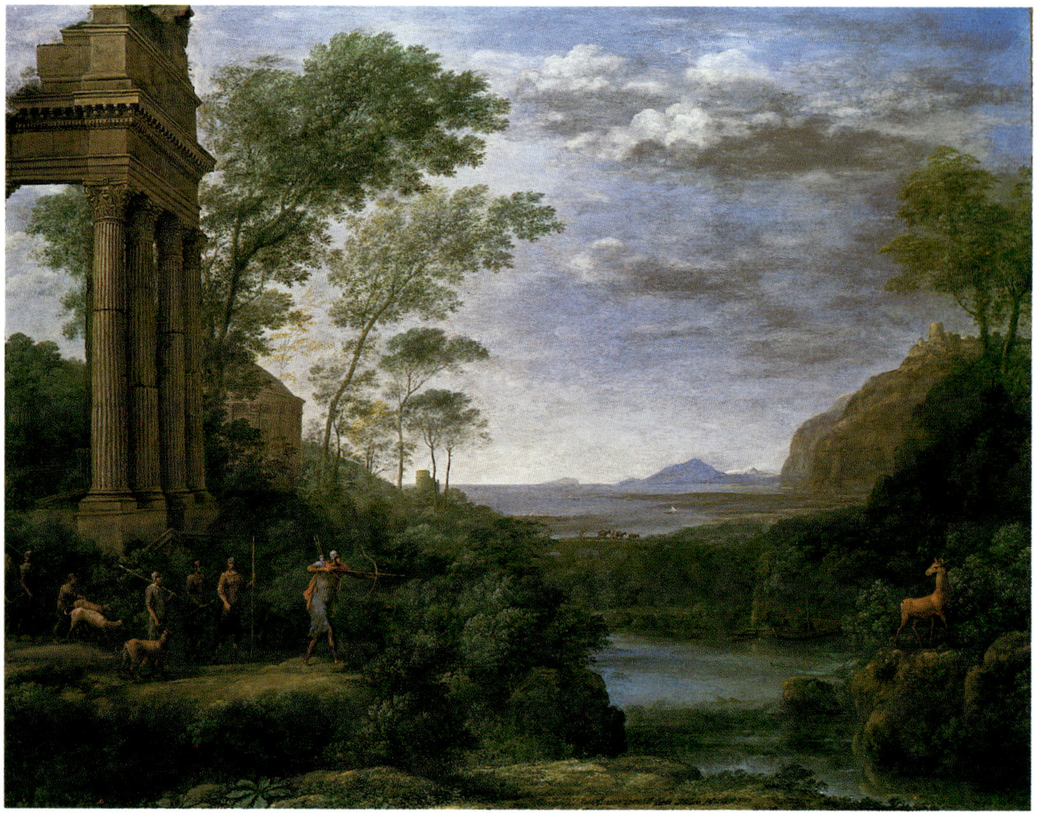

Bibliography

The standard for work on Claude's paintings is the *catalogue raisonné* by Marcel Röthlisberger: *Claude Lorrain—The Paintings*, New Haven, 1961. Some new information was incorporated in Marcel Röthlisberger and Doretta Cecchi, *L'opera completa di Claude Lorrain*, Milan, 1975. The specialist literature on Claude's paintings has concentrated on newly discovered early works and on pictures in British collections. Especially useful is the exhibition catalogue by Michael Kitson, Newcastle upon Tyne, Laing Art Gallery, and London, Hayward Gallery, *Claude Lorrain*, 1969. The standard work on the drawings is Marcel Röthlisberger, *Claude Lorrain—The Drawings*, Berkeley, 1968. The most useful new contribution to Claude studies with a complete reassessment of his graphic work is H. Diane Russel, in the exhibition catalogue, *Claude Gellée*, Washington, National Gallery, Paris, Grand Palais, 1982–3. Claude's influence on two centuries of painters of different nationalities was admirably demonstrated in the exhibition catalogue *Im Licht von Claude Lorrain*, Munich, Haus der Kunst, 1983.

Nicolas Colombel

Sotteville (near Rouen) 1646–Paris 1717

Almost all Colombel's pictures are severe renderings of Poussin's compositions and themes. Colombel was a pupil of Eustache Le Sueur in Paris, and then studied in Rome, not returning to Paris until 1694. His pictures have been confused with the work of many other artists, including Benjamin West.

Collections

Baroda (India), Museum
The Magdalen before Christ

Budapest, Szépmüvészeti Múzeum
Hagar and the Angel

Cherbourg, Musée Thomas Henry
Pyramus and Thisbe (attribution)

Greenville (South Carolina), Bob Jones University
The Finding of Moses

Los Angeles, County Museum
Christ and the Woman Taken in Adultery

New Orleans, Museum of Art
Adoration of the Kings

Paris, École des Beaux-Arts
Mars and Rhea Sylvia

Paris, Louvre
St Hyacinthe Saving the Statue of the Virgin from the Enemies of Christianity

Phoenix (Arizona), Art Museum
Haman Begs for his Life (attribution)

Rouen, Musée des Beaux-Arts
St Cecilia

Saint Louis (Missouri), Art Museum
Christ Healing the Blind
Christ Driving the Money Changers from the Temple

Salzburg, Residenzgalerie
Christ and the Samaritan Woman

Stanford (California), University Art Museum
Moses and the Daughters of Jethro

Villeneuve-lès-Avignon, Museum
St Bruno

Wilton House (Wiltshire), Earl of Pembroke
Narcissus

Bibliography

The only recent study of all the known works, with a number of new attributions, is Anthony Blunt, 'Nicolas Colombel', *Revue de l'Art*, 1970, pp.27–36.

Meiffren Conte

Marseilles ?c.1630–Marseilles 1705

Conte's long career was spent in Provence, and only in recent years has his considerable *oeuvre* been identified. Almost all his pictures are of elaborately chased gold and silver vessels placed in sumptuous arrangements. The reason for the neglect, when similar pictures by Dutch artists continued to be esteemed, was his curious naïvety in the depiction of objects, which nevertheless lacked the primitive vision of Stoskopff, who can still delight today.

Collections

Arles, Musée Réattu
Young Woman at the Mirror
Pitcher, Chinese Vase and Red Draperies

Béziers, private collection
Pitcher, Gourd, Flowers and Shells

France, private collections
Pitchers, Fruits and Shells
Pitchers, Flowers and Shells
Pitchers and Vase of Flowers
Pitchers, Flowers, Fruit and Shells
Pitcher, Oval Dish and Shells
Miniature Chest, Chinese Vase, Oval Dish and Violin
Pitcher, Dish of Fruit, Shells and Grapes
Perfume Burner, Flambeau of Hercules, Pitchers, Porphyry Vase with Flowers and Blue Drapery

Karlsruhe, Staatliche Kunsthalle
Pitcher, Flambeau of Hercules, Armorial and Shells against a Landscape Background (fig. 51)

Marseilles, Palais Longchamp
Pitcher, Dagger, Flowers and Shells
Perfume Burner and Book, Lemon and Shells

Marseilles, Gastaut collection
Needle Box, Pyx, Mirror and Flowers
Pitcher, Shells and Armorial (signed)
Pitcher, Oval Dish, Flowers and Shells
Needle Box, Flowers, Parrot and Engraving

Marseilles, private collection
Pitchers and Overturned Vases

Paris, Musée des Arts Décoratifs
Vases, Pitchers and Shells
Pitcher, Perfume Burner, Flambeau of Hercules Shells and Flowers

Paris, J. P. Cholet collection
Pitchers, Flowers, Shells and a Parrot against a Landscape Background
Pitchers, Vases, Fruits and Shells against a Landscape Background

Paris, P. Seghers collection
Vase of Flowers, Map of the World and Silver on a Carpet

Paris, with Heim Gallery
Pitcher, Oval Dish and Flambeau of Hercules
Pitcher, Plate and Basket of Flowers

Paris, private collections
Miniature Chest, Oval Dish, Pitcher and Shells
Pitchers, Flowers and Fruit against the Sky
Perfume Burner, Pitcher, Miniature Chest and Shells
Silver, Shells, Books and Violin
Pitchers and Flambeau of Hercules
Pitchers, Oval Dish and Flambeau of Hercules, Fruit and Shells against a Landscape Background
Pitcher, Miniature Chest, Flowers, Fruit and Shells against a Landscape Background
Pitcher, Lute, Open Book, Watch, Flowers and Blue Drapery
Miniature Chest, Bronze Statuette, Watch and Red Drapery

Private collection
Perfume Burner, Vase, Shells and Medallion

Quimper, Musée des Beaux-Arts
Pitchers, Flute and Shells

Saint-Étienne, Musée d'Art et d'Industrie
Pitcher, Perfume Burner, Sword and Shells

Switzerland, private collection
Pitcher, Gourd, Vase, Perfume Burner, Sword, Fruit and Shells against a Landscape Background

Toulon, Musée d'Art et d'Archéologie
Pitcher and Overturned Vases

Valenciennes, Musée des Beaux-Arts
Pitcher, Gourd, Clock, Flowers, Fruit and Shells

Warsaw, National Museum
Pitcher, Oval Plate, Marble Vase and Shells
Pitchers, Vase, Miniature Chest and Fruit

Bibliography

Michel Faré
Le grand siècle de la nature morte en France, 1974, pp.205–33.
Nathalie Voille
in the exhibition catalogue, Marseilles, Palais Longchamp, *La peinture en Provence au XVIIe siècle*, 1978, pp.17–25.

Jean-Baptiste Corneille

Paris 1649–Paris 1695

Pupil of his father Michel Corneille I, Jean-Baptiste was received into the French Academy in Paris in 1675. His *Resurrection of Lazarus* at Rouen was painted for the Paris Charterhouse, in a style which was very much up to date for the time, probably the 1680s, when the artist's style was close to that of Charles de La Fosse.

Collections

Brest, Musée des Beaux-Arts
Venus and Vulcan
(monogrammed)

Dijon, Musée des Beaux-Arts
The Guardian Angel
The Death of Cato (signed and dated 1687)
The Appearance of the Virgin to St Bernard
The Burning of Troy

Dijon, Musée Magnin
The Assassination of Archimedes

Les Andelys, Le Grand Andely, Church
The Resurrection of Lazarus
(replica)

Rouen, Musée des Beaux-Arts
The Resurrection of Lazarus
(signed)

Tournai, Musée des Beaux-Arts
Martyrdom of a Bishop

Bibliography

There is no recent literature on this artist, but see Pierre Rosenberg in Rouen, Musée des Beaux-Arts, *Tableaux français du XVIIe siècle ...*, 1966, p.15.

Michel Corneille I

Orléans 1602–Paris 1664

Corneille's *Esau and Jacob* at Orléans is an altogether exceptional picture because it shows the artist to have been preoccupied with a realism exactly paralleled in the work of the young Rembrandt.

Collections

Arras, Palais Saint-Vaast
St Paul and St Barnabas at Lystra
(signed and dated 1644)

Le Mans, Musée de Tessé
The Visitation (signed and dated 1650)

Orléans, Musée des Beaux-Arts
Esau Selling his Birthright to Jacob
(signed and dated 1630) (fig. 61)

Toulouse, Saint-Pierre
The Baptism of the Centurion
(dated 1658)

Tours, Musée des Beaux-Arts
The Massacre of the Innocents

Bibliography

Charles Sterling in the exhibition catalogue, Paris, Orangerie, *Les peintres de la réalité*, 1934, pp.30–32.

Michel Corneille II

Paris 1642–Paris 1708

Corneille II was a pupil of Charles Le Brun, and his style reflects that fact. He was received into the French Academy in Paris in 1663; and he executed an enormous number of engravings after both French and Italian artists.

Collections

Angers, Musée des Beaux-Arts
Virgin and Child and St John
(documented 1672)

Arras, Palais Saint-Vaast
The Calling of St Peter and St Andrew

Chantilly, Musée Condé
Allegory of Repentance
(documented 1691)

Dijon, Musée des Beaux-Arts
Assumption of the Virgin

Florence, Uffizi
The Finding of Zenobia
(attribution)

Greenville (South Carolina), Bob Jones University
Holy Family with St Joseph
(attribution)

Leningrad, Hermitage
Holy Family

Nantes, Musée des Beaux-Arts
St Genevieve Receiving a Palm from St Médard

Orléans, Musée des Beaux-Arts
St Jerome and the Angel

Paris, Louvre
The Celestial Glory (reduced copy of Mignard's decoration of the cupola of the Val-de-Grâce, Paris)
Rest on the Flight into Egypt

Rennes, Musée des Beaux-Arts
The Calling of St Peter and St Andrew

Stuttgart, Staatsgalerie
Holy Family with Marble Vases

Versailles, Château
Portrait of Philippe de France, 'Monsieur'
Allegory of the Glory of Louis XIV
Isis and Jupiter
Day
Evening
Judgment of Midas
Zephyrus and Flora
Acis and Galatea
Decoration of the *Salon des Nobles de la Reine*
Night
Mars

Bibliography

There is no recent literature on this artist.

Guillaume Courtois (Guglielmo Cortese)

Saint Hippolyte (Doubs) 1628–Rome 1679

Guillaume collaborated with his brother, Jacques Courtois, the specialist painter of battle scenes, but his work is distinguishable from his brother's by a concentration on subject pictures in an Italian Baroque style.

Collections

Greenville (South Carolina), Bob Jones University
Sarah Carried towards the House of Abimelech

Leningrad, Hermitage
The Martyrdom of St Peter Dominic

Princeton, Art Museum
The Flight into Egypt

Stockholm, Nationalmuseum
Christ in the House of Mary and Martha

Bibliography

There is no recent literature on this artist.

Jacques Courtois (called Le Bourguignon or Il Borgognone)

Saint Hippolyte (Doubs) 1621–Rome 1676

Courtois is an example of a painter who has escaped notice in terms of art history, because of both his isolation from his native Franche Comté (incorporated into France by Louis XIV) and his lack of association with Italian art, even though he spent his whole career in Rome. Courtois evolved the archetypal small battle piece, depicting plenty of violence and the smoke of combat, a format that was to remain standard right up to the end of the eighteenth century, though few of its exponents were French. Authentic works by Courtois frequently appear on the art market, but much of his *oeuvre* has still to be identified.

Collections

Ansbach, Residenzgalerie
Cavalry Battle
Infantry

Baltimore, Walters Art Gallery
Review of Cavalry

Bayreuth, Neues Schloss
Battle between Cavalry and Turks

Besançon, Musée des Beaux-Arts
Battle Piece
Cavalry Combat
Cavalry Crossing a Bridge
Cavalry Battle

Boston, Museum of Fine Arts
Battle Scene

Brest, Musée des Beaux-Arts
Battle Piece (2)

Caen, Musée des Beaux-Arts
Battle Piece

Chalon-sur-Saône, Musée Denon
Cavalry Combat

Darmstadt, Hessisches Landesmuseum
Cavalry Battle

Detroit, Institute of Arts
Battle Scene

Dijon, Musée des Beaux-Arts
Cavalry Combat (2)
Battle Piece (2)

Dunkirk, Musée des Beaux-Arts
Cavalry Battle

Edinburgh, National Gallery of Scotland
Battle Piece

Edinburgh, University
A Skirmish

Ellingen, Schloss
Moses and the Amalekites
Four Battle Scenes
After the Battle

Épinal, Musée Départemental des Vosges
Battle Piece

Florence, Galleria Pitti
Conversion of St Paul
Battle Scene

Florence, Uffizi
Self-portrait
The Battle of Mongiovino (plate 25)

Gray, Musée Baron Martin
Cavalry Combat (2)

The Hague, Mauritshuis
Cavalry Engagement

Karlsruhe, Staatliche Kunsthalle
Battle Piece (2) (attribution)

Kassel, Staatliche Gemäldegalerie
Battle Piece

Leeds, Temple Newsam House
Battle Piece (attribution)

Leningrad, Hermitage
Cavalry Battle
Battle between the French and Spanish
Cavalry
Cavalry Skirmish
Battlefield
Cavalry and Infantry Battle
Cavalry Battle

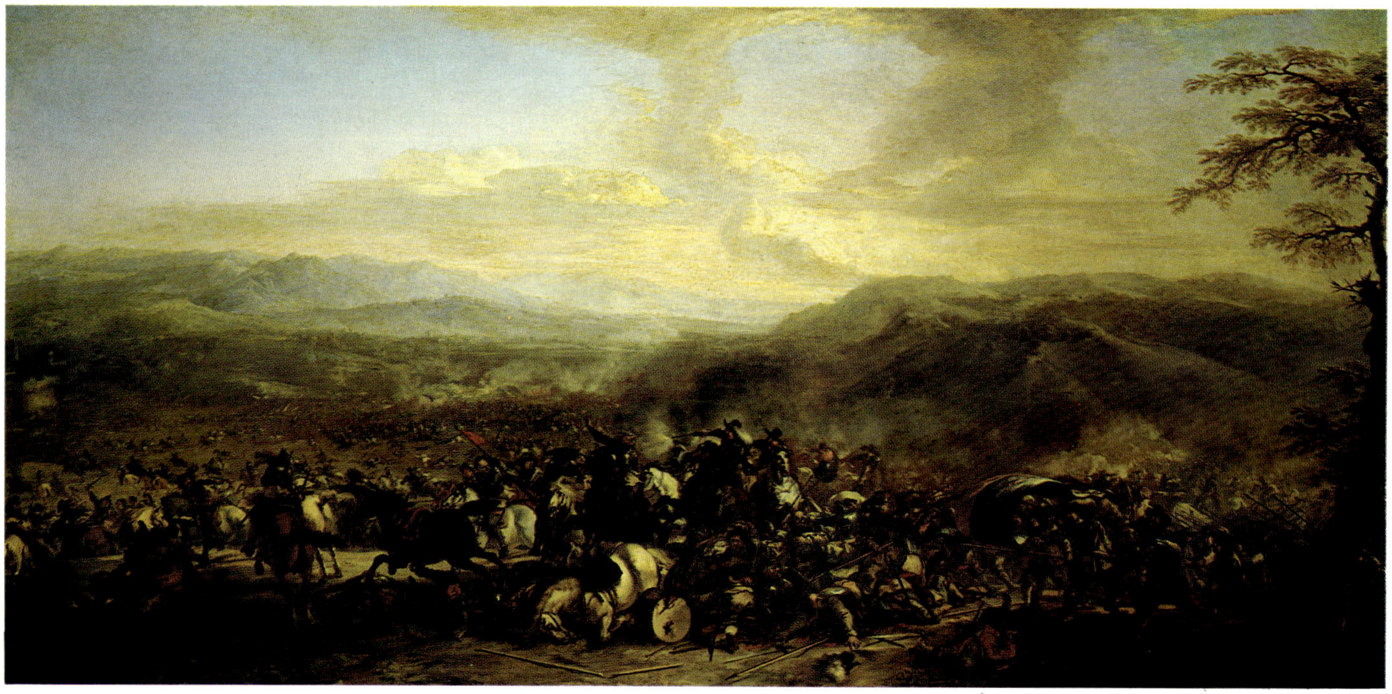

PLATE 25
Jacques Courtois
The Battle of Mongiovino
Canvas, 138 × 276 cm. Signed centre: Iacomo Cortesi
Florence, Uffizi
In the collection of Don Mattias de' Medici, brother of the Grand Duke Ferdinand II, by 1659. Transferred from the Pitti to the Uffizi in 1773.

One of a series of battle pieces representing the victories of the patron, in this instance against the troops of Pope Urban VIII in 1643.

Battle
Cavalry Skirmish
Landscape with Horsemen on the Road

Lexington, Washington and Lee University
Battle Scene

Madrid, Prado
Battle between Christians and Turks
Battle for Possession of a Fortress
Cavalry Charge
Cavalry Battle

Nancy, Musée des Beaux-Arts
Cavalry near a Bridge

Nantes, Musée des Beaux-Arts
Battle Piece (attribution)
Battlefield after Combat (attribution)

New York, Brooklyn Museum
Battle Scene (attribution)

Oxford, Christ Church
Cavalry Skirmish

Paris, Louvre
Joshua Defeating the Amalekites
Joshua Commanding the Sun to Stand Still
Cavalry Encounter
Engagement with Turkish Cavalry
Cavalry Combat

Phoenix (Arizona), Art Museum
Meeting of Cavaliers

Portland (Oregon), Art Museum
Battle Piece (attribution)

Princeton, Art Museum
Conversion of St Paul (attribution)

San Francisco, Art Museums
'After the Battle'

Shawnee (Oklahoma), Mabee-Gerrer Museum
Battle Scene

Stockholm, Nationalmuseum
Battle Piece
Battle on a Bridge
Cavalry Battle

Stourhead House (Wiltshire), National Trust
Battle Scene

Tours, Musée des Beaux-Arts
Cavalry Combat

Versailles, Château
Cavalry Combat
March of the Troops
Battle of Arbela

Warsaw, National Museum
Battle Scene

Bibliography

Charles Sterling in the exhibition catalogue, Paris, Orangerie, *Les peintres de la réalité*, 1934, pp.32–4.
A good general article is E. Holt, '*The Jesuit battle painter Jacques Courtois*', *Apollo*, March 1969, pp.212–23.

Noël Coypel

Paris 1628–Paris 1707

Coypel's active career spanned almost fifty years. He replaced Le Sueur in the decoration of the Royal apartments in Paris in 1655. At this time his work was strongly influenced by Poussin. He became a member of the Academy in 1663, and in 1672 Louis XIV made him director of the French Academy in Rome. Although the influence of Poussin is always detectable, Coypel's colours were much closer to Rubens. His *Cain and Abel* of 1663, the Academy reception piece, is also close to Le Brun.

Collections

Angers, Musée des Beaux-Arts
Zephyr and Flora

Avignon, Musée Calvet
Apollo

Besançon, Musée des Beaux-Arts
The Painter and his Daughter

Bordeaux, Musée des Beaux-Arts
The Triumph of Apollo

Chalon-sur-Saône, Musée Denon
Orpheus and Euridice

Dijon, Musée des Beaux-Arts
St Genevieve Receiving a Medal from St Germain

Dublin, National Gallery of Ireland
Neptune and Amphitrite (attribution)

Fontainebleau, Château
Apollo Crowned by Minerva

Le Mans, Musée de Tessé
Ariadne Abandoned by Theseus on the Isle of Naxos
The Nymph Galatea

Le Puy, Musée Crozatier
Ecce Homo

Lille, Palais des Beaux-Arts
Hercules Fighting Achelous

Lyons, Musée des Beaux-Arts
Earth

Marseilles, Palais Longchamp
Apollo and Marsyas
Mercury and Endymion

Montpellier, Musée Fabre
Christ Healing a Blind Man

Norfolk (Virginia), Chrysler Museum
The Emperor Trajan Giving a Public Audience (attribution)

Notre Dame (Indiana), University Art Gallery
The Resurrection

Paris, Louvre
Solon Proposing the Justice of his Laws against the Objections of the Athenians (documented 1699)
Ptolemy Philadelphus Giving Liberty to the Jews (documented 1699)
The Emperor Trajan Giving a Public Audience (documented 1699)
Alexander Severus Distributing Grain to the People of Rome during the Famine (documented 1699)
The Reproof of Cain after the Death of Abel (documented 1663)
Apollo Crowned by Victory
Apollo Crowned by Minerva
Triumph of Minerva
Triumph of Mars
Triumph of Bacchus
Triumph of Apollo

Rennes, Musée des Beaux-Arts
The Resurrection (signed and dated 1700)

Rouen, Musée des Beaux-Arts
The Emperor Trajan giving a Public Audience (attribution)

Tournus, Musée Greuze
Achilles Recognized by Ulysses in the House of Lycomedes

Versailles, Château
Decoration of the Salle des Gardes de la Reine
Apollo Vanquishing the Serpent Python
Apollo and Mercury
Allegorical Figure
Hercules Sacrificing to Jupiter
Jupiter Appearing to Hercules
Deianira Sending the Poisoned Shirt of Nessus to Hercules
Hercules and Achelous
Hercules and Nessus
Abundance
Apollo Crowned by Victory
Nymphs Presenting a Cornucopia to Amalthea
Apotheosis of Hercules

Bibliography

There is no recent literature on this artist.

Pierre Louis Cretey

1645?–Paris 1721

Apparently Cretey worked in Lyons, where he is documented in the 1680s. His *Nativity* at Detroit appears to be influenced by Charles Le Brun.

Collection

Detroit Institute of Arts
The Nativity

Bibliography

There is no recent literature on this artist.

Jean-Pierre Crozier

Marseilles 1623/1626?–Aix-en-Provence ?1658

Crozier was totally out of touch with his times, painting in a 'natural' style unaffected by either the Baroque or Caravaggism. The composition of his one surviving picture seems like an inept version of an Italian sixteenth-century altarpiece.

Collection

Aix-en-Provence, Musée des Tapisseries
The Holy Innocents Resuscitated by the Infant Christ (signed and dated 1654)

Bibliography

Marie-Christine Gloton in the exhibition catalogue, Marseilles, Palais Longchamp, *La peinture en Provence au XVIIe siècle*, 1978, pp.25–6.

Jean-Claude Cundier

Aix-en-Provence 1650–Aix-en-Provence 1718

Cundier continued the style of Laurent Fauchier at Aix in the last years of the seventeenth century, but his portraits were much weaker than those of Fauchier.

Collections

Aix-en-Provence, Musée Granet
A Woman with a Pearl Necklace (signed and dated on the reverse 1670)
An Old Woman

Lanson, Church
Assumption of the Virgin (signed and dated 1690)

Luynes, Centre de Protection Civile
Presumed Portrait of Madeleine de Trets and her Daughter (signed)

Marseilles, Palais Longchamp
Charles de Grimaldi

Saint-Maximin, Basilique
The Magdalen with the Pot of Ointment (signed and dated 1703)

Ventabren, Church
Holy Family (signed)

Vitrolles, Church
Assumption of the Virgin (signed)

Bibliography

Henri Wytenhove in the exhibition catalogue, Marseilles, Palais Longchamp, *La peinture en Provence au XVIIe siècle*, 1978, pp.27–8.

Jean Daret

Brussels 1613 or 1615?–Aix-en-Provence 1668

Daret, the most promising of all the painters to settle in Aix-en-Provence, had arrived there by 1637. He became the most important painter and decorative artist in Aix in the middle years of the century, and his later style was much influenced by the Italian Baroque, especially Domenichino. His best-known but least typical work is the *Self-portrait* of 1636 in The Hermitage, Leningrad, which has always been considered to be Caravaggesque in inspiration. The influences on him can also be seen to come from artists in northern Italy, especially Moretto da Bescia and Lorenzo Lotto.

Collections

Aix-en-Provence, Musée Granet
Guitar Player

Aix-en-Provence, Saint-Esprit
Pentecost (signed and dated 1653)

Aix-en-Provence, La Madeleine
St Saveur Saving All Those under the Influence of the Devil (signed and dated 1637)
St Theresa Receiving the Order from the Hand of the Virgin and St Joseph who is Giving her the White Habit (signed and dated 1641)

Aix-en-Provence, Saint-Saveur
Christ on the Cross with the Virgin of Sorrows and St Peter and St Anthony (signed and dated 1640)

Aix-en-Provence, private collection
View of Aix-en-Provence Besieged by the Comte Allari
Education of Christ (signed and dated 165(5)?)
Dead Christ and St Joseph of Arimathea (signed and dated 1658)

Apt, Cathedral
Holy Family with St John the Baptist (signed and dated 1666 or 1668)

Aups, Church
Scenes from the Life of St Bartholomew (documented 1641)

Cavaillon, Cathedral
Deposition with the Virgin, Magdalen and St John (signed and dated 1658)

Grasse, Musée Fragonard
The Virgin with the Magdalen and St Catherine Offering to the Monks the Image of St Dominic

Grenoble, private collection
Allegory of Spring (signed and dated 1641 or 1661)

Lambesc, Church
Death of St Joseph

Leningrad, Hermitage
Self-portrait (signed and dated 1636) (fig.13)

Manosque, Château de Rousset, de Saporta Collection
Holy Family (signed and dated 1645)

Marseilles, Palais Longchamp
A Magistrate (signed and dated 1638)

New Haven (Connecticut), Yale University Art Gallery
The Lute Player

New York, art market, 1982
Pomona (signed and dated 1643)

Pertuis, Church
Presentation of the Virgin in the Temple

Saint-Chamas, Church
Pietà, St Leger and St Andrew and the Holy Sacrament and two Angels

Saint-Paul-de-Vence, Church
St Matthew and the Angel,
St Anthony of Padua with the Christ Child and the Blessed Pierre de Luxembourg (signed and dated 1661)

Salon, Saint-Michel
Annunciation with St Augustine and St Ursula (documented 1642)

Bibliography

Pierre Rosenberg in the exhibition catalogue, Marseilles, Palais Longchamp, *La peinture en Provence au XVIIe siècle*, 1978, pp.34–53.

Charles Dauphin

Lorraine c.1620–Turin 1693

Dauphin worked exclusively for the House of Savoy at Turin and in the churches there. His style is a softer version of the Baroque, of the type favoured by Simon Vouet.

Collections

Nantes, Musée des Beaux-Arts
The Holy Family

Racconigi, Castello
Allegorical Portrait of Christine of France

Turin, Duomo
St Luke Painting the Virgin
Jesus Giving the Communion to St Honorius

Turin, Istituto Bancario San Paolo
The Ecstasy of St Paul

Turin, San Carlo Borromeo
St Joseph Holding the Infant Jesus in his Arms

Turin, San Francesco di Paolo
St Francis Walking on the Water
Louise of Savoy, Duchesse d'Angoulême, Invoking St Francis de Paul

Turin, Palazzo Reale
Christine de Fleury and Emmanuel Philibert of Savoy-Carignan

Bibliography

Michela di Macco in the exhibition catalogue, Rome, Villa Medici, and Nancy, Musée des Beaux-Arts, *Claude Gellée et les peintres lorrains en Italie au XVIIe siècle, 1982*, pp.376–419.

Degant (or Degart)

Working mid-seventeenth century

Nothing is known of this painter, whose style is close to that of Charles Emmanuel Bizet.

Collections

Paris, A. Seligmann collection
Still Life of Books: The Dream of Endymion (signed)

Paris, private collection
Still Life of Books: The Death of Actaeon

Bibliography

Michel Faré
Le grand siècle de la nature morte en France, 1974, pp.151–2.

Claude Deruet

Nancy 1588–Nancy 1662

As a young man Deruet went to Italy, where he executed a small fresco in the Villa Borghese, Rome. He seems to have learned little from his Italian sojourn, however, and almost all the influences on his style are traceable to his native Lorraine. He was the favourite court painter of Duke Henry II of Lorraine and also of Louis XIII of France, whose drawing master he became. A touching record of this latter relationship survives in the drawing by Louis XIII of Deruet in the Musée Historique Lorrain at Nancy. None of Deruet's important decorations for the Lorraine court survive, and his frescoes for the Carmelite church were destroyed with the building during the Revolution of 1789. Deruet had the distinction of being the master of Claude Lorrain for the year 1626–27. The contract of Claude's apprenticeship survives, but it was only on the completion of that year that Deruet began the Carmelite frescoes. Claude almost certainly left immediately, as he is recorded in Rome a few months later.

The only important commissioned pictures from Deruet's hand to survive are the four vast canvasses of *Elements* at Orléans, commissioned by Cardinal Richelieu, and the *Rape of the Sabines* (Munich) offered to La Ferté in 1651 by the municipality of Nancy.

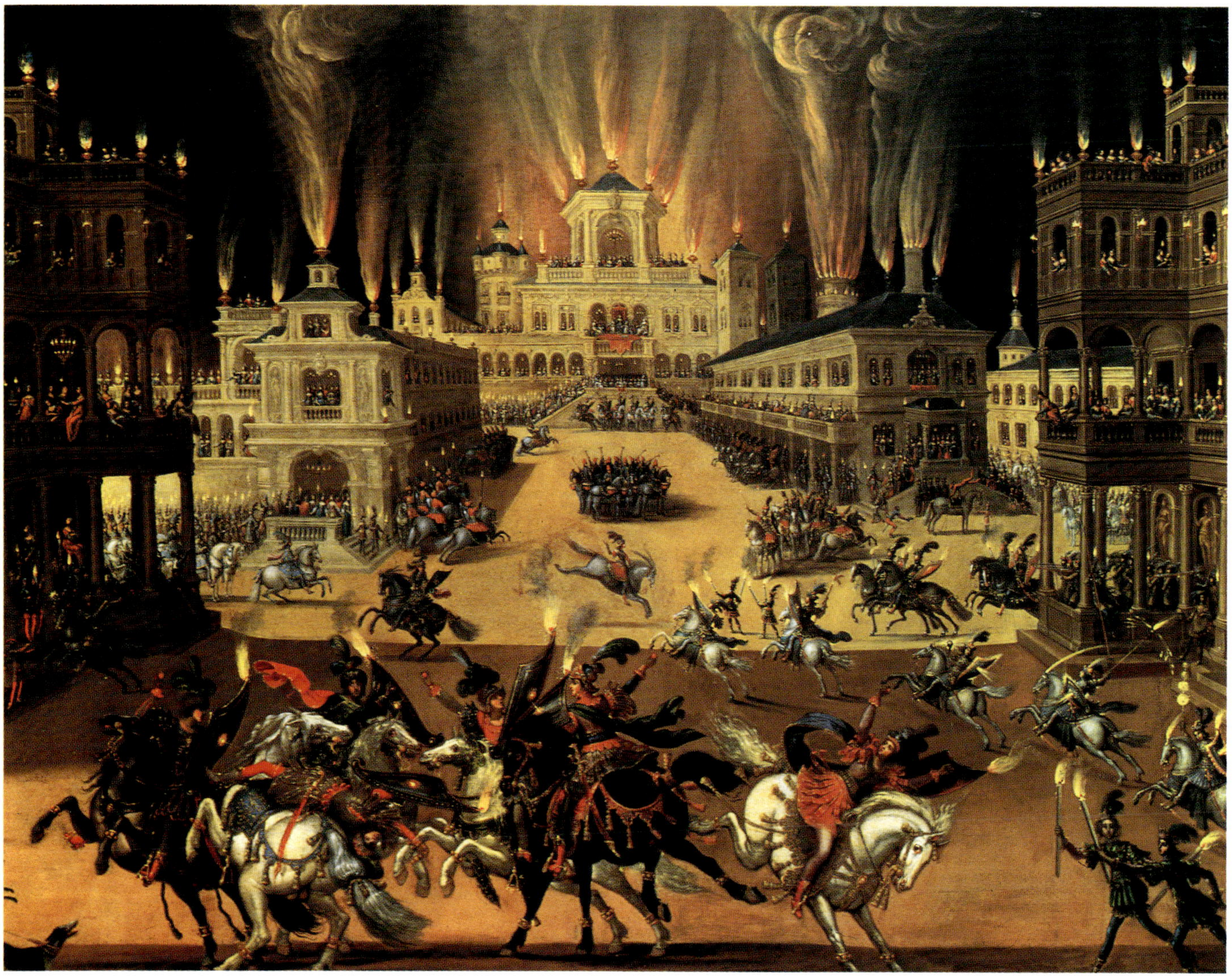

PLATE 26
Claude Deruet
Fire (detail of figure 22)
Orléans, Musée des Beaux-Arts

Collections

Chartres, Musée des Beaux-Arts
Air (or *The Duchesse de Lorraine at the Hunt*) (replica of the picture at Orléans)

La Fère, Musée Jeanne d'Aboville
Two Scenes from the Story of the Amazons

Mainz, Mittelrheinisches Landesmuseum
Christ on the Cross

Munich, Alte Pinakothek
The Rape of the Sabines

Nancy, Musée Historique Lorrain
The Artist's Daughter Elisabeth
Mme de Saint-Baslmont on Horseback (fig.19)
The Archangel Michael
Three Goddesses
St Elizabeth of Hungary
A Woman Disguised as Pallas
Virgin and Child in a Garland (signed)

New York, Metropolitan Museum
The Departure of the Amazons
The Combat of the Amazons and the Greeks

Orléans, Musée des Beaux-Arts
Air (documented 1653) (fig.20)
Earth (documented 1653) (fig.21)
Fire (documented 1653) (fig.22, plate 26)
Water (documented 1653) (fig.23)
Portrait of Louis XIV as a Child
Allegorical Composition (attribution)

Paris, Musée Carnavalet
Mme de Saint Baslmont on Horseback

Strasbourg, Musée des Beaux-Arts
Julie d'Argenue
Four Scenes from the Story of the Amazons

Versailles, Château
The Duchesse de Chevreuse
The Triumph of Louis XIII

Bibliography

The old study of Deruet is that of Albert Jacquot, *Notes sur Claude Deruet*, Paris, 1894, in which the artist's inventory is published and there is also a short biography. A more up-to-date survey is by Jacques Thuillier in the exhibition catalogue, Rome, Villa Medici, and Nancy, Musée des Beaux-Arts, *Claude Lorrain e i pittori lorenesi in Italia nel XVII secolo*, 1982, pp.104–33.

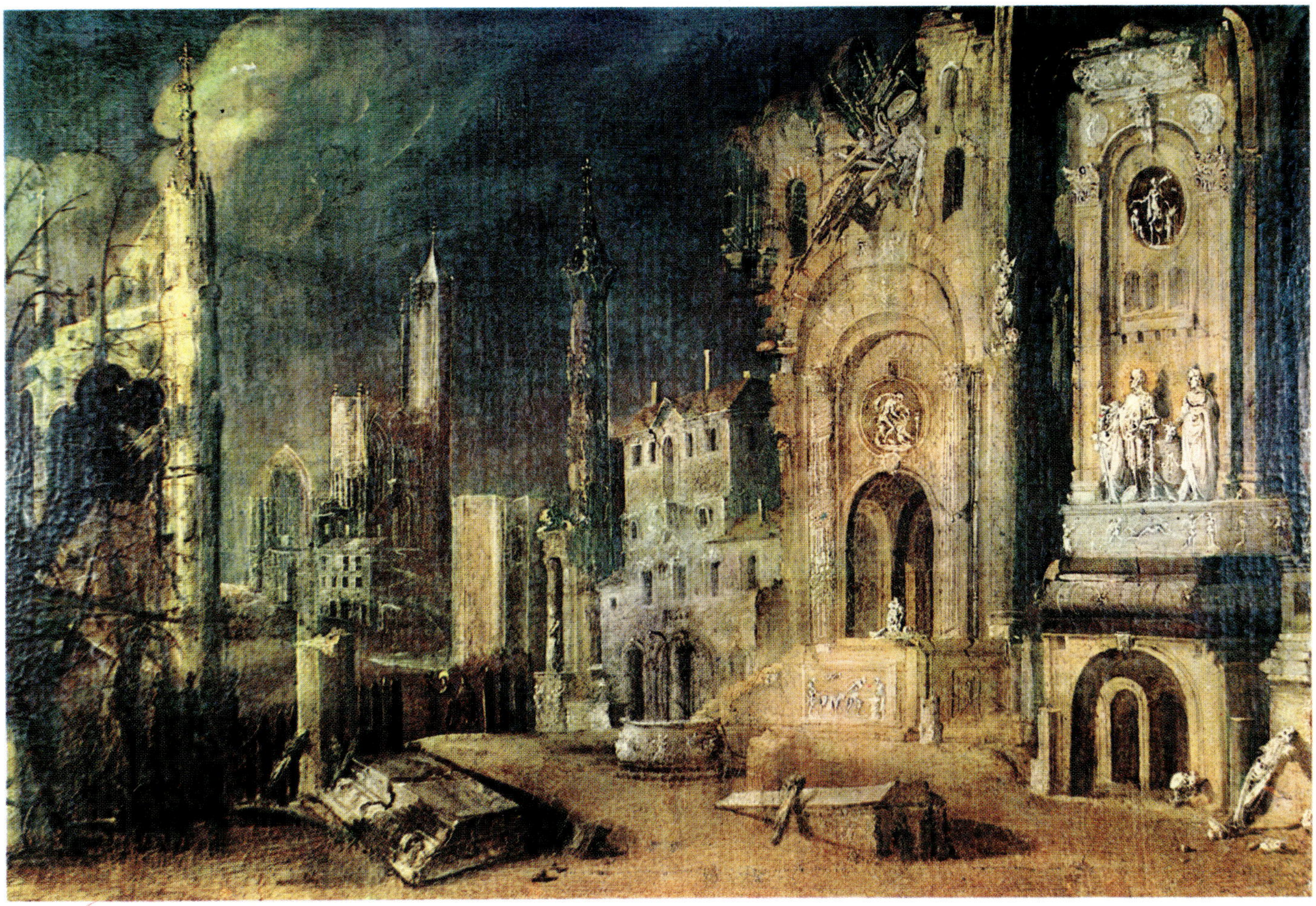

PLATE 27
Monsù Desiderio
Martyrdom of a Saint
Canvas, 46 × 70 cm.
Paris, Musée des Arts Décoratifs

Many of the artist's pictures are scenes of martyrdom against an architectural background. The saint or saints involved have often not been identified.

'Monsù Desiderio'
Didier Barra

Metz 1590–working Naples until 1644

François de Nomé

Metz 1593–working Naples 1644

It is only in recent years that 'Monsù Desiderio' has been separated into two artists, who occasionally collaborated. Didier Barra usually painted topographical views, chiefly of Naples. François de Nomé was the more adventurous of the two, concentrating on the bizarre. Both painters spent their entire careers in Naples but never assimilated any local influences; they both retained a form of archaizing Mannerism of a similar type to that of Claude Deruet. At their best, François de Nomé's pictures excite by their power of expression, even though they seem flagrantly to disobey almost every rule of art.

Collections

Baltimore, Walters Art Gallery
St Paul Preaching
The Head of St John the Baptist Presented to Salome

Basle, Dreyfus collection
Martyrdom of a Bishop Saint

Besançon, Musée des Beaux-Arts
Vision of Hell (1622)

Budapest, Szépmüvészeti Múzeum
Interior of a Gothic Church

Cambridge, Fitzwilliam Museum
King Asa of Judah Destroying the Idols (plate 28)

Dijon, Musée des Beaux-Arts
King Jeroboam in the Temple of the Pagan Gods

Florence, Uffizi
Lot Fleeing from Sodom (dated 1619)

Florence, private collection
Jael and Sisera

Glasgow, Pollok House
Church Interior

Gothenburg, Konstmuseum
A City in Ruins

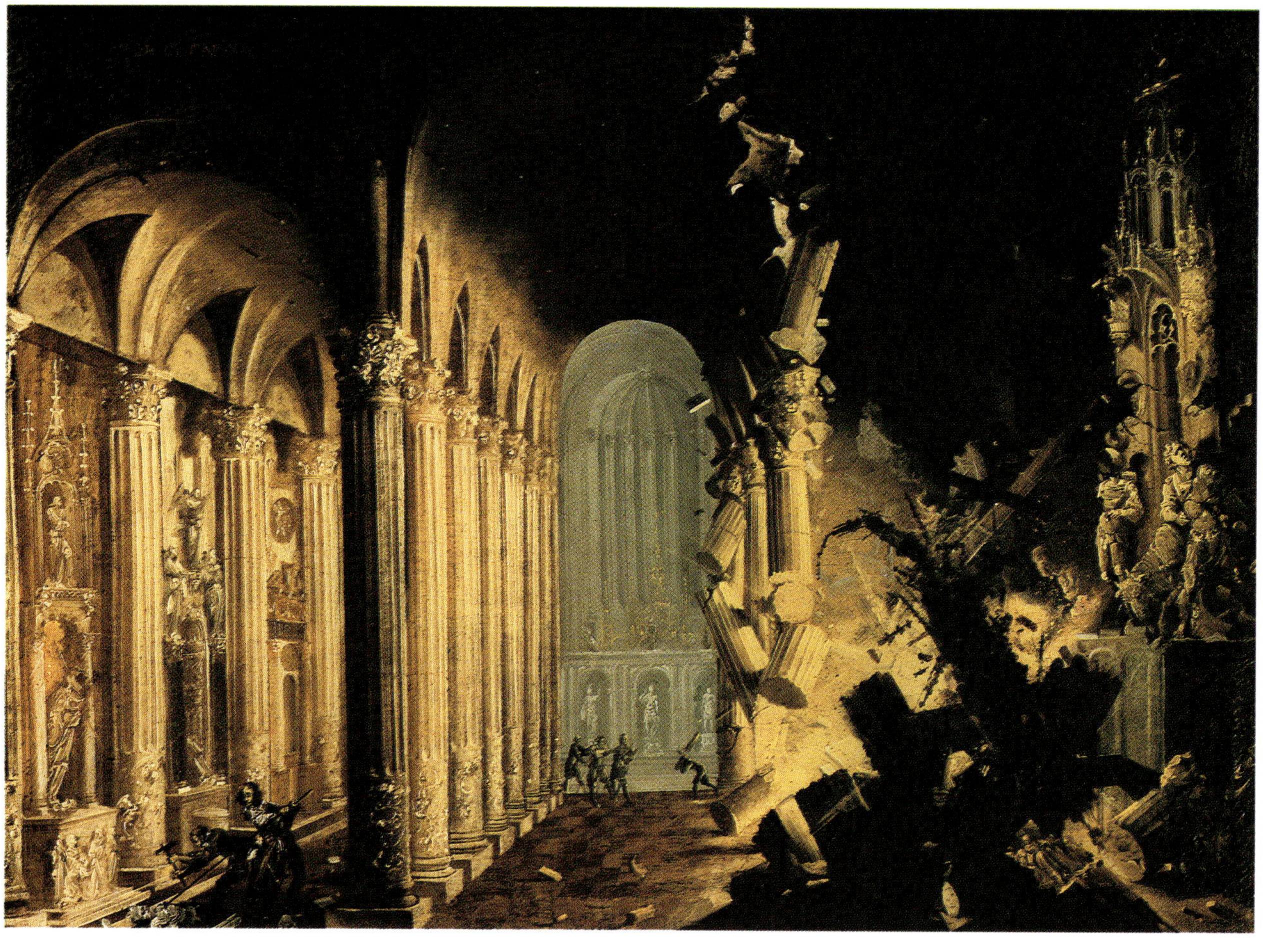

PLATE 28
Monsù Desiderio
King Asa of Juda Destroying the Idols
Canvas, 82.5 × 126 cm.
Cambridge, Fitzwilliam Museum (reproduced by permission of the Syndics)
Recorded before 1950 and bequeathed by F. F. Madan to the museum.

Although the subject is taken from the Old Testament, the picture is an excuse for one of the artist's dramatic effects. No other artist of the seventeenth century had such a sense of theatricality.

Hartford (Connecticut), Wadsworth Athenaeum
Belshazzar's Feast

Houston (Texas), Museum of Fine Arts
The Flight into Egypt

Houston (Texas), private collection
Interior of a Cathedral

London, National Gallery
St Augustine by the Seashore (dated 1623)

Louisville (Kentucky), Speed Art Museum
A Cathedral by Moonlight

Montreal, Museum of Fine Arts
Destruction of Sodom

Nancy, Musée Historique Lorrain
Sodom and Gomorrah

Nantes, Musée des Beaux-Arts
The Beheading of St Januarius and his Companions

Naples, Capodimonte
The Emperor Titus Destroying the Temple of Jerusalem

Naples, Museo di San Martino
Panorama of Naples (signed Didier Barra and dated 1647 on the reverse)
The Castello dell'Ovo at Posillipo

New Haven (Connecticut), Yale University Art Gallery
The Circumcision (signed François Didnomé and dated 1623)

Orléans, Musée des Beaux-Arts
Street Scene

Oxford, Ashmolean Museum
Decapitation of a Female Saint

Paris, Louvre
Architectural Fantasy

Paris, Musée des Arts Décoratifs
The Flight into Egypt (dated 1624)
Martyrdom of a Saint (plate 27)

Ponce (Puerto Rico), Museo de Arte
Scene with Ruins (*The Arrest of Christ?*)

Raleigh, North Carolina Museum of Art
Martyrdom of St Januarius (dated 1622)

Sarasota (Florida), John and Mable Ringling Museum
Martyrdom of St Januarius

Southampton, Art Gallery
Martyrdom of St Catherine (possibly dated 1617)

Vienna, Graf Harrachsch' Gemäldegalerie (Schloss Rohrau)
Gothic and Renaissance Palace
St George in Front of Richly Sculptured Buildings
Feeding the Sick
Martyrdom of St Barbara
Interior of a Church

Warsaw, National Museum
Ruined City

Würzburg, Martin von Wagner Museum
Christ and the Woman Taken in Adultery
David in the Temple

Bibliography

The standard monograph, although this is now rather out of date, is F. Sluys, *Monsù Desiderio*, 1961. A more up-to-date survey is by Jacques Thuillier in the exhibition catalogue, Rome, Villa Medici, and Nancy, Musée des Beaux-Arts, *Claude Lorrain e i pittori lorenesi in Italia nel XVII secolo*, 1982, pp.180–205. A general book with outstanding illustrations is Pierre Seghers, *Monsù Desiderio ou le Théâtre de la fin du Monde*, Paris, 1981.

Luc Despeches

d. Dijon 1648/1659

Nothing seems to be known about this painter, who was active in Dijon in the middle years of the seventeenth century.

Collection

Dijon, Musée des Beaux-Arts
The Young Christ Having the Vision of the Passion (signed)

Bibliography

There is no recent literature on this artist.

Michel Dorigny

St Quentin 1617–Paris 1665

Dorigny was one of Simon Vouet's most important pupils, in the sense that he was able to assimilate his master's style. He engraved much of Vouet's work, and the engravings are especially valuable because they record much of what has been lost. Many of Dorigny's pictures are still confused with those of Vouet.

Collections

Florence, Uffizi
Annunciation

Madrid, Prado
The Triumph of Prudence

Narbonne, Musée des Beaux-Arts
Burial of St Petronilla

Paris, Louvre
Christ on the Cross (formerly attributed to Simon Vouet)
Pan and Syrinx
Ceiling Decoration of *Europe, Asia, Africa and America*
Ceiling Decorations, *Genius Holding the Arms of Anne of Austria*
Force and Prudence
Temperance

Quebec, Saint Michel-de-Sillery
Annunciation (attribution)

Bibliography

Pierre Rosenberg in the exhibition catalogue, Florence, Galleria Pitti, *Pittura francese nelle collezioni pubbliche fiorentine*, 1977, p.106.

Paul Dorival

Grenoble 1604–Grenoble 1684

Without the signature, this artist's surviving work would be attributed to an east French follower of Jacques Linard. The accomplished level of this work is proof that competent still-life painting existed outside the orbit of Paris.

Collections

Paris, Mestrallet collection
Basket of Grapes (signed and dated 1660)

Private collection
Basket of Fruit (signed and dated 1661)
Basket of Fruit

Bibliography

Michel Faré
Le grand siècle de la nature morte en France, 1974, pp.144–5.

Jean Dubois

Avon (Seine-et-Marne) 1604–Fontainebleau 1676

Son of the Fontainebleau School painter Ambroise Dubois, Jean was patronized by Louis XIII, both at Fontainebleau and the Louvre.

Collections

Fontainebleau, Château
Felicity

Paris, Louvre
Felicity (documented 1642)

Bibliography

There is no recent literature on this artist.

René Dudot

Working Rouen 1653–1659

Dudot's work is close to the lyrical pictures of Nicolas Loir and also to Sébastien Bourdon, with whom he has been confused. In 1659 he executed the 'May' for Notre Dame in Paris, but it does not survive.

Collections

Florence, Uffizi
Rest on the Flight into Egypt
(signed)

Rouen, Musée des Beaux-Arts
Rest on the Flight into Egypt
(signed)

Bibliography

Pierre Rosenberg
in the exhibition catalogue, Florence, Galleria Pitti, *Pittura francese nelle collezioni pubbliche fiorentine*, 1977, p.103.

Charles-Alphonse Dufresnoy

Paris 1611–Villiers-le-Bel (Val de l'Oise) 1668

Dufresnoy was a pupil of Simon Vouet in Paris for a short time in about 1630; in 1633 he went to Italy, where he spent about twenty years; and he was in Paris from 1656 until his death. Dufresnoy's art was a livelier version of the classicism of François Perrier, whose pupil he also was. His fame rests on the treatise *De Arte Graphica*.

Collections

Caen, Musée des Beaux-Arts
The Drunkenness of Noah

Copenhagen, Statens Museum for Kunst
Self-portrait

Dijon, Musée Magnin
Landscape with the Prodigal Son

Épinal, Musée Départemental des Vosges
Landscape (attribution)

Evreux, Musée de l'Ancien Evêché
St Margaret (dated 1656)

Florence, Uffizi
The Death of Socrates
(attribution)

Paris, Louvre
Alexander at the Tomb of Achilles

Salzburg, Residenzgalerie
The Dream of Nausicae

Troyes, Musée des Beaux-Arts
A Man

Bibliography

Jacques Thuillier
in *Miscellanea Friedlaender, 1965*.
Pierre Rosenberg
in the exhibition catalogue, Florence, Galleria Pitti, *Pittura francese nelle collezioni pubbliche fiorentine*, 1977, p.105.

Gaspard Dughet (sometimes known as Gaspard Poussin)

Rome 1613–Rome 1675

Dughet is one of the most difficult seventeenth-century artists to identify and define, even though he achieved success in his lifetime and his pictures continued to be in demand for two centuries after his death. Born in Rome of French parents, he became associated with Nicolas Poussin at an early age because Poussin married Gaspard's sister, Anne-Marie Dughet, in 1630. It is assumed that Gaspard was taught to paint by his illustrious brother-in-law in the early 1630s, in spite of the fact that Poussin at that time was totally preoccupied with mythological and religious subject-matter, and had not turned his attention to landscapes. It is likely, therefore, as nothing but landscapes survive from Gaspard's hand, that he was the initiator of the classical landscape painting. These earliest essays may well be the group of pictures formerly put together as 'The Silver Birch Master', although there is now a theory that these works represent Poussin's earliest landscapes. The best-documented works by Gaspard are some landscape frescoes in the Roman church of S. Martino ai Monti, dating from the early 1650s. The superb series of landscapes in gouache in the Colonna Gallery in Rome show him at the height of his powers as a decorator. It has always been thought that Gaspard's cold, stylized pictures with intense blues and dark trees are his later works, all painted under the influence of Nicolas Poussin's classical landscapes of about 1650.

PLATE 29
Gaspard Dughet
View of Tivoli
Canvas, 31 × 46.5 cm.
Bologna, Maestro Francesco Molinari Pradelli collection

This is one of Dughet's many paintings of the same site, which was one much favoured by artists of the time who were in search of the picturesque.

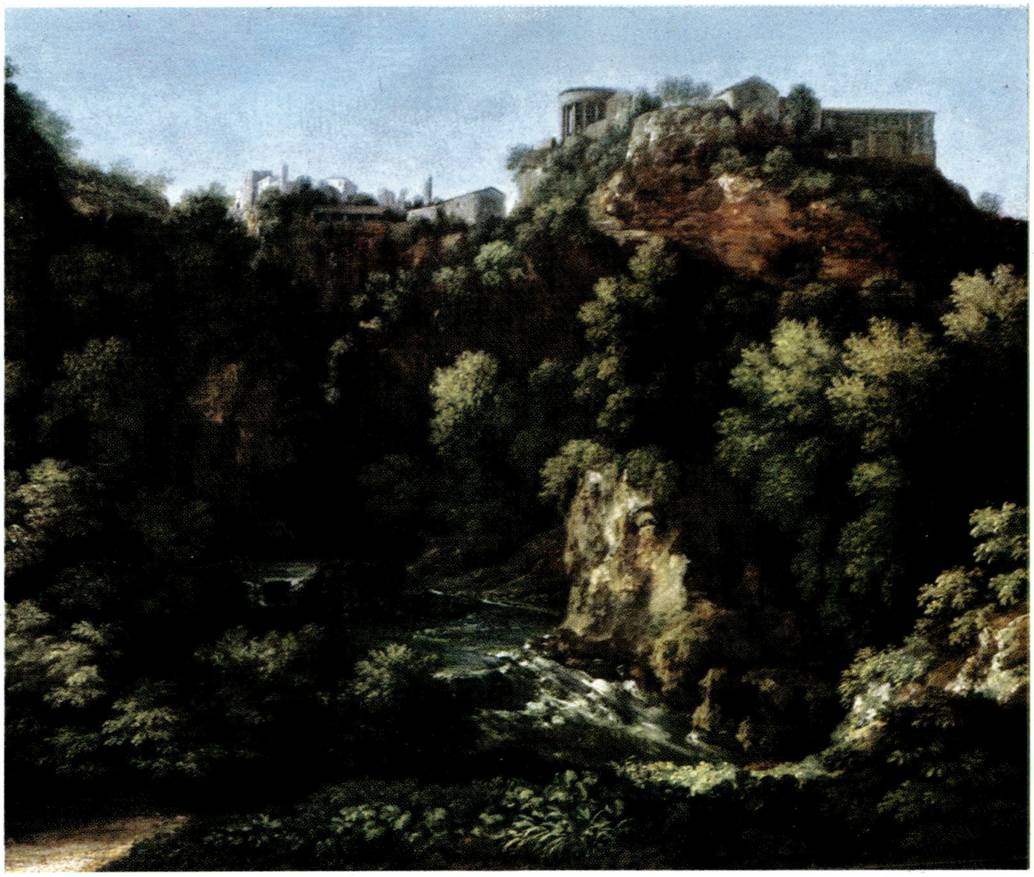

Collections

Amsterdam, Rijksmuseum
Landscape (3)

Arras, Palais Saint-Vaast
Landscape with Figures Washing

Avignon, Musée Calvet
Landscape

Barnsley, Cooper Art Gallery
Landscape

Birmingham, Barber Institute
Classical Landscape

Birmingham, City Art Gallery
Classical Landscape

Bologna, Molinari Pradelli collection
View of Tivoli (plate 29)

Boston (Massachusetts), Museum of Fine Arts
River and Mountain Landscape
Landscape with St Jerome

Budapest, Szépmüvészeti Múzeum
Landscape with Ruins

Cambridge, Fitzwilliam Museum
Landscape (3)

Cardiff, National Museum of Wales
Landscape

Chantilly, Musée Condé
Landscape in the Roman Campagna

Chartres, Musée des Beaux-Arts
Landscape

Cherry Valley (California), Edward Dean Museum
Landscape with a Fortified Hill Town

Chicago, Art Institute
Landscape

Cleveland (Ohio), Museum of Art
Landscape with Hunters

Cologne, Wallraf-Richartz Museum
Landscape with a Hill Town

Dijon, Musée Magnin
Landscape with a Castle
Two Landscapes

Dresden, Gemäldegalerie
Rocky Landscape

Dublin, National Gallery of Ireland
Landscape

Edinburgh, National Gallery of Scotland
Landscape with a Pool

Florence, Academia
Landscape with Men Fishing

Florence, Longhi Foundation
Rocky Landscape

Florence, Galleria Pitti
Landscape with Nymphs and Figures
Landscape with Animals
Landscape with Shepherds and Fishermen
Landscape with Shepherds (2)
Landscape with Satyrs Dancing
Landscape with a Ruined Temple

Glasgow, Art Gallery
Landscape (2)

Hamburg, Kunsthalle
Landscape with Tivoli

Hanover, Niedersächsisches Landesmuseum
Ideal Landscape

Lawrence (Kansas), University Art Museum
Landscape

Le Havre, Musée des Beaux-Arts
Landscape: the Disobedient Prophet

Le Mans, Musée de Tessé
Landscape (attribution)

Leningrad, Hermitage
Landscape with Lightning
Forest Landscape
Mountain Landscape
Landscape with Shepherd and Sheep
Landscape with Angler
Landscape with a Road
Landscape

Liverpool, Walker Art Gallery
Landscape with Pyramus

London, National Gallery
Landscape with a Storm
View of Ariccia
Landscape with Dido and Aeneas (fig.39)
Abraham and Isaac
Landscape with Moses and the Angel

London, Wallace Collection
View of Tivoli

Lyons, Musée des Beaux-Arts
Landscape

Madison (Wisconsin), Elvehjem Museum of Art
Landscape

Madrid, Prado
Landscape with the Penitent Magdalen
Landscape with St John
Landscape with a Storm (2)
Landscape
Landscape with the Penitent Magdalen (in collaboration with Carlo Maratta)

Manchester, City Art Gallery
Landscape

Manchester, Whitworth Art Gallery
Landscape with Tivoli

Minneapolis, University of Minnesota Art Gallery
The Heron Hunt

Nancy, Musée des Beaux-Arts
Landscape (attribution)

Nantes, Musée des Beaux-Arts
Landscape (3) (attribution)

Narbonne, Musée des Beaux-Arts
Landscape

New York, Metropolitan Museum
Classical Landscape

Nîmes, Musée des Beaux-Arts
Landscape

Oxford, Ashmolean Museum
Landscape with Tivoli

Oxford, Christ Church
Landscape

Paris, Louvre
Landscape
Landscape in the Roman Campagna
Landscape with Shepherds

Pittsburgh, Art Museum
Landscape

Ponce (Puerto Rico), Museo de Arte
The Cascade at Tivoli

Reims, Musée Saint-Denis
Landscape: Storm

Rome, Galleria Borghese
Cycle of Landscape Frescoes

Rome, Galleria Colonna
Landscape (12)

Rome, Galleria Doria
Landscape with Animals
Landscape with Ruins
Landscape with the Flight into Egypt
Landscape (7)

Rome, Galleria Spada
Landscape (2)

Rome, San Martino ai Monti
Series of Frescoes: *Landscapes with Scenes from the Lives of Elijah, Elisha and St Simon Stock*

Salzburg, Residenzgalerie
Heroic Landscape (signed)

Sarasota (Florida), John and Mable Ringling Art Museum
Landscape

Schleissheim, Schloss
Landscape (attribution)
Storm at Sea (attribution)

Seattle, Art Museum
View of Tivoli

Southampton, Art Gallery
Landscape

Stockholm, Nationalmuseum
Landscape with a Circular Temple
Landscape with a Circular Temple (attribution)
Rocky Landscape (attribution)
Landscape with a Waterfall (attribution)
Landscape (attribution)

Strasbourg, Musée des Beaux-Arts
Landscape

Turin, Galleria Sabauda
Landscape with a Waterfall (2)

Vienna, Akademie der bildenden Künste
Landscape with Diana and Actaeon

Vienna, Kunsthistorisches Museum
Landscape

Warsaw, National Museum
Landscape: the Roman Campagna (2)

Bibliography

A carefully thought-out discussion of the problems surrounding Dughet's art is Denis Sutton, 'Gaspard Dughet. Some Aspects of his Art', *Gazette des Beaux-Arts*, 1962, pp.269–312.

The most recent article is Marie-Nicole Boisclair, 'Gaspard Dughet, une chronologie revisée', *Revue de l'Art*, 1976, no.34, pp.29–56. The same author's 'Documents inédits relatifs à Gaspard Dughet', *Bulletin de la Société de l'Histoire de l'Art français, 1973*, 1974, pp.75–85, is also useful. A full biography and *catalogue raisonné* by Marie-Nicole Boisclair is in preparation.

Daniel Dumoustier

Paris 1574–Paris 1646

Dumoustier was primarily a portraitist, specializing in crayons (see under Louis XIII for an example of this technique). A few oil paintings have been attributed to him, chiefly on the grounds that they are painted versions of the drawings. Dumoustier's long career was extremely successful with the French court.

Collections

Paris, Louvre
A Woman (attribution)

Rennes, Musée des Beaux-Arts
A Woman Holding a String of Pearls

Bibliography

There is no recent literature on the artist's paintings.

PLATE 30
Pierre Dupuys
Basket of Grapes
Canvas, 50 × 60 cm.
Paris, Louvre
Acquired by the museum in 1951.

The influence of Moillon and Linard is visible in this humble but beautifully painted picture.

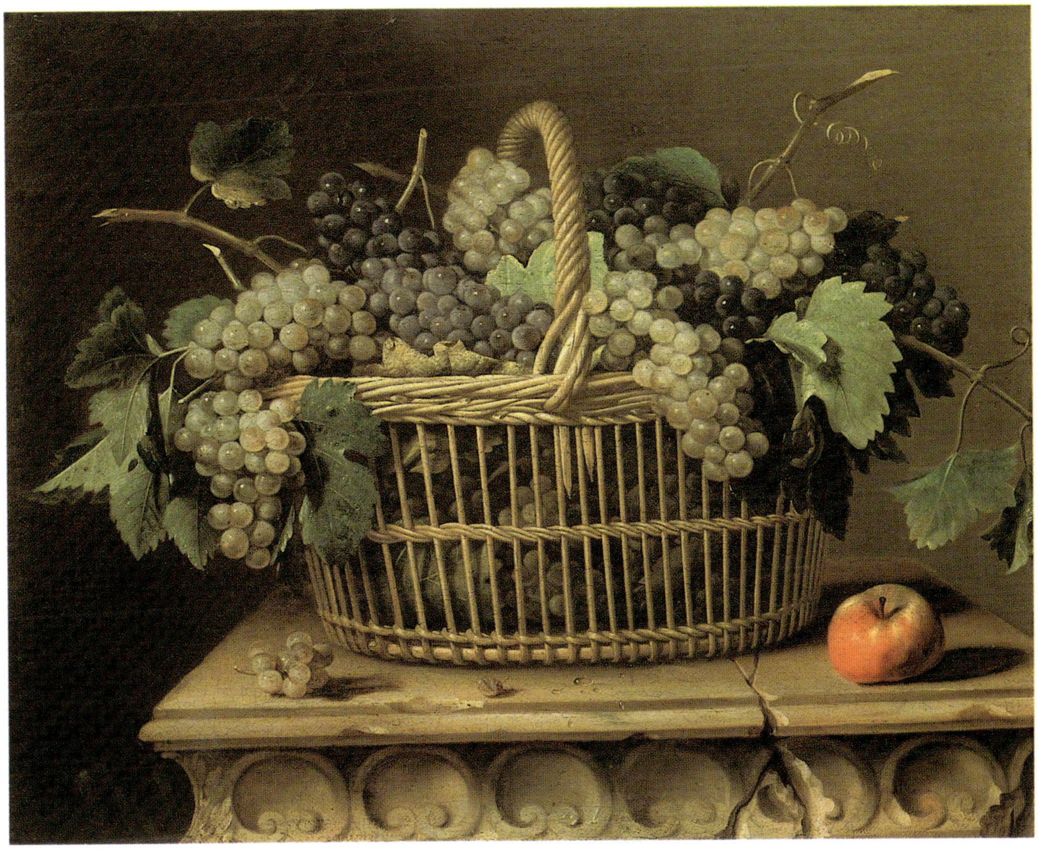

Pierre Dupuys

Montfort l'Amaury (Seine-et-Oise) 1610–Paris 1682

All Dupuys' dated pictures are from the second part of his career, and indicate by their style that he was deeply influenced by his contemporary Louise Moillon, though his pictures are usually a little less precise and crisp than that celebrated painter's work. Three of his pictures were recorded in the seventeenth century in the collection of the Archduke Leopold Wilhelm at Brussels. Dupuys was received into the French Academy in Paris in 1663.

Collections

Algiers, Musée des Beaux-Arts
Plate of Peaches and Apples on a Sculptured Entablature (monogram)

France, private collection
Basket of Fruit and an Open Pomegranate (signed)

La Fère, Musée Jeanne d'Aboville
Basket of Plums

Munich, formerly Scharnowski collection
Fruit and Flowers on an Entablature (attribution)

Narbonne, Musée des Beaux-Arts
Basket of Fruit and Silver Vases (close to Ephraim Conte)

Paris, Louvre
Basket of Grapes (plate 30)
Plums and Peaches (signed and dated 1650)

Paris, François Heim collection
Dish of Peaches

Paris, F.M. collection
Peaches and Grapes (monogram)

Paris, N. Leeb collection
Dish of Peaches and Melon before a Landscape

Paris, private collection
Basket of Fruit and Two Grey Pigeons

Paris, private collection
Basket of Peaches and Grapes

Paris, private collection
Basket of Peaches

Strasbourg, Musée des Beaux-Arts
Plums and Peaches (monogrammed and dated 1664)

USA private collection
Basket of Fruit and Dead Game (signed)

Bibliography

Michel Faré
Le grand siècle de la nature morte en France, 1974, pp.198–204.

Louis-Ferdinand Elle the Elder

Paris 1612–Paris 1689

One of the fourteen founder-members of the French Academy in Paris in 1648, Elle was expelled in 1681, along with Jean Michelin, for his Protestantism. He returned to the Academy in 1686, having become a Catholic. His work, although in the realistic Flemish tradition brought to France by Frans Pourbus II, preserves a certain provincial naïvety not dissimilar to that of the brothers Beaubrun.

Collections

Bordeaux, Musée des Beaux-Arts
A Woman (attribution)

Bristol, City Art Gallery
Head of an Elderly Man (attribution)

Florence, Uffizi
A Young Woman (attribution)

London, Chiswick House
Louis XIII

Marseilles, Musée Grobet Labadié
A Woman as Minerva (dated 1655)

Reims, Musée Saint-Denis
François d'Épinay-St-Luc

Bibliography

There is no recent literature on this artist.

Charles Errard

Nantes 1606–Rome 1689

Better known as an engraver and architect than as a painter, Errard spent much of his career in Rome. He was one of the fourteen founder-members of the French Academy in Paris in 1648.

Collection

Rennes, Musée des Beaux-Arts
Allegory of Prudence

Bibliography

There is no recent literature on this artist.

Martin Faber

Emden 1587?–Emden 1648

A contemporary of the Bruges painter Louis Finson, Faber was working in Aix-en-Provence and Arles from 1613 onwards. His *Self-portrait* at Marseilles was painted as a pendant to the one by Finson, also at Marseilles. Many of his pictures have only recently been separated from those of Finson.

Collections

Beauvallon, Church
Martyrdom of St John the Baptist (signed and dated 1616)

Brunswick, Herzog Anton-Ulrich Museum
Martyrdom of St John the Baptist

Lyons, Saint-Jean
St Sebastian

Marseilles, Palais Longchamp
Self-portrait (signed and dated 1614)

Paris, private collection
Samson and Delilah

Valenciennes, private collection
Delivery of St Peter (signed and dated 1622)

Vienna, Sale, Dorotheum, no.617, 1978, no.31
Adoration of the Shepherds

Whereabouts unknown
Salome

Bibliography

Maurice Pettex-Sabarot in the exhibition catalogue, Marseilles, Palais Longchamp, *La peinture en Provence au XVIIe siècle*, 1978, pp.53–8.

Laurent Fauchier

Aix-en-Provence 1643–Aix-en-Provence 1672

From his few surviving works, it can be seen that Fauchier was a provincial painter of considerable talent. His portraits are well observed, and avoid the elaborate props of the Baroque, which was already becoming an influential style in Paris under the direction of Louis XIV.

Collections

Marseilles, Palais Longchamp
Portrait of a Priest

Montpellier, Musée Ather
Portrait of the Painter J. B. de la Rose (attribution)

Paris, Louvre
A Man Playing the Lute (presumed portrait of d'Imbert, *greffier* (clerk of the court) of the Aix *parlement*)

Pau, Musée des Beaux-Arts
Man with a Lute

Bibliography

Marielle Latour in the exhibition catalogue, Marseilles, Palais Longchamp, *La peinture en Provence au XVIIe siècle*, 1978, pp.59–60.

Jean-Baptiste de Faudran

Marseilles 1611–Marseilles 1669

Along with that of Pierre Puget, Faudran's art is the earliest example of a fully developed Baroque style imported from Italy. His altarpieces are reminiscent of Domenichino and Lanfranco.

Collections

Lambesc, Church
Holy Family (signed and dated 1643)

La-Penne-sur-Huveaune, Church
St Bernard in Prayer before the Virgin

Marseilles, Musée du Vieux Marseille
Apotheosis of Marseilles

Saint-Maximin, Basilique
Vision of St Dominic

Whereabouts unknown
Adoration of the Kings (signed)

Bibliography

Marie-Claude Homet in the exhibition catalogue, Marseilles, Palais Longchamp, *La peinture en Provence au XVIIe siècle*, 1978, pp.61–3.

Louis Finson

Bruges before 1578–Amsterdam 1617

Although he only spent a short time in Provence, in the period 1613–15, Finson's surviving output is largely preserved there. His is a rare example of the type of painting immensely popular in the second decade of the century, a curious mix of sixteenth-century Mannerism with a few references to the stylistic changes brought about by Caravaggio. A few of Finson's pictures, such as the Marseilles *Magdalen*, are almost caricatures of Caravaggio's art, they are so extreme in style.

Collections

Aix-en-Provence, Saint-Jean de Malte
Resurrection of Christ (signed and dated 1610)

Aix-en-Provence, Saint-Saveur
Incredulity of St Thomas (signed and dated 1613)

Aix-en-Provence, Musée des Tapisseries
Paul Hurault de l'Hôpital (signed and dated 1613)

Aix-en-Provence, Château de la Calade
Crucifixion (signed and dated 1613)

Andenne, Sainte-Begge
Massacre of the Innocents (signed)

Arles, Saint-Trophîme
Stoning of Stephen (signed and dated 1614)
Adoration of the Kings (signed and dated 1614)
Annunciation (signed and dated 1614)

Avignon, Aubanel collection
Annunciation to the Pinchinats (signed and dated 1612)

Berlin, Jagdschloss Grünewald
Angelica and Medor

Brunswick, Herzog Anton-Ulrich Museum
The Concert

Dijon, Musée Magnin
Self-portrait (attribution)

Ermenonville, Church
The Charity of St Martin (signed and dated 1615)

Hazebrouck, Musée Municipal
Beheading of St John the Baptist (attribution)

Lille, Saint-Catherine
Christ Bound

London, with Brian Sewell
David and Goliath

Madrid, Prado
Annunciation to Celes (signed)

Marseilles, Palais Longchamp
The Dying Magdalen (signed)

Marseilles, Église du Château-Gombert
Resurrection of Lazarus (signed and dated 1613)

Naples, Capodimonte
Annunciation (signed and dated 1612)

New York, private collection
St Januarius

Paris, private collection
Samson and Delilah

Paris, Saint-Nicolas-des-Champs
The Circumcision

Poitiers, Chapelle du Lycée
The Circumcision (signed and dated 1615)

Potsdam, Sans Souci (formerly)
Christ and the Adulteress (destroyed)

Rome, Accademia di San Luca
A Gentleman (signed and dated 1613)

Rougiers (Var), Church
Martyrdom of St Sebastian (signed and dated 1615)

France, private collection
St Sebastian
St Jerome

Switzerland, private collection
Crucifixion of St Andrew

Bibliography

The standard reference work, with *catalogue raisonné* and exhaustive bibliography, is Didier Bodart, *Louis Finson*, 1970. This was brought up to date by Jacques Thuillier in the exhibition catalogue, Marseilles, Palais Longchamp, *La peinture en Provence au XVIIe siècle*, 1978, pp.66–75. A still longer list of pictures was given by Benedict Nicolson in *The International Caravaggesque Movement*, 1979, pp.47–8.

Guy François

Le Puy c.1578/9–Le Puy 1650

François was known to be in Rome as early as 1608 and to be back in his native Puy-de-Dôme by 1613. He seems to have spent the rest of his long career in and around Le Puy, with an undocumented visit to Toulouse at an indeterminate date, probably in the 1620s. Most of the artist's pictures remain in the obscurity of the parish churches for which they were painted, and it is clear that he had ceased to experiment by about 1630. One of his most important pictures is at Bourg-en-Bresse, the largest altarpiece *The Holy Family with St Bruno and St Elizabeth* of 1626, which shows the artist's careful assimilation of the style of the Roman painter Carlo Saraceni.

There is now a dispute as to whether some pictures are by Saraceni or Guy François, notably the *Holy Family* in the Wadsworth Athenaeum, Hartford, which seems characteristic of both artists. Unlike Tournier, François never showed any passion in his art; his pictures always retained a Saracenesque smoothness and elegance.

Collections

Bordeaux, Saint-Bruno
St Bruno

Bourg-en-Bresse, Musée de L'Ain
Holy Family with St Bruno and St Elizabeth (1626) (plate 31)

Céaux d'Allegre (Haute-Loire), Church
Virgin of Pity

Craponne-sur-Arzon, Church
Virgin of Pity (1640)

Gannat (Allier), Church
Adoration of the Shepherds (1630)

Langeac, Church
Coronation of the Virgin

Le Puy, Église des Carmes
Apparition of the Virgin to St Felix of Catalice (1629)

Le Puy, Église du Collège
Christ on the Cross
Adoration of the Shepherds (1621)

Le Puy, Saint-Laurent
Virgin of the Rosary (1619)
Incredulity of St Thomas
Miracle of St Hyacinthe

Massiac (Cantal), Church
Adoration of the Shepherds (1633)

Montpellier, Notre Dame des Tables
Christ on the Cross

Pontgibaud, Church
Adoration of the Shepherds (1643)
Adoration of the Kings (1646)

Saint-Bonnet, Church
Adoration of the Shepherds (1643)

Saint-Rambert sur Loire, Church
Virgin of Pity

Tournon (Ardèche), Church
The Presentation in the Temple (1645)

Vienne (Isère), Saint-André-le-Haut
Adoration of the Kings

Bibliography

All the available information was brought together in the excellent exhibition catalogue by Marie-Félicie Perez, *Guy François*, Le Puy, Musée Crozatier, Saint-Étienne, Musée d'Art et d'Industrie, 1974.

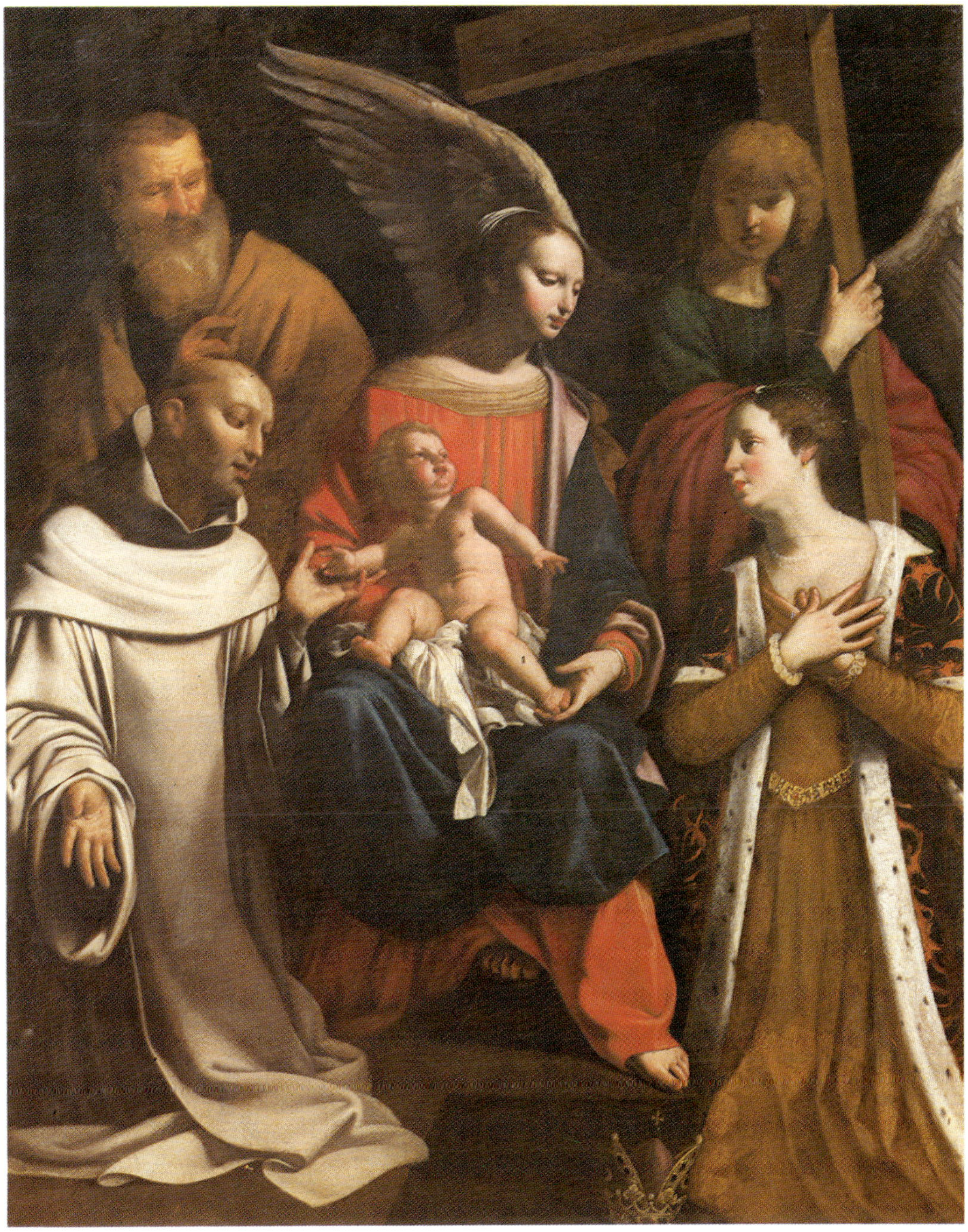

PLATE 31
Guy François
Holy Family with St Bruno and St Elisabeth
Canvas, 210 × 153 cm. Signed lower centre:
GUIDO FRANCISCUS ANCIENSIS
Bourg-en-Bresse, Musée de l'Ain
Given to the museum in 1857. Earlier history unknown.

St Bruno was canonized in 1623, and so appeared frequently at that time in paintings from throughout southern Europe.

Ambroise Frédeau

Paris c.1620–Toulouse 1673

Although a pupil of Vouet in Paris, Frédeau remained faithful to the Mannerist style. He became an Augustinian monk at Toulouse.

Collections

Toulouse, Musée des Augustins
St Nicholas of Tolentino Consoled by the Angels (dated 1650)
St Augustine Presenting his Heart to the Virgin

Toulouse, Saint-Pierre
The Risen Christ Appearing to the Virgin

Bibliography

There is no recent literature on this artist.

French School (Narbonne)

Collection

Narbonne, Musée des Beaux-Arts
Consuls for the Year 1596 (dated 1596)
Consuls for the Year 1600 (dated 1600)
Consuls for the Year 1603 (dated 1603) (fig.2)
Consuls for the Year 1607 (dated 1607)
Consuls for the Year 1626
Consuls for the Year 1643 (dated 1643)

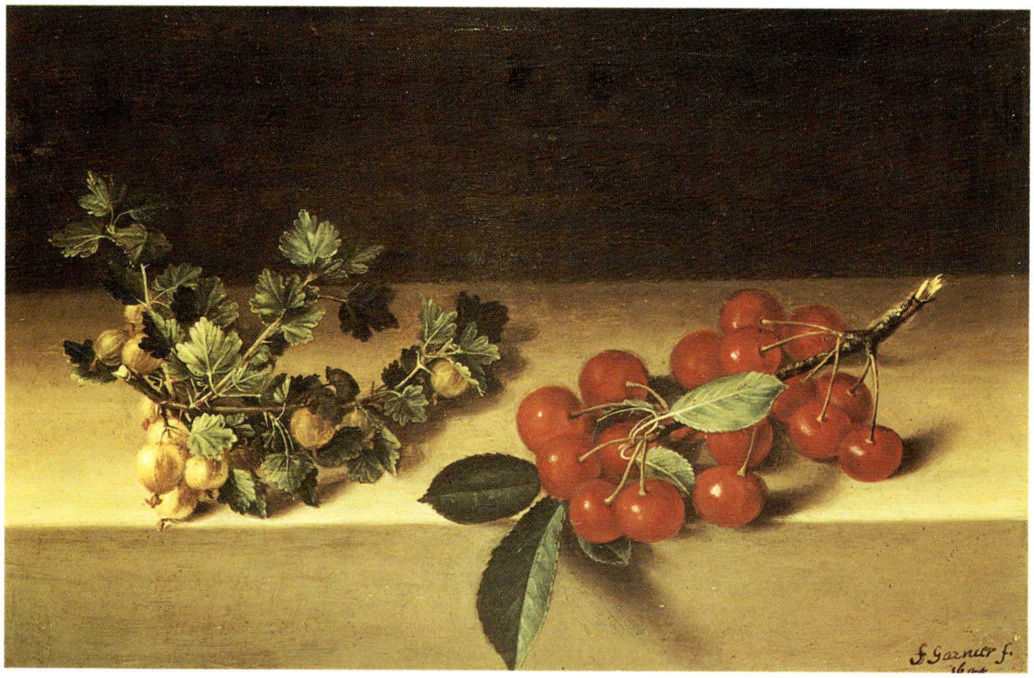

PLATE 32
François Garnier
Cherries and Gooseberries on a Table
Panel, 24 × 35 cm. Signed and dated: F. Garnier f.1644.
Paris, Louvre
Given to the museum by Charles Sterling in 1952.

François Garnier

d.Paris 1672

Garnier was first recorded in Paris in 1627. The celebrated Louise Moillon was his daughter-in-law. Garnier's work is careful and realistic, and close to that of Jacques Linard. His type of realism can also be found much later in the century, in the work of the equally obscure Dutch artist, Adriaen Coorte.

Collections

Algiers, Musée des Beaux-Arts
Basket of Cherries and Bowl of Strawberries

Grenoble, L. collection
Basket of Cherries and Bowl of Strawberries
Dish of Cherries on a Chip-wood Box

Paris, Louvre
Cherries and Gooseberries on a Table (signed and dated 1644) (plate 32)
Bowl of Strawberries and Basket of Cherries (attribution)

Paris, formerly with Pardo
Bowl of Strawberries and Gooseberries (signed and dated 1637)
Bowl of Strawberries and a Basket of Raspberries
Bowl of Cherries
Bowl of Strawberries and Lily-of-the-Valley

Paris, private collection
Basket of Plums
Basket of Cherries and a Bowl of Red and White Currants

Bibliography

Michel Faré
Le grand siècle de la nature morte en France, 1974, pp.44–8.

Jean-Baptiste Garnier

Meaux 1633–Paris 1705

A portraitist and still-life painter, Garnier was received into the French Academy in Paris in 1671. He had a successful career in both his specialist genres.

Collections

Paris, G. B. collection
Celestial Globe and Attributes of the Arts
Apricots and Plums (monogram)

Versailles, Château
Louis XIV with Musical Instruments, Flowers and Fruits (documented 1672)

Bibliography

Michel Faré
Le grand siècle de la nature morte en France, 1974, pp.249–53.

Henri Gascars

Paris 1634–Rome 1701

Gascars was one of the two French painters of the period (the other being Bourdon) to pursue his career with success in several different countries, including England. His style of portraiture was close to that of Pierre Mignard, but there was always a certain provincial stiffness in his approach to his sitters.

Collections

Munich, Residenzmuseum
Adelheid of Savoy
Max Emanuel with Maria Anna as a Child

Nuremberg, Germanisches Nationalmuseum
A Woman as Diana
A Monk

Providence (Rhode Island), Brown University
The Duchess of Grafton

Bibliography

There is no recent literature on this artist.

Andreas Gellée

Working Arras 1628

Gellée is a rare example of an artist who worked in northern France in a provincial style.

Collections

Arras, Palais Saint-Vaast
Christ on the Cross with St Martin and St Sebastian (signed and dated 1628)

Bibliography

The picture at Arras is listed in the exhibition catalogue, Dunkirk/Valenciennes/Lille, *La peinture française aux XVIIe et XVIIIe siècles*, 1980, p.174.

Abiah Gibbens

Working Paris 1629

Possibly of Netherlandish origin, Gibbens worked in a strongly realistic style reminiscent of Jacques Linard and François Garnier.

Collections

Lucerne, F. Steinmeyer collection
Bowl of Fruit and Horseradish (signed and dated 1635)

Paris, private collection
Bowl of Cherries and a Finch

Bibliography

Michel Faré
Le grand siècle de la nature morte en France, 1974, pp.79–80.

PLATE 33
Michel Gobin
Young Man with a Candle
Canvas, 121 × 116 cm. Signed on the left below the cock and dated: M^{el} Gobin f. 1681.
Orléans, Musée des Beaux-Arts
Early history unknown. Given to the museum in 1825 by M. Peteau-Lasneau.

Many authorities believe that this picture is an allegory of study and vigilance, rather than a genre scene without any specific meaning.

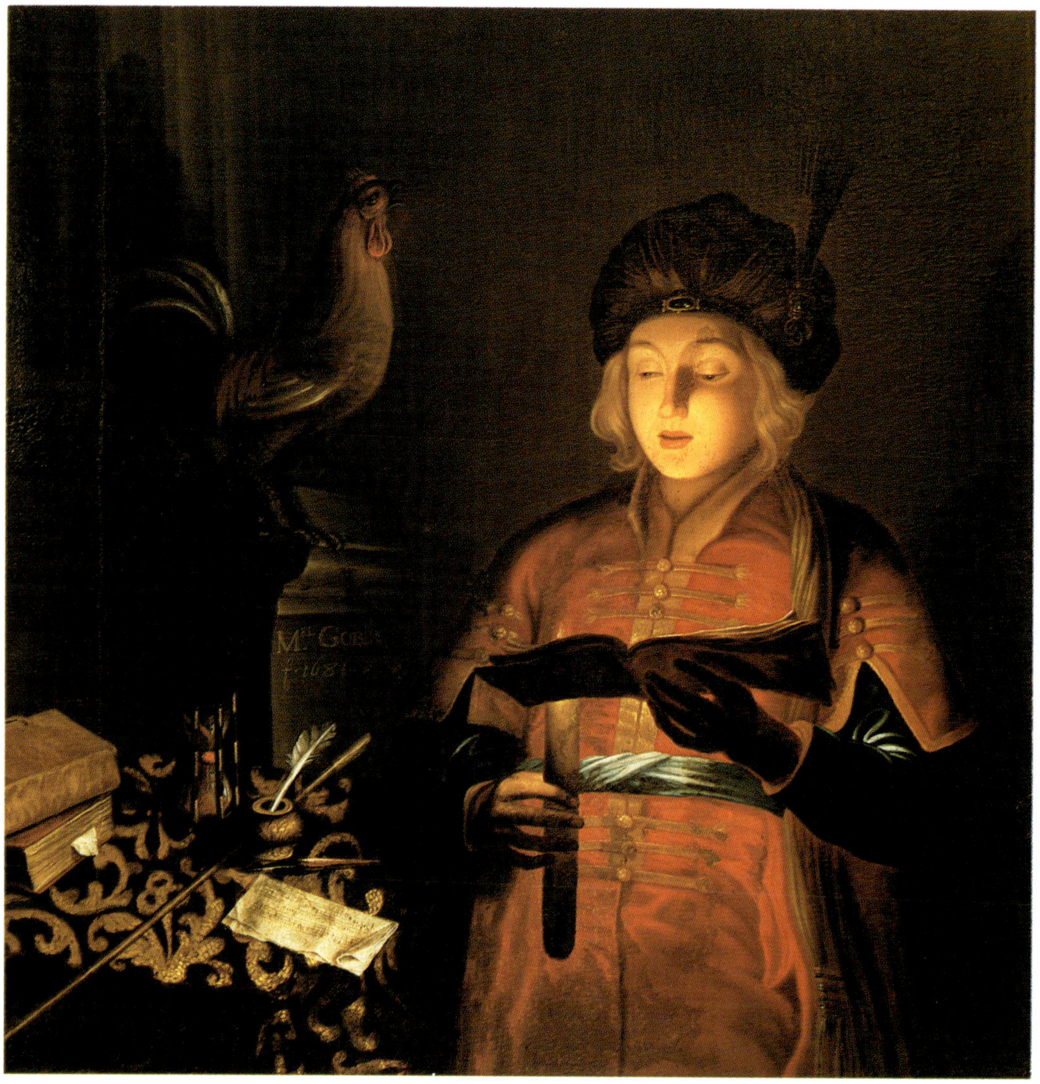

Michel Gobin

Working Orléans 1681

Gobin's *Young Man with a Candle* of 1681 (Orléans) is remarkable proof of the long continuation of the early seventeenth-century tenebrist tradition; only the handling of the still life is any indication of the late date of this picture. It is assumed that Gobin worked at Orléans. He was also a still-life painter, and it is likely that his work is still confused with that of Meiffren Conte.

Collections

Budapest, Szépmüvészeti Múzeum
Boy Smoking a Pipe (attribution)

Orléans, Musée des Beaux-Arts
Young Man with a Candle (signed and dated 1681) (plate 33)
Still Life with Flowers and Silver (signed and dated 1681; after Meiffren Conte)

Bibliography

Charles Sterling in the exhibition catalogue, Paris, Orangerie, *Les peintres de la réalité*, 1934, pp.50–51.

F. Habert

Nothing is known about this painter of genre scenes and flower pictures, although it is reasonable to assume that he worked in France in the middle years of the seventeenth century. He was one of the very few painters of the time who were interested in depicting large banquet pieces.

Collections

Crans-sur-Sierre (Switzerland), A. S. collection
Bowl of Spring Flowers and Butterflies (signed)

France, private collection
Basket of Flowers and an Orange Tree (signed and dated 1649)

France, private collection
Banquet Piece (monogrammed)
Flowers and Fruit (signed)

Munich, P. Griebert collection
Fish, Meat, Kitchen Utensils and Asparagus (monogrammed)

Paris, private collection
Still Life with a Pack of Cards (signed and dated 1649)

Paris, private collection
Flowers, Fruit and Fish (signed)

Bibliography

Michel Faré
Le grand siècle de la nature morte en France, 1974, pp.272–7.

Daniel Hallé

Rouen 1614–Paris 1676

Most of Hallé's career was spent in Paris, where he painted large altarpieces for the main churches, including Notre Dame. He was strongly influenced by Charles Le Brun in his compositions.

Collections

Clermont-Ferrand, Musée Bargoin
St John at the Latin Gate (dated 1662)

Paris, Saint-Germain-des-Prés
The Martyrdom of St Symphorian

Rouen, Musée des Beaux-Arts
The Nativity (signed and dated 1669)

Rouen, Saint-Ouen
The Miracle of the Loaves and Fishes (signed and dated 1664)

Bibliography

There is no recent literature, but see Pierre Rosenberg in Rouen, Musée des Beaux-Arts, *Tableaux français du XVIIe siècle* . . ., 1966, p.47.

Jean Hellart

Reims 1618–Reims 1685

Apart from a brief visit to Italy, Hellart spent his whole career in the relative isolation of Reims.

Collections

Reims, Saint-Denis
The Death of Ananias
St Peter and St Andrew
The Preaching of St Peter

Reims, Saint-Rémi
Reception of Clovis by St Rémi at Reims

Bibliography

E.C. Bénézit
Dictionnaire des peintres . . ., 1976, ed., vol.5, pp.470–2, devotes a long and virtually incomprehensible passage to the artist's personal life.

Jacques Hupin

Working mid-seventeenth century

It is not known exactly when this artist worked, but his elaborate pictures, which concentrate on heavily chased silver and patterned carpets, are close to those of Meiffren Conte.

Collections

Auxerre, Musée des Beaux-Arts
Still Life with Silver and a Carpet (signed)

Caen, Musée des Beaux-Arts
Still Life

Carcassonne, Musée des Beaux-Arts
Still Life

France, private collection
Silver and a Carpet

France, private collection
Silver and Fruit on a Carpet

France, private collection
Silver on a Carpet

Paris, Louvre
Still Life with a Carpet (signed)

Paris, private collection
Vanitas (signed)

Tours, Musée des Beaux-Arts
Still Life with Apples, Silver and a Carpet

Bibliography

Michel Faré
Le grand siècle de la nature morte en France, 1974, pp.238–42.

Georges de La Chapelle

Working Caen, mid-seventeenth century

La Chapelle was one of the very few French artists to be completely influenced by the realistic tradition in Dutch seventeenth-century painting, especially as practised by artists such as Jan van Goyen, who was not at that time appreciated in France.

Collection

Paris, Louvre
Landscape (signed and dated 1646)

Bibliography

There is no recent literature on this artist.

Charles de La Fosse

Paris 1636–Paris 1716

A pupil of Charles Le Brun, La Fosse was one of the most important decorators of the period, although his major work, the dome of Les Invalides in Paris, was not executed until the end of the century. Of the five years he lived in Italy, three were spent in Venice. The rich colouring characteristic of sixteenth-century art is obvious in his work. La Fosse was the artist least influenced by Poussin, and all his main works have a curiously eighteenth-century air, on account of their lightness of composition and swirling movement. Most of his major work was executed for Parisian churches. He became a member of the French Academy in Paris in 1673.

Collections

Agen, Musée des Beaux-Arts
Triumph of Galatea

Algiers, Musée des Beaux-Arts
Neptune Chasing the Wind

Amiens, Musée de Picardie
Virgin and Child

Barnard Castle, Bowes Museum
Sketch for a ceiling decoration

Brest, Musée des Beaux-Arts
Venus Presenting Arms to Aeneas

Chartres, Musée des Beaux-Arts
Thetis Imploring Jupiter

Cherbourg, Musée Thomas-Henry
Presentation in the Temple
Dormition of the Virgin

Dijon, Musée des Beaux-Arts
Bacchus and Ariadne (dated 1699)

Dijon, Musée Magnin
Apollo and Daphne
Apollo and Marsyas
Assumption of the Virgin

Dunkirk, Musée des Beaux-Arts
God and the Father Supported by Angels and Evangelists

Grenoble, Musée de Peinture et de Sculpture
Christ in the Wilderness
Hope and Temperance
Faith and Charity (signed)

Le Havre, Musée des Beaux-Arts
Consecration of the Virgin

Leningrad, Hermitage
Hagar in the Desert

Lyons, Sainte-Blandine
The Visitation

Madrid, Prado
Acis and Galatea

Marseilles, Palais Longchamp
Sketch: *The Rising of the Sun*

Montfort-l'Amaury, Church
Christ on the Cross

Moscow, Pushkin Museum
Christ Appearing to the Holy Women

Nancy, Musée des Beaux-Arts
Assumption of the Virgin

Nantes, Musée des Beaux-Arts
Aeneas, Venus and Vulcan

Nevers, Musée des Beaux-Arts
Hercules between Vice and Virtue

Orléans, Musée des Beaux-Arts
Christ on the Cross
Apollo and Daphne
Pan and Syrinx

Paris, École des Beaux-Arts
Rape of Proserpine

Paris, Louvre
Annunciation (in a *Garland of Flowers* by Jean-Baptiste Monnoyer)
Marriage of the Virgin
Triumph of Bacchus (documented 1700)
The Finding of Moses (documented 1701)
Adoration of the Kings (documented 1715)

Potsdam, Sans Souci
Venus Presenting Arms to Aeneas

Rouen, Musée des Beaux-Arts
Sketch: *The Rising of the Sun*
Coronation of the Virgin
Time Discovering Truth

Saint-Quentin, Musée Antoine Lecuyer
Incredulity of St Thomas

Toulouse, Musée des Augustins
Presentation in the Temple (dated 1682)
Venus and Vulcan

Tours, Musée des Beaux-Arts
The Duc de Richelieu on Horseback
The Visitation (ruined)

Vendôme, Musée Municipal
Sacrifice of Iphigenia

Versailles, Château
Decoration in the Vault of the Chapel Royal
Decorations in the Salon de Diane
Decorations in the Salon d'Apollon
Sacrifice of Iphigenia
Clytie Changed into a Sunflower
Apollo and Thetis
St Mark
St Luke
The Chariot of Apollo
The Chariot of Apollo (attribution)

Bibliography

The standard article is M. Stuffman, 'Charles de La Fosse et sa position dans la peinture française à la fin du XVIIe siècle', *Gazette des Beaux-Arts*, ii, 1964, pp.1–121.

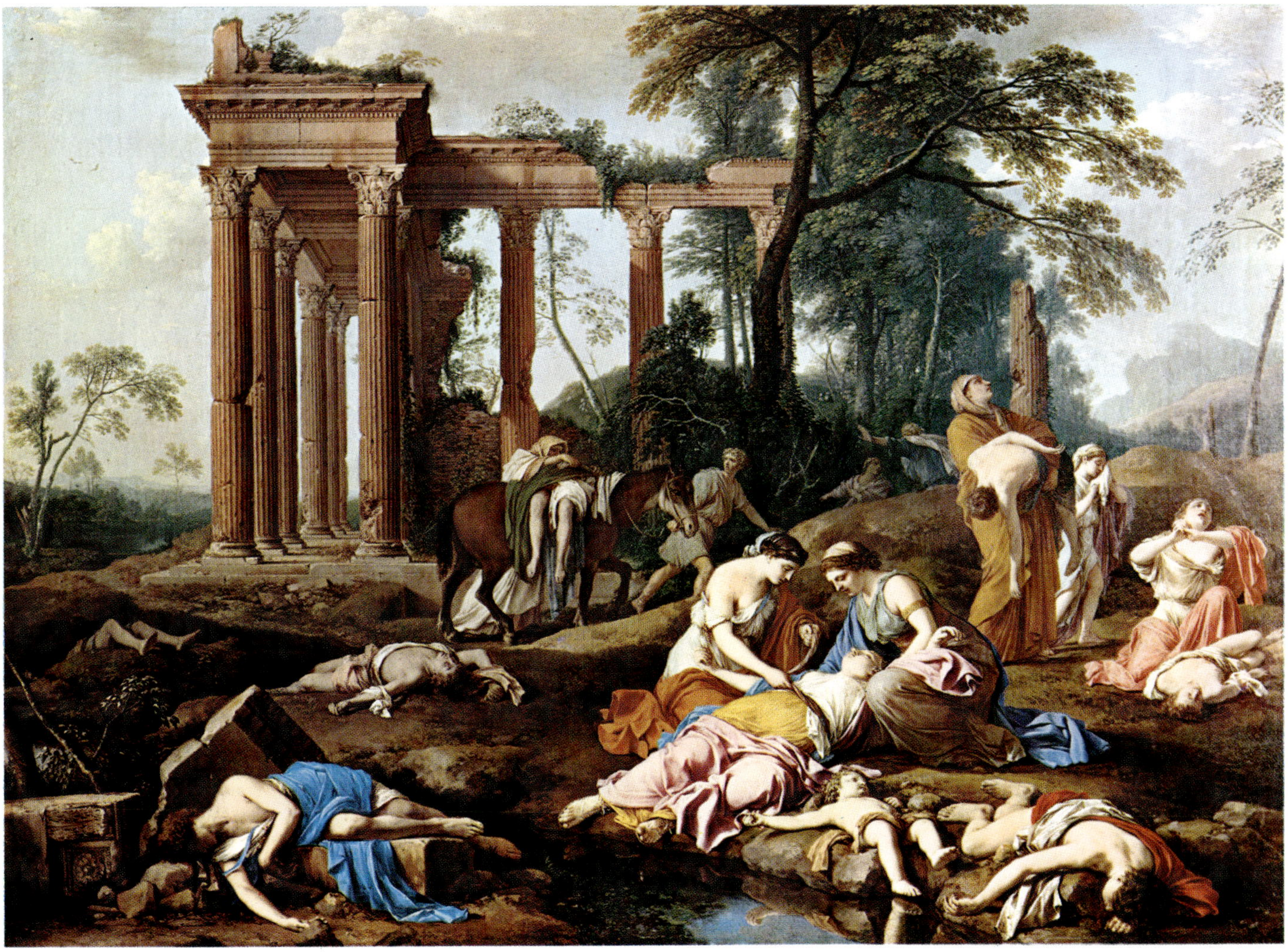

PLATE 34
Laurent de La Hyre
The Children of Bethel Mourned by their Mothers
Canvas, 97 × 129 cm. Signed and dated: L. de La Hyre in et F. 1653
Arras, Palais Saint-Vaast
In 1805 in the collection of Lucien Bonaparte. Acquired by the museum in 1938.

Laurent de La Hyre

Paris 1606–Paris 1656

La Hyre never went to Italy, and his style was formed in Paris under the Mannerist Georges Lallemant. All La Hyre's leanings towards classical antiquity were therefore learned at second hand, particularly from the work of Nicolas Poussin. As early as 1630, however, a certain coldness was detectable in his art, probably derived from Vouet, who had recently returned from Rome. Although most of La Hyre's work is of many-figured compositions executed in bright, bold colours, he is best remembered for his contribution to the development of landscape painting: his few surviving landscapes seem to amalgamate the limpid light of Claude Lorraine with the antiquarian interests of Nicolas Poussin. As there was so little landscape painting in Paris in the middle years of the century, the works of La Hyre form an illuminating example of the way that taste was turning towards the dry and formal. He was one of the fourteen founder-members of the Academy in Paris in 1648.

Collections

Aix-en-Provence, Musée Granet
'Maternité'
The Dead Christ

Arras, Palais Saint-Vaast
Assumption of the Virgin (signed and dated 1635)
A Dog Guarding its Prey (signed and dated 1632)
The Children of Bethel Mourned by their Mothers (signed and dated 1653) (plate 34)

Berlin-Dahlem Staatliche Museen
Holy Family in a Landscape

Boulogne-sur-Mer, Musée des Beaux-Arts
A Woman

Budapest, Szépmüvészeti Múzeum
Theseus at Trézène
Virgin and Child
Cornelia Refusing the Crown of Ptolemy (signed and dated 1646)

Bürgenstock (Switzerland), Schloss
Rhetoric (signed and dated 1650)
Philosophy (signed and dated 1650)

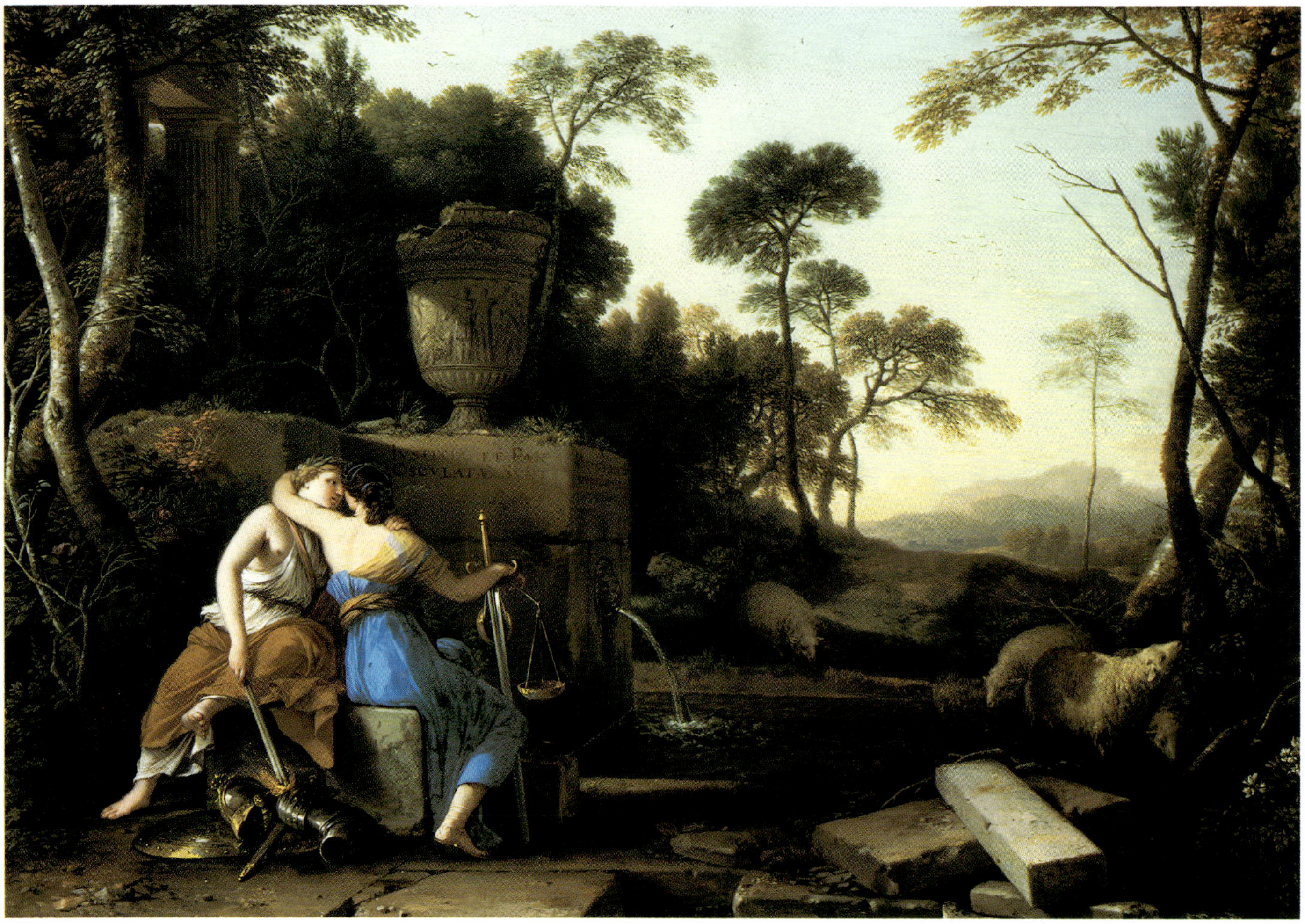

PLATE 35
Laurent de La Hyre
Landscape with Peace and Justice Embracing
Canvas, 55 × 76 cm. Signed and dated lower right: L. De La Hyre in et F. 1654.
Inscribed in the centre: Iusticia et Pax/osculatae sunt
Cleveland (Ohio), Museum of Art
First recorded in the eighteenth century in the collection of Evrard Titon du Tillet, Paris. Acquired by the museum in 1971 (purchase John L. Severance Fund)

It is unusual for the subject of a picture to be inscribed so clearly on the painting.

Chalon-sur-Saône, Musée Denon
Called *Comtesse de Beauvais as Diana*

Chicago, Art Institute
Cyrus and Araspe

Cleveland (Ohio), Museum of Art
Landscape with Peace and Justice Embracing (signed and dated 1654) (plate 35)

Detroit, Institute of Arts
The Finding of Moses
The Sacrifice of Isaac (attribution)

Dijon, Musée Magnin
Allegory of Love with a Violin
Allegory of Love with Music
Presentation in the Temple

Épinal, Musée Départemental des Vosges
Mercury and Herse

Florence, Uffizi
St Peter Healing the Sick

France, private collection
Geometry (signed and dated 1650)

Grenoble, Musée de Peinture et de Sculpture
Noli me Tangere (signed and dated 1656)
The Disciples at Emmaus (signed and dated 1656)

Heino, Kasteel Het Nijenhuis Hannema-de-Stuers Fundatie
Arithmetic

Houston (Texas), Museum of Fine Arts
The Rape of Europa (dated 1644)

Karlsruhe, Staatliche Kunsthalle
Virgin and Child in a Landscape

La Fère, Musée Jeanne d'Aboville
Landscape

Le Mans, Musée de Tessé
Christ in the Garden of Olives

Leningrad, Hermitage
The Birth of Bacchus (dated 1638)

Lille, Palais des Beaux-Arts
Landscape

London, National Gallery
Allegory of Grammar (signed and dated 1650)

Louisville (Kentucky), Speed Art Museum
The Rest on the Flight into Egypt (signed and dated 1648)

Lyons, Musée des Beaux-Arts
The Trinity

Malibu (California), J. Paul Getty Museum
Diana and her Nymphs in a Landscape (signed and dated 1644)

Marseilles, Palais Longchamp
Angelica and Medor

Montluçon, Musée du Vieux-Château
The Arrival of Panthée before Cyrus

Montpellier, Musée Fabre
Pastoral Landscape (signed and dated 1647)

Montreal, Museum of Fine Arts
Landscape

Nantes, Musée des Beaux-Arts
Rest on the Flight into Egypt (signed and dated 1641)

New York, Metropolitan Museum
Allegory of Music (signed and dated 1648)

Norfolk (Virginia), Chrysler Museum
Job

Orléans, Musée des Beaux-Arts
Astronomy (signed and dated 1649)
St Francis Giving the Cord of the Third Estate to Louis XIII (attribution)

Paris, Louvre
Pope Nicolas V in 1449 Opening the Tomb of St Francis of Assisi (signed and dated 1630)
St Peter Curing the Sick with his Shadow
Virgin and Child (signed and dated 1642)
Rest on the Flight into Egypt
Laban Seeking the Idols in the Baggage of Jacob (signed and dated 1647)
Landscape with Shepherds (signed and dated 1649)
Landscape with Bathers (signed and dated 1653)
Christ Appearing to the Three Marys

Paris, Note Dame
St Peter Healing the Sick

Paris, Saint-Germain-des-Prés
Entry of Christ into Jerusalem

Paris, Saint-Thomas d'Aquin
Conversion of St Paul (signed and dated 1637)

Ponce (Puerto Rico), Museo de Arte
Two Nymphs (signed and dated 1636)

Poughkeepsie (New York), Vassar College Art Gallery
Holy Family (signed and dated 1646)

Rennes, Musée des Beaux-Arts
The Meeting of Abraham and Melchisedeck
Elias Nourished by the Angel

Rouen, Musée des Beaux-Arts
Adoration of the Shepherds (signed and dated 1635)
Descent from the Cross (signed and dated 1655)
The Education of the Virgin (attribution)

Toledo (Ohio), Museum of Art
Allegory of Geometry (signed and dated 1649)

Troyes, Musée des Beaux-Arts
Leda Bathing with her Companions (attribution)
Landscape: the Torrent

Versailles, Château
Allegory of the Peace of Westphalia, 1648 (signed and dated 1648)

Bibliography

A monograph with *catalogue raisonné* by Pierre Rosenberg and Jacques Thuillier has been in preparation for some years. A useful summary with extensive discussion of individual pictures is found in the exhibition catalogue, Pierre Rosenberg, Paris, Grand Palais, *La peinture française du XVIIe siècle dans les collections américaines*, 1982, pp.247–52.

Louis de La Hyre

Paris 1629–Paris 1653

The younger brother of Laurent de La Hyre, Louis painted in the former's style.

Collections

Baltimore, Walters Art Gallery
Grammar (after Laurent de La Hyre; signed and dated 1650)
Arithmetic (after Laurent de La Hyre; signed and dated 1650)

Rouen, Musée des Beaux-Arts
The Vow of the Virgin (signed and dated 1651)

Bibliography

Jacques Thuillier
in the exhibition catalogue, Rouen, Musée des Beaux-Arts, *Nicolas Poussin et son temps*, 1961, pp.20–21.

De La Jeinsière

Working Lyons, mid-seventeenth century

The influence of Stoskopff is visible in the naïve style of this painter's work.

Collection

Paris, L.L. collection
Still Life with a Curtain (signed)

Bibliography

Michel Faré
Le grand siècle de la nature morte en France, 1974, p.144.

Georges Lallemant

Nancy c.1575/76–Paris 1636

The most important teacher of his generation, Lallemant taught Nicolas Poussin, Philippe de Champaigne and Laurent de La Hyre. His own style, concentrating on bold compositions with bright colour, seems scarcely to have influenced his pupils. His most important surviving work, *The Échevins of Paris* in the Musée Carnavalet, Paris, is a rare example of a group portrait from the period.

PLATE 36
Georges Lallemant
The Échevins of Paris Praying before St Geneviève
Canvas, 200 × 250 cm. Dated 1611
Paris, Musée Carnavalet

One of the few surviving group portraits for the city of Paris (the other is by Philippe de Champaigne).

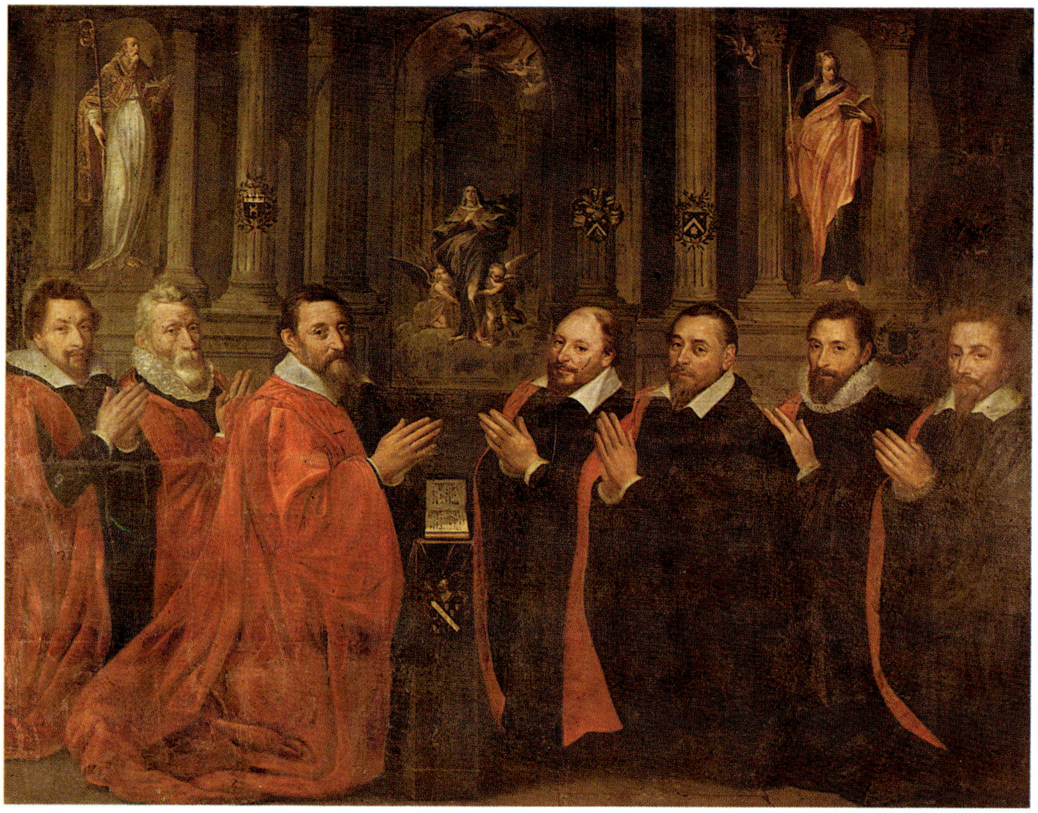

Collections

Leningrad, Hermitage
Adoration of the Kings

Lille, Palais des Beaux-Arts
Adoration of the Kings

Norfolk, (Virginia), Chrysler Museum
Christ Mourned by Two Angels

Paris, Musée Carnavalet
The Échevins of Paris Praying before St Geneviève (dated 1611) (plate 36)

Paris, Petit Palais
St Martin Parting his Cloak

Paris, Saint-Nicolas-des-Champs
Pietà

Bibliography

There is no recent literature on this artist, but two pictures were published by M. Dargand, *Bulletin de la Société de l'Histoire de l'Art Français*, 1974, p.17.

Philippe Lallement

Reims 1636–Paris 1716

Received into the Academy in 1672 with the two portraits at Versailles, Lallement was apparently a portrait specialist, although the rest of his work has not been identified.

Collections

Versailles, Château
Charles Perrault (documented 1672)
Gedeon Berber du Metz (documented 1672)

Bibliography

There is no recent literature on this artist.

Florent de La Mare-Richart

Bayeux c.1630–Versailles 1718

This portrait painter was received into the Academy in Paris in 1677.

Collections

Chantilly, Musée Condé
Group of Children Symbolizing Summer (signed and dated 1697)

Versailles, Château
Portrait of Noël Coypel (documented 1677)
Antoine Paillet (documented 1677)

Bibliography

There is no recent literature on this artist.

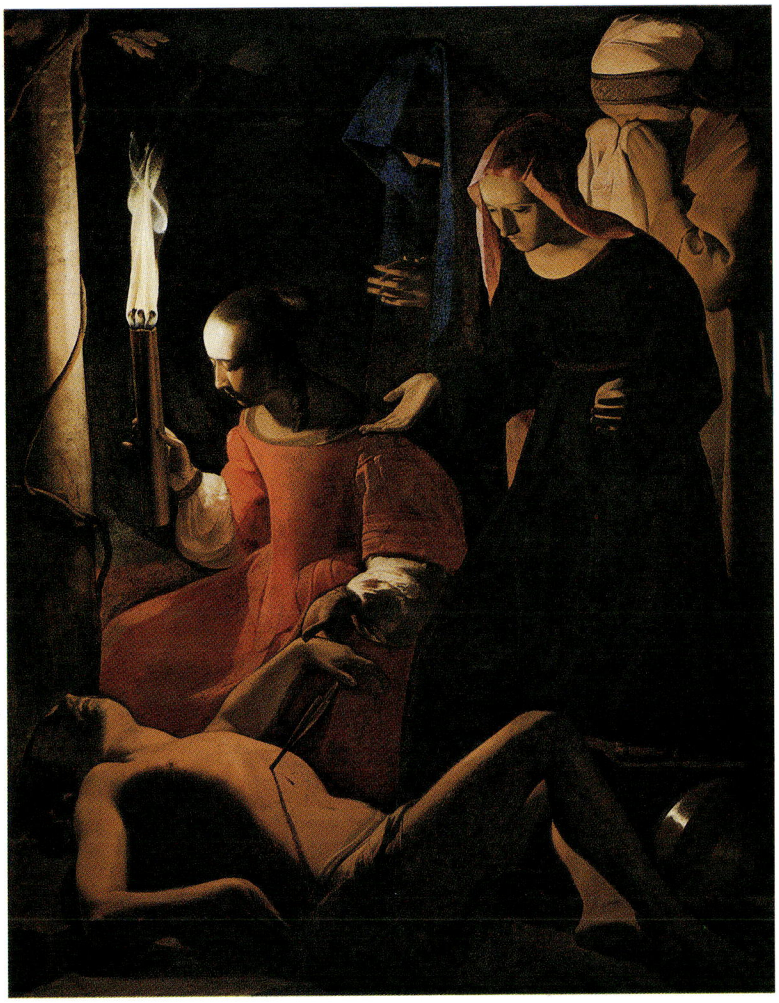

PLATE 37
Attributed to Étienne de La Tour
St Sebastian Tended by the Holy Irene
Canvas, 167 × 130 cm.
Paris, Louvre
First discovered in 1945 in the small church of Bois-Anzeray in the Eure. Acquired by the Louvre recently.

The subject was especially popular in the seventeenth century and Étienne de La Tour's treatment of it is unusual for its lack of gruesome detail. St Sebastian was thought to ward off the Plague, hence the popularity of the image. The painting is attributed to Georges de La Tour by all other authorities.

Jean-Baptiste de La Rose

Marseilles c.1612–Toulon 1687

The two surviving signed works of La Rose show that he was one of the earliest French painters of marines, somewhat in the manner of those by Salvator Rosa. He was to influence Claude-Joseph Vernet a century later.

Collections

Paris, Musée National de la Marine
The Port of La Ciotat (signed and dated 1664)

Versailles, Château
The Building of the Galère Royale (attribution)

Bibliography

Marielle La Tour in the exhibition catalogue, Marseilles, Palais Longchamp, *La peinture en Provence au XVIIe siècle*, 1978, pp.81–2.

Étienne de La Tour

Lunéville (Meurthe-et-Moselle) 1621–Lunéville 1692

It appears that Étienne de La Tour, son of Georges, was taken into his father's studio at an early age, and there learned to paint in careful imitation of Georges de La Tour's work. The few surviving documents imply that after the latter's death in 1652 Étienne gave up painting in order to concentrate on his business interests in property. One signed painting by him survives, and it is likely that many of the copies and variants of the elder La Tour's late style are also from his hand, especially as these pictures almost always vary slightly from one another, implying that they are not merely accurate copies executed outside La Tour's studio.

Collections

Berlin-Dahlem, Staatliche Museen
St Sebastian Tended by the Holy Irene (attribution)

Dublin, National Gallery of Ireland
St Alexis (attribution)

Nancy, Musée Historique Lorrain
The Smoker (attribution)
St Alexis (attribution)

New York, Frick Collection
The Education of the Virgin (signed) (fig.28)

Orléans, Musée des Beaux-Arts
St Sebastian Tended by the Holy Irene (attribution)

Paris, Louvre
St Sebastian Tended by the Holy Irene (attribution) (plate 37)

Paris, private collection
St Sebastian Tended by the Holy Irene (attribution)

Rome, Ottavio Poggi collection
St Sebastian Tended by the Holy Irene (attribution)

Rouen, Musée des Beaux-Arts
St Sebastian Tended by the Holy Irene (attribution)

Saint Louis, Art Museum
The Smoker (attribution)

Bibliography

The identification of the signature on the Frick Collection picture was made by Christopher Wright, 'A suggestion for Étienne de La Tour', *The Burlington Magazine*, May 1969, pp.295–6. Most of the documents appear in Benedict Nicolson and Christopher Wright, *Georges de La Tour*, London, 1974, pp.217–19.

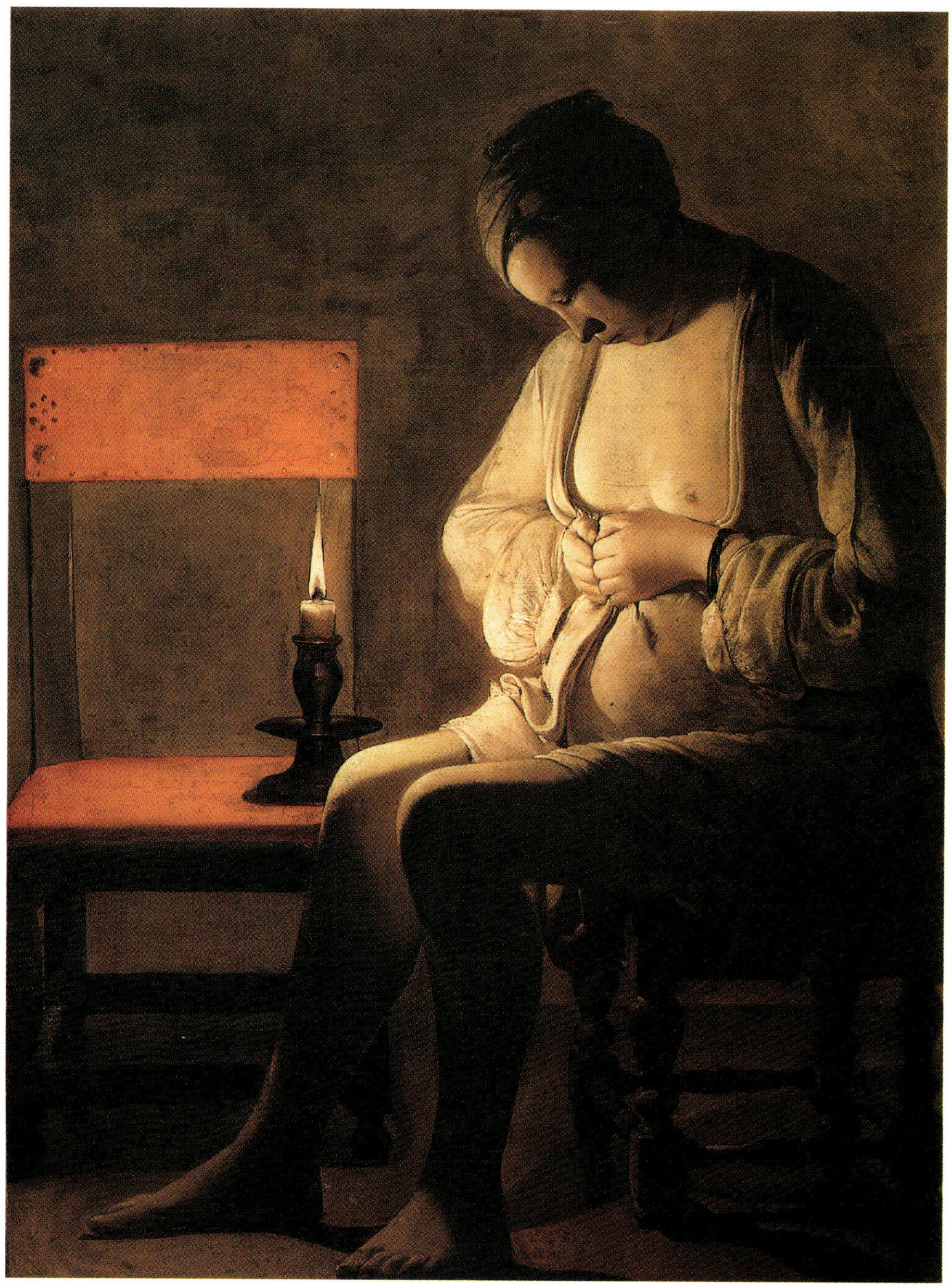

PLATE 38
Georges de La Tour
'*The Woman with the Flea*'
(*The Virgin Awaiting the Light of the World?*)
Canvas, 120 × 90 cm.
Nancy, Musée Historique Lorrain
Not certainly recorded until 1955, in which year acquired by the museum.

For the subject, see page 46.

Georges de La Tour

Vic-sur-Seille (Moselle) 1593–Lunéville (Meurthe-et-Moselle) 1652

The known facts of La Tour's life are few, and they relate but little to his enigmatic art. The son of a baker, he is first documented as a painter in his native Vic at the time of his marriage contract in 1617. Three years later he moved to Lunéville, where he seems to have remained for the rest of his life. A few commissions and contracts for pictures are recorded, but none of them can with certainty be associated with pictures known today. In 1623/4 La Tour provided two pictures for the Duke of Lorraine. More complete records survive for the years 1645–51, when La Tour executed a series of religious pictures for the town of Lunéville, which were intended as presentations to the French occupying governor at Nancy, the maréchal de La Ferté.

Nothing is known of La Tour's artistic education, but it is certain that he had apprentices in his studio in the years after 1620. Although his style was continued by his

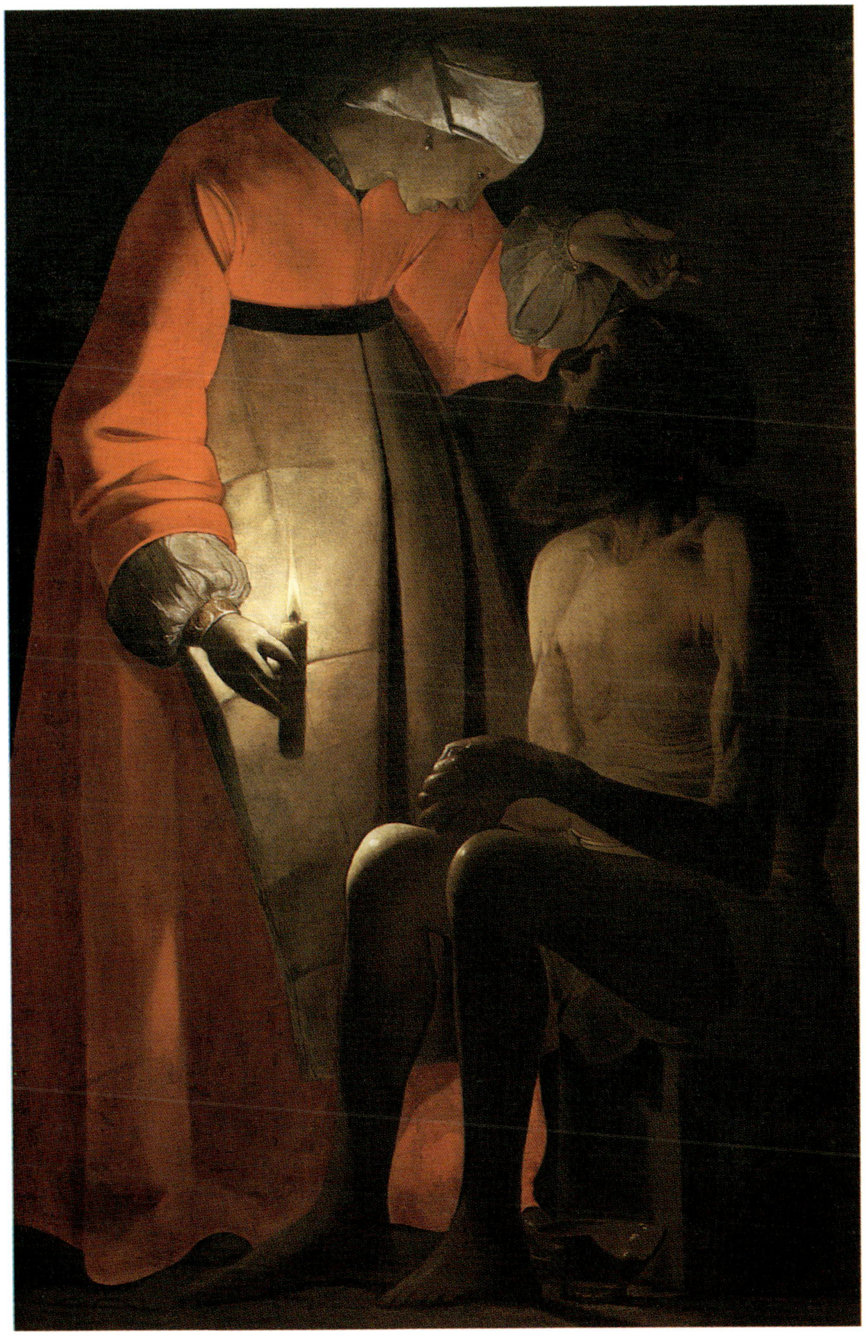

PLATE 39
Georges de La Tour
Job Mocked by his Wife
Canvas, 145 × 97 cm. Signed indistinctly, lower right: De La Tour fecit
Épinal, Musée Départemental des Vosges
First certainly recorded in 1825 when acquired by the duc de Choiseul from the collection of a local painter called Krantz. Acquired by the museum in 1829.

The subject is a rare one, and La Tour has introduced a special pathos into Job's sufferings.

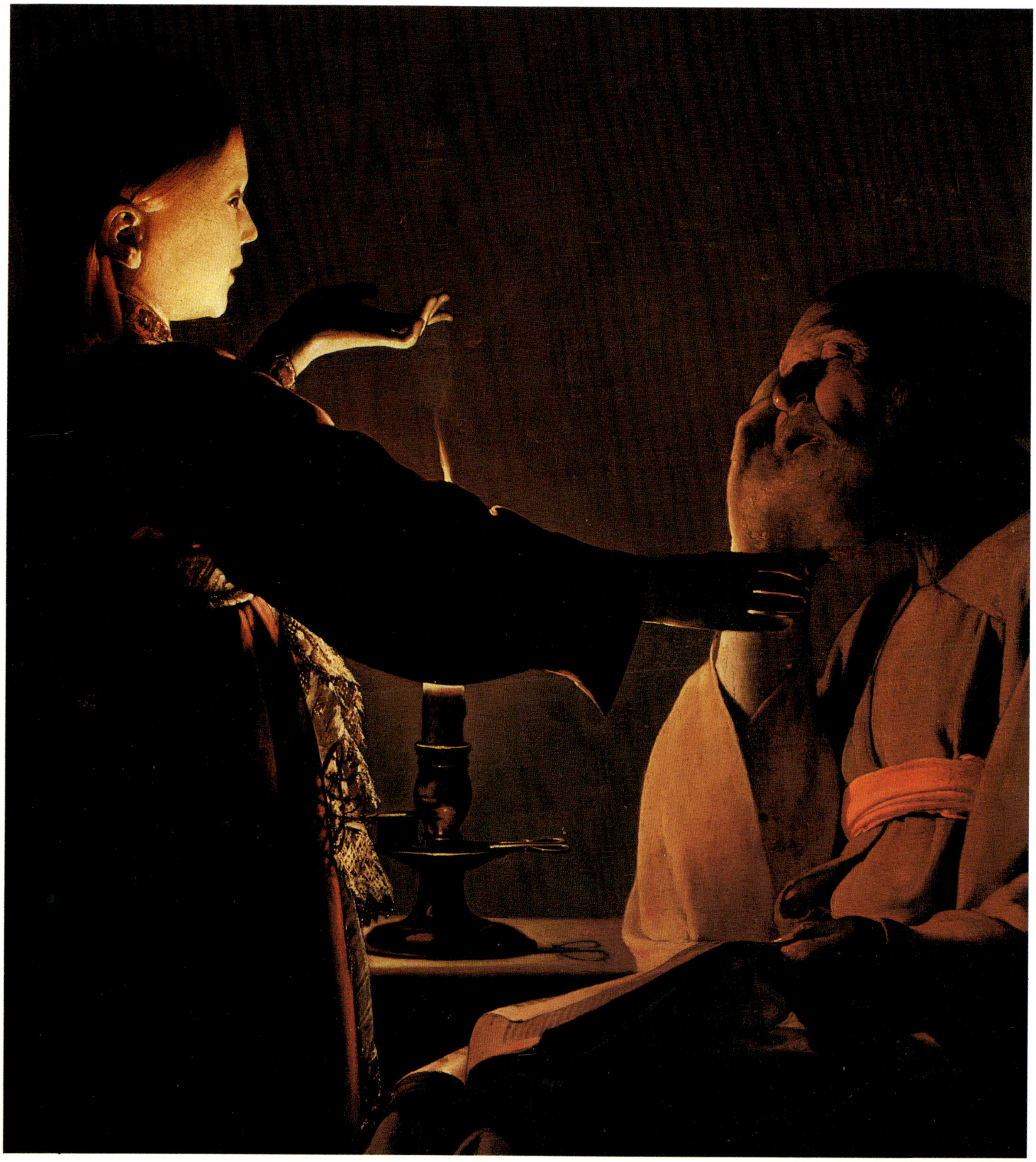

son Étienne, La Tour's reputation was lost immediately after his death, not to be revived until the twentieth century. A few of the biographical documents were discovered in the nineteenth century, but it was not until 1915 that a small group of pictures was assembled (by Herman Voss) under his name. From that date until 1972 the number of attributed pictures gradually increased. Many authorities continue to attribute to La Tour the two versions of *The Cheat* (Paris, Louvre, and Fort Worth, Kimbell Art Museum) and the *Fortune Teller* (New York, Metropolitan Museum).

PLATE 40 (left)
Georges de La Tour
'The Dream of Joseph'
(*Samuel and Eli*) (detail)
Canvas, 93 × 81 cm (cut on the right). Signed upper right hand corner: Gˢ De La Tour
Nantes, Musée des Beaux-Arts
First recorded in 1810 when acquired by the museum from the collection of François Cacault. One of the first pictures to be identified as by Georges de La Tour as early as 1915.

For a discussion of the subject, see page 46.

PLATE 41 (right)
Georges de La Tour
Christ in the Carpenter's Shop
Canvas, 137 × 101 cm.
Paris, Louvre
Given to the museum by Percy Moore Turner, 1948.
Its earliest history is unknown. It had been turned down by the National Gallery in London.

The subject was used by the Netherlandish Caravaggesques; especially close is Honthorst's treatment as a nocturne which was formerly in the church at Montecompatri.

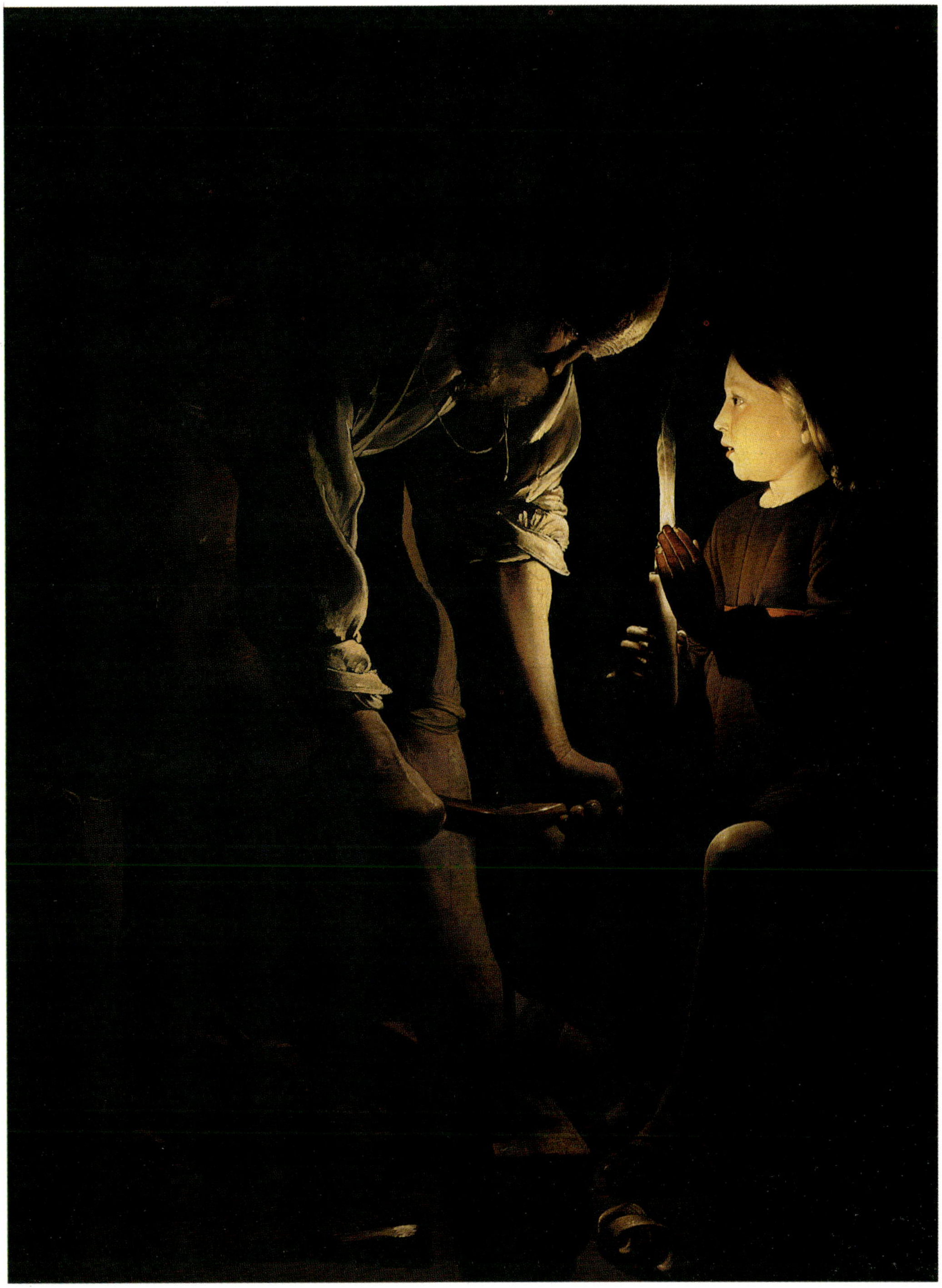

Collections

Bremen, private collection
The Girl with the Brazier (signed)

Cleveland (Ohio), Museum of Art
The Penitent St Peter (signed and dated 1645) (fig.26)

Detroit, Institute of Arts
The Education of the Virgin (fragment)

Dijon, Musée des Beaux-Arts
Boy Blowing on a Charcoal Stick (attribution)

Épinal, Musée Départemental des Vosges
Job Mocked by his Wife (signed) (plate 39)

Hampton Court Palace (Middlesex), Royal Collection
St Jerome

Leicester, Leicestershire County Museums
The Choirboy

Le Mans, Musée de Tessé
The Two Monks (attribution) (fig.25)

Los Angeles, County Museum of Art
The Penitent Magdalen (signed)

Lvov, Museum
The Payment of Dues (signed and dated 1634) (fig.24)

Montreal, private collection
Virgin and Child with St Anne (fragment)

Nancy, Musée Historique Lorrain
'The Woman with the Flea' (*The Virgin Awaiting the Light of the World?*) (plate 38)

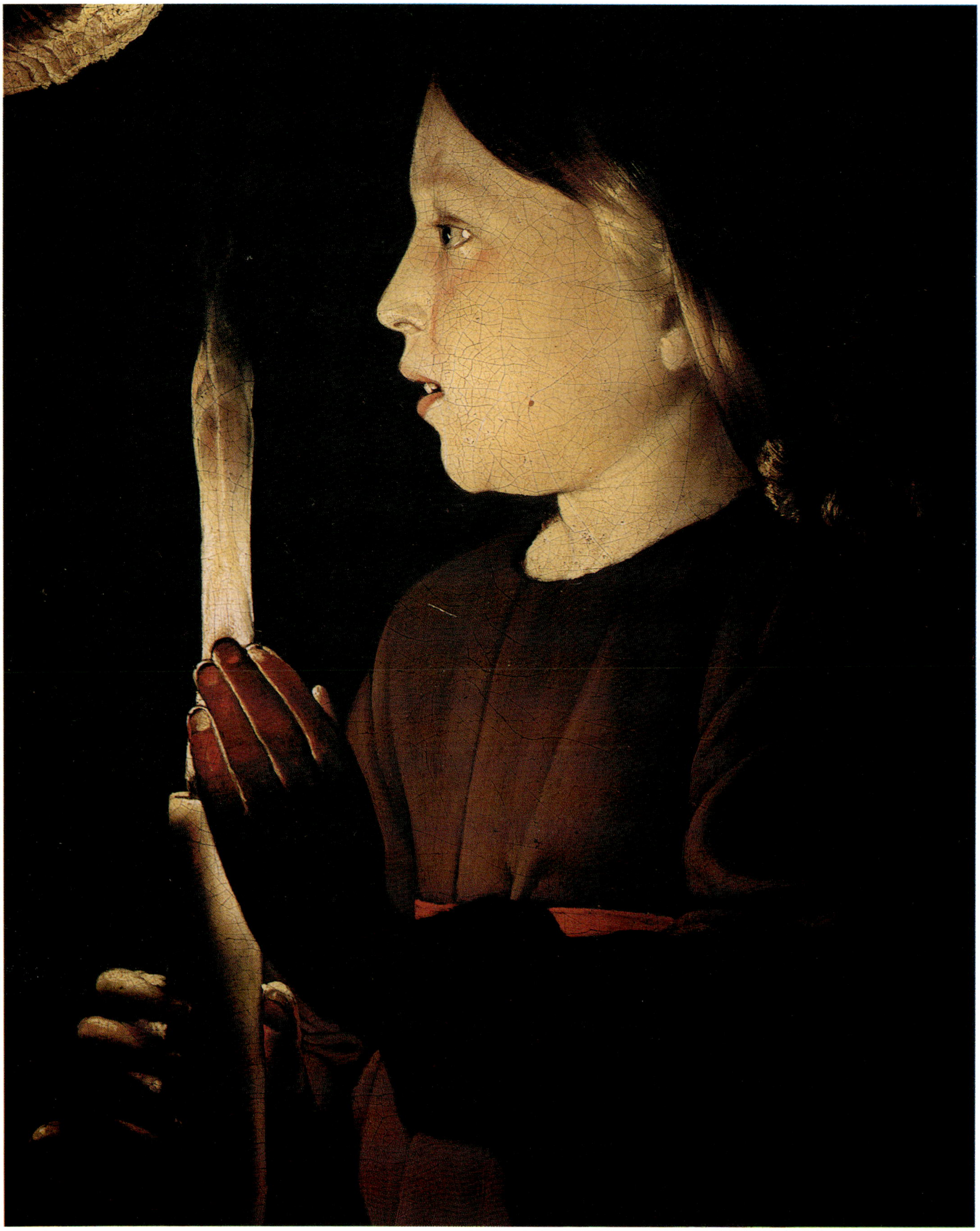

PLATE 42
Georges de La Tour
Christ in the Carpenter's Shop
(detail)
Paris, Louvre

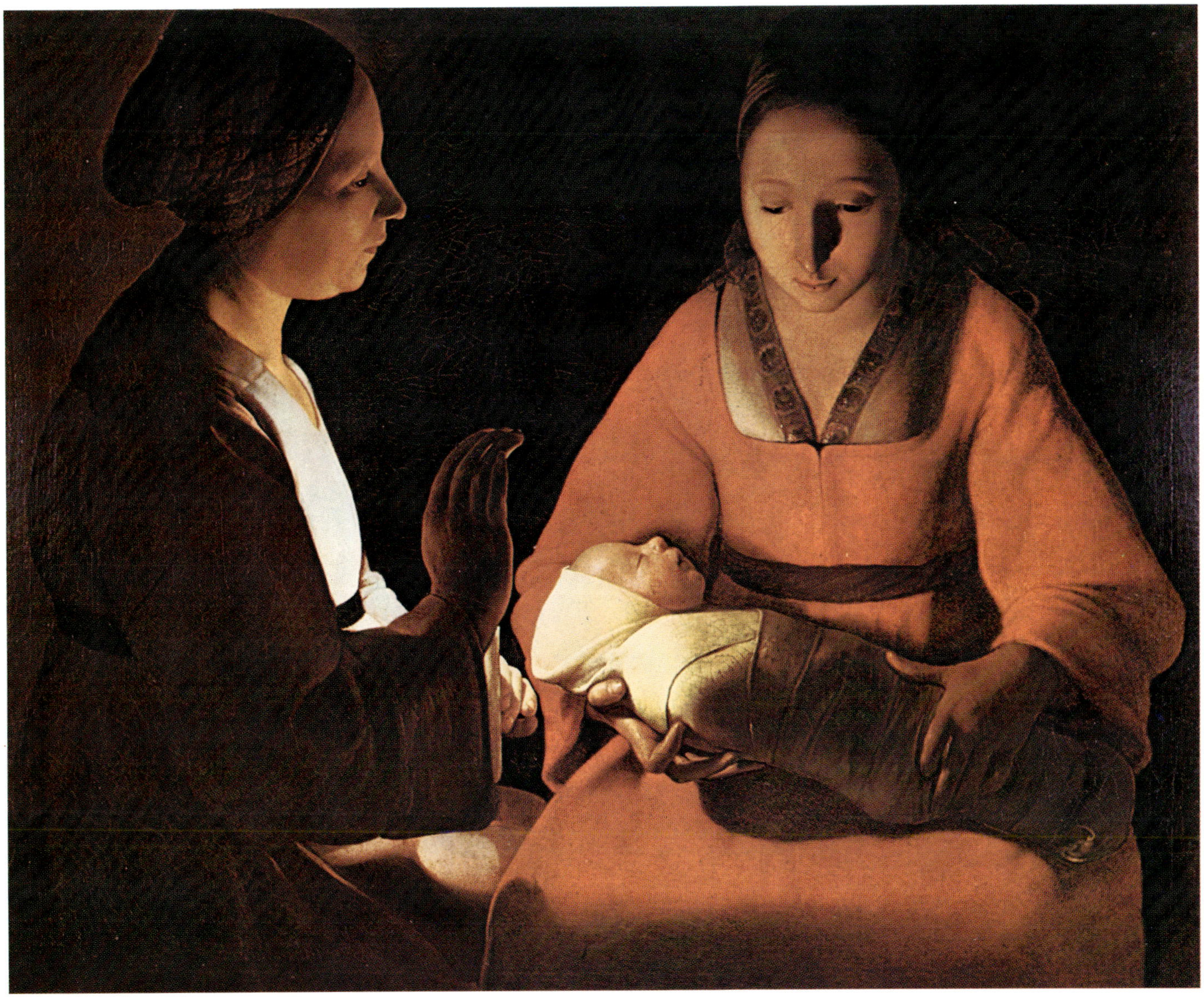

PLATE 43
Georges de La Tour
The New-born
Canvas, 76 × 91 cm.
Rennes, Musée des Beaux-Arts
First recorded at Rennes in 1794 at the time of the foundation of the museum there.

The subject is ambiguous because the spectator is uncertain whether it is a simple genre scene or whether it represents the Virgin, St Anne and the Christ Child.

Nantes, Musée des Beaux-Arts
'The Dream of Joseph' (*Samuel and Eli*) (signed) (plate 40)
The Denial of Peter (signed and dated 1650)

Paris, formerly with Cailleux
The Smoker (signed)

Paris, Louvre
Christ in the Carpenter's Shop (plates 41 and 42)
The Adoration of the Shepherds (plate 45)
The Penitent Magdalen (signed)

Paris, private collection
The Ecstasy of St Francis (attribution)

Rennes, Musée des Beaux-Arts
The New-born (plates 43 and 44)

San Francisco, California Palace of the Legion of Honor
A Peasant Man (attribution)
A Peasant Woman (attribution)

Stockton-on-Tees, Preston Manor
The Dice Players (signed) (fig.27)

Washington, National Gallery
The Penitent Magdalen

Bibliography

The best summary of the vast amount of twentieth-century literature is still the exhibition catalogue by Jacques Thuillier and Pierre Rosenberg, Paris, Orangerie, *Georges de La Tour*, 1972. All the books published immediately after the exhibition are modelled on it, but present slightly different points of view. The most sensible of them are Jacques Thuillier, *L'opera completa di La Tour*, Milan, 1973 (French edition, Paris, 1973, with slight changes) and Pierre Rosenberg, *Georges de La Tour*, Freiburg, 1973. The most detailed catalogue is found in Benedict Nicolson and Christopher Wright, *Georges de La Tour*, London, 1974. A revised list, with the addition of a few more attributions, was provided by Benedict Nicolson in *The International Caravaggesque Movement*, 1979, pp.63–6. New information concerning La Tour's visit to Paris in 1639 was published by Michel Antoine, 'Un séjour en France de Georges de La Tour en 1639', *Annales de l'Est*, 1979, I, pp.17–26. A useful summary of the present (and still controversial) state of La Tour studies is by Pierre Rosenberg in the exhibition catalogue, Paris, Grand Palais, *La peinture française du XVIIe siècle dans les collections américaines*, 1982, pp.253–8.

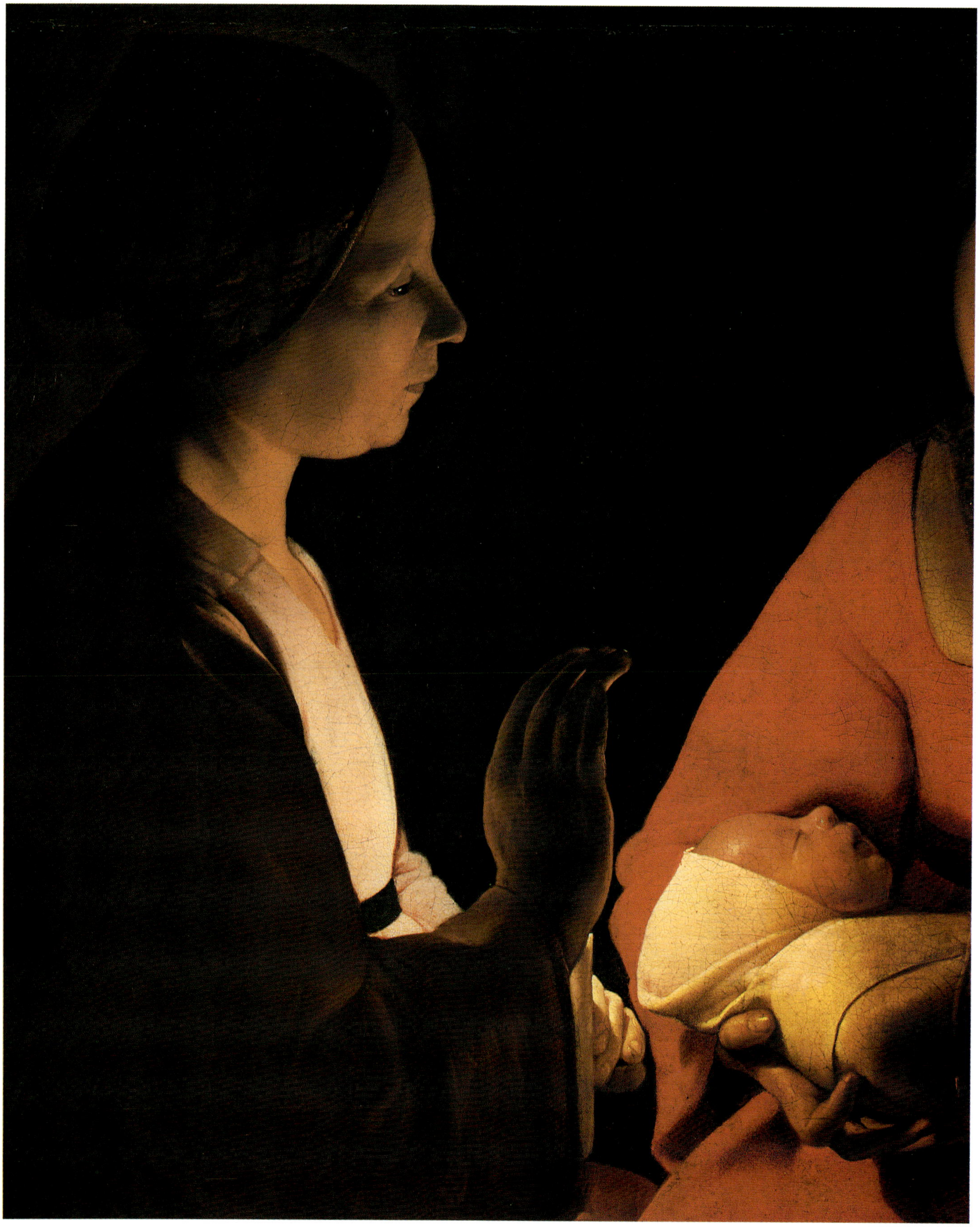

PLATE 44
Georges de La Tour
The New-born (detail)
Rennes, Musée des Beaux-Arts

PLATE 45
Georges de La Tour
The Adoration of the Shepherds
Canvas, 107 × 137 cm.
Paris, Louvre
Bought by the museum in 1926. No earlier history known.

This is one of the most frequently painted subjects in western art, but La Tour is unique in the realism of his treatment: the shepherds are entirely convincing.

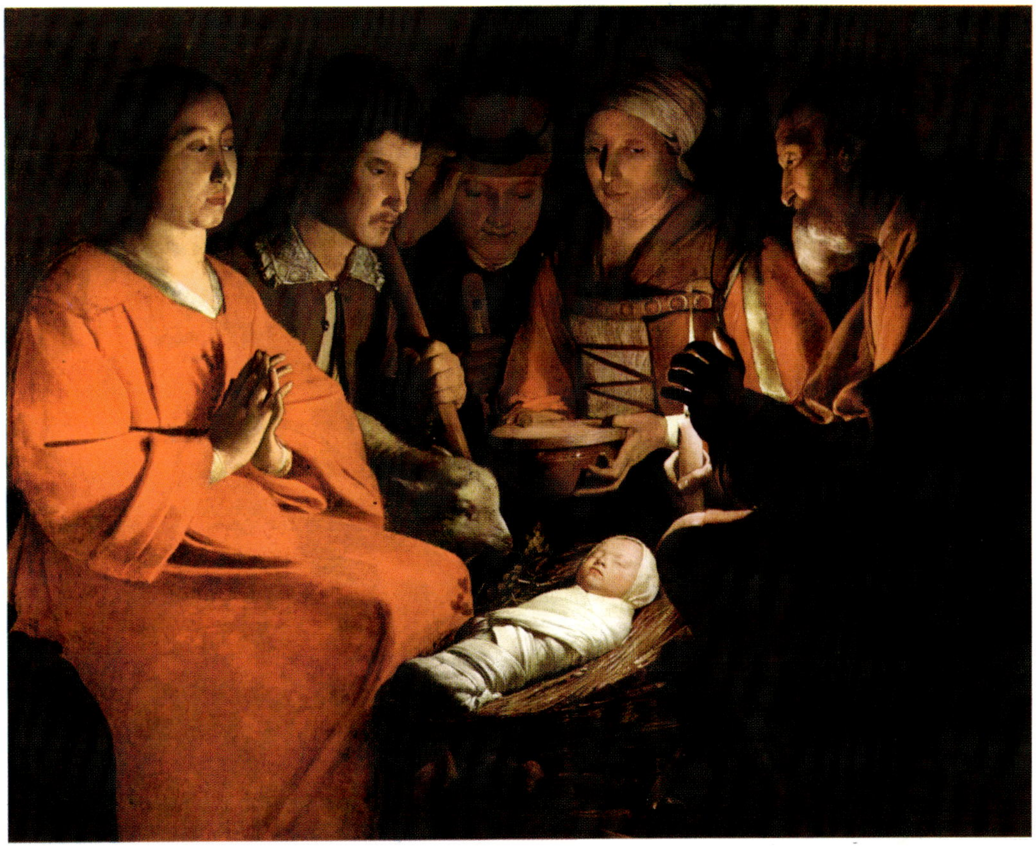

It is possible that a whole group of pictures has been wrongly attributed to Georges de La Tour, most of them since 1934. They form a coherent group: none is signed, dated or documented, and none of them is a night scene. They have strong links with Netherlandish art, especially Terbrugghen, and may well turn out not to be French. Those at Albi, Bergues and Grenoble have been in France since at least the eighteenth century, at which time they were attributed to a variety of painters, including Annibale Caracci.

Collections

Albi, Musée Toulouse-Lautrec
St Judas Thaddeus
St James the Less

Bergues, Musée Municipal
The Hurdy-gurdy Player

Berlin, Staatliche Museen, Berlin-Dahlem
The Vegetable Eaters

Grenoble, Musée de Peinture et de Sculpture
St Jerome

Malibu (California), J. Paul Getty Museum
The Beggars' Brawl

Nantes, Musée des Beaux-Arts
The Hurdy-gurdy Player

Norfolk (Virginia), Chrysler Museum
St Philip

Remiremont (Vosges), Musée Charles Friry
The Hurdy-gurdy Player

Stockholm, Nationalmuseum
St Jerome

Horace Le Blanc

Lyons before c.1580–Lyons 1637

Le Blanc is an example of a provincial artist painting in a Mannerist style during the first quarter of the century. He was patronized by Louis XIII.

Collections

Grenoble, Saint-André
The Mocking of Christ (signed and dated 1621)

Rome, San Giuseppe dei Falegnani
Marriage of the Virgin

Rouen, Musée des Beaux-Arts
Martyrdom of St Sebastian (signed and dated 1624)

Bibliography

Charles Sterling in the exhibition catalogue, Paris, Orangerie, *Les peintres de la réalité*, 1934, pp.80–82. See also Pierre Rosenberg in the catalogue, Rouen, Musée des Beaux-Arts, *Tableaux français du XVIIe siècle . . .*, 1966, p.78.

André Lebre

Toulouse 1629–Toulouse 1700

This minor painter continued the tradition of painting the *capitouls* of Toulouse which had been begun by Chalette.

Collections

Béziers, Musée Fabrégat
Sleeping Child

Paris, Louvre
Abraham and the Three Angels

Toulouse, Musée des Augustins
The Capitouls of 1692
St John on Patmos (dated 1695)
St Martin
St Rosa of Lima
Infant Christ Asleep on the Cross
St Roch

Bibliography

There is no recent literature on this artist.

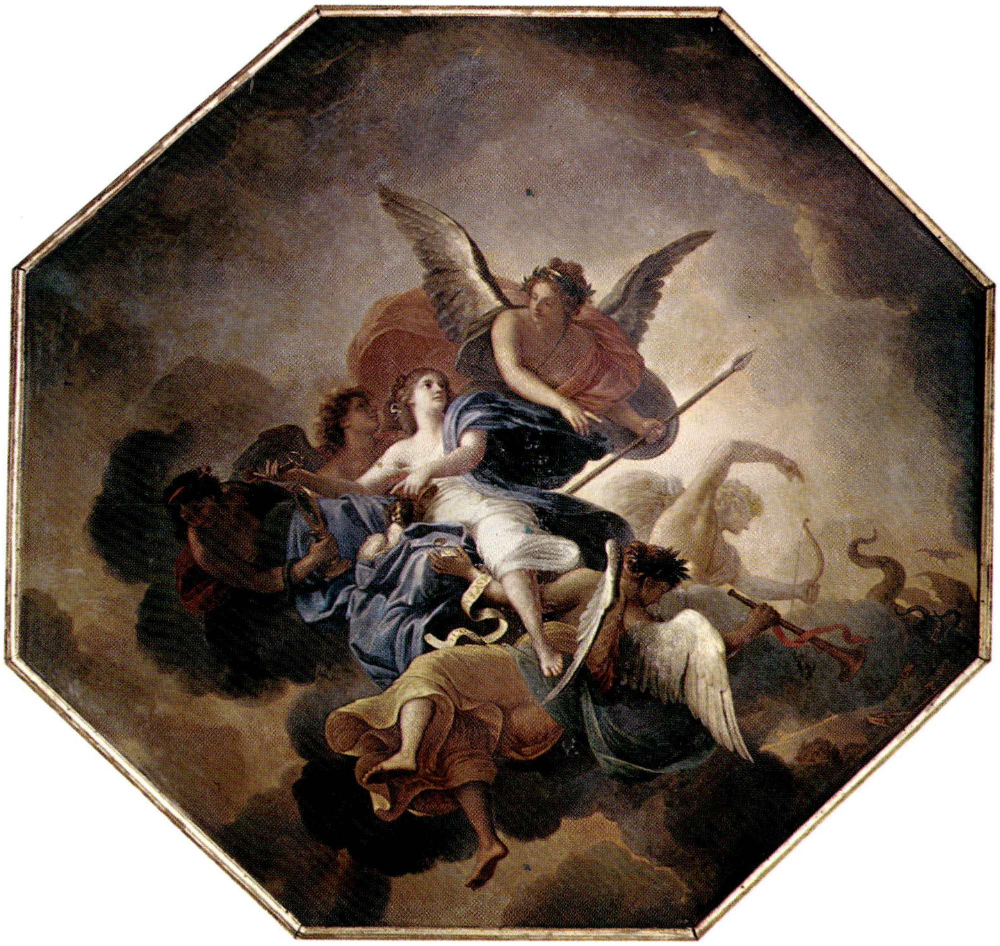

PLATE 46
Charles Le Brun
The Triumph of Faith
Vaux-le-Vicomte, Château
The decoration for the newly constructed château was begun by Le Brun in 1658, and was probably completed by 1660.

Charles Le Brun

Paris 1619–Paris 1690

Le Brun was the dominant painter of the reign of Louis XIV from 1661 onwards. A pupil of both François Perrier and Simon Vouet, Le Brun, aged twenty-three, accompanied Poussin on his return to Rome in 1642. He came back to Paris four years later, having been exposed to two opposing trends—the mature Baroque of Rome and the mature work of Poussin, particularly the first set of *Sacraments*. The first important stage in Le Brun's career was his decoration of the château at Vaux-le-Vicomte for Fouquet in the years 1658–61, after which he was employed by Louis XIV to decorate the ceilings of Versailles, his principal achievement. He took a secondary interest in easel painting, and his work of this nature can be divided into two categories. Half his pictures were

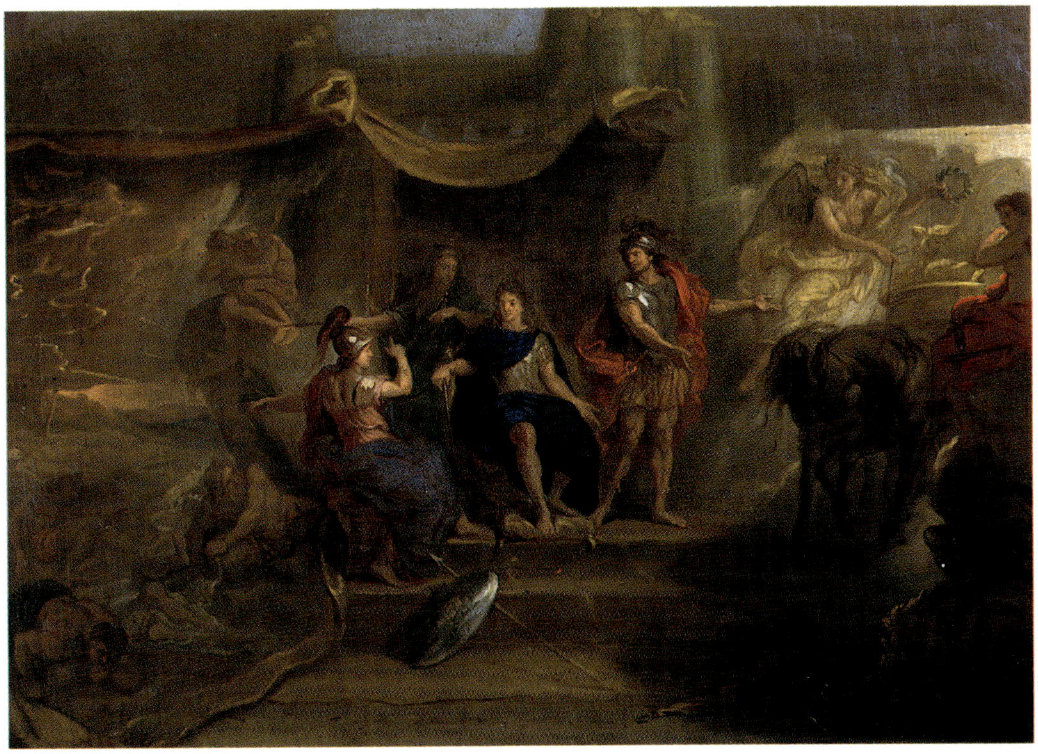

PLATE 47
Charles Le Brun
The Resolution of Louis XIV to Make War on the Dutch Republic, 1671
Canvas, 72 × 98 cm.
Auxerre, Musée des Beaux-Arts
This sketch for the ceiling of the Galerie des Glaces at Versailles apparently remained, along with others, in the French royal collection until the Revolution of 1789. It was bought by the museum in 1825.

The moment depicted is one of great importance in the history of the period: Louis XIV was eventually defeated by the Dutch.

official commissions—large altarpieces and battle pieces—and the other half were intimate portraits or sketches for grand designs. Le Brun has always been regarded as the archetypal academic painter, and although his enormous reputation died with him, his historical importance has never been in doubt. His best pictures stand comparison with those of any of his contemporaries.

Collections

Althorp (Northamptonshire), formerly Earl Spencer
Crucifixion of St Andrew

Arras, Palais Saint-Vaast
The Suicide of Cato (documented 1646) (fig.70)

Auxerre, Musée des Beaux-Arts
The Resolution of Louis XIV to Wage War on the Dutch Republic, 1671 (plate 47)
The King Armed on Land and Sea, 1672

Bristol, City Art Gallery
The Brazen Serpent (fig.72)

Budapest, Szépmüvészeti Múzeum
Apotheosis of Louis XIV

Cambridge, Fitzwilliam Museum
Holy Family (attribution)

Château-Gontier, Musée Municipal
The Battle of Constantine

Compiègne, Musée Vivenel
The Seven Provinces Declaring Peace, 1678

Darmstadt, Hessisches Landesmuseum
Flora
The Magdalen and the Cross

Detroit, Institute of Arts
The Purification (dated 1645)

Dijon, Musée des Beaux-Arts
The Fall of the Rebel Angels

Douai, Musée de la Chartreuse
The Dead Christ
Louis XIV on Horseback (attribution)

Florence, Uffizi
The Sacrifice of Jephthah
Self-portrait (documented 1684)

France, Silvestre collection
Henriette Selincart (dated 1680)

Greenville (South Carolina), Bob Jones University
Pentecost (attribution)

Houston (Texas), Menil Foundation collection
Holy Family (attribution)

Karlsruhe, Staatliche Kunsthalle
Hercules and Hesion

Langres, Musée Saint-Didier
The Fall of the Rebel Angels (attribution)

Le Mans, Musée de Tessé
God in Glory

Leningrad, Hermitage
Christ and the Sacrament
Daedalus and Icarus

Liverpool, Walker Art Gallery
Atalanta and Meleager

London, Dulwich College Picture Gallery
Horatius Coclus at the Subiacan Bridge
The Massacre of the Innocents

London, Victoria and Albert Museum
The Descent from the Cross (attribution)

Lyons, Musée des Beaux-Arts
The Resurrection of Christ (documented 1676)

Mâcon, Musée des Ursulines
Mucius Scaevola before Porsena

Minneapolis, Institute of Arts
Holy Family

Modena, Galleria Estense
Moses Defending the Daughters of Jethro (documented 1686)
Moses Marrying Sephora, Daughter of Jethro (documented 1687)

Montreal, Museum of Fine Arts
Deification of Aeneas

Moscow, Pushkin Museum
Christ on the Cross (signed and dated 1637)

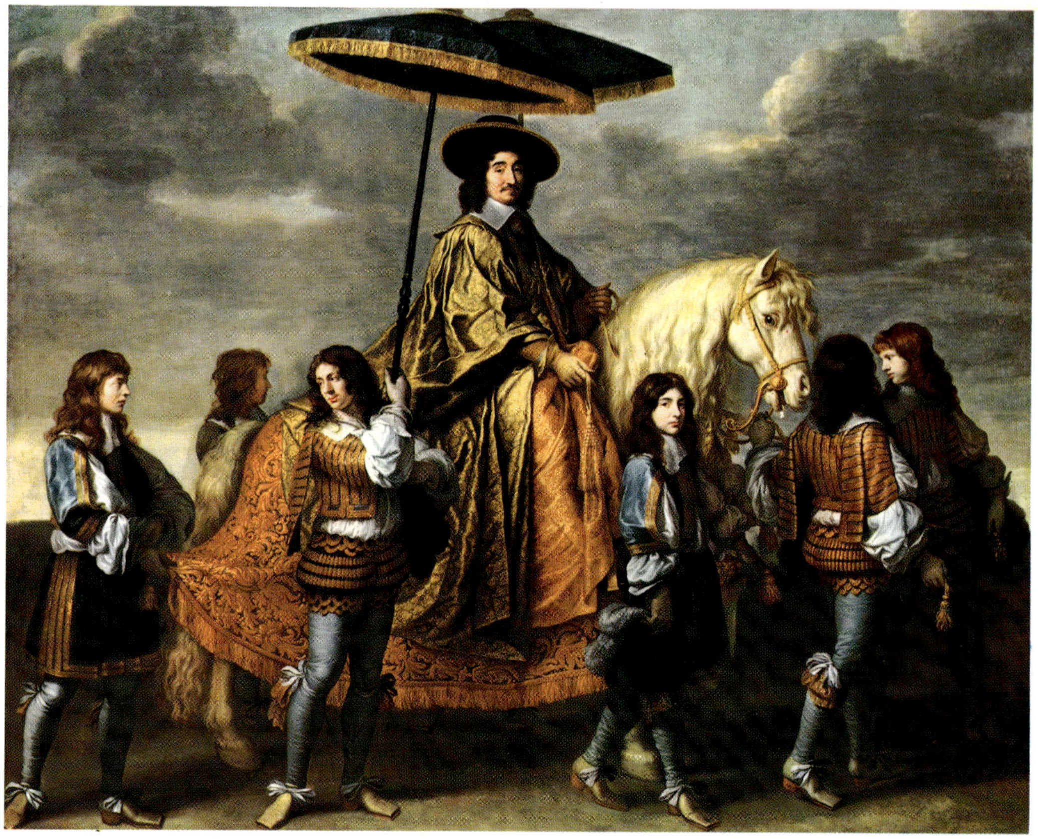

PLATE 48
Charles Le Brun
The Chancellor Séguier
Canvas, 295 × 357 cm.
Paris, Louvre
Acquired by the museum from the descendants of the sitter in 1942. The picture appears not to have been recorded until 1764. It is now thought that the picture was executed in the 1650s.

Munich, Bayerisches Staatsgemäldesammlungen
Head of an Old Woman

Nottingham, Castle Museum
Hercules and Diomedes (signed) (fig.71)

Paris, Musée Carnavalet
Psyche Elevated to Heaven (documented 1652/3)

Paris, Louvre
Dead Christ on the Knees of the Virgin
Charles Alphonse Dufresnoy
Louis Testelin
Moses Striking the Rock
Christ in the Desert Succoured by Angels
The Sleep of the Infant Christ (signed and dated 1655)
The Chancellor Séguier (plate 48)
Crucifixion with Angels
Holy Family
Pentecost
The Penitent Magdalen
The Hunt of Meleager and Atalanta
The Death of Meleager (documented 1672)
The Battle of Arbela (documented 1673)
Passage of the Granicus (documented 1673)
Alexander and Porus (documented 1673)
Entry of Alexander into Babylon (documented 1673)
Christ Carrying the Cross (documented 1688)
Adoration of the Shepherds (documented 1689)
Adoration of the Shepherds

Paris, Saint-Nicolas du Chardonnet
St Charles Borromeo
Martyrdom of St John the Evangelist (documented 1642)

Paris, Note Dame
The Martyrdom of St Andrew (documented 1647)
The Martyrdom of St Stephen (signed and dated 1651)

Paris, private collection
Lamentation over Dead Christ

Paris, private collection
The Tomb of Seneca

Paris, private collection
Hercules and Diomedes (sketch)

Ponce (Puerto Rico), Museo de Arte
Venus Clipping Cupid's Wings

Prague, Národni Galeri
Descent from the Cross

Rennes, Musée des Beaux-Arts
Descent from the Cross

Salzburg, Residenzgalerie
Portrait of a Sculptor (attribution)

Saint-Étienne, Musée de l'Art et d'Industrie
Entry of Christ into Jerusalem (documented 1688/9)

Schleissheim, Schloss
The Magdalen

Troyes, Musée des Beaux-Arts
Taking of the Town and Citadel of Ghent in Six Days, 1678
Christ Elevated on the Cross (documented 1685)

Vaux-le-Vicomte, Château
The Triumph of Faith (plate 46)

Venice, Accademia
The Feast in the House of Simon

Versailles, Château
The Queens of Persia at the Feet of Alexander (documented 1660/1)
Portrait of Turenne
The Conquest of the Franche-Comté 1674
Ceiling of the Galerie des Glaces
Decorations in the Salon de la Reine
Decorations in the Salon de la Guerre
Sketches: *The Fall of the Rebel Angels*
The Conquest of the Franche-Comté for the Second Time
St John the Evangelist
God the Father Adored by Angels
Bellona in Fury
Germany
Holland

Bibliography

The standard work is the exhibition catalogue by Jacques Thuillier, Versailles, Château, *Le Brun*, 1963. At the exhibition most of the artist's easel paintings were on display.

Jean Le Clerc

Nancy c.1585/87–Nancy 1633

Because of the lack of securely documented pictures, Le Clerc is difficult to assess, although he was the leading painter at the court of the dukes of Lorraine in the 1620s. He spent the first part of his career in Italy, first in Rome and then in Venice, where he worked in collaboration with Carlo Saraceni. A picture signed by both artists, the *Doge Enrico Dandalo Inciting the Crusade*, is in the Doge's Palace, Venice.

By 1622 Le Clerc had returned to his native Lorraine, where he was immediately honoured by Duke Henry II. Commissions poured in, both from the court and from the Church, for the adornment of the numerous churches of Nancy. Because all but one of these churches was destroyed during the 1789 Revolution, attributions to Le Clerc have to be cautious. For instance, a *St Sebastian*, documented as a commission for the church of St Sebastian (rebuilt in the early eighteenth century), was described in the eighteenth century, yet the St Sebastian in the church today is far too small to be the commissioned picture.

Le Clerc was also an engraver, making an etching of Saraceni's most popular composition, the *Death of the Virgin*. Le Clerc also made an etching of his own Munich *Concert*, the only known print of which is in the Albertina, Vienna. Had none of his pictures survived, it would still be reasonable to assume from his engravings that Le Clerc brought Saraceni's style back to Lorraine, where it died with him in 1633.

Collections

Boston, Museum of Fine Arts
St Stephen Mourned by Gamaliel and Nicodemus (attribution)

Bouxières-aux-Dames (Meurthe-et-Moselle), Church
The Ecstasy of St Francis (based on a Saraceni composition; attribution)

Chaumont, Église Collégiale
The Banquet of Herodias (fig.17)

Florence, Galleria Corsini
The Denial of Peter (attribution)

Langres, Musée Saint-Didier
The Adoration of the Shepherds

Nancy, Saint-Nicholas
The Nativity (attribution)
The Preaching of St Francis Xavier

Nancy, Saint-Sébastien
The Martyrdom of St Sebastian (attribution)

Palm Beach (Florida), private collection
The Adoration of the Shepherds

Piazzola sul Brenta, Villa Simes
The Shipwreck

Santa Giustina, Church
The Annunciation (by Saraceni, but completed and inscribed by Le Clerc)

Schleissheim, Schloss
The Concert (attribution based on the etching signed by the artist) (fig.18)

Stuttgart, Staatsgalerie
The Denial of Peter (attribution)

Venice, Doge's Palace
Doge Enrico Dandalo Inciting the Crusade (signed; with Saraceni)

Bibliography

The only article devoted to Le Clerc's Lorraine period, and now obsolete, is F.G. Pariset, 'Note sur Jean Le Clerc', *Revue des Arts*, 1958. A summary of his Italian period appears in Arnauld Brejon de Lavergnée and Jean-Pierre Cuzin, exhibition catalogue, Paris, Grand Palais, *Les Caravagesques français*, 1974, pp.46–52 and 249. A list of the artist's whole output is given in Benedict Nicolson, *The International Caravaggesque Movement*, 1979, pp.66–7. A more up-to-date survey of the artist's career is by Jacques Thuillier in the exhibition catalogue, Rome, Villa Medici, and Nancy, Musée des Beaux-Arts, *Claude Lorrain e i pittori lorenesi in Italia nel XVII secolo*, 1982, pp.71–102.

Claude Lefebvre

Fontainebleau 1637–Paris 1675

An enigmatic portrait painter, Lefebvre was received into the Academy in Paris in 1663. His surviving works are all attributions. The portraits associated with his name have the softness of those of Bourdon combined with the stronger realism of Philippe de Champaigne, and it appears that Lefebvre achieved a considerable reputation in his lifetime. It is in fact unlikely that all the pictures listed here are by the same hand.

Collections

Barnard Castle, Bowes Museum
A Gentleman (attribution)

Caen, Musée des Beaux-Arts
A Man

Chantilly, Musée Condé
Portrait of La Chapelle (attribution) (fig.65)

Cheshire, private collection
A Man (attribution)

Dijon, Musée des Beaux-Arts
Jacques de Saulx-Tavannes (attribution)

Dijon, Musée Magnin
Portrait of a Magistrate (attribution)

PLATE 49
Claude Lefebvre
A Teacher and his Pupil
Canvas, 135 × 111 cm.
Paris, Louvre
Acquired by the museum in 1810.

An unusual portrait, on account of the obvious intimacy between master and pupil.

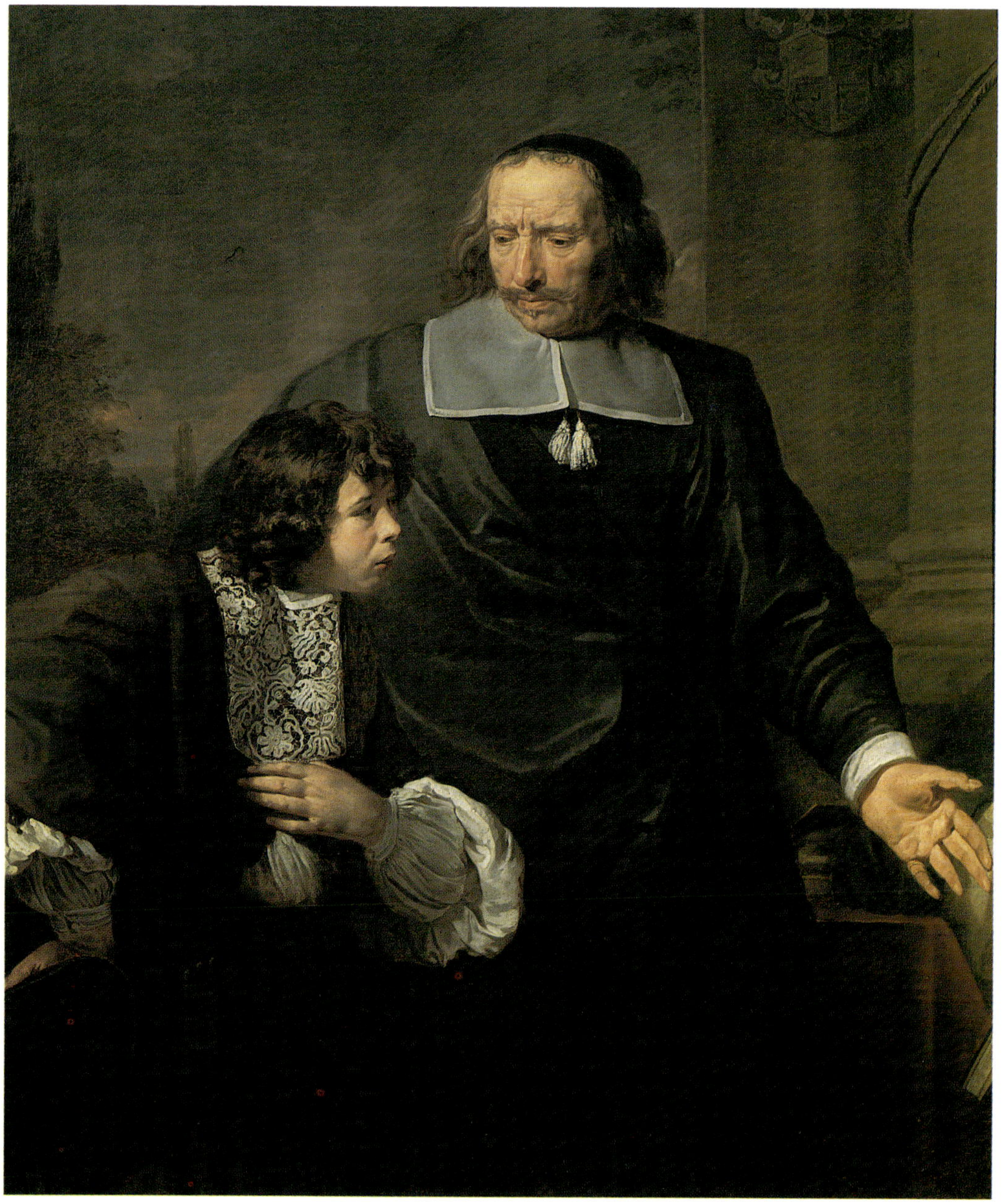

Metz, Musée Central
Nicolas-Edmund Olivier (dated 1661)

Narbonne, Musée des Beaux-Arts
Vicomte de Turenne (attribution)

New Orleans, Museum of Art
Louis XIV (attribution)

Paris, Louvre
A Teacher and his Pupil (attribution) (plate 49)
A Man (attribution)

Strasbourg, Musée des Beaux-Arts
Hugues de Lione (attribution)

Versailles, Château
Charles Couperin with the Artist's Daughter
Jean-Baptiste Colbert (documented 1666)
Duchesse de la Vallière
Prince de Condé

Bibliography

Charles Sterling
in the exhibition catalogue, Paris, Orangerie, *Les peintres de la réalité*, 1934, pp.85–7.

Rolland Lefebvre

Bagneux, near Saumur 1608–London 1677

A painter whose style was formed in Italy, Rolland Lefebvre specialized in portraits, though few are identifiable today.

Collections

Leningrad, Hermitage
Esther before Ahasuerus

Narbonne, Musée des Beaux-Arts
Portrait (attribution)

Bibliography

Charles Sterling in the exhibition catalogue, Paris, Orangerie, *Les peintres de la réalité*, 1934, pp.88–9.

François Lemaire

Maison-Rouge (Seine-et-Marne) 1620–1688

From the evidence of the portrait he submitted to the French Academy in Paris in 1657, François Lemaire was an archaizing provincial. Such a work would have been an anathema to the young Louis XIV, and it may have been the presence there of such painters as Lemaire that persuaded him to reform the Academy.

Collection

Versailles, Château
Portrait of the Sculptor Jacques Sarrazin (documented 1657)

Bibliography

Charles Sterling in the exhibition catalogue, Paris, Orangerie, *Les peintres de la réalité*, 1934, pp.89–90.

Jean Lemaire

Dammartin (Seine-et-Marne) 1598–Gaillon (Eure) 1659

Jean Lemaire's chief claim to distinction is the fact that he collaborated with Nicolas Poussin for the architectural backgrounds of some of the latter's pictures. There is still some dispute as to which these are, but the best-known is Poussin's *Theseus Recovering his Father's Shield* in the Musée Condé at Chantilly. Most of the second half of Lemaire's career was spent in Paris.

Collections

Arras, Palais Saint-Vaast
Roman Ruins (attribution)

Compiègne, Musée Vivenel
Gathering Flowers in Antique Ruins (attribution)

Dublin, National Gallery of Ireland
The Youthful Romulus

Fontainebleau, Château
Nymphs Dancing before a Temple
Peristyle before a Palace in Ruins

Leningrad, Hermitage
Architectural Scene
Landscape with a Sarcophagus

London, formerly Anthony Blunt collection
Pasiphae (fig.40)

Los Angeles, County Museum
Achilles and the Daughters of Lycomedes

Montauban, Musée Ingres
Landscape

Paris, Louvre
Antique Monuments (2)
Pasiphae

Rennes, Musée des Beaux-Arts
Landscape with Antique Ruins

Bibliography

The essential study is Anthony Blunt, 'Jean Lemaire, painter of architectural fantasies', *The Burlington Magazine*, 1943, pp.241–6. Blunt later added more pictures in 'Poussin studies IX: additions to the work of Jean Lemaire', *The Burlington Magazine*, 1959, pp.440–43. Further works were added by A. Busiri Vici, 'Opere romane inédite di Jean Lemaire', *Palatino*, 1965, nos.8–12, pp.161–8.

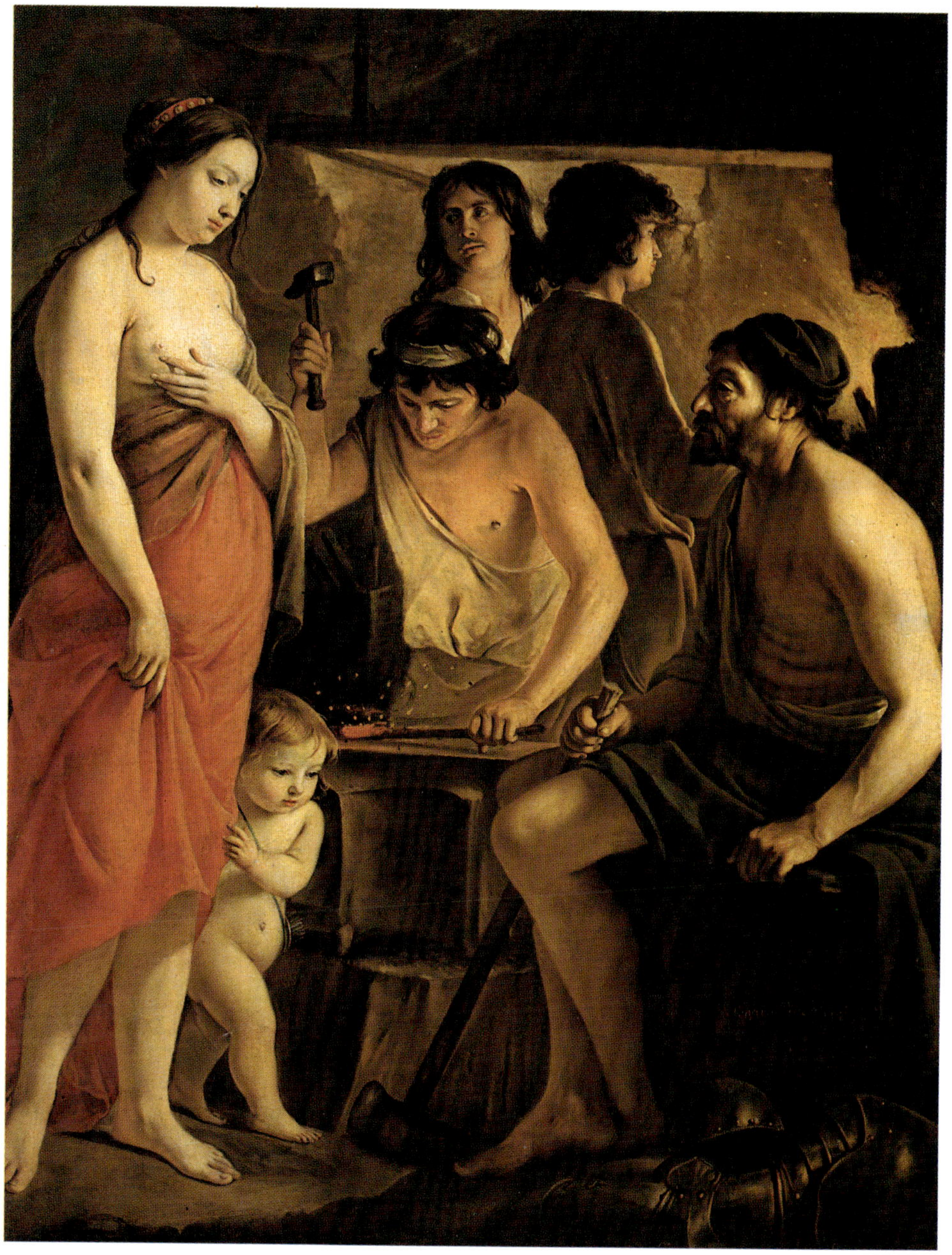

PLATE 50
Le Nain brothers
Venus at the Forge of Vulcan
Canvas, 150 × 116.8 cm. Signed and dated lower right: Lenain Pin A° 1641
Reims, Musée Saint-Denis
First recorded in 1918 in a Brussels sale. Acquired by the museum in 1922.

It is unusual for this often repeated mythological subject to be treated as a genre piece, although this occurs in Velasquez's celebrated picture in the Prado, Madrid.

Antoine Le Nain

Laon c.1600/10–Paris 1648

Louis Le Nain

Laon c.1600/10–Paris 1648

Mathieu Le Nain

Laon c.1607–Paris 1677

The activity of the three Le Nain brothers has always posed one of the most difficult problems of connoisseurship of the whole period, even though the known facts about them are simple. All three were born in Laon in the first decade of the seventeenth century. Antoine and Louis arrived in Paris in 1629, and in 1633 Mathieu was recorded as 'peintre ordinaire de la ville de Paris'. Until the deaths of Louis and Antoine in 1648, all three brothers lived together and collaborated on their pictures, probably in a variety of combinations. Mathieu survived the other two brothers for almost thirty

PLATE 51
Le Nain brothers
The Forge
Canvas, 69 × 57 cm.
Paris, Louvre
First recorded in the collection of the duc de Choiseul in 1772. Seized at the time of the Revolution in 1794 and since then in the Louvre.

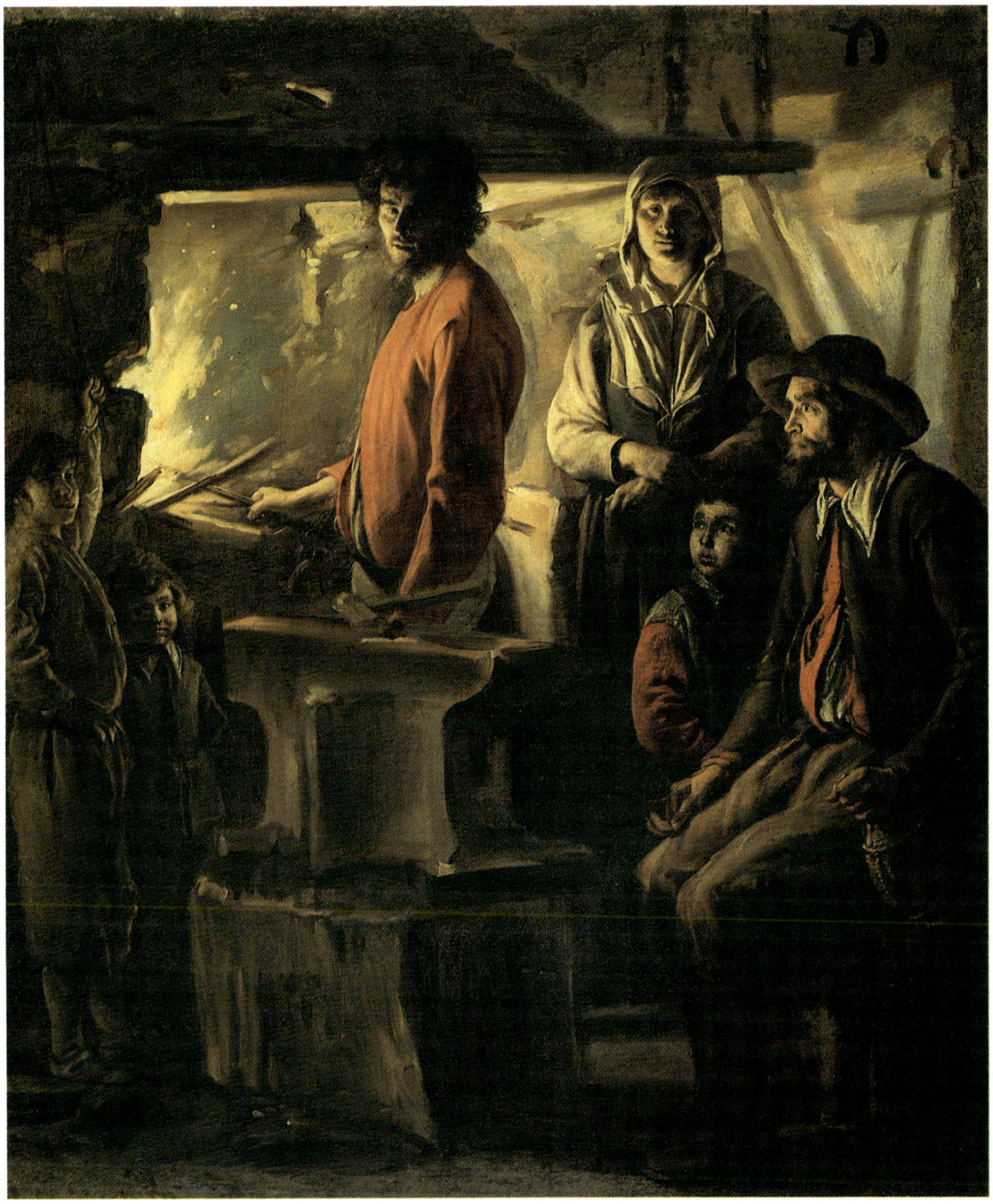

years, thus giving historians a chance of isolating his work from that of the other two. In spite of the great Le Nain exhibition held in Paris in 1978, the regroupings made then remain unsatisfactory because the pictures which do not fit into the groups have been given to such artificially created figures as 'Le Maître des Cortèges'.

The style of the three painters may be interchangeable, but their pictures fall into different categories of subject-matter. Working in Paris in the 1640s, the Le Nain brothers were the chief exponents of genre painting, so familiar in the Netherlands and so rare in France. Their religious and mythological pictures are painted in a variety of styles, whereas their peasant scenes are much more homogenous, falling into two groups, either small interiors with dominating figures or much broader pictures, often with landscape backgrounds. They also painted a few, more refined, middle-class genre scenes and portraits. The fact that all three brothers pursued successful careers, being founder-members of the Academy in 1648, shows that their art was appreciated by Parisian patrons. It was only after the reorganization of the Academy under Louis XIV, when the hierarchy of the genres was to become important, that history and religious painting took precedence over all the others, including the 'low-life' pictures at which the brothers were most successful.

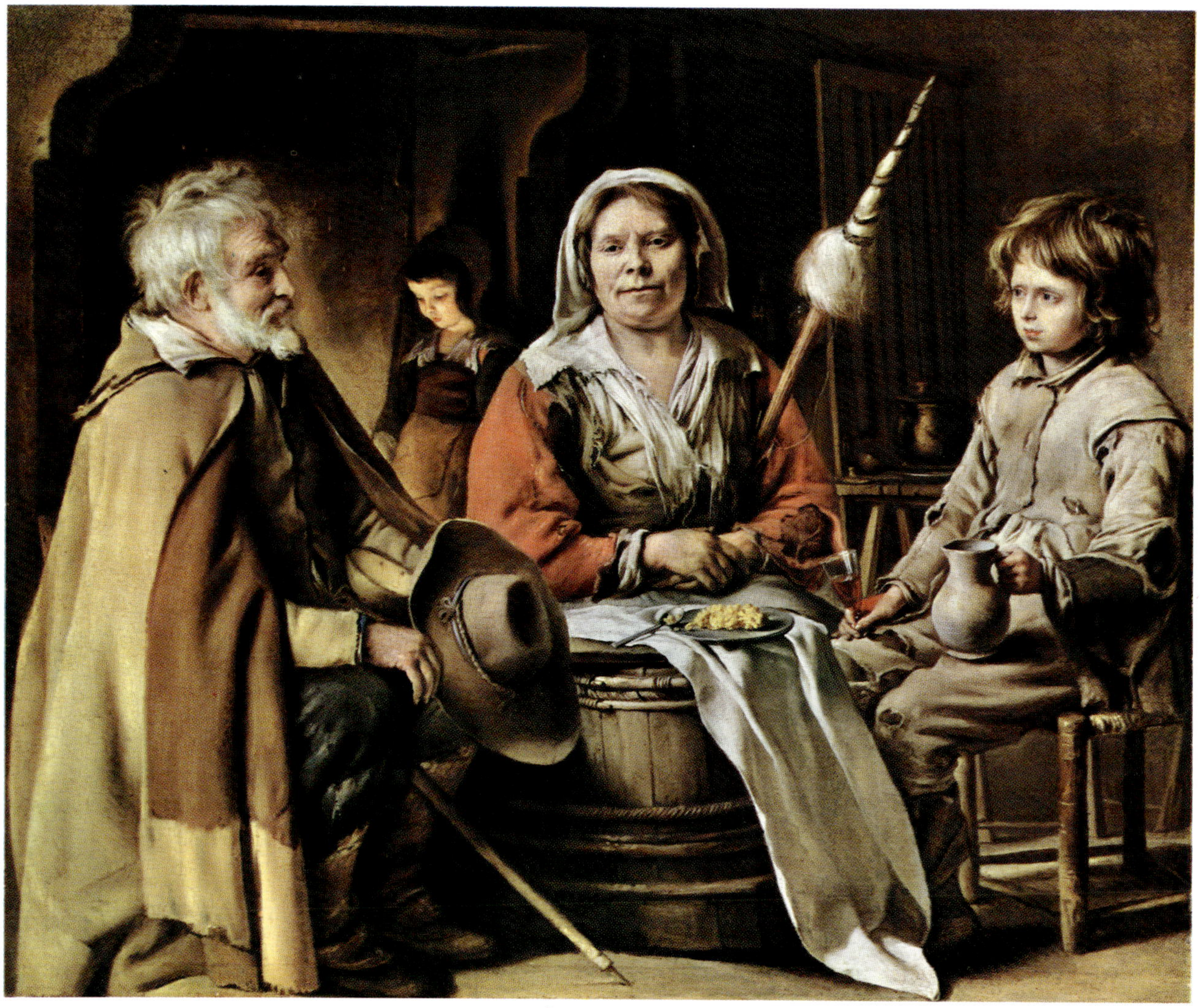

PLATE 52
Le Nain brothers
Peasant Interior
Canvas, 55.6 × 64.7 cm.
Washington, National Gallery of Art
First recorded in the collection of the Duke of Leeds in 1902. Given to the museum as part of the Samuel H. Kress collection, 1952.

Collections

Aix-en-Provence, Musée Granet
The Card Players

Amsterdam, Rijksmuseum
The Dice Players

Avignon, Musée Calvet
Portrait of an Old Woman (signed and dated 1644; attribution disputed)

Berlin, Staatliche Museen, Berlin-Dahlem
Adoration of the Shepherds

Birmingham, Barber Institute
Soldiers Playing Cards (fig.59)

Boston, Museum of Fine Arts
The Entombment

Cardiff, National Museum of Wales
The Brawl (signed and dated 164..)

Cleveland (Ohio), Museum of Art
Dance of Children
The Family Meal

Cologne, Wallraf-Richartz Museum
The Garden (fragments of signature)

Darmstadt, Hessisches Landesmuseum
Lamentation Over the Dead Christ

Detroit, Institute of Arts
The Old Flageolet Player (signed and dated 1642)
The Rustic Meal

Dublin, National Gallery of Ireland
Adoration of the Shepherds (signed and dated 1644)

Hartford (Connecticut), Wadsworth Athenaeum
Landscape with Peasants and a Chapel (plate 54)

Kansas City, Nelson Gallery
The Preparations for the Dance (attribution)

Karlsruhe, Staatliche Kunsthalle
Children with a Cage
The Preparations for the Dance

Leningrad, Hermitage
Peasants with a Young Flageolet Player
The Donkey

Le Puy, Musée Crozatier
Portrait of a Soldier

London, National Gallery
Adoration of the Shepherds
A Woman with Five Children (signed and dated 1642)
The Three Ages
Portrait of Three Men (unfinished)

London, Royal Collection
The Little Card Players

London, Victoria and Albert Museum
The Halt of the Cavalier

Los Angeles, County Museum of Art
Three Young Musicians

Lugano, Thyssen collection
The Young Musicians

Meudon, Benedictines du Saint-Sacrement
Presentation of the Virgin in the Temple

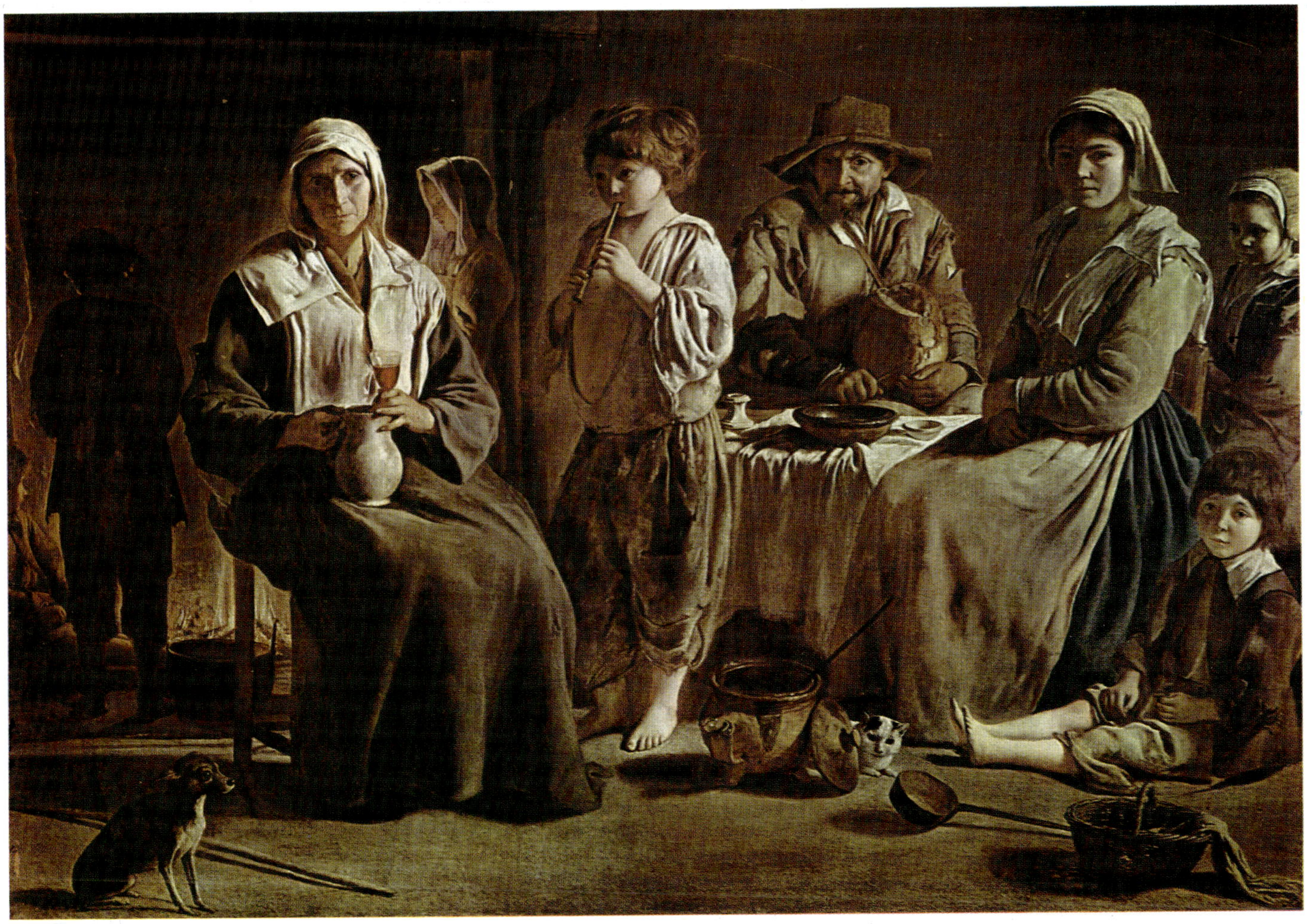

PLATE 53 (above)
Le Nain brothers
Peasant Family
Canvas, 113.3 × 159.5 cm.
Paris, Louvre
First recorded in a Paris sale in 1914. Acquired by the Louvre the following year.

PLATE 54 (right)
Le Nain brothers
Landscape with Peasants and a Chapel
Canvas, 41 × 55 cm.
Hartford (Connecticut), Wadsworth Athenaeum
First recorded in the Wilbraham collection, Northwich, in 1839. Acquired by the museum in 1931.

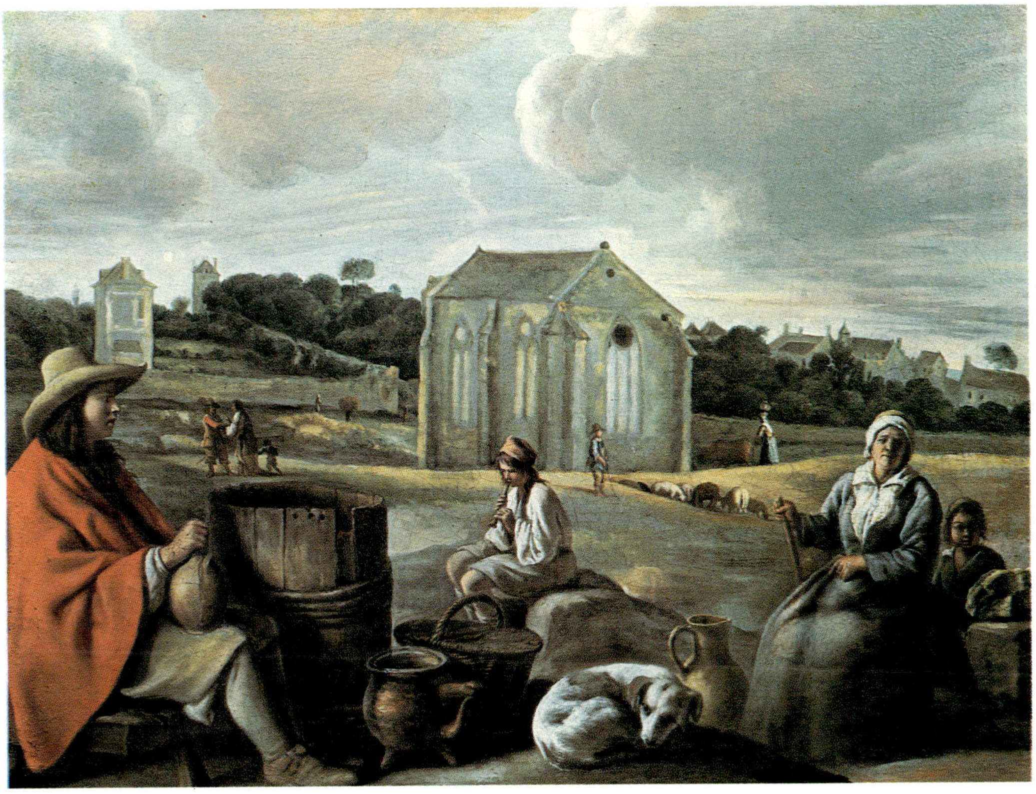

PLATE 55
Le Nain brothers
Smokers in an Interior
Canvas, 117 × 137 cm. Signed and dated lower right:
Le Nain. fecit 1643.
Paris, Louvre
Probably recorded in a Paris sale in 1778. Acquired by the Louvre in 1969 from the collection of the Baronne de Berckheim.

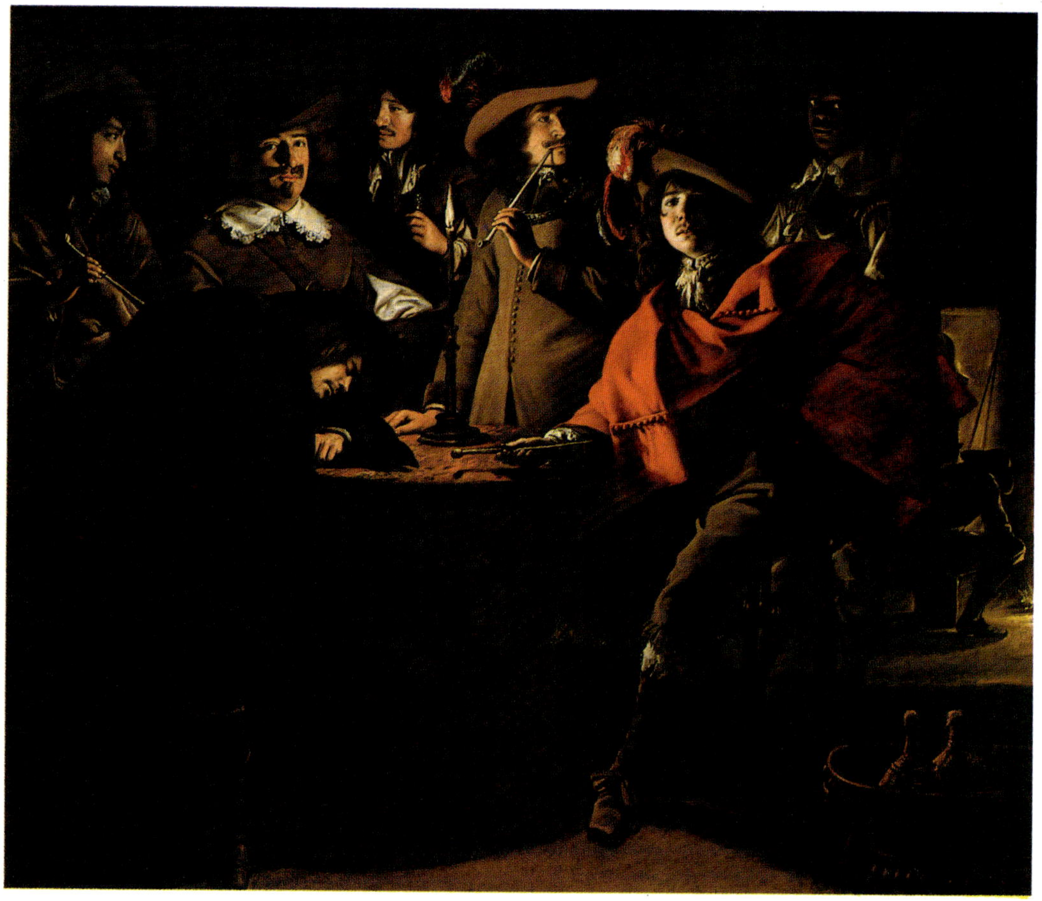

Nevers, Saint-Pierre
St Michael Dedicating his Arms to the Virgin

New York, Farkes Foundation
Nativity

New York, with Wildenstein
Holy Family

Orléans, Musée des Beaux-Arts
Bacchus and Ariadne

Paris, Louvre
Allegory of Victory (signed)
Nativity
The Pilgrims to Emmaus
The Little Card Players
The Happy Family (signed and dated 1642)
The Peasant Meal (signed and dated 1642)
Peasant Family (plate 53)
The Forge (plate 51)
The Hay Cart (signed and dated 1641)
The Pontifical Mass
The Musical Reunion (signed and dated 1642)
Portraits in an Interior (signed and dated 1647)
The Academy
Smokers in an Interior (signed and dated 1643) (plates 55&56)
The Tric-trac Players

Paris, Notre Dame
Nativity of the Virgin

Paris, Saint-Jacques du Haut Pas
Annunciation

Petworth House (Sussex), National Trust
Peasants (signed and dated 1642)

Pittsburgh, Frick Art Museum
Saying Grace

Reims, Musée Saint-Denis
Venis at the Forge of Vulcan (signed and dated 1641) (plate 50)
The Card Sharp

Rennes, Musée des Beaux-Arts
The Virgin with the Glass of Wine

Saint-Denis de Pile, Church
The Visitation

San Francisco (California), Palace of the Legion of Honor
Peasants before their House (fig.58)

Scotland, The Marquess of Bute
The Artist's Studio

Springfield (Massachusetts), Art Museum
The Brawl (attribution)

Stockholm, Nationalmuseum
Man with a Hat

Toledo (Ohio), Museum of Art
The Family Meal

Washington, National Gallery
Peasant Interior (plate 52)
Peasants in a Landscape

Williamstown (Massachusetts), The Sterling and Francine Clark Art Institute
The Little Card Players

Worcester (Massachusetts), Art Museum
The Little Card Players (attribution)

Whereabouts unknown
The Preparation for the Dance (signed and dated 1643)
The Magdalen

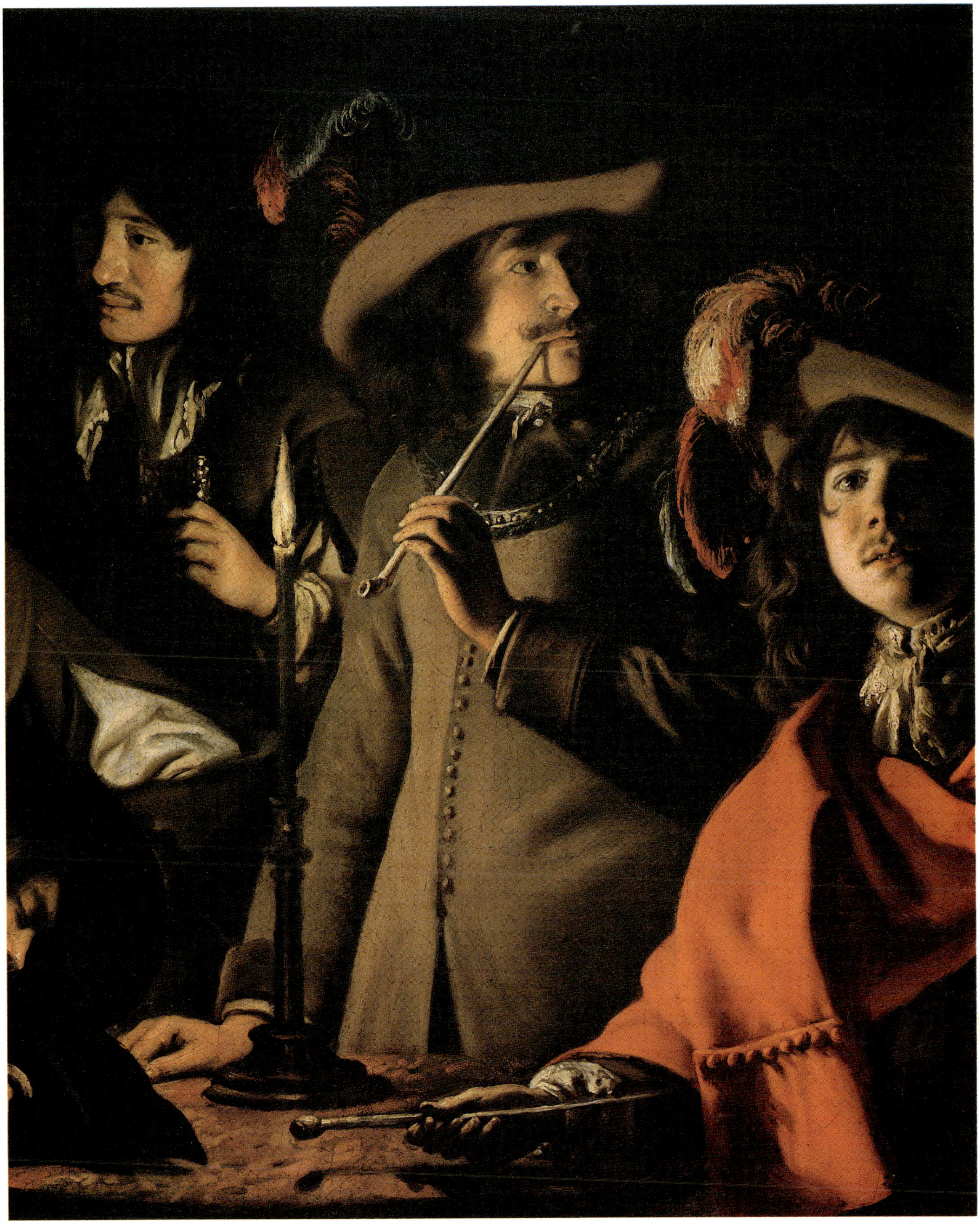

PLATE 56
Le Nain brothers
Smokers in an Interior (detail)
Paris, Louvre

The following are paintings whose attribution is in doubt or dispute, but which owe their composition or style, or both, to the work of the Le Nain brothers.

Collections

Abbéville, Musée Boucher de Perthes
Adoration of the Kings

Chicago, Art Institute
Peasants at the Well

Cleveland (Ohio), Museum of Art
Dance of Village Children
Peasant Scene

Glasgow University
Peasants at the Well

Hagerstown, Washington County Museum of Fine Arts
Portrait of Cinq-Mars

Laon, Musée Municipal
Peasant Interior (probably a copy of a lost work)
Stable Interior (probably a copy of a lost work)

Lille, Musée des Beaux-Arts
Peasants

London, Dulwich College Picture Gallery
The Musicians

Moscow, Pushkin Museum
Village Scene

New York, Metropolitan Museum
Charity

Norfolk (Virginia), Chrysler Museum
A Man

Paris, Louvre
The Last Supper
The Village Meal
The Watering Place

Poughkeepsie (New York), Vassar College Art Gallery
The Artist's Studio

Princeton, University Art Museum
Peasant Family

Reims, Musée Saint-Denis
Ecce Homo

Rennes, Musée des Beaux-Arts
The Virgin with the Glass of Wine

Sens, Musée Municipal
Double Portrait of a Young Girl

The following paintings in the style of the Le Nain brothers were temporarily grouped at the time of the Paris exhibition under the title 'Le Maître des Cortèges':

Collections

Bristol, City Art Gallery
Peasant Interior

Jacksonville (Florida), Cummer Gallery Exhibition, 1969
The Marriage Contract

Minneapolis, Institute of Arts
Assembly with the Hurdy-gurdy Player

Moscow, Pushkin Museum
Battle of Harnesses

Paris, Louvre
'Le Cortège du Boeuf'

Philadelphia, Museum of Art
'Le Cortège du Belin'

Bibliography

The essential bibliography is the exhibition catalogue by Jacques Thuillier, Paris, Grand Palais, *Les frères Le Nain*, 1978/9. In this publication the results of a century of research and rehabilitation were collated, and new assessments were made.

Jeremie Le Pileur

Working Tours 1623–38

Le Pileur is an example of a painter working in the Mannerist tradition, away from the influence of Rubens and Vouet in Paris.

Collections

Paris, Louvre
Gideon Setting Fire to the Camp of the Midianites (signed and dated 1630)

Rouen, Musée des Beaux-Arts
Christ in the Garden of Gethsemane (signed and dated 1625)

Saumur, Notre Dame des Ardilliers
Vow of the Town of Saint-Aignan (signed and dated 1631)

Tours, Musée des Beaux-Arts
The Crowning with Thorns
Christ on the Cross (signed and dated 1627)

Bibliography

There is no recent literature on this artist.

A. Le Roy

Working mid-seventeenth century

Nothing is known of this naïve painter, whose only known work suggests that he was active in the east of France or Alsace.

Collection

Paris, J. Leegenhoeck collection
The Meal of Herrings (signed)

Bibliography

Michel Faré
Le grand siècle de la nature morte en France, 1974, pp.142–3.

PLATE 57
Jacques de L'Estin
Self-portrait
Canvas, 63 × 52 cm.
Troyes, Musée des Beaux-Arts
Bequeathed to the museum by Mme Pigeotte, 1900.

Self-portraits are rare for most French seventeenth-century artists. This one shows the influence of Simon Vouet.

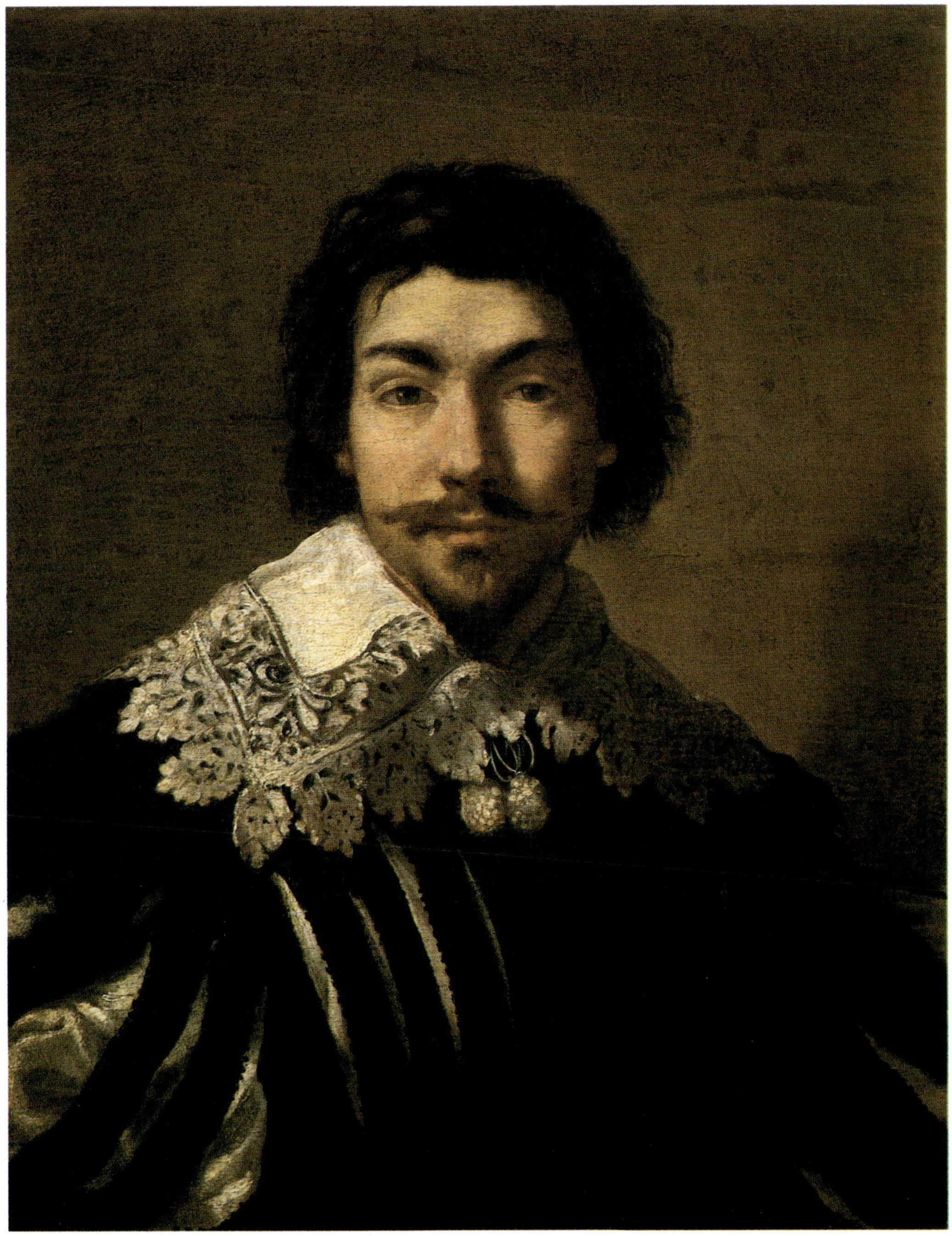

Jacques de L'Estin

Troyes 1597–Troyes 1661

The career of Jacques de L'Estin can be traced in some detail. His early life was spent in his native Troyes. By 1622, when he was twenty-five years old, he was in Rome, where he remained for about four years. In 1626 he was back in Troyes, and the following year he received commissions for pictures for Troyes Cathedral, which no longer survive. In 1634 he moved to Paris, where he executed (in 1636) a 'May' for Notre Dame, which was an annual commission for the cathedral. Three years later he again returned to Troyes, where he seems to have spent most of the rest of his career, except for a brief visit to Paris in 1656.

Both in style and accomplishment, L'Estin was close to his near contemporary Guy François in Le Puy. In Rome in their impressionable youth, both painters rapidly assimilated the popular style, and both were incapable in their maturity of developing this style in their native provinces. L'Estin was still painting in the Baroque manner, which had been fashionable in 1630 under the dominance of Vouet, thirty years after it had gone out of date. His stylish *Self-portrait* at Troyes shows him to have had an affinity with Vouet, whom he would have known in Rome. Most of L'Estin's surviving pictures are in the churches of the Troyes region for which they were originally painted.

Collections

Aix-en-Oth, L'Assomption
Institution of the Rosary

Chavagnes, Saint-Georges
Institution of the Rosary

Corsham Court (Wiltshire), Lord Methuen
The Pope St Clement Ordaining St Denis

Coutances, Musée Municipal
Institution of the Eucharist (attribution)

Fontivanne, Saint-Alban
The Flight into Egypt

Les Loges-Margueron, Saint-Robert
Apparition of the Virgin and Child to St Robert

Moscow, Pushkin Museum
Death of Virginia (formerly attributed to Simon Vouet and to Jacques Blanchard)

Nevers, Saint-Pierre
Presentation of Christ in the Temple (signed)

Orléans, Cathedral
Agony of Christ
The Flagellation
Carrying of the Cross
Crucifixion

Paris, Saint-Paul Saint-Louis
St Louis Dying of the Plague at Tunis (signed)

Provins, Hôpital Général
Adoration of the Kings (signed)
Altarpiece of the Cordeliers of Mont Saint Sulpice

Ricey-Haute-Rive, Saint-Jean-Baptiste
Institution of the Rosary

Troyes, Musée des Beaux-Arts
Adoration of the Shepherds
The Visitation
Lycergas giving a Constitution to Sparta
Self-portrait (plate 57)
Deposition from the Cross
Presentation of the Virgin in the Temple (from S. Nizier)
Martyrdom of St Ursula (from S. Nizier)

Troyes, Association Diocesaine
Virgin and St John

Troyes, Saint-Madeleine
St Augustine Exorcising Heresy

Troyes, Saint-Martin-les-Vignes
Deposition from the Cross

Troyes, Saint-Nicolas
St Nicholas Consecrated Bishop of Myra

Troyes, Saint-Pantaleon
Christ in the Garden of Gethsemane

Troyes, Saint-Rémi
Adoration of the Shepherds (signed)
Institution of the Rosary
Assumption of the Virgin (signed)
Christ at the Pool of Bethesda
Virgin and Child
Marriage of the Virgin
Deposition from the Cross

Bibliography

All the available information is to be found in the excellent exhibition catalogue, Troyes, Musée des Beaux-Arts, *Jacques de L'Estin, 1976*, introduction by Jacques Thuillier, catalogue by Jean-Pierre Sainte-Marie.

Eustache Le Sueur

Paris 1616–Paris 1655

Le Sueur's early style was formed in the Paris studio of Simon Vouet, but he soon rejected it in favour of a much colder and more classically inspired manner, influenced chiefly by Nicolas Poussin, whose visit to Paris (1640–42) meant that his work was more readily available to Parisian artists for study in the original. The fact that Le Sueur was able to establish a purely personal style of classicism, quite independent of his contemporaries Philippe de Champaigne and Laurent de La Hyre, indicates the level of his ability: his subsequent reputation in France in the eighteenth and nineteenth centuries was second only to that of Poussin. His *St Bruno* series in the Louvre is one of the main surviving examples of a religious cycle by a French artist of the period. He was a founder-member of the Academy in Paris in 1648.

Collections

Alençon, Musée des Beaux-Arts
Subject from the Hypnerotomachia Poliphii

Berlin-Dahlem, Staatliche Museen
St Bruno in his Cell

Besançon, Musée des Beaux-Arts
Dead Christ
Minerva
Fortune

Birmingham, Barber Institute
Solomon and the Queen of Sheba

Bloomington (Indiana), University Art Museum
Joseph Searching for his Brothers

Boston (Massachusetts), Museum of Fine Arts
A Sacrifice to Diana
Bacchus and Ariadne

Budapest, Szépmüvészeti Múzeum
The Young Tobias

Chartres, Musée des Beaux-Arts
The Archangel Raphael

Chicago, Art Institute
A Beatitude

Coutances, Musée Municipal
The Last Supper

Dayton (Ohio), Art Institute
Allegory of Magnificence

Dijon, Musée Magnin
Poliphilus in the Bath of the Nymphs

Dublin, National Gallery of Ireland
Christ in the House of Martha and Mary

Dunkirk, Musée des Beaux-Arts
Allegory of a Perfect Minister, or *The Minister of State with his Attributes* (1653)

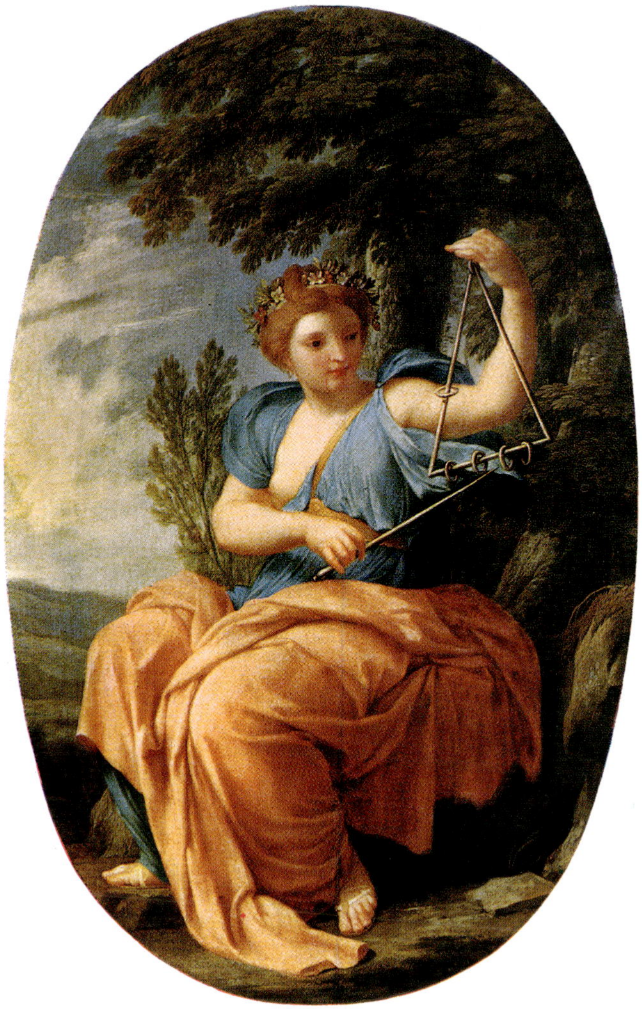

PLATE 58
Eustache Le Sueur
The Muse Terpsichore
Panel, 116 × 74 cm.
Paris, Louvre
Part of the decoration of the Chambre des Muses for the Hôtel Lambert, Paris. Acquired by Louis XVI in 1776.

Grenoble, Musée de Peinture et de Sculpture
The Angel Leaving Tobias

Guéret, Musée Municipal
Portrait of M. Albert
(inscribed on the back and dated 1641) (fig.57)

La Rochelle, Musée des Beaux-Arts
Adoration of the Shepherds
(documented 1653)

Lawrence (Kansas), University Art Museum
Allegorical Scene (attribution)

Le Mans, Musée de Tessé
Poliphilus Assisting the Triumph of Bacchus

Leningrad, Hermitage
Diana at the Hunt (attribution)
The Presentation in the Temple
Moses Saved from the Water
Two Scenes from the Life of Cincinnatus (attribution)

Lille, Palais des Beaux-Arts
The Penitent Magdalen
St Bruno Constructing the Grande Chartreuse

London, National Gallery
St Paul Preaching at Ephesus

Lyons, Palais des Beaux-Arts
The Martyrdom of St Gervais and St Protais

Malibu (California), J. Paul Getty Museum
The Sea Gods before Cythera

Marseilles, Palais Longchamp
Presentation in the Temple

Montpellier, Musée Fabre
The Wedding Night of Tobias

Munich, Alte Pinakothek
Christ in the House of Martha and Mary

Nantes, Musée des Beaux-Arts
The Rising of Aurora

Norfolk (Virginia), Chrysler Museum
Holy Family

Paris, Louvre
The Muses Clio, Euterpe and Thalie
The Muses Melopomene, Erato and Polymena
The Muse Uranie
The Muse Terpsichore (plate 58)
The Muse Calliope
Phaeton Asking Apollo to Drive the Chariot of Heaven
Christ Appearing to the Magdalen
St Gervais and St Protais, Brought before Astasius, Refuse to Sacrifice to Jupiter
Christ Carrying the Cross
Descent from the Cross
Appearance of the Virgin, Accompanied by St Agnes and St Thecle, to St Martin (documented 1654)
Mass of St Martin (documented 1654)
Angels Saluting the Virgin
The Young Tobias Receiving Instructions from his Mother (attribution)
Reunion of Friends
Return of Tobias
Life of St Bruno (documented 1645–8):
St Bruno Assisting at the Sermon of Raymond Diocres
Death of Raymond Diocres
Raymond Diocres Replying after his Death
St Bruno in Prayer
St Bruno Teaching Theology in the Schools of Reims
St Bruno Persuading his Disciples and Friends to Leave the World
Dream of St Bruno
St Bruno and his Companions Before Departing for Grenoble Distributing their Goods to the Poor
Arrival of St Bruno at Grenoble
Voyage to the Charterhouse
St Bruno Constructing the Monastery
St Bruno taking the Monastic Habit
Pope Victor III Confirming the Institution of the Charterhouse
St Bruno Giving the Monk's Habit to Several People
St Bruno Receiving a Message from the Pope
Arrival of St Bruno in Rome
St Bruno Refusing the Archbishopric of Reggio Offered by Urban II
St Bruno in Prayer in his Oratory
Meeting of St Bruno and Count Roger (lost)
Appearance of St Bruno to Count Roger
Death of St Bruno, 6th October, 1101
St Bruno Carried to Heaven
St Bruno Examining a Drawing of the Baths of Diocletian
Plan of the Charterhouse of Paris Carried by Two Angels
Dedication of a Carthusian Church
Decoration of the Hôtel Lambert:
The Birth of Cupid
Venus, Cupid and Jupiter
Cupid Reprimanded by his Mother
Taking Refuge in the Arms of Ceres

Cupid Receiving Homage of Diana, Apollo and Mercury
Cupid Ordering Mercury to Announce his Power to the Universe
Cupid and Jupiter
Ganymede Carried off by Jupiter

Paris, Notre Dame
St Paul at Ephesus

Paris, Saint-Germain-en-Auxerrois
Martyrdom of St Lawrence

Paris, Saint-Roch
Christ Resuscitating the Son of the Widow of Zarepath

Potsdam, Sans Souci
Christ Healing the Blind

Rennes, Musée des Beaux-Arts
Hagar and the Angel

Rouen, Musée des Beaux-Arts
Poliphilus Before Queen Eleutherylda

San Francisco, Art Museums
Sleeping Venus Surprised by Cupid

Toledo (Ohio), Museum of Art
The Annunciation (fig.56)

Toulouse, Musée des Augustins
The Sacrifice of Manoah

Tours, Musée des Beaux-Arts
St Sebastian Succoured by the Holy Irene
St Louis Helping the Sick (1654)

Vienna, formerly Czernin collection
Picture from the *Poliphilus* series

Bibliography

The work for the Hôtel Lambert was studied by C. Lastic in the exhibition catalogue, Paris, Louvre, *Le cabinet de l'amour de l'Hôtel Lambert*, 1972. A new biography by Alain Mérot is in preparation.

Pierre Le Tellier

Vernon 1614–Rouen after 1680

Apart from a brief visit to Rome where he came under the influence of Nicolas Poussin, Le Tellier spent his career in Rouen. He produced numerous altarpieces for the local churches.

Collection

Rouen, Musée des Beaux-Arts
The Rest on the Flight into Egypt (signed and dated 1658)
The Marriage of the Virgin (attribution)
Christ Giving the Keys to Peter
St Joseph and the Infant Christ
St Bernard before the Virgin, Child and St Joseph (signed and dated 1678)
Three Half-figures of Angels
The Farewell of St Paul and Sylas (signed and dated 1680)
Christ of Pity
Virgin of Pity
The Ascension
Assumption of the Virgin
Presentation in the Temple (attribution)

Bibliography

Jacques Thuillier in the exhibition catalogue, Rouen, Musée des Beaux-Arts, *Nicolas Poussin et son temps*, 1961, p.26.
Pierre Rosenberg in the catalogue, Rouen, Musée des Beaux-Arts, *Tableaux français du XVIIe siècle ...*, 1966, pp.82–9.

Reynaud Levieux

Nîmes 1613–Rome ? after 1694

Most of the work of Levieux was executed in Provence. The fact that he had worked in Rome, copying Raphael's frescoes, is reflected in the careful order of his compositions and their great clarity of lighting.

Collections

Aix-en-Provence, Musée Granet
Study for the Crucifix of Fournes

Aix-en-Provence, Musée d'Histoire Naturelle
The Four Seasons (dated 1666)

Aix-en-Provence, C.E.S. Mignet, Chapelle
Assumption (dated 1662)

Aix-en-Provence, Cours Sainte-Catherine de Sienne
Presentation of the Virgin (signed and dated 1660)
Nativity (dated 1660)

Aix-en-Provence, Saint-Jean de Malte
St Bruno (signed and dated 1665)

Aix-en-Provence, La Madeleine
The Visitation (dated 1660)

Aix-en-Provence, Hôpital Saint-Jacques, Chapel
Adoration of the Shepherds

Aix-en-Provence, private collection
Head of the Virgin

Amherst, College Art Museum
Holy Family with St John the Baptist

Avignon, Musée Calvet
The Sauvan Crucifix
Jacob and Laban
Zacharias Blessing St John the Baptist
Zacharias and the Angel (signed and dated 1663)

Avignon, Cathedral
Purification of the Virgin (signed and dated 1654)

Avignon, Pénitents Noirs
St Anne, the Virgin and the Christ Child
St John the Baptist Conducted to the Desert by Angels
St William of Acquitaine
The Baptism of Christ (signed and dated 1694)

Avignon, private collection
Herodias Receiving the Head of St John the Baptist
Flowers and Fruit with a Red Parrot
Flowers and Fruits with a Small Spaniel

Caromb (Vaucluse), Church
Virgin Adored by Saints

Cassis, Chapelle des Pénitents
St Louis and St Catherine at the Feet of the Virgin

Isle-sur-Sorgue, Church
Assumption of the Virgin (signed and dated 1680)

Jacksonville (Florida), Cummer Gallery
Theseus Discovering his Father's Sword (attribution)

Lambesc, Church
Our Lady of the Rose (signed and dated 1663)

London, private collection
The Sleep of the Infant Jesus

Marsillargues (Hérault), Church
Holy Family

Montpellier, Cathedral
Holy Family

Montpellier, Pénitents Blancs
Holy Family

Nîmes, Musée des Beaux-Arts
Beheading of St John the Baptist (signed and dated 1656)
St John the Baptist Taken to Prison (signed)
St John the Baptist and Herod (signed)

Paris, Hôpital de la Saltpétrière
Zacharias Blessing St John the Baptist

Rome, San Luigi de Francesi
The Miracle of the Blind Man

Serra San Bruno, Chiesa del'Addolorata
Death of St Anne

Ventabren, Church
The Virgin of the Seven Sorrows

Villeneuve-lès-Avignon, Museum
Crucifixion of the Hospice
Mourning of Christ by the Angels

Villeneuve-lès-Avignon, Collégiale
Crucifix de Fournes
Holy Family (signed and dated 1651)

Viviers, Cathedral
The Flight into Egypt

Bibliography

Henri Wytenhove
in the exhibition catalogue, Marseilles, Palais Longchamp, *La peinture en Provence au XVIIe siècle*, 1977, pp.84–90.

Jacques L'Homme

Troyes 1600–?

L'Homme was apparently a pupil of Simon Vouet.

Collection

Troyes, Musée des Beaux-Arts
Vanitas (signed and dated 1641)

Bibliography

There is no recent literature on this artist.

Louis Licherie

Houdan or Dreux 1629–Paris 1687

Although he did not enter the French Academy in Paris until 1679, Licherie had been a pupil of Charles Le Brun and a teacher at the Gobelins School until 1670. His pictures are in the style of his master, although more cold and dry.

Collections

Besançon, Musée des Beaux-Arts
Calvary

Cherbourg, Musée Thomas Henry
Holy Family

Nantes, Musée des Beaux-Arts
Death of St Joseph

Paris, École des Beaux-Arts
Abigail Bringing Presents to King David

Paris, Louvre
Miraculous Cure of Don Carlos by St Diego of Alcala

Bibliography

There is no recent literature on this artist.

Paul Liégois

Working Paris mid-seventeenth century

Probably of Flemish origin from Liège, he worked in Paris in the style of Louise Moillon but with a little less precision. His work is still confused with that of Moillon or classified with anonymous Flemish work.

Collections

Besançon, Musée des Beaux-Arts
Peaches

Dijon, Musée des Beaux-Arts
Plums and Pears on a Ledge (attribution)

Florence, Uffizi
Peaches, Figs and Grapes on a Blue Cloth

France, private collection
Peaches and Grapes on a Blue Carpet

France, private collection
Peaches and Grapes

France, private collection
Plums on a Carpet and a Ledge

Paris, with Pardo
Peaches and Grapes
Plums and Apricots on a Carpet with a Fringe

Paris, private collection
Dish of Peaches, Pears and Mushrooms (signed and dated 1666)

Paris, private collection
Peaches and Grapes (signed)

Paris, private collection
Fruit on a Ledge (signed)

Paris, private collection
Peaches, Grapes and Figs
Apricots, Plums and Cherries

Pasadena (California), Norton Simon Museum
Still Life with Grapes

Rouen, Musée des Beaux-Arts
Still Life with Peaches and Grapes

Bibliography

Michel Faré
Le grand siècle de la nature morte en France, 1974, pp.72–8.

Jacques Linard

Paris ?c.1600–Paris 1645

A still-life painter, Linard spent his career in Paris. In 1631 he was named as a 'valet de chambre' of Louis XIII. His pictures are strongly influenced by the Antwerp school of still-life painters, especially Jan Brueghel. Linard delights by his use of bright colour, his painstaking work and a curiously powerful juxtaposition of boxes and flowers. His present status is only slightly below that of Moillon, Bauguin and Stoskopff.

Collections

Amsterdam, with De Boer
The Five Senses and a Portrait (signed and dated 1639)

Athens, Pinacoteca Nazionale
Plums and Pears on a Pewter Plate (signed and dated 1629)
Dish of Plums

Barnard Castle, Bowes Museum
Still Life of Peaches, Plums and Melon (dated 1642) (fig.55)

Indianapolis, Museum of Art
The Five Senses and Birds (signed)

Karlsruhe, Staatliche Kunsthalle
Flowers in a Vase

Lugano, Thyssen collection
Chinese Bowl with Flowers (signed and dated 1640)

Madrid, Prado
Vanitas with a Carnation

Paris, Louvre
Basket of Flowers (signed) (plate 59)
Basket of Pomegranates and Grapes (signed)
The Five Senses and the Four Elements (signed and dated 1627)

Paris, formerly B. collection
Plums, Cherries and a Fig
Plate of Cherries and Strawberries
Polyanthus in a Basket
Apricots and Moths (signed and dated 1631)

Paris, F.M. collection
The Flower Arranger

Paris, J.F. collection
Bowl of Peaches (signed and dated 1634)
Vanitas with a Moth (signed and dated 1634)

Paris, J.R. collection
Basket of Plums (signed and dated 1638)

Paris, formerly with Pardo
Vases of Flowers, Lobster and Oysters (signed)

Paris, P.L. collection
Oysters and Lemon (signed)

Paris, R.P. collection
The Five Senses
Basket of Fruit and Melon (signed and dated 1642)

Paris, private collection
Basket of Flowers

Paris, private collection
The Flower Arranger

Pasadena (California), Norton Simon Museum
Still Life: the Five Senses (signed and dated 1639)

Snowshill Manor (Gloucestershire), National Trust
Still Life: Basket of Fruit

Strasbourg, Musée des Beaux-Arts
Vase of Tulips (signed and dated 1639)
The Five Senses and a Landscape (signed and dated 1638)

Bibliography

Michel Faré
Le grand siècle de la nature morte en France, 1974, pp.17–40.

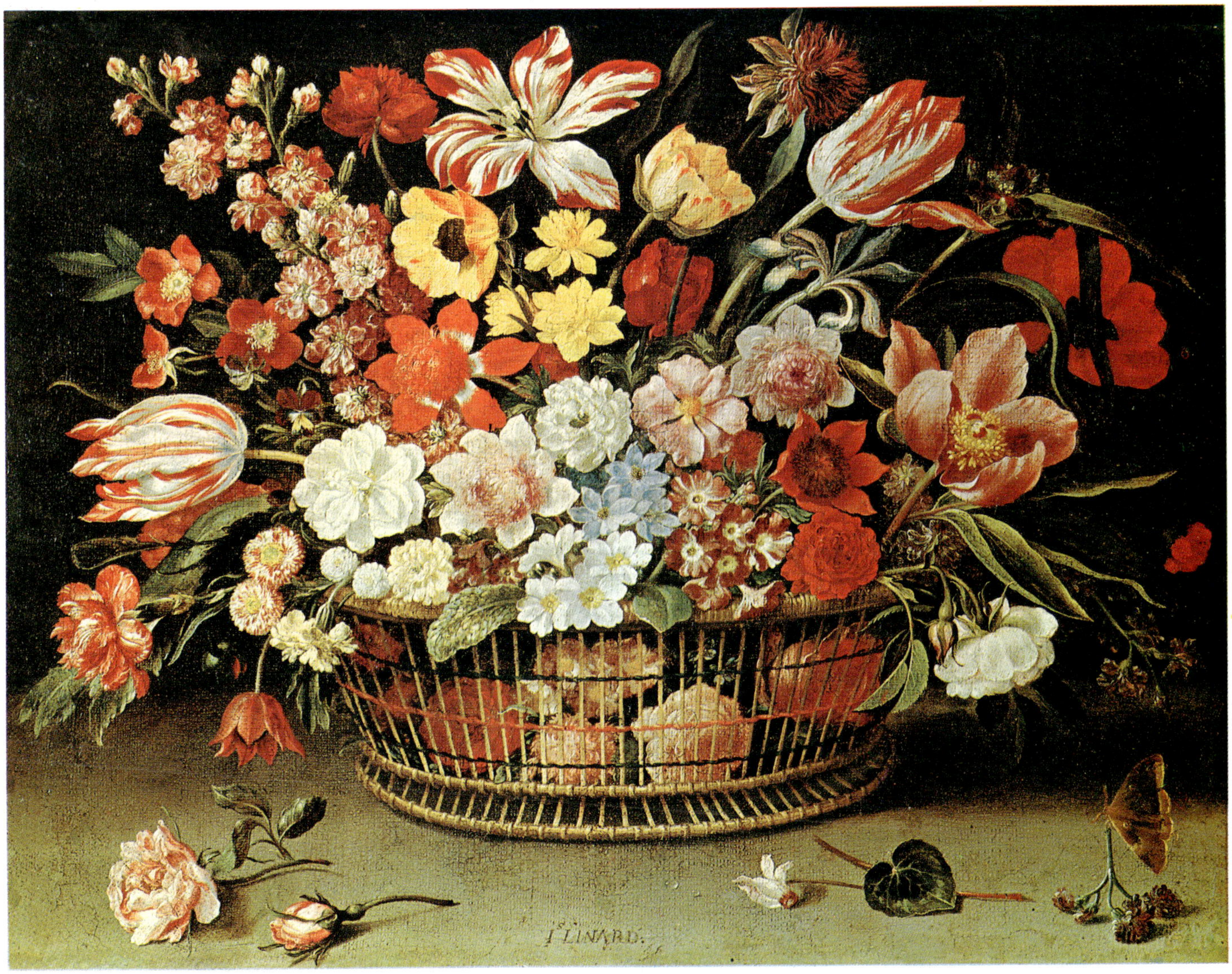

PLATE 59
Jacques Linard
Basket of Flowers
Canvas, 48 × 60.5 cm. Signed
Paris, Louvre
Acquired by the museum in 1935.

Nicolas Loir

Paris 1624?–Paris 1679

Although a pupil of Sébastien Bourdon, Loir preferred to imitate the work of Nicolas Poussin. He made two visits to Rome, one in the 1630s and one in the 1640s, and became a member of the French Academy in Paris in 1663. Although he was strongly influenced by Poussin, the greater lyricism in his work could well be derived from Pietro da Cortona.

Collections

Angers, Musée des Beaux-Arts
The Finding of Moses
Eleazer and Rebecca

Besançon, Musée des Beaux-Arts
Sleep of the Infant Christ

Budapest, Szépmüvészeti Múzeum
Cleobis and Biton

Cambridge (Massachusetts), Fogg Art Museum
Virgin and Child with St John the Baptist (1666)

Compiègne, Musée Vivenel
Royal Allegory

Dijon, Musée des Beaux-Arts
Pan and Syrinx

Florence, Uffizi
Virgin and Child with St John the Baptist

Grenoble, Musée de Peinture et de Sculpture
Time

Leningrad, Hermitage
Hagar in the Wilderness
Hagar and Ishmael in the Wilderness
Holy Family in a Garland of Flowers

Louisville (Kentucky), Speed Art Museum
Rebecca Hiding her Father's Idols

Lyons, Musée des Beaux-Arts
Diana and Endymion

Marseilles, Palais Longchamp
St Mary of Egypt

Montpellier, Musée Fabre
Annunciation

Nancy, Musée des Beaux-Arts
Triumph of Flora

Northampton (Massachusetts), Smith College
Eleazer and Rebecca

Paris, Louvre
St William of Acquitaine
Taking the Habit
A Queen Addressing Soldiers

Quimper, Musée des Beaux-Arts
The Finding of Moses
(attribution)

Bibliography

Georges Wildenstein
'Les vierges de Nicolas Loir', *Gazette des Beaux-Arts*, 1959, pp.145–52.
Jacques Thuillier
in the exhibition catalogue, Rouen, Musée des Beaux-Arts, *Nicolas Poussin et son temps*, 1961, pp.27–8.

Louis XIII of France

Fontainebleau 1601–Paris 1643

An amateur, Louis was taught to draw by Claude Deruet.

Collection

Nancy, Musée Historique Lorrain
Portrait of Claude Deruet (pastel) (fig.1)

Bibliography

François-Georges Pariset
Les peintres et graveurs Lorrains du XVIIe siècle, not dated but c.1955, pp.15, 18.

Charles Martin

Paris c.1562–Paris 1646

Martin was one of many now-obscure painters working in Paris at the end of the sixteenth and in the early seventeenth century.

Collection

Blois, Museum
Louis XIII as a Child and Marie de Medici (dated 1603)

Bibliography

There is no recent literature on this artist.

Master of the Judgment of Solomon

Probably working in Rome, 1620s

A small number of pictures has been grouped round the *Judgment of Solomon* in the Galleria Borghese, Rome. The *Judgment* is clearly French, and was probably influenced by the work of Le Valentin. One of the eccentric characteristics of the painting is the depicting of slanting eyes, a marked feature of the work of Jean Tassel of Langres during his French period. The whole group has often been associated with Gerard Douffet of Liège, but in style it is much closer to Tassel. No picture from Tassel's Roman period has yet been identified, and these pictures may turn out to be by him.

Collections

Budapest, Szépmüvészeti Múzeum
St Thomas

Catania, Museo dei Benedetti
A Prophet

Florence, Longhi collection
St Paul
St Philip
St Bartholomew
St Matthias
St Judas Thaddeus

Florence, Florentine Galleries
Two Saints

Langres, Saint-Martin
Christ among the Doctors

London, with Colnaghi's (formerly)
St Peter and St Paul

Milan, Chiesa collection (formerly)
Origen

Munich, with Julius Böhler, 1967
St James

Naples, Capodimonte
St Matthew
St James the Less

Naples, Certosa di San Martino
St Matthew

Paris, Michel Laclotte collection
Denial of Peter

Paris, with Jean Néger (formerly)
St James the Less

Rome, Galleria Borghese
The Judgment of Solomon

Rome, Galleria Corsini
Denial of Peter

Rome, Nunes collection, 1943
Christ Mocked

Saint Omer, Musée de l'Hôtel Sandelin
Two Philosophers

Torella dei Lombardi, Ruspoli collection
Philosopher

Unknown location
David with the Head of Goliath

Bibliography

The two most recent assessments of this artist, reflecting the current state of knowledge, are Arnauld Brejon de Lavergnée and Jean-Pierre Cuzin in the exhibition catalogue, Paris, Grand Palais, *Le Valentin et les caravagesques français*, 1974, and Benedict Nicolson, *The International Caravaggesque Movement*, 1979, pp.73–4. The authors give slightly different versions of the artist's *oeuvre*, and a compromise between the two lists has been made here. Gerard Douffet is still the favourite candidate for the group, although the pictures currently attributed to Douffet are by a very different hand.

Thomas Mather

Working 1671

On stylistic grounds, it is possible that Mather worked under the influence of Sébastien Stoskopff in Alsace. Nothing is known about his life.

Collections

Nantes, Musée des Beaux-Arts
Still Life of Fish (signed and dated 1671)
Still Life of Dead Games (signed and dated 1671)

Paris, private collection
Chicken, Artichoke and Dead Duck in a Basket (attribution)

Paris, private collection
Basket of Grapes and an Artichoke (attribution)

Bibliography

Michel Faré
Le grand siècle de la nature morte en France, 1974, p.136.

PLATE 60
Attributed to Henri Mauperché
Landscape with Jephthah and his Daughter
Canvas, 122 × 111 cm.
Birmingham, City Art Gallery
Acquired by the museum in 1967 as by Pierre Patel the Elder. The attribution to Mauperché was made by Pierre Rosenberg in 1969.

The subject plays an insignificant role in this essentially decorative canvas. The perspective implies that it was meant to be placed relatively high up.

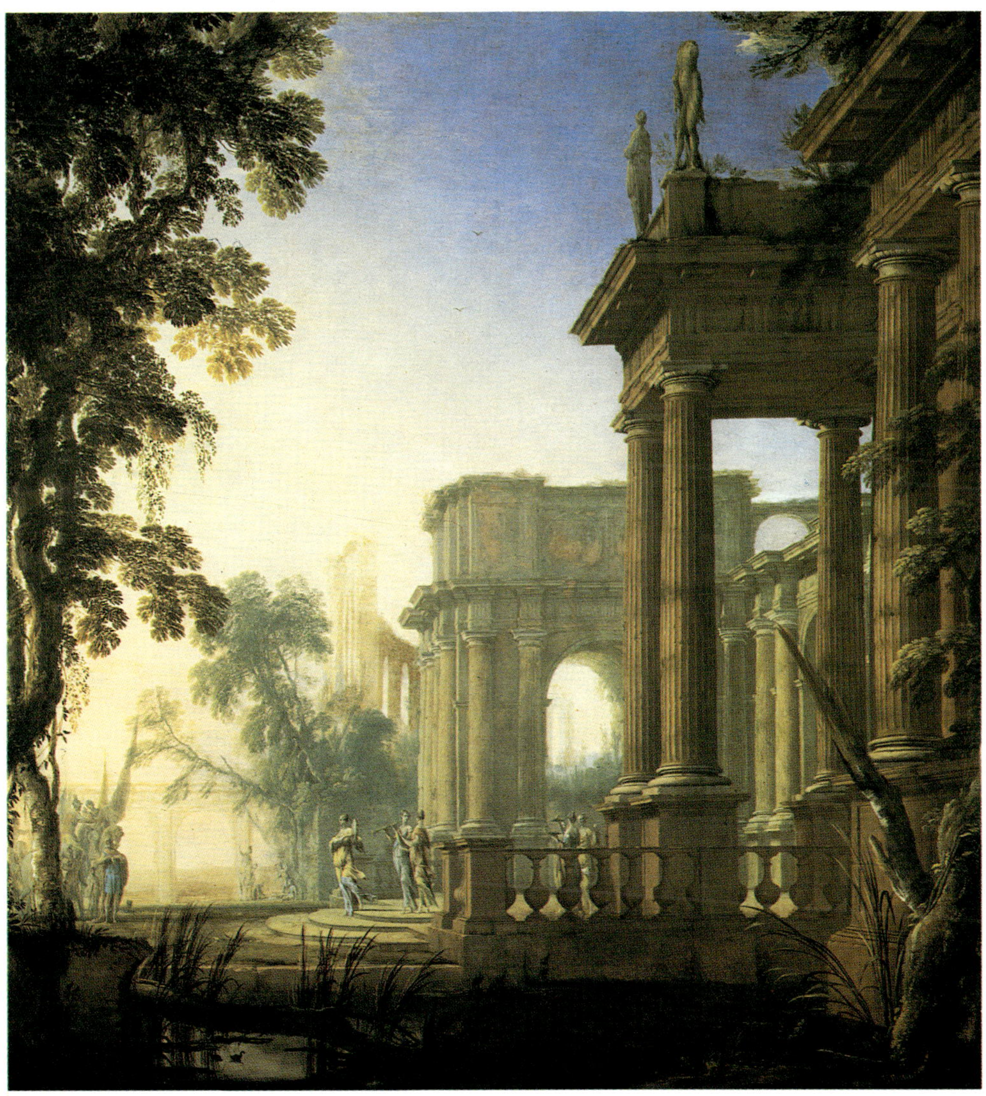

Henri Mauperché

Paris 1602–Paris 1686

This artist's work is still misunderstood, as, along with Pierre Patel the Elder, he was one of the few imitators of Claude Lorraine to work in France. In Rome from 1634 onwards, he came under the influence of the Bamboccianti. In 1648 he was one of the fourteen founder-members of the French Academy in Paris.

Collections

Birmingham, City Art Gallery
Landscape with Jephthah and his Daughter (attribution) (plate 60)

Bourges, Musée du Berry
Landscape with the Ass of Balaam

Florence, Uffizi
Landscape with Shepherds (attribution)

Leningrad, Hermitage
Landscape with Drovers

Nantes, Musée des Beaux-Arts
The Broken Rock (attribution)

New York, Metropolitan Museum
Landscape with Ruins

Paris, Saint-Étienne du Mont
Tobias and the Angel

Paris, Louvre
Landscape with a Bridge
Landscape with the Rest on the Flight into Egypt (signed and dated 1671)

Bibliography

Jacques Thuillier in the exhibition catalogue, Rouen, Musée des Beaux-Arts, *Nicolas Poussin et son temps*, 1961, pp.29–30.

(Du) Mélezet

Recorded Grenoble 1639

Apart from his appearance at Grenoble in 1639, nothing is known about Mélezet. His one surviving picture shows him to have been familiar with the style of Louise Moillon and Jacques Linard.

Collection

Atlanta (Georgia), Mrs Francis Storza
Bowl of Wild Strawberries (inscribed on the reverse)

Bibliography

Pierre Rosenberg in the exhibition catalogue, Paris, Grand Palais, *La peinture française du XVIIe siècle dans les collections américaines*, 1982, pp.284–5.

Claude Mellan

Abbeville 1598–Paris 1688

Best known as a draughtsman and engraver, especially of portraits, Mellan spent a short time in Rome with Simon Vouet from 1624 onwards.

Collections

Besançon, Musée des Beaux-Arts
St John (attribution)

Montpellier, Musée Fabre
Herodias

Rome, Galleria Borghese
Joseph Interpreting Dreams

Sarasota (Florida), John and Mable Ringling Museum
St Bruno (attribution)

Bibliography

The current state of knowledge is summed up by Benedict Nicolson in *The International Caravaggesque Movement*, 1979, p.74.

Charles Mellin

Nancy c.1597–Rome 1649

Mellin is one of the most enigmatic artists of the period, because of the difficulty of identifying his work and separating it from that of Nicolas Poussin. It is known that Mellin copied Poussin, and it is possible that there has been some confusion between the two artists, especially for the work of the late 1620s and early 1630s. The known work of Mellin is brightly coloured, has great facility and is more akin to that of Vouet than to Poussin.

Collections

Compiègne, Château
St Bartholomew

Geneva, Musée d'Art et d'Histoire
Roman Charity

Macon, Musée des Ursulines
Roman Charity

Mainz, private collection
Love and Faith

Nancy, Musée Historique Lorrain
St Francis de Paul at Prayer

Naples, Tempio dell'Incoronata del Buon Consiglio
The Annunciation
The Assumption

Plessis-lez-Tours, Château
St Francis de Paul at the Feet of Sixtus V

Ponce (Puerto Rico), Museo de Arte
Assumption of the Virgin (formerly attributed to Simon Vouet)

Rome, San Luigi dei Francesi
The Annunciation

Rome, Santa Trinità de Monti
Fresco: *St Francis de Paul before Sixtus V*

Valenciennes, Musée des Beaux-Arts
St Stephen in Prayer

Viterbo, Palazzo Vescovile
The Glory of St Dominic

Bibliography

The artist's biography was deciphered by Jacques Bousquet, 'Charles Mellin', in *Annales de l'Est*, 1955, pp.1–35. A more up-to-date survey is by Jacques Thuillier in the exhibition catalogue, Rome, Villa Medici, and Nancy, Musée des Beaux-Arts, *Claude Lorrain e i pittori lorenesi in Italia nel XVII secolo*, 1982, pp.208–74.

Pierre Mellin

d. Paris 1662

Documented as working in Paris in the 1630s and 1640s, Pierre Mellin appears to have been primarily a decorative artist, involved in producing ephemeral scenery for such events as the triumphal entry of important persons into towns.

Collection

Caen, Saint-Étienne
The Stoning of Stephen (attribution)

Bibliography

Jacques Thuillier in the exhibition catalogue, Rouen, Musée des Beaux-Arts, *Nicolas Poussin et son temps*, 1961, pp.30–31.

Jean Michelin

Langres 1623–Isle of Jersey 1696

Michelin's few surviving pictures show that he was a competent imitator of the Le Nain brothers, although he lacked their force of observation and tended to be more anecdotal. Received into the Academy in Paris in 1660, he was forced to leave it in 1681, presumably because he was a Protestant. He worked for Georg-Wilhelm, Duke of Brunswick-Lüneburg.

Collections

Bordeaux, Musée des Beaux-Arts
Peasant Scene

Dublin, National Gallery of Ireland
Peasant Family

Moscow, Pushkin Museum
Peasant Family

New York, Metropolitan Museum
The Baker's Cart (signed and dated 1656) (fig.60)

Paris, Louvre
Adoration of the Shepherds (signed and dated 163(5 or 6))
The Bread Merchant and Water Carriers (signed and dated 165(0 or 6)
Soldiers at an Inn

Portland (Oregon), Art Museum
The Poultry Merchant

Raleigh (North Carolina), Museum of Art
The Poultry Merchant (signed and dated 165(2 or 6)

Strasbourg, Musée des Beaux-Arts
The Poultry Merchant

Tarbes, Musée Massey
Adoration of the Shepherds

Bibliography

An excellent summary is by Jacques Thuillier in the catalogue, Paris, Grand Palais, *Les Frères Le Nain*, 1979, pp.339–480.

Nicolas Mignard

Troyes 1606–Paris 1688

Elder brother of the much better-known Pierre Mignard, Nicolas Mignard executed most of his work in Provence. His style was colder and drier than that of his brother, but showed the same attention to drawing. His compositions tended to be based on Italian models.

Collections

Aix-en-Provence, Musée Granet
Mars and Venus (signed and dated 1658)

Aix-en-Provence, Saint-Jean de Malte
The Virgin and St Simon Stock (signed and dated 1648)

Aix-en-Provence, La Madeleine
The Nativity (signed and dated 1657)

Apt, Cathedral
Holy Family with St Anne (signed and dated 1634)

Aubignan (Vaucluse), Church
The Resurrected Christ Appearing to the Virgin and St Anne (signed and dated 1641)

Avignon, Musée Calvet
St Bruno (signed and dated 1638)
The Virgin and St Simon Stock (signed and dated 1644)
Pietà (signed and dated 1655)
Nativity
St John
Vow of Vice-legate Sforza (signed)

Avignon, Palais des Papes
The Visitation

Avignon, Cathedral
Assumption of the Virgin (signed and dated 1633)
The Visitation (signed and dated 1636)
The Annunciation (signed and dated 1637)
Adoration of the Shepherds (signed and dated 1654)
Presentation of the Virgin in the Temple (signed and dated 1657)

Avignon, Pénitents Gris
The Visitation (signed and dated 1639)
Virgin and Child with Angels
St Benedict
St Ignatius

Avignon, Pénitents Noirs
The Visitation
Christ on the Cross
Head of St John the Baptist
Assumption of the Virgin (signed and dated 1663)

Avignon, Saint-Agricol
Adoration of the Shepherds (signed and dated 1654)

Avignon, Saint-Pierre
St Barbara and St Margaret (signed and dated 163?)
Holy Family with St Anne
The Virgin and St Simon Stock (signed and dated 165(7))

Avignon, Hôpital Sainte-Marthe
Death of St Joseph (signed and dated 1654)

Bedarrides (Vaucluse), Church
The Vision of Soriano
The Virgin appearing to St Dominic

Carcassonne, Saint-Vincent
Christ on the Cross with the Virgin and St John (signed and dated 1644)

Carpentras, Cathedral
The Nourishment of St Bernard in the Presence of St Helen and St Louis (signed and dated 1640)

Cavaillon, Cathedral
Nativity
The Annunciation
The Education of the Virgin with St Blaise and St Margaret

Châteaurenard, Church
St Eloi and the Miracle of the Horse's Cut Foot (signed and dated 1645)
The Virgin Presenting the Christ Child to St Anthony of Padua in the Presence of St Francis (signed and dated 1656)

Dallas, Museum of Fine Arts
Faustulus Bringing Romulus and Remus back to his Wife (signed and dated 1654)

Lambesc, Church
The Vision of St John of Matha (signed and dated 1630)

Lille, Palais des Beaux-Arts
The Judgment of Midas

L'Isle-sur-la-Sorgue, Church
Presentation in the Temple (signed and dated 1665)

Montpellier, Cathedral
The Angel Ordering Joseph to take Flight (signed and dated 1664)

Mormoiron (Vaucluse), Church
Assumption of the Virgin (signed and dated 1642)

Nîmes, Musée Vieux Nîmes
Assumption of the Virgin

Paris, Musée de la Comédie Française
Molière as César in 'La morte de Pampée'

Paris, private collection
Still Life with Silver and Musical Instruments
Still Life with a Perfume Burner

Paris, private collection
Still Life with Fruit and Vanitas

Pierrelatte, private collection
Holy Family (signed and dated 1659)

Rochefort du Gard, Chapelle Nôtre Dame de Grace
St Joseph with the Christ Child and St Benedict and Scolastica (signed and dated 1645)

Santa Fe (New Mexico), Museum of Fine Arts
Holy Family (signed and dated 1659)

Sisteron, Cathedral
God the Father
Virgin and Child with St Joseph and Music-making Angels

Tarascon, Sainte-Marthe
Jesus Arriving at Bethany (signed and dated 1640)
Assumption of the Virgin (signed and dated 1643)

Troyes, Musée des Beaux-Arts
Christ on the Cross (signed and dated 16(36?))

Versailles, Château
Ex-Voto of Louis XIV (attribution)

Villeneuve-lès-Avignon, Museum
Christ among the Doctors (signed and dated 1649)
Annunciation with St Charles Borromeo (signed and dated 1652)

Villeneuve-lès-Avignon, Notre Dame
St Anne, the Virgin and St Bruno (signed and dated 1639)
The Mystic Marriage of St Catherine (signed and dated 1651)
St Bruno

Visan (Vaucluse), Church
The Virgin of the Seven Sorrows (signed and dated 1659)

Viviers (Ardèche), Cathedral
The Annunciation (signed and dated 1642)

Whereabouts unknown
Holy Family with St Bruno
Virgin and Child with the Infant St John the Baptist (signed and dated 1654)

Bibliography

Antoine Schapper in the exhibition catalogue, Marseilles, Palais Longchamp, *La peinture en Provence au XVIIe siècle*, 1978, pp.90–100. Michel Faré in *Le grand siècle de la nature morte en France*, 1974, pp.235–7, drew attention to the still-life pictures of this artist. There is a complete study of the artist by Antoine Schnapper in the exhibition catalogue, Avignon, Palais des Papes, *Nicolas Mignard d'Avignon, 1606–68*, 1979.

Paul Mignard

Avignon 1641–Lyons 1691

Son and pupil of Nicolas Mignard, Paul was received into the French Academy in Paris in 1672. Most of his career was spent working as a portraitist for different European courts, and his portrait style was influenced by that of his uncle, Pierre Mignard.

Collections

Lyons, Musée des Beaux-Arts
Nicolas Mignard (signed)
Anne Marguerite d'Acigné, Duchesse de Richelieu

Orléans, Musée des Beaux-Arts
Anne Marguerite d'Acigné, Duchesse de Richelieu (attribution)

Bibliography

Charles Sterling in the exhibition catalogue, Paris, Orangerie, *Les peintres de la réalité*, 1934, pp.87–8.

Pierre Mignard I

Troyes 1612–Paris 1695

Pierre Mignard I was a pupil of Jean Boucher of Bourges, who had been influenced by Simon Vouet, before entering the studio of Vouet himself. From 1635 to 1658 he was in Rome, assimilating almost all the numerous influences possible from both French and Italian artists. Correggio seems to have played an important part in his development, as he had done with the Italian Lanfranco. Mignard was also influenced in Rome by his French contemporary Le Brun, even though in France they were to be bitter rivals. Only on Le Brun's death in 1690 was Mignard received into the French Academy in Paris. Mignard had great facility as a decorator—he painted the cupola of the Val-de-Grâce in Paris in 1663—his portrait style was perceptive and his bust-length pictures were much copied and imitated. In his lifetime his reputation ranked with that of Nicolas Poussin and Le Brun.

Collections

Angers, Musée des Beaux-Arts
Virgin and Child with St John

Arras, Palais Saint-Vaast
Bacchanal (attribution)

Avignon, Musée Calvet
The Duc de Berri as a Child
Mme de Montespan and the Duc de Maine (copy?)

Barnard Castle, Bowes Museum
A Lady as St Catherine (attribution)

Besançon, Musée des Beaux-Arts
A Lady
Mme de Saint-Germain

Blois, Museum
Elisabeth d'Orléans

Bourges, Musée du Berry
A Young Woman

Bremen, Kunsthalle
Venus and Mars (attribution)

Brussels, Musées Royaux des Beaux-Arts
A Woman as Diana

Budapest, Szépmüvészeti Múzeum
The Muse Clio (signed and dated 1689)

Cambrai, Musée Municipal
The Duc de Berri as a Child (attribution)

Cambridge (Massachusetts), Fogg Art Museum
A Lady holding an Oval Portrait of a Man

Chantilly, Musée Condé
Cardinal Mazarin
Mme Deshoulières
Molière (fig.69)

Columbus (Ohio), Museum of Fine Arts
Louis XIV (attribution)

Darmstadt, Hessisches Landesmuseum
Louis XIV with his Mistresses

Dayton (Ohio), Art Institute
A Woman

Dijon, Musée des Beaux-Arts
An Artist (Charles-Alphonse Dufresnoy?)

Dijon, Musée Magnin
La Grande Mademoiselle (attribution)

Dinan, Museum
Fragment of Decoration for Versailles

Dôle, Musée Municipal
A Lady with her Son

Dublin, National Gallery of Ireland
The Way to Calvary (attribution)

Dunkirk, Musée des Beaux-Arts
Claude Leblanc

Edinburgh, Scottish National Portrait Gallery
Duchesse d'Orléans (attribution)

Épinal, Musée Départemental des Vosges
Louis-Auguste de Bourbon, Duc de Maine

France, Comtesse de Rouge
Mme de Montespan

Ghent, Mme B. Thouand collection
Elisabeth-Charlotte de Bavière, Duchesse d'Orléans (1678)

Glasgow, Pollok House
Marie-Thérèse, Wife of Louis XIV (attribution)

Greenville (South Carolina), Bob Jones University
Head of Christ (attribution)

Grenoble, Musée de Peinture et de Sculpture
The Antique and the Modern Idyll

Hanover, Niedersächsisches Landesmuseum
Elisabeth-Charlotte d'Orléans

Honolulu, Academy of Fine Arts
The Children of the Duc de Bouillon

Le Mans, Musée de Tessé
The Duc de Berri as a Child (documented 1692–5)

Leningrad, Hermitage
The Return of Jephthah
The Magnanimity of Alexander the Great
Death of Cleopatra
Mlle de La Vallière (attribution)
Duchesse de Mazarin

Le Puy, Musée Crozatier
A Duchess of Savoy (attribution)

Lille, Palais des Beaux-Arts
Fortune

London, National Gallery
Marquise de Seignelay and her Two Children (1691)

London, National Portrait Gallery
Duchess of Portsmouth (1682)

Louisville (Kentucky), Speed Art Museum
Maréchal de Schomberg

Madrid, Prado
Philippe d'Orléans, Regent of France
St John the Baptist
Maria-Theresa of Austria and the Grand Dauphin (attribution)
Philippe de France, Duc d'Orléans (attribution)
Henrietta Maria of England, Duchesse d'Orléans (attribution)

Marseilles, Palais Longchamp
Mlle de La Vallière (attribution)

Monaco, National Museum of Fine Arts
Anne de Foudras

Montauban, Musée Ingres
Allegory of Painting (1684)

Montserrat (Spain), Pinacoteca
Mme Jeanne de La Fontaine

Nancy, Musée des Beaux-Arts
Virgin and Child
Mme Claude des Salles de Malpierre (signed)

Narbonne, Musée des Beaux-Arts
St Charles Borromeo and the Plague-stricken of Milan

New Orleans, Gallier Hall
Figure of Glory holding a Medallion of Louis XIV (attribution)

New York, Historical Society
Mme Dufresnoy (?)

Nîmes, Musée des Beaux-Arts
A Man
A Man

Norfolk (Virginia), Chrysler Museum
Virgin and Child (attribution)

Orléans, Musée des Beaux-Arts
Louis XIV (attribution)
A Woman (signed)

Paris, Musée Carnavalet
Françoise-Marguerite de Sevigné, Comtesse de Grignan

Paris, Louvre
Equestrian Portrait of Louis XIV
The Virgin and Child
Christ on the Way to Calvary (signed and dated 1684)
Mlle de Blois
Christ and the Samaritan Woman (signed and dated 1690)
Self-portrait
St Cecilia Singing to the Saviour (signed and dated 1691)
Mme de Maintenon (documented 1691)

Paris, Comte de Lastic
Maria Mancini (?)

Paris, Paul Levy collection
Comte de Vermandois and Mlle de Blois

Pavlovsk, Castle
Christ and the Samaritan Woman (dated 1691)

Prague, National Gallery
A Man (Senator Marco Peruta?)

Quimper, Musée des Beaux-Arts
Faith (dated 1692)
Hope (dated 1692)

Raleigh, North Carolina Museum of Art
Christ and the Samaritan Woman

Reims, Musée Saint-Denis
Louvois (*Michel Le Tellier*)
Charles-Maurice Le Tellier

Rouen, Musée des Beaux-Arts
Ecce Homo (signed and dated 1690)

Stockholm, Nationalmuseum
Magistrate of Toulouse (attribution)

Toulouse, Musée des Augustins
Christ with the Rosary
Eloquence and Knowledge
Science

Troyes, Musée des Beaux-Arts
Anne of Austria
Mme de Montespan (1668?)
St Luke Painting the Virgin (1695)
Head of a Man

Turin, Galleria Sabauda
The Duc de Berri as a Child (copy?)

Valetta (Malta), San Anton Palace
Commandeur des Vieux, Ambassador of Malta to Rome

Versailles, Château
Catherine Marguerite Mignard
The Duc d'Anjou
Louis XIV on Horseback Crowned by Victory
Edouard Colbert, Marquis de Villacerf
Mlle de Blois, Duchesse d'Orléans
Louis-Alexandre de Bourbon
Mme de Maintenon (replica)
Comtesse de Fouquières
Mme de Montespan and her Children
The Family of the Grand Dauphin
Louis XIV Crowned by Victory (attribution)
President Jacques Tubeuf (1663)
Comte de Toulouse as Love Asleep

Bibliography

Jean-Claude Boyer, 'L'Inventaire après décès de l'atelier de Pierre Mignard', *Bulletin de la Société de l'Histoire de l'Art français*, 1980, pp.137–65.
Georges de Lastic, 'Contribution à l'oeuvre de Pierre Mignard', *Bulletin de la Société de l'Histoire de l'Art français*, 1980, pp.167–76.
Lada Nikolenko, *Pierre Mignard, The Portrait Painter of the Grand Siècle*, Munich, 1983. The portraits accepted by this authority have been reduced to only thirty (all reproduced). The remaining hundreds of rejected attributions are inadequately discussed.

Pierre Mignard II

Avignon 1640–Avignon 1725

Eldest son of Nicolas Mignard and brother of Paul Mignard, Pierre continued the style of his father into the eighteenth century.

Collections

Avignon, Cathedral
Assumption

Avignon, Hôtel Galeans des Issarts
Ceiling paintings: *Bacchus and Ariadne, Venus Arming Aeneas, Time in his Chariot* (one signed)

Isle-sur-Sorgue, Church
Ascension of Christ and the Doctors of the Church (signed and dated 1675)

Saint-Gilles, Church
Saint Gilles

Villeneuve-lès-Avignon, Museum
St Casarie

Bibliography

Henry Wytenhove in the exhibition catalogue, Marseilles, Palais Longchamp, *La peinture en Provence au XVIIe siècle*, 1978, pp.101–2.

Philippe Millereau

d. Paris 1610

Apparently Millereau worked in a Mannerist tradition in Paris.

Collections

Châlons-sur-Marne, Musée Municipal
Ceres and Bacchus

Reims, Musée Saint-Denis
Vulcan, Venus and Cupid (signed and dated 1609)

Bibliography

There is no recent literature on this artist.

Jean-François (Francisque) Millet

Antwerp 1642–Paris 1679

Millet was received into the French Academy in Paris in 1673, after having worked in the Low Countries and in England. He can lay claim to being the best interpreter of Nicolas Poussin's classical landscapes, retaining the formality and dignity of his models without loss of subtlety. Like those of Gaspard Dughet, his pictures are largely attributions on purely stylistic grounds, there being no sure documentation.

Collections

Aix-en-Provence, Musée Granet
Landscape

Avignon, Musée Calvet
Landscape

Baltimore, Museum of Art
Landscape with Classical Buildings

Berkeley, University of California
Landscape with Shepherds

Besançon, Musée des Beaux-Arts
Landscape with an Ancient City

Birmingham, City Art Gallery
Regulus Returning to Carthage

Bordeaux, Musée des Beaux-Arts
Landscape

Budapest, Szépmüvészeti Múzeum
Classical Landscape

Châlon-sur-Saône, Musée Denon
Landscape

Cherbourg, Musée Thomas Henry
Landscape

Chicago, Art Institute
Landscape with Three Women on a Road

Darmstadt, Hessisches Landesmuseum
Ideal Landscape
Rocky Landscape

Dijon, Musée Magnin
Landscape

Douai, Musée de La Chartreuse
Landscape

Glasgow University
Tomb of Phaeton

Grenoble, Musée de Peinture et de Sculpture
Landscape

Hamburg, Kunsthalle
Heroic Landscape
Ideal Landscape
Landscape

Hanover, Niedersächsisches Landesmuseum
Rocky Landscape (attribution)

Kassel, Staatliche Kunsthalle
Landscape

La Fère, Musée Jeanne d'Aboville
Landscape

Le Mans, Musée de Tessé
Landscape

Leningrad, Hermitage
A Harbour
Landscape with a Fountain
Landscape with Christ and the Disciples
Landscape with the Expulsion of Hagar

London, National Gallery
Mountainous Landscape with Lightning

Montpellier, Musée Fabre
Landscape

Munich, Alte Pinakothek
Italian Coastal Landscape

Nantes, Musée des Beaux-Arts
Landscape with Figures

Newcastle upon Tyne, Hatton Gallery
Landscape with a Burning City

New York, Metropolitan Museum
Landscape with Mercury and Battus

Norfolk (Virginia), Chrysler Museum
Landscape

Orléans, Musée des Beaux-Arts
Landscape: Mercury and Battus

Oxford, Ashmolean Museum
Mountainous Landscape with a Citadel

Paris, Louvre
Pastoral Scene (attribution)
Landscape (attribution)

Pau, Musée des Beaux-Arts
Landscape with Tobias and the Angel

Raleigh, North Carolina Museum of Art
Landscape with Two Travellers

Petworth House (Sussex), National Trust
Landscape with a Shrine

Ponce (Puerto Rico), Museo de Arte
Landscape with a Fountain

Reims, Musée Saint-Denis
Landscape

Schleissheim, Schloss, Staatsgalerie
Italian Landscape

Southampton, Art Gallery
Landscape with Regulus returning to Exile

Strasbourg, Musée des Beaux-Arts
Landscape

Toledo (Ohio), Museum of Art
Landscape with Christ and the Woman of Samaria

Toulouse, Musée des Augustins
Landscape

Tourcoing, Musée des Beaux-Arts
The Rest on the Flight into Egypt

Warsaw, National Museum
Landscape (2) (attributions)

Würzburg, Marten von Wagner Museum
Landscape
Landscape with the Flight into Egypt

York, City Art Gallery
The Noblemen of Capernaum (fig.68)
Classical Landscape

Bibliography

Martin Davis, 'A note on Francisque Millet', in *Bulletin de la Société Poussin*, II, December 1948, pp.13–26.

Nicolas Moellon (Moillon)

d. Reims 1627

Father of Louise Moillon, Nicolas Moellon painted in a sixteenth-century style influenced by North Italian artists, especially those of Brescia. It is possible that he was a still-life painter as well as a portraitist.

Collections

Paris, J.F. collection
The Utensils of the Smoker (monogrammed NM)

Reims, Musée Saint-Denis
Eustache de La Salle (signed and dated 1613)

Bibliography

Charles Sterling in the exhibition catalogue, Paris, Orangerie, *Les peintres de la réalité*, 1934, pp.125–6. The possibility that Moillon was also a still-life painter was suggested by Michel Faré in *Le grand siècle de la nature morte en France*, 1974, pp.152–3.

Louise Moillon

Paris 1616–Paris after 1674

Louise Moillon, the greatest still-life painter of the French seventeenth century, spent her long career in Paris, specializing specifically in still-life pictures with the occasional figure. Her technique was extremely refined, and this led, in later centuries, to the confusion of her work with Dutch, Flemish and even German painters. Since four still-life pictures at Grenoble, one given to Moillon, have been (sensibly) reattributed to the Flemish artist Osias Beert, Moillon's art has been redefined. Her best pictures have a stillness combined with acute powers of observation, notably of the texture of exotic fruit, which have never been surpassed.

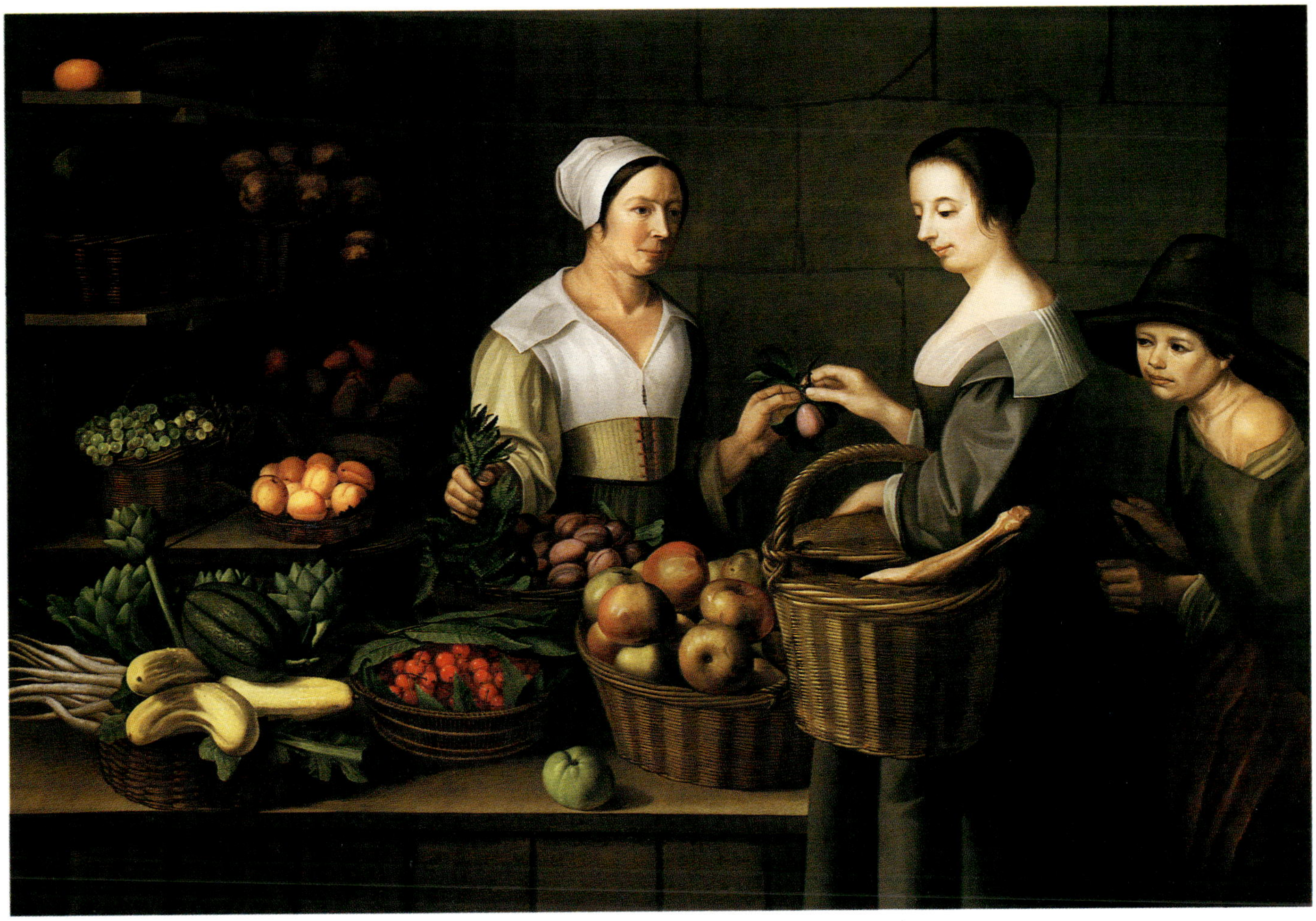

PLATE 61
Louise Moillon
Market Scene with a Pick-pocket
Canvas, 116 × 165.5 cm.
London, private collection
Probably first recorded in a Paris sale in 1786.

Collections

Amsterdam, with de Boer
Apricots on a Blue Porcelain Plate

Chicago, Art Institute
Basket of Fruit and Asparagus (signed and dated 1630)
Grapes, Apples and Melons (signed and dated 1637)

Dessau, Schloss
Bowl of Peaches and Grapes (signed and dated 1641)

France, A.C. collection
The Meal

Grand Rapids (Michigan), Art Museum
Basket of Raspberries on a Chip-wood Box

Karlsruhe, Staatliche Kunsthalle
Basket of Peaches and Grapes (signed and dated 1631)

London, private collection
Market Scene with a Pick-pocket (plate 61)

London, formerly with Leonard Koetser
Bowl of Peaches and Grapes (signed and dated 1634)

Lugano, Thyssen collection
Fruit and Vegetables (signed and dated 1637)

New York, formerly with Knoedler
Basket of Peaches, Asparagus and Artichokes (signed and dated 1637)
Basket of Plums and Blackberries on a Chip-wood Box

New York, A.R. Lander collection
Basket, Bowl of Fruit and Open Pomegranate

New York, J. Lowenthal collection
Bunches of Grapes in a Bowl and Figs (signed and dated 1631)

New York, with Wildenstein
The Fruit Seller (signed and dated 1629)

Paris, Louvre
The Fruit and Vegetable Seller (signed and dated 1630)
Still Life of Peaches and Pears
Bowl of Cherries and Melon (signed and dated 1633)

Paris, A.B. collection
Apricots and Plums (signed and dated 1634)

Paris, with Cailleux
Bowl of Cherries and Bunch of Gooseberries (signed and dated 1634)

Paris, with François Heim
Basket of Apricots
Bunches of Grapes (signed and dated 1637)

Paris, with Heim-Gairac
Basket of Oranges and Cut-open Pomegranate

Paris, formerly J.R. collection
Basket of Cherries and Bunch of Apricots

Paris, R.D. collection
Bunch of Grapes

Paris, R. Lebel collection
Bowl of Peaches on a Chip-wood Box (signed and dated 1634)

Paris, Michelson collection
Basket of Grapes

Paris, formerly Vicomtesse d'Origny collection
Basket of Apricots and Basket of Plums (signed and dated 1636)

Paris, with Pardo
Basket of Cherries
Basket of Cherries and Bowl of Apricots

Paris, D.W. collection
Bowl of Plums

Paris, private collection
Bowl of Peaches, Plums and Grapes

Paris, private collection
Bowl of Grapes and Figs

Paris, private collection
Exotic Fruits (signed and dated 1634)

Paris, private collection
Peaches, Plums and Red Currants in a Porcelain Bowl

Paris, private collection
Bowl of Apricots

Pasadena (California), Norton Simon Museum
Cherries on a Plate, Basket of Gooseberries and a Bowl of Strawberries (signed and dated 1630) (fig.54)
Still-life with a Bowl of Curaçao Oranges (signed and dated 1634)

Strasbourg, Musée des Beaux-Arts
Dish of Plums on a Chip-wood Box (signed and dated 1632)

Sweden, Steenman collection
The Fruit Seller, a Basket on her Head Holding Artichokes

Switzerland, A.S. collection
Dish of Purple Plums (signed)

Toulouse, Musée des Augustins
Peaches, Apricots, Grapes and Strawberries (signed and dated 1672) (fig.53)
Bowl of Strawberries and a Bowl of Fruit
Plums and a Basket of Apricots (signed and dated 1674) (fig.62)
Basket of Blackberries

Bibliography

Michel Faré
Le grand siècle de la nature morte en France, 1974, pp.48–69.

Jean-Baptiste Mole

Besançon 1616–Rome 1661

Mole's early career was spent as a pupil of Simon Vouet in Paris. He then went to Italy where he settled permanently, painting in a style similar to that of the Italian Baroque painter Pier Francesco Mola.

Collections

Bergamo, Accademia Carrara
The Magdalen

Florence, Uffizi
Nymphs and Cupids Sacrificing to Flora

Liège, Musée des Beaux-Arts
St Bruno in Ecstasy
St Francis Receiving the Stigmata

Paris, Louvre
The Players of Bowls (signed and dated 1633)

Stockholm, Nationalmuseum
St Jerome

Bibliography

There is no recent literature on this artist.

Jean-Baptiste Monnoyer

Lille 1636?–London 1699

The most successful specialist in flower painting of this period, Monnoyer lived in Paris in the 1660s, when he worked on the decoration of numerous royal palaces. There are influences in his art which show his Flemish background, especially in the Baroque arrangement of his flowers. The second half of his career was spent in London, where the Duke of Montagu was his main patron (many of the pictures commissioned by the Duke are still in the family collection at Boughton House, Northamptonshire). Monnoyer was received into the Academy in 1665. Many pictures have been wrongly attributed to him, and his *oeuvre* is difficult to define because of the lack of signed and dated pictures.

Collections

Amboise, Hôtel de Ville
Basket of Flowers
Metal Bowl of Flowers

Amiens, Musée de Picardie
Bouquet of Flowers

Arles, Musée Réattu
Flowers Against Carved Stonework

Arras, Palais-Saint-Vaast
Flowers in a Pitcher

Atlanta (Georgia), Art Association
Flowers in a Wicker Basket

Avignon, Musée Calvet
Vase of Flowers

Barnard Castle, Bowes Museum
Vases of Flowers

Bayeux, Musée des Beaux-Arts
Still Life of Flowers

Bedford, Cecil Higgins Museum
Flowers in a Silver Dish

Besançon, Musée des Beaux-Arts
Bouquet of Flowers (attribution)

Boughton House (Northamptonshire), The Duke of Buccleuch
Series of pictures painted for Montagu House, London:
Bowl of Flowers
Infant Christ and St John Encircled with Flowers (in collaboration with Charles de La Fosse)
Infant Christ and the Divine Lamb Encircled with a Floral Wreath (in collaboration with Charles de La Fosse)
Still Life with a Carved Stone Screen on a Pedestal

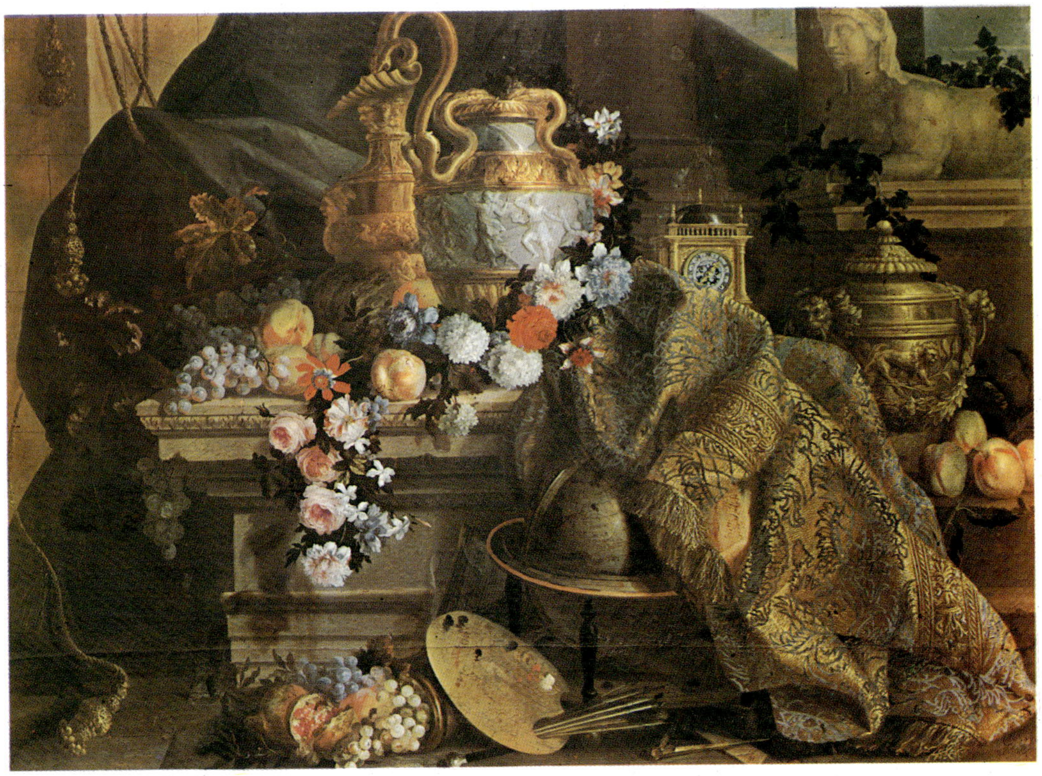

PLATE 62
Jean-Baptiste Monnoyer
Still Life of Flowers, Fruits and Objets d'Art
Canvas, 146 × 190 cm.
Montpellier, Musée Fabre
Painted in 1665 and submitted to the Academy at the time of his admission in the same year. Following the upheavals of the Revolution of 1789, deposited at Montpellier in 1804.

Vase of Flowers
Still Life of Vases of Flowers
Flowers on a Sculptured Urn
Sculptured Urn of Flowers (signed and dated 1698)
Vase of Flowers
Bowl of Flowers
Bowl of Flowers
Thirty-seven other *Flower Pieces*

Brighton, Art Gallery
Spring Flowers in a Vase

Bristol, City Art Gallery
Flower Piece

Budapest, Szépmüvészeti Múzeum
Vase of Flowers

Burghley House (Northamptonshire), The Marquess of Exeter
Bowl of Flowers
Vase of Flowers
Flowers in an Urn
Flowers in an Urn
Flowers in an Urn
Basket of Flowers

Caen, Musée des Beaux-Arts
Vase of Flowers

Cambridge, Fitzwilliam Museum
Urn with Flowers (signed and dated 1698)
Flowers in a Metal Vase
Vase of Flowers

Chalon-sur-Saône, Musée Denon
Flowers on a Table

Cincinnati (Ohio), Art Museum
Vase of Flowers (signed and dated 1696)

Detroit, Institute of Arts
Vase of Flowers
Vase of Flowers

Dôle, Musée Municipal
Vase of Flowers

Douai, Musée de La Chartreuse
Vase of Flowers

Dublin, National Gallery of Ireland
Flower Piece (2)

Dyrham Park (Gloucestershire), National Trust
Flower Piece

Fontainbleau, Château
Vase of Flowers, Fruit and Garland of Flowers
Vase, Orange Tree and Garland of Flowers

Grenoble, Musée de Peinture et de Sculpture
Vase of Flowers

Hanover, Niedersächsisches Landesmuseum
Flowers around an Urn

Hatchlands (Surrey), National Trust
Flower Piece

Hatfield House, Marquess of Salisbury
Vase of Flowers
Vase of Flowers
Vase of Flowers

Karlsruhe, Staatliche Kunsthalle
Flowers in a Vase (signed)
Flowers in a Vase

La Fère, Musée Jeanne d'Aboville
Still Life of Flowers

Leeds, Temple Newsam House
Flowers in a Stone Vase (attribution)

Le Mans, Musée de Tessé
Flowers and Fruit on a Balustrade
Flowers and Fruit

Leningrad, Hermitage
Flowers and Fruit on a Table

Lille, Palais des Beaux-Arts
Flowers and Birds
Vase of Flowers
Vase of Flowers
Vase of Flowers

London, Chiswick House
Cupid and Flowers

Lyons, Musée des Beaux-Arts
Flower Piece (signed)
Flower Piece (signed)

Marseilles, Musée Grobet-Labadié
Vase of Flowers

Melbourne Hall, Derbyshire, Marquess of Lothian
Vase of Flowers

Milwaukee, Marquette University
Vase of Flowers (attribution)

Montpellier, Musée Fabre
Still Life of Flowers, Fruits and Objets d'Art (documented 1665) (plate 62)

Montpellier, private collection
Flowers in a Sculptured Vase

Nancy, Musée des Beaux-Arts
Still Life of Flowers and a Carpet

Nantes, Musée des Beaux-Arts
Pomegranates, Peaches and Apples

Narbonne, Musée des Beaux-Arts
Vase of Flowers
Vase of Flowers

New York, Queen's College
Vase of Flowers (attribution)

Norfolk (Virginia), Chrysler Museum
Vase of Flowers (signed)

Orléans, Musée des Beaux-Arts
Still Life with Flowers and Fruit

Oslo, Nasjionalgalleriet
Bowl of Flowers

Palm Beach (Florida), Mrs David Annan
Sprig of Lilac (signed)

Paris, Louvre
Flower Piece (signed)

Paris, private collection
Vase of Flowers (2)

Paris, private collection
Vase of Flowers

Paris, private collection
Bouquet of Flowers in a Silver Vase (signed and dated 1686)

Paris, with Pardo
Roses and Garland of Flowers round an Urn

Paris, W. collection
Portrait of the Artist and his Wife with Flowers

Poitiers, Musée des Beaux-Arts
Sculptured Vase of Flowers (signed)

Prague, Národni Galeri
Bowl of Flowers

Provo (Utah), Brigham Young University
Vase of Flowers

Rennes, Musée des Beaux-Arts
Basket of Flowers and Fruits
Vase of Flowers and Fruits

Rouen, Musée des Beaux-Arts
Cupids Playing with Flowers
Cupids Playing with Flowers
Flowers in a Metal Vase (attribution)

Schleissheim, Schloss
Still Life with Flowers

Stockholm, Nationalmuseum
Vase of Flowers
Sculptured Vase of Flowers

Stourhead House (Wiltshire), National Trust
Flower Piece
Flower Piece
Flower Piece

Toulon, Musée des Beaux-Arts
Basket of Flowers
Basket of Flowers
Vase of Flowers

Toulouse, Musée des Augustins
Vase of Flowers (fig.66)

Tours, Musée des Beaux-Arts
Flowers in an Alabaster Vase

Uppsala, University collection
Vase of Flowers
Bowl of Flowers (2)

Valenciennes, Musée des Beaux-Arts
Vase of Flowers (2)

Versailles, Château
Vase of Flowers and a Cassolette
Vase of Flowers (7)
Vase and Flowers
Golden Ewer of Flowers and Fruits
Vase of Flowers and Fruits
Basket of Flowers (4)
Golden Vase Full of Flowers
Bouquet of Flowers with a Large Lily Branch
Jardinière of Flowers in an Architectural Setting
Golden Ewer and Flowers in an Architectural Setting

Warsaw, National Museum (formerly)
Flowers and Fruits in a Landscape (signed and dated 1682)

Wellesley College (Massachusetts), Jewett Art Center
Vase of Flowers

Bibliography

The only book is Sidney H. Pavière, *Jean-Baptiste Monnoyer*, 1966, which includes a catalogue. Although there is a good corpus of plates, the book is unreliable, as many pictures unrelated to Monnoyer are included. A good general account is found in Michel Faré, *Le grand siècle de la nature morte en France*, 1974, pp.290–316.

Pierre Montallier

Paris c.1643–?1697

Montallier was one of the few artists working in the second half of the seventeenth century to be influenced by the work of the Le Nain brothers. He was received into the Academy in 1676 and became 'Peintre ordinaire du Roy'.

Collection

Leningrad, Hermitage
The Works of Mercy (signed)

Bibliography

There is no recent literature on this artist.

Jean Mosnier

Blois 1600?–Blois 1656

Mosnier was a stained-glass painter as well as an artist, and most of his work was executed for churches in and around Chartres and Blois.

Collections

Blois, Museum
Allegory
The Échevin Jean Martin (dated 1654)

Toledo (Ohio), Museum of Art
Decorated Room from the Château of Chenailles

Bibliography

There is no recent literature on this artist.

Pierre Mosnier

Blois 1641–Paris 1703

Son of Jean Mosnier, Pierre was a pupil of Sébastien Bourdon in Paris. He was received into the French Academy in Paris in 1674.

Collection

Arras, Palais Saint-Vaast
Dance of Shepherds and Shepherdesses

Bibliography

There is no recent literature on this artist.

P. Nichon

Working Dijon c.1626–c.1655

Nichon was probably a pupil of Sébastien Stoskopff in Strasbourg, but no documentation about this artist survives.

Collections

Boston, Museum of Fine Arts
The Carp (signed) (attributed to Stoskopff)

Dijon, Notre Dame
The Crucifixion (signed)

Paris, private collection
Still Life of Fish (signed)

Bibliography

A brief summary is made by Pierre Rosenberg in the exhibition catalogue, Paris, Grand Palais, *La peinture française du XVIIe siècle dans les collections américaines*, 1982, pp.293–4. The artist was tentatively identified with the Dijon painter Pierre Nichon by Sylvan Laveissière, 'Pierre Nichon identified', *The Burlington Magazine*, 1982, p.704.

Jean Nocret

Nancy 1617–Paris 1672

Nocret was a portrait painter who, like the Beaubrun brothers, achieved a considerable reputation with the French court. He was an archaizing artist, much influenced by Frans Pourbus the Younger.

Collections

Baltimore, Museum of Art
François de Vendôme, Duc de Beaufort

Madrid, Prado
Philippe of France, Duc d'Orléans (2)

Versailles, Château
The Family of Louis XIV
Anne of Austria
Marie-Thérèse, wife of Louis XIV
Duchesse de La Vallière

Bibliography

There is no recent literature on this artist.

Jean-Charles Nocret

Paris 1647–Paris 1719

Son of Jean Nocret, Jean-Charles continued his father's tradition of official portraiture.

Collections

Brest, Musée des Beaux-Arts
The Renunciation of Louise de La Valière

Versailles, Château
Portrait of the Artist's Father, Jean Nocret

Bibliography

There is no recent literature on this artist.

François de Nomé

See under Monsù Desiderio.

René Nourrisson

Paris ?c.1610–Paris ?c.1650

As this painter's work is close in style and composition to that of Jacques Linard, it is possible that unsigned pictures have been wrongly attributed. Nourrisson is recorded as having been in Paris in the 1630s and 1640s.

Collections

Bordeaux, H.B. collection
Basket of Peaches and a Bowl of Strawberries

New York, with Wildenstein
Basket of Fruit, Flagon and Chip-wood box

Paris, formerly C.B. collection
Basket of Peaches, Quince and Pears (signed)

Bibliography

Michel Faré
Le grand siècle de la nature morte en France, 1974, pp.40–42.

Hilaire Pader

Toulouse 1617–Toulouse 1677

A pupil of Jean Chalette in Toulouse, Pader painted in a provincial Baroque style showing the influence of Vouet. His *Triumph of Joseph* in Toulouse Cathedral is particularly elaborate, with its numerous figures in excited poses pulling Joseph's chariot.

Collections

Toulouse, Musée des Augustins
The Flagellation of Christ

Toulouse, Cathedral
The Triumph of Joseph
Samson Struggling against the Philistines
The Sacrifice of Abraham

Bibliography

There is no recent literature on this artist.

Antoine Paillet

Paris 1626–Paris 1701

Pupil of Sébastien Bourdon in Paris, Paillet became a member of the Academy there in 1659. He executed numerous decorations for Versailles, as well as religious pictures for Notre Dame.

Collection

Toulouse, Musée des Augustins
Annunciation

Bibliography

There is no recent literature on this artist.

Joseph Parrocel

Brignoles (Var) 1646–Paris 1704

A specialist in battle pieces, Parrocel was received into the Academy in 1676 with his *Siege of Maastricht* (Versailles).

Collections

Aix-en-Provence, Musée Granet
Battle on a Bridge

Besançon, Musée des Beaux-Arts
Cavalry Combat (2)

Caen, Musée des Beaux-Arts
Sobieski before Vienna

Chalon-sur-Saône, Musée Denon
Cavalry Combat before a Fortress

Épinal, Musée Départemental des Vosges
Cavalry Combat

Florence, Uffizi
Cavalry Combat

Hanover, Niedersächsisches Landesmuseum
Hunting Scene
Battle Piece

Leningrad, Hermitage
Battle near a Windmill
Battery Attack
Battle
Landscape with Horsemen

Lyons, Musée des Beaux-Arts
Cavalry Officers Resting

Paris, Louvre
The Passage of the Rhine (documented 1699)

Tours, Musée des Beaux-Arts
Group of Cavalry Officers

Versailles, Château
Battle Scene (6)
Cavalry Combat (4)
The Battle of Lenze, 1691
Siege of Maastricht
Halt of the Cavaliers

Bibliography

There is no recent literature on this artist.

Pierre Patel (the Elder)

Picardie c.1605–Paris 1676

Primarily a decorative painter of landscape, Patel was a pupil of Vouet. The main influence on his art was that of Claude Lorraine, whose compositions and golden lighting Patel imitated. His most significant work was the decoration of the Hôtel Lambert in Paris, on which he collaborated with Le Sueur.

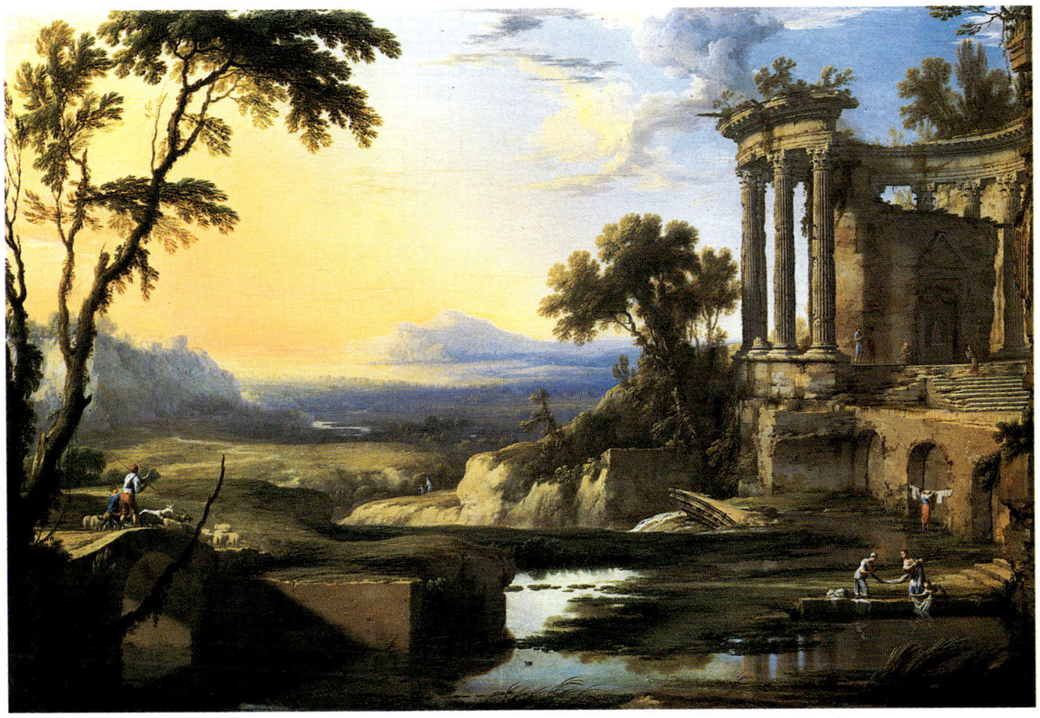

PLATE 63
Pierre Patel
Landscape with Ruins
Canvas, 59 × 85.5 cm.
Springfield (Massachusetts), Art Museum (James Philip Gray collection)
First recorded in the collection of the chevalier de Damery before 1763. Acquired by the museum in 1967.

Collections

Aix-en-Provence, Musée Granet
Moses Saved from the Water
Landscape

Besançon, Musée des Beaux-Arts
Landscape with Ruins

Caen, Musée des Beaux-Arts
Landscape

Cambridge, Fitzwilliam Museum
River Landscape
Landscape with Classical Ruins (fig.67)

Cherbourg, Musée Thomas Henry
Landscape

Dinton Park (Wiltshire), National Trust
Cybele and Atys

Dunkirk, Musée des Beaux-Arts
Landscape with Monuments and Figures (2)

La Fère, Musée Jeanne d'Aboville
Landscape

Le Mans, Musée de Tessé
Landscape

Leningrad, Hermitage
Landscape (signed and dated 1652)
Landscape

Narbonne, Musée des Beaux-Arts
Landscape (2)

Norfolk (Virginia), Chrysler Museum
Landscape with the Pilgrims to Emmaus

Orléans, Musée des Beaux-Arts
Landscape with Ruins on the Left
Landscape with Ruins on the Right

Paris, Louvre
Landscape: the Traveller
Landscape with Antique Ruins
Josabeth Exposing Moses on the Nile (signed and dated 1660)
Moses Burying beneath the Sand the Egyptian he had Killed (signed and dated 1660)
The Rest on the Flight into Egypt (signed and dated 1673)

Poitiers, Musée des Beaux-Arts
Landscape

Quimper, Musée des Beaux-Arts
Landscape

Sheffield, Graves Art Gallery
The Flight into Egypt

Springfield (Massachusetts), Art Museum
Landscape with Ruins (plate 63)

Valenciennes, Musée des Beaux-Arts
Landscape
Landscape

Versailles, Château
View of Versailles (dated 1668)

Wallington (Northumberland), National Trust
Landscape

Warsaw, National Museum
Figures in a Landscape (signed)

Bibliography

A short summary is in the exhibition catalogue, Munich, Hans der Kunst, *Im Licht von Claude Lorrain*, 1983, pp.217–18.

Gabriel Perelle

Vernon-sur-Seine 1604–Paris 1677

A pupil of Simon Vouet, Perelle specialized in classical landscapes not dissimilar to those of Francisque Millet, although more obviously decorative.

Collections

Orléans, Musée des Beaux-Arts
Landscape (attribution)

Sibiu (Rumania), Bruckenthal Museum
Park Scene (2)

Bibliography

There is no recent literature on this artist.

Nicolas Perelle

Paris 1631–Paris 1695?

Eldest son of Gabriel Perelle, Nicolas also concentrated on landscapes in a classical style. He was a pupil of both his father and Simon Vouet.

Collections

Florence, Galleria Pitti
Landscape with St John the Baptist

Marseilles, Palais Longchamp
Ruins with Figures

Orléans, Musée des Beaux-Arts
St Francis de Paul Resuscitating a Child (signed and dated 1683)

Bibliography

There is no recent literature on this artist.

François Perrier

Saint-Jean de Losne (Burgundy) c.1590–Paris 1650

Perrier's paintings are complex because of the enormous number of different influences evident in his art; he had two sojourns in Rome and was Vouet's pupil in Paris for a short time. He was one of the fourteen founder-members of the French Academy in Paris in 1648. Most of his pictures are stylistically close to the early work in Rome of Charles Le Brun, and it is likely that they were both influenced by the same artists, such as Pietro da Cortona who worked in the Roman Baroque style.

Collections

Caen, Saint-Étienne
The Stoning of Stephen

Carcassonne, Musée des Beaux-Arts
The Triumph of Amphitrite

Dijon, Musée Magnin
The Brazen Serpent
Venus and Adonis

Épinal, Musée Départemental des Vosges
Venus and Neptune

Lewisburg (Pennsylvania), Bucknell University
Polyphemus and Galatea

Lyons, Musée des Beaux-Arts
David and Goliath

Montauban, Musée Ingres
The Rape of Proserpine
The Neriades Carrying the Body of Leander

Paris, Musée Carnavalet
The Awakening of Aurora

Paris, Louvre
Orpheus before Pluto and Proserpine
Acis and Galatea
Aeneas and his Companion fighting the Harpies

Ponce (Puerto Rico), Museo de Arte
Assumption of the Virgin (attribution)

Rennes, Musée des Beaux-Arts
The Farewell of St Peter and St Paul

Weilburg, Schlossmuseum
The Death of Cicero

Bibliography

There is no recent literature on this artist.

Jean-Michel Picart

Antwerp 1600–Paris 1682

Although almost all Picart's career was spent in Paris, his art remained close to the general style of flower painting practised in Antwerp, especially that of Jan van Kessel. Most of his best pictures have a certain austerity, and are quite the opposite of the extravagant and opulent treatment given by Monnoyer.

Collections

Amsterdam, with de Boer
Bouquet of Flowers in a Vase

Amsterdam, Dr J.A. van Dongen
Fruit, Bouquet of Flowers, and Bowl of Flowers on a Chip-wood Box

Cambridge, Fitzwilliam Museum (Broughton Collection)
Vase of Flowers (signed)
Vase of Flowers

Karlsruhe, Staatliche Kunsthalle
Basket of Peaches and Grapes
Flowers in a Vase (signed and dated 1653)

Paris, with Cailleux
Vase of Flowers on a Sculptured Ledge

Paris, C.B. collection
Roses and a Bowl of Strawberries

Paris, with François Heim
Vase of Flowers and a Basket of Medlars and Cherries

Paris, J.M. collection
Dish of Fruit and Vase of Flowers

Paris, J.R. collection
Fruits and Bowl of Flowers on a Chip-wood Box

Paris, K. collection
Basket of Flowers and Fruit on a Sculptured Entablature

Paris, Landry collection
Vase of Flowers on a Chip-wood Box

Paris, M. collection
Basket of Peaches

Paris, R.D. collection
Flowers in a Glass Vase

Paris, W. collection
Vase of Flowers and Plums

Paris, private collection
Bouquet of Flowers in a Stone Vase

Paris, private collection
Bouquet of Flowers with a Parrot (signed)

Saint-Étienne, Musée d'Art et d'Industrie
Flowers in a Glass Vase
Flowers in a Vase

Switzerland, private collection
Bowl of Flowers and Cherries

Bibliography

Michel Faré
Le grand siècle de la nature morte en France, 1974, pp.84–98.

Nicolas Pinson

Valence 1635–Rome 1681

Pinson spent seventeen years in Rome, and his few surviving pictures show the influence of Pier Francesco Mola and Giovanni Lanfranco. The rest of his career was spent in Provence.

Collections

Aix-en-Provence, Hôpital Saint-Jacques
St John giving Communion to the Virgin (recently disintegrated)

Aix-en-Provence, Saint-Jean-de-Malte
Christ on the Cross between the Virgin, St John and the Magdalen
The Judgment of Solomon
Christ and the Woman Taken in Adultery

Avignon, Musée Calvet
Rest on the Flight into Egypt (signed)

Rome, San Luigi dei Francesi
Catherine de Medici Presenting to St Louis the Drawings of the New Church (signed and dated 1680)

Bibliography

Marie-Christine Gloton
in the exhibition catalogue, Marseilles, Palais Longchamp, *La peinture en Provence au XVIIe siècle*, 1978, pp.109–11.

Nicolas Plattemontagne

Paris 1631–Paris 1706

A pupil of both Philippe de Champaigne and Charles Le Brun, Plattemontagne is known chiefly as an engraver, mostly of Champaigne's portraits. His painting in the Louvre, although damaged, is both dramatic and severe, as might be expected from an artist whose two teachers were so different from one another.

Collection

Paris, Louvre
Conversion of the Gaoler of St Paul (signed and dated 1666)

Bibliography

There is no recent literature on this artist.

Charles Poërson

Vic-sur-Seille (Moselle) 1609–Paris 1667

A pupil of Simon Vouet, Poërson continued his master's style, painting large altarpieces in a broad Baroque manner. He executed the annual 'May' commission for Notre Dame in Paris twice (1642 and 1653). He was received into the Academy in 1651, three years after its foundation.

Collections

Arras, Palais Saint-Vaast
Tapestry cartoon: *The Annunciation*

Cologne, Wallraf-Richartz Museum
The Rest on the Flight into Egypt

Dublin, National Gallery of Ireland
Assumption of the Virgin

Le Mans, Musée de Tessé
Two Scenes from the Life of Cincinnatus (2)

Metz, Musée Central
The Poisoning of Camme and Simonix

Paris, Louvre
The Nativity (signed)

Perpignan, Musée Rigaud
The Marriage at Cana

Rouen, Musée des Beaux-Arts
Adoration of the Shepherds (attribution)

Bibliography

There is no recent literature on this artist.

Pierre Poncet

Orléans 1574–?1640

Poncet was a pupil of Simon Vouet, and his Orléans picture seems to be his only known surviving work.

Collection

Orléans, Musée des Beaux-Arts
Andreas Vesalius (signed)

Bibliography

There is no recent literature on this artist.

Nicolas Poussin

Les Andelys 1594–Rome 1665

Considering Poussin's fame in Rome during his middle age, and the vast amount written about him by people who knew him, it is surprising that the first half of his life, until about 1630, is shrouded in mystery. He appears to have spent his youth in his birthplace, the small town of Les Andelys, near Rouen. In about 1612 he went to Rouen, where he worked in the studio of Noël Jouvenet. Soon afterwards he left for Paris, where he worked in various studios, notably those of Ferdinand Elle and Georges Lallemant. It appears that, when still a young, immature artist, he made two unsuccessful attempts to go to Rome. No picture has been identified with certainty from this period. In the years 1622–3 the first official success in Paris came his way, when he was commissioned, along with Philippe de Champaigne, to help with the decoration of the Luxembourg Palace. He also painted a *Death of the Virgin*, now lost, for Notre Dame.

By 1624 Poussin had arrived in Rome, where he received the patronage and protection of Cavaliere Marino and for whom he executed a series of drawings, most probably those now at Windsor Castle, although they have been disputed in recent years. Marino introduced Poussin to Cardinal Sachetti and Francesco Barberini, but then unfortunately died the following year, leaving Poussin unprotected, vulnerable to the enormous competition from his contemporaries. It must have been at this time that Poussin met Cassiano dal Pozzo, the antiquarian and patron of art, who was to be the most important single influence on his life. Cassiano may well have commissioned Poussin to add the central motifs to two garlands of flowers (now lost) painted by Daniel Seghers. These centrepieces by the still-hesitant painter survive (Brighton and Cherbourg), though in a mutilated state. Poussin was living with the Flemish artist François Duquesnoy, who specialized in making lively Cupids and putti in marble, and it is generally considered that the proliferation of such figures in Poussin's early work comes from Duquesnoy's influence. The first important commissions came to Poussin in 1627, when Cardinal Barberini asked him to execute the *Death of Germanicus* (Minneapolis),

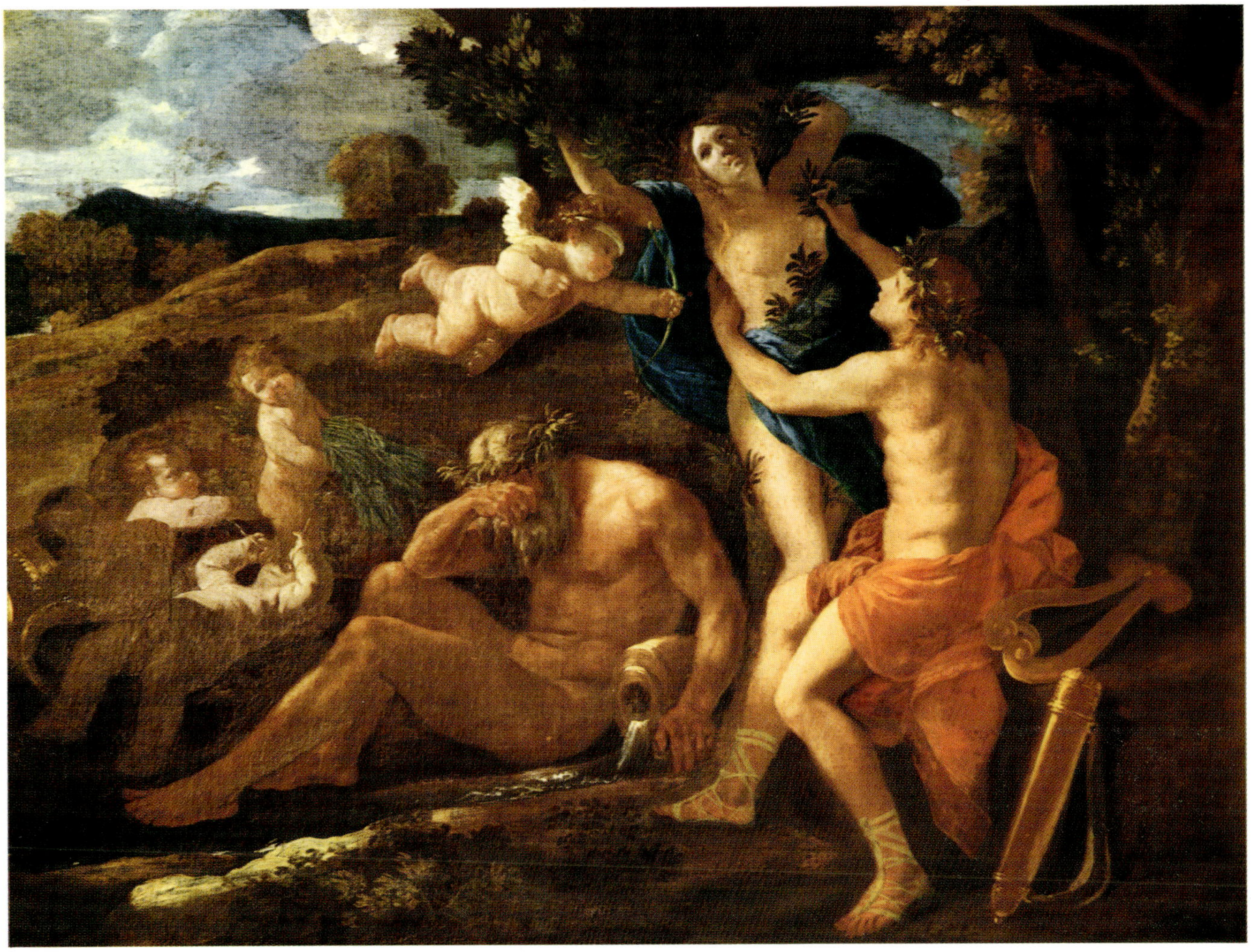

PLATE 64
Nicolas Poussin
Apollo and Daphne
Canvas, 97 × 131 cm.
Munich, Alte Pinakothek
First recorded in the collection of the Elector of Bavaria in 1781.

Daphne is changed into a laurel tree in order to escape from Apollo's clutches.

completed the following year. The enormous *Martyrdom of St Erasmus* was also completed in 1628, for St Peter's, and placed opposite Le Valentin's *Martyrdom of St Processus and St Martinian*. The *St Erasmus* made it clear that Poussin was not really suited to the execution of large and imposing decorations, a fact that was to prove his undoing a few years later in Paris.

In 1630 Poussin married Anne-Marie Dughet, the sister of Gaspard Dughet (who later adopted the name of Poussin), and this alliance was to be of enormous significance: until 1635, both painters shared a studio. The exact artistic relationship between them has never been explained, through lack of evidence about the dates when their pictures were painted. Although the point of their closest contact is known to be in the 1630s, it was not until the late 1640s that Poussin turned to painting pure landscapes, much influenced by the style of Gaspard Dughet. (In Dughet's later years the influence is reversed.)

From 1630 onwards, Poussin began to acquire a variety of patrons, including Fabrizio Valguarnera who commissioned the *Plague of Ashdod* (Louvre) in 1631 and the *Empire of Flora* (Dresden). Poussin's name became known in France, and he produced the two *Bacchanals* (Kansas City and London) for Cardinal Richelieu in 1636. His need for patrons was particularly important, because his pictures were so completely out of step with contemporary trends in Rome that they were very difficult to sell on the open market. In his later years his output declined, and it appears that almost all his later pictures were commissioned.

After the *Bacchanals*, Poussin, already over forty, entered his mature phase. He began the first series of *Sacraments* (Belvoir Castle and Washington) for Cassiano dal Pozzo, which was not completed until 1640, by which time he had arrived in Paris. This journey was made with some reluctance at the insistence of Louis XIII. The King

PLATE 65
Nicolas Poussin
Bacchanal: the Andrians
Canvas, 121 × 175 cm.
Paris, Louvre
In the collection of Louis XIV by 1683.

The picture was the subject of a lecture by Jean-Baptiste de Champaigne to the Academy in 1674.

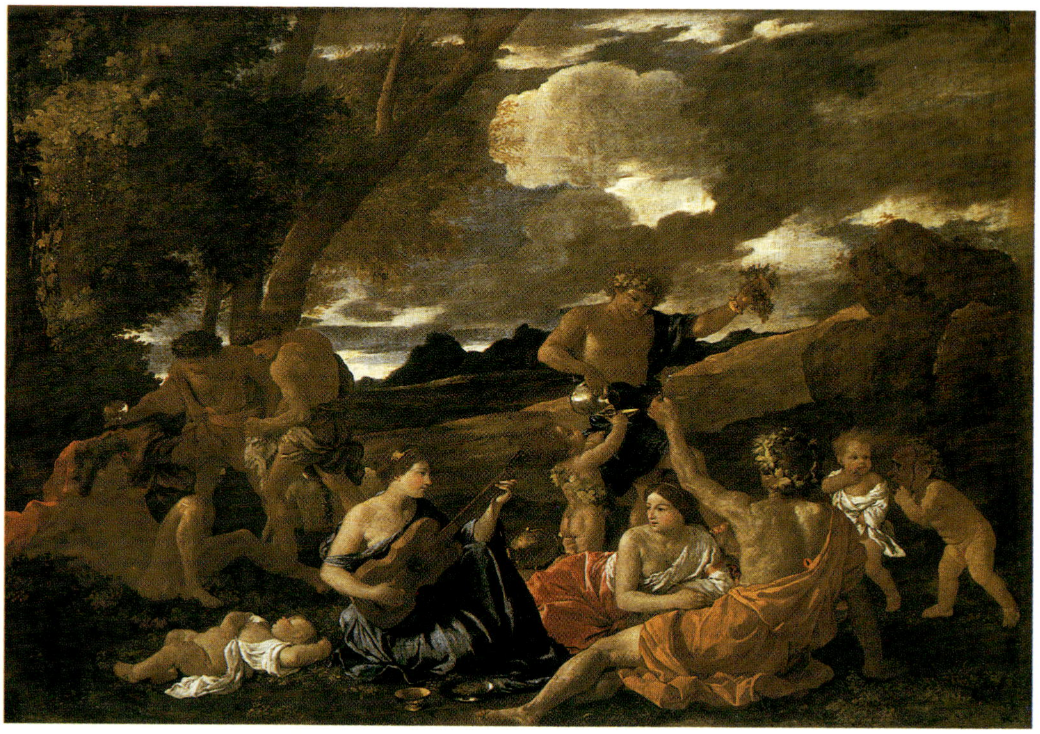

PLATE 66
Nicolas Poussin
The Triumph of Flora
Canvas, 165 × 241 cm.
Paris, Louvre
In the collection of Louis XIV by 1684–5.

The composition was directly inspired by the Venetian painter Titian.

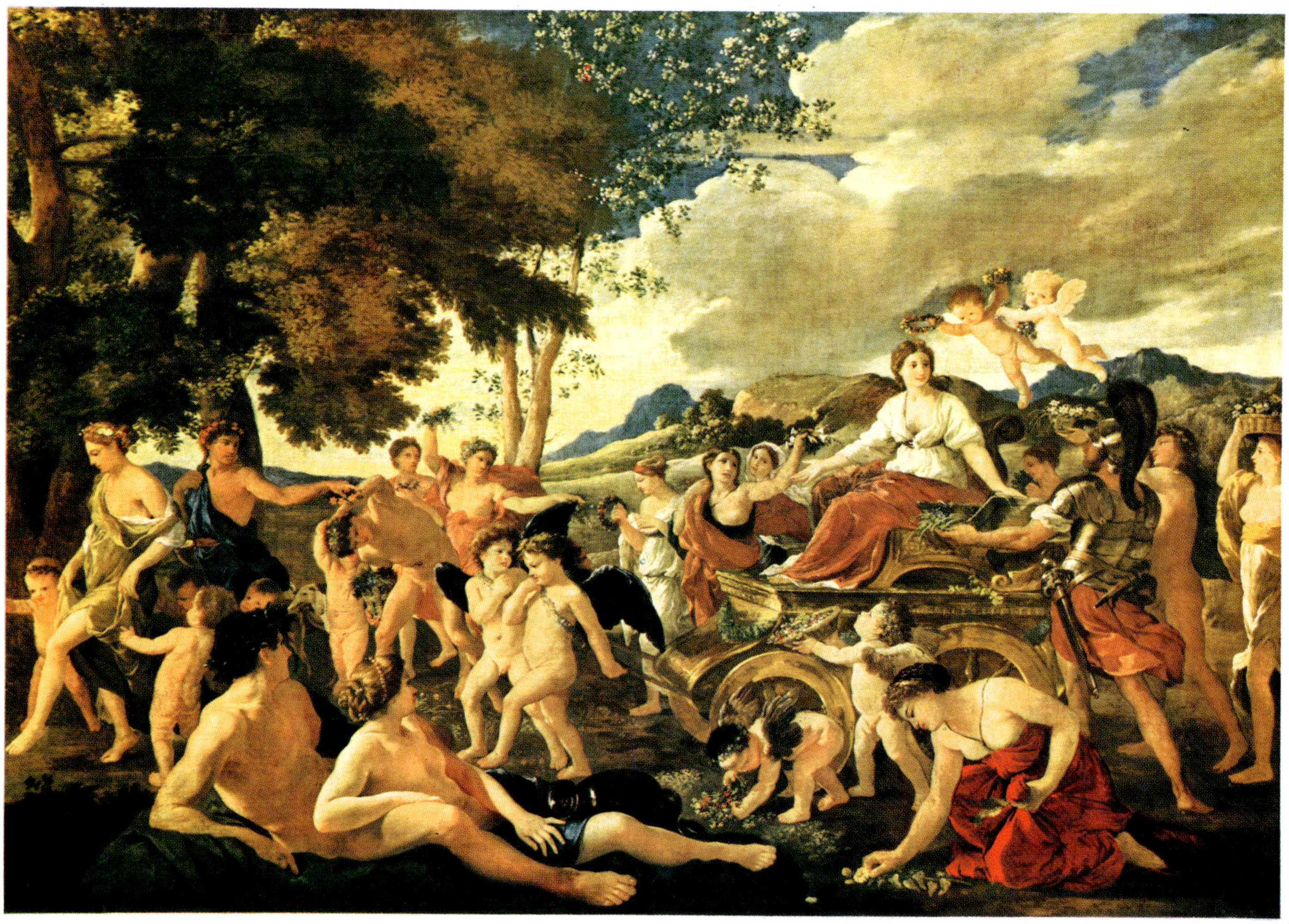

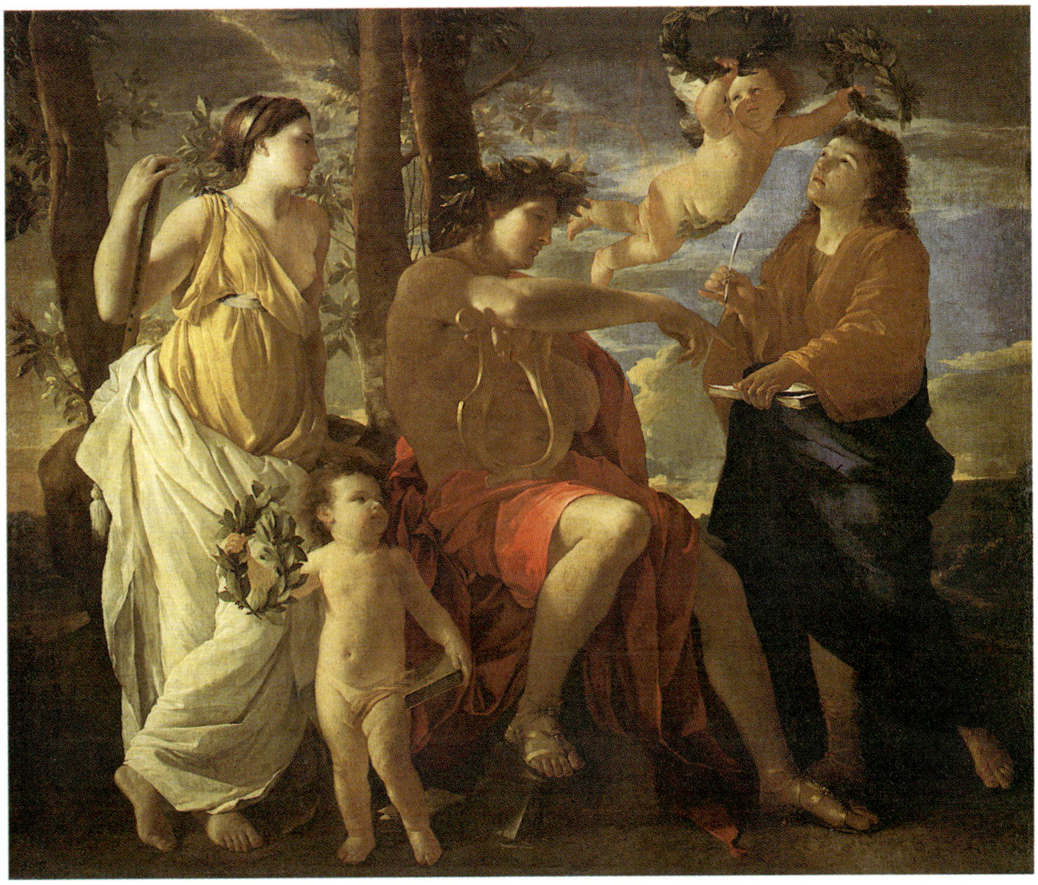

PLATE 67
Nicolas Poussin
The Inspiration of the Poet
Canvas, 182.5 × 213 cm.
Paris, Louvre
Not recorded certainly until 1824. Acquired by the Louvre in 1911.

The appearance of the muse Calliope has led to the suggestion that the picture was painted in honour of a recently dead poet.

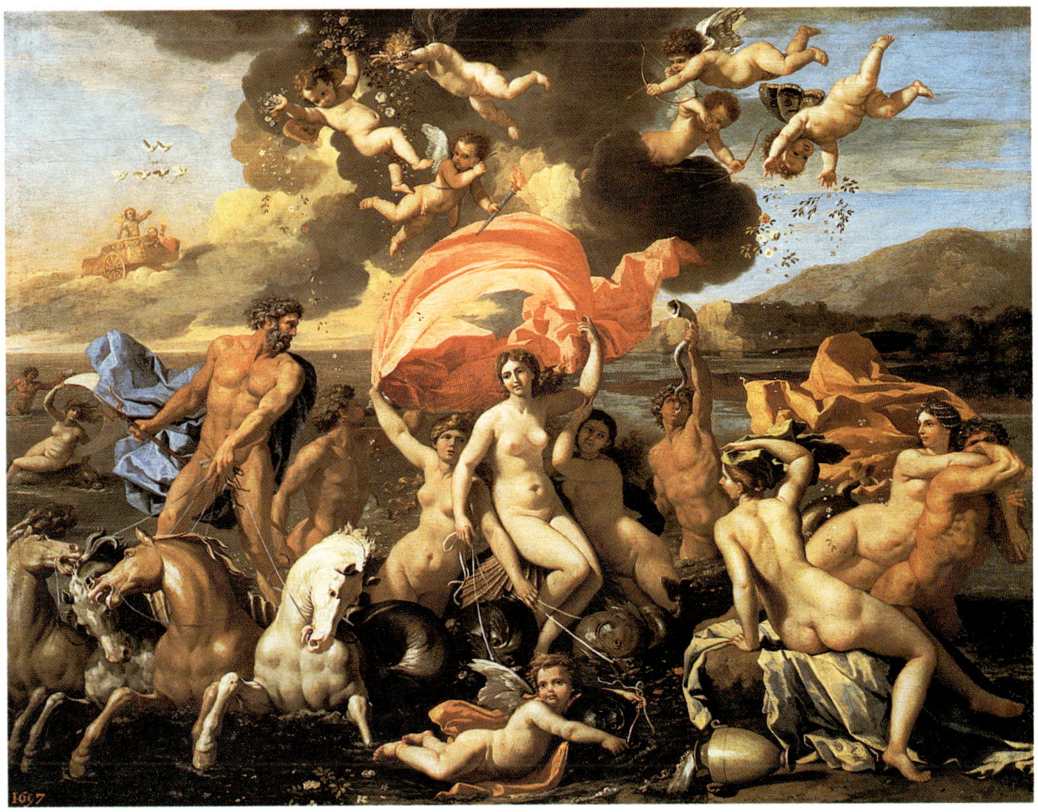

PLATE 68
Nicolas Poussin
The Triumph of Neptune
Canvas, 114 × 146 cm.
Philadelphia, Museum of Art (George W. Elkins collection)
First recorded in the Crozat collection in Paris in 1755. Acquired by Catherine the Great of Russia in 1771. Sold by the Stalinist authorities in 1930 and acquired by the museum soon afterwards.

Probably painted for Cardinal Richelieu, the picture has been subject to widely differing interpretations.

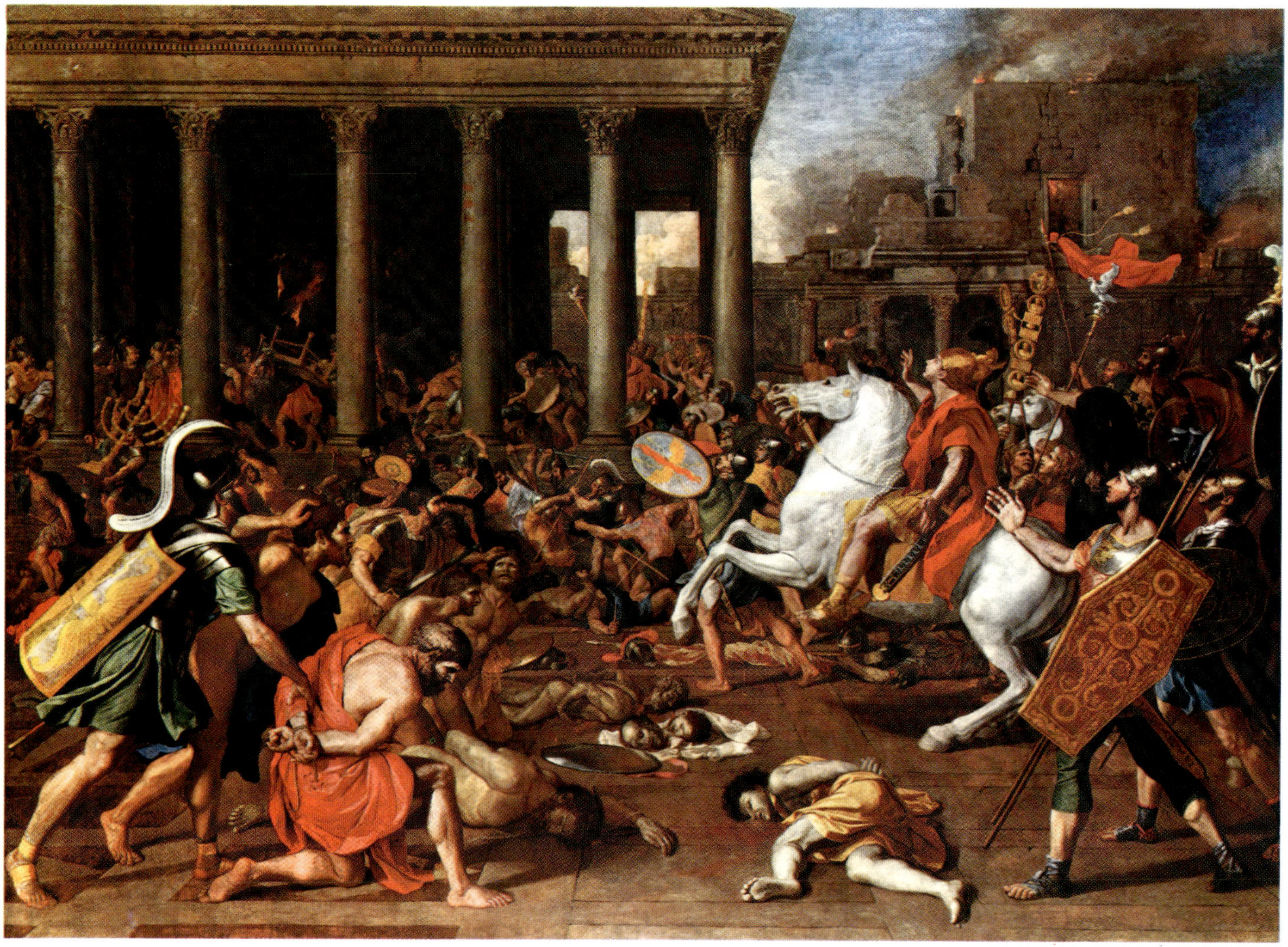

PLATE 69 (above)
Nicolas Poussin
The Destruction of the Temple at Jerusalem
Canvas, 147 × 198.5 cm. Signed: NI. PUSIN FEC.
Vienna, Kunsthistorisches Museum
Commissioned by Cardinal Francesco Barberini in 1637. Given by him to Prince Eggenberg in 1638. Then by descent in the Austrian Imperial Collection.

In this depiction of the final destruction of the temple, Poussin was striving for historical accuracy.

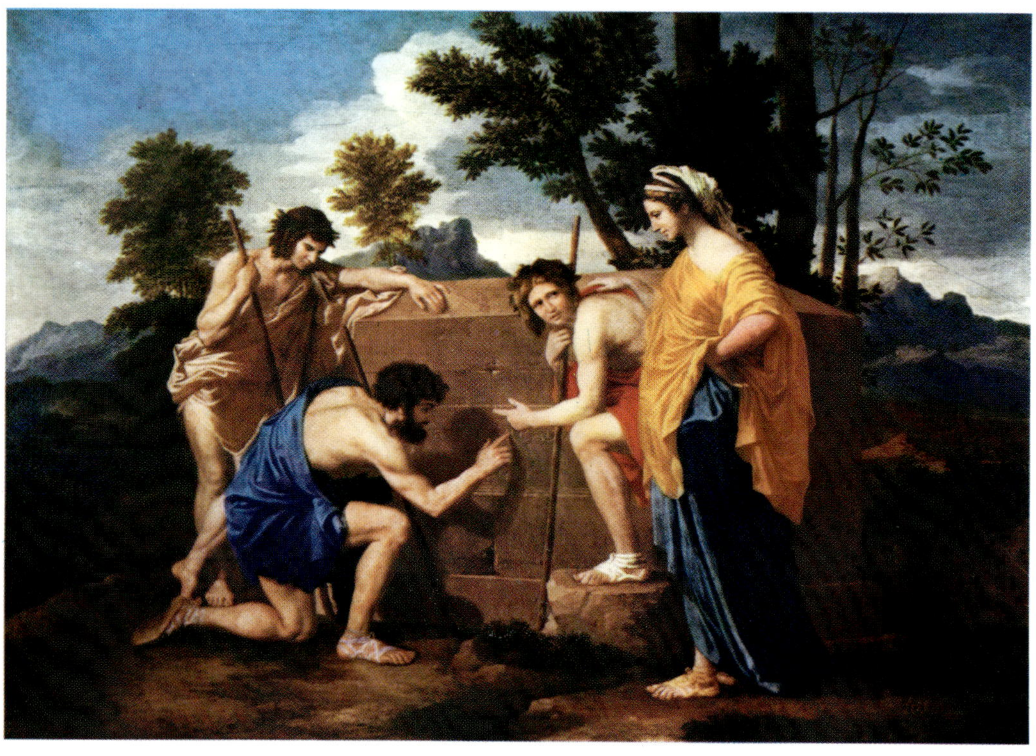

PLATE 70 (right)
Nicolas Poussin
'Et in Arcadia Ego'
Canvas, 185 × 121 cm.
Paris, Louvre
Acquired by Louis XIV in 1685.

This is a much more severe treatment of the subject also depicted in the Chatsworth picture (figure 34).

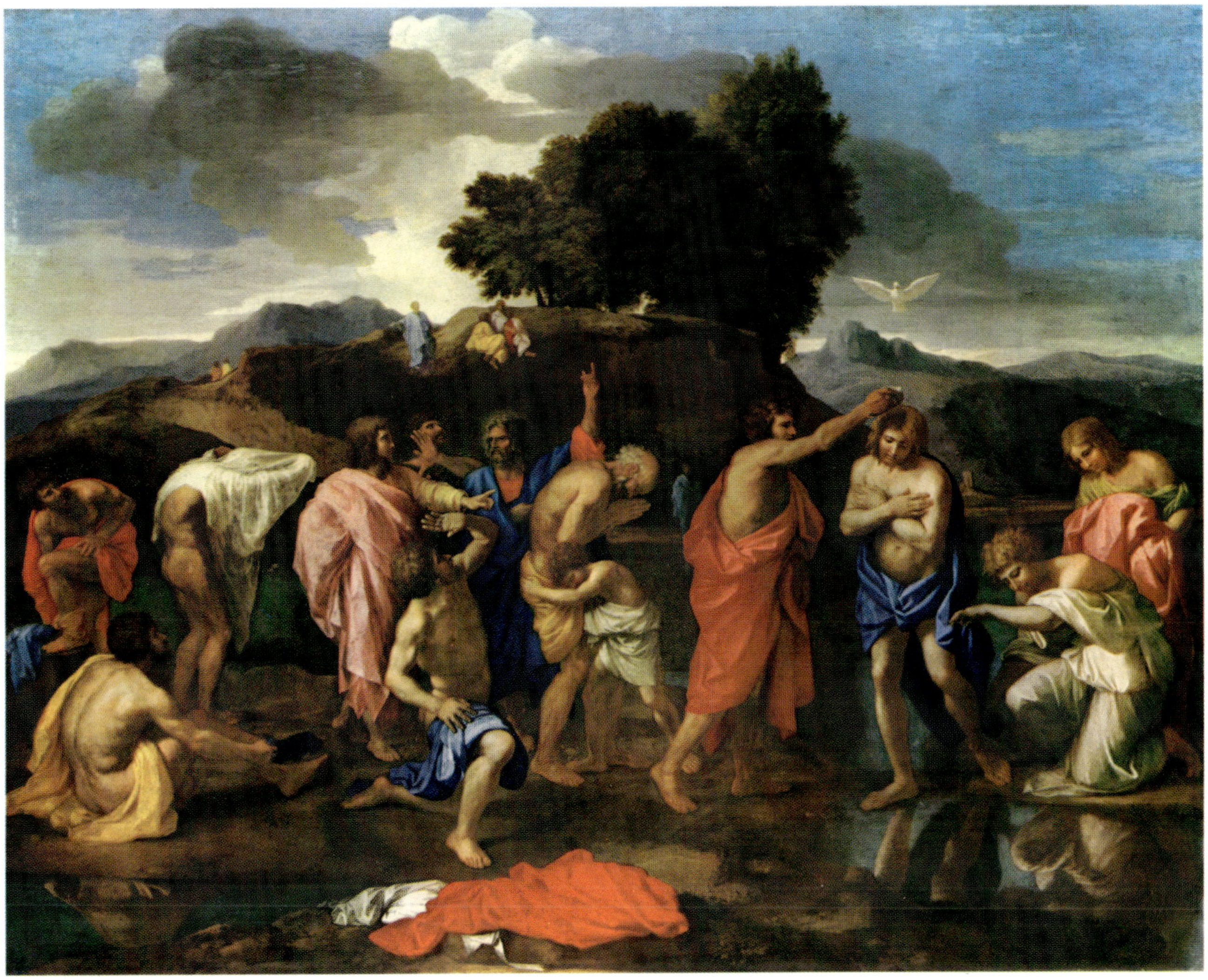

PLATE 71
Nicolas Poussin
The Sacrament of Baptism
Canvas, 95.3 × 121.6 cm.
Washington, National Gallery of Art
Given to the Museum as part of the Samuel H. Kress collection in 1946.

One of the first set of *Sacraments*, painted for Cassiano dal Pozzo. The picture was the last of the set to be completed, in 1642, and is quite unlike the other surviving five.

commissioned the *Institution of the Eucharist* (Louvre) for the chapel in the château at St Germain, and several other pictures. Most important, however, was the idea that Poussin should decorate the vast Grande Galerie of the Louvre. Some drawings survive of Poussin's ideas to cover the walls and ceiling with a variety of classical figures, many of them in roundels. (Jacques Foucquières had previously been commissioned to decorate the Grande Galerie, and had planned a series of views of French towns, but had progressed but slowly.) Poussin was singularly unsuitable by temperament for such a vast project, however, and his unease was turned into discontent by the intrigues of other painters in Paris. He returned to Rome late in 1642, never to return to France.

The remaining twenty-three years of his career show a certain homogeneity. Poussin was already revered in artistic circles in both Rome and Paris. He began a second series of *Sacraments* (Edinburgh) for Chantelou in 1644, and in 1648 painted the two *Phocion* landscapes (Liverpool and Cardiff) which mark the peak of his career. His late style developed almost imperceptibly out of his maturity, and is seen at its best in the second set of *Sacraments*. The London *Annunciation* of 1657 shows how far Poussin's application of theory had taken him: he had arrived at an extreme where his thought overwhelmed his vision. The artist's last years were clouded with ill-health and an increasingly shaky hand, as his drawings show, and yet, in his very last pictures, especially the *Seasons* (Louvre), which represent the furthest point of his extremism, he rose above his self-imposed conventions and produced landscapes with an unusual depth of feeling.

Collections

Ajaccio, Musée Fesch
Midas at the Source of the Pactolus

Baltimore, Walters Art Gallery
Moses Sweetening the Bitter Waters of Mara (attribution)

Belgrade, Palace of the President
Landscape with Three Monks

PLATE 72
Nicolas Poussin
Self-portrait
Canvas, 78 × 94 cm. Signed and dated: EFFIGIES NICOLAI POUSSINI ANDELGENSIS PICTORIS, ANNO AETA FIS 56. ROMAE ANNO JUBILEI 1650
Paris, Louvre
Acquired by Louis XIV from the duc de Richelieu in 1665.

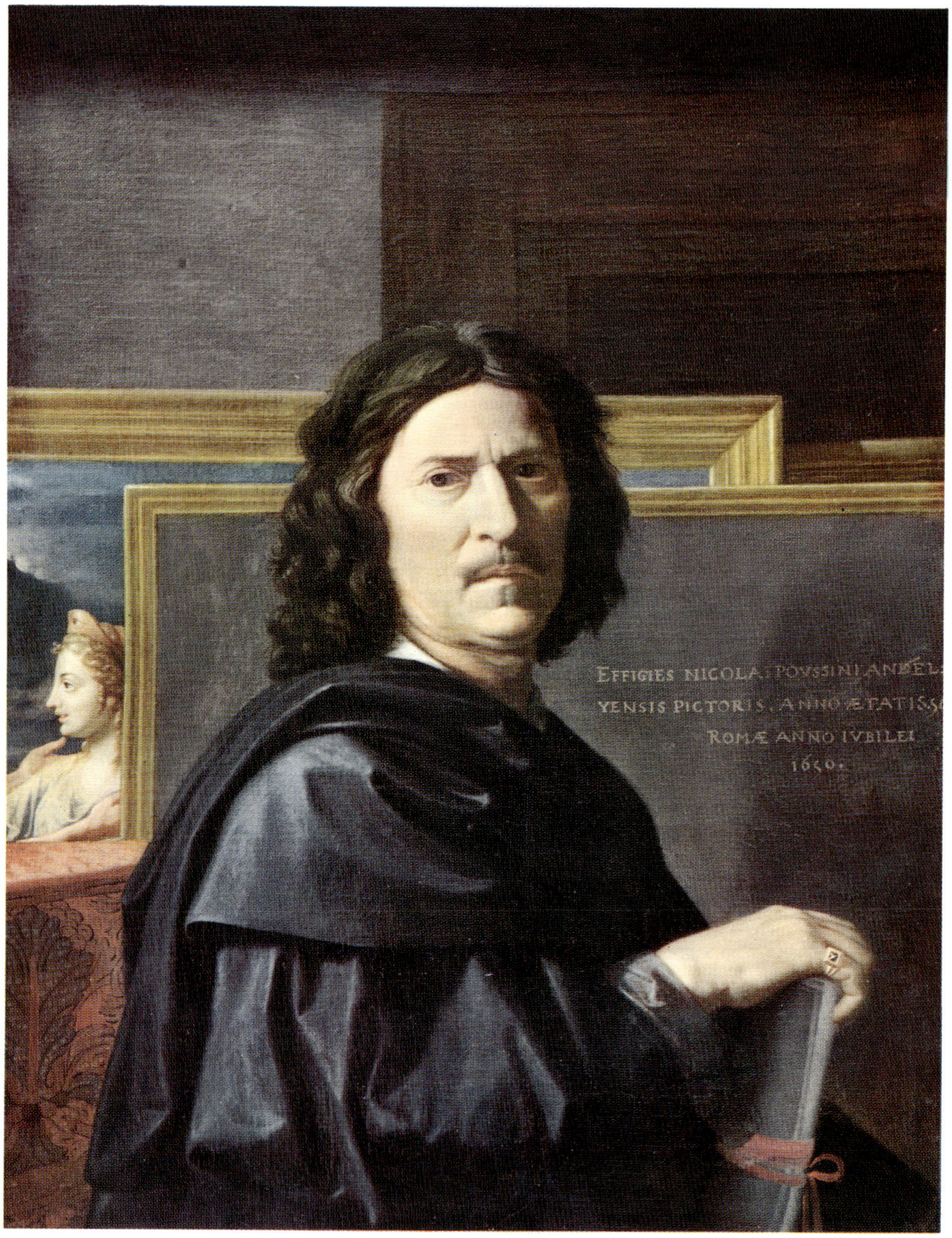

Belvoir Castle (Leicestershire), Duke of Rutland
The Sacrament of Marriage (documented 1636–40)
The Sacrament of Extreme Unction (documented 1636–40) (fig.36)
The Sacrament of Confirmation (documented 1636–40)
The Sacrament of Ordination (documented 1636–40)
The Sacrament of the Eucharist (documented 1636–40)

Berlin, East, Bode Museum
Landscape with Juno and Argus
Self-portrait (signed and dated 1649)

Berlin-Dahlem, Staatliche Museen
Helios and Phaethon
The Nurture of Jupiter
Landscape with St Matthew (documented 1641)
Rinaldo and Armida (attribution)

Birmingham, Barber Institute
Tancred and Erminia

Boston, Museum of Fine Arts
Venus and Mars
Achilles and the Daughters of Lycomedes

Brighton, Preston Manor (lent to Brighton Art Gallery)
Virgin and Child (fragment of *Garland of Flowers* by Daniel Seghers) (fig.33)

Caen, Musée des Beaux-Arts
Venus Lamenting over Adonis

Cambridge, Fitzwilliam Museum
Rebecca at the Well

Cambridge (Massachusetts), Fogg Art Museum
Holy Family with Saints
The Birth of Bacchus (documented 1657)
Hannibal Crossing the Alps

Cardiff, National Museum of Wales (lent by the Earl of Plymouth)
Landscape with the Funeral of Phocion (documented 1648)

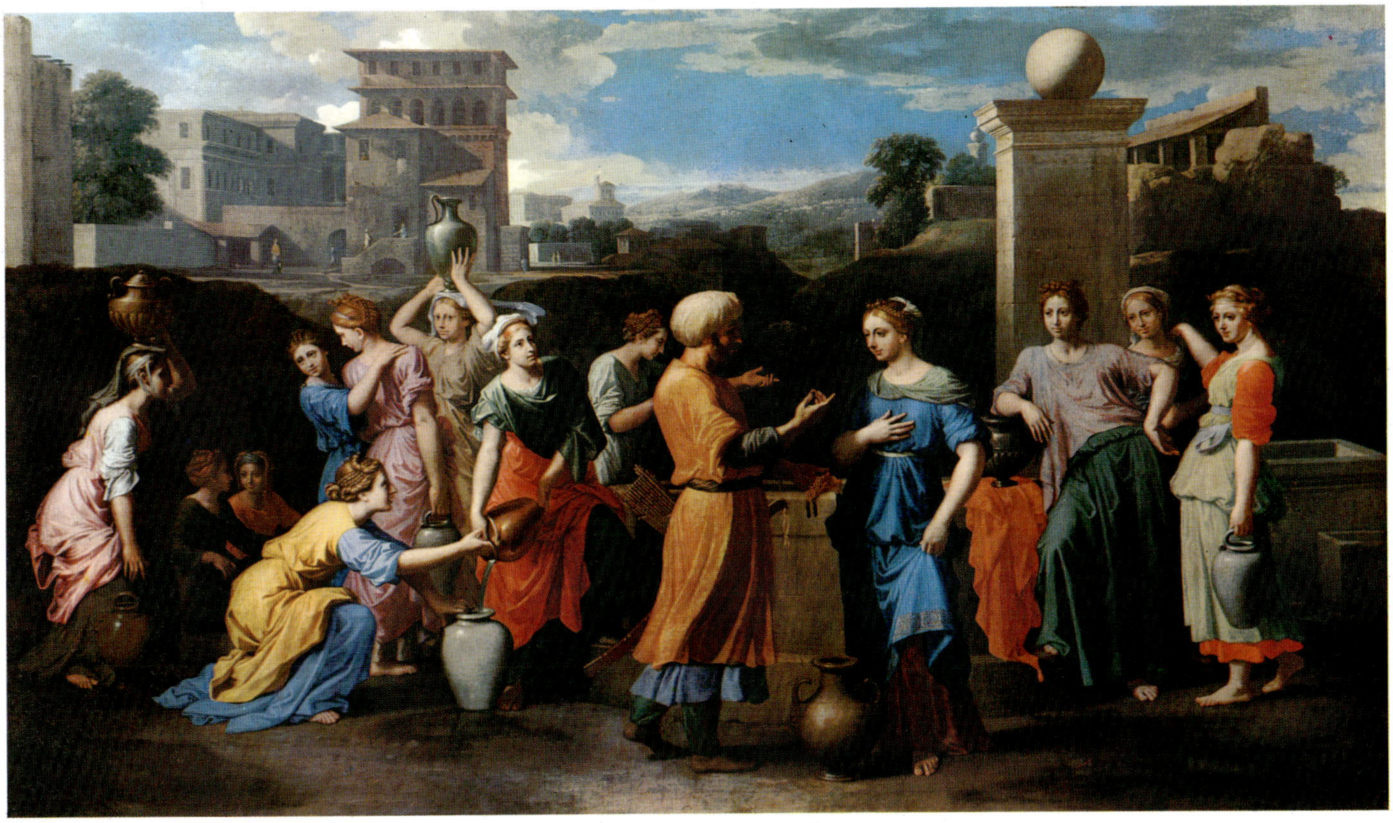

PLATE 73
Nicolas Poussin
Rebecca at the Well
Canvas, 118 × 199 cm.
Paris, Louvre
Documented 1648; acquired by Louis XIV from the duc de Richelieu in 1665.

Chantilly, Musée Condé
The Massacre of the Innocents
The Annunciation
The Youth of Bacchus
Theseus Recovering his Father's Shield
Landscape with Two Nymphs
Landscape with Numa Pompilius and the Nymph Egeria
Holy Family

Chatsworth (Derbyshire), Trustees of the Chatsworth Settlement
The Arcadian Shepherds (fig.34)

Cherbourg, Musée Thomas Henry
Pietà (fragment of *Garland of Flowers* by Daniel Seghers)

Chicago, Art Institute
Landscape with St John on Patmos (documented 1640)

Cleveland (Ohio), Museum of Art
The Return from Egypt
'Amor Vincit Omnia'
The Madonna of the Steps

Copenhagen, Statens Museum for Kunst
Moses and the Burning Bush (documented 1641)
The Testament of Eudamidas

Detroit, Institute of Arts
Diana and Endymion
Holy Family (*The Roccatagliata Madonna*)

Dorking (Surrey), Schreiber collection
Moses Saved from the Water (documented 1651)

Dresden, Gemäldegalerie
Moses Saved from the Water
The Kingdom of Flora (documented 1631)
The Adoration of the Shepherds (signed and dated 1633)
Pan and Syrinx
Venus and the Shepherds (attribution)

Dublin, National Gallery of Ireland
Acis and Galatea
Holy Family with Saints (documented 1649)
Lamentation over the Dead Christ (fig.37)
Nymphs and Satyrs Drinking (attribution)

Edinburgh, National Gallery of Scotland
Mystic Marriage of St Catherine
Sutherland loan:
Moses Striking Water from the Rock
The Sacrament of Extreme Unction (documented 1644)
The Sacrament of Confirmation (documented 1645)
The Sacrament of Baptism (documented 1646)
The Sacrament of Confession (documented 1647)
The Sacrament of Ordination (documented 1647)
The Sacrament of the Eucharist (documented 1647)
The Sacrament of Marriage (documented 1647–8)

Fort Worth (Texas), Kimbell Art Museum
Venus and Adonis

Frankfurt-am-Main, Städelsches Kunstinstitut
Landscape with Pyramus and Thisbe (documented 1651)

Hanover, Niedersächsisches Landesmuseum
The Inspiration of the Poet

Hartford (Connecticut), Wadsworth Athenaeum
The Crucifixion

Hovingham Hall (Yorkshire), Sir William Worsley
Cephalus and Aurora

Kansas City, Nelson Gallery
The Triumph of Bacchus

Karlsruhe, Staatliche Kunsthalle
Holy Family with St John the Baptist

Kassel, Staatliche Gemäldegalerie
Nymphs being Carried by Satyrs

Leningrad, Hermitage
The Battle of Joshua against the Amalekites
The Deposition from the Cross
Tancred and Erminia
Seven Cupids Playing

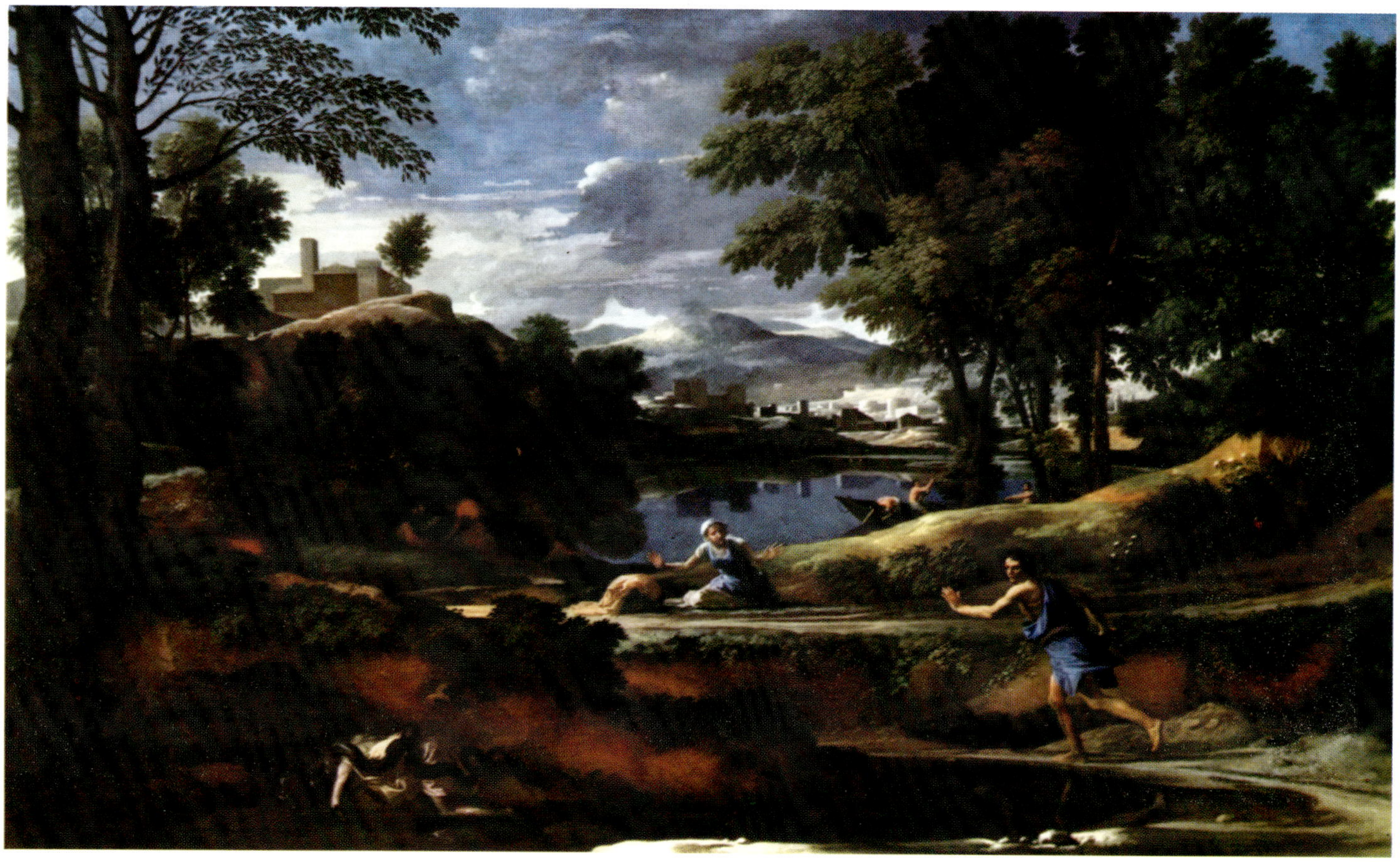

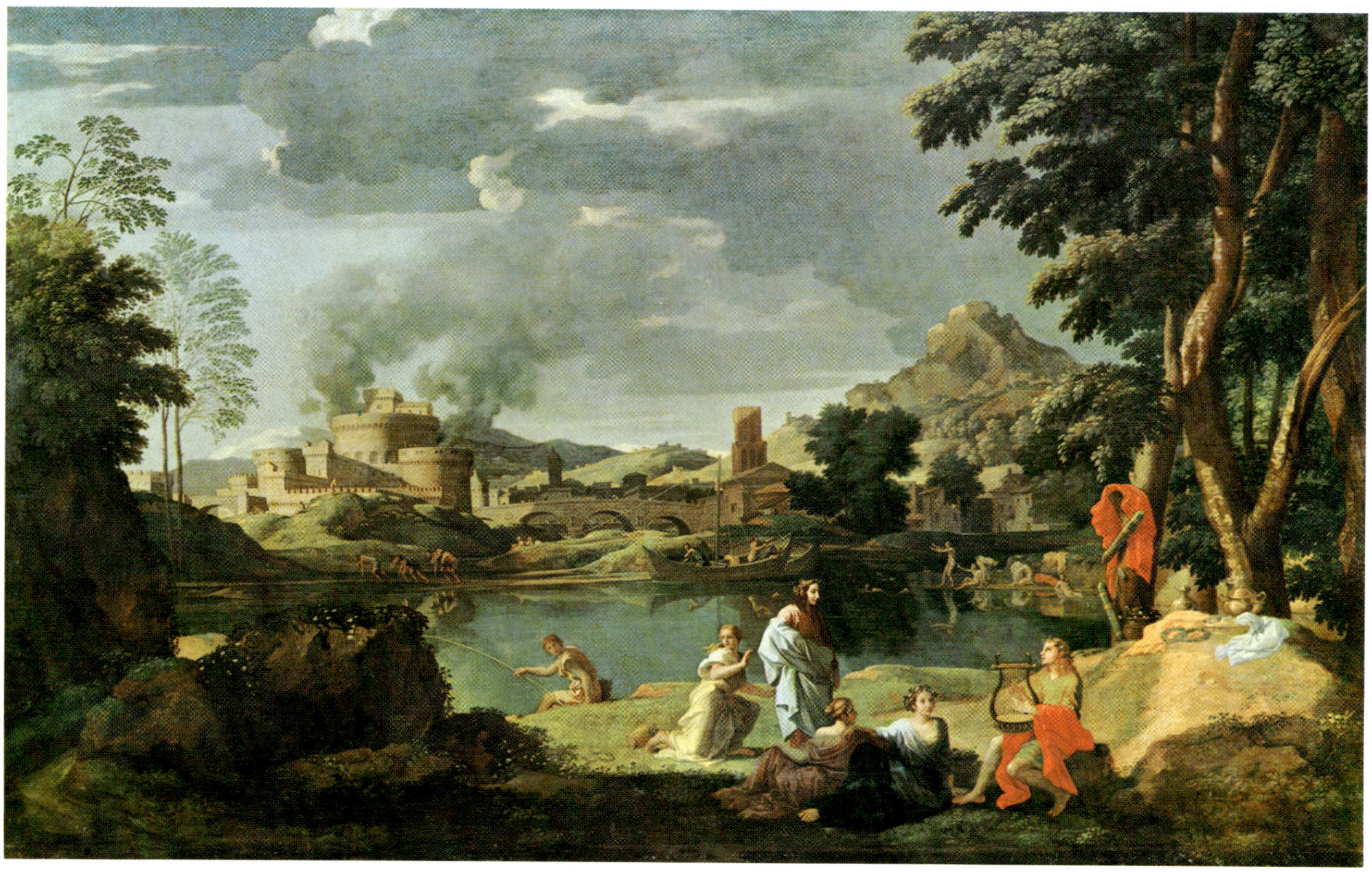

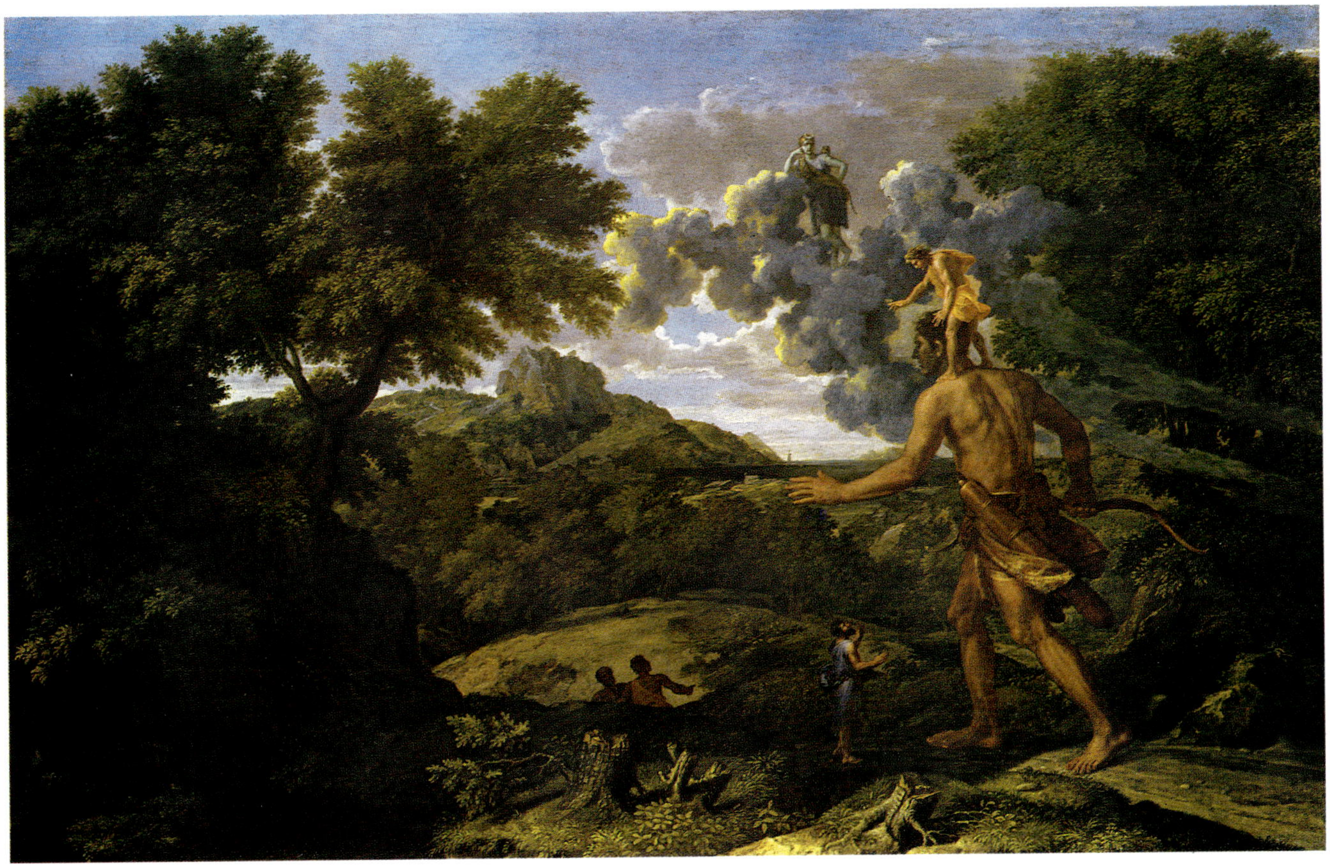

PLATE 74 (top left)
Nicolas Poussin
Landscape with a Man Killed by a Snake
Canvas, 119.4 × 198.8 cm.
London, National Gallery
Probably painted for one of Poussin's main patrons, Pointel, in 1648. Bought by the National Gallery in 1947, the picture has been in England since c.1773.

PLATE 75 (bottom left)
Nicolas Poussin
Landscape with Orpheus and Euridice
Canvas, 124 × 200 cm.
Paris, Louvre
Acquired by Louis XIV in 1685.

One of Poussin's most formal compositions.

PLATE 76 (above)
Nicolas Poussin
Landscape with Diana and Orion (The Blind Orion Searching for the Rising Sun)
Canvas, 119 × 183 cm.
New York, Metropolitan Museum of Art
Painted in 1658. Acquired by the museum in 1924 from the Methuen collection.

There has been controversy over the subject, which Poussin has treated in a personal way.

Nymphs on the Back of a Goat
Moses Striking Water from the Rock
Landscape with Polyphemus (documented 1649)
Esther before Ahasuerus
Holy Family with Saints
Rest on the Flight into Egypt (documented 1655–7)
Landscape with Hercules and Cacus
The Queen Zenobia (attribution)

Les Andelys, Hôtel de Ville
Coriolanus

Lisbon, Gulbenkian Foundation
Cupids Playing (attribution)

Liverpool, Walker Art Gallery
Landscape with Nymphs and Satyrs
Landscape with the Gathering of the Ashes of Phocion (documented 1648)

London, Dulwich College Picture Gallery
Rinaldo and Armida
Venus and Mercury
The Triumph of David (fig.41)
The Return from Egypt
St Rita of Cascia
The Nurture of Jupiter (frontispiece)
Landscape with a Roman Road (documented 1648)

London, National Gallery
Cephalus and Aurora
The Nurture of Bacchus
Adoration of the Shepherds (signed)
Adoration of the Golden Calf (fig.35)
Bacchanalian Revel before a Term of Pan
Landscape with a Man Killed by a Snake (plate 74)
Landscape with Bandits in Repose
Landscape with a Man Drinking
Landscape with a Man Washing his Feet
The Annunciation (signed and dated 1657)
The Triumph of Pan

London, Wallace Collection
Dance to the Music of Time

London, Denis Mahon Collection
Rebecca at the Well

Madrid, Prado
Nymphs and Satyrs Drinking
David Victorious
Landscape with St Jerome
Landscape with Three Figures
Apollo and the Muses (Parnassus)
Noli me tangere
St Cecilia
Martyrdom of St Lawrence (attribution)

Malibu (California), J. Paul Getty Museum
St John Baptizing the People
Holy Family with Saints in a Landscape (shared with Pasadena, Norton Simon Museum)

Melbourne, National Gallery of Victoria
The Crossing of the Red Sea

Minneapolis, Institute of Arts
The Death of Germanicus (documented as completed 1628)

Montpellier, Musée Fabre
Landscape with Venus and Adonis

Montreal, Museum of Fine Arts
Landscape with a Man Pursued by a Snake

Moscow, Pushkin Museum
Rinaldo and Armida
Battle of Joshua against the Amorites
Nymphs and Satyrs Drinking
The Continence of Scipio (documented 1640)

Munich, Alte Pinakothek
Lamentation over Dead Christ
Apollo and Daphne (plate 64)
Midas and Bacchus
Annunciation
Nativity

Nancy, Musée des Beaux-Arts
The Entry of Christ into Jerusalem

New York, Heinemann collection
Holy Family

New York, Metropolitan Museum
Midas Washing Himself in the Pactolus

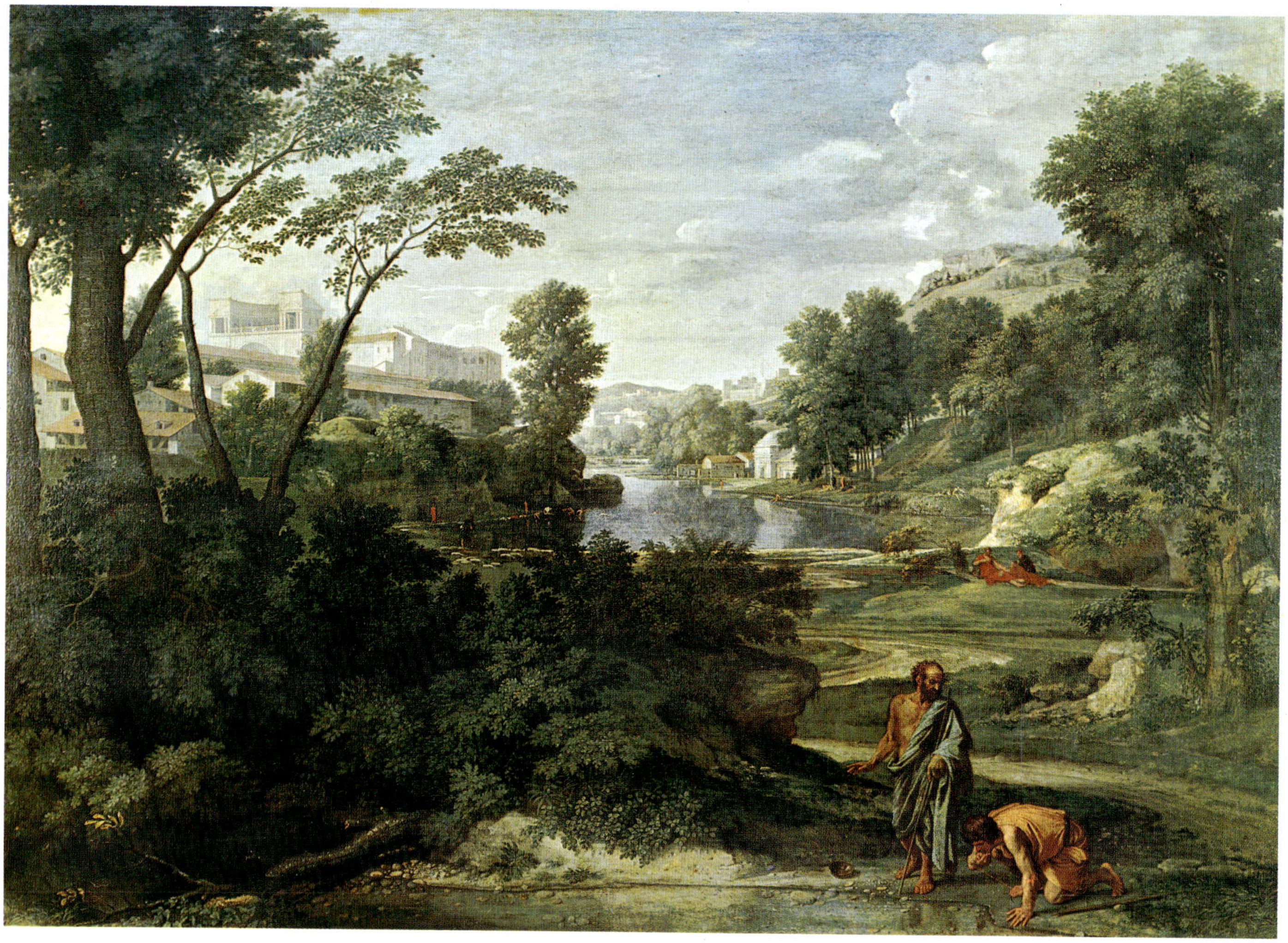

PLATE 77
Nicolas Poussin
Landscape with Diogenes
Canvas, 160 × 221 cm.
Paris, Louvre
Acquired by Louis XIV from the duc de Richelieu in 1665. Documented 1648, and probably painted c.1647 or 1648.

Diogenes throws away his drinking cup after seeing a man drinking by cupping his hands.

The Rape of the Sabines
St Peter and St John Healing a Sick Man (documented 1655)
Landscape with Diana and Orion (documented 1658) (plate 76)
The Companions of Rinaldo

Ottawa, National Gallery of Canada
The Martyrdom of St Erasmus
Landscape with a Woman Washing her Feet (documented 1650)

Oxford, Ashmolean Museum
The Exposition of Moses

Paris, École des Beaux-Arts
Mercury, Herse and Aglauros

Paris, Louvre
Putti (fragment of the Dulwich *Venus and Mercury*)
Marsyas and Olympus
Bacchus Nurtured by the Nymphs
Bacchanal: the Andrians (plate 65)
The Triumph of Flora (plate 66)
Echo and Narcissus
Appearance of the Virgin to St James
The Inspiration of the Poet (plate 67)
The Plague of Ashdod (documented 1630–31)
St John the Baptist Baptizing the People
The Saving of the Pyhrric Boy (documented 1634)
Camillus and the Schoolmaster of the Falerii (documented 1637)
The Rape of the Sabines
'Et in Arcadia Ego' (plate 70)
Moses Saved from the Waters (documented 1638)
The Gathering of the Manna (documented 1639)
The Institution of the Eucharist (documented 1640)
The Miracle of St Francis Xavier (documented 1641)
Time and Truth Destroying Envy and Discord (documented 1641)
Moses Saved from the Water (documented 1647)
Moses Trampling on Pharaoh's Crown
Moses and Aaron Dining with Pharaoh
Rebecca at the Well (documented 1648) (plate 73)
Landscape with Diogenes (documented 1648) (plate 77)
The Judgment of Solomon (documented 1649)
The Assumption (documented 1650)
The Ecstasy of St Paul (documented 1650)
Self-portrait (signed and dated 1650) (plate 72)
Landscape with Orpheus and Euridice (plate 75)
Christ Healing the Blind (documented 1650)
Holy Family with Saints
Christ and the Woman taken in Adultery (documented 1653)
The Death of Sapphira
Holy Family with Saints
Spring (documented 1660–64)
Summer (documented 1660–64) (plate 78)
Autumn (documented 1660–64)
Winter (documented 1660–64) (fig.38)
Apollo and Daphne

Paris, Petit Palais
The Massacre of the Innocents

Pasadena (California), Norton Simon Museum
Camillus and the Schoolmaster of the Falerii
Holy Family with Saints in a Landscape (see also under Malibu, J. Paul Getty Museum)

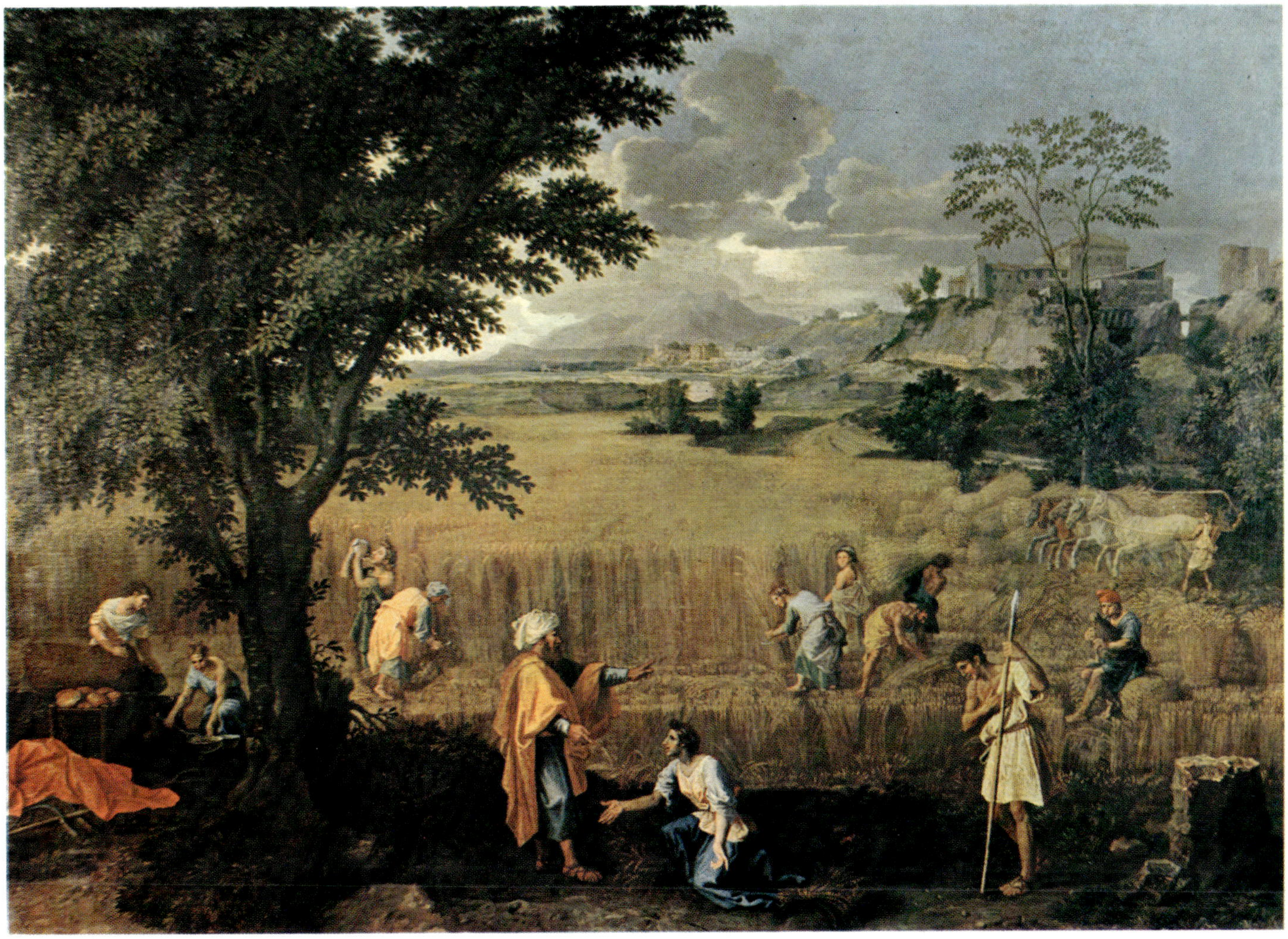

PLATE 78
Nicolas Poussin
Summer (Ruth and Boaz)
Canvas, 118 × 160 cm.
Paris, Louvre
Documented 1660–64; acquired by Louis XIV from the duc de Richelieu in 1665.

Philadelphia, Museum of Art
The Triumph of Neptune (plate 68)

Philadelphia, John G. Johnson Collection
The Baptism of Christ

Providence, Rhode Island School of Design
Venus and Adonis

Richmond, Virginia Museum of Fine Arts
Achilles and the Daughters of Lycomedes (documented 1656; may be a copy)

Rome, Palazzo Altieri
Landscape with Hagar and the Angel

Rome, Galleria Nazionale
Bacchanal of Putti (2)

Rome, Pinacoteca Vaticana
Battle of Gideon against the Midianites
The Martyrdom of St Erasmus (signed; documented as completed 1629) (fig.5)

Rouen, Musée des Beaux-Arts
Venus Presenting Arms to Aeneas (documented 1639)
Landscape—Storm

Sarasota (Florida), John and Mable Ringling Museum
The Ecstasy of St Paul (documented 1643)
Holy Family (documented 1655)

Schleissheim, Schloss, Staatsgalerie
Adoration of the Shepherds

Stockholm, Nationalmuseum
Bacchus/Apollo

Stourhead (Wiltshire), National Trust
The Choice of Hercules

Switzerland, private collection
The Baptism of Christ

Tatton Park (Cheshire), National Trust
The Sacrifice of Noah (damaged)

Toledo (Ohio), Museum of Art
Dido and Aeneas
The Holy Family (attribution)

Toronto, Art Gallery of Ontario
Venus Presenting Arms to Aeneas

Turin, Galleria Sabauda
St Margaret

Vienna, Kunsthistorisches Museum
The Destruction of the Temple at Jerusalem (signed) (plate 69)

Washington, National Gallery
The Sacrament of Baptism (documented as completed 1642) (plate 71)
The Madonna of the Steps (documented 1648; attribution of this version disputed)
The Assumption
The Nurture of Jupiter

Winterthur (Switzerland), Oskar Reinhardt collection
The Rest on the Flight into Egypt

Woburn Abbey (Bedfordshire), Marquess of Tavistock
Moses Trampling on Pharaoh's Crown

Worcester (Massachusetts), Art Museum
The Flight into Egypt

Zurich, Kunsthaus
Venus Surprised by Satyrs (attribution)

The following pictures are painted in a style very close to Poussin's, and none of them has yet been assigned convincingly to his followers.

Amherst (Massachusetts), College Art Museum
Narcissus and Two Nymphs

Brunswick, Herzog-Anton Ulrich Museum
Apollo and Diana at the Hunt

Budapest, Szépmüvészeti Múzeum
Holy Family

Dresden, Gemäldegalerie
The Sacrifice of Noah
Echo and Narcissus

Hovingham Hall (Yorkshire), Sir William Worsley
Leda

London, National Gallery
Perseus and Finea

London, Victoria and Albert Museum
Figures before Antique Buildings

Madrid, Prado
Bacchus and Ariadne
Mercury, Herse and Aglauros
Meleager and Atalanta

Montpellier, Musée Fabre
Baptism of Christ

New York, Metropolitan Museum
Landscape with Orpheus and Euridice

Ottawa, National Gallery of Canada
Augustus and Cleopatra

Reims, Musée Saint-Denis
Achilles with the Daughters of Lycomedes

Rome, Galleria Nazionale (Palazzo Corsini)
The Triumph of Ovid

São Paolo, Museu de Arte
Dance in Honour of Priapus

Woburn Abbey (Bedfordshire), Marquess of Tavistock
Bathsheba

Bibliography

I EARLY BIOGRAPHIES

The most important early biography is that of Giovanni Pietro Bellori, which appeared in his celebrated *Vite de' pittore, scultore ed architetti moderni*, Rome, 1672 (a convenient French translation: Geneva, 1947).

A rather more detailed biography is that of André Félibien which appeared in his *Entretiens sur les vies at les ouvrages des plus excellents peintres*, Vol.II, Paris, 1685. On these two biographies all subsequent work has been based.

II GENERAL STUDIES

All the early sources, both minor and important, were collated by Jacques Thuillier, 'Per un Corpus Poussinianum', in *Actes du colloque Poussin*, Paris, 1960, Vol.II, pp.49–238. The best modern individual studies are the series of articles, 'Poussin Studies' I–XIV, 1947–64, by Anthony Blunt, which appeared in *The Burlington Magazine*. Many of the ideas in these articles were expanded and elaborated in his Mellon Lectures at Washington, finally published as *Nicolas Poussin*, 2 Vols., London/New York, 1967. A very different approach, concentrating on Poussin the painter, is Walter Friedländer, *Nicolas Poussin*, New York, 1966.

III CATALOGUES

The first *catalogue raisonné* is that of John Smith, in his *Catalogue Raisonné of the Most Eminent Dutch, French and Flemish Painters*, 9 Vols., London, 1829–42. After a gap of almost a century, two conflicting catalogues were produced, both of them now out of date: Emile Magne, *Nicolas Poussin: premier peintre du roi*, Brussels/Paris, 1914 and Otto Grautoff, *Nicolas Poussin: sein Werk und sein Leben*, Munich, 1914. The most detailed of all the catalogues is that of Anthony Blunt, *The Painting of Nicolas Poussin: A Critical Catalogue*, London, 1966. This catalogue puts a highly personal point of view which was strongly challenged by Jacques Thuillier in *L'opera completa di Nicolas Poussin*, Milan/Paris, 1974. A general introduction with *catalogue raisonné* is Christopher Wright, *Nicolas Poussin*, London, 1985.

IV INDIVIDUAL STUDIES

The literature on Poussin is one of the largest in the history of art. Blunt published a list of over 1400 items in 1966, and a few stand out, either for their charm as period pieces or because they seek to challenge long-established views. Of importance in the history of taste is Delacroix, 'Essai sur Nicolas Poussin', reprinted from the artist's *Journal*, Geneva, 1966. Also of interest, because unexpected, is Doris Wild's study, 'Charles Mellin ou Nicolas Poussin' in *Gazette des Beaux-Arts*, October 1966 and January 1967, in which she maintained that many well-known early works were in fact by Mellin. Of more recent date and seriousness is Pierre Rosenberg's 'La mort de Germanicus de Poussin', *Les dossiers du Département des Peintures*, Paris, Louvre, 1973, which represents an approach which is both more scientific and sympathetic.

V EXHIBITIONS

The most comprehensive exhibition to date was that held in Paris, Louvre, *Nicolas Poussin*, 1960, catalogue by Anthony Blunt and Charles Sterling. (Many of the views expressed in that catalogue were challenged by Denis Mahon in 'Poussiniana', *Gazette des Beaux-Arts*, July/August, 1962.) Although only a small selection of pictures by Poussin was on view in the exhibition at Rouen, Musée des Beaux-Arts, *Nicolas Poussin et son temps*, 1961 (catalogue by Pierre Rosenberg), he was well placed in the context of his contemporaries, especially those whom he influenced. The most recent exhibition, mainly incorporating newly discovered or recently cleaned pictures, was Rome, Palazzo Medici, and Düsseldorf, Kunstmuseum, *Nicolas Poussin*, 1978, catalogue by Pierre Rosenberg.

VI LETTERS

Poussin's letters were fully published by Charles Jouanny, 'Correspondence de Nicolas Poussin publiée d'après les originaux', *Archives de l'art français*, Vol.v, Paris, 1911. An edited selection of the more interesting ones was published by Anthony Blunt, *Nicolas Poussin, Lettres et propos sur l'art*, Paris, 1964.

P. du Pré

Working mid-seventeenth century

Nothing is known of this painter, whose one surviving picture is close in style to the work of Jacques Linard.

Collection

Château-Gontier, private collection
Basket of Apricots and Bowl of Plums (signed)

Bibliography

Michel Faré
Le grand siècle de la nature morte en France, 1974, pp.43–4.

François Puget

Toulon 1651–Marseilles 1707

Son of the painter and sculptor Pierre Puget, François' style is very similar to his father's, especially in the directness and realism of his portraits. Like his father, he was influenced by the Genoese Baroque.

Collections

Aix-en-Provence, Musée Granet
Guintrand, Échevin of Marseilles
Madame Guintrand

Château-Gombert, Saint-Matthieu
The Calling of Matthew

Clermont-Ferrand, Musée Bargoin
Portrait of Pierre Puget

Marseilles, Palais Longchamp
Seated Man
The Visitation

Marseilles, Musée Grobet-Labadié
An Old Man
Judgment of St Barbara
Torture of St Barbara

Paris, Louvre
Concert Party (signed and dated 1688)
The Sculptor Pierre Puget

Bibliography

Marie-Christine Gloton
in the exhibition catalogue, Marseilles, Palais Longchamp, *La peinture en Provence au XVIIe siècle*, 1978, pp.133–7.

Pierre Puget

Marseilles 1620–Marseilles 1694

Puget was one of the great baroque sculptors, whose work remains too little known outside specialist circles. Like the outstanding figure of the Italian Baroque, Gianlorenzo Bernini, he also executed a few paintings, many of which have a freshness and directness only paralleled by Bernini himself. The *Self-portrait* at Aix-en-Provence is especially brilliant. Puget worked much in Italy, specifically Genoa, and the influence of Genoese baroque painting can be seen in his work.

Collections

Aix-en-Provence, Musée Granet
The Visitation
Self-portrait

Aix-en-Provence, Musée des Tapisseries
Annunciation

Marseilles, Palais Longchamp
St Cecilia (signed and dated 1651)
The Battle of Constantine (signed)
The Baptism of Clovis
The Sacrifice of Noah
The Saviour of the World
Gaspard Puget (?)
The Education of Achilles
The Sleep of the Infant Jesus

Nîmes, private collection
The Virgin Teaching the Christ Child to Read
The Artist's Mother

Puy-Sainte-Reparade, private collection
Holy Family

Quebec, Laval University
David with the Head of Goliath (signed and dated 1671)

Toulon, Cathedral
Appearance of the Virgin to St Felix of Cantalice
The Annunciation

Toulon, private collection
Head of St John the Baptist (signed)

Bibliography

Marie-Christine Gloton
in the exhibition catalogue, Marseilles, Palais Longchamp, *La peinture en Provence au XVIIe siècle*, 1978, pp.112–23.

Philippe Quantin

?c.1600–Dijon 1636

Quantin's style was consistently Caravaggesque, and he died young before his art could become completely unfashionable, unlike his near-contemporary Jean Tassel, who lived thirty years longer. Quantin is documented as working for the Bishop of Langres in 1617, and it seems that most of his pictures were painted for churches in Dijon.

Collections

Autun, Musée Rolin
The Beheading of St John the Baptist

Dijon, Cathédrale Saint-Bénigne
The Mystic Marriage of St Catherine of Siena
St Anthony and the Gardener
St Thomas Writing According to the Dictation of St Peter and St Paul

Dijon, Hôpital Général
The Annunciation
The Education of the Virgin

Dijon, Saint-Michel
The Annunciation

Dijon, Musée des Beaux-Arts
Adoration of the Shepherds
Triptych: *St Margaret, The Circumcision, Miracle of St Claude* (signed and dated 1635)
The Mystic Communion of St Catherine of Siena
The Visitation
St Bernard Writing

La Rochepot (Côte d'Or), Church
The Entombment

Bibliography

Charles Sterling
in the exhibition catalogue, Paris, Orangerie, *Les peintres de la réalité*, 1934, pp.136–8.

Marguerite Guillaume
'A propos de Philippe Quantin, essai de catalogue raisonné', *Bulletin de la Société de l'Histoire de l'Art français*, 1980, pp.101–25.

Augustin Quesnel I

Paris 1595–Paris ?1661

Quesnel was a portrait painter whose style was rather archaic and similar to the engravings of Abraham Bosses. The Budapest picture is a rare surviving example of a middle-class portrait of the time. Most of his other pictures continue the sixteenth-century naturalistic tradition begun by the Clouet family.

Collections

Budapest, Szépmüvészeti Múzeum
A Young Woman Playing the Guitar (signed and dated 1635)

Chantilly, Musée Condé
Nicolas Sieur de Mollais (monogrammed and dated 1651)

Le Puy, Musée Crozatier
Portrait of a Man (attribution)

Paris, Louvre
Jacob Bunel (signed)
A Man (signed and dated 1652)

Bibliography

Charles Sterling
in the exhibition catalogue, Paris, Orangeries, *Les peintres de la réalité*, 1934, pp.138–9.

'Remy'

Working late seventeenth century

Nothing is known about this painter, who is presumed to be French on grounds of style.

Collection

Orléans, Musée des Beaux-Arts
Allegory of Vigilance (signed)

Bibliography

Mary O'Neill, Orléans, Musée des Beaux-Arts, *Catalogue critique: Les peintures de l'école française des XVIIe et XVIIIe siècles*, 1981, p.120.

Simon Renard de Saint-André

Paris 1613–Paris 1677

This artist specialized in complex *Vanitas* pieces of dramatic clarity. The general influence on his art is Netherlandish, and it is likely that his unsigned pictures are still classified under the Northern schools. Most of his pictures are dominated by a grisly

PLATE 79
Simon Renard de Saint-André
Vanitas
Canvas, 52 × 44 cm.
Marseilles, Palais Longchamp (Musée des Beaux-Arts)

An unusual subject in French seventeenth-century painting (cf. Philippe de Champaigne).

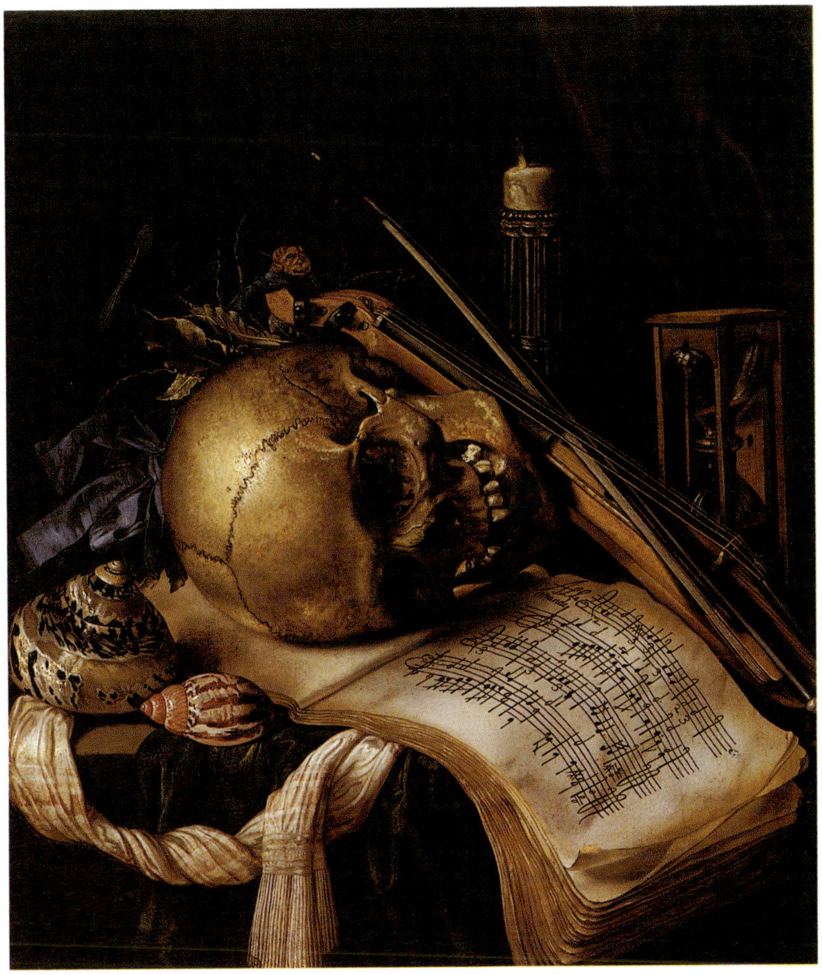

skull surrounded by numerous other indications of the brevity of life. He was received into the French Academy in 1663 as a portraitist.

Collections

France, private collection
Vanitas

France, private collection
Still Life with a Lute

France, private collection
Still Life with a Lacquer Coffer

France, private collection
The Vanities of the World

Lyons, Musée des Beaux-Arts
Vanitas

Marseilles, Palais Longchamp
Vanitas (plate 79)

Munich, Alte Pinakothek
Silver and Porcelain

Niort, Musée des Beaux-Arts
Still Life

Paris, A. and O.W. collection
Vanitas

Paris, Leegenhoek collection
Still Life with Coral

Paris, private collection
The Vanities of the World

Pontoise, Musée Tavet
Vanitas (signed)

Bibliography

Michel Faré
Le grand siècle de la nature morte en France, 1974, pp.168–74.

Jean-Pierre Rivalz

La Bastide d'Anjou c.1625–Toulouse 1706

Rivalz, a painter and architect, became town painter of Toulouse in the tradition exemplified by Chalette earlier in the century. Rivalz's Toulouse *Self-portrait* shows the strong Italian influence on his work, and the forceful result is similar to the work of Pierre Puget.

Collection

Toulouse, Musée des Augustins
Clemence Isaure (dated 1678)
Self-portrait

Bibliography

Charles Sterling
in the exhibition catalogue, Paris, Orangerie, *Les peintres de la réalité*, 1934, pp.144–5.

Jacques Rousseau

Paris 1630–London 1693

Much of this artist's career was spent in England, where he worked in a classically inspired landscape style, somewhat akin to that of Jean-François Millet.

Collections

Birmingham, Aston Hall
Landscape (attribution)

Hampton Court Palace (Middlesex), Royal Collection
Landscape

Versailles, Château
Four *Landscapes* decorating the Salon de Venus

Bibliography

There is no recent literature on this artist.

Adrien Sacquespée

Caudebec c.1629–Rouen after 1688

Though primarily a history painter, in Paris Sacquespée was the pupil of the still-life artist François Garnier, the father-in-law of Louise Moillon. Most of Sacquespée's career was spent in Rouen, painting in a style similar to that of Laurent de La Hyre and Eustache Le Sueur.

Collections

Paris, Saint-Nicolas du Chardonnet
St Bernard at the Council of Étampes
The Death of Ananias (signed and dated 1668)

Rouen, Musée des Beaux-Arts
The Martyrdom of St Andrew (signed and dated 1659)
Appearance of Christ to St Peter (signed and dated 1667)
The Eternal Father
St Bruno in Blessing (signed and dated 1671)
The Carthusians of Mont St Bernard in the Snow
Lamentation over the Dead Christ
Self-portrait (?)
Annunciation (attribution)

Paris, private collection
Self-portrait (signed and dated 1660)

Bibliography

Pierre Rosenberg
in the catalogue, Rouen, Musée des Beaux-Arts, *Tableaux français du XVIIe siècle* . . ., 1966, pp.114–17.

Jean de Saint-Igny

Rouen c.1595/1600–Rouen after 1647

Saint-Igny was one of the few artists of the period whose work was similar in its mannered extravagance to that of Claude Vignon. After a short stay in Paris in c.1629/31, Saint-Igny returned to his native Rouen where he spent the rest of his career. Many engravings and some drawings survive from his hand.

Collections

Dunkirk, Musée des Beaux-Arts
Adoration of the Kings
The Presentation in the Temple
Episode in the Life of St Bruno (?)

Nîmes, Musée des Beaux-Arts
Equestrian Portrait of Louis XIV as a Child (identification uncertain)

Paris, Musée de Cluny
Seven Scenes from Roman Antiquity

Poughkeepsie (New York), Vassar College Art Gallery
Triumphal Procession of Anne of Austria and the Young Louis XIV

Rouen, Musée des Beaux-Arts
Adoration of the Kings (signed)
Adoration of the Shepherds (signed and dated 1636)
Air

Valenciennes, Musée des Beaux-Arts
St Bernard and the Duke of Aquitaine (attribution)

Bibliography

Charles Sterling
in the exhibition catalogue, Paris, Orangerie, *Les peintres de la réalité*, 1934, pp.145–7.

Jean Senelle

Meaux 1603–Paris ? before 1671

Senelle was probably a pupil of Le Valentin, presumably in Rome.

Collections

Meaux, Musée Bossuet
Preaching of St John the Baptist (dated 1629)

Orléans, Musée des Beaux-Arts
Pope Nicolas V before the Body of St Francis of Assisi

Bibliography

There is no recent literature on this artist.

Gilbert de Sève

Moulins 1615–Paris 1698

One of the fourteen founder-members of the French Academy in Paris in 1648, de Sève painted in a style not easily distinguishable from the standard subject pictures executed in the middle years of the century.

Collections

Paris, Louvre
Nitocris, Queen of Syria, Constructing a Bridge over the Euphrates
Rhodope, Queen of Egypt, Looking at the Pyramid she had Constructed
Dido Building Carthage

Versailles, Château
Anne of Austria under a Figure of Wisdom
Mademoiselle de Montpensier (La Grande Mademoiselle)

Bibliography

There is no recent literature on this artist.

Pierre de Sève

Moulins 1623–Paris 1695

Brother of Gilbert de Sève, Pierre became a member of the French Academy in Paris in 1663.

Collections

Paris, Louvre
Cupid's Hunters
Cupid's Musicians

Versailles, Château
Renewal of the Alliance between France and Switzerland, 1663
The Passage of the Rhine (after Le Brun)
Siege of Tournai, 1667
Louis XIV Visiting the Gobelins

Bibliography

There is no recent literature on this artist.

Antoine Bouzonnet Stella

Lyons 1637–Paris 1682

Nephew of Jacques Stella, Antoine went to Rome where he was well received by Nicolas Poussin because of the latter's friendship with his uncle. He returned to Paris in 1664 and became a member of the Academy in 1666. His pictures are similar in style to those of Jacques Stella.

Collection

Paris, École des Beaux-Arts
The Pythian Games

Bibliography

There is no recent literature on this artist.

Claudine Bouzonnet Stella

Lyons 1636–Paris 1697

Niece and pupil of Jacques Stella, this artist was chiefly distinguished as an engraver, mostly after Nicolas Poussin and Jacques Stella.

Collections

Leningrad, Hermitage
Christ Appearing to a Centurion (signed and dated 1666)

Norfolk (Virginia), Chrysler Museum
Mystic Marriage of St Catherine (attribution)

Bibliography

There is no recent literature on this artist.

Jacques Stella

Lyons 1596–Paris 1657

Stella is an example of a painter who enjoyed great esteem in his lifetime, both as an artist and a patron (of Nicolas Poussin), but whose work is no longer appreciated. Most of the early part of his career was spent in Italy, both in Florence and Rome, and he must have been strongly influenced by the small *Madonnas* of Raphael. He became a friend of Poussin in Rome and acquired numerous pictures by him, including the *Venus and Aeneas* now at Rouen. Poussin influenced Stella's sweetly decorative style (which is similar in scale and charm to that of Lubin Baugin) to the point where his pictures became cold and hard and lacking in sentimentality. Unusually for a Frenchman, Stella sometimes painted on a precious ground such as lapis-lazuli or marble, allowing the pattern of the stone to form part of the composition.

Collections

Alençon, Musée des Beaux-Arts
Sacrifice of Abraham

Angers, Musée des Beaux-Arts
Holy Family

Barnard Castle (Co. Durham), Bowes Museum
Adoration of the Child (fig.41)

Béziers, Musée Fabrégat
Presentation of the Virgin in the Temple

Budapest, Szépmüvészeti Múzeum
Marriage of the Virgin

Caen, Musée des Beaux-Arts
The School of Athens

Cambridge (Massachusetts), Fogg Art Museum
The Liberality of Titus

Chantilly, Musée Condé
Louis II de Bourbon, Duc d'Enghien

Dijon, Musée Magnin
Eleazer and Rebecca

Épinal, Musée Départemental des Vosges
Virgin and Child

Florence, Uffizi
Virgin and Child with St John
Christ in the Wilderness Nourished by Angels

Fontainebleau, Château
Cloelia Traversing the Tiber with her Companions
Minerva and the Muses

Glasgow, University, Hunterian Collection
Rest on the Flight into Egypt

Greenville (South Carolina), Bob Jones University
Adoration of the Shepherds

Grenoble, Musée de Peinture et de Sculpture
Christ and the Samaritan Woman
Rachel

Hartford (Connecticut), Wadsworth Athenaeum
The Judgment of Paris

Le Havre, Musée des Beaux-Arts
Virgin and Child (attribution)

Le Mans, Musée de Tessé
The Infant Christ Adored by Angels

Leningrad, Hermitage
Holy Family
Venus and Adonis
Lucius Albinus Gives his Carriage to the Vestal Virgins
Angels

Limoges, Musée des Beaux-Arts
Mater Dolorosa

Lisbon, National Museum
Virgin and Child

Lyons, Musée des Beaux-Arts
Adoration of the Angels (signed and dated 1635)

Madrid, Prado
Rest on the Flight into Egypt (signed and dated 1652)

Montpellier, Musée Fabre
Christ and the Samaritan Woman

Munich, Bayerisches Nationalmuseum
The Magdalen (dated 1630)

Nantes, Musée des Beaux-Arts
Assumption of the Virgin (signed and dated 1627)

Oldenburg, Landesmuseum
Diana and her Nymphs

Paris, Louvre
Christ Receiving the Virgin in Heaven
St Cecilia Playing the Organ
Cloelia Passing the Tiber

Paris, Notre-Dame-de-Bercy
Christ and the Samaritan Woman

Philadelphia (Pennsylvania), Museum of Art
Christ at the Column

Princeton (New Jersey), Art Museum
Rape of the Sabines

Richmond (Surrey), Ham House
Salome with the Head of St John the Baptist
Virgin and Child with St John the Baptist

Rouen, Musée des Beaux-Arts
St Anne and the Virgin (signed)

Sarasota (Florida), John and Mable Ringling Museum
Candaulus Showing his Wife to Gyges

Toulouse, Musée des Augustins
Holy Family
Holy Family
Marriage of the Virgin
Communion of St Peter

Versailles, Château
Triumph of Louis XIII over the Enemies of Religion (signed and dated 1642)

Vienna, Kunsthistorisches Museum
The Judgment of Solomon

Bibliography

For the artist's Roman period, see Liliana Barroero, 'Una tracia per gli anni romani di Jacques Stella', *Paragone*, no.347, 1979, pp.3–24.

PLATE 80
Sébastien Stoskopff
Still Life of Glasses in a Basket
Canvas, 51 × 62 cm. Signed and dated lower left: STOSKOPFF 1644
Strasbourg, Musée de l'Oeuvre de Notre Dame
Acquired by the museum in 1931 from a Paris collection.

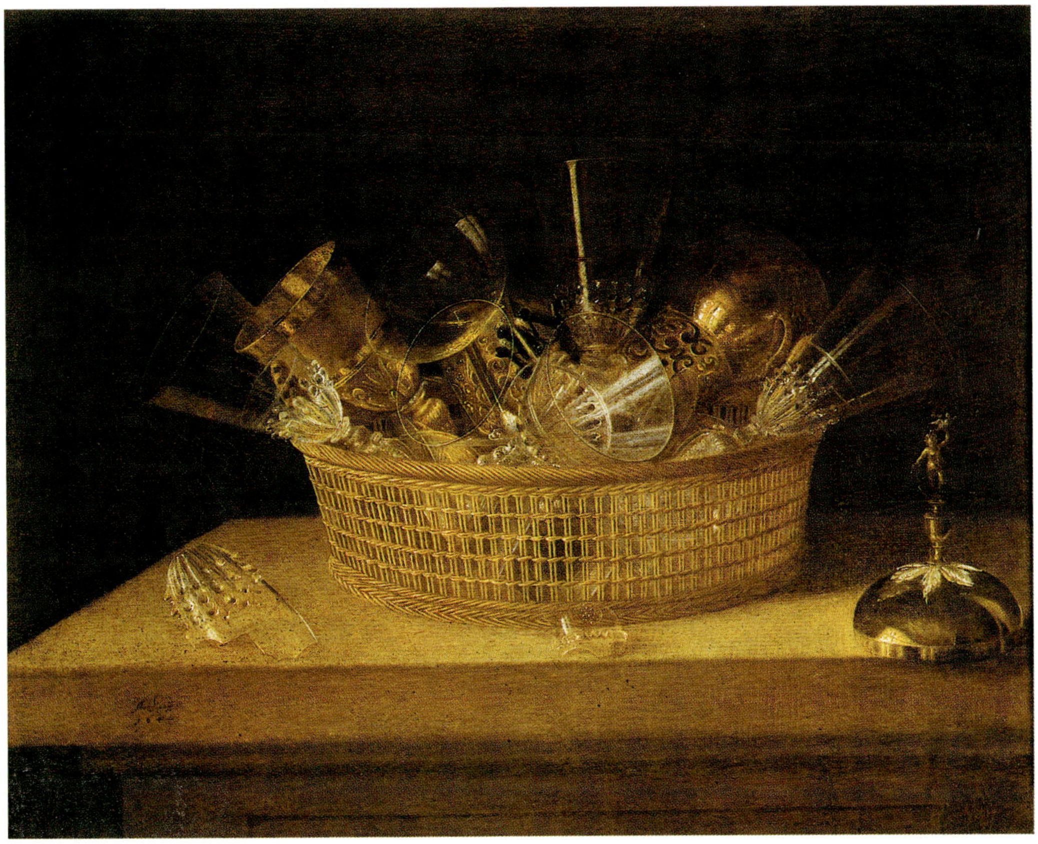

Sébastien Stoskopff

Strasbourg 1597–Idstein 1657

Exclusively a still-life painter, Stoskopff was old-fashioned in his style. Working most of his life in Strasbourg, he visited both Venice and Paris, clearly ignoring what he had seen there. His art was totally uninfluenced by the Baroque. Most of his pictures have been identified in recent years: at the time of the exhibition *Les peintres de la réalité* in 1934, only five were known. Stoskopff's realism, combined with the naïvety of his compositions, appeals very strongly to modern tastes.

Collections

Amsterdam, with de Boer
Basket of Glasses (signed and dated 1644)

Arras, Palais Saint-Vaast
Pheasants, Partridge and Pigeons (signed)

Balte, private collection
Wine Holder, Bread and Wine Glass (signed)

Basle, Öffentliche Kunstsammlung
Carp in a Wooden Bucket

Berlin-Dahlem, Staatliche Museen
Still Life

Chaumont, Musée Municipal
Warmer, Salt Pot and Cornet of Pepper (fig.49)

Clamecy, Musée Municipal
Carp on a Chip-wood Box (signed)

Cologne, Wallraf Richartzmuseum
Still Life

Detroit (Michigan), Institute of Arts
Still Life of Books with a Rembrandt Etching

Karlsruhe, Staatliche Kunsthalle
Basket of Glasses and a Copper Basin

Le Havre, Musée des Beaux-Arts
Pewter Plates, Cheese, Bread and Fruits (signed)
Pewter Plates, Prawns and Lemon (signed)

Lyons, Musée des Beaux-Arts
Still Life with a Carp and Earthenware Pot

Montbéliard, P. Jouffroy collection
Carp on a Chip-wood box and Beer Mug (signed)

Munich, Alte Pinakothek
Still Life (2)

Munich, formerly Scharnowski collection
Still Life with a Fish

New York, formerly with Knoedler
Still Life with an Earthenware Pot (signed)

Nuremberg, Germanisches Nationalmuseum
Still Life

Paris, Bernier collection
Small Tarts on a Dish

Paris, D. collection
Vanitas

Paris, K. collection
Still Life with Dead Game and a Parrot

Paris, R. Lebel collection
Pewter Dish, Rummer, Apple and Bread (signed and dated 1644)
Still Life of Books

Paris, Louvre
Books, Candle and Bronze Statuette
Statuette, Books, Chip-wood Box and Shells

Paris, private collection
Vanitas Piece with a Miniature Sundial

Paris, private collection
Chicken, Salt Pot and Wine Glass (signed)

Paris, private collection
Strawberries on a Pewter Plate on a Carpet

Paris, private collection
Warmer, Leg of Lamb and Bread

Paris, private collection
Warmer, Oysters and Wine Glasses

Pasadena (California), Norton Simon Museum
Still Life with Empty Glasses (signed and dated 1644)

Princeton, Art Museum
Shells and Statuette of Minerva

Rotterdam, Museum Boymans-van Beuningen
Open Book with a Callot Etching and Candle (signed and dated 1625) (fig.48)

Saarbrücken, Saarland-Museum
Still Life with a Calf's Head (signed and dated 1640)

Strasbourg, Musée de l'Oeuvre de Notre Dame
Vase of Flowers (signed)
Dish of Strawberries (signed)
Still Life of Glasses in a Basket (signed) (plate 80)
The Five Senses with Table Clock (fragments of signature)
The Banquet Served
Winter, or the Four Elements
Allegory of Summer, or the Five Senses (signed and dated 1633)
Nautilus Shell and Coral (signed)
Large Vanitas (signed and dated 1641)
Basket of Glasses (signed and dated 1644)

United States of America, D. Rust collection
Dead Heron (signed and dated 1646)

Vienna, Kunsthistorisches Museum
Trompe l'Oeil with an Engraving by Michel Dorigny

Zurich, Dr Nathan collection
Still Life with a Basket of Glasses and Six Goblets

Bibliography

Michel Faré
Le grand siècle de la nature morte en France, 1974, pp.115–34.

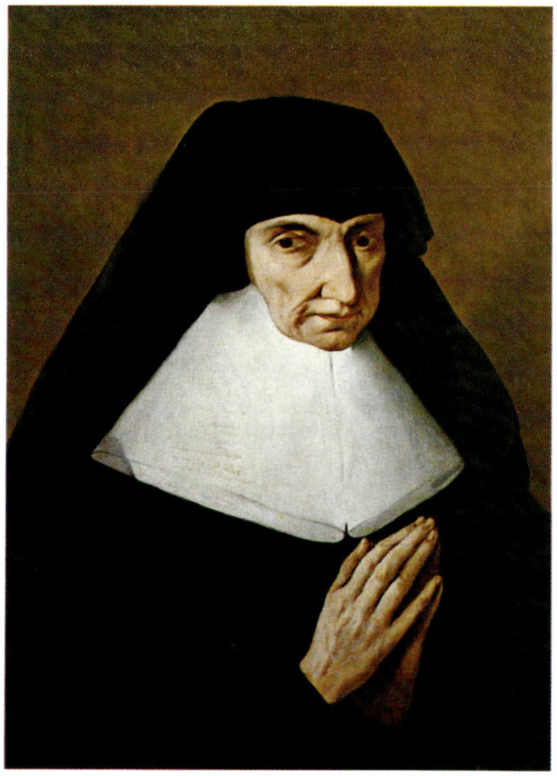

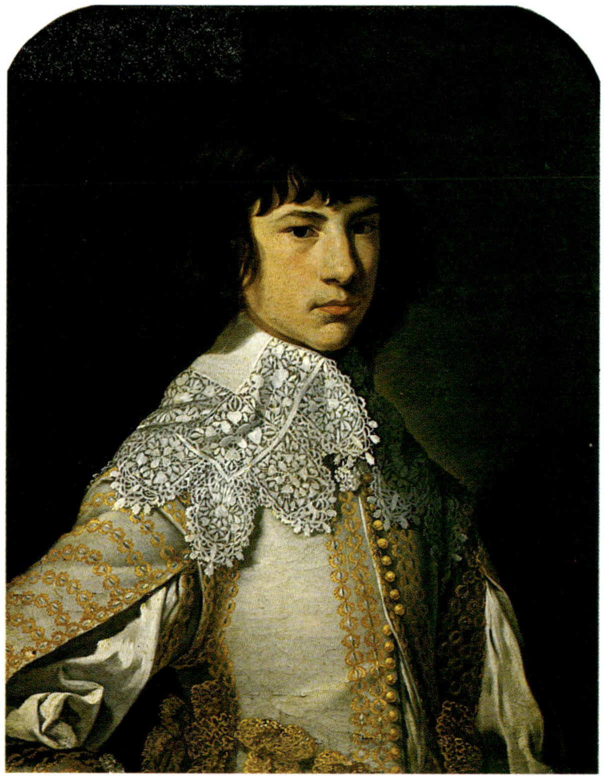

Jean Tassel

Langres 1608–Langres 1667

Son of the painter Richard Tassel, Jean Tassel began his career in Italy. No picture from his Italian period has yet been identified with certainty, but it may well be that the small group of pictures at present called 'The Master of the Judgment of Solomon' could be by Tassel, showing him to be more cosmopolitan than usual. The picture of *Christ among the Doctors* in the church of Saint-Martin at Langres, given to 'The Master of the Judgment of Solomon', provides a local link, although the provenance of this picture appears uncertain.

On his return to France, Tassel worked in Troyes, Dijon and his native Langres, where he received a number of commissions towards the end of his life. He acquired considerable skill in Italy, but his style remained totally out of touch with developments, even in the rest of France. The fascination of his work lies in his ability to create a mood of brooding and exaggeration, partly through his trick of painting his figures with slanting eyes. Only one portrait, the *Catherine de Montholon* at Dijon, is given to him with any certainty, but the *Portrait of a Young Man* at Avignon, long considered to be from the circle of the Le Nain brothers, could well be by him.

Collections

Avignon, Musée Calvet
Portrait of a Young Man (attribution dated ?1632) (plate 82)

Burghley House (Northamptonshire), The Marquess of Exeter
Virgin and Child

Chaumont, Musée Municipal
The Flight into Egypt

Chaumont, Saint-Jean-le Baptiste
The Annunciation (documented 1653)

Dijon, Musée des Beaux-Arts
St James
Presentation of the Virgin in the Temple
Presentation of Christ in the Temple
Tobias and the Angel
The Return of Tobias
Crowning of the Virgin by the Infant Christ
Portrait of Catherine de Montholon (plate 81)
Adoration of the Kings
Three Nymphs
Christ as a Boy
Christ of Pity
The Magdalen (after Gentileschi)
The Virgin of Sorrow
Martyrdom of St Stephen (dated 1666)
The Descent from the Cross
Head of the Virgin
Woman Holding a Stone in her Hand

Dôle, Musée Municipal
Christ and the Pilgrims
St Bernard Giving Communion

Florence, Uffizi
Landscape with Walkers

The Hague, Museum Bredius
The Wheelwright
Three Soldiers in an Inn
Moses Striking the Rock

Hartford (Connecticut), Wadsworth Athenaeum
Virgin and Child

Kassel, Staatliche Kunsthalle
The Quartet

Langres, Musée Saint Didier
St James
The Last Supper
The Brigands (*Les Maraudeurs*) (fig. 15)
Virgin and Child
Moses Striking the Rock
Death of St Joseph
St Michael Defeating the Dragon
Martyrdom of St Martine (signed and dated 1663)
Holy Family

Langres, Cathedral
The Departure of the Prodigal Son
The Return of the Prodigal Son
S. Mammès
The Nativity (after Jean Le Clerc; in the Musée Saint Didier, Langres)

Langres, Société Historique et Archéologique
Head of the Virgin

Lyons, Musée des Beaux-Arts
Virgin and Child (fig. 16)

Meaux, Cathedral
Adoration of the Kings (signed and dated 1636)

Paris, Louvre
Adoration of the Kings
The Rape of Helen

Sarasota (Florida), John and Mable Ringling Museum
The Judgment of Solomon

San Sebastian, Museo di San Telmo
Adoration of the Kings

Sète, Musée Paul Valéry
Diana and Venus

Toulouse, Musée des Augustins
Virgin and Child

Troyes, Musée des Beaux-Arts
The Just Horace (attribution)
The Tree of Jesse
Holy Family
The Rest on the Flight into Egypt
St John in the Desert
St John in the Desert
The Resurrection
Head of the Virgin (attribution)
The Pilgrims to Emmaus

Warsaw, National Museum
A Hold Up

Bibliography

All Tassel studies in recent years have been made by Dr H. Ronot, and reflect a gradual accumulation of information about the artist. Tassel has not yet been subjected to scrutiny outside his locality. Dr H. Ronot, 'La vie d'une famille de peintres provinciaux du XVIIe siècle; les Tassel de Langres', *Annales de Bourgogne*, 1954.

Most of Tassel's pictures in French collections were brought together at the exhibition, Dijon, Musée des Beaux-Arts, *Le Tassel*, 1955. A more recent study by Dr Ronot is 'A la découverte d'un peintre langrois du XVIIe siècle', *Médicine de France*, No. 158, Jan. 1965.

PLATE 81 (far left)
Jean Tassel
Portrait of Catherine de Montholon
Canvas, 54 × 40 cm.
Dijon, Musée des Beaux-Arts
Seized from the convent of the Ursulines, Dijon, during the Revolution.

Widow of René Le Beau, Seigneur de Sanzette, the sitter was founder of the Ursulines of Dijon and died in 1650.

PLATE 82 (left)
Attributed to Jean Tassel
Portrait of a Young Man
Canvas, 56 × 44 cm. Apparently dated upper right: 1632
Avignon, Musée Calvet
Acquired by the museum in 1864 from the painter Evariste de Valernes.

The attribution to Tassel is based on stylistic comparison. The old attribution to the Le Nain brothers has long since been abandoned.

Richard Tassel

Langres 1583–Langres 1666

Until recently, Richard Tassel was confused with his son Jean, and even now only one picture can be ascribed to Richard with certainty. It is likely, however, that a number of pictures still attributed to Jean are by his father. Richard is thought to have gone to Bologna at an early age, to work in the studio of Guido Reni. He then returned to Langres, where he seems to have worked for the rest of his long life. From the evidence of his one certain picture, he seems to have been little affected by his sojourn in Italy, and to have continued painting in an out-of-date provincial style.

Collection

Dijon, Musée des Beaux-Arts
The Triumph of the Virgin in Heaven (signed and dated 1617) (fig.14)

Bibliography

Dr H. Ronot, 'A la découverte d'un peintre langrois du XVIIe siècle', *Médecine de France*, No.158, Jan. 1965.

Henri Testelin

Paris 1616–The Hague 1695

Pupil of Simon Vouet and brother of Louis, Henri Testelin was one of the fourteen founder-members of the Academy in 1648. His portraits tend to be rather formal, and show the influence of Philippe de Champaigne.

Collections

Baltimore, Walters Art Gallery
Louis XIV (fragment)

Gray, Musée Baron Martin
Louis XIV at the Age of Ten (attribution)

Madrid, Prado
The Triumph of Caesar (attribution)

Newport, Marble House
Louis XIV in Coronation Robes

Valenciennes, Musée des Beaux-Arts
Portrait of Louis XIV (attribution)

Versailles, Château
Louis XIV (signed and dated 1648)
Siege of Dôle (dated 1668)
The Keys of Marsal Returned to the King (dated 1663)
Establishment of the Academy of Science and the Foundation of the Observatory
Marriage of Louis XIV and Marie-Thérèse
Chancellor Séguier
Louis XIV (2)
Louis XIV Founding the Academy of Sciences and the Observatory

Bibliography

There is no recent literature on this artist.

Louis Testelin

Paris 1615–Paris 1665

A pupil of Vouet, Louis Testelin was extremely successful at gaining official commissions. His *Resurrection of Tabitha*, now at Arras, was one of the annual 'Mays' for the Notre Dame Cathedral, Paris.

Collections

Arras, Palais Saint-Vaast
The Resurrection of Tabitha (dated 1652)

Dijon, Musée Magnin
The Division of the Promised Land
Death of Tancred

Grenoble, Musée de Peinture et de Sculpture
The Magdalen in the Wilderness

Bibliography

There is no recent literature on this artist.

Jean Tiger

Falaise 1623–Paris 1698

Tiger was a pupil of Pierre Mignard, and became a member of the Academy in 1675.

Collection

Versailles, Château
Portrait of Henri Testelin (?) (documented 1675)
Portrait of Nicolas Loir (?) (documented 1675)

Bibliography

There is no recent literature on this artist.

François Tortebat

Paris 1616–Paris 1690

A pupil of Vouet, Tortebat's portrait of his master was his reception piece for the Academy in 1665.

Collection

Versailles, Château
Portrait of Simon Vouet
(documented 1665)

Bibliography

There is no recent literature on this artist.

Nicolas Tournier

Montbéliard 1590–Toulouse in or before 1639

Nicolas Tournier was the most faithful follower of Caravaggio in France. Little is known about his career. He came from a Protestant family that, it is believed, had moved south to the Narbonne area by 1600. Tournier is certainly recorded in Rome by 1619, and he stayed there until at least 1626, but the rest of his career was spent in France (he was recorded in Carcassonne in 1627 and in Toulouse from 1632 onwards).

No picture from the artist's Roman period can be identified with certainty, although a considerable group of pictures has been associated with his name for that time, almost all of them concert parties in the Caravaggesque manner of Manfredi. Few pictures survive from Tournier's French period, partly because of the destruction of his work in the 1789 Revolution. *The Battle of Constantine* at Toulouse, astonishingly, is derived in its composition from the fifteenth-century Pierro della Francesca, who was completely ignored in Tournier's time as there was little or no interest in quattrocento painting. The remainder of Tournier's pictures are directly dependent on Caravaggio, both for their lighting and emotional intensity.

Collections

Nantes, Musée des Beaux-Arts
Christ at Emmaus (attribution)

Narbonne, Cathedral
The Guardian Angel (attribution)

Narbonne, Saint-Serge
Crucifixion with the Virgin and St Joseph of Arimathea

Paris, Louvre
Crucifixion with the Virgin, the Magdalen, St John and St François de Paul (dated 1628)
The Concert

Toulouse, Musée des Augustins
The Battle of Constantine (fig.12)
Deposition from the Cross (fig.10)
Entombment (fig.11, plate 83)
Virgin and Child

The following pictures are frequently considered to be the work of Tournier, executed during the years he spent in Rome. They are likely to be by a painter who was strongly influenced by Manfredi and also possibly Le Valentin, but are very different, both in handling and general style, to those Tournier certainly executed when he was in Toulouse.

Attingham Park, Shropshire, National Trust
Dice Players

Belgrade, Novakovic collection, 1938
Man with a Lute

Belgrade, National Museum
Concert

Bourges, Musée du Berry
Concert

Brescia, Pinacoteca Tosio e Martinengo
Flautist

Budapest, Szépmüvészeti Múzeum
Concert

Catton Hall (Derbyshire), Anson collection
Dice Players

Caracas, Rafael Ramirez collection
Tobias

Claremont (California), Pomona College
Young Man in a Plumed Hat

Dresden, Gemäldegalerie
Card and Dice Players
Denial of Peter

Florence, Florentine Galleries
The Parable of the Mote and the Beam

Le Mans, Musée de Tessé
Concert

Leningrad, Hermitage
Lute Player

London, private collection
St Paul Writing

London, private collection
Dice Players

London, Barlow collection (formerly)
Abraham and Hagar

Madrid, Prado
Denial of Peter

Madrid, private collection
Banquet

PLATE 83
Nicolas Tournier
Entombment
Canvas, 305 × 154 cm.
Toulouse, Musée des Augustins
Painted for the chapel of the Pénitents Noirs, Toulouse.

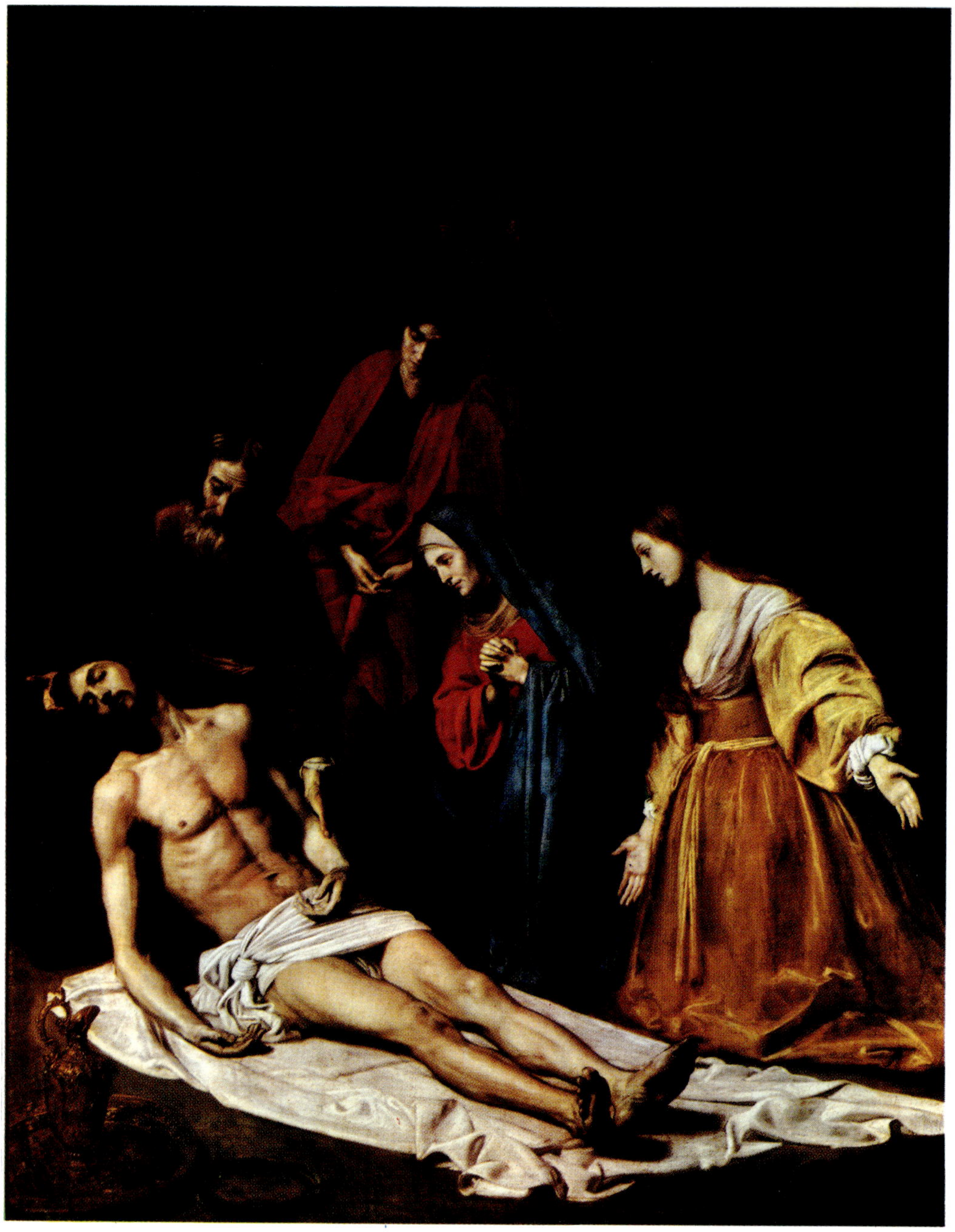

Modena, Galleria Estense
Drinker

Munich, with Silvano Lodi, 1972
Denial of Peter

Paris, private collection
Bust of a Soldier

Pommersfelden, Schloss Schönborn
Judgment of Solomon

Providence, Rhode Island School of Design
Flagellation of Christ

Rome, Galleria Corsini
David with the Head of Goliath
'Sinite Parvulos'

Rome, Galleria Spada
St John the Evangelist

Rome, with Nino Salocchi, 1965
Denial of Peter

Rome, Chigi collection (formerly)
Joseph Explaining his Dreams

Saint Louis, Art Museum
Concert

Sarasota (Florida), John and Mable Ringling Museum
Tobias Leaving his Parents

Stockholm, sold Bukowski 1966
Concert

Warsaw, National Museum
David

Bibliography

The standard article, now out of date, is R. Mesuret, 'L'oeuvre peinte de Nicolas Tournier', *Gazette des Beaux-Arts*, December 1957. A recent summary of the artist's revised biography and a list of all the pictures by and attributed to him is to be found in Benedict Nicolson, *The International Caravaggesque Movement*, Oxford, 1979, pp.102–3.

Pierre Toutain
Le Mans 1645–Paris 1686

Toutain worked on the decoration of Versailles under Le Brun.

Collection

Paris, Louvre
Jason Presenting the Toison d'Or in the Temple of Jupiter (documented 1681)

Bibliography

There is no recent literature on this artist.

Henri Traivoel
? Working Rome 1622

An artist of this name is documented as being a pupil of Simon Vouet in Rome in 1622. An old inscription on the reverse of a superb Vouet-like portrait of a young man records Traivoel as its author.

Collection

Neuilly-sur-Seine, Richers collection
A Young Man (self-portrait?)

Bibliography

See Arnauld Bréjon de Lavergnée and Jean-Pierre Cuzin in the exhibition catalogue, Paris, Grand Palais, *Le Valentin et les caravagesques français*, pp.122–3.

Antoine de Troy
Toulouse 1608–Toulouse 1684

Almost all this artist's works were destroyed in the Revolution of 1789. A pupil of Chalette, de Troy specialized in portraiture.

Collection

Toulouse, Musée des Augustins
Peire Godolin

Bibliography

There is no recent literature on this artist.

Jean de Troy
Toulouse 1638–Montpellier 1691

Elder son of Antoine de Troy, Jean de Troy founded the École des Beaux-Arts at Montpellier. He followed in his father's tradition of portrait painting.

Collections

France, Marquis de Beaumont collection
A Magistrate

France, Latecoere collection
Jeanne de Juliard, Dame de Mondonville

Montpellier, Musée Fabre
Elisabeth de Bonzi, Marquise de Castries

Toulouse, Musée du Vieux Toulouse
Jean-Louis Fontanilles (signed and dated 1674)

Bibliography

There is no recent literature on this artist.

Le Valentin
Coulommiers ?1590s–Rome 1634

Le Valentin was the most original of all the Caravaggesque French painters working in Rome after about 1615. His career is largely undocumented, except for a commission for the altarpiece for St Peter's in Rome, *The Martyrdom of St Processus and St Martinian*, which was painted c.1629/30 as a pendant to Nicolas Poussin's *Martyrdom of St Erasmus* of 1628. Le Valentin's chronology has to be worked out on a stylistic basis, and only the broadest generalizations can be made at present. His earliest pictures, mostly concert

PLATE 84
Le Valentin
The Fortune Teller
Canvas, 125 × 175 cm.
Paris, Louvre
In the collection of Louis XIV.

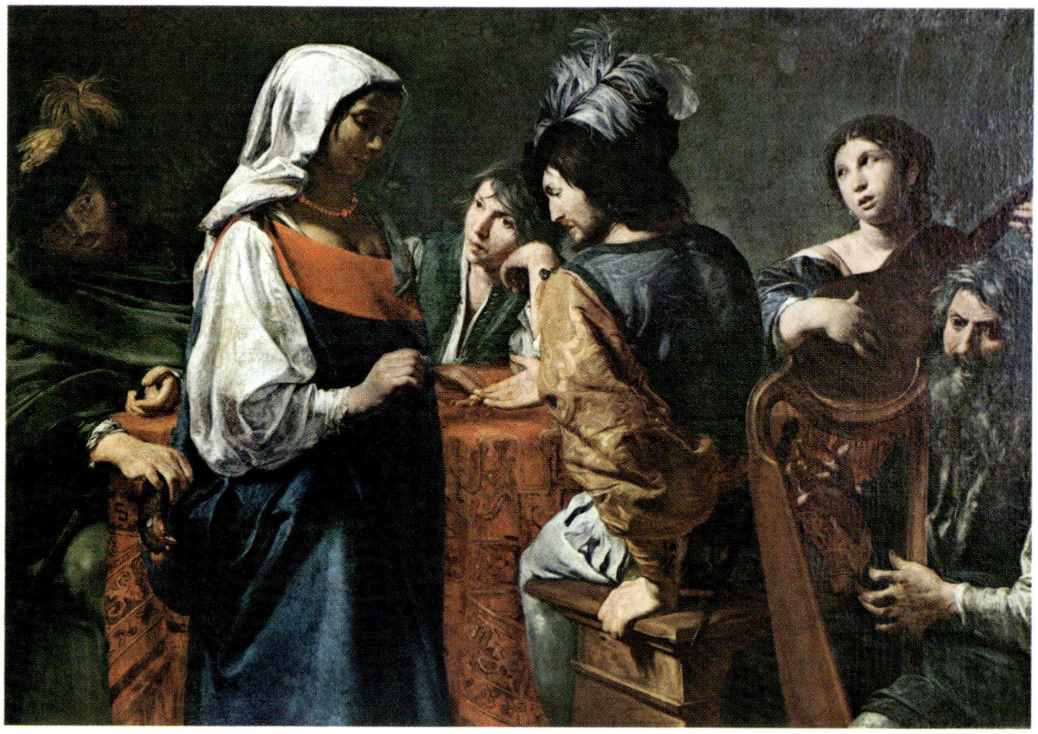

parties, rely heavily on pictures of the same subject by one of the most faithful of Caravaggio's followers, Bartolomeo Manfredi, who certainly influenced a wide variety of painters in Rome. In the 1620s Le Valentin's style became much softer, and he started to use smoky blues and soft reds which make his mature work unmistakable. The Vatican picture is different because of the nature of the commission, but right up to the artist's early death in Rome in 1634 there was no indication that he was about to change his already old-fashioned style.

Collections

Althorp (Northamptonshire), formerly Earl Spencer
Erminia and the Shepherds

Apiro, San Urbano
St John the Baptist

Beauvais, Musée Départemental de l'Oise
St Paul

Cambridge (Massachusetts), Fogg Art Museum
Crowning with Thorns

Camerino, Santa Maria in Via
St John the Baptist

Chapel Hill (North Carolina), Ackland Memorial Art Center
St John the Evangelist

Cleveland (Ohio), Museum of Art
Samson

Copenhagen, Statens Museum for Kunst
The Fortune Teller

Dresden, Gemäldegalerie
The Card Sharps (fig.6)

Florence, Longhi Foundation
The Denial of Peter

Florence, Sala collection, 1958
The Return of the Prodigal Son

Indianapolis (Indiana), Museum of Art
Soldiers and Gypsies

Italy, private collection
Christ and the Samaritan Woman

Italy, private collection
St John the Baptist

La Valletta, Malta Museum
Judith and Holofernes

Leningrad, Hermitage
Christ Driving the Money-changers from the Temple

London, National Gallery
The Four Ages of Man

Lugano, Thyssen collection
David with the Head of Goliath

Milan, Rainoldi collection, 1958
Crowning with Thorns

Montreal, Museum of Fine Arts
Sacrifice of Isaac

Moscow, Pushkin Museum
Denial of Peter

Munich, Alte Pinakothek
Crowning with Thorns
Crowning with Thorns
Erminia and the Shepherds

New York, with Wildenstein
Concert

Paris, Louvre
The Fortune Teller (plate 84)
Reunion in a Tavern
Concert with an Antique Bas-relief
The Innocence of Susanna
The Judgment of Solomon
Concert

Paris, Heim collection
St Jerome

Paris, private collection
The Lute-player

Perugia, Galleria Nazionale
Noli Me Tangere

Pommersfelden, Schloss Schönborn
The Fortune Teller

Rome, Galleria Corsini
Christ Driving the Money-changers from the Temple
The Last Supper
The Judgment of Solomon

Rome, Galleria Spada
Holy Family
Salome

Rome, Villa Lante
Allegory of Rome

Rome, Pinacoteca Vaticana
Martyrdom of St Processus and St Martinian (in place 1630) (fig.4)

Rome, private collection, 1958
St Peter in Prison

Rome, private collection
Card Players and Musicians

Rome, private collection, 1958
St Jerome

Strasbourg, Musée des Beaux-Arts
Musicians and Drinkers

Toledo (Ohio), Museum of Art
Fortune Teller with Drinkers

Toulouse, Musée des Augustins
Judith

Turin, Galleria Sabauda
St Jerome

Venice, Accademia
Martyrdom of St Bartholomew

Versailles, Château
The Tribute to Caesar
St Matthew
St Mark
St Luke
St John

Vienna, Kunsthistorisches Museum
Moses and the Tables of the Law

Wellesley (Massachusetts), Jewett Art Center
St Jerome

Bibliography

The most comprehensive list is found in Benedict Nicolson, *The International Caravaggesque Movement*, 1979, pp.103–6.

Quentin Varin

Beauvais c.1570–Paris 1634

Varin worked chiefly in Beauvais and Paris. It has always been assumed that his work for the Church of the Grand Andely must have influenced the young Nicolas Poussin, who was born at Les Andelys. Varin never departed from his out-of-date but powerful Mannerist style.

Collections

Beauvais, Cathedral
The Flagellation of Christ (signed)

Beauvais, Musée Départemental de l'Oise
Presentation in the Temple (signed)
The Flagellation
Martyrdom of a Saint

Les Andelys, Le Grand Andely, Church
Martyrdom of St Vincent (signed and dated 1612)
Martyrdom of St Clare (signed)

Paris, Louvre
Lamentation over the Dead Christ (signed)

Rennes, Musée des Beaux-Arts
The Marriage at Cana

Rouen, Musée des Beaux-Arts
Picture of Cébès (signed)

Bibliography

Jacques Thuillier
in the exhibition catalogue, Rouen, Musée des Beaux-Arts, *Nicolas Poussin et son temps*, 1961, pp.64–6.

Claude Vignon

Tours 1593–Paris 1670

The facts of Vignon's career are simple enough: he went to Rome at an early age—he was probably there by 1616—and by about 1627 he had returned to France and settled in Paris, where he remained for the rest of his long life. Vignon's stylistic development, on the other hand, is complex and fascinating. His earliest pictures are predictable, in the sense that they follow the expected style and themes of late Mannerist painters in France; and it is not surprising that, once in Rome, he came under the spell of Caravaggio, like almost all the painters who arrived there before about 1625. After his return to France, however, Vignon reverted to a kind of backward-looking Mannerism full of his own idiosyncrasies in the form of extravagant colour-schemes. Lime-greens clash with lilacs and cherry-reds, and the broken surfaces of his paintings seem to shimmer and glitter with inappropriate colours. The only parallel with his work in the seventeenth century is found in a late follower of Rembrandt, Aert de Gelder; and the very extravagance of Vignon's art in the 1620s has led to him being described as a 'precursor of Rembrandt'. In fact, his return to Mannerism in the 1620s is exactly paralleled by another Dutchman, Pieter Lastman of Amsterdam, whose colour and handling are very close to Vignon's. The similarities between Rembrandt and Vignon have been pointed out because Rembrandt was briefly but effectively influenced by Lastman during his first stay in Amsterdam in the years 1625–6.

PLATE 85
Claude Vignon
Esther before Ahasuerus
Canvas, 80 × 119 cm. Signed and dated: Vignon in. fe. 1624
Paris, Louvre
Acquired by the museum in 1933.
The picture has also been identified as depicting Solomon and the Queen of Sheba.

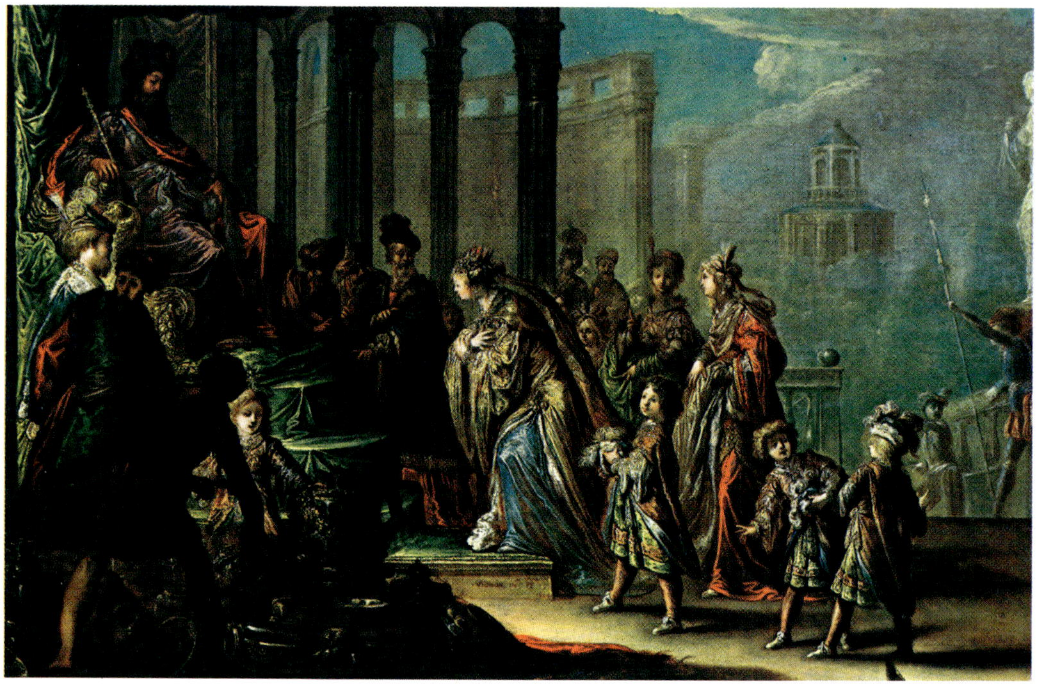

Although Vignon was not much imitated in his time, he was patronized by the court of Louis XIII, and executed many decorations for private clients, all of which have perished. The last of these to disappear, during the last war, was the decoration of the château at Torigny-sur-Vire. Vignon was received into the Academy in 1651, three years after its foundation. By this time dates seem to have disappeared from his pictures, but it can reasonably be assumed that for the rest of his life he continued to paint in the manner he had perfected in the 1620s.

Collections

Algiers, Musée des Beaux-Arts
Adoration of the Kings

Amsterdam, Rijksmuseum
Christ Commanding St Peter: Feed my Lambs

Angoulême, Saint-André
St Wolfgang Appearing to St Henry (signed and dated 1627)

Arc-et-Senans, Church
Presentation in the Temple

Arras, Palais Saint-Vaast
Martyrdom of St Matthew (signed and dated 1617)

Barnard Castle (Co. Durham), Bowes Museum
Croesus and Solon (fragment) (fig. 3)

Binghamton (New York), University Art Gallery
Allegory of Peace and War

Blois, Musée du Château
The Suicide of Dido

Bouconvilliers (Oise), Church
Holy Family

Caen, Musée des Beaux-Arts
Dido

Caen, Abbaye-aux-hommes
Adoration of the Kings (signed)

Châtillon-Cologny (Loiret), Church
The Assumption (dated 1629)
The Transfiguration (dated 1624)

Copenhagen, Statens Museum for Kunst
Lot and his Daughters

Dayton (Ohio), Art Institute
Adoration of the Kings (dated 1619)

Dieppe, Saint-Jacques
St Henry before the Crucifix

Dijon, Musée des Beaux-Arts
The Delphic Sybil (copy)

Dijon, Musée Magnin
The Departure
A Pregnant Woman Imploring Justice from a King

Dunkirk, Musée des Beaux-Arts
The Feast in the House of Simon

Épinal, Musée Départemental des Vosges
St Paul the Hermit and St Anthony

Esnoms (Haute-Marne), Church
Denial of Peter

France, Carmelite collection
The Prophet Elias

Gentilly, Church
Adoration of the Kings (signed and dated 1625)

Greenville (South Carolina), Bob Jones University
Esther before Ahasuerus
The Circumcision (signed and dated 1652)
St Jerome
Croesus and Solon

Grenoble, Musée des Beaux-Arts
Christ among the Doctors (signed and dated 1623)

Hartford (Connecticut), Wadsworth Athenaeum
The Banquet of Antony and Cleopatra

La Fère, Musée Jeanne d'Aboville
Adoration of the Kings

La Grasse (Aude), Church
St Jerome Reading

Le Puy, Cathedral
Adoration of the Kings

Limoges, Chapelle du Lycée
Christ and St Ignatius (signed and dated 1643)

London, with Speelman
Joseph Explaining Dreams (signed and dated 162 .)

London, Stepney Public Library
The Sacrifice of Isaac

Los Angeles, Solomon collection
Solomon Adoring the Idols of Baal (fragment, signed and dated 1626) (fig.32)

Lyons, Cathedral
The Circumcision (signed and dated 1627)

Milwaukee (Wisconsin), Marquette University
Adoration of the Kings

Minneapolis (Minnesota), Institute of Arts
St Ambrose (signed and dated 1623)

Munich, Alte Pinakothek
The Entombment

Nantes, Musée des Beaux-Arts
The Washing of the Disciples' Feet (signed and dated 1653)

Norfolk (Virginia), Chrysler Museum
Solomon Sacrificing to the Idols (signed and dated 1626)

Orléans, Musée des Beaux-Arts
The Triumph of St Ignatius (signed and dated 1628)
The Judgment of Solomon
St Jerome Reading
The Prophet Jeremiah
Head of a Man

Paris, Louvre
Esther before Ahasuerus (signed and dated 1624) (plate 85)
Death of St Anthony (signed and dated 16..)
The Young Singer
The Death of Seneca (signed and dated 1623)

Paris, Saint-Gervais
The Beheading of St John the Baptist

Paris, Saint-Roch
The Victory of Godfroy Bouillon

Ponce (Puerto Rico), Museo de Arte
Allegory of the Catholic Faith

Potsdam, Sans Souci
Marriage at Cana (destroyed)

Quebec, Université de Laval
St Jerome in the Desert

Richmond (Virginia), Museum of Fine Arts
Adoration of the Kings

Rouen, Musée des Beaux-Arts
Samuel
Moses and the Tables of the Law
Joseph Interpreting the Dreams of the Baker

Sarasota (Florida), John and Mable Ringling Museum
Anthony and Cleopatra

Semur-en-Auxois, Musée Municipal
St Anthony

Southill Park (Bedfordshire), Major Whitbread
Two Drinkers

Stanford (California), University Museum
The Penitent St Peter

Stockholm, Nationalmuseum
St Jerome
A Man

Tours, Musée des Beaux-Arts
Croesus Receiving Tribute from a Lydian Peasant (signed and dated 1629) (fig.31)
An Allegory

Turin, Museo Civico
St Paul

Turin, Galleria Sabauda
Adoration of the Kings

Vienne (Isère), Musée des Beaux-Arts
Lot and his Daughters

Williamsburg (Virginia), The Colonial Williamsburg Foundation
St John the Evangelist

Bibliography

The standard study is Wolfgang Fischer, 'Claude Vignon', *Nederlands Kunsthistorisches Jahrboeck*, 1962, pp.105–48, 1963, pp.137–82. This two-part study contains a full stylistic analysis and *catalogue raisonné*.

Some new information and attributions, especially of the Rome period, can be found in the exhibition catalogue by Arnauld Bréjon de Lavergnée and Jean-Pierre Cuzin, Paris, Grand Palais, *Valentin et les caravagesques français*, 1974.

Charlotte Vignon

Paris 1639–?

Daughter of Claude Vignon, Charlotte seems to have been influenced by the complex pictures of Louise Moillon, in which there is an interplay between leaves and fruits.

Collections

Cambridge, Ward collection
Bunch of Grapes (signed)

Paris, J.R. collection
Bowl of Fruit
Peaches and Grapes

Bibliography

Michel Faré
Le grand siècle de la nature morte en France, 1974, pp.70–1.

Claude-François Vignon

Paris 1633–Paris 1703

Son of Claude Vignon, Claude-François became a member of the Paris Academy in 1667. He worked in a style influenced more by Le Brun than that of his father.

Collections

Paris, Louvre
Hercules Chastening Vice and Ignorance in the Presence of Minerva (documented 1667)

Versailles, Château
Decoration of the *Ante-chambre de la Reine*

Bibliography

There is no recent literature on this artist.

Philippe Vignon

Paris 1638–Paris 1701

Son of Claude Vignon, Philippe became a member of the Academy in Paris in 1687.

Collections

Balleroy, Château
Judgment of Paris (signed and dated 1665)

Tours, Musée des Beaux-Arts
Presumed Portrait of Mlle de Blois (attribution)

Versailles, Château
Portrait of Henri Mauperché (documented 1687)
Mlle de Blois, afterwards Duchesse d'Orléans and Mlle de Nantes, afterwards la Princesse de Condé (signed)
Philippe de Buyster (documented 1687)

Bibliography

There is no recent literature on this artist.

Étienne Villequin

Ferrière-en-Brie (Seine-et-Marne) 1619–Paris 1688

Villequin became a member of the Academy in Paris in 1663. Like so many of his contemporaries, he was influenced by Le Brun.

Collections

Douai, Musée de la Chartreuse
The Family of the Virgin (signed and dated 1668)

Paris, Louvre
Christ Healing the Blind of Jericho

Bibliography

There is no recent literature on this artist.

Aubin Vouet

Paris 1599–Paris 1641

Aubin Vouet was the younger brother and pupil of Simon Vouet, and his pictures are only in recent years being disentangled from those of his master, whom he resembled in style. Some of his work was engraved, which has aided its identification.

Collections

Arras, Palais Saint-Vaast
Lamentation over the Dead Christ

Lyons, Musée des Beaux-Arts
St Paul giving Alms

Nantes, Musée des Beaux-Arts
Peace (attribution)

Paris, Notre Dame
The Centurion Cornelius at the Feet of St Peter

Rennes, Musée des Beaux-Arts
The Hunt of Meleager

Rouen, Musée des Beaux-Arts
The Death of Sapphiro and of Ananias (signed, documented 1632)

Toulouse, Musée des Augustins
Deliverance of St Peter from Prison

Versailles, Château
Christ on the Cross, with St John, the Magdalen and the Virgin (signed and dated 1626)

Bibliography

There is no recent literature on this artist.

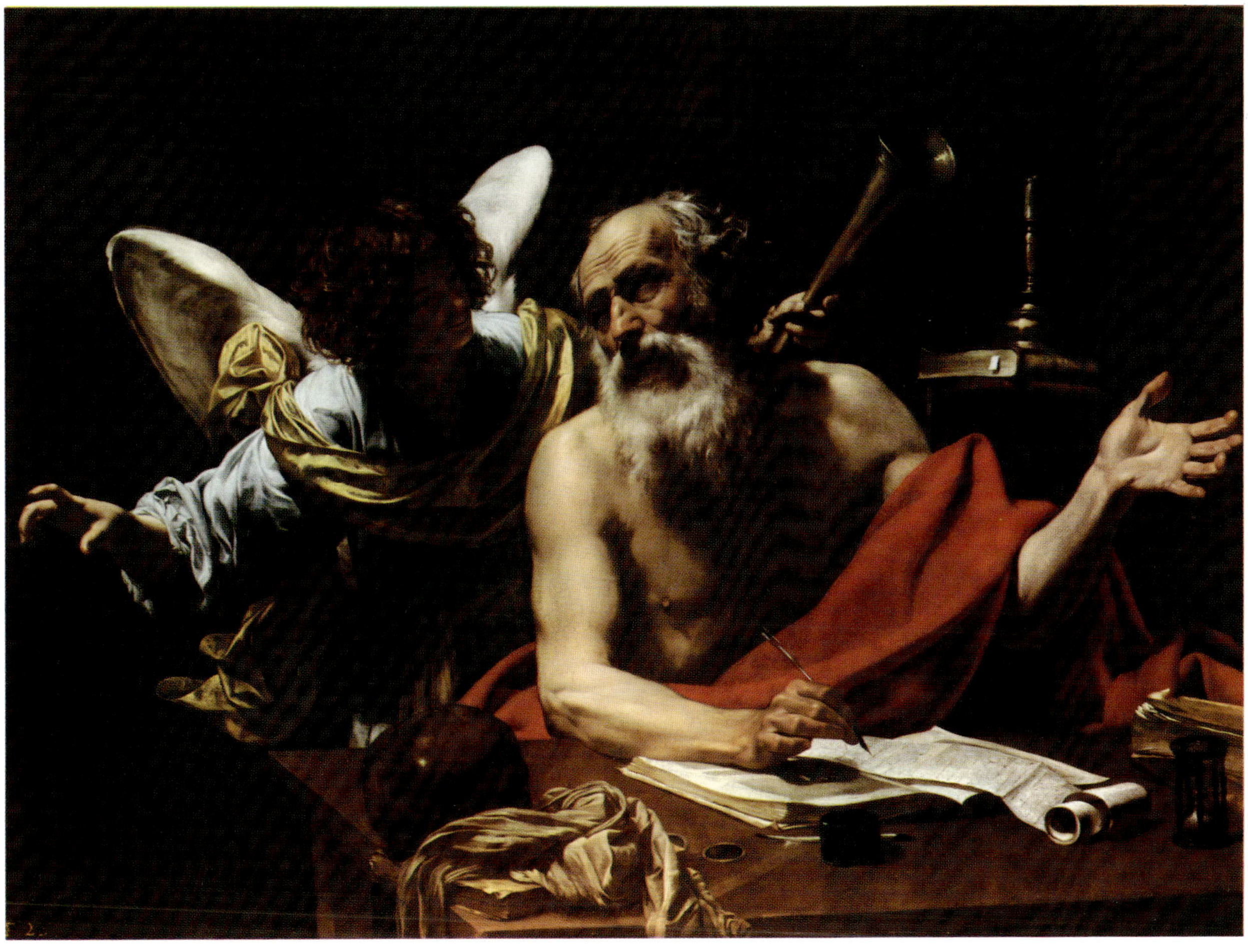

PLATE 86
Simon Vouet
St Jerome and the Angel
Canvas, 144.8 × 179.8 cm.
Washington, National Gallery of Art
Given to the museum as part of the Samuel H. Kress collection in 1961. Formerly in the Barberini collection in Rome.

Simon Vouet

Paris 1590–Paris 1649

Simon Vouet was the most active painter of the whole century, and also one of the most influential, but his present reputation does little to indicate the fact. The majority of his major decorative cycles, for which he was most famous in his lifetime, are either lost or dispersed. His early career in Rome in the 1620s has much in common with those of his French contemporaries Le Valentin and Vignon—like them, he was influenced by Manfredi in his earliest pictures—but he neither softened his style when in Rome, as Le Valentin did later, nor reverted to Mannerism, as did Vignon. Vouet travelled much more extensively in Italy than other French artists, absorbing much more of the general Italian painting tradition, and executed works in Naples and Genoa.

It was only on his return to France in 1627 that Vouet's abilities as a decorator, and his abrupt change of style into a fully fledged Baroque painter, became apparent, and he quickly became successful at the court of Louis XIII. Vouet's artistic dichotomy has led to much misunderstanding of his work: on the one hand he is seen as a Caravaggesque but without the subtlety of Le Valentin, on the other as a decorator who had fully assimilated the Italian Baroque but who lacked the strength and grandeur of Le Brun. It is only when these disparate stylistic elements are put together and Vouet's career is seen as a whole that his importance in historical terms emerges. The reasons for his success at court were his energy and his ability (learned in Italy) to coordinate assistants in the creation of large decorations. It was Vouet who, virtually single-handed, introduced the Italian studio system into France, and he trained a large number of pupils in his methods, including Le Sueur, La Hyre and Le Brun. Most of the pictures Vouet painted in France owe a great debt to the Italian Baroque rather than the Caravaggesque style, which he excluded from his art after the mid-1620s.

PLATE 87
Simon Vouet
Presentation in the Temple
Canvas, 393 × 250 cm.
Paris, Louvre
Given by Cardinal Richelieu to the Church of the Jesuits, Paris. From 1764 in the collection of the Academy, following the suppression of the Jesuits in 1763.

This is one of the most Baroque of all Vouet's compositions.

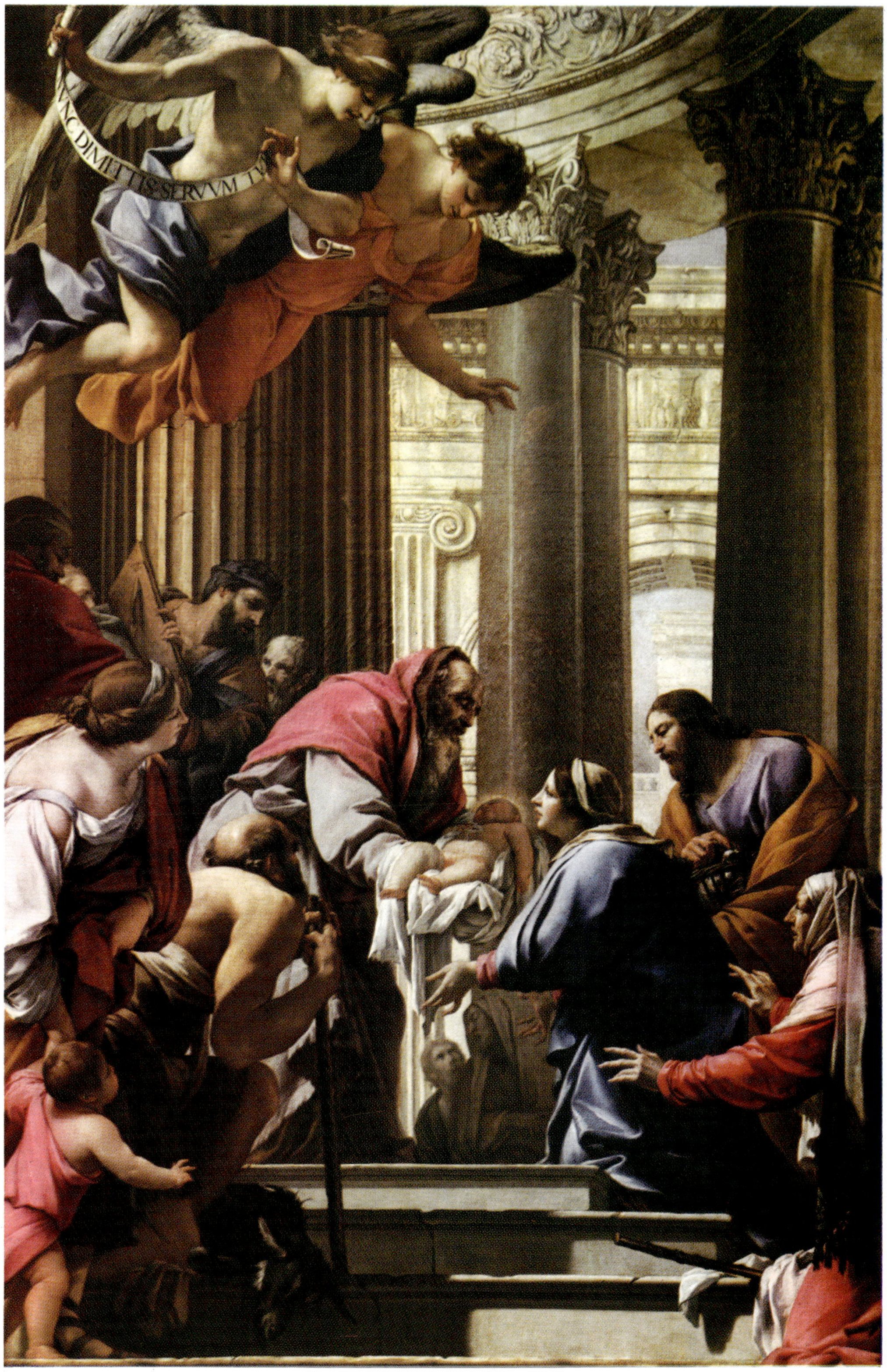

Collections

Algiers, Musée National des Beaux-Arts
St William of Aquitaine

Amiens, Musée de Picardie
The Magdalen

Arles, Musée Réattu
Self-portrait (?)

Bayonne, Musée Bonnat
Roman Charity

Besançon, Musée des Beaux-Arts
Ecstasy of the Magdalen
Angels with Instruments of the Passion

Bourges, Musée du Berry
Times Defeated
The Magdalen: Saint with a Sword (attribution)

Bremen, Kunsthalle
The Holy Family

Brunswick, Herzog Anton-Ulrich Museum
A Bravo

Budapest, Szépmüvészeti Múzeum
Apollo and the Muses
Sleeping Venus

Caen, Musée des Beaux-Arts
The Man with the Fig (attribution)

Cambridge, Fitzwilliam Museum
Entombment of Christ

Chapel Hill (North Carolina), Ackland Art Gallery
A Man in Armour (attribution)

Chatsworth (Derbyshire), Trustees of the Chatsworth Settlement
Venus and Adonis

Cherbourg, Musée Thomas Henry
Ceres Vanquishing the Attributes of War

Chicago, Art Institute
Christ on the Cross (attribution)

Chilly-Mazarin, Church
Lamentation over the Dead Christ

Cincinnati (Ohio), Art Museum
Toilet of Venus

Cleveland (Ohio), Museum of Art
Rest on the Flight into Egypt (attribution)

Dayton (Ohio), Art Museum
Halberdier

Dôle, Musée Municipal
Death of Dido

Dublin, National Gallery of Ireland
The Four Seasons

Épinal, Musée Départemental des Vosges
Entombment of Christ

Florence, Accademia
Virgin and Child

Florence, Uffizi
Self-portrait (attribution)

France, Carmelite collection
Mère Marguerite du Sacrement (1630)

Genoa, Palazzo Bianco
David

Genoa, Sant' Ambrogio
Crucifixion

Genoa, private collection
St Catherine (signed and dated 1621)

Greenville (South Carolina), Bob Jones University
Salome with the Head of St John the Baptist (attribution)
David Playing the Harp (attribution)

Grenoble, Musée de Peinture et de Sculpture
Temptation of St Anthony
Holy Family in Egypt

Hampton Court Palace (Middlesex), Royal Collection
Diana (signed and dated 1637) (fig.30)

Hartford (Connecticut), Wadsworth Athenaeum
St Martha (attribution)
St Ursula

Hovingham Hall (Yorkshire), Sir Marcus Worsley
Adoration of the Cross

Indianapolis (Indiana), Museum of Art
Allegory of Victory

Karlsruhe, Staatliche Kunsthalle
The Muse Clio

Kassel, Staatliche Gemäldegalerie
Sophonisba Receiving the Poison Cup

Le Havre, Musée des Beaux-Arts
Entombment of Christ

Le Mans, Musée de Tessé
St Veronica

Leningrad, Hermitage
Virgin and Child
Allegorical Portrait of Anne of Austria
Crucifixion
Venus and Adonis
Virgin and Child

London, National Gallery
Landscape

London, formerly Tomàs Harris collection
Mater Dolorosa

London, private collection
Groups of Angels (2)

London, private collection
Virgin Adoring the Christ Child

Longjumeau, Church
The Last Supper

Lons-le-Saunier, Musée Municipal
Woman with a Tambourine

Lugano, Thyssen collectio
The Rape of Europa

Lyons, Musée des Beaux-Arts
Self-portrait

Madrid, Prado
Virgin and Child with St Elizabeth, St John the Baptist and St Catherine
Time Defeated (signed and dated 1627)

Mainz, Gemäldegalerie
St Apollonia (attribution)

Malibu (California), J. Paul Getty Museum
Cupid and Psyche (attribution)
Venus and Adonis

Milan, Brera
A Young Woman

Milan, private collection
Marc Antonio Doria

Minneapolis (Minnesota), Institute of Arts
Angels Carrying the Instruments of the Passion (2)

Montpellier, Musée Fabre
Prudence

Munich, Alte Pinakothek
Judith (attribution)

Nancy, Musée des Beaux-Arts
St Paul in Prison
Nymph and Cupid (2)

Nantes, Musée des Beaux-Arts
The Family of St Eustace Carried to Heaven

Naples, Certosa di San Martino
Appearance of the Virgin to St Bruno (signed and dated 1620)

Naples, Capodimonte
Angel Carrying a Lance
Angel Carrying the Dice and the Tunic of Christ

Naples, Sant' Angelo a Segno
The Circumcision (signed and dated 1623)

New York, Welden collection
A Man

New York, with Wildenstein
Rest on the Flight into Egypt

New York, private collection
St Cecilia

Norfolk (Virginia), Chrysler Museum
Virgin and Child

Ottawa, National Gallery
The Fortune Teller

Oxford, Ashmolean Museum
Virgin and Child

Paris, with Cailleux
The Muse Euterpe

Paris, Louvre
Louis XIII between France and Navarre (fig.29)
The Entombment
Gaucher de Châtillon
Christ on the Cross
Faith
Wealth
Victory
Presentation in the Temple (plate 87)
Prudence Leading Peace and Abundance
Polhymnia, the Muse of Eloquence

Pittsburgh (Pennsylvania), Art Museum
The Toilet of Venus

Rome, Museo Capitolino
Memory, Intelligence and Bounty

Rome, Palazzo Barberini
Allegory of the Fine Arts

Rome, Galleria Corsini
Salome (attribution)

Rome, San Francesco a Ripa
The Birth of the Virgin

Rome, San Lorenzo in Lucina
The Clothing of St Francis
The Temptation of St Francis

Rome, formerly Busiri Vici collection, 1971
Bust of the Virgin

Rome, Condorelli collection
St Sebastian Succoured by Irene

Rome, Pallavicini collection
A Young Man

Rouen, Musée des Beaux-Arts
Apotheosis of St Louis

San Francisco (California), Art Museums
Holy Family

San Simeon (California), Hearst Historical Monument
Diana and Endymion
Neptune and Amphitrite

Sarasota (Florida), John and Mable Ringling Museum
Time, Love, Mars and Venus

Strasbourg, Musée des Beaux-Arts
Lot and his Daughters (dated 1633)

Toulouse, Musée des Augustins
The Brazen Serpent
The Invention of the Cross

Turin, Accademia Albertina
Achilles at Scyros (attribution)

Versailles, Château
Allegory of Justice
Allegory of Temperance
Allegory of Force
Allegory of Prudence

Vienna, Kunsthistorisches Museum
Judith with the Head of Holofernes (attribution)

Warsaw, National Museum
Vanitas (attribution)

Washington, National Gallery of Art
St Jerome and the Angel (plate 86)
The Muses Urania and Calliope

Bibliography

The standard work, with *catalogue raisonné*, is William R. Crelly, *The Painting of Simon Vouet*, New Haven, 1962. As this was a pioneering study and much new work has since been done, especially on the Roman period, it is in many respects out of date, but still useful. The essential study on the Roman period is Georgette Dargent and Jacques Thuillier, 'Simon Vouet en Italie' in *Saggi e memorie di storia dell'arte*, no.4, Venice 1965, pp.25–63, 143–66. This was further brought up to date by Arnauld Bréjon de Lavergnée and Jean Pierre Cuzin in the exhibition catalogue, Paris, Grand Palais, *Le Valentin et les caravagesques français*, 1974, pp.202–33, 254–8.

General Bibliography

This bibliography covers all the books and articles of general interest. Where they refer to a specific artist they are included in the bibliography of the relevant painter. Each section is in alphabetical order of either author or, in the case of museum and exhibition catalogues, institution.

Source material

Bellori, Giovan Pietro, *Le vite de pittori, scultori e architetti moderni* (recent edition edited by Evelina Borea, Turin, 1976).

Chennevières-Pointel, Philippe de, *Recherches sur la vie et les ouvrages de quelques peintres provinciaux de l'ancien France*, 4 vols, Paris, 1847–62.

Dezallier d'Argenville, Antoine-Joseph, *Abrégé de la vie des plus fameux peintres*, 4 vols, Paris, 1862.

Books and articles covering general aspects of French seventeenth-century painting

Auzas, Pierre-Marie, 'Les Grands "Mays" de Notre Dame de Paris', *Gazette des Beaux-Arts*, October–December 1949, pp.177–200.
An important article covering the annual commissions for Notre Dame of a large picture with a religious theme. Some of the surviving paintings are in the Palais Saint-Vaast at Arras.

Blunt, Anthony, *Art and Architecture in France, 1500–1700*, Harmondsworth, 1953.
The only general survey of the whole field in English. The treatment is inevitably brief, as two centuries (and also architecture) are covered. The essays on Claude and Poussin have become standard summaries.

Bousquet, Jacques, *Recherches sur le séjour des peintres français à Rome au XVIIe siècle*, Montpellier, 1980.
A book especially rich in source material, giving a clear account of the large number of French painters in Rome. It has few illustrations.

Boyer, Jean, 'La peinture et la gravure à Aix-en-Provence au XVIe, XVIIe et XVIIIe siècles (1530–1790)', *Gazette des Beaux-Arts*, July–September 1971, pp.5–187.
An article which paved the way for the exhibition, bringing together the work of a large number of almost-forgotten painters working in the Aix–Marseilles area.

Châtelet, Albert, and Thuillier, Jacques, i. *La peinture francaise de Foukuet à Poussin*, Geneva, 1963; ii. *La peinture française de Le Nain à Fragonard*, Geneva, 1964.
These two beautifully illustrated volumes complement one another. Although they begin earlier and end later than the seventeenth century, they form one of the few comprehensive general surveys of the period.

Dimier, Louis, *Histoire de la peinture française du retour de Vouet à la mort de Le Brun, 1627 à 1690*, 2 vols, Paris–Brussels, 1926–7.
Now out of date, but in its time an exceptionally thorough survey concentrating on the mainstream in Paris.

Erlanger, Philippe, *Les peintres de la réalité*, Paris, 1946.
A short book taking up the theme of the 'Peintres de la réalité' exhibition held in Paris in 1934, and illuminating for the realist tradition in French seventeenth-century painting.

Faré, Michel, *Le grand siècle de la nature morte en France*, 2nd edition, 1974.
A standard work; nothing else has been written on the subject. The book is superbly illustrated, but the author has covered up the lack of documentation by his eloquence.

Weisbach, Werner, *Französische Malerei des XVII Jahrhunderts*, Berlin, 1932.
In its time a thorough general survey.

L'art baroque à Lyon, Actes du colloque, 1972, Lyons, 1975.
A thoroughly documented study of a neglected area.

Lists of paintings

Isarlo, Georges, *Caravage et le caravagisme européen*, Aix-en-Provence, 1941.
Although now completely out of date, this was a pioneering work which listed an enormous number of French seventeenth-century pictures derived from old sale catalogues and exhibitions. Many of these pictures are not now traceable.

Nicolson, Benedict, *The International Caravaggesque Movement*, Oxford, 1979.
The lists given here are complete for some French seventeenth-century painters, and the book also records copies and other versions of well-known pictures. The bibliography is especially useful, as it contains many little-known items.

Schweers, Hans F., *Gemälde in Deutschen Museen*, Vol.I, A–K, 1981, Vol.2, L–Z, 1982.
In these two volumes, the pictures are listed strictly according to the attributions of their owners.

Vergnet-Ruiz, Jean, and Laclotte, Michel, *Petits et grands musées de France*, Paris, 1962.
This immensely useful book lists most of the major pictures in the French provincial museums. The attributions are in most cases the old ones, however, and therefore the book must be used with caution.

Wright, Christopher, *Old Master Paintings in Britain*, London, 1976; *Paintings in Dutch Museums*, London, 1980.
Pictures listed strictly according to the attributions of their owners.

Two exhibition catalogues contain indispensable lists:
Rome, Académie de France and Paris, Grand Palais, *Le Valentin et les caravagesques français*, 1974. French Caravaggesque paintings in Rome.
Paris, Grand Palais, New York, Metropolitan Museum, Chicago, Art Institute, *La peinture française du XVII siècle dans les collections américaines*, 1982.
All the French seventeenth-century paintings in American public collections.

Museum Catalogues

Budapest, Szépmüvészeti Múzeum, *Peintures françaises des XVIIe et XVIIIe siècles*, 1976, by Agnes Szigethi.
A well-illustrated survey of a little-known collection.

Chantilly, Musée Condé, *Peintures de l'école française XVe–XVIIe siècle*, 1970, by François-Georges Pariset.
A fully illustrated, specialist catalogue of a collection distinguished for a group of Poussins and a large number of portraits.

Dijon, Musée des Beaux-Arts, *Catalogue des peintures françaises*, 1968, by Pierre Quarré.
Brief notes and a few illustrations of a large collection.

Karlsruhe, Staatliche Kunsthalle, *Katalog Alte Meister*, 2 vols, 1966, by Jan Lauts.
The largest collection of French seventeenth-century pictures in Germany.

Le Mans, Musée de Tessé, *Peintures françaises du XVIIe siècle*, 1982, by Elizabeth Foucart-Walter.
One of a recent series of very well-documented catalogues dealing with specific aspects of one collection (see also Rouen and Tours).

Leningrad, Hermitage, *Catalogue I, Italy, Spain, France, Switzerland*, 1976 (in Russian).
The largest collection in existence outside the Louvre. Short notices on all the pictures and a few illustrations.

London, National Gallery, *The French School*, 1957, by Martin Davies.
Fully documented entries on the outstanding collection of pictures by Poussin and Claude.

Madrid, Prado, *Catalogo de las Pinturas*, 1972.
Summary catalogue of an interesting and underestimated collection, most of it not exhibited.

Munich, Alte Pinakothek, *Französische und Spanische Malerei*, 1972.
Full entries and illustrations of this small but high-quality collection.

New York, Metropolitan Museum, *A Catalogue of French Paintings, XV–XVIII Centuries*, 1955, by Charles Sterling.
Now out of date because of many more acquisitions, but very thorough and all works illustrated.

Orléans, Musée des Beaux-Arts, *Les peintures de l'école française des XVIIe et XVIIIe siècles*, 1980, 2 vols, by Mary O'Neill.
The best catalogue to date of any French seventeenth-century pictures. The Orléans collection is particularly varied, although neither Claude nor Poussin is represented.

Paris, Musée du Louvre, *Catalogue illustré, école française XVIIe et XVIIIe siècles*, 1974, by Pierre Rosenberg, Nicole Reynaud and Isobelle Compin.
Completely illustrated, but the entries are without full bibliographies. The greatest collection of French seventeenth-century paintings still lacks a fully documented catalogue.

Rennes, Musée des Beaux-Arts, *Bulletin des Amis du Musée de Rennes*, No.3, 1979, 'Catalogue des peintures de l'école française du XVIIe siècle', by François Bergot and Patrick Ramade.
A very thorough study of an interesting collection.

Rouen, Musée des Beaux-Arts, *Tableaux français du XVIIe siècle et italiens des XVIIe et XVIIIe siècles*, 1966, by Pierre Rosenberg.
One of the best catalogues in existence in the field. Rosenberg was especially thorough with the early documentation and cautious with the attributions.

Strasbourg, Musée des Beaux-Arts, *Natures mortes: catalogue de la collection du Musée des Beaux-Arts*, 1964, by Hans Haug.
Short entries and some illustrations on the only significant collection of still-life paintings in France.

Tours, Musée des Beaux-Arts, *Tableaux français et italiens du XVIIe siècle*, 1982, by Robert Fohr.
Part of a series of well-documented catalogues dealing with specific aspects of a single collection.

Some of the major collections of French seventeenth-century paintings in France have no museum catalogue. There have been no studies of the following important collections since before 1914: Aix-en-Provence, Arras, Lille, Montpellier, Nantes, Nancy and Toulouse.

Exhibition Catalogues

This is the most important section of the general bibliography, since almost all the significant research in the field over the last thirty years has been published in exhibition catalogues.

Dunkirk, Musée des Beaux-Arts, Valenciennes, Musée des Beaux-Arts, Lille, Palais des Beaux-Arts, *La peinture française au XVIIe et XVIIIe siècles*, 1980.
Part of a series of exhibitions covering the holdings of the museums of northern France. All the French seventeenth-century paintings in the area are listed, and most of the more interesting ones are reproduced.

Florence, Gallerie Pitti, *Pittura francese nelle collezioni pubbliche fiorentine*, 1977.
A comprehensive catalogue with particular reference to the history of the Medici collections. Every painting reproduced.

Lille, Palais des Beaux-Arts, *Au temps du roi soleil, les peintres de Louis XIV, 1660–1715*, 1968.
Survey of the painters of the period with important loans from French collections, all discussed in the catalogue.

London, Royal Academy, *The Age of Louis XIV*, 1958.
The most comprehensive exhibition of French seventeenth-century painting held to date. All the loans were from French provincial museums, and the reign of Louis XIII was especially well covered.

Marseilles, Palais Longchamp, *La peinture en Provence au XVIIe siècle*, 1973.
A pioneering exhibition that established the oeuvre of dozens of painters active in Provence during the period.

Naples, Palazzo Reale, *Arte francese a Napoli*, 1967.
Useful information on French pictures in Neapolitan collections.

Paris, Orangerie des Tuileries, *Les peintres de la réalité*, 1934.
A pioneering exhibition that brought Georges de La Tour to light for the first time, and rehabilitated many of his contemporaries. The catalogue by Charles Sterling is still a useful work of reference.

Paris, Orangerie des Tuileries, *L'age d'or de la peinture toulousaine*, 1947.
One of those small exhibitions that disappear without trace. The only coverage of the considerable school of Toulouse painters, especially Tournier.

Paris, Grand Palais, *La peinture française du XVIIe siècle dans les collections américaines* (also New York, Metropolitan Museum, Chicago Art Institute with a few changes), 1982.
An exhibition with many masterpieces drawn from American collections. Useful historical surveys and introductions to certain categories of painting.

Paris, Petit Palais, *L'art du XVIIe siècle dans les Carmes de France*, 1982–3.
A surprising exhibition of mainly anonymous French seventeenth-century pictures which showed the large extent of Carmelite patronage.

Rouen, Musée des Beaux-Arts, *Nicolas Poussin et son temps*, 1961.
The only exhibition ever to be held on the theme of Poussin's influence, bringing together a considerable number of pictures from obscure French provincial collections.

Rome, Académie de France and Paris, Grand Palais, *Le Valentin et les caravagesques français*, 1973/4.
The most thoroughly documented and brilliantly thought-out exhibition on a specific theme to be held in recent years. The stylistic unity of French Caravaggesque painters was convincingly demonstrated.

Rome, Villa Medici and Nancy, Musée des Beaux-Arts, *Claude Gellée et les peintres lorrains en Italie au XVIIe siècle*, 1982.
Richly documented catalogue by Jacques Thuillier.

Index of Locations

This index lists all known paintings in public collections. A star indicates an outstanding picture or group of pictures by an individual artist; a location given in bold type indicates a collection generally representative in terms of quality.

Detroit, Institute of Arts
Jacques Blanchard; *Jean-Baptiste de Champaigne*; *Claude* 2; *Jacques Courtois*; *Cretey*; *Laurent de La Hyre*; *Georges de La Tour*; *Le Brun*; *Le Nain brothers* 2; *Monnoyer* 2; *Poussin* 2; *Stoskopff*

Dieppe, Saint-Jacques
Claude Vignon

Dijon, Musée des Beaux-Arts
Boucher; *Bourdon*; *Philippe de Champaigne* 2; *Jean-Baptiste Corneille* 5; *Michel Corneille* 2; *Jacques Courtois* 4; *Noël Coypel*; *'Monsu Desiderio'*; *Despeches*; *La Fosse*; *Georges de La Tour*; *Le Brun*; *Claude Lefebvre*; *Liégois*; *Loir*; *Pierre Mignard*; *Quantin* 4; *Jean Tassel* 17*; *Richard Tassel*; *Claude Vignon*

Dijon, Musée Magnin
Lubin Baugin 2; *Boucher*; *Bourdon* 3; *Jean-Baptiste de Champaigne*; *Chaperon*; *Jean-Baptiste Corneille*; *Dufresnoy*; *Dughet* 3; *Finson*; *La Fosse* 3; *Laurent de La Hyre* 3; *Claude Lefebvre*; *Le Sueur*; *Pierre Mignard*; *Millet*; *Perrier*; *Jacques Stella*; *Henri Testelin* 2; *Claude Vignon* 2

Dijon, Hôpital Général
Quantin

Dijon, Cathédrale Saint-Bénigne
Quantin 4

Dijon, Saint-Michel
Quantin

Dinan, Musée Municipal
Pierre Mignard

Dinton Park (Wiltshire), National Trust
Patel

Dôle, Musée Municipal
Pierre Mignard; *Monnoyer*; *Jean Tassel* 2; *Simon Vouet*

Douai, Musée de La Chartreuse
Le Brun; *Millet*; *Monnoyer*; *Villequin*

Dresden, Gemäldegalerie
Claude, 2; *Dughet*; *Poussin* 5,* (attributions) 2; *Tournier* (attributions) 2; *Le Valentin**

Dublin, National Gallery of Ireland
Claude; *Noël Coypel*; *Dughet*; *Étienne de La Tour*; *Jean Lemaire*; *Le Nain brothers*; *Le Sueur*; *Michelin*; *Pierre Mignard*; *Monnoyer*; *Poërson*; *Poussin* 4; *Simon Vouet*

Dunkirk, Musée des Beaux-Arts
Bourdon 2; *Jacques Courtois*; *La Fosse*; *Le Sueur*; *Pierre Mignard*; *Patel* 2; *Saint-Igny* 3; *Vignon*

Dyrham Park (Gloucestershire), National Trust
Monnoyer

Edinburgh, National Gallery of Scotland
Claude; *Jacques Courtois*; *Dughet*; *Poussin*, *Poussin* (loan 8)*

Edinburgh, Scottish National Portrait Gallery
Pierre Mignard

Edinburgh, University, Torrie Collection
Jacques Courtois

Éguilles, Hôtel de Ville
Bigot ?

Elmira (New York), Arnot Art Museum
Jean-Baptiste de Champaigne; *Claude*

Épinal, Musée Départemental des Vosges
Bassot; *Bourdon*; *Claude*; *Jacques Courtois*; *Dufresnoy*; *Laurent de La Hyre*;* *Georges de La Tour**; *Pierre Mignard*; *Parrocel*; *Perrier*; *Jacques Stella*; *Claude Vignon*; *Simon Vouet*

Ermenonville, Church
Finson

Esnoms (Haute-Marne), Church
Claude Vignon

Evreux, Musée de L'Ancien Evêché
Dufresnoy

Flers-bourg, Church
Bergaigne

Florence, Accademia
Dughet; *Simon Vouet*

Florence, Florentine Galleries
'Master of the Judgment of Solomon'; *Tournier* (attribution)

Florence, Longhi Foundation
Dughet; *'Master of the Judgment of Solomon* 5; *Le Valentin*

Florence, Galleria Pitti
Beaubrun brothers; *Philippe de Champaigne*; *Jacques Courtois* 2; *Dughet* 7; *Nicolas Perelle*

Florence, Uffizi
Bodan; *Bourdon*; *Claude* 2; *Michel Corneille II*; *Jacques Courtois*; *'Monsu Desiderio'*; *Dorigny*; *Dudot*; *Dufresnoy*; *Elle*; *La Hyre*; *Le Brun* 2; *Liégois*; *Loir*; *Mauperché*; *Mole*; *Parrocel* 2; *Jacques Stella* 2; *Jean Tassel*; *Simon Vouet*

Fontainebleau, Château
Noël Coypel; *Dubois*; *Jean Lemaire* 2; *Monnoyer* 2; *Jacques Stella*

Fontvanne, Saint-Alban
L'Estin

Fort Worth (Texas), Kimbell Art Museum
Claude 2* *Poussin*

Frankfurt-am-Main, Städelsches Kunstinstitut
Claude 2; *Poussin*

Freiburg-im-Breisgau, Augustinermuseum
Bourdon

Gannat, Church
François

Geneva, Musée d'Art et d'Histoire
Bergaigne; *Boucle*; *Philippe de Champaigne*; *Charles Mellin*

Genoa, Palazzo Bianco
Simon Vouet

Genoa, Sant-Ambrogio
Simon Vouet

Gentilly, Church
Claude Vignon

Ghent, Museum voor Schone Kunsten
Philippe de Champaigne

Glasgow, Art Gallery
Dughet

Glasgow, Pollok House
'Monsu Desiderio'; *Pierre Mignard*

Glasgow, University
Millet; *Jacques Stella*

Gothenburg, Konstmuseum
'Monsu Desiderio'

Grand Rapids (Michigan), Art Museum
Moillon

Grasse, Musée Fragonard
Daret

Gray, Musée Baron Martin
Jacques Courtois 2; *Henri Testelin*

Greenville (South Carolina), Bob Jones University
Bigot ?; *Jacques Blanchard*; *Bourdon* 2; *Philippe de Champaigne*; *Colombel*; *Michel Corneille* 2; *Guillaume Courtois*; *Le Brun*; *Pierre Mignard*; *Jacques Stella*; *Claude Vignon* 4; *Simon Vouet* 3

Grenoble, Musée de Peinture et de Sculpture
Bourdon; *Philippe de Champaigne* 6; *Claude*; *La Fosse* 3; *Laurent de La Hyre* 2; *Georges de La Tour* (attribution); *Le Sueur*; *Loir*; *Pierre Mignard*; *Millet*; *Monnoyer*; *Jacques Stella* 2; *Louis Testelin*; *Claude Vignon*; *Simon Vouet* 2

Guéret, Musée Municipal
Le Sueur

Hagerstown (Maryland), Washington County Museum of Fine Arts
Le Nain brothers

The Hague, Museum Bredius
Jean Tassel 3

The Hague, Mauritshuis
Jacques Courtois

The Hague, Schilderijenzaal Prins Willem V
Claude

Hamburg, Kunsthalle
Philippe de Champaigne; *Claude*; *Dughet*; *Millet*

Hampton Court Palace (Middlesex), Royal Collection
Bigot II; *Philippe de Champaigne*; *Georges de La Tour*; *Rousseau*; *Simon Vouet*

Hanover, Niedersächsisches Landesmuseum
Dughet; *Pierre Mignard*; *Millet*; *Monnoyer*; *Parrocel*; *Poussin*

Hartford (Connecticut), Wadsworth Athenaeum
Bourdon; *Claude*; *'Monsu Desiderio'*; *Le Nain brothers*;* *Poussin*; *Jacques Stella*; *Jean Tassel*; *Claude Vignon*; *Simon Vouet* 2

Hatchlands (Surrey), National Trust
Monnoyer

Hazebrouck, Musée Municipal
Finson

Heidelberg, Kurpfälzisches Museum
Jacques Blanchard

Heino, Kastel Het Nijenhuis, Hannema-De Stuers Fundatie
Laurent de La Hyre

Honolulu, Academy of Fine Arts
Pierre Mignard

Houston (Texas), Museum of Fine Arts
Bourdon; *Philippe de Champaigne*; *Chaperon*; *Claude*; *'Monsu Desiderio'*; *Laurent de La Hyre*

Hull, Ferens Art Gallery
Philippe de Champaigne

Indianapolis, Museum of Art
Jean-Baptiste Blanchard; *Claude*; *Linard*; *Le Valentin*; *Simon Vouet*

Jacksonville (Florida), Cummer Gallery
Claude; *Le Nain brothers* (attribution); *Levieux*

Jassy (Rumania), Art Museum
Philippe de Champaigne

Kansas City, Nelson Gallery-Atkins Museum
Philippe de Champaigne; *Claude* 2; *Le Nain brothers*; *Poussin*

Karlsruhe, Staatliche Kunsthalle
Lubin Baugin; *Bellange*; *Jacques Blanchard*; *Bouman*; *Philippe de Champaigne*; *Claude*; *Jacques Courtois* 2; *Laurent de La Hyre*; *Le Brun*; *Le Nain brothers* 2; *Linard*; *Moillon*; *Monnoyer* 2; *Picart* 2; *Poussin*; *Stoskopff*; *Simon Vouet*

Kassel, Staatliche Gemäldegalerie
Jacques Courtois; *Millet*; *Poussin*; *Jean Tassel*; *Simon Vouet*

Kiel, Stiftung Pommern
Bourdon

La Grasse (Aude), Church
Claude Vignon

La Fère, Musée Jeanne d'Aboville
Deruet; *Dupuys*; *Laurent de La Hyre*; *Millet*; *Monnoyer*; *Patel*; *Claude Vignon*

Lambesc, Church
Daret; *Faudran*; *Levieux*; *Nicolas Mignard*

Langeac, Church
François

Langres, Musée Saint-Didier
Le Brun; *Le Clerc*; *Jean Tassel* 9

Langres, Société Historique et Archéologique
Jean Tassel

Langres, Cathedral
Jean Tassel 4

Langres, Saint-Martin
'Master of the Judgment of Solomon'

Lanson, Church
Cundier

Montpellier, Cathedral
Bourdon; Levieux; Nicolas Mignard

Montpellier, Notre Dames des Tables
François

Montpellier, Pénitents Blancs
Levieux

Montreal, Museum of Fine Arts
'Monsu Desiderio'; Le Brun; Poussin; Le Valentin

Montrésor, Church
Philippe de Champaigne

Montserrat (Spain), Pinacoteca
Pierre Mignard

Morlaix, Musée des Jacobins
Bourdon

Mormoiron, Church
Nicolas Mignard

Moscow, Pushkin Museum
Jacques Blanchard; Claude 3; *La Fosse; Le Brun; Le Nain brothers* 2; *L'Estin; Michelin; Poussin* 4; *Le Valentin*

Mulhouse, Musée des Beaux-Arts
Bodan

Munich, Alte Pinakothek
Bellange (attribution); *Bourdon* 2; *Philippe de Champaigne; Claude* 3; *Deruet; Le Sueur; Millet; Poussin* 5; *Renard de Saint-André; Stoskopff; Le Valentin* 3; *Vignon; Simon Vouet*

Munich, Bayerisches Nationalmuseum
Jacques Stella

Munich, Bayerische Staatsgemäldesammlungen
Le Brun

Munich, Residenzmuseum
Gascars

Nancy, Musée des Beaux-Arts
Lubin Baugin; Jacques Blanchard; Jean-Baptiste de Champaigne; Philippe de Champaigne; Claude; Jacques Courtois; Dughet; La Fosse; Loir; Pierre Mignard 2; *Monnoyer; Poussin; Simon Vouet* 3

Nancy, Musée Historique Lorrain
Bellange (attribution); *Deruet* 7; *'Monsu Desiderio'; Étienne de La Tour; Georges de La Tour;* Louis XIII; Charles Mellin*

Nancy, Saint-Nicolas
Le Clerc

Nancy, Saint-Sébastien
Le Clerc

Nantes, Musée des Beaux-Arts
Bizet; Bourdon; Philippe de Champaigne; Michel Corneille II; Jacques Courtois 2; *Dauphin; 'Monsu Desiderio'; Dughet* 3; *La Fosse; Laurent de La Hyre* 3; *Georges de La Tour* 2,* (attribution);* *Le Sueur; Licherie; Mather* 2; *Mauperché; Millet; Monnoyer; Jacques Stella; Tournier; Claude Vignon; Aubin Vouet; Simon Vouet*

Naples, Capodimonte
Claude; 'Monsu Desiderio'; Finson; 'Master of the Judgment of Solomon'; Simon Vouet

Naples, Museo di San Martino
'Monsu Desiderio' 2

Naples, Certosa di San Martino
Simon Vouet

Naples, Sant'Angelo a Segno
Simon Vouet

Naples, Santa Maria di Donna Regina Nuova
Charles Mellin 2

Narbonne, Musée des Beaux-Arts
Audran II; Boucle; Bourdon 3; *Brocard; Philippe de Champaigne* 3; *Dorigny; Dughet; Dupuys; Claude Lefebvre; Rolland Lefebvre; Monnoyer* 2; *Patel* 2

Narbonne, Cathedral
Tournier

Narbonne, Saint-Serge
Tournier

Nevers, Musée des Beaux-Arts
La Fosse

Nevers, Saint-Pierre
L'Estin

New Bern (North Carolina), Tryon Palace
Claude

Newcastle upon Tyne, Hatton Gallery
Millet

New Haven (Connecticut), Yale University
Bourdon; Claude; Daret; 'Monsu Desiderio'

New Orleans, Museum of Art
Claude; Colombel; Claude Lefebvre

New Orleans, Gallier Hall
Pierre Mignard

Newport, Marble House
Henri Testelin

New York, Brooklyn Museum
Jacques Courtois

New York, Frick Collection
Claude; Étienne de La Tour

New York, Historical Society
Philippe de Champaigne 2; *Pierre Mignard*

New York, Metropolitan Museum
Bellange (attribution); *Jacques Blanchard; Philippe de Champaigne; Claude* 5; *Deruet* 2; *Dughet; Laurent de La Hyre; Le Nain brothers* (attribution); *Mauperché; Michelin; Millet; Poussin* 4;* (attribution)

New York, Queen's College
Monnoyer

Nîmes, Musée des Beaux-Arts
Dughet; Levieux 3; *Pierre Mignard; Saint-Igny*

Nîmes, Musée du Vieux Nîmes
Nicolas Mignard

Niort, Musée des Beaux-Arts
Renard de Saint-André

Nivagaard (Denmark), Hage collection
Claude

Norfolk (Virginia), Chrysler Museum
Lubin Baugin; Claude; Noël Coypel; Laurent de La Hyre; Georges Lallement; Georges de La Tour (attribution); *Le Nain brothers* (attribution); *Le Sueur; Pierre Mignard; Millet; Monnoyer; Patel; Claudine Bouzonnet Stella; Claude Vignon; Simon Vignon*

Northampton (Massachusetts), Smith College
Bourdon; Loir

Notre Dame (Indiana), University Art Gallery
Boucle; Claude; Noël Coypel

Nottingham, Castle Museum
*Le Brun**

Nuremberg, Germanisches Nationalmuseum
Gascars; Stoskopff

Oberlin (Ohio), Allen Memorial Art Museum
Bourdon

Oldenburg, Landesmuseum
Jacques Stella

Omaha (Nebraska), Joslyn Art Museum
Claude

Omaha (Nebraska), Creighton University
Beaubrun brothers

Orléans, Musée des Beaux-Arts
Lubin Baugin 2; *Jacques Blanchard; Bourdon; Philippe de Champaigne; Michel Corneille I; Michel Corneille II; Deruet* 5;* *'Monsu Desiderio'; Gobin* 2; *La Fosse* 2; *Laurent de La Hyre; Étienne de La Tour; Le Nain brothers; Paul Mignard; Pierre Mignard; Millet; Monnoyer; Patel* 2; *Gabriel Perelle; Nicolas Perelle; Poncet; 'Remy'; Senelle; Claude Vignon* 5

Orléans, Cathedral
L'Estin 4

Ottawa, National Gallery of Canada
Bigot ?; Philippe de Champaigne; Claude; Poussin 2; (attribution); *Simon Vouet*

Oslo, Nasjonalgalleriet
Monnoyer

Oxford, Ashmolean Museum
Bigot ?; Claude 2; *'Monsu Desiderio'; Dughet; Millet; Poussin; Simon Vouet*

Oxford, Christ Church
Jacques Courtois; Dughet

Paris, Musée des Arts Décoratifs
Conte 2; *'Monsu Desiderio'* 2

Paris, École des Beaux-Arts
Blanchet; Colombel; La Fosse; Licherie 2; *Poussin; Antoine Bouzonnet Stella*

Paris, Musée Carnavalet
Philippe de Champaigne; Deruet; Georges Lallement; Le Brun; Pierre Mignard; Perrier

Paris, Musée de La Comédie Française
Nicolas Mignard

Paris, Musée de Cluny
Saint-Igny

Paris, Musée Jacquemart-André
Philippe de Champaigne

Paris, Louvre
Audran II; Baugin 2;* *Lubin Baugin* 2; *Gabriel Blanchard* 2; *Jacques Blanchard* 4; *Jean-Baptiste Blanchard; Louis de Boullongne I; Bourdon* 13; *Jean-Baptiste de Champaigne* 3; *Philippe de Champaigne* 24;* *Claude* 15;* *Colombel; Michel Corneille II* 2; *Jacques Courtois* 5; *Noël Coypel* 11; *'Monsu Desiderio'; Dorigny* 5; *Dubois; Dufresnoy; Dughet* 3; *Dumoustier; Dupuys* 2; *Fauchier; François Garnier* 2;* *La Chapelle; La Fosse* 4; *Laurent de La Hyre* 7; *Étienne de La Tour;* Georges de La Tour* (3);* *Lebre; Le Brun* 20;* *Claude Lefebvre* 2; *Jean Lemaire* 2; *Le Nain brothers* 15,* (attributions) 3; *Le Pileur; Le Sueur* 47;* *Licherie; Linard* 3; *Loir* 2; *Mauperché* 2; *Michelin* 3; *Pierre Mignard* 5; *Millet* 2; *Moillon* 3; *Mole; Monnoyer; Parrocel; Patel* 5; *Perrier* 3; *Plattemontagne; Poërson; Poussin* 39;* *François Puget; Quesnel* 2; *Gilbert de Sève* 3; *Pierre de Sève* 2; *Jacques Stella* 3; *Stoskopff* 2; *Jean Tassel* 2; *Tournier* 2; *Toutain; Le Valentin* 6;* *Varin; Claude Vignon* 4; *Claude-François Vignon; Villequin; Simon Vouet* 11

Paris, Musée de La Marine
La Rose

Paris, Petit Palais
Claude; Georges Lallement; Poussin

Paris, Saint-Étienne du Mont
Philippe de Champaigne; Mauperché

Paris, Sainte-Geneviève du Mont
Philippe de Champaigne

Paris, Saint-Germain en Auxerrois
Le Sueur

Paris, Saint-Germain des Près
Hallé; Laurent de La Hyre

Paris, Saint-Gervais
Claude Vignon

Paris, Saint-Jacques du Haut Pas
Bourdon; Le Nain brothers

Paris, Saint-Leu Saint-Gilles
Bigot ?; Philippe de Champaigne

Paris, Saint-Médard
Philippe de Champaigne

Paris, Saint-Nicolas des Champs
Finson; Georges Lallemant

Paris, Saint-Nicolas du Chardonnet
Le Brun 2; *Saquespée* 2

Paris, Notre Dame
Lubin Baugin 2; *Jacques Blanchard; Bourdon; Laurent de La Hyre; Le Brun* 2; *Le Nain brothers; Le Sueur; Aubin Vouet*

Paris, Notre Dame de Bercy
Jacques Stella

Paris, Saint-Paul Saint-Louis
L'Estin

General Index

Figures in bold refer to main entries; those in italics to captions of illustrations.

Picture Acknowledgments

Photographs were supplied by the museums, galleries and collections to which the paintings belong, with the exception of the following: Archivio IGDA 143 bottom, 148 top left, 148, top right, 156 top right, 156 bottom, 165 top, 183, 187, 196, 197, 198, 199, 201, 202, 204, 207, 210, 212, 213, 216, 217, 218, 247 top, 263, 264 left; Bulloz 23 bottom, 41, 56, 95 bottom, 102 right; Courtauld Institute of Art 28, 29, 30 top right, 30 bottom, 31, 34, 65, 68, 99 top, 118 right; Photographie Giraudon 44, 58 top, 110, 118 left, 121, 122; Réunion Des Musées Nationaux 43, 116; Scala 23 top left, 23 top right.